INTERNATIONAL STUDIES

Sara Miller McCune founded SAGE Publishing in 1965 to support the dissemination of usable knowledge and educate a global community. SAGE publishes more than 1000 journals and over 800 new books each year, spanning a wide range of subject areas. Our growing selection of library products includes archives, data, case studies and video. SAGE remains majority owned by our founder and after her lifetime will become owned by a charitable trust that secures the company's continued independence.

Los Angeles | London | New Delhi | Singapore | Washington DC | Melbourne

INTERNATIONAL STUDIES

Global Forces, Interactions, and Tensions

Scott Straus

The University of Wisconsin—Madison

Barry Driscoll

Grinnell College

FOR INFORMATION:

CQ Press

An Imprint of SAGE Publications, Inc.

2455 Teller Road

Thousand Oaks, California 91320

E-mail: order@sagepub.com

SAGE Publications Ltd.

1 Oliver's Yard

55 City Road

London EC1Y 1SP

United Kingdom

SAGE Publications India Pvt. Ltd.

B 1/I 1 Mohan Cooperative Industrial Area

Mathura Road, New Delhi 110 044

India

SAGE Publications Asia-Pacific Pte. Ltd.

3 Church Street

#10-04 Samsung Hub

Singapore 049483

Acquisitions Editor: Scott Greenan

Development Editor: Elise Frasier

Editorial Assistant: Sarah Christensen

Production Editor: David Felts

Copy Editor: Sheree Van Vreede

Typesetter: Hurix Digital

Proofreader: Scott Oney

Indexer: Diggs Publication Services

Cover Designer: Gail Buschman

Marketing Manager: Jennifer Jones

Library of Congress Cataloging-in-Publication Data

Names: Straus, Scott, author. | Driscoll, Barry (Political scientist), author.

Title: International studies : global forces, interactions, and tensions / Scott Straus, Barry Driscoll.

Description: Los Angeles : SAGE, 2019. | Includes bibliographical references and index.

Identifiers: LCCN 2018023430 | ISBN 978-1-4522-4119-7 (pbk. : alk. paper)

Subjects: LCSH: International relations. | Globallization.

Classification: LCC JZ1318 .S765 2019 | DDC 327—dc23 LC record available at https://lccn.loc.gov/2018023430

This book is printed on acid-free paper.

18 19 20 21 22 10 9 8 7 6 5 4 3 2 1

Brief Contents

Detailed Contents

PART I   FOUNDATIONS

CHAPTER 1   **The Making of Our Global Age: Forces, Interactions, and Tensions Since 1800**   **21**

CHAPTER 8   **Human Rights: The Challenge of Setting and Enforcing Global Norms**   **208**

Preface

International Studies is a relatively new addition to many universities. Students are flocking to the field as they discover how exciting and relevant it can be; indeed, the major has become one of the most popular at many large universities. At the same time, anyone who has put together a syllabus for the introductory course has had to confront the inherent challenge of the field: it can be, frankly, a little amorphous. What exactly is International Studies? How is it different from International Relations? Is there some kind of framework that can make the course more coherent?

The origins of this book stem from more than a decade of teaching the large Introduction to International Studies lecture course at The University of Wisconsin–Madison, where we asked ourselves those same questions right from the start. When it came time for us to put meat on the bones of that course, we had trouble defining International Studies beyond the core concepts of "interdisciplinary" and "global." Colleagues from other disciplines gently teased that International Studies was "Political Science light"; others dismissed the field as not serious. When we looked for guidance in some existing textbooks, International Studies seemed like a parade of disciplines, anchored around the concept of globalization. It often amounted to how an Anthropologist, a Sociologist, and a Geographer—and others—would approach globalization in all its many facets. There was nothing per se wrong with these approaches, but we craved a program of study that had stronger conceptual foundations and analytical cohesion.

In our search for something more satisfying, our students were our inspiration. We knew that fundamentally they wanted to understand the world around them. We also knew that they did not care primarily about disciplinarity or interdisciplinarity. Over time, we learned that they were drawn to the course for two main reasons. First, they wanted a course of study that provided insight into the complex and fascinating world in which they lived. Many fashioned themselves as students of global issues and aspiring global travelers. Others sought a career with strong international dimensions. They wanted a course of study that gave them purchase on their world. This textbook, therefore, takes a "problems first" approach. We place issues front and center, drawing on social scientific research to help students understand issues, but not as a means of introducing the disciplines themselves.

Second, they wanted flexibility in course selection; they came from a wide variety of backgrounds, had a diverse set of interests, and did not want to be confined to a particular discipline. Many of our students intended to, or had, studied abroad; others wanted a way to combine their core interests in, say, a language, literature, business, health sciences, anthropology, or political science with a dedicated *international* course of study. With a wide lens, this book pays tribute to the broad range of interests that draw students to International Studies.

Framework

International Studies: Global Forces, Interactions, and Tensions is our long answer to the question of what International Studies is. The book introduces students to four interrelated themes that run throughout: in *International Studies* we focus on *global interactions*, the *tensions* produced by those interactions, the *global forces* that animate interactions, and the *outside-in and inside-out* dynamics that shape interactions. These are not new ideas, but we think taken together they usefully organize the field in a way that is pedagogically manageable, intellectually stimulating, and discipline-agnostic. We say more about each of the themes below.

First, **global interactions** are the myriad ways in which people, things, information, and ideas intersect in our world. The concept of interactions allows us to capture under one umbrella a broad range of exchanges—economic, political, environmental, informational, and cultural—that take place within and across borders. International studies can claim all these interactions as part of its purview because it is interdisciplinary. A typical international studies course or program will therefore encompass a broad range of topics, from global governance, to global economics, to culture and language, to human rights, to migration, to the environment, to global health. The lens is wide. What can unite it is the study of interactions. Each instructor will craft their course to emphasize particular themes and topics; we designed our framework to be flexible but concrete enough to accommodate different ways of organizing an International Studies introductory class.

Second, **global tensions** are the unintended resentments, frustrations, and conflicts that arise from global interactions. While our interconnected world creates many new kinds of opportunities and possibilities, global interactions also create winners and losers. New ideas and new ways of living rub against more traditional ones. While greater oversight from intergovernmental organizations can help solve collective problems and bring stability, such governance can make ordinary people and local politicians feel like they are losing control. While increased mobility in the world is exciting, the influx of populations from one place to another can spawn raw feelings of losing one's community and identity. These are among the many ways that interactions stimulate tension, a perspective that we think is essential to understand our contemporary world.

Third, **global forces** are powerful, cross-cutting drivers of global interactions and tensions. We focus attention on four primary forces that shape interactions and matter for almost any contemporary global challenge. *Global markets* is the reach and depth of supply and demand across borders. *Information and communications technology* power global online interactions and speed the spread and reach of ideas and information. *Shifting centers of power in the world* reflects how large, developing countries are rising to assert their power on a global stage in new and significant ways. *Global governance* is the way in which multiple institutions and actors seek to manage complex international issues by making and enforcing rules. Examine nearly any global problem that faces our world today, and we argue that these forces are fundamental to how the issue plays out and to how solutions could be crafted.

The idea of *inside-out and outside-in* interactions focuses attention not only on exchanges across borders. Interactions across borders, or from the outside-in, is clearly one dimension of International Studies. But actors, institutions, and ideas from *within* countries exert influence on the world, and they often shape and reshape products and meanings that come from outside traditional boundaries of state or nation. Disciplines that focus on the micro-level, such as Anthropology, are especially attentive to these inside-out dimensions. International Studies as the study of outside-in and inside-out interactions is, therefore, a concrete and relatable way of incorporating interdisciplinarity without highlighting interdisciplinarity per se.

The Organization of the Book

International Studies has two major parts. *Part 1: Foundations* introduces core concepts and major actors that appear throughout the textbook, including multinational corporations, states, markets, intergovernmental organizations, and civil society. Chapters in *Part 1* are intended to be short. The goal is not to downplay the importance of social scientific concepts—indeed, their importance is very much *the point* of this entire endeavor—but rather to provide students with a basic understanding of core concepts and terms in order to get the most out of later chapters. We also believe that International Studies students need that conceptual foundation; moving away from disciplines does not mean abandoning rigor.

There are six chapters in the Foundations section. *Chapter 1: The Making of Our Global Age* provides students with a broad chronological account of the first and second global ages, spanning the mid-1800s to the early 1900s and post-1990s, respectively. We explain to students that our present global age is not new, inevitable, or irreversible. We incorporate a variety of examples, including Reddit, colonialism, the Gold Standard, and China's (re)emergence.

Chapter 2: States contends that states have been, and remain, the key actors in the world. Understanding what states are, where they came from, and how they work in theory and in practice is crucial for understanding the subsequent chapters, especially chapters on intergovernmental organizations as well as civil society.

Chapter 3: Intergovernmental Organizations (IGOs) introduces students to the concepts of realism, liberalism and constructivism, and places IGOs in relation to other international actors. We explain to students what roles IGOs perform and we provide a detailed case study of United Nations bodies.

Chapter 4: Civil Society introduces students to the Tocquevillian and Gramscian views of civil society, which helps frame debates concerning the nature and impact of transnational advocacy networks and global social movements. We draw examples from anti-poverty, LGBT, and animal rights movements.

Chapter 5: Social Identities and Culture focuses attention on how ideas, meanings, and identities are fundamental to how people behave and how the world works. We introduce students to some of the most important social identities and how they matter; we also discuss major traditions in the study of culture and why culture matters. We draw on examples from hip-hop, food, and women's health in Zambia, among others.

Chapter 6: Money introduces students to major concepts, trends, and debates in international trade, finance, and monetary systems. Topics include how global capitalism in the 21st century differs from what came before, and how trade is relatively simple in theory but controversial in practice. We draw examples from the 2007–08 Global Financial Crisis, the Trans-Pacific Partnership, the World Trade Organization, and the International Monetary Fund.

Part II of the book moves away from foundations to global challenges. In this section of the book, we focus on contemporary problems in the world that interest many students. These Global Challenges chapters are a little longer than the Foundations ones. We summarize major debates about the problems, but we also provide a number of examples and present data trends where possible. We also weave our framework and the material from the foundations section into our discussion of these contemporary global challenges, showing how the first half of the book illuminates an understanding of global problems.

Chapter 7: Democracy and Representation is about the struggle for freedom. We introduce students to the basic ways that democracy is defined and measured, to the historical trends in democratization, and to theories of why democracies survive or lapse into authoritarianism. We draw examples from the Arab uprisings, the Umbrella movement in Hong Kong, Mexico, and election tampering in the United States.

Chapter 8: Human Rights introduces students to the global human rights regime. That regime includes human rights treaties, institutions, regional bodies, and non-governmental organizations. We discuss broad debates about what kind of power the human rights regime has, and we draw examples from Myanmar, United Nations reporting on Eritrea, abortion in Ireland, and the Save Darfur movement.

Chapter 9: Development provides an overview of important terms in the study of development, such as purchasing power parity, human development, and the Gini Index of Inequality. We contrast explanations for the poverty of some countries through an exploration of markets and states, and we introduce students to ideas and research on modernization theory, dependency theory, development states, neoliberalism, and good governance, as well as debates around foreign aid. We bring in a variety of examples, such as research on cash transfers, the use of randomized controlled trials in development research, and the operations of the World Bank.

Chapter 10: Civil Wars and Terrorism introduces students to the contemporary security threats beyond interstate war. The chapter discusses major explanations of civil war onset, patterns and trends in warfare around the world, and the consequences of such wars. The chapter also discusses patterns and causes of terrorism as well as ways to counter it. The chapter ends with a discussion of cybersecurity issues. The chapter draws on examples from Syria and the Democratic Republic of Congo, primarily.

Chapter 11: Migration clarifies the difference between a refugee, a migrant, an asylum seeker, and a stateless person. We provide an overview of trends in migration over time and between countries. We guide students through debates concerning "brain drain" versus "brain gain" and through the controversial topic of how immigrants affect host countries. We also introduce topics including sex trafficking, modern slavery, and child labor, and we describe the patchy nature of global governance in the area.

Chapter 12: Global Health provides an overview of major health issues around the world. The chapter opens by making some fundamental distinctions about how global health is conceptualized. The chapter then discusses global health outcomes, and disparities in them, from maternal health, to infectious disease, to heart disease. The chapter takes a deeper dive on the global HIV and AIDS pandemic, tracing both the devastation it has caused and also the progress made in the area.

Chapter 13: Global Environment introduces students to some global environmental challenges, such as invasive species, but quickly turns to climate change as the most pressing contemporary environmental challenge. The chapter details the main causes of climate change, the effects of it, and the human and nonhuman consequences of it. Examples are drawn from around the world, but there is sustained discussion of the effects of climate change on access to clean water in the Himalayas.

Chapter 14: Global Food links the major theories of global food control to the food-versus-fuel debate. We explain the difference between the food security and food sovereignty approaches to global hunger. Our examples include global cocoa/chocolate commodity chains, the 2007 Global Food Crisis, Malthus, and *La Via Campesina*.

The Features of the Book

In addition to summarizing arguments and being careful about concepts, the book aims to be empirically rich. As the chapter summaries indicate, we thread case examples throughout the chapters. We also look for empirical trends and outcomes as well as ways to present them visually. The result, we hope, is a thick description, through words, tables, and figures, of the world around us.

We also introduce features that aim to illuminate our framework. Every chapter has at least one figure that plots the forces, interactions, and tensions under discussion. The feature is designed to help students conceptualize and make concrete the International Studies framework that anchors the book. Each chapter also has at least one International Studies from the Inside-out or Outside-in box. These boxes focus on a particular issue in a particular place and describe how inside-out or outside-in (or both) forces shape that issue.

Support for Instructors and Students

SAGE edge offers a robust online environment featuring an impressive array of free tools and resources for review, study, and further exploration, keeping both instructors and students on the cutting edge of teaching and learning. Learn more at **edge.sagepub.com/straus1e.**

SAGE edge for Students provides a personalized approach to help students accomplish their coursework goals in an easy-to-use learning environment.

- Mobile-friendly **eFlashcards** strengthen understanding of key terms and concepts.

- Mobile-friendly practice **quizzes** allow for independent assessment by students of their mastery of course material.

- **Learning objectives** reinforce the most important material.

SAGE edge for Instructors supports your teaching by making it easy to integrate quality content and create a rich learning environment for students.

- **Test banks** provide a diverse range of pre-written options as well as the opportunity to edit any question and/or insert your own personalized questions to effectively assess students' progress and understanding.

- Editable, chapter-specific **PowerPoint® slides** offer complete flexibility for creating a multimedia presentation for your course.

- **Instructor Manual** for each chapter includes a chapter summary, outline, learning objectives, discussion questions, and in-class activities.

About the Authors

Scott Straus: My first deep international experience, like many undergraduates, took place on a foreign study program. In my case, the program was in Kenya, where I studied the balancing act between pressing needs for development and the environmental demands to preserve Kenya's extraordinary patrimony of open space. I was interested in politics, and my program placed me in a family heavily involved in opposition politics. At that time, Kenya was undergoing a rapid transition from authoritarian, one-party rule to a more competitive process of multi-party competition. I had a life-changing experience in Kenya. I never knew how much politics could matter. I could feel the intense yearning of people all around me to be free from dictatorship and to live better lives. From my comfortable life in the United States, I had little to prepare me for police beating demonstrators and for the intense poverty we experienced in parts of Kenya, where an antibiotic eyedrop could make a huge difference in a child's life or a meal with meat was considered a luxury.

After graduating college, I traveled across Africa and eventually became a freelance journalist based in Nairobi, Kenya's capital. I began covering a range of topics, from politics, to the HIV crisis, to urban planning, to business, to conflict, and to reconciliation after wars ended. I ended up spending a good deal of time in the Great Lakes region of Africa, in particular in the countries of Rwanda, Burundi, and the Democratic Republic of Congo. That region was in the throes of some of the worst political violence seen in the world since the end of the Cold War. Rwanda had experienced a genocide in 1994. The Democratic Republic of Congo was undergoing the first of two massive wars that devastated the country. My experiences with violence and suffering in these countries, as well as the exceptionally difficult process of rebuilding states and repairing societies after war, also had a profound impact on me. I went on to graduate school in Political Science in which I wrote a dissertation that examined the sources of genocide in Rwanda.

After becoming a professor, I continued my focus on armed conflict, human rights, and genocide. I expanded my field research into West and Central Africa. But as my interest in International Studies developed, I also traveled to other world regions—in Latin America, Europe, Asia, and the South Pacific. The more that I observed, the more that I read, and the more that I understood, the more convinced I became of the awesome complexity and fluidity of the world in which we live. International Studies offers a unique approach to understanding that complexity and to capturing how exciting and sometimes scary the world can be.

 **Barry Driscoll:** My first memorable international experience was traveling from my home in Ireland to see the embalmed corpse of Mao Zedong, Chairman of the Chinese Communist Party, in his final resting place in Tiananmen Square. Before visiting, I had read that even the current government admitted that "grave mistakes" were made during Mao's time, but to my surprise I encountered emotional and tearful crowds of mostly elderly Chinese mourning the deceased leader. Later that afternoon, I tucked into a burger and fries at an A&W restaurant, a U.S. fast-food chain that had recently opened its doors in China. *Burgers & Mao* could easily have been the title of any number of books on globalization I read at the time.

Over time, through travel and work with international governmental and non-governmental organizations, in countries as dissimilar as Mongolia and Madagascar, I developed my interest in the problem of global poverty. Today I teach at Grinnell College, an undergraduate liberal arts college. Despite its setting in a small Midwestern town, the student body is highly diverse: one in four students come from outside the United States, and one in five students are U.S. students of color.

All college instructors know how hard it can be to put oneself in the mind of a 19-year-old from Indiana or Arizona, not to mention Pakistan or Brazil. It can be hard to visualize what undergraduates know, what they would like to know, or what they "ought" to know. But class discussions in small groups with Grinnell's diverse student body helped me appreciate something that guided my writing: students already know the world is complex. What they need help with is making the world appear less bewildering or chaotic.

Years ago, I found myself in conversation with Scott about the kind of textbook we wanted to see. I wanted a textbook that understood its primary mission to be excellence in covering basic terms, concepts, and debates. The textbook should not be complex, ideological, or discipline-specific, yet it should embrace nuance and expose students to leading social scientific research. Looking back, I see what seemed a modest set of aims was actually a high bar. I hope readers will appreciate the book's ambition and feel it succeeded.

Acknowledgments

We learned and benefited from many in the course of writing this book. A huge thank-you to Elise Frasier, who commissioned and developed this book; Elise has a remarkable eye for snappy phrases and compelling ideas. She has been a joy with whom to work from start to finish. We also deeply appreciate the editorial and production team at CQ Press, including Scott Greenan, Sarah Christensen, Sheree Van Vreede, David Felts, Jennifer Jones, and others. They have exercised much good judgment and professionalism in the process. We would also like to acknowledge those who contributed their feedback throughout the lengthy review process, including Mneesha Gellman, Emerson College; Michael Greenwald, Texas A&M University; Brandon Kendhammer, Ohio University; Judy Krutky, Baldwin Wallace University; Timothy Lim, California State University–Los Angeles; Cecilia Manrique, University of Wisconsin–La Crosse; Anna Meyendorff, University of Michigan; Carrie Mott, University of Louisville; Sarah Muir, City College, CUNY; Philip Nash, Pennsylvania State University–Shenango; Farzeen Nasri, Ventura College; Bora Pajo, Mercyhurst College; Nancy Stefureak, Brock University; David Swanz, Colby-Sawyer College; Faedah Totah, Virginia Commonwealth University; Daniel Weiner, Ohio University; Jonathan Weiler, University of North Carolina; and Roland Wilson, George Mason University. Last, Kate Carter, Kyra Fox, and Emma Sayner all contributed research assistance to the book, and we thank them for it.

Introduction

GLOBAL INTERACTIONS AND GLOBAL TENSIONS

Fur Pelts for Sale

Flickr user Joe Ross, https://www.flickr.com/photos/joeross/6743972159. Licensed under CC BY-SA 2.0, https://creativecommons.org/licenses/by-sa/2.0/.

In rural Wisconsin, near to one of our homes, lives a middle-aged man named Jim. Jim is a trapper. He traps raccoons, beavers, and coyotes, among other animals. When working, he prefers to wear camouflage outfits bought from a local superstore that caters to farmers, a Farm and Fleet, and he drives a highly accessorized Ranger all-terrain vehicle (ATV) that is the envy of many of his neighbors.

At one level, Jim would seem cut off from the rest of the world. Rural Wisconsin is not cosmopolitan New York, Shanghai, Paris, or Rio de Janeiro. Jim's town has a few thousand residents; it is fairly isolated. The main issues of the day are local, such as whether to issue a bond for a new public school in the area. Jim lives off the land. But ask Jim about trapping, as one of us did recently, and he was quick to answer that business was really bad. Why? His answer opined on the state of the economy in

Russia and China. It turns out the price of fur pelts depends on demand in those countries, which in turn is connected to the global price of oil (in Russia) and global consumer demand (in China).

The global connections do not stop there. The company Polaris makes Jim's Ranger. Based near Minneapolis, Minnesota, Polaris is a manufacturer of snowmobiles, ATVs, motorcycles, and a variety of other motorized equipment. Polaris conducts business worldwide. The company has distributers in countries on all five continents, from Algeria and Afghanistan to Tanzania and Venezuela. Although its main manufacturing sites are in the United States, Polaris also makes vehicles in India, China, France, Mexico, and Poland. At our local Farm and Fleet, the clothing for sale—socks, T-shirts, dress shirts, hats, and boots, in addition to Jim's waders and camouflage jacket—is made in factories around the world, from Bangladesh and Sri Lanka to Morocco and Mauritius.

The reality is that our lives—even the most local ones—are embedded in international networks (see Figure Intro.1). This is the case in North America and other parts of what scholars call the "Global North," which in addition to Canada and the United States loosely includes most of Europe and the most developed parts of East Asia, in particular, Japan. Not only are the vehicles we drive, the oil with which we supply them, and the clothes we wear often sourced from around the world, but so is much of the food and drink that we consume. Our colleges and universities attract students from around the world, and students in turn elect to study in many parts of the globe. Our phones instantly connect us to a global online supply of information.

FIGURE INTRO.1

Mapping Our International Networks

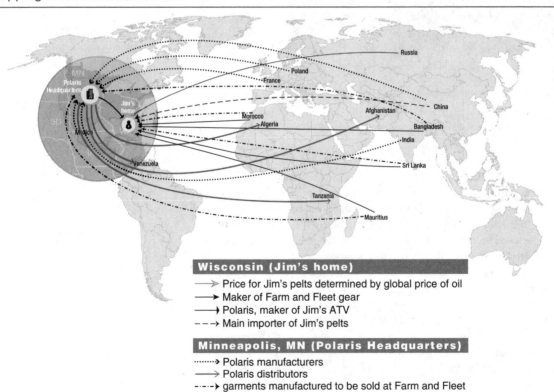

Wisconsin (Jim's home)
⟶➤ Price for Jim's pelts determined by global price of oil
⟶➤ Maker of Farm and Fleet gear
⟶➤ Polaris, maker of Jim's ATV
- - -➤ Main importer of Jim's pelts

Minneapolis, MN (Polaris Headquarters)
·······➤ Polaris manufacturers
⟶➤ Polaris distributors
-·-·-➤ garments manufactured to be sold at Farm and Fleet

The situation is similar in the Global South. In the most dynamic economies, such as in China, India, and Brazil, people's lives are buzzing with both global and local influences. On the one hand, their consumer goods are the same as those in the United States. Indians use cars, motorcycles, computers, refrigerators, and kettles made in India and other countries. Indians watch television with stations from around the world. Their news is both global and local, as it is for those of us in the United States.

Many citizens in these countries own cell phones or smartphones. In fact, Apple recently sold more than 60 million iPhones every three months, and more were sold in China than in any other country.[1] Citizens all over the Global South thus have access to content on websites like Facebook and Twitter that is generated from people and organizations around the world. Mobile phones around the world are not just for watching cats playing piano. They have become

M-Pesa

essential tools in the management of everyday life. In Kenya, for example, mobile banking—whereby even at a stall in an open market you can pay with a mobile phone for rice or fruit—has taken the country by storm. The mobile money transfer system initially developed in East Africa now has spread to countries in Europe, the Middle East, South Asia, and other parts of Africa. This is just one example.

The field of international studies pays particular attention to these forms of global interconnections. They are part of our lives—and people's lives all around the world—in many visible and invisible ways. Start to ask questions about the objects, the tools, and the information around you in your daily life, and you will see very quickly how internationally embedded your everyday life is. The same is true today for people around the world. The dense, deep, and constant global interactions are at the heart of international studies.

International studies, however, does not consider our world and the interactions that structure it as uniformly positive. Our interconnections also produce tension, conflict, and new forms of domination. Consider information technology. The power and reach of information technology provide governments with a newfound ability to surveil, control, and censor. While mobile banking has taken off in Kenya, in nearby Ethiopia, the government has purchased technology that allows it to spy on opposition political forces. The international connections run deeper. An Italian company, Hacking Team, sold it to Ethiopia, and we know this because other global actors, in this case Wikileaks, published a record of the relationship between the private Italian technology company and the Ethiopian government.[2]

International studies recognizes that global interactions can be fraught with tension and bad outcomes. The power of states to exploit information technology to control and spy is one example. Another is employment dislocation. As global economic interdependence deepens, companies find it easier to relocate factories to places where production is cheaper. That might lower costs for consumers, but factory relocation often puts people out of work. In our globally connected world, migration has become easier. Yet migrants who look different and have different customs from the majority population in a country can become targets of resentment and hatred. Our interconnected world creates many new possibilities, but it also creates many new tensions and problems, often in invisible and complex ways.

These examples point to the interconnected and complicated world in which we live. It is a world marked by **globalization**, which through markets and information shrinks the space that separates people and connects them through products and ideas. It is a world with tremendous possibility and opportunity, in which technological advances and the flows of information, people, and material can improve and even transform lives. But it is also a world with winners and losers, where global markets and other global forces can negatively impact lives and reinforce inequality.

As a body of thought and teaching, international studies invites students to learn about and, in particular, to analyze and make sense of our complex world. At the same time, international studies can seem vague. What is international studies? What is an international studies approach? In this book, we develop a new approach, one that we hope will help you understand your world better and provide you with the analytic foundations for a lifetime of learning. It is that framework and the core ideas in international studies that we detail in the remainder of the chapter.

A FRAMEWORK FOR INTERNATIONAL STUDIES

International studies is the study of global interactions, the tensions those interactions produce, and the forces and actors that play a role in them. **Global interactions** are the myriad ways in which people, things, information, and ideas intersect in our world. Global interactions are the raw material of international studies. By focusing on global interactions, we can start asking a specific set of questions about issues or events taking place in the world. Who and what is interacting? From where do those interactions come? What are the policies and institutions that facilitate and govern those interactions?

International studies is concerned with the **global tensions** that result from these interactions. Our world and the interactions that structure it are not only a source of commonality and community but also rife with tension and conflict. Inequality is baked into our world order. Millions suffer who need not. Billions live on a dollar a day while others jet around the world on private planes. Many of the global challenges we discuss in this textbook are actually *tensions*, such as climate change or civil war, that have resulted from *interactions*.

We describe international studies as providing an **inside-out and outside-in perspective**. This means that we consider actors and events at the global level—such as the United Nations, the Organization of American States, or human trafficking—to be no more or no less important than actors and events that occur within states—such as domestic politics, ethnic groups, labor unions, or life in slums. It is important to understand how "the local" affects "the global" as well as how "the global" affects "the local."

Last, international studies is primarily interested in contemporary issues and challenges. International studies is not a single scholarly discipline, such as sociology or history. Rather, we are primarily concerned with the global challenges of the day, and we draw from across established scholarly disciplines for the analytical tools to help understand them. See Figure Intro.2 for an illustration of how all of these pieces of the framework fit together.

In the sections that follow, we will further explore these concepts by illustrating what we mean by interactions leading to tensions, and we will explain the necessity for taking both "inside-out" and "outside-in" views of global issues and challenges—an exploration that will take us back to Wisconsin, and Jim.

globalization: multidimensional and transnational ways in which people, things, information, and ideas interact and are interconnected across space and time.

international studies: study of global interactions, the tensions those interactions produce, and the forces and actors that play a role in them.

global interactions: ways in which people, things, information, and ideas intersect across and within borders.

global tensions: resentments, frustrations, and conflicts that arise from global interactions.

inside-out and outside-in perspective: approach that emphasizes looking at bottom-up, within-country processes and looking at top-down, international processes that cut across national borders.

International Studies Framework

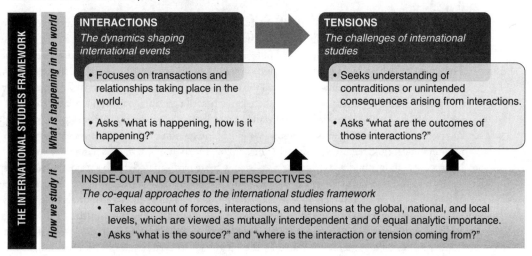

International studies is the study of global interactions, the tensions those interactions produce, and the forces and actors that shape them. It seeks to explain those interactions and tensions by analyzing them from both "outside-in" and "inside-out" perspectives.

THE INTERNATIONAL STUDIES FRAMEWORK

What is happening in the world

INTERACTIONS
The dynamics shaping international events

- Focuses on transactions and relationships taking place in the world.
- Asks "what is happening, how is it happening?"

TENSIONS
The challenges of international studies

- Seeks understanding of contradictions or unintended consequences arising from interactions.
- Asks "what are the outcomes of those interactions?"

How we study it

INSIDE-OUT AND OUTSIDE-IN PERSPECTIVES
The co-equal approaches to the international studies framework
- Takes account of forces, interactions, and tensions at the global, national, and local levels, which are viewed as mutually interdependent and of equal analytic importance.
- Asks "what is the source?" and "where is the interaction or tension coming from?"

GLOBAL INTERACTIONS

Interactions occur whenever people come into contact, whenever they share ideas, or whenever they exchange objects with others. So, for instance, interactions can be about the movement of people across borders—as economic migrants, as refugees, as tourists, or as students. Interactions can be about the movement of goods and services across borders—from the food we eat, to the clothing we wear, to the music we hear, to the movies we watch, to the cars that we drive. Interactions can be about the movement of ideas across borders—ideas about gender equality, about the value of free markets, or about religion. Interactions can be about the movement of money across borders—from huge sums of currency or stock market trades, to small remittances of migrants in one country to their families back home. Interactions can also be social and political. They include the ways in which activists in one country may lobby on behalf of people in another country or the way in which intergovernmental organizations (IGOs) like the United Nations may deploy troops from many countries to help stabilize another country. In sum, by focusing on interactions, international studies allows us to study the multiple, overlapping types of exchanges that take place across and within national borders.

To return to the earlier examples, international studies illuminates the web of international relationships that influence Jim's life. One perspective might see Jim as someone who lives a life shorn of international interactions. He does not travel internationally. He rarely uses e-mail. But an international studies perspective draws our attention to the ways that his life is nonetheless entwined in international webs of interactions.

As noted, global interactions are not always benign. Connecting people through migration, goods, information, and ideas creates tension and friction alongside possibility and opportunity. Ignoring the tensions provides a one-sided and misleading view of our contemporary world and the dynamics that drive it.

What counts as a tension? When the price of subsistence food or even water is subjected to global markets (an interaction), that can lead to real hardship and ultimately to protest, as it has in places such as Mexico and Bolivia. Those economic outcomes and the political protests are examples of tensions. The airing of certain movies and television shows in which women dress in short sleeves and skirts (an interaction) can unintentionally offend the tastes of traditionalists (a tension). To some observers, the rise of *jihadist* organizations such as the Islamic State (a tension) points to a backlash against the forces of globalization (an interaction). Islamic State leaders proclaim an aversion to Western values and power as domineering and dangerous, via global interactions, to Islamic values. At the same time, to communicate and recruit, the Islamic State employs the tools of international interactions: YouTube, Internet chat rooms, and texting connect an Islamic State partisan in Syria to a resident in Minneapolis, while global transportation networks enable the movement of would-be militants from England to Yemen. As you can see, interactions give rise to tensions, which give rise to other interactions, and so on.

Let's consider another example of how tensions—in both positive and negative forms—can flow from interactions: the International Criminal Court (ICC). The ICC is at one level a pinnacle for human rights on a global scale. Based in the Hague (Netherlands), the ICC tries individuals for crimes of genocide, crimes against humanity, and war crimes when domestic courts are unable or unwilling to prosecute such crimes. The premise is that these are global crimes, crimes that offend a universal sense of humanity. The ICC is one of the most potent symbols of the global reach of intergovernmental organizations. States around the world become members of the ICC, and the court's jurisdiction in turn extends to those states and in some cases beyond. The court itself is a site of multiple interactions—of lawyers and investigators from around the world, of members state from around the world, and of ideas of international human rights that in theory apply to all people everywhere. In some cases, the court has taken bold measures. For example, the court issued an arrest warrant for Omar al-Bashir, the president of Sudan, on charges of committing genocide and crimes against humanity. Think about that for a moment: An international court based in the Netherlands indicted a sitting president of Sudan for massive crimes against civilians. For some, such a move is the epitome of the promise of human rights: to declare some crimes so horrible that they shock humanity and should be punishable in an international court.

When considered from another perspective, however, how would you feel if the president of your country were indicted by an international court? Perhaps not surprisingly, the court has aroused significant opposition among leaders in Africa and the Philippines, where to date the court has focused most of its cases. As a result, although some human rights activists see the ICC as the institution that can finally hold the perpetrators of the worst human rights crimes accountable for the worst human rights crimes, others in Africa and elsewhere see the court as an example of colonial-style power of the powerful over the weak. They see the court as imposing values on African states and disallowing Africans to solve their own problems—even if many African states had previously endorsed the court. In short, the ICC inspires tension and friction even while for some advocates it is the realization of a dream of universal punishment for the worst crimes. The examples are many. An international studies perspective brings these possible tensions into focus.

International Studies and Globalization

WHAT IS THE DIFFERENCE?

Is international studies any different from the study of globalization? They certainly overlap. In general, we are relaxed about using the two terms throughout the book, but we argue that they are not the same. The first problem with the term "globalization" is that it has come to mean many things to many people. To some, globalization represents Americanization or McDonaldization, which means it is a process by which American actors, especially U.S. corporations and the U.S. military, and American ideas, including consumerism and individualism, extend their domination across the world at the expense of non-U.S. societies. But to others, globalization is a new age of reason, in which oppressive governments and poverty are becoming things of the past, and the fruits of which are globally minded citizens connected online and feeling unbound by national borders. For our purposes, however, a term that can mean such different things, while being so provocative, is not useful.

Second, globalization usually refers to a specific historical period. Our current global era is probably only a few decades old. Societies go through phases of lesser or greater connectivity and interaction. International studies focuses on big global issues, but it is not tied to a specific historical period. So, globalization is a period in time, while international studies is an approach to studying the world at any time.

To make this point highlights the ways in which the history of the world is not marching progressively forward in some linear fashion. Our interconnected world also creates tension and conflict, sometimes in unpredictable ways, between actors within and across states.

AN INSIDE-OUT/OUTSIDE-IN APPROACH

International studies has a predominant focus on global issues. In that, international studies shares much with other fields of study, such as the international relations subfield of political science. Whereas international relations focuses mostly on what states are doing internationally and how that affects people within borders (i.e., from the outside-in), an international studies approach looks *also* at global processes from the inside-out, where "inside" means within a country. In other words, international studies takes seriously domestic, grassroots actors and bottom-up interactions in particular places, and the international studies approach seeks to adopt their perspectives on global problems as well.

International studies pays close attention to local context and to local meanings with the understanding that global processes and globalization occur in particular places. For example, human trafficking is global, yet each instance of a trafficked human does not take place "in a globe," but in a specific location, and that specific location has a specific history and culture. If the topic is climate change, global health, or global poverty, an international studies approach will take seriously not only the global forces at work in shaping these issues but also how livelihoods and attitudes in particular places are fundamentally important.

To return to the examples at the start of the chapter, one aspect of the spread of global markets is the spread of information technology. One approach to understanding that phenomenon would be to examine the global supply chains, the global flow of goods and services across borders, and the global financial markets that contribute to the production of an iPhone and that allow it to be sold all over the world. Indeed, different parts of the iPhone are made in different parts of the world, even if designed in California, and sold in almost every country of the world. These are outside-in perspectives: to look at how global markets shape consumer choices around the world and are embedded in global supply chains, underpinned by economic policy that allows capital and goods to move easily across borders. International studies examines these processes, as we do later in the book.

But international studies also takes much more domestic, locally rooted processes into account. For example, on the question of iPhones, how do people in different countries use their technology? How do they inflect their own values, ideas, and priorities into their uses of smartphones? To Indians in New Delhi, are iPhones used in the same ways that New Yorkers in the United States use their iPhones? Are they used for social purposes, like connecting with friends or finding dates? Are they used for economic purposes, like selling in online marketplaces or checking market information like crop prices? Or are they used for purposes of identity, such as the desire to be seen with a smartphone? Moreover, an inside-out perspective might disaggregate the category of "Indians" to look at differences among economic classes, among religions, among language groups, or among gender groups. Those bottom-up, micro-level considerations that ground disciplines such as anthropology and sociology are as important as the top-down, macro-level concerns that often ground international relations or international political economy. This focus on *both* outside-in and inside-out processes *defines* international studies.

GLOBAL FORCES

As you know by now, international studies is all about global interactions and the tensions that result. But what is driving these interactions? We focus on four specific global forces, which we argue are major influences on the contemporary world and matter for every global problem described throughout the book. These **global forces** structure interactions that drive change in the world. The four forces are as follows:

global forces: particularly powerful, cross-cutting drivers of global interactions and tensions. Global forces matter on almost any global issue. They are specific to our present global age.

- *Global markets.* This is the reach and depth of supply and demand across borders. Through changes in communication, transportation, government policy, and computer technology, global markets are deep and powerful and they play a major role in all of our lives, as the examples of Jim and smartphone users in New Delhi make clear.

- *Information and communications technology.* Whereas much of the world was once cut off and limited from communication outside their home areas, today cell phone penetration is nearly universal. Information and communications technology power global online interactions, reshape the spread of information, and even impact security and elections around the world. These developments intersect with global markets, but information and communications technology are a distinct force shaping the world today.

- *Shifting centers of power in the world.* In the past, the highly industrialized states of the global north—in western Europe, North America, and Japan—dominated world politics and global economics. That is no longer the case. Now global affairs are affected by the rise of large, developing countries, such as China, Russia, Brazil, India, Indonesia, Iran, Turkey, Mexico, Vietnam, Nigeria, and South Africa. While the advanced industrialized countries remain influential, to be sure, several countries with immense populations are growing economically and asserting their power on a global stage in new and significant ways.

- *Global governance.* This is the way in which multiple institutions and actors seek to manage complex international issues by making and enforcing rules. Global governance includes creating institutions to make rules as well as to monitor and enforce those rules across borders. We make two observations. First, global governance is *crowded*. Rule-making, rule enforcement, and rule management for global issues is no longer the unique purview of states. Today, a large range of actors enter into that process of governance— intergovernmental organizations, nongovernmental organizations (NGOs), advocacy networks, businesses, and even citizens are shaping public discourse about how to manage global issues. Second, global governance is *uneven*: There are major global issues where global governance is present, such as trade and nuclear weapons, as well as areas where there is no global agreement or governing authority, such as climate change or global finance.

Let's look at these global forces in greater detail. Figure Intro.3 also shows how our global forces fit into the overall framework.

FIGURE INTRO.3

Global Forces

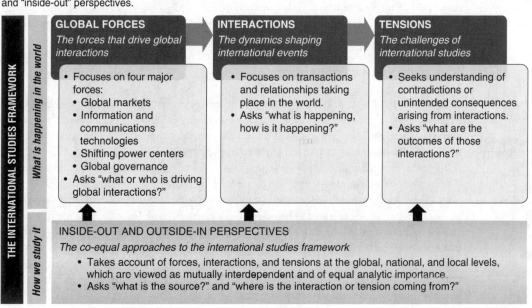

International studies is the study of global interactions, the tensions those interactions produce, and the forces and actors that shape them. It seeks to explain those interactions and tensions by analyzing them from both "outside-in" and "inside-out" perspectives.

THE INTERNATIONAL STUDIES FRAMEWORK

What is happening in the world

GLOBAL FORCES
The forces that drive global interactions

- Focuses on four major forces:
  - Global markets
  - Information and communications technologies
  - Shifting power centers
  - Global governance
- Asks "what or who is driving global interactions?"

INTERACTIONS
The dynamics shaping international events

- Focuses on transactions and relationships taking place in the world.
- Asks "what is happening, how is it happening?"

TENSIONS
The challenges of international studies

- Seeks understanding of contradictions or unintended consequences arising from interactions.
- Asks "what are the outcomes of those interactions?"

How we study it

INSIDE-OUT AND OUTSIDE-IN PERSPECTIVES
The co-equal approaches to the international studies framework

- Takes account of forces, interactions, and tensions at the global, national, and local levels, which are viewed as mutually interdependent and of equal analytic importance.
- Asks "what is the source?" and "where is the interaction or tension coming from?"

Global Markets

global markets: arena in which goods and services are traded across borders.

Our first global force driving interactions is **global markets** or what some people call "economic globalization." Several elements of global markets—trade, finance, and production—each drive interactions between societies, and each can produce tensions.

global trade: buying and selling of goods and services across borders.

Growth of Trade. The first way economic globalization constitutes a global force that drives interactions is the enormity of **global trade**, which we can think of as the cross-border movement of commercial goods (i.e., physical things for sale). The volume of that trade has exploded over time. In 1953, world merchandise trade was worth $84 billion in U.S. dollars, but in 2008, it was worth $15.7 *trillion*.[3] Because economies are so interconnected, and because of the speed with which goods, money, and information can flow, economic events in one corner of the globe have ripple effects that are felt far away.

For example, when China made its currency cheaper in 2015, it raised unemployment in Zambia. Why? Because investors knew that China devaluing its currency meant China was worried about its future economic growth. Investors then speculated that China's trading partners, like Zambia, would suffer as a result, so they sold their investments in copper, which is Zambia's major export. Lower prices for copper meant lower profitability for copper mining companies in Zambia, which responded by laying off workers. This all happened in the space of one month. While China represented an export market for Zambia, it also increased Zambia's sensitivity (or vulnerability) to developments in China.

distributional effects: how distinct people or places are differentially affected by an event, such as a change in taxation or import of a product.

Trade also acts as a global force because of what are called **distributional effects** within countries, meaning that there are winners and losers from trade. For example, many of western Europe's manufacturing industries moved to Southeast Asia over the past decades. Although some people have moved from factories to office jobs in things like finance or insurance, it also led to unemployment and political agitation by working-class voters who were harmed. In some countries, unions that represented the workers became staunch opponents of trade liberalization, including the free movement of migrant workers. Today, many industrialized countries have strong anti-immigrant and xenophobic political parties. So, when boats carrying Arab or African refugees capsize off the Italian coast, we should see the connection between a decline in European manufacturing decades ago, the decline in public support for immigration that resulted, and reluctance in Europe today to help even the most desperate migrants.

financial globalization: how people and places are linked through the cross-border flow of finance, such as foreign direct investment or the trading of stocks and bonds.

Growth of Finance. The growth of global finance or what some call **financial globalization** refers to flows of money around the world. This activity is centered on the world's major stock markets, where one can buy shares in a Chinese company through the Shanghai stock market, where a Costa Rican can buy shares in Germany's heavy industries, or where a German can buy and sell the currencies of Canada or Japan. Up until a few decades ago, however, one could not simply invest in whichever country one pleased. Many countries, including developed economies, placed limits on how much money could come in and out of their economy. But today about 75% of countries have stock markets.[4] The value of all the shares traded is in the tens of trillions of dollars. This does not even include bond markets, in which investors trade in loans to governments or corporations, which itself involves tens of billions in annual transactions. Although most countries, rich or poor, seek investment, not all money flowing into an economy is good. Let's look at two examples of how money floating about in the international economy can produce tensions when it moves in and out of a state's borders.

The price of oil was high in the 2000s. This was good news for oil-exporting countries like Saudi Arabia and Russia. As they exported billions of barrels of oil, the world repaid them by pumping billions of dollars into their government bank accounts. Oil exporters then deposited the money in the world's largest private banks to earn interest. Eager to put the money to work, banks in turn loaned this money elsewhere, creating "easy money," meaning loans (credit) that were cheap for borrowers. Some of it was loaned to developing countries hungry for investment, but it was also loaned to consumers in places like Dublin and Arizona who were happy to have low interest rates on mortgages and credit cards. But once some borrowers could not repay—such as home owners in Cincinnati or the government of Greece—banks announced that they had loaned out too much money. It is tempting to think of the U.S. mortgage crisis of 2008 as being caused when people irresponsibly took out mortgages they could not afford. But there were deeper causes to be found in the growth of global finance, in which banks eager to loan their money engaged in risky lending.

The second example of tensions arising from the force of global finance comes with currency speculation. Imagine you took out a loan of just £1 from a British bank, which is $1 in U.S. dollars. If the British pound declines in value ($1 now buys you £2), then paying back that loan becomes slightly cheaper. You took out the loan for $1, but repaying a £1 loan now costs you only 50 U.S. cents, since $1 equals £2. You just made 50 cents! Now imagine you did this with $1 *billion*. This economic activity is so large it makes the news. People know you took out the loan because you think the value of the British currency is about to go down (that is, depreciate), and you are such an enormous economic actor that your actions affect the market. This is one way a currency speculator can make money.

Scaled up, this kind of behavior can have dramatic negative consequences and generate a great deal of tension. In the late 1990s, currency speculation crashed several Asian economies. That prompted the Malaysian prime minister to complain that "society must be protected from unscrupulous profiteers. Currency traders have become rich—very, very rich—through making other people poor."[5] He was referring to the ability of foreigners to buy and sell bits of Malaysia—in this case, its currency—with no intention of investing but buying and selling for quick gain. This is why some describe the growth of global finance as financial *hyper* globalization because excessive global finance imperils the ability of countries to manage their own affairs.[6]

Internationalization of Production. The internationalization of production means the proliferation of business activity across the globe. When a company expands abroad by building or buying a factory in a foreign country, that activity is called **foreign direct investment (FDI)**, and the company is then a **multinational corporation (MNC)**. The world's stock of FDI—the total amount of foreign investment everywhere in the world—went from less than $1 billion in 1980 to over $26 *trillion* in 2008.[7] The MNCs engaged in these investments number in the tens of thousands, and they employ almost 100 million people worldwide. But they are overwhelmingly headquartered in industrialized countries: 92 of the largest 100 MNCs are headquartered in just the United States, western Europe, or Japan.[8]

Although we are aware of global U.S. companies like Coca Cola and General Electric, you might be surprised to know that some of the largest public companies in the world are Chinese, and that many products we think of as American are not: Budweiser (Belgium), 7-Eleven (Japan), Popsicle (England). So the internationalization of production is not a U.S. phenomenon. Moreover, about half of all goods imported into the United States are "intra-firm," which is when a company trades with itself. For example, when a car manufacturer in Kentucky imports tires from a rubber factory it owns in Malaysia, that is an intra-firm trade.

foreign direct investment (FDI): ownership and management of a productive asset in another country, such as owning a factory or farm.

multinational corporation (MNC): corporation that undertakes production in more than one country. Also known as a *transnational corporation (TNC).*

expropriation: when a government seizes a privately owned company, sometimes by force and often with little or no compensation.

race to the bottom: theory that countries competitively lower their labor and environmental standards in order to attract foreign investment.

information and communications technology (ICT): information technology plus a variety of audio and visual communications technology, such as smartphones and television networks.

information flows: spread of knowledge, ideas, words, and images across borders.

Over the past few decades, most FDI has gone from one developed country to another, not to developing countries. In recent years, however, this has started to change, with developing countries receiving almost half of all FDI, with most going to Asia and especially China. FDI also creates major tensions within developing countries. In return for companies investing billions to construct heavy machinery to extract these materials, and for paying the highly educated engineers to operate them, governments offer things like no taxation of company profits for several years, relocation of local people from the area, or relaxation of environmental or labor standards.

Two tensions commonly result. First, the risk of **expropriation**, meaning government seizes the MNC's assets (its mines, equipment, machines, etc.) and requires it to be publicly owned. Such nationalization was common in developing countries several decades ago, especially with utilities like electric plants and with natural resources like oil and gas. Second, some scholars are concerned about a **race to the bottom** among developing countries, who are eager to weaken labor laws and environmental protections in order to attract investment.

Information and Communications Technology

At different points in international history, new forms of **information and communications technology (ICT)** have shrunk time and space, bringing people around the world closer together. Items such as the Morse Code, the telegraph, the radio, the printing press, a global postal system, and of course the telephone allowed people around the world to communicate with each other more efficiently and cheaply than ever before. The contemporary period, however, differs from previous ones in the scale and intensity of the effects of ICT. During the last 50 years, investment and development in these technologies have been massive, and the result has been the availability of more efficient, cheaper, faster, and more sophisticated devices.

Also crucial is the distribution of ICT. In previous periods, the global elite had the primary access to technologies such as the telegraph or the printing press. True, the Bible and the Koran reached large audiences via the printing press, and radio was a cheap means of communication with widespread adoption. But today advanced ICT touches all parts of the world. The Internet provides a remarkably cheap and instantaneous mechanism for communication within and across borders. In sum, advances in technology are having, and are likely to continue to have, significant implications on the lives of most human beings on the planet and on many global problems. Many observers consider ours the "information age" and our society a "network society."[9] These terms reflect the significance of ICT in the contemporary globe.

In recent decades, there has been a remarkable expansion of access to ICT, as well as an expansion of cross-border **information flows**. The parents of many students enrolled in college today did not grow up with a computer in their home or a cell phone. When they did get them, their first computers were likely clunky, slow, and heavy pieces of equipment that had primitive access to information, primarily through floppy disks. Computers then—until the mid-1990s—did not have access to the Internet and e-mail; when they did, it was through a dial-up modem.

That was only some 20 years ago. How things have changed! Today in the United States most families will have access to at least one computer—some 84% of households own at least one computer and 75% of households use the Internet.[10] Most high school and college students have their own personal computers as well. To be sure, these statistics are averages; they mask inequalities that often present in terms of income, as well as in terms of race and ethnicity—the lower the household income, the less likely will be computer ownership and Internet usage, and the less English spoken at home, the less computer usage there is, to take two examples. Still, on a relative basis, these technologies have extremely wide usage and adoption.

But that story is not just one that applies to the United States. The rapid expansion has been replicated on the global stage. In the contemporary world, more than one third of the adults in the world regularly access the Internet. About three quarters of adults own a cell phone or have regular access to one. These numbers represent an extraordinary pace of increase, given that mobile phone subscriptions essentially began in the mid-1990s. Some 20 years later, the World Bank estimates that there are more than 6 billion mobile phone subscriptions worldwide. An infographic that the World Bank produced in 2012 tells the story very well (see Figure Intro.4). The graphic plots the number of mobile and landline subscriptions globally, compared with the global population growth and the history of the telephone. The Bank says that the spread of mobile technology is "unmatched in the history of technology."[11]

The global implications of this surge in access to mobile and Internet communications are huge. We are witnessing a remarkable **democratization of information**. Although Internet access is correlated to income level, the reality is that even the poorest in the lowest income countries today have access to cell phones. In contrast to centralized information systems, such as radio and television, the spread of ICT in the contemporary world is decentralized. Information is moving in literally millions of directions at any one moment in time, rather than information flowing from a central point to points of reception, which is the case with traditional forms of media. At the most basic level, people

democratization of information: ease and decentralized nature of how individuals may access and disseminate information using modern technology.

FIGURE INTRO.4

Sharp Global Increase in Mobile Phone Use

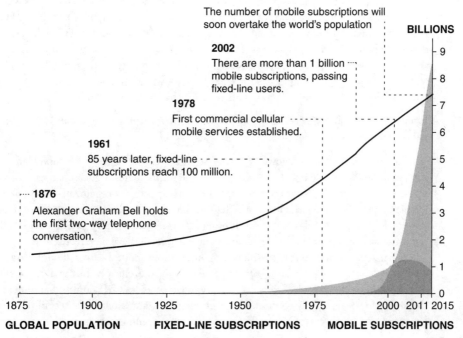

The number of mobile subscriptions will soon overtake the world's population

BILLIONS

2002
There are more than 1 billion mobile subscriptions, passing fixed-line users.

1978
First commercial cellular mobile services established.

1961
85 years later, fixed-line subscriptions reach 100 million.

1876
Alexander Graham Bell holds the first two-way telephone conversation.

1875 · 1900 · 1925 · 1950 · 1975 · 2000 · 2011 · 2015

9 · 8 · 7 · 6 · 5 · 4 · 3 · 2 · 1 · 0

GLOBAL POPULATION · **FIXED-LINE SUBSCRIPTIONS** · **MOBILE SUBSCRIPTIONS**

Source: World Bank, 2012. *Information and Communications for Development 2012: Maximizing Mobile*. Washington, DC: World Bank, http://www.worldbank.org/ict/IC4D2012, licensed under CC BY 3.0 https://creativecommons.org/licenses/by/3.0/.

cost of information: price to access and disseminate information; modern information and communications technology reduces the price drastically.

speed of information: rate at which information may be accessed and disseminated.

technology optimists: those who believe that technology will have broad and positive impacts on society, culture, and politics.

can communicate much more easily with each other, whether through texting or more sophisticated social networking sites. They can "self-communicate" as users of Facebook know well. People around the globe have the ability to access information from anywhere around the world instantaneously and cheaply. That is, the **cost of information** has decreased so remarkably that information is almost free to many Internet users around the world. With Google or some other search engine, millions of bits of information are available in a second or two. In other words, in addition to the cost, the **speed of information** flows has increased exponentially. People can "self-inform."

Global connectivity has the potential to affect many sectors. In politics, the ability to control information has become much more difficult. When repression takes place, people know—and they can communicate it almost instantaneously. Citizens can organize more effectively. They can coordinate protests through Twitter accounts and film atrocities if the police crack down on them. ICT should democratize the world. Information is power, and many now have low-cost access to it.

We can identify these views as those of **technology optimists**. They look at the world, and they see that whole swaths of the global population—some five billion people—will now have information connectivity that they never had before. In the optimists' view, the changes will be massive. In economics, people will be more productive than ever before. In finance, ordinary citizens and mega investors can affect trades immediately or move money around the world with great ease. In agriculture, local farmers can know through a text message what the market price of their product is. In health, consumers can research medicines and treatments without necessarily relying on physicians; they can receive text messages about when to take certain medications. Businesses can coordinate global supply chains in dozens of countries through sophisticated software. The depth of change is from politics, to finance, to agriculture, to health, to name a few. Soon computers will drive us to work and school! These are some of the key ideas that Eric Schmidt, the co-founder of Google, and Jared Cohen, a former adviser to the U.S. State Department and founder of Google Ideas, stressed in their 2013 book, *The New Digital Age: Transforming Nations, Businesses, and Our Lives.* In their words, the new age will see "every crime and atrocity caught on camera," "pills that tell your phone what's wrong with your body," "digital insurgencies bring down autocratic leaders," and "unprecedented power in the hands of people," among other major changes.

Watch Schmidt and Cohen at https://www.youtube.com/watch?v=QK9V5APXhTY or www.newdigitalage.com.

Technological advances, however, have also increased the capacity for surveillance, which can have profoundly anti-democratic effects. The same technologies that can harness people power to organize protests to challenge dictatorships also can help terrorist organizations recruit or radicalize people online. The same search engines that provide cheap access to streams of useful information also can lead to unhelpful or incorrect information. Yes, the Internet can help people self-diagnose, but it can also lead people to try crackpot therapies that will have no effectiveness.

Social networking applications allow us to know more about the lives of our friends and family; we can also be in touch with each other more quickly and cheaply. But in a major study, Sherry Turkle (2011), a professor of Science and Technology Studies at MIT, finds that humans are losing the ability to meaningfully connect with each other. We are "alone together" in the sense that we have removed ourselves and do not know how to have meaningful conversations with one another.

Compare Sherry Turkle's TED Talk to Jared Cohen's: https://www.ted.com/talks/sherry_ turkle_alone_together? language=en.

There are other, more skeptical voices in the technology debate. Like those who argue that the effects of markets will be to widen economic inequalities between populations around the globe, some claim that technology will benefit those who already have the skills and education to take advantage of such technology. Rather than leveling differences, as Cohen and Schmidt argue, information and communications technology will benefit the wealthy while doing little for the poor. The rich will get richer, and the lives of the rich will get even better, while the poor will remain in a steady state. Rather than being a source of innovation, according to some, the power of information and communications technology will allow big corporations to monitor, track, and target consumers better. In the end, big business will benefit. As with global markets, technology may undercut jobs. Where once humans did the work, now machines will. Last, in the realm of human rights, although it may be true that citizens around the world will know more and can harness that information to generate public pressure, such cyberactivism is often shallow. Will retweeting a page on atrocities in Myanmar make a difference to the human rights in that country? Does the information that recirculates make violence a show, distribute naive recommendations, and ultimately harm victims? These are the kinds of questions that some scholars have begun to ask.[12]

Shifting Centers of Global Power

The third global force reshaping the world is a reorganization of power. As we proceed through the 21st century, power will essentially shift from being concentrated in the hands of old, industrialized states in western Europe, North America, and Japan to a broader array of states as well as to other types of organizations, such as intergovernmental organizations, nongovernmental organizations, and multinational corporations. Some authors and politicians frame the issue as "American decline." Rather, alongside some other influential thinkers, we think the right framework is the diffusion of power rather than the decline of any one state in absolute terms. Rather than being the sole, dominant superpower, the United States will share the global stage increasingly with other states and organizations that have gained power compared with their power in the 20th century.

In the 18th, 19th, and 20th centuries, global power was divided between several European states and eventually the United States. Power was divided between several European states and eventually the United States. The major European powers were Britain, France, Germany, and to a lesser extent Spain and Portugal. There also were the key multinational empires: the Austro-Hungarian and the Ottoman empires, in particular. No one state dominated international relations, although Germany sought to establish worldwide domination in the two world wars, especially the second. After World War II, the world was primarily **bipolar**, or split between two major states—the United States and the Soviet Union. This period was also known as the Cold War because the two countries sought for primacy and prepared for war but never fought against each other directly. Then after the Soviet Union, we lived in a **unipolar** world in which the United States was hegemonic.

One central way that analysts express the coming global shift is the **rise of the rest**.[13] The main idea is that in the contemporary era, we shall witness the sustained growth and increased power of many large, developing countries. They are large both in terms of land mass but especially in terms of their population sizes. Central here is the rise of China, a country of some 1.38 billion people that has experienced a period of astonishing and consistent growth during the past three decades. Also key is the rise of India and Brazil, countries with 1.32 billion and 208 million people, respectively, where growth also has been sustained. Also in the mix are countries such as Indonesia, with 261 million people, Nigeria, Turkey, and others.

bipolar: idea that global power is bifurcated between two primary holders, e.g., between the United States and the Soviet Union during the Cold War.

unipolar: idea that a single power holder is dominant globally.

rise of the rest: expression indicating that nontraditionally dominant powers are rising in power and status globally.

BRIC or BRICS:
expression to capture four or five large countries that are rising in global power and status; BRIC stands for Brazil, Russia, India, and China; the S stands for South Africa.

next 11 or N-11:
like BRICS, N-11 refers to rising powers globally, in this case Bangladesh, Egypt, Indonesia, Iran, Mexico, Nigeria, Pakistan, the Philippines, Turkey, South Korea, and Vietnam.

nonpolarity: a world in which there is no dominant power.

global governance:
the formal and informal institutions, systems or relationships that manage affairs that cut across national boundaries.

A few acronyms speak to these changes. Many scholars and journalists employ the acronym **BRIC or BRICS** to shorthand the rising power of new countries. A term first introduced by an analyst from Goldman Sachs, an investment firm, BRIC stands for Brazil, Russia, India, and China. The added "S," which some include and some do not, refers to South Africa. One estimate captures the expected change nicely. In 2010, the five largest economies in the world were the United States, China, Japan, Germany, and France. By 2050, the expected five will be China, the United States, India, Brazil, and Russia.[14] When these shifts will take place is uncertain, but many economists project that China will have the largest economy, measured by gross domestic product, by the mid- to late 2020s.

Goldman Sachs also has introduced the numeronym **next 11 or N-11** to refer to other developing countries that were rising in power and market share: Bangladesh, Egypt, Indonesia, Iran, Mexico, Nigeria, Pakistan, the Philippines, Turkey, South Korea, and Vietnam. These countries are poised, according to the investment firm, to become the next BRICs. They have large populations, increasingly urbanized populations, macroeconomic stability, and the human capital and technology to become a major part of the world economy in the next 50 years. Despite whether these in fact will be the "next 11," the term indicates the rising relative power of many states that a generation ago were not seen as major world players.

How to characterize the contemporary era beyond the "rise of the rest" remains a question. Fareed Zakaria coins the idea of a "Post-American World." In his account, the United States remains dominant, especially in military terms, but the rest of the world is catching up. In another influential book, political scientist Charles Kupchan employs the term "No One's World," which is synonymous with **nonpolarity**. He sees a world in which no one country will dominate. Even more crucially, Kupchan argues that the coming world will not be fashioned in the image of the West, which emphasizes liberal democracy, secular nationalism, and industrial capitalism. "The Chinese ship of state will not dock in the Western harbor," writes Kupchan. The new world is one with proliferating ideologies and value systems, new economic models, and new ways to imagine the relationship between state and society.

Kupchan's thesis underlines one of the themes of the book: Although the rise of the rest represents an exceptional moment of change and opportunity for literally billions of people worldwide, the tectonic shift could engender conflict and tension.

Global Governance

Our final global force is global governance. **Global governance** refers to how something is managed: which actors are involved, what the rules are, and how strong the enforcement is. Every part of life involves some governance. In a typical Western, nuclear family, the governance structure involves parents who set rules. In a typical corporation, the board of directors establish rewards systems like pay and bonuses. But even parts of life in which no one is necessarily in charge involve governance. For example, when friends go camping, there is no parent or CEO, but there is some unspoken understanding that no one person gets to call all the shots. Campers discuss who will gather firewood, who will clean dishes, and so on. While government is about authority, governance is about common management of an issue.

States engage in governance-making all the time. They meet to discuss highly specific things like how many miles out into the sea our "state" extends or how we should compensate the postal service in another country for delivering letters paid with our stamps. Any cross-border issue you can possibly conceive of, there is either some governance activity in the form of a United Nations (UN) treaty or convention, or there is a group trying to introduce some governance. Global governance does not mean global government; in fact, a major reason we are interested in global governance is because *there is no global government*. As we will see, there is extensive global governance of some issues but not of others.

One issue in which we find extensive global governance is human rights, which we discuss in Chapter 8. The key actors are states but also intergovernmental organizations, like the UN High Commissioner for Human Rights and the European Court of Human Rights, as well as civil society organizations such as Amnesty International and Physicians for Human Rights. The key rules are established in things like the Universal Declaration of Human Rights or the Convention on the Rights of the Child. These agreements often represent the formalization of what were once norms, meaning unwritten rules about desirable behavior. One can speak of a "global human rights regime" because this issue is attended to by a multitude of actors, and a multitude of types of actors, and they together monitor, shape, and enforce formal and informal rules.

An issue with weak global governance is climate change. There are international civil society actors in the form of NGOs like Friends of the Earth and Greenpeace. These nongovernmental organizations are on the ground doing research, and making environmentally destructive behavior by states and companies known to the world. They have been effective in disseminating norms about environmentally sustainable behavior, but they have no legal power to punish bad behavior. Corporations are also involved in the area through the UN Global Compact, which allows corporations to publicly commit themselves to certain labor and environmental practices. But participation is voluntary, and the "only" punishment is public shaming. As we detail in Chapter 13, however, fashioning a global treaty to which all states of the world adhere has been difficult. There is the United Nations Framework Convention on Climate Change, but some key states, including the United States, Russia, and China, at various times have refused to ratify it.

These examples show us that global governance is a patchwork. On issues such as human rights there is significant activity by states, IGOs, NGOs, and even MNCs. Yet on issues such as climate change and the global environment, there is limited governance. The examples also reveal there are more levels of governance than just states and IGOs. Indeed, some speak of "multilevel" governance that simultaneously takes place at subnational (think megacities like Los Angeles or Lagos), state, regional (think European Union), or global levels (think UN).

Last, global governance does not have to be state-led. For example, on the issue of climate change, in the face of weak state action, nongovernmental groups, including NGOs and corporations, formed the Forest Stewardship Council (FSC) to ensure the sustainable management of forests. The nonprofit's membership comprises approximately 800 civil society actors from around the world, including NGOs and individuals, with thousands of corporations holding FSC certificates.[15] Outlets like Home Depot display the FSC stamp, which certifies that their materials were responsibly sourced. No states or intergovernmental organizations are involved in any of this. There are no fines, invasions, or jail time for violating the code, but a company could lose certification, suffer public shaming, and lose market share as a result. Even in the face of weak governance at a global level, actors across multiple levels are jointly managing an issue of common concern.

These four global forces are dominant in our world today. They are the forces that are making and remaking our globe; they are driving the interactions and the tensions that are at the heart of this book. Highlighting them will help you understand the world around you and the forces that impact the issues about which you care.

WHAT IS INTERNATIONAL STUDIES GOOD FOR?

This book provides an introduction to the field of international studies, and as we've explored, our goal in this Introduction has been to outline a framework that will allow you to understand better today's critical global challenges as you work your way through the book. But many students may rightfully ask what the practical purpose of such a course is.

First, our reality for today and the foreseeable future is global. The international intrudes on our daily lives in all kinds of ways. As students, teachers, and citizens, it is incumbent on us to understand those processes—to understand the forces that influence our lives. A course such as this provides you with an intellectual foundation by which to understand global forces that shape our world.

Second, this book should help you develop a global awareness. Although much of the book is about how the global affects us, the book also should help you understand that which is unfamiliar. That might mean coral reefs in Australia, human rights in Eritrea, protests in Bolivia, or AIDS in Botswana. In other words, the book should help you to understand the world in which you live and provide you with the tools to make sense of it. We hope that stimulates a lifetime of learning and curiosity about our world.

Last, in ways that may be of immediate concern to many, international issues shape many careers. The labor pool is increasingly a global one. From manufacturing, to service, to sports, music, and academics, the people who compete for positions often come from all parts of the world. Most businesses today—should they look to expand their markets—often play or aim to play on the international scene. The market for entertainment may be largest in the United States, but anyone in the business—from cinema, to gaming, to basketball—will tell you how global the market is. International studies is a fantastic gateway for a student interested in a globally engaged career, such as in international finance, humanitarian relief, or global health. And it is also useful for students who may not want a globally engaged career but wish to nonetheless understand how global affairs will relate to their lives. Whether you wish to be an organic potato farmer in Idaho, a ceramicist in New York City, a real estate agent in Chicago, a chef in New Orleans, a Lyft driver in Arizona, or a tech entrepreneur in San Francisco, your professional development will be strengthened with an appreciation for how you affect and will be affected by oil prices, climate change, free trade, or global food production.

In sum, understanding the international in as holistic a way as possible is an essential part of your education today, and this course will give you a core training in that subject from an interdisciplinary perspective.

KEY TERMS

QUESTIONS FOR REVIEW

1. What are three ways in which global interactions affect your life?

2. Have you or anyone in your family experienced a negative outcome from a global interaction?

3. What is an outside-in and inside-out framework? What are some examples of each?

4. What are the four major global forces outlined in this chapter? Consider an issue you care most about (e.g., global health or climate change). Which forces matter and how for that issue?

LEARN MORE

Charles Kupchan, *No One's World: The West, the Rising Rest, and the Coming Global Turn* (New York, NY: Oxford University Press, 2012).

Dani Rodrik, *The Globalization Paradox: Why Global Markets, States, and Democracy Can't Coexist* (Oxford, U.K.: Oxford University Press, 2011).

Deborah D. Avant et al. (eds.), *Who Governs the Globe?* (Cambridge, U.K.: Cambridge University Press, 2010).

Saskia Sassen, "Global Cities," in *The Encyclopedia of Global Studies* (Thousand Oaks, CA: Sage, 2012).

Global Policy, an interdisciplinary academic journal analyzing global problems and solutions. https://www.globalpolicyjournal.com.

Council on Foreign Relations, Explainers, series focused on explaining issues of concern to U.S. foreign policy. https://www.cfr.org/explainers.

Textbook Notes, Carnegie Council, provides videos and podcasts on issues of interest to international studies. https://www.carnegiecouncil.org/education/006.

NOTES

1. Tim Higgins, "Apple iPhone Sales in China Outsells the U.S. for the First Time," *Bloomberg Technology*, April 27, 2015. http://www.bloomberg.com/news/articles/2015-04-27/apple-s-iphones-sales-in-china-outsell-the-u-s-for-first-time.

2. Andrea Peterson, "What It Took for Ethiopia to Lose Access to Hacking Tools It Used Against Journalists in the US," *The Washington Post*, July 12, 2015. https://www.washingtonpost.com/blogs/the-switch/wp/2015/07/12/what-it-took-for-

ethiopia-to-lose-access-to-hacking-tools-it-used-against-journalists-in-the-u-s/.

3. Thomas Oatley, *International Political Economy*, 5th edition (Boston, MA: Routledge, 2015), 21.

4. Shalifay, "List of Countries Without Stock Exchanges," *Investment Frontier* (blog), July 28, 2014. http://www.investmentfrontier.com/2014/07/28/list-countries-without-stock-exchanges/.

5. *Manila Standard*, September 22, 1997.

6. Dani Rodrik, *The Globalization Paradox: Why Global Markets, States, and Democracy Can't Coexist* (Oxford, U.K.: Oxford University Press, 2011).

7. UNCTAD, "World Investment Report 2015," 2015.

8. Oatley, *International Political Economy*, 162.

9. Manuel Castells, *The Rise of the Network Society* (Cambridge, MA: Blackwell, 1996); M. Castells, *End of Millennium* (New York, NY: Wiley-Blackwell, 2000).

10. Based on U.S. Census data from 2013: http://www.census.gov/hhes/computer/.

11. The World Bank, http://siteresources.worldbank.org/EXTINFORMATIONANDCOMMUNICATIONANDTECHNOLOGIES/Resources/IC4D_Infographic-1.png.

12. Fuyuki Kurasawa, "The Aporias of New Technologies for Human Rights Activism," in Steve Stern and Scott Straus, eds., *The Human Rights Paradox: Universality and Its Discontents* (Madison: University of Wisconsin Press, 2014), 177–203.

13. Fareed Zakaria, *The Post-American World* (New York, NY: W.W. Norton, 2008).

14. Charles Kupchan, *No One's World: The West, the Rising Rest, and the Coming Global Turn* (New York, NY: Oxford University Press, 2012).

15. FSC member search database, http://memberportal.fsc.org.

The Making of Our Global Age

FORCES, INTERACTIONS, AND TENSIONS SINCE 1800

SAMUEL KUBANI/AFP/Getty Images

LEARNING OBJECTIVES

After finishing this chapter, you should be able to:

- Articulate the main features of the first and second global ages.

- Describe events leading to the decline of the first global age.

- Contrast major actors in the first and second global ages.

- Identify the historical roots of today's global challenges.

Steve Huffman, Reddit's CEO and co-founder, underwent laser eye surgery in 2015. But he did not do it because he disliked the look of glasses or the feel of contact lenses. He did it to improve his chances of surviving a massive disaster. As he told *The New Yorker*, "If the world ends—and not even if the world ends, but if we have trouble—getting contacts or glasses is going to be a huge pain in the ass."[1] Huffman is part of a broad community who prepare themselves for withstanding global chaos. They are known as survivalists or doomsday preppers. National Geographic Channel's "Doomsday Preppers" was a reality TV show centered on this community, and it became the most popular show in the channel's history. The show may have entertained some, but it seemed to speak to many: In one survey, 40% of Americans said stocking supplies or building a bomb shelter was a wiser investment than a retirement savings account.

Exactly what is being prepared for varies widely, from economic collapse in the United States to a global power grab by a "One World Order." Companies such as Survivalist101.com describe one "doomsday scenario that could wipe out our way of life and set our civilization back a couple of centuries. . . . The world is edging closer to a time when rogue nations will have the capability of detonating a nuclear bomb over Washington, DC. All they need is a barge anchored 100 miles off the coast, a missile launcher and a nuclear tipped missile."[2] While some preppers fear war, others fear chaos brought on by economic crisis. As Robert Richardson of Off Grid Survival warned: "Economies around the world are crashing, countries are drowning in record amounts of debt, and governments continue to pile on new debt like there's no tomorrow. At some point this debt train is going to come to a screeching halt; when that happens we are going to see panic and chaos like nothing we've ever seen before."[3] Prepper companies sell peace of mind for a fee, and their market is experiencing rapid growth.[4] Even household names such as Costco have joined the market, selling a product with 36,000 servings of food for $6,000.

These businesses are not just engaged in simple fear mongering. They are tapping into a more general anxiety with the tensions that came with global interactions and the speed of global change in the 21st century: in the global economy, communications technologies, the environment, and cultural influences. The complex interactions that characterize the world today, and the tensions that result from them, are driven by some of the major global forces discussed in our Introduction. At the turn of the 21st century, multinational corporations (MNCs) like Alcoa, Wal-Mart, and JP Morgan had vastly greater clout compared with many smaller states. These MNCs, in turn, struggled against other international actors, such as global civil society groups like Amnesty International or Save the Children, that monitored the behavior of MNCs and used social media to influence the companies' behavior.

In the 1990s, technological and economic changes seemed to outpace humanity's ability to govern them. Genocides in Yugoslavia, Rwanda, and Sudan, and terrorist groups taking control of towns and cities in the Middle East added to a sense that a rapidly changing world was beyond anyone's ability to manage. This gave rise to a flurry of popular books on globalization. Figure 1.1 shows the rapid increase in the 1990s in use of the word "globalization" as a percentage of all English language books.

Our current era of globalization is not new, however. A century ago, societies were also undergoing changes that seemed stunning at the time. The global forces driving intensified interaction included scientific advances such as the manufacture of steel in the late Industrial Revolution, which made it possible to build enormous buildings, reliable railways, and larger ships. Politically, Europe had experienced the growth of nation-states and the decline of monarchies, whereas the spread of colonial rule brought many societies into production for global markets and into political organizations called "states," some for the first time. A woman born in Lagos in 1830 would by 1901 find herself in a newly invented state called "Nigeria" and a legal subject of the British Empire. A woman born into slavery in Louisiana in 1830 would by 1901 find herself legally free. Ships could travel further than humans had ever imagined, and two people could exchange messages over distances more immense than their ancestors could have ever conceived. More and more men—and, soon, women—could vote irrespective of their property or education.

So, our present global age—this remarkably integrated world—is not new. Ours is not the first period in which humans have had a truly global economy. Such a thing existed more than a century ago. This first age of globalization spanned the mid-1800s to the early 1900s. The second age of globalization took off in the 1990s, and we are still experiencing it. But what happened in between? Why did the first global age end?

FIGURE 1.1

Growing Use of "Globalization" in English-Language Books

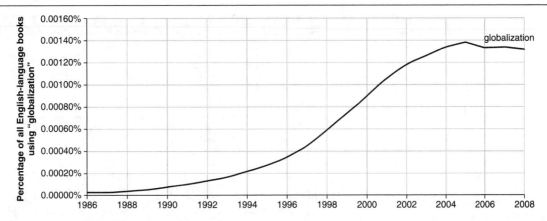

Source: Google Books Ngram Viewer. https://books.google.com/ngrams/graph? content=globalization&year_start=1986&
year_end=2008&corpus=15&smoothing=2&share=&direct_url=t1%3B%2Cglobalization%3B%.

This chapter provides a broad overview of major global events spanning recent centuries, with an emphasis on recent decades. Understanding this basic history is foundational for the remainder of this textbook. The chapter goes in chronological order, introducing major events that will help contextualize the international news you read today, tying them to our major global forces (like shifting world power and related changes in global governance, transformations in the global economy, and the rise of new technologies). We start in the early 1800s, but not because it marked the start of global history. Rather, it marked the first time people started to perceive the world as truly globally connected (see Figure 1.2).

THE FIRST GLOBAL AGE: INCREASING GLOBAL INTERACTIONS

The first global age can be loosely located in the early 1800s. A world emerged with more global interactions than ever before. Some of these interactions were voluntary, such as economic agreements and international scholarly travel. But some were anything but voluntary, such as slavery and colonialism. The effect was to bring people together in ways that shape our present. This section describes this first global age. (Figure 1.3 puts the First Global Age in our international studies framework.)

Global Stability Under Pax Britannica: 1815–1914

The year 1900 seemed to be one of dizzying change because western Europe and North America had experienced the fastest economic growth in history. Their economies had grown about eightfold in size in recent decades. The growth achieved in the previous 1,000 years had taken 100 years.[5] Yet, the 1800s were not without conflict. A civil war had ravaged the United States; elsewhere, indigenous people faced massive suppression as they attempted to resist colonial domination. Nevertheless, the

FIGURE 1.2

Making of the Modern World: Timeline of Global Forces and Interactions

Major political events	Period to 1918	Major economic events
Era of empires	1500–1750	Mercantilism
Napoleonic Wars	1803–1815	
Pax Britannica	1815–1914	
Unipolar system	1815–1900	
	1690 (Locke), 1776 (Smith), Ricardo (1817), "still relatively new by" 1900	Liberalism/Free Trade
	1800s	Continuation of protectionist economic policies
	1800s to early 1900s	Colonies forced to export raw materials
	1870–1914	Gold Standard
Rise of strong industrial state powers	1900	
Multipolar system	early 1900s	
Universal suffrage	1900–1930	
	1914	Collapse of the Gold Standard
World War I	**1914–1918**	
League of Nations	1920–1945	
	1929	Great Depression
	1930s	Latin American countries shift toward industrialization
	1930s	Rise of protectionism
Rise of Fascism and communism	1930s	
World War II	**1939–1945**	
United Nations	1945–today	
United States and the Soviet Union emerge as superpowers	1945	
Bipolar system	1945–1991	

Cold War	Late 1940s–1991	
	1944–1973	Bretton Woods System
North Atlantic Treaty Organization	1949	
Warsaw Pact	1955–1991	
	1958–1961	China's Great Leap Forward
Decolonization and independence movements gain traction	1945–today	
	1960	Organization of Oil Exporting States (OPEC)
Rise of the Non-Aligned Movement	1961	
	1970s	New International Economic Order
	1970s	Price of oil spikes
	1973	U.S. leaves Bretton Woods Monetary System
	1980s	Capital controls lifted
Number of dictatorships worldwide declines	1980s–1990s	
	1982	Recession in U.S., end of petrodollar cycle
Berlin Wall dismantled	1989	
Soviet Union dissolved	1991	
Unipolar system	1990s	
Asian Financial Crisis	1997	
	2000	Dot Com bubble burst
9/11 terror attacks	2001	
War on Terror	**2001-today**	
	2007	Global Financial Crisis
Multipolar or nonpolar system	2000s–today	
Arab Spring	2010	

Pax Britannica:
meaning
"British Peace,"
the period of
Britain's global
dominance from
1815 to 1914,
during which
Britain's interest
in increasing
international
trade allowed
for economic
cooperation
between major
countries.

period was notable for the absence of large-scale war involving major powers. The period is referred to as the **Pax Britannica** ("British Peace") because Great Britain was the undisputed globally dominant force. In the 99 years between Napoleon's defeat at Waterloo in 1815 to the start of World War I (WWI) in 1914, Britain's self-interest in economic integration across its colonies and with other trading partners provided the military and diplomatic support for a gradual increase in cross-border trade.

The idea of free trade was still new by 1900. The previous 300 to 400 years was a time of mercantilism rather than of liberalism and free trade. During the earlier mercantilist period, countries like France and Britain had not believed they could benefit by trading with one another. But this was precisely the idea of comparative advantage that is at the heart of the theory of free trade: If you and your trading partner both trade what you each produce most efficiently, you both gain from trade. See Chapter 6 for more on these economic concepts.

By the mid-1800s, Britain had started to reduce some of the tariffs that it had once used to protect industries from foreign imports. In the second half of the 1800s, other major economies followed suit. They began to import what they produced less efficiently. The mercantilist idea that trade was zero-sum—that I will be worse off if I sell my rival something they need—was losing favor.

But the rise of Britain as a superpower (see definition provided later in the chapter), and the emergence of several other countries as industrialized nation-states, was not a simple matter of them embracing free trade. First, major powers like Britain, Germany, Japan, and the United States all used protectionist policies for many decades while they were industrializing. This means they made it hard for foreign competition to enter their markets.[6] While they liberalized some industries, they protected others. Second, for the great swathe of humanity that lived as colonial subjects, global markets were not experienced as a liberating thing. Colonies were forced to sell their raw materials like timber or palm oil directly to their colonial master for less than they could get if the global economy were truly free. In addition, colonialism often forced people pay taxes in cash, which meant leaving their small farms where they engaged in subsistence agriculture to enter waged labor in cities, forests, and mines. Subsistence agriculture gave families some stability and control in managing their own economic fortunes. In wage labor, however, colonial subjects lost power over their own production.

Around the beginning of the Industrial Revolution in the mid-1700s, industrial activity in Asia and Latin America was similar to that in Europe. In previous centuries, the center of the world economy was not Europe or North America but China and India. By 1900, however, Europe had experienced a sixfold increase in industrial activity while Asia and Latin America had declined to one third of their initial level.[7] Because they were not allowed to protect their infant industries, as Europe and the United States had done, all they could offer to the world was their raw commodities, meaning either their natural resources, like gold, or their agricultural products, like cocoa.

An international division of labor thus began to emerge: Industrializing countries in Europe and North America continued to industrialize, and wealth turned into a virtuous circle of even greater human capital; stronger militaries, stronger states, and better universities; and thus more wealth. Conversely, in Asia, Latin America, and much of Africa, the colonized were *de*industrialized, and they became reliant on exporting raw commodities to the wealthy world, earning little of the profit that occurred at the manufacturing stage, and suffering the whims of global fluctuations in prices for their goods.

Global Cooperation and the Gold Standard

One reason for economic growth was the political cooperation on economic issues. The world's major economies participated in the **Gold Standard**, which was an agreement between states lasting from about 1870 to 1914 in which participants agreed to fix the value of their currencies to a

Gold Standard:
agreement
between
countries from
1870 to 1914 that
each member's
currency could
be exchanged
for a specified
amount of
gold. It lasted
until the early
to mid-1930s,
but its heyday
was 1870–1914
because it was
associated
with significant
international
trade.

specific amount of gold. (Today, the exchange rates of the world's currencies generally float freely, meaning the value of currencies goes up and down according to world demand for that currency.) Under the Gold Standard, major economies agreed that if you had X amount of their currency, you could walk into a bank and exchange that for a set amount of gold. This provided tremendous stability to international prices, which was good for long-term and long-distance trade.

iStock/LeeYiuTung

World War I (1914–1918)

By 1900, rapid economic growth led to shifting power among major European states. Three empires— Russia, Ottoman, and Austria-Hungary—were declining economically and experiencing political dissent within their borders. On the rise were Germany, Japan, and the United States. Britain was being outpaced by German industrial innovation. States and societies in sub-Saharan Africa were victims of these tensions.[8] At the Berlin Conference of 1884, major European powers agreed on the principles governing their division of African territories, transforming Africans into colonial subjects. Germany also sought to bring Europe's other German-speaking populations into its newly formed borders. Under Pax Britannica, there would have been less fear of this occurring, but without a globally dominant state to impose its will, Europeans grew concerned in the early 1900s that Germany desired more European land and that Britain might not be able to stop them.

This competition between European powers, together with enormous military buildups, was the backdrop for a series of small events that led to war in 1914. On one side were the Central Powers: Germany, Austria-Hungary, and the Ottomans.[9] On the other were the Allies: Britain, France, and Russia. The war birthed trench warfare, in which both sides dug long, deep trenches and became stuck in a bloody stalemate. In just five months of the Battle of the Somme in 1916, more than one million British, French, and German men died. Many of these were in fact non-European colonial subjects from places like Canada and Australia.

FIGURE 1.3

Global Forces, Interactions, and Tensions in the First Global Age: A Synopsis

GLOBAL FORCES	INTERACTIONS	TENSIONS
• Global markets: Increasing global economic cooperation but with economically dependent and disempowered colonies. • Shifting global powers: Pax Britannica.	• Major economies participate in the Gold Standard. • Britain's status as global leader threatened by rise of Germany and others. • Decolonization in Latin America but new colonization in Africa and Asia.	• The Global North industrializes, the Global South deindustrializes. • World War I divides Allies vs. the Central Powers.

The devastation ended when the United States entered the war, tipping the balance in favor of the Allies. The war had been far costlier, and lasted far longer, than any could have imagined. Major European wars of the past had not featured tanks, airplanes, trenches, and chemical weapons. In all, about 15 million people died, half of them civilians.

BETWEEN THE FIRST AND SECOND GLOBAL AGES: WARS, HOT AND COLD, AND NEW INTERACTIONS

Pax Britannica and the first period of globalization ended in 1914 as the world entered 30 years of war and financial collapse. World War I was the largest and most devastating conflict in world history. After it came the Great Depression of the 1930s, the rise of Fascism in Germany, the rise of Communism in the Soviet Union, and a second World War (WWII). Two major global forces that drove interactions a few decades earlier were absent at this time: Major powers became less interested in free trade and became more protectionist, and global cooperation on things like exchange rates failed. In the colonized world, independence movements were growing in popularity just as the popularity of colonialism itself was declining within the colonial powers.

The Aftermath of War

World War I had been devastating for all, and especially for those on the losing side. The Russian and Austria-Hungarian empires broke apart. The Ottoman Empire lost much of the Arab Middle East and became the state of Turkey. Germany lost its non-European colonies, as well as many German-speaking populations in Europe (see Figure 1.4) Germany then suffered further under the Treaty of Versailles, in which the Allied powers laid out the terms of German surrender. The outcome was enormous debts that Germany was to pay to the war's victors. France needed Germany to repay because France had borrowed heavily during the war from the United States, which was unwilling to forgive loans. Germany's war-torn economy was hobbled further when it experienced hyperinflation. This meant one German mark might buy a loaf of bread one day, but the bread might cost 10 marks the next day, and 10,000 marks a year later. People with marks in the bank saw their savings turn to dust as marks became worthless.

Universal Suffrage for Europe and North America

Universal suffrage was among the most significant social and political changes happening across Europe at this time. For most of the 1800s, the few places in Europe and North America that were democratic restricted the right to vote to educated men. But in the early 1900s, thanks in part to the organizing activities of labor unions and socialists, the working classes in most of the industrialized world were beginning to assert themselves politically. In the first three decades of the 20th century, universal suffrage, inclusive of all men and women, was won in Norway, Finland, Denmark, Germany, Sweden, Holland, Ireland, Britain, Canada, and (in law if not in practice) the United States. The effect of this electoral empowerment of entire populations cannot be overstated. To win power and stay in office, governments now had to be much more responsive on issues like worker safety and unemployment than ever before.

FIGURE 1.4

Europe Before and After World War I

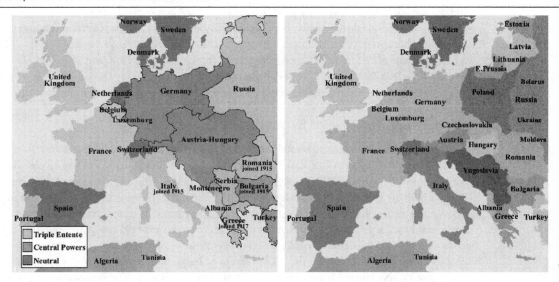

Source: National Archives, http://www.nationalarchives.gov.uk/pathways/firstworldwar/maps/maps.htm.

The Global Depression of 1929

The Global Depression that started in 1929 was longer, more widespread, and more destructive than any other economic crisis in living memory. Since the world had become increasingly interconnected and economically interdependent, few corners of the globe could escape the effects of major economies imploding. Colonial economies, which had been developed to export raw materials for industrial centers in the Global North, saw their export-driven economies collapse.[10]

The result in many Latin American countries was a turn away from the global economy. The idea that the global economy was something to be feared rather than embraced was a tremendously powerful notion that came to dominate much of the developing world. Many developing countries started to use the power of their own states to move away from a reliance on exporting raw materials, and toward industrializing themselves. Their models at the time were Germany and the Soviet Union, countries that had grown at then-unheard-of rates thanks to the government actively intervening in the economy to help it industrialize. This distrust of global markets and free trade, and embrace of a state that actively develops its own economy, would exert a powerful influence on the world in the decades that followed.[11]

The Gold Standard had facilitated international trade for several decades, but it collapsed in the 1930s. For it to work, countries had to agree to keep their currencies set at a specific value, as well as agree to exchange each other's currencies for a set amount. But this prevented any single country from changing the value of its currency to make its exports more competitive. In other words, the system required states to *desire* cooperation. When economies struggled to get out of the depression, international agreements to honor fixed currencies became too much to bear.

The general decline in international cooperation was not just economic. An intergovernmental project was developed to make sure states cooperated and engaged with one another, but it did not last. U.S. president Woodrow Wilson had proposed the creation of the League of Nations, which would have looked a little like the United Nations (UN) today. The League of Nations was created after WWI, but it was Wilson himself who was unable to convince the Republican Party, which was not in favor of deepening U.S. engagement in foreign affairs, to join the organization. The League of Nations lived on, without much effect, until it was replaced by the UN in 1945. Rather than cooperate, major economies turned inward, away from free trade, toward protectionism.

World War II: The Rise of Extremism

At the same time, domestically, politicians were coming to power on the basis of provocative and divisive visions of the world. Germany's Fascists came to power arguing that Germany's problem was that nonethnic Germans (non-Aryans) had grown too powerful within Germany and could not be trusted. Elsewhere, socialists came to power arguing that the problem was instead capitalists in the form of bosses and owners, and that public control of the economy would be better for workers than private control of things like power grids and factories. Political extremism grew in Europe in the 1930s, culminating in WWII and the efforts of world powers to stop Hitler's attempts to expand Germany's borders.

This time the two sides were the Axis (Germany, Italy, and Japan along with their colonies) against the Allies (United States, Britain, and the Soviet Union). The balance was tipped in favor of the Allies after a succession of victories. Russia turned Germany back from Stalingrad in 1943. British and American forces recaptured territory in North Africa, Italy, and France in

FIGURE 1.5

The United States Emerged From World War II an Economic Powerhouse

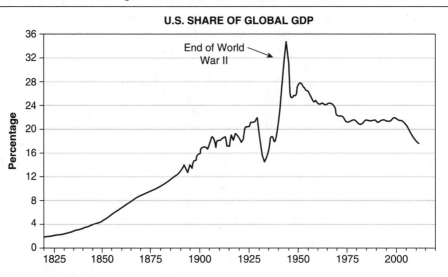

Source: Data from Angus Maddison, IMF, CIM.

1943–1944. U.S. forces bombed Japan into surrender in 1945 with use of the world's first nuclear bombs, leaving more than 100,000 civilians dead. Perhaps the greatest toll was paid by Russians, between 15 and 20 million of whom died in WWII, but casualties were staggeringly high on all sides, and among soldiers and civilians. All told, about 60 million civilians and soldiers died, including some six million in the Holocaust. The physical infrastructure of Europe was destroyed for both the victorious and the defeated.

Although the United States also suffered enormous casualties, with approximately 400,000 killed, it emerged from the war as a **superpower**. At war's end, the United States alone accounted for an estimated one third of global gross domestic product (GDP; Figure 1.5). WWII had been a boom time for the United States as European states relied on U.S. weapons manufacturing, and the United States, in large part, avoided damage to its physical infrastructure, thanks to its oceans preventing land invasions. In the few years after the war, it would play an instrumental role in devising international institutions spanning issues of trade and security that are with us today.

The end of WWII also saw changes in the status of two superpowers: the decline of Britain and the rise of the Soviet Union. Even before the war, Britain had lost its economic and military supremacy. WWII seemed to confirm and hasten the decline. By the 1960s, British colonial occupation in Africa and the Middle East had ended, and it has never regained the global position it occupied in the 1800s. At the same time, the Bolsheviks who took over Russia in 1917 began a project of enormous state-driven transformation. Politically, the Soviet Union was formed in 1922 when Russia was combined with several neighboring territories, such as modern Georgia and Ukraine. What became of the Union of Soviet Socialist Republics (USSR, aka the "Soviet Union" or "Russia") was transformed from a poor and rural place into an industrial and scientific leader.

The Cold War: A Bipolar World

Bipolarity—a system with two centers of power—reigned in the aftermath of World War II. Although the United States and the USSR were joined in their fight against Hitler, by the end of the 1940s, these two economic and military giants agreed on very little. The United States had a democratically elected government that presided over a market-based economy. The Soviet Union was a one-party state that directly controlled its economy. It was an interventionist state that built factories and heavy industry. All workers worked for the state, whether they were trash collectors or machinists. The Soviets had a centrally planned economy, in which the central government allocated resources like people, equipment, and materials to different sectors and different regions to meet growth targets.

Each superpower led alliances of like-minded states. Western states formed a military alliance, the North Atlantic Treaty Organization (NATO), in 1949. NATO still exists and in recent years has had operations in Afghanistan and Libya. The Soviet version was the Warsaw Pact, an alliance of Communist countries lasting from 1955 to 1991. Although the two superpowers never fought a major war—hence the name *Cold War*—their opposition to one another was felt across the world through proxy wars, support for dictators, and propagation of the nuclear arms race. Proxy wars, in which two states fight one another by backing opposing sides in someone else's war, were often fought in the world's poorest countries. In wars in Laos, Cambodia, Vietnam, and El Salvador, the United States supported the government while the Soviet Union funded and armed rebel groups. The opposite occurred in Afghanistan, Nicaragua, and Angola, with the United States supporting rebels against Soviet-backed governments. Precisely because of the support of powerful external actors, these sorts of conflicts are some of the most difficult to resolve.[12]

Although the next 50 years of international relations was characterized as a Cold War that divided "capitalist West" against "communist East," there was significant international cooperation in the form of the United Nations, which as mentioned was created in 1945. Unlike NATO or the Warsaw Pact, the UN was inclusive of all countries. One important part of the UN, the Security Council, likely helped avoid major war between superpowers during the Cold War. We discuss intergovernmental organizations in Chapter 3.

Bretton Woods System (1944–1973): Compromise and Cooperation

As the Great Depression lay waste to economies in the early 1930s, classic economic thinking held that if an economy was doing poorly, governments should spend less and wages should be allowed to fall such that the economy becomes competitive again. British economist John Maynard Keynes challenged this idea. He said that during bad times, governments should increase spending and keep interest rates low to keep the economy moving. Why? Because of the paradox of thrift: What is the rational thing to do when you are threatened with unemployment? You will spend less and save more. When everyone thinks a recession is coming, they all spend less and save more. But this becomes a self-fulfilling prophecy: You think a crisis is coming, so you change your behavior, and this makes the crisis happen. Keynes said investors will not invest if there is no prospect for rising demand, no matter how low wages or interest rates go.

By the late 1940s, there was growing acceptance of the Keynesian idea that markets were not self-regulating and that governments had to manage their economies. This was not socialism, however, since Keynes wanted to understand how markets worked precisely so they could be made even more effective.

This helps us understand why industrialized countries emerging from WWII wanted to create an international economic system that would allow them to manage their own economies while simultaneously avoiding the protectionism and anti–free trade policies of the 1930s. They did this by creating the **Bretton Woods System (BWS)**, named after the place in New Hampshire where 44 Allied states met in 1944.

Bretton Woods System (BWS): economic order among mostly Western industrialized nations after World War II, providing for lower barriers to trade and investment while safeguarding the ability of member states to manage their economies even at the expense of international economic activity.

First, the states created a compromise system in which they all agreed to use a fixed exchange rate, but they were allowed to change the price at which their currency was fixed on occasion if they needed to manage their own economy. For example, a country might wish to raise the value of its currency if it wanted to be able to import foreign goods more cheaply, which would make consumers happy. This was the Bretton Woods Monetary Regime, explained in greater detail in Chapter 6.

Second, the states created the Bretton Woods Institutions (BWIs). This is where the World Bank (WB), World Trade Organization (WTO), and International Monetary Fund (IMF) all come from. The WB was originally designed to provide cheap loans to European states trying to rebuild after WWII. Today, the purpose of the WB is to help developing countries lift their people out of poverty. The WTO began as the General Agreement on Tariffs and Trade (GATT) and became the WTO about 50 years later. The GATT was created to enforce trade deals and resolve trade disputes between its members. Last, the IMF was created to ensure global financial stability by acting as a "lender of last resort." When countries find themselves in crisis with no banks or governments willing to lend to them, the IMF is supposed to ensure that the country does not collapse.

The Bretton Woods System was a success, with rapid economic growth in the 1950s and 1960s. When people talk about this golden age of American prosperity, this is partly why. The share of

FIGURE 1.6

Economic Growth Under the Bretton Woods System (1950–1973)

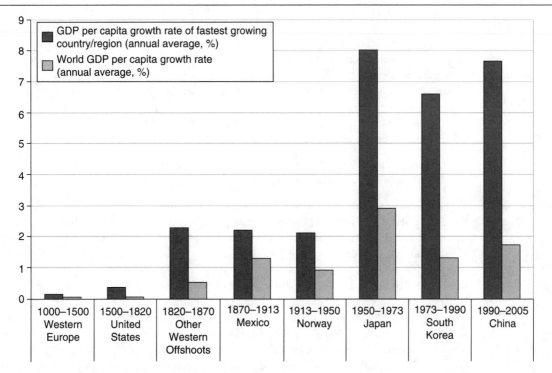

Source: Dani Rodrik, "Are the Good Times Really Over?" Dani Rodrik's Weblog, http://rodrik.typepad.com/dani_rodriks_weblog/2009/04/are-the-good-times-really-over.html.

global GDP that came from trade doubled, meaning more and more of the world's economic activity was centered on trading with one another, exactly as the BWS planned.

Figure 1.6 shows economic growth in distinct periods. The darker bars show the growth rate of the fastest growing country. The lighter bars show the economic growth rate for the whole world. We see that in the 1950–1973 period—the period of the Bretton Woods System—global growth was higher than it had ever been before, and indeed, it was higher than it has ever been since. Growth was also broad based, meaning the economic gains did not just accrue to the top 10% to 20%, but there was expansion of the middle classes in industrialized countries. And in northern Europe, several states developed extensive social welfare systems, where states taxed citizens heavily and in return provided excellent childcare, healthcare, education, pensions, and unemployment compensation and retraining assistance.

Decolonization and Dependency

By the end of WWII, nationalist and independence movements were growing in most colonial states. Most of Spain's colonial possessions in the Americas had been independent since the early to mid-1800s, so anti-colonial struggles after WWII developed in Africa, the Middle East, and Asia. Prominent figures included Kwame Nkrumah of Ghana, Julius Nyerere of Tanzania, Léopold Senghor of Senegal, and Mahatma Mohandas Gandhi and Jawaharlal Nehru of India. These anti-colonial leaders were not "mere" politicians: They were thought leaders. People like Senghor were respected intellectuals in their own right. They constructed a worldview that explained how the world "really" worked. Their ideas overlapped with many of the ideas of what became known as *dependency theory*, or **structuralist theory**, of the world economy. In this view, the world is not simply one of many independent states freely pursuing what they think is best for them. Instead, the world has been *intentionally structured* to benefit the wealthy, industrialized, white world at the expense of the poor, agricultural, nonwhite world. In this view, for example, Britain did not get wealthy despite Kenya being poor: Britain got wealthy *because it made Kenya poor*.

See dependency and structuralist theories applied to today's global challenges at Third World Network, https://www.twn.my/.

Independence generally came much more quickly than the colonial powers expected. In 1946, the United States gave up control of the Philippines. The next year, Britain left India, from which Pakistan emerged, and from which Bangladesh emerged decades later. One year after the British left the Palestine Mandate, Israel declared itself a state. In 1949, Indonesia gained independence from the Netherlands. In the 1950s, waves of independence swept Africa, first in North Africa with Libya, Tunisia, and Morocco all independent by 1956. In 1957, Ghana became the first sub-Saharan African country to gain independence. Decolonization spread rapidly in Africa thereafter, with major states like Nigeria, Ivory Coast, Zaire/Democratic Republic of the Congo, and Kenya all gaining independence. Some struggles for independence were long and violent, especially where independence movements were opposed by white settler populations (like Zimbabwe) or Cold War powers (like Vietnam). In other cases, superpowers fueled conflict between indigenous populations seeking to control a newly independent state, such as the Angolan Civil War (1975–2002).

The 1950s and 1960s were a period of tremendous excitement and optimism in many developing countries. Countries that had not even existed a few decades before colonialism invented them were now legally free, and those in power felt the right and the duty to use the state to modernize their societies. The state, rather than the market, played a major role in their plans because dominant political thinking held that global markets and trading with wealthy countries were what held poor countries back. Rather than look to the economic models of the United States or United Kingdom, many developing countries looked instead to the East. Soviet economic stagnation set in gradually over the coming decades, but in the 1950s, they were admired by independence leaders for having cast off their imperial rulers and for turning poor and agricultural Russia into an industrialized and advanced socialist powerhouse. Moreover, the Soviets had claimed the first victory in the emerging space age by successfully sending a human into orbit in 1961.

Many developing countries tried to resist being dominated by what they called the "first world" (capitalist states led by the United States and the United Kingdom) or the "second world" (communist states led by Russia). Instead, they identified as the "third world," a group of like-minded countries that had common experiences as postcolonial developing countries. Prominent states like Indonesia, Egypt, and India formed the Non-Aligned Movement in 1961 in an effort to present a united front in international forums like the UN General Assembly. In the 1970s, they advanced an agenda for a New International Economic Order, centered on improving terms of trade for developing countries, increasing development aid, and improving access to the markets of wealthy

structuralist theory: also known as "dependency" theory; theory that wealthy countries got rich by making others poor. One variant, structural Marxism, believes elites in wealthy and poor countries all share a commitment to the survival of capitalism, and thus, states are tools used to ensure the dominance of capitalism.

countries. The group still exists with 120 member states, but it has recorded few successes. One effort by developing countries to self-organize was successful, however. The Organization of Petroleum Exporting Countries (OPEC) was created in 1960 by five oil-producing countries trying to command a greater share of their oil wealth that had hitherto been controlled by the multinational oil companies.[13] Through its control of energy prices, OPEC has played an important role in the global economy for more than 50 years.

The End of the Bretton Woods System

The optimism of the 1950s and 1960s that had come from space exploration, growth in the Bretton Woods economies, and the widespread ending of colonialism began to dwindle into the 1970s. The Bretton Woods Institutions (WB/IMF/WTO) lived on, but the fixed exchange rate that had been part of the West's prosperity in the previous 20 years was to end. U.S. president Richard Nixon needed to spend heavily for the Vietnam War, but the Monetary Regime required other countries to believe that the United States had enough physical gold supplies to be able to convert any amount of dollars for gold. As Nixon printed more dollars to pay for the war, people doubted whether the United States could honor the exchange rate commitment, and so Nixon left the Bretton Woods Monetary Regime in 1973.

The 1970s was also notable for spikes in oil prices that led to recessions in many industrialized countries. The welfare states of northern Europe struggled to sustain generous maternity leaves and pensions as tax revenues dwindled and welfare demand rose. But higher oil prices were precisely what OPEC wanted, and oil-producing countries had more cash than they could even invest in their own countries. The consequence was that oil producers deposited enormous amounts of dollars (oil contracts were priced in U.S. dollars) in major banks in Europe and the United States. Flush with cash, these banks found willing borrowers in developing countries eager to borrow money to build railways, ports, electricity grids, and schools. While industrialized economies suffered under high energy prices, oil producers prospered, and developing countries borrowed heavily.

This recycling of petrodollars came to a screeching halt when in 1982 Mexico announced that it would not be able to pay its debts to international banks. The precipitating event was a recession in the United States, when the U.S. Federal Reserve had raised interest rates to make it expensive to borrow from banks. President Ronald Reagan did this because he wanted to reduce spending in the economy to bring down inflation. The knock-on effect, however, was that he sent the United States and many other economies into recession. This reduced global demand for exports from developing countries, while the rise in interest rates increased the debt burden for developing countries. Worse, the value of the dollar rose, so loans that were in U.S. dollars now became enormous. By 1983, 27 countries owing $239 billion had rescheduled their debts or were in the process of doing so: 16 of these were in Latin America.

The Rise of Neoliberalism and the Fall of Communism

It was at this time that the IMF began to expand its activities significantly. As the "lender of last resort," it was the organization countries turned to when no one else would loan to them. Countries like Mexico were in such a position. In return for loaning massive sums of money to developing countries to pay their debts, the IMF required that developing countries make significant changes to their economies. The logic behind these changes (known as "conditionality") was inspired by ideological developments in the United States and the United Kingdom especially, where Keynesianism

neoliberalism:
ideological belief that free markets are desirable in an economy and in society as a whole.

and state involvement in the economy had come under attack. In its place was **neoliberalism,** an ideology that preferred market-based solutions to problems, whether they be financial crises, climate change, or even how to pay for public schools. Intellectually, these ideas were represented in the work of Milton Friedman and Friedrich Hayek and politically by U.S. president Ronald Reagan and U.K. prime minister Margaret Thatcher.

These pro-market ideas were also influential among intergovernmental organizations engaged in lifting developing countries out of poverty. When developing countries came to the WB and IMF in crisis, therefore, the message they received was that their states were too involved in their economies. They had to liberalize, deregulate, and privatize. This was the beginning of structural adjustment programs (SAPs). In many countries in Latin America and sub-Saharan Africa, cutbacks in government spending on health and education services made poverty worse in the 1980s, a period known as the "Lost Decade." This was especially disastrous in Southern Africa where the HIV/AIDS epidemic was begging to explode, just as health facilities were being defunded (see Figure 1.7).

FIGURE 1.7

Latin America's Lost Decade

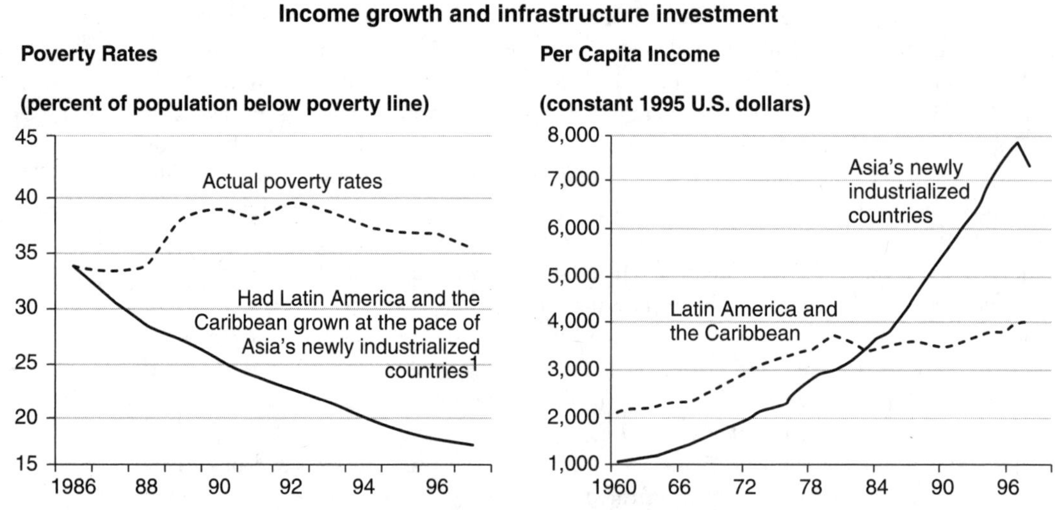

Income growth and infrastructure investment

Poverty Rates

(percent of population below poverty line)

Actual poverty rates

Had Latin America and the Caribbean grown at the pace of Asia's newly industrialized countries[1]

Per Capita Income

(constant 1995 U.S. dollars)

Asia's newly industrialized countries

Latin America and the Caribbean

[1]Asia's newly industrialized countries grew 5.8 percent a year, on average, during 1986–97.

These graphs illustrate why the 1980s is called a lost decade for Latin America. On the left, we see the percentage of the population below the poverty line. The top line shows an increase in the percentage of the populations of the Caribbean and Latin America below the poverty line. By the mid-1990s, these populations were back to where they had been in the mid-1980s. The line below it shows what this poverty rate would have been had these economies grown at the pace of Asia's newly industrialized countries. You can think of the gap between the two lines as the Lost Decade. On the right, we see per capita income from 1960 to 1996 in Asia and Latin America/Caribbean. Both lines go up over time, meaning per capita income increased. But the difference between the two becomes extreme as Latin America and the Caribbean enter the Lost Decade.

Source: Danny Leipziger, "The Unfinished Poverty Agenda: Why Latin America and the Caribbean Lag Behind," *Finance and Development,* March 2001 (3:1), http://www.imf.org/external/pubs/ft/fandd/2001/03/leipzige.htm.

The 1980s were not only a period of economic decline for the world's poorest countries. The Soviet Union was also beginning to show signs of significant weakness. Starting in 1979, the Soviets had been involved in a lengthy and an expensive invasion of Afghanistan. Since 1981, the Reagan administration had dramatically increased U.S. military spending in an attempt to entice the Soviets to follow suit and bankrupt themselves in the process. The Soviet Union was falling behind militarily and economically. Although it had once made great leaps in industrial production, it had failed to innovate and move beyond heavy industry. Under Mikhail Gorbachev in 1985, the Soviet Union attempted to improve relations with the United States, while introducing economic and political reforms within the USSR. By the end of the 1980s, the Soviets had reduced their control over, and support for, other communist regimes. The Berlin Wall, the literal and symbolic dividing line between East and West, fell in 1989. When the Soviet Union dissolved in 1991, 15 newly independent states emerged.

Why did the Cold War end? One theory holds that U.S. military spending forced the USSR into bankruptcy in an effort to keep pace, whereas a variant says the stagnant Soviet economic model would likely have collapsed without foreign pressure. Yet another says that Soviet *ideas* changed. Specifically, Gorbachev had new ideas for how to build a stronger Soviet Union. In this reading, the Cold War ended because communism was found not to work. Although the former explanations for the end of the Cold War had to do with material things like declining economic strength, this latter explanation had to do with ideas, which are nonmaterial. As we will see later, this reflects a division in how social scientists see the world: Some think people do things for material reasons (i.e., they want money, or they fear violence); others think people do things for nonmaterial reasons (i.e., a "good state" is one that bans land mines or allows women to vote).

THE SECOND GLOBAL AGE: AN EXPLOSION OF GLOBAL FINANCE, INTERNATIONAL INTERACTIONS, AND NEW TENSIONS

The world entered its current rate of tremendous economic growth and relative geopolitical stability in the 1990s. Exact dating of the beginning of this second global age is not possible because the intensity or depth of interactions around the world has developed unevenly. Certainly, global trade and telecommunications innovations advanced in the 1990s. But two significant drivers of globalization began before that. The first was China's move to become an export powerhouse. The second was the growth of global finance. We will begin this section by looking at developments in China and global finance that began before the 1990s. Thereafter, we will discuss four important developments since the 1990s that bring us up to today: the global spread of elected government; explosive growth of the Internet; terrorism and the politics of waging wars against it; and faster economic growth in developing countries than in the developed world, with a resulting shift of many countries from the ranks of the world's poorest to the ranks of middle-income countries.

China (Re)emerges

China under Mao Zedong attempted to imitate the remarkable industrialization witnessed in the Soviet Union. Mao's Great Leap Forward (1958–1961) tried to move China from a rural, agrarian economy into a modern, urban society rapidly through the use of industrialization and forced collectivization, which banned private farming. One result was a famine that killed 20 million people. After Mao's death in 1973, Deng Xiaoping began a series of economic reforms that continue today. Special economic zones were set up in which private firms were allowed to operate. Limited foreign investment was also allowed. The result was a flood of multinational corporations building factories in China to take advantage of low labor costs, political stability, and export infrastructure in the form of railways and ports. These reforms are often labeled "liberalization," but that is not accurate. Politically, the Chinese Communist Party is highly authoritarian, repressive, and invasive. Economically, there is tremendous state involvement in the economy, which is why the three biggest banks in the world are all Chinese state banks, the largest of which has $3.3 *trillion* in assets.[14]

It is more accurate to speak of China's reemergence than of its rise. There has been a functioning state in China for at least 2,000 years. Compare that with states in Africa, many of which are at most one century old, and states in Europe, many of which are only about 200 years old. While European societies were technological backwaters more than 1,000 years ago, China had already invented modern forms of bureaucracy, standardized building codes, piped gas, steel, and even playing cards and toilet paper. This is why people refer to the recent rise of China as the *return* of China. It is the reemergence of perhaps the oldest and most sophisticated continuously existing social and political system in the world.[15] China's rapid economic growth is shown in Figure 1.8.

FIGURE 1.8

China's Booming Economy

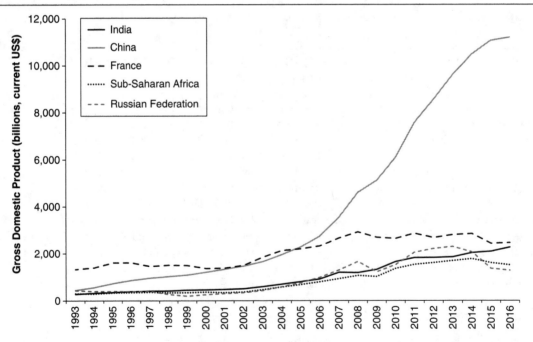

China's economy is now larger than that of India, France, and Russia, as well as of all sub-Saharan African countries combined.

Source: Data are from the World Bank, World Development Indicators.

IS From the Outside-In

WHY DID CHINA EMBRACE THE GLOBAL ECONOMY?

Most accounts of China's embrace of the global economy start with gradual economic reforms enacted by Deng Xiaoping in 1979. After the economic disaster of Mao's communism, Deng declared "to get rich is glorious!" Farmers were allowed to market a portion of their crops privately rather than produce only to meet government quotas. The introduction of township and village enterprises (TVEs) encouraged local governments to invest in businesses that were right for their local context. Importantly, profits could be returned to the local government officials, giving officials an incentive to see local businesses do well. And foreign firms were encouraged to come to invest and build factories.[16] The results were a quadrupling of the country's output in 20 years. China surpassed Japan as the world's second largest economy in 1992.

International studies helps us see our global age with inside-out and outside-in perspectives. In the case of Deng, accounts stress his political leadership, pragmatism, and courage. In introducing limited market reforms, in enabling Chinese to move about more freely within China, and by implicitly tolerating some inequality, Deng marked a real break from his predecessor, Chairman Mao. As to whether this turn to markets was a betrayal of communism, Deng, the pragmatist, famously replied, "If a cat catches mice, what does it matter if it's black or white?" This is an Inside-Out view because we start from the local and ask how it affected or was experienced by the global. But an Outside-In perspective is also possible.

China's economic reforms were influenced by ideas and experiences beyond its own borders. For example, Deng learned from Japan's export-oriented economic model as well as from its emphasis on technological upgrading. In the West, people often assume China grew by using its abundant cheap labor. Certainly that played a part, but

it also misleads. Indeed, China did not stay in the business of exporting low-tech consumer goods. Rather, the government borrowed economic policy ideas from neighbors such as Japan and South Korea who supported native companies while taxing foreign goods coming into the country. The policy was designed to move the economy up the value-added ladder, away from producing low-tech goods such as jeans, and toward hi-tech industries such as consumer electronics.

China borrowed from other neighbors too. From Taiwan, China copied the idea of a *free trade zone*. From Singapore, it got the idea of encouraging investment from multinational corporations. These companies would bring capital, expertise, and links to global markets. From Hong Kong, China saw that tourism could help the economy. Deng also learned from India how useful diasporas can be. For example, he embraced Y. K. Pao, a Chinese financier who had fled to Hong Kong after the Communist Revolution. Pao told Deng of his intent to invest in the new China, saying, "I was born in China. My roots are in China. I will do what I can to help the motherland to develop."[17]

An Outside-In perspective also alerts us to the historical moment in which China began to globalize. Because of its limited engagement with the global economy, China avoided the 1980s debt crisis that shook many developing countries. China also benefited from having a large diaspora (Chinese living abroad), especially in the United States. This would prove useful in forging links between importers and exporters. And in the 1990s, China's export orientation was able to meet a global appetite for cheap consumer goods, irrespective of the working conditions involved in their production. Historians Niall Ferguson and Moritz Schularick used the term "Chimerica" to refer to the relationship in which Chinese workers manufacture goods that American consumers

(Continued)

(Continued)

import, and the money exchanged is then recycled by China as credit to enable further American consumerism.[18]

Deng's economic policy was also shaped by his sense of China's place in the world. He sought a low-profile foreign policy precisely because China was not strong enough for anything else. As we learn in Chapter 3, realists think international relations is a self-help system in which states have to carefully guard their very existence.

This is why Deng said, "If we do not develop, then we will be bullied."[19]

Reflect

One interaction we saw in this example was between China and the Chinese diaspora. How many more interactions can you identify? Interactions can be between two actors within one country, between two international actors, or between one international and one domestic actor.

The Extraordinary Growth of Global Finance

Financial globalization refers to the massive amount of money that is exchanged daily on global markets. Under the Bretton Woods Monetary System (1944–1973), major economies limited the amount of money that could move in and out of their economy (known as "capital controls"). They did this because huge amounts of investment or speculative market activity would have made it difficult to manage their own economies. Once the Bretton Woods Monetary System ended, however, money began to move more freely between countries. As wealthy countries removed these restrictions throughout the 1980s, investors and speculators moved billions around the global economy.

The sums were enormous. In 1973, $160 billion was available for lending on international markets. By the early 1990s, they held over $5 *trillion*.[20] In the 1980s, the global financial system accounted for less than 5% of global GDP. Today it is over 15%. In 1975, international lending by banks was about $100 billion. In 2012, it was worth $20 *trillion*. In 1986, about $850 billion was traded in currencies every day in international foreign exchange markets. Today, about $5 *trillion* worth of currencies are traded every day (see Figure 1.9). Most of that currency trade is buying and selling euros for U.S. dollars since trade between the two is so enormous. You and everyone you know are probably intimately involved in this. When you buy something made in the European Union (EU) on Amazon, a currency trade occurs to allow you to pay in dollars and for the seller to get paid in euros.

Global finance has exploded for a few reasons. First, many countries removed legal limits to the buying and selling of currency and to the movement of money across borders. Second, there was liberalization of financial centers like The City in London, which is Britain's Wall Street. The City had once been the leader in global finance, meaning the place where companies and governments could come to borrow, but it had fallen behind Wall Street. Prime Minister Margaret Thatcher (1979–1990) responded by removing restrictions on how market traders and investors could operate. It was in The City that complex financial instruments like derivatives markets were invented, which unleashed billions that would eventually be loaned out around the world.

Communications and transport technology also made it possible for large firms to be active in global markets 24/7. International flights, high-speed Internet, and advances in shipping technology made it possible for light bulb manufacturers and currency speculators to factor wars, weather, or commodity prices millions of miles away into their investment decisions. The real cost of air travel fell 90% from 1930 to 2000. In the 1920s, a five-minute phone call from New York to London would

FIGURE 1.9

Daily Trades in Global Foreign Exchange Markets

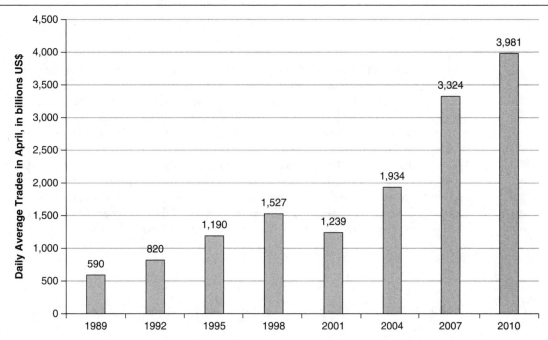

Source: Data are from Andriy Moraru, "Forex Market Turnover Infographics #1," December 2, 2013, http://www.earnforex.com/blog/forex-market-turnover-infographics-1/.

cost an American worker three weeks wages. By 2000, it would cost 15 minutes' worth of wages.[21] Meanwhile, growth in the financial sector made available ever larger sums for them to expand their economic activities. Today international trade is worth about $18 trillion per year. There are approximately 63,000 multinational companies with one quarter of total global production, one third of world trade, and 86 million employees.[22]

This financial globalization had two important consequences. First, enormous sums of money became available for countries, including developing countries, to borrow. Capital flows to developing countries went from $60 billion in 1990 to about $1 trillion today and funded the construction of factories, airports, railways, mines, roads, and houses. Second, these enormous amounts of money threatened the financial systems of many newly liberalized economies, which is why financial globalization was intimately tied to multiple financial crises in Latin America, Russia, and Southeast Asia that were intensely destructive and made life worse for millions. This is also partly why U.S. homeowners and credit card holders were able to borrow so much before the 2007 housing market bubble burst and the global economy crashed.

Watch: Inside Job (2010), a documentary placing the U.S. mortgage crisis in global context, http://www.sonyclassics.com/insidejob/.

The Spread of Elected Government

After decades of U.S.- and Soviet-backed dictatorships, a wave of regime change had spread throughout Africa in the early 1990s. Like the optimism that greeted independence decades earlier, people were excited to watch African states move from dictatorships to multiparty electoral systems. This sense of change was embodied in the release from prison of Nelson Mandela in South Africa, as well as in that country's mostly peaceful transition from a racist apartheid government to a peaceful, multiparty democracy. This wave of political reform was not restricted to Africa. In the 1980s and 1990s, military and one-party dictatorships fell throughout Latin America, Central Europe, and East Asia. By 2000, most countries in the world had governments elected by the majority of their populations, which was a first for humanity. Figure 1.10 shows data from a widely used dataset in political science. The red line shows a decline in the number of countries considered autocratic and a rise in the number considered democratic (blue line), starting around 1990. Democratization processes are discussed in more detail in Chapter 7.

By the end of the 1990s, however, Afro-optimism turned to Afro-pessimism. Many states experienced protracted civil wars, which in places like Somalia and Liberia led to a total collapse of state authority. The entire neighborhood of countries in central Africa was engulfed in a multicountry conflict in the Democratic Republic of Congo, a country four times the size of France, in a conflict

FIGURE 1.10

Global Democracy and Autocracy, 1946–2016

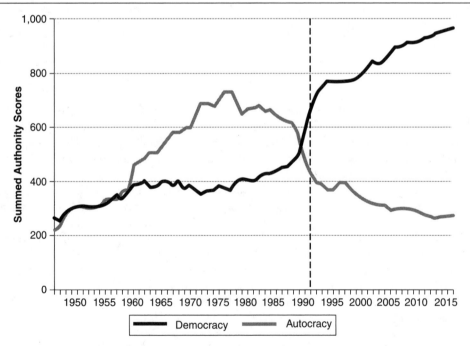

Source: The Center for Systemic Peace, "Global Conflict Trends," Figure 14, "Global Democracy and Autocracy, 1946-2016," http://www.systemicpeace.org/conflicttrends.html.

that killed millions. Added to the Rwandan Genocide in 1994 in which more than 600,000 civilians were killed in three months, the international image of Africa was one of disorder and backwardness.

The mass violence, in particular significant civilian deaths, added to growing calls to reconsider the very idea of state sovereignty: the idea that no government may intervene in the domestic affairs of another. Not only were there mass atrocities in some African states, but there also was ethnic cleansing and genocide in southern Europe as Yugoslavia broke up. The idea of humanitarian intervention gained support even though it was not a new idea. Powerful states formulated a plan called "Responsibility to Protect" (R2P) that called for the UN to commit to playing a role in managing conflict, thus expanding humanitarian efforts enormously in the 1990s.[23]

Today, the image of Africa is much more mixed. States like Ghana, Botswana, and South Africa are politically open and growing economically. States like Ethiopia and Rwanda are stable and growing economically, although they remain politically repressive. On the other hand, governments in Chad, Somalia, and Nigeria cannot control effectively swathes of their own territory. Figure 1.11 compares life expectancy at birth in Ethiopia, Ghana, and Chad, as well as provides the average for sub-Saharan Africa as a whole. We see that the sub-Saharan Africa average has generally increased since the turn of the century, but some countries have progressed faster than others.

The Internet Age

The Internet is a hallmark of this second global age, yet the impact of the Internet in the 1990s is easily romanticized. As late as 1998, only one quarter of U.S. households had computers,

FIGURE 1.11

Life Expectancy at Birth in Three African Countries

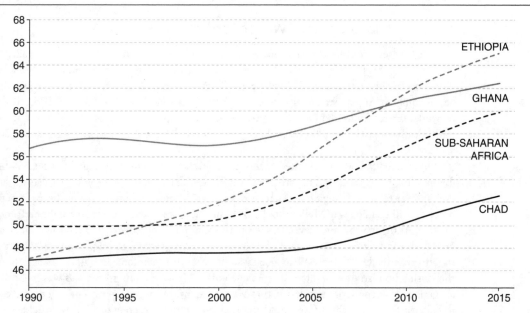

Source: World Bank. Life Expectancy at Birth, total years, https://data.worldbank.org/indicator/SP.DYN.LE00.IN?contextual=default& end=2015&locations=ZG-GH-TD-ET&start=1990. Licensed under CC BY 4.0 https://creativecommons.org/licenses/by/4.0/.

and not all of those were online.[24] According to the International Telecommunications Union, the percentage of the global population with Internet access never went above 10% that entire decade.[25]

The remarkable online takeoff in the 1990s was less in actual usage and more so in the speculative bubble that developed around new Web companies that dreamed of reaching billions of people in a totally new commercial model. The growth model used by websites such as Boo, GeoCities, and Lycos featured rapid expansion of the customer base, even at the expense of actual revenue. Investors bought into Web companies that reported millions of visitors but no profit whatsoever. Dallas Mavericks owner Mark Cuban was made a billionaire when Yahoo! paid almost $6 billion for Internet radio company broadcast.com in 1999. The site was discontinued only three years later. The talk of the 2000 Super Bowl was the number of websites that bought expensive ads, something that was novel at the time: 16 websites bought ads at a cost of about $2 million each. The stock market crash that started in 2000 wiped about $5 trillion off the worth of the NASDAQ.

Whereas the world's largest companies in 1900 were involved in oil, steel, and mining, today finance and technology companies are major players. Of the top ten most valuable publically traded companies in the world, only two are energy companies,[26] while three are computer companies,[27] two are pharmaceuticals,[28] and three are financial institutions.[29, 30] Apple's market value in early 2015 was $700 billion, twice that of oil giant ExxonMobil. The Internet age has not only created new economic giants, but it has also connected people in vast online social networks, as well as in transnational production networks.[31] In the case of Apple, international production includes software development by a multinational company in California, miners digging for tin ore in Indonesia, and factory workers assembling iPhones in China, all transported on Greek-owned ships. See the Introduction for more on the importance of the Internet.

The Long Shadow of the "War on Terror"

The next seismic event in this second global age involved the events leading to the so-called "War on Terror." On September 11, 2001, 19 men—15 from U.S. ally Saudi Arabia—hijacked four planes, ultimately leading to the death of 2,996 people. Twenty-six days later, the United States and Britain began bombing Afghanistan in an effort to capture Osama bin Laden and dismantle the al-Qaeda network that had sponsored the attacks. Over a decade later, it is the longest ever U.S. war. It has led to the deaths of just over 2,000 U.S. soldiers, and almost 100,000 Afghans, including almost 30,000 civilians.

On March 19, 2003, the United States led an invasion of Iraq after many months of a highly divisive diplomatic campaign to gather support for war. The *Guinness Book of Records* lists the largest ever antiwar rally occurring on February 15, 2003, when three million people in Rome gathered to protest the impending war. Millions took part in similar protests across the world in the early months of 2003. At the international level, UN weapons inspectors entered Iraq and reported "no evidence or plausible indication of the revival of a nuclear weapons program in Iraq."[32] But the report came months after the U.S. Congress had already authorized the use of force in Iraq. The suggestion that the Bush administration wanted to remove Saddam Hussein from power, and was merely using allegations of weapons of mass destruction as a pretext, has only grown over time. For example, aides to Defense Secretary Donald Rumsfeld reported that on the afternoon of 9/11, Rumsfeld asked for intelligence information that would be "good enough [to] hit Saddam Hussein at [the] same time. Not only Osama bin Laden."[33]

Since the Iraq war started, roughly 150,000 Iraqi civilians have been killed, in addition to approximately 50,000 Iraqi armed fighters. When researchers include deaths resulting from things like destroyed health infrastructure, the number of dead Iraqis is approximately half a million. Over 4,000 U.S. soldiers died in combat. In 2013, the U.S. Department of Veterans Affairs reported that, on average from 1999 to 2010, one veteran committed suicide every hour.[34]

Although military action was successful in removing Saddam Hussein and Osama bin Laden, it led to a significant destabilizing of the entire region. Governments in Afghanistan and Iraq were defeated in just a few weeks, but what followed were decades-long civil wars in which various ethnic and religious groups fought against the United States and against one another for control of the state. The United States and its allies have spent the past decade in protracted wars, but not against other states. Instead, they have been fighting nonstate actors, like al-Qaeda, the Taliban, and the Islamic State of Iraq and Syria (ISIS, or "the Islamic State").

By the end of the first decade of the 2000s, the Middle East was in upheaval, as a wave of anti-authoritarian protests rocked the Arab world. Protests that started in Tunisia in late 2010 saw the fall of government in Tunisia, Egypt, Libya, and Yemen about one year later, as well as uprisings in Bahrain and Syria, and street protests in almost every other Arab-majority country. The popular revolts seemed to reflect the times: a global norm that unelected government was illegitimate; the use of social media to connect disparate groups; and the interconnectedness of global markets, as biofuels drove up the price of staple foods in developing countries.[35] The outcomes of the Arab Uprisings have been highly varied: Tunisia has an elected government; Egypt once again has a military ruler; governments in Libya and Yemen appear unable to control their own territory. Elsewhere, protests have been brutally repressed, and civil wars are ongoing. In the chaos and struggles for power, nonstate actors like the Islamic State briefly governed territory covering millions of Iraqis and Syrians.

The Rise of New Powers

In the past two decades, many poor countries have made significant economic strides. There are four major reasons for this. First, many emerged from lengthy and costly civil wars, and political stability is essential for growth. Second, commodity prices have been high, which has helped spur growth in countries with abundant natural energy resources, such as Brazil and Russia. Third, investors have been excited by the potentially large returns offered by emerging economies, and as a result, poorer countries can now avail themselves of significant amounts of investment. Fourth, a poor country can take advantage of available technology to jump-start its growth because it does not need to reinvent the wheel. Consider malaria. A poor country suffering from malaria has at its disposal the knowledge of the world about where malaria comes from, how it is spread, how it can be treated, and how it can be prevented. The same goes for road-building technology, telecommunications technology, food technology, and so on.

The second global age has witnessed a reversal of a much longer trend in global inequality.[36] Although inequality between countries generally grew in the past 200 years, it has narrowed in the past 20 or so years. The initial divergence was mainly because of the rapid development of the Industrial Revolution and the growth of strong states in the Western world, followed by the spread of colonialism, in which these increasingly wealthy countries retarded the progress of societies that had weak or not-yet-strong-enough economic and political systems to resist domination. Nobel-prize-winning economist Michael Spence says that the 200-year period leading up to 1940 was a "breakout period for a minority of the world's population, with some 750 million people living in industrializing countries and the remaining 4-plus billion left behind."[37]

Over the past two decades, however, the opposite is true: Developing countries have had much stronger economic growth than developed countries. Countries like Brazil and China have raised tens of millions of people out of poverty. But wealth is still highly concentrated in the world. In Figure 1.12, the human population is shown from left to right, and wealth is shown on the vertical axis. The dotted line shows the average per capita wealth for all countries is $13,460. We see that only a small share of humanity is above this line and that a tiny share is far above it. China and India are especially notable for the size of their populations. Figure 1.13 provides an overview of the interactions and tensions that have resulted from this second global age.

FIGURE 1.12

Share of Wealth in the Global Population

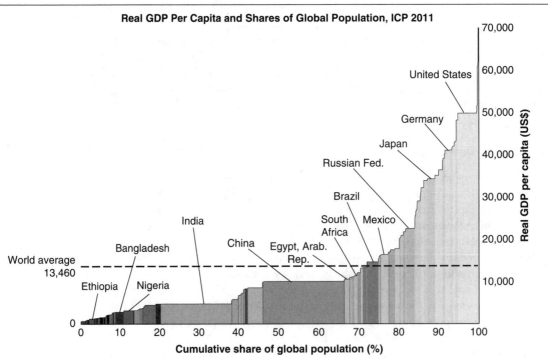

Source: World Bank, 2015. *Purchasing Power Parities and Real Expenditures of World Economics : A Comprehensive Report of the 2011 International Comparison Program.* Washington, DC. © World Bank. https://openknowledge.worldbank.org/handle/10986/20526 License: CC BY 3.0 IGO.

FIGURE 1.13

Global Forces, Interactions, and Tensions in the Second Global Age: A Synopsis

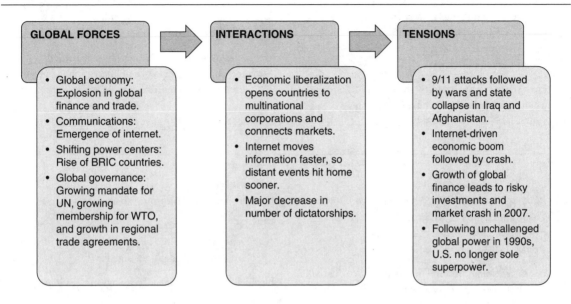

GLOBAL FORCES

- Global economy: Explosion in global finance and trade.
- Communications: Emergence of internet.
- Shifting power centers: Rise of BRIC countries.
- Global governance: Growing mandate for UN, growing membership for WTO, and growth in regional trade agreements.

INTERACTIONS

- Economic liberalization opens countries to multinational corporations and connects markets.
- Internet moves information faster, so distant events hit home sooner.
- Major decrease in number of dictatorships.

TENSIONS

- 9/11 attacks followed by wars and state collapse in Iraq and Afghanistan.
- Internet-driven economic boom followed by crash.
- Growth of global finance leads to risky investments and market crash in 2007.
- Following unchallenged global power in 1990s, U.S. no longer sole superpower.

SUMMARY

One could fill a library covering each paragraph of this chapter, so sweeping have we needed to be. Although a "complete" telling of all historical events is not possible, this chapter has provided you with enough basic background knowledge to begin making sense of the next chapters. We have seen how the international actors and events that interest us in this book do not emerge from thin air. They emerge from, and through, history. More specifically, we have seen that our present global age is not unique. The world witnessed unprecedented integration and connection in the 19th century. In acknowledging this first global age, we also can appreciate that its decline means the present second global age is neither inevitable nor irrevocable. In other words, our global age is the product of decisions made by human action. Our world is not something that simply "happened" to us. Every act to make our lives more global can also be undone. Any global age can be made and unmade.

KEY TERMS

Bretton Woods System (BWS) 32
Gold Standard 26

neoliberalism 36
Pax Britannica 26

structuralist theory 34
superpower 31

QUESTIONS FOR REVIEW

1. Choose one international story from the front page of a major newspaper. Identify one specific event discussed in this chapter that improves our understanding of the news story.

2. How resilient and durable is the Second Global Age when compared with the First Global Age?

3. Of our four Global Forces, rank the Forces that best explain the rise of China.

4. In international studies, tensions are sometimes the unintended consequence of interactions. Can you identify one example of an unintended consequence in the chapter?

LEARN MORE

Cold War International History Project, The Woodrow Wilson International Center for Scholars, https://www.wilsoncenter.org/program/cold-war-international-history-project

African Studies Center, Boston University Pardee School of Global Studies, http://www.bu.edu/africa/outreach/colonialism/

Further resources for learning about colonialism and decolonization:

Gold Standard, Economic History Association, https://eh.net/encyclopedia/gold-standard/

Detailed description of the workings of the Gold Standard

NOTES

1. This section draws on Evan Osnos, "Doomsday Prep for the Super-Rich," *The New Yorker*, January 23, 2017, http://www.newyorker.com/magazine/2017/01/30/doomsday-prep-for-the-super-rich.

2. Survivalist101.com, "Financial Survival for Domesday Preppers," http://survivalist101.com/tutorials/financial-prepping-101/financial-survival-for-doomsday-preppers/.

3. Survivalist101.com, "Financial Survival for Domesday Preppers."

4. Carly Stec, "The Doom Boom: Inside the Survival Industry's Explosive Growth," HubSpot, August 14, 2017, https://blog.hubspot.com/marketing/survival-industry-growth.

5. Angus Maddison, "The World Economy: A Millennial Perspective," Development Centre Studies (Paris, France: OECD, 2001).

6. H.-J. Chang, *Kicking Away the Ladder: Development Strategy in Historical Perspective* (London, U.K.: Anthem Press, 2002).

7. Dani Rodrik, *The Globalization Paradox: Why Global Markets, States, and Democracy Can't Coexist* (Oxford, U.K.: Oxford University Press, 2011), 141.

8. Thomas Packenham, *The Scramble for Africa, 1876–1912* (New York, NY: Random House, 1991).

9. At the time, the German Empire included much of present-day Poland; Austria-Hungary included present Austria, Czech Republic, Slovakia, Hungary, Slovenia, Croatia, Bosnia, and some of Romania, Serbia, and

Ukraine. The Ottoman Empire spanned present-day Turkey and much of the Arab Middle East.

10. Charles Poor Kindleberger, *The World in Depression 1929–1939 40th Anniversary of a Classic in Economic History* (Berkeley: University of California Press, 2013).

11. Barry J. Eichengreen, *Hall of Mirrors: The Great Depression, the Great Recession, and the Uses—and Misuses—of History*, 2016. F. H. Cardoso and E. Faletto, *Dependency and Development in Latin America* (Berkeley: University of California Press, 1979).

12. Patrick M. Regan, *Civil Wars and Foreign Powers: Outside Intervention in Intrastate Conflict*, 2002. Patrick M. Regan, "Third-Party Interventions and the Duration of Intrastate Conflicts," *The Journal of Conflict Resolution* 46, no. 1 (February 2002): 55–73.

13. The founding members were from Kuwait, Saudi Arabia, Venezuela, Iran, and Iraq.

14. As of July 27, 2015, these are the Industrial & Commerce Bank of China, China Construction Bank Corporation, and Agricultural Bank of China Limited. *Source:* http://www.forbes.com/sites/liyanchen/2015/05/06/2015-global-2000-the-worlds-largest-banks/.

15. John M. Hobson, *The Eastern Origins of Western Civilisation* (Cambridge, U.K.: Cambridge University Press, 2004). Janet L. Abu-Lughod, *Before European Hegemony: The World System A.D. 1250–1350* (Oxford, U.K.: Oxford University Press, 2006).

16. Lawrence J. Lau, Yingyi Qian, and Gerard Roland, "Reform Without Losers: An Interpretation of China's Dual-Track Approach to Transition," *Journal of Political Economy* 108, no. 1 (February 1, 2000): 120–143. Barry Naughton, *The Chinese Economy: Transitions and Growth*, vol. 1 (Cambridge, MA: The MIT Press, 2007). Chenggang Xu, "The Fundamental Institutions of China's Reforms and Development," *Journal of Economic Literature* 49, no. 4 (December 2011): 1076–1151, https://doi.org/10.1257/jel.49.4.1076. Loren Brandt, Debin

Ma, and Thomas G. Rawski, "From Divergence to Convergence: Reevaluating the History Behind China's Economic Boom," *Journal of Economic Literature* 52, no. 1 (March 2014): 45–123, https://doi.org/10.1257/jel.52.1.45.

17. Min Ye, *Diasporas and Foreign Direct Investment in China and India* (Cambridge, U.K.: Cambridge University Press, 2014), 53.

18. Niall Ferguson and Moritz Schularick, "'Chimerica' and the Global Asset Market Boom," *International Finance* 10, no. 3 (December 1, 2007): 215–239.

19. Sandra Heep, *China in Global Finance: Domestic Financial Repression and International Financial Power* (New York, NY: Springer Science & Business Media, 2014), 12.

20. J. A. Frieden, *Global Capitalism: Its Fall and Rise in the Twentieth Century* (New York, NY: W.W. Norton, 2006), 380.

21. Frieden, 395.

22. Thomas Oatley, *International Political Economy*, 5th edition (Boston, MA: Routledge, 2015), 4.

23. Thomas G. Weiss and Pallavi Roy, "The UN and the Global South, 1945 and 2015: Past as Prelude?," *Third World Quarterly* 37, no. 7 (July 2, 2016): 1147–1155, https://doi.org/10.1080/01436597.2016.1154436.

24. U.S. Department of Commerce, "Falling Through the Net: Toward Digital Inclusion," A report on Americans' access to technology tools (Washington, DC: U.S. Department of Commerce, 2000).

25. International Telecommunications Union, "ICT Statistics," http://www.itu.int/ITU-D/ict/statistics/ict/.

26. Exxon Mobil, Petro China.

27. Apple, Google, Microsoft.

28. Johnson & Johnson, Novartis.

29. Berkshire Hathaway, Wells Fargo, Bank of China.

30. According to https://www.forbes.com/global2000/list/#tab: overall.

31. Manuel Castells, *The Rise of the Network Society* (Cambridge, MA: Blackwell, 1996).

32. "The Status of Nuclear Inspections in Iraq: An Update," Text, March 7, 2003, https://www.iaea.org/newscenter/statements/status-nuclear-inspections-iraq-update.

33. CBS News, "Plans For Iraq Attack Began On 9/11," September 4, 2002, http://www.cbsnews.com/news/plans-for-iraq-attack-began-on-9-11/.

34. http://www.reuters.com/article/2013/02/02/us-usa-veterans-suicide-idUSBRE9101E320130202

35. Tim Rice, "Biofuels Are Driving Food Prices Higher | Tim Rice," *The Guardian*, http://www.theguardian.com/global-development/poverty-matters/2011/jun/01/biofuels-driving-food-prices-higher.

36. Branko Milanovic, *Global Inequality: A New Approach for the Age of Globalization* (Cambridge, MA: Belknap Press, 2016).

37. Michael Spence, *The Next Convergence: The Future of Economic Growth in a Multispeed World* (New York, NY: Macmillan, 2011), 4.

States

SHAPERS AND SUBJECTS OF GLOBAL INTERACTIONS

Kurdish YPG Fighters

Flickr user Kurdishstruggle, https://www.flickr.com/photos/kurdishstruggle/13164543633/.
Licensed under CC BY 2.0, https://creativecommons.org/licenses/by/2.0/legalcode.

LEARNING OBJECTIVES

After finishing this chapter, you should be able to:

- Define a state and be able to explain the definition's components.

- Distinguish between states, nations, governments, and regimes.

- Situate today's states in terms of the historical emergence of states.

- Identify the role of states in contemporary domestic and international issues.

- Articulate differences between states in terms of states' strengths or weaknesses.

THE AGE OF STATES: BORN FROM A CYCLE OF INTERACTIONS

In movies and TV, we see images of medieval life under kings. From his throne, the king commands his jester to dance, his executioner to kill, and his peasants to bow. But in reality, kings did not have much power beyond the castle walls. A king may order his peasants 100 miles away to bow, but in practice, he had little ability to make them do so. Moreover, the peasants may have been "subjects" of many rulers, not just one. This was an age before states, in which rulers did not have the administrative ability to control people far away, nor did they assume they alone could claim the loyalty of communities. They did not have territorial control. They did not claim to monopolize authority.

But today we live in the age of states. For most of history, people have lived in a huge variety of political communities, such as kingdoms, chiefdoms, or stateless tribes. Over the past 300 years or so, a type of political entity called a **state** emerged. Today, practically every square inch of land on the earth is controlled by a state. So widespread is the reach of states that we often take them for granted and don't even notice they're there. You do not simply live in some "place." You, and almost every other human, lives inside an organization called a "state."

state: sovereign organization with compulsory membership that claims a monopoly on the legitimate use of violence within a territory.

It is only when states fail that their importance is cast into stark relief. States are such important actors in the world today that many argue that they made globalization possible. This can be confusing since others say that globalization is putting an end to the state as we know it. Can they both be right? In this chapter, we start by clarifying what states are, what they do, and where they come from. We then learn about the difference between strong and weak states and assess the arguments made about states and globalization. This leads to some of the biggest questions of our time. Should every nation have its own state? Why are some states supposedly "strong" while others are "weak" or "failed"? What becomes of states when a few corporations are wealthier than many states and when diseases, terrorists, and media freely move through borders? Will these things called "states" even exist in decades to come?

States are perfect examples of how the world is shaped through complex *interactions*. States emerged as distinct types of political systems over hundreds of years as a result of interactions with other political systems. Just as today's global events are the outcome of states interacting, states are simultaneously shaped by the actions of other states. Even powerful states like China or the United States are constrained by the actions of other states. In addition, groups within states—whether they be religious, economic, environmental, or military groups—are constantly trying to shape and control the state, yet they are also affected by those already in control of the state. Just as with the global level, domestically (internally) states affect their societies and are a product of them. At all levels, states are products of interaction.

States also affect, and are affected by, our *global forces*. First, global markets are in part a result of the actions states have taken to forge trade deals and connect financial systems, but economic globalization also constrains the ability of many states to do what their citizens would like. Second, states make investment in undersea cables and satellites that make information technology a global force, but the free movement of information has made it hard for states to control their media. States have been instrumental in the spectacular economic growth seen and poverty reduction in emerging powers such as China and India. In both countries, states have been heavily involved in providing loans to agricultural and industrial producers, and both have managed their exchange rates in order to make their exports competitively priced. Fourth, global governance. Nonstate actors, as defined later in this chapter, challenge the ability of states to control global governance. Organizations like the United Nations are state organizations. They were created by states to serve states. But now the ability of states to shape the global agenda is being challenged by global corporations, civil society actors, and militants (see Figure 2.1).

FIGURE 2.1

Global Forces, Interactions, and Tensions in the Age of States

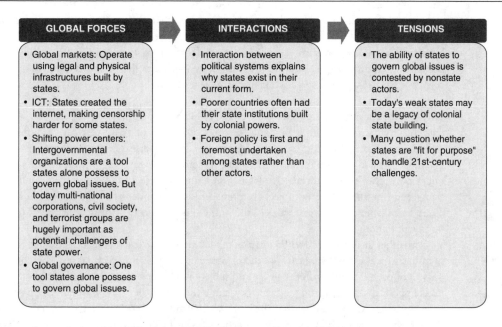

GLOBAL FORCES	INTERACTIONS	TENSIONS
• Global markets: Operate using legal and physical infrastructures built by states. • ICT: States created the internet, making censorship harder for some states. • Shifting power centers: Intergovernmental organizations are a tool states alone possess to govern global issues. But today multi-national corporations, civil society, and terrorist groups are hugely important as potential challengers of state power. • Global governance: One tool states alone possess to govern global issues.	• Interaction between political systems explains why states exist in their current form. • Poorer countries often had their state institutions built by colonial powers. • Foreign policy is first and foremost undertaken among states rather than other actors.	• The ability of states to govern global issues is contested by nonstate actors. • Today's weak states may be a legacy of colonial state building. • Many question whether states are "fit for purpose" to handle 21st-century challenges.

What Is a State? An Organization That Monopolizes Violence

The most popular definition of a state comes from the German sociologist Max Weber. He defined a state as "the form of human community that (successfully) lays claim to the *monopoly of legitimate physical violence* within a particular territory."[1] The key words are monopoly, legitimate, violence, and territory. Let's look at each in turn.

Monopoly. A state monopolizes—or takes for itself—the sole right to rule in a territory. Before states, rulers often shared power with other powerful actors, like landowners, religious leaders, or clan elders. But today, states claim a **monopoly** on the right to govern in their territory. No one but the U.S. government, for example, claims the right to pass laws or put people on trial in the United States.

monopoly: sole ownership.

Legitimacy. Citizens sometimes kill one another and armed groups sometimes rebel against the government, but states say violence is only legitimately used when they use it. Only they can use violence with **legitimacy**. Citizens may be permitted to kill other citizens—for example, in self-defense—but only if the state passes laws to legalize it. A state can always kill in self-defense, despite whether it has passed a law to allow it.

legitimacy: perception that something is appropriate or natural, even if not preferred.

Violence. This may seem like a strange thing to include in a definition, but **violence** is what makes states unique compared with all other types of organizations. Pastors cannot kill their

violence (or coercion): use or threat of physical harm.

followers, and companies cannot execute their workers, but states are allowed to kill their own people (capital punishment or suppressing rebellions). Although most scholars define states in terms of violence, others use the term "coercion," which is a more general term that includes the use or threats to use force. Whether you like it or not, the state can force you by threats of jail or fines to wear a seatbelt, vaccinate your child, or recycle, or draft you to go to war and kill on its behalf. As we will see in our chapter on human rights, most states now agree to things they will not do to their own people, such as use chemical weapons. But even this is a new thing, and a state can always leave any such agreements it may have made.

Territory. The difference between this type of political organization and organizations like a church is that a state's claim is first and foremost a claim to rule over **territory**, whereas a church defines its authority in terms of people.[2] Catholics are subject to the moral authority of the Pope no matter where they are in the world, but everyone and everything within a state's territory is under the authority of that state. An Iranian in China is subject to Chinese law even if, as a practicing Muslim, the person is subject to moral and ethical codes of his or her Imam back home. Thus, there is no escape from states. Only in the middle of oceans or in space can a person truly be free of the rule of a state.[3]

territory: physical space including land and water.

Two other qualities set states apart from other types of political organizations. First, **compulsory membership**. You can voluntarily opt out of your gym membership without punishment, but if you opt out of your U.S. citizenship, you are still subject to U.S. law while in the United States. Second, unlike political systems throughout history, and unlike any other type of organization today, states have **sovereignty**. This means that they are the final authority in their territory, and no one or no thing is above them. Chile, for example, participates at the United Nations (UN) and signs treaties just like other states. But it can never be legally forced to sign a treaty, and no other state or international organization can do anything within its territory without the approval of the Chilean state. When we talk about the "sovereign state," therefore, we mean organizations that have the ultimate authority in their territory.

compulsory membership: subject to an organization's rules irrespective of consent.

sovereignty: principle that states have supreme authority within their territory.

What Is Not a State? Regimes, Governments, Countries, and Nations

A lot of other terms are used interchangeably with states in the media and popular culture, so let's clarify what they mean. First, states within the United States like Alabama or Michigan are units in the federal structure of a much bigger thing, the United States of America. But in social science, a state is the sovereign entity that can make treaties with other states, represent itself at the UN, and have the final say on what happens in its territory. A **regime** is the rules governing how people get into power and how government works. The regime in Botswana is democratic, but in Myanmar (Burma), it is military. If Myanmar becomes a democracy, the regime would be democratic, but the Republic of the Union of Myanmar would be unchanged.

regime: rules governing how people get into power and how government works.

A **government** is the people or political parties that govern, make laws, sign treaties, and so on. In the United States, we often refer to the government as "the administration," such as the "Carter administration." That is just another way of talking about who currently heads. But the police, judges, and Department of Motor Vehicles (DMV) or Motor Vehicle Administration (MVA) employees that work for the U.S. state do not change after an election. The U.S. government changes, but the state does not. A country, meanwhile, is an ambiguous term that scholars avoid

government: people or political parties that govern and make laws.

when they want to be precise since depending on the culture and language spoken, "country" can mean state, nation, or territory.

A **nation** is a group that thinks of itself as a political community. Not all groups think of themselves as political. For example, amateur bowlers generally do not think that fellow amateur bowlers comprise a political group. A nation, by contrast, is a group that thinks of itself as a political community. Why does this matter for states? Some people talk about the rise of the state in the past 300 years in terms of the emergence of the **nation-state**. This is a political system where the state and the nation are one and the same, that is, where leaders come from the same group as most of the citizens. For example, most people who think of themselves as Icelandic live in the territory controlled by the Icelandic state. We might call Iceland a nation-state, therefore, because the nation (Icelanders) and the state (Republic of Iceland) are indistinguishable.

But not all states are nations, and not all nations are states. For example, Canada is a state. It is a sovereign entity that engages in international relations with other sovereign states. But some Canadians in Quebec identify more strongly with their French roots than with an identity as a Canadian. Nevertheless, even though not all Canadian citizens "feel" Canadian, the Canadian state is still a state, and even if some in Quebec identify with their nation rather than with the Canadian state, the fact is they live in the Canadian state, and have no sovereign state of their own. Finally, not all nations are states. In the United States, native Americans consider themselves nations—they are a group of people who identify a shared past with one another—but they do not have a state. They have significant legal autonomy *within* the United States, but they are not a state.

To use all of these terms correctly, let's say that the Kingdom of the Netherlands (the state) is a democracy (its regime), led by Prime Minister Mark Rutte (the government), who is elected by the Dutch people (the nation). Since the nation broadly corresponds to who controls the state and who is subject to the state, we can also say the Netherlands is a nation-state.

A Site of Interaction: What Is "Inside" a State?

We should not think of states as coherent, unified "things" that have an existence of their own. We hear in the news about "the Indonesian" or "the Lebanese state," as though these were monolithic things, but we would not say that the "United States is anti-gun control" since a range of viewpoints exists across citizens and groups within the United States. We would instead say, "Some powerful groups and many active voters lobby to protect existing gun laws in the United States." This statement *disaggregates the state*, which means we understand a state is composed of many different actors, many of whom have conflicting interests. A state does not "think" or "desire" something any more than an ocean does. An ocean has structure and patterns we can analyze, but it is not one being. It is made up of billions of small things that try to push it in a way that helps them survive.

Similarly, states are hugely complex organizations covering vast territories. They are made up of **state actors** and **nonstate actors**. State actors could include traffic cops, financial regulators, nuclear technicians, judges, or teachers. Typically a state actor's ultimate authority and resources (salary, equipment, etc.) come from the fact that they work for, or in, a state. State actors can be domestic/internal, such as an elected official, or international, such as an ambassador to the UN. Nonstate actors do not get their resources and power by virtue of their connection to a state, and they are also diverse: parents, unions, farmers, priests, anarchists, religious extremists, and so on.

nation: group that thinks of itself as a political community.

nation-state: where the state governs, and is governed by, people of one nation.

state actors: person, group, or organization whose ultimate authority and resources (salary, equipment, etc.) typically come from the fact that they work for, or in, a state.

nonstate actors: any person, group, or organization— whether within a state or across state boundaries—that does not work in or for a state.

Kurds often describe themselves as the world's largest ethnic group without its own state (on ethnicity, see Chapter 5). Kurdistan refers to an area rather than a state. It is the area inhabited by ethnic Kurds that spans Turkey, Syria, Iran, and Iraq. Iraqi Kurdistan is an autonomous region with about five million people in northern Iraq. It is a functioning *de facto* state that is not recognized within the larger dysfunctional state of Iraq. Repeated attempts to gain their independence were brutally suppressed

FIGURE 2.2

Kurdish Regions in Iraq, Iran, Syria, and Turkey

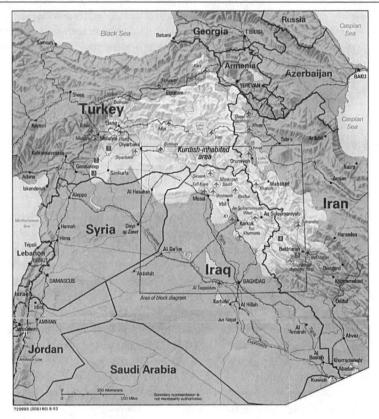

Source: Based on map drawn by U.S. Central Intelligence Agency, located at the Perry-Castañeda Library Map Collection at The University of Texas at Austin http://www.lib.utexas.edu/maps/middle_east_and_asia/kurdish_lands_92.jpg. Linked from Perry-Castañeda Library Map Collection at The University of Texas at Austin, Public Domain, https://commons.wikimedia.org/w/index.php?curid=1656189.

by former Iraqi president Saddam Hussein. The Iraqi Kurds are mostly Sunni Muslim, but they define themselves as much by their cultural heritage as Kurds as they do as Muslims, and Kurdish is its own language. As Iraq went through multiple implosions over the past decade, Kurdish leaders have secured greater independence for the region, and in 2014, they even began exporting their own oil.[4]

Iraqi Kurds hoped powerful states would back their 2017 independence referendum since they helped Western countries fight against the Islamic State of Iraq and Syria (ISIS, or "the Islamic State"). But they miscalculated. Although the referendum passed, major powers did not support the claim, each for its own geopolitical reasons. But the United States maintains a "one Iraq" policy, meaning no breakup of Iraq will be considered, so full Kurdish independence may not come any time soon. From the perspective of Iraqi Kurds, they are condemned to remain subjects of the dysfunctional and violent Iraqi state (see Figure 2.2).

Should Iraqi Kurdistan get its own state? On the one hand, the principle of self-determination—that each nation should govern itself—has historically been an important idea for liberals and human rights advocates, who used it to rail against colonial rule (see Chapter 7). There are hundreds, if not thousands, of groups around the world that would like to form their own country (secessionism), leave and join another country (irredentism), or simply become autonomous within their state (federalism). The people in Iraq's Kurdish region probably do a better job of governing themselves than does the Iraqi state. But not only is the "mother state" unwilling to lose some of its territory, states in general also have been reluctant to recognize claims of statehood over the past few decades for fear that it could ignite a series of secessionist claims.

It is not only states that tend to oppose the creation of new states. Some scholars say that the "one nation, one state" idea also mistakenly assumes that nations are set in stone. For example, America's identity as an English-speaking country was something that was cultivated over time: Both the Bible (1743) and the Declaration of Independence (1776) appeared in wide circulation in German before they appeared in English![5] Nations, in other words, are not unchanging "things," so it does not make sense to give each nation its own state. This is why critics fear that if every nation has its own state, this would not prevent nations themselves from splintering over generations, with ever smaller entities calling themselves nations and seeking new states. These critics say the solution is to have states so large that no one race, religion, or ethnicity can come close to a majority.

Reflect

What global forces are at play in preventing Kurds from having their own sovereign state?

WHAT DOES A STATE DO?

Most states play important roles in controlling, protecting, monitoring, and investing in people and things.

A State Controls

States control movement and activity. First, states try to control movement within and across their borders. This includes the movement of goods like pigs, guns, and trucks, but also it includes people in the form of controls on citizenship and migration. In many places in the world, before states, there were few legal restrictions on migration. But today, states try to control who comes and goes through their ports and airports through physical infrastructure, like checkpoints, and legal infrastructure, in the form of laws and regulations that legalize some behaviors while criminalizing others.

Second, states try to control activity. States can legalize markets, like enacting laws to protect the property of slave owners. States can create markets, like financial derivatives. States can disrupt markets, like anti-trust or anti-monopoly laws. And states can criminalize markets, like slavery, eventually.

Groups want to control their state because of this power, which can be put to very different ends. The apartheid state of South Africa used its regulatory power to create racist laws in all areas of life (work, housing, voting, health) to contain and suppress the majority black population. The "Pass Laws" were like an internal passport, under which nonwhites were only allowed to leave their designated areas to work in the (white) cities. Thus, the white population used its control of the state's powers to oppress another group.

If used correctly, however, states can use their ability to control behavior toward positive ends. For instance, they can ensure the strength and vitality of markets by preventing monopolies. If the French company Orange developed the world's greatest laptop and all competing manufacturers went out of business, Orange would be the sole actor in the laptop market. To maximize profits, it would make sense for Orange to cut back on research and development and simply raise prices, which it could do in the absence of competition. If a small number of actors can control a market, innovation will slow down and the public as a whole loses. What is good for the company can harm consumers and the economy overall. This is why countries developed strong anti-trust (anti-monopoly) laws one century ago. Consumers need the state to serve as a kind of third party to make sure that markets stay competitive.

A State Protects

States are supposed to protect the life and property of everyone within their borders. But this is a *normative* quality of states—a quality we would like states to have but that they don't always possess. The reality is highly variable around the world. In some states, people who are formally recognized as members (i.e., citizens) are entitled to special treatment: An immigrant can easily be thrown into jail without due process, whereas a citizen cannot. In these states, laws constrain the state's ability to arbitrarily detain or search people. These are places with the **rule of law**, meaning laws apply even to the most powerful in society, even to the state itself. In many other states, however, people have little power to stop states from invading their privacy, discriminating against them on grounds of sex or race, or stealing their assets. Sometimes this discriminatory behavior is official state policy—like a law on racial segregation—or sometimes it is just the behavior of a state official over whom a person has no control—like a corrupt cop.

A state that protects people and property can be beneficial for prosperity. In fact, corporations have their origin in this activity. The oldest documented corporation in the world is Stora, a Swedish copper mining company created in 1228. Stora was a legal entity that was backed by the Swedish Crown.[6] The king endorsed Stora's contracts, meaning that if Stora or the contracting party did not abide by the signed contract, the guilty party would be punished by the king. This willingness of a ruler to act as a third party in a relationship in which he was not primarily involved enabled things like large contracts to exist. Without a third party willing to punish rule-breakers, complex economic or social activity becomes too risky and few are willing to do it. Almost one millennium later, Stora Enso is a multinational corporation worth more than the gross domestic product (GDP) of most countries.

A State Monitors

States collect information on people and things. Economic data that are crucial for the smooth functioning of markets are provided by states, such as rates of inflation, economic growth, or

rule of law: expectation that all citizens are equally subject to laws, regardless of their power or status.

migration. The economic statistics we hear about in the news, or that investors use every day, rely on some state worker gathering data on the average price of eggs, the number of people coming and going through ports, or the number of birth certificates issued. Even before the Internet, states collected extraordinary amounts of information about their territory and all within it, including data on soil quality, sending satellites into space for better weather prediction, and monitoring the spread of diseases. All of these things make states data-rich organizations. They are uniquely able—and often uniquely willing—to collect data that are beneficial to the public, and their territorial presence makes this possible. But states can use their monitoring powers for different ends. The mass violence seen in Nazi Germany was made possible in part because the state was present in every neighborhood. It had information on people through their bank accounts, passports, birth certificates, or business licenses, which allowed the state to target specific homes and businesses for persecution.

A State Invests

One of the most important roles states play is solving what is known as the **free rider (or public goods) problem**.[7] This occurs when something everyone wants fails to be provided because everyone thinks others will provide it, even if they don't personally contribute. If a community needs a bridge, for example, even those who do not contribute to its construction could still use it (i.e., they will free ride), so they stay at home in the belief that others will build the bridge. The problem is that *everyone* thinks like this, so the public good—the bridge—does not get built. These problems are everywhere in society. Modern economies require a variety of public investments, like university systems, police, or protections for working parents or rivers near commercial farms. Each individual in society has an interest in better education, security, child rearing, or drinking water, but he or she won't pay higher taxes for it unless everyone does. By forcing everyone to pay taxes—to pay for things we want but would rather someone else pay for—states serve as third-party investors.

free rider (or public goods) problem: benefiting from someone else's work, such as using a bridge without paying for its construction.

WHERE DO STATES COME FROM? FORCES SHAPING THE MODERN STATE

Most modern states grew first in Europe over the past 300 years or so, and then they were spread around the world, usually by colonial Europeans. Europeans did not invent the idea of the state, however. Such a thing existed in China for over 2,000 years. Nor was Europe unique in having successful and enduring political systems that governed large territories. At one time or another, major empires have covered great expanses of land and population, for example, around modern India (Mughal Empire from the 1500s), southern Europe (Ancient Greece), the Middle East and Central Asia (Achaemenid Empire from 600 BCE), West Africa (Mali Empire from 1230), and the Americas (Aztecs, Inca, Maya). Indeed, around the 1400s to 1500s, the global centers of innovation and prosperity were not in Europe but in India and China. Europe was a poor place. It was not dominated by one type of political system as it is today. It had *hundreds* of small political systems, which were a mixture of city-states, communes, and kingdoms, and borders between them were not firm. Indeed, for most of human history, even outside of Europe, there were vast ungoverned spaces in which humans could live without being regulated, monitored, controlled, or licensed by a centralized government. How did the economically poor and organizationally weak European political systems around 1500 transform into powerful states today? War played a key role.

War, Sovereignty, and the Modern State System

Europe's mixture of political systems—city-states, communes, and kingdoms—were gradually replaced by a new type of organization: states. The process played out over centuries in a Darwinian, survival-of-the-fittest way, in which states became better at winning wars and growing their economies than did other political systems. An enhanced fighting ability meant a stronger state, which meant a stronger fighting ability, and so on. This is why political scientist Charles Tilly said, "[W]ar made the state and the state made war."[8] But how exactly did this happen?

First, kings who were formerly dependent on lords to rule their territory began to centralize power. In the 1600s and 1700s, Europe was becoming ever more dominated by powerful kings, which we call **absolutist states**.[9] In an absolutist state, all political power is invested in one person (usually a king), such that there is no discernable difference between the state and its ruler. King Louis XIV of France famously said "*l'état c'est moi,*" meaning "I am the state." Absolutism meant despotic and brutal rule for the people, but the long-term consequence of building strong war machines was investment in taxation systems needed to pay for the military, professionalized armies that required competent bureaucracies, systems of courts, and the growing use of state law to regulate everyday economic interaction. The emergence of a system of states was then deeply interactive: When a neighboring kingdom developed its military power, another kingdom was obliged to develop its military. The incentive to centralize power in the hands of the king and to develop complex and modern systems of taxation with professional bureaucracies spread throughout the continent.[10]

Second, as states became better at fighting wars, some legitimized their power by granting their societies more of a role in everyday governance and they grew wealthier through private property and investments in health, education, infrastructure, and science and by protecting their industries. The notion of liberalism grew in importance, in which individuals, not just kings, were said to have rights. The idea that the king himself should be subject to laws also emerged, and for the first time, people began to think of the king and the state as different things, where before they were inseparable. In the 1700s and 1800s especially, many people in the Western world went from being subjects to citizens. Where once the absolutist King Louis XIV said "I am the state," people began to say "the state is us."

Finally, fighting between Europe's political systems reached an important turning point with the 1648 Treaty of Westphalia, which ended a series of religious wars known as the Thirty Years War (1618–1648). The Treaty placed the principle of sovereignty at the heart of states' interactions with one another. Under this principle, rulers agreed to not interfere in the religious practices of other monarchies. Today, the concept has come to mean a more general agreement that states do not have the right to interfere in the internal affairs of other states. Although sovereignty is a norm rather than an international law—the Treaty did not establish a law of sovereignty—it began the modern international system based on the *principle* of state sovereignty we know today. The Treaty was a product of the interactions between states, and it continues to shape states' interactions today.

Colonial States

Perhaps the most important historical factor that has shaped the fortunes of poor and wealthy countries was the creation of colonial states. Most states outside of Europe were creations of European colonialism, including the United States. From the 1500s to the 1900s, only a tiny fraction of the world evaded control by European powers.[11] The state as a model of political organization was exported by Europeans to the Americas from the 1500s, and to Africa and Asia in the 1800s. As colonies contributed to prosperity in Europe, rivalries between European powers intensified in the

absolutist state: state where there is no rule of law, since the ruler is not subject to any laws.

Almost all of today's weak states were once colonies. They are often described in terms of their "postcolonial pathologies," meaning their dysfunction or abnormality results from once being colonized. We can see the roots of their present problems (or pathologies) in their distant (colonial) past, and that many of these former colonies experience the world today in ways similar to one another. Let's look at the Philippines.

When the Philippines became independent in 1946, its economy was not so dissimilar to that in South Korea. But over the next few decades, as South Korea's boomed, the Philippine economy stumbled as the country went from dictatorship to coups. Today, per capita income in the Philippines is at the level of Nicaragua and the Republic of Congo, and on the Human Development Index, it is at the level of Uzbekistan and Mongolia, a full 102 places below South Korea. Why was the Philippine postcolonial experience so disastrous? Let's look from the inside-out perspective, meaning from within the country.

Corruption and cronyism seem to be a major contributor to the state's weakness. The country is known for the dominance of political dynasties: in 2007, 60% of its members of congress had a relative who was previously in congress; in the United States, the figure was 7%.[12] Half of all the provincial governors are related to someone in congress. Thus, one explanation for the weakness of the Philippine state is that it is "captured" by a small group of elite families that rule in their own interest. This is a "state versus society" way of seeing weak states, in which "strong" social actors prevent a weak state from becoming a "strong" state.[13]

But look more closely at Philippine history and you will see that the Philippine state was often *the reason* such families emerged in the first place. Here we can use an outside-in perspective and see how external colonial powers shaped local circumstances. The Spanish extended their control over the modern Philippines from the 1500s and used the Catholic Church rather than Spanish officials to govern. The Spanish invested little in developing the country economically or in cultivating a sense of Filipino identity: Despite some 300 to 400 years of colonialism, no more than 5% of the population spoke Spanish at the time of U.S. occupation in 1898 after the Spanish-American War (see Figure 2.3).[14]

The United States suppressed Filipino independence struggles with a brutal counterinsurgency campaign, and the Philippines remained a U.S. colony until 1946. The United States introduced elections at all levels of the Philippine state with expanded suffrage in the early 20th century. Importantly, elections were introduced before the creation of a professional bureaucracy, which meant that politicians were able to politicize all types of public offices, like police chiefs, court clerks, and health inspectors.[15] In the first elections, a candidate had to come from a set of families that were recognized by the United States. This incentivized politicians to come together as families and rewarded those who could do so. The state also controlled most of the land in the country, so political forces were able to use this to reward their supporters and punish their opponents.

Businesses that were allied with the "right" factions were able to use state-owned banks to get cheap loans and used their connections to buy land cheaply and set up massive sugar plantations. They were then able to mix their economic power with their political power. They used profits from these plantations to put their candidates in office, and thus, they ensured the state would exist to benefit them. The state allowed these powerful groups to set up monopolies and to punish their competitors. In this view, the dynasties that eventually came to be seen as the enemy to progress in the Philippines thus became powerful *because* of the colonial state.

Today the Philippines is a democracy, but observers say the main political forces really just

(Continued)

(Continued)

FIGURE 2.3

Dynasty in Philippine Politics

Source: Jose V. Abueva, "Dynasties Threat to Democracy," *Philippine Daily Inquirer,* November 3, 2012. Retrieved from http://opinion.inquirer.net/40084/dynasties-threat-to-democracy.

represent powerful families.[16] So, when we describe a developing country as a postcolonial country, we are really saying that this country's weaknesses must be understood in light of its colonial experience.

Reflect

What tensions—or unintended consequences—arising from global interactions are evident in this example?

late 1800s and sparked a new wave of colonization that targeted Africa and Asia. Unlike the previous wave, however, this new wave saw limited settlement by Europeans, so the colonists were much less interested in the quality of life in these new colonies. This means they did not build effective bureaucracies, roads, courts, or laws to protect property or limit the power of the state. Instead, colonial powers often tried to rule their subjects on a shoestring by using local or indigenous groups to rule on their behalf in a system known as *indirect rule*.[17]

Shortly after World War II, most colonial states became independent. These newly independent states faced three major problems, however. Economically, many were heavily dependent on the export of a few commodities, like raw (unprocessed) agricultural or energy products. This left a country's economy heavily exposed to fluctuating global prices. Since developing countries exported these "primary commodities," they did not reap the profits that come from *processing* commodities, which happened in Europe. Politically, colonial powers left behind states in which the president had strong executive powers, civil liberties either did not exist or were easily dismantled, and the civil service was not equipped to administer a modern state. When Belgium gave up on decades of plundering Zaire in 1960, it left behind only a handful of college-educated Zairians to govern an area about four times the size of Texas. Socially, colonial powers often invented their colonial states with complete disregard for precolonial borders, such that some societies were separated by an international

FIGURE 2.4

Global Forces, Interactions, and Tensions in the Growth of States

GLOBAL FORCES	INTERACTIONS	TENSIONS
• Markets: European kings needed taxes to pay for war, so they invested in their economies, thereby strengthening their states while growing their economies. Outside of Europe, the search for gold and silver brought the Spanish and Portuguese to the Americas, the search for spices brought the Dutch to Southeast Asia, and the search for cotton brought the English to India. Goods could be traded for slaves in Africa.	• As one European king strengthened their state's ability to fight wars, neighboring kings were compelled to follow or face extinction. This competitive pressure led kingdoms to build large bureaucracies, professional armies, and modern systems of mass taxation. • Competition between European states for colonial possessions saw great swathes of Africa and Asia colonized in the late 1800s. Most existing states have their origins in this period.	• After centuries of conflict, European states agreed to respect the principle of sovereignty, which may be the key feature of international law. But this creates tensions, as any one state can prevent responses to cross-border challenges by invoking the principle. • Weak states are a legacy of colonial-era state building, because colonists did not want to invest in building effective states or strong economies. • Wars among industrialized nations left some too weak to prevent colonies from gaining indepedence. The Ottomans and Germans lost their colonial possessions after WWI, followed by Britain and France after WWII.

border, while other societies found themselves lumped together with people they did not consider part of their community. Although the idea of a nation-state had developed over hundreds of years in Europe—in which the political unit and the people are one and the same—colonialism left many of today's poor countries with little sense of any common identity (see Figure 2.4).

THE STRENGTHS AND WEAKNESSES OF STATES

state capacity: effective ability of a state to develop and execute laws and policies throughout its territory.

States can be strong externally—they can shape the world in their own interests, and make other states do things they would otherwise not do—or internally, which is the concept of **state capacity**. The strength of a state says nothing about whether it is democratic or authoritarian; only about whether it is capable of governing (see Figure 2.5).

Some states are strong domestically—the government is effective, and people obey the law—but weak internationally, while others are the reverse. In Figure 2.5, we see that a "strong state" internationally is not the same as a "strong state" domestically. On the horizontal axis, we proxy the international strength of a state using the size of its economy since the world's most powerful countries tend to be those with the largest economies. On the vertical axis, we have government effectiveness, which is a proxy for a state's capacity within its own borders. The measure comes from a widely used expert survey developed by the World Bank.[18] We have selected just a few countries to illustrate the point that

FIGURE 2.5

Internal and External Strength of States

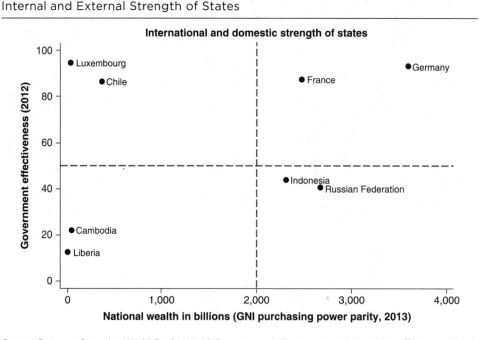

Source: Data are from the World Bank, World Governance Indicators. Located at https://data.worldbank.org/data-catalog/worldwide-governance-indicators, wgi.csv, 2by2.gph, 2by2.png.

states vary in their internal and external strength. In the top left, Luxembourg and Chile are effective domestically but not influential internationally. They have good internal state capacity, but globally they are not powerful. Indonesia and Russia are influential internationally without being strong domestically, while France and Germany fare well on both counts, with Cambodia and Liberia the opposite.

External Power: Global Influence

When you hear about "strong states," you probably think of states that are militarily strong. This is **hard power**: a state's ability to *force* other states to do something. But there is another type of power: **soft power**, which is a state's ability to *influence* what other states do.

hard power: state's ability to force actors to change their behavior.

soft power: state's ability to influence actors' behavior.

Hard Power. We often think of relations between states as undertaken at gunpoint. In this view, the world is run by major powers who bully lesser powers into doing what they want: Russia recently took Crimea from Ukraine because it was strong enough to do so; the United States toppled Saddam Hussein because it did not like him. This is not a world of justice but of force. But, when we compare this time in history with what came before, we see that war between states is becoming *less* common (see Chapter 10). Although military spending is very high in the United States, Russia, and China, it does not seem to be the case that modern states associate military strength with a strong modern state.

Figure 2.6 shows military expenditure as a percentage of GDP by regional average. Keep in mind that GDP has also risen over time, so what we observe is that military expenditure is not becoming more important for states. Look at the thick solid line in Figure 2.6: Total global military expenditure as a share of global GDP has *decreased* over the past two decades, even though the raw amount of expenditure has increased, and even though superpowers like China, Russia, and the United States still spend a lot on their military. Many states today are less concerned with being invaded and more concerned with growing their economies.

Most states are not ramping up their military expenditure. States now try to influence the world by means which are nonmilitary. This is true of the world's most powerful states as well, who try to use organizations like the International Monetary Fund (IMF), UN, or World Trade Organization (WTO) to shape the world the way they want it. They also try to influence other countries through the use of development aid, as we discuss in Chapter 9.

Soft Power. Hard power means you do want I want because I threaten or bribe you. In contrast, soft power means I get you to *want* what I want.[19] A state's soft power is all the things that make it attractive to other states. This could include its wealth, civil liberties, or scientific progress. China's soft power might be its model of economic growth, which has lifted millions out of poverty by explicitly not following Western models of growth. Britain's soft power might be the publicly funded BBC, which broadcasts high-quality journalism around the world.

Read "The Decline of America's Soft Power," by Joseph Nye. Foreign Affairs, 83/16 (2004) at http://www.foreignaffairs.com/articles/59888/joseph-s-nye-jr/the-decline-of-americas-soft-power.

The important thing about soft power is that states are not the only ones that can use it. Nonstate actors like NGOs and McDonald's can also wield soft power by influencing people's ideas or by influencing global markets. This means "soft power" is less something states possess than something

FIGURE 2.6
Global Military Expenditure

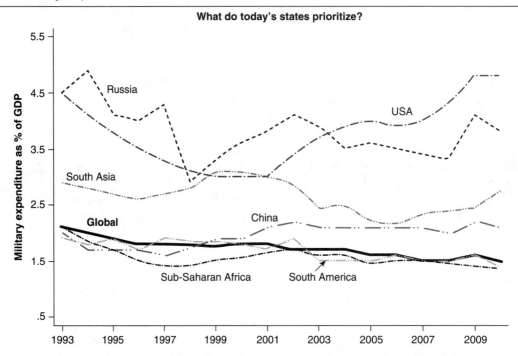

What do today's states prioritize?

Source: Data from the Stockholm International Peace Research Institute (SIPRI) Military Expenditure Database, https://www.sipri.org/databases/milex.sipri_military_data.csv.

their society possesses and they can take advantage of. Thus, it is sometimes hard for states to use their soft power in an instrumental way. For example, a globally powerful actor might affect its own country's global image in a way that the state does not want. Perhaps a U.S. oil giant is responsible for environmental damage in a developing country, and this reflects poorly on the U.S. government even though the company is directly responsible. Another example might be people in the U.S. entertainment industry mocking U.S. government officials in full view of global audiences.

See which country ranks highest on the Monocle's Soft Power Survey at https://monocle .com/film/affairs/soft-power-survey-2016-17/.

Internal Power: State Capacity

We take it for granted that when our government enacts a new law, civil servants and police will implement it. We expect laws to matter. But many people around the world—perhaps most people—are born into states in which laws are not applied equally or at all. In some places, governments have very little ability to enforce their own laws. They cannot detect tax evasion, stop their coastlines from being used by drug smugglers, or vaccinate newborn babies. Sometimes they struggle to control even their own state officials. These are places with low state capacity, which means the government has a weak ability to develop and implement its own laws.

In Figure 2.7, we see that the most effective states in the world also tend to be the wealthiest. The variables on the horizontal and vertical axes are the same as those used in Figure 2.5, but now we look at all countries for which we have data. The countries that are wealthier than we would expect given the effectiveness of their state are oil states (Kuwait, Qatar, Equatorial Guinea). Other states are more effective than we would expect given their wealth. Rwanda shows that a state can be well run even if it is not wealthy, but the general pattern is that poorer states tend to be less effective.

But does state effectiveness lead to wealth, or does a state have to be wealthy before it can become effective? Social scientists debate this a lot. The likely answer is somewhere in the middle: For an economy to grow, an effective state is necessary to preserve law and order, to enforce contracts, to invest in human and physical capital, and to regulate markets. In the right conditions, a growing economy can then feed back into a more effective state, with better educated civil servants and better resourced police, soldiers, and judges.

We can think of the internal (domestic) strength of states along a continuum.[20] **Strong states** like France tend to have strong economies, low corruption, and stable government. **Weak states** like Thailand do a poor job of providing public services or are prone to instability or coups. In **failed states** like Libya, the government does not control all of its territory. Some call these "fragile" states. Constant battling to control the state and its territory means these places are usually violent. **Collapsed states** are extreme versions of failed states because they may not even have a government. Most states are weak, but few are failed, and even fewer are collapsed.

strong states: high state capacity with rule of law. Common in, but not exclusive to, wealthy countries.

weak states: lower state capacity and some violation of rule of law. Common.

failed states: significant territory not under state control. A minority of countries.

collapsed states: most territory not under state control, and maybe no government. Very rare.

FIGURE 2.7

Wealth and State Capacity

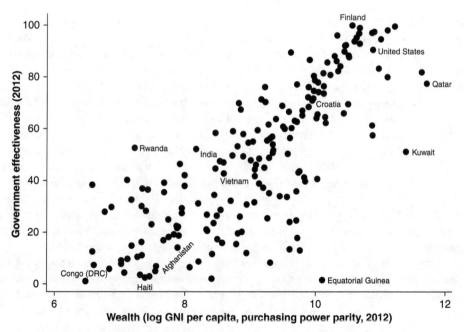

Source: Data are from World Bank, World Governance Indicators.

Read Robert Rotberg's blog on the different categories of state weakness at http://robertrotberg.wordpress.com/2013/02/11/failed-and-weak-states-defined/.

Read "10 Reasons Countries Fall Apart," by Daron Acemoglu and James A. Robinson. Foreign Policy, July/August 2012 at https://foreignpolicy.com/2012/06/18/10-reasons-countries-fall-apart/.

quasi-states:
states that are legally recognized but in reality do not function because they are failed or collapsed. They exist largely "on paper."

Observers wonder whether the problem of weak and failed states is helped or hindered by the international system. Because we live in the age of sovereign states in which states agree not to attack each other, failed states persist because their legal existence is not threatened. Scholars sometimes call these **quasi-states:** They are states that are legally recognized by other states, but they have little if any control over their people or territory. In the time before the modern state, these quasi-states would have been invaded by more powerful neighbors, and their people and territory incorporated into the more successful state. But today, entities like Afghanistan and Somalia are allowed to continue existing. During the Cold War, many states that were oppressive and did little to improve people's welfare were supported diplomatically, militarily, and financially by the United States or the Union of Soviet Socialist Republics (USSR, aka the "Soviet Union" or "Russia"). But once the Cold War ended, many of these states lost their support. The USSR fell apart, and the United States had no need to keep supporting dictatorial governments around the world. Without their patrons, these weak "client" states fell apart. Yet even though they failed, they are still recognized as states. The international system never removes entirely its recognition of one state. Notice again how interactive is the world of states: We cannot understand why states rise and fall without putting them in the context of a *world* of states.

But why are some states weaker than others in the first place? Let's look at two major explanations: legitimacy and identity.

Legitimacy: The State as a Negotiation. The paradox of the world's strongest states is that they are *politically* weak. Why? Imagine a king wants to build a palace but doesn't have any oil or gold to sell. He'd like to tax his people, but he doesn't know where they keep their money, and when they tell him how much they have, he can't tell if they are lying. His state has a low capacity to monitor people, to pry into their personal lives in order to gather data. What does he do? One option would be to smash down their doors and turn up their mattresses to find the cash. But he would need a sizable army to accomplish that and the negative reaction will probably make it even less likely the public will trust him in the long run. A better option is to make people willing to show what is under their mattress or, better yet, willing to pay more tax because they think they will get something in return.

politically constrained:
when a state is logistically able do all types of things, but it is not *allowed* to do them.

quasi-voluntary compliance:
unspoken agreement between rulers and ruled in which the ruled agree to be taxed in return for service provided by the ruler, such as police or schools.

This is why the states that are strongest—those that could, if they were allowed, eavesdrop when you Skype with your nephew—are usually those that are **politically constrained,** meaning the state is logistically able do all types of things, but it is not *allowed* to do them. Part of the reason the U.S. government is able to monitor the calls and e-mails of its own people is that people have let it. Social scientists call this **quasi-voluntary compliance.**[21] In this explanation, strong states are negotiated agreements between rulers and society. This means elites in business, media, churches, or labor, as well as "ordinary people" share an informal understanding of what people get in return for taxes paid. This informal understanding is often intertwined with people's sense of what a government can legitimately do. This helps us make sense of countries where there are no such negotiated agreements. For example, when a government can raise revenue by selling oil or gas or can rely on international aid, it may be less responsive to its citizens, on whom it does not depend for revenue. In oil-rich dictatorships like Gabon, the government may feel little pressure to build better roads or schools.

IS From the Outside-In and the Inside-Out

STATE FAILURE IN AFGHANISTAN

We have heard a lot about failed or collapsed states since 9/11. They are described as lawless places where terrorist groups can gain strength. Examples in recent history include Sierra Leone and Liberia in the 1990s, and Somalia and Afghanistan over the past two decades. How and why does a state fail or even completely collapse? Let's look at Afghanistan. Pay attention to two recurring themes: internally (from the inside-out), the inability of the government to monopolize violence in the territory; and externally (from the outside-in), how international factors can turn weak states into failed or collapsed states.

In the 19th century, Afghanistan was caught in the middle of what was called the "Great Game," in which Russia and British-held India battled for regional supremacy. The last Afghan king attempted to modernize the country in the early to mid-20th century, but a series of coups in the 1970s and then a Soviet invasion put the state on a very different path. The Soviet Union had invaded in 1979 to support a pro-communist government fighting an Islamist insurgency group called the *mujahedeen*. Huge numbers of civilians were killed, and millions of refugees fled to Pakistan and Iran. With the help of President Ronald Reagan's government in the United States, the mujahedeen successfully fought the Soviets and pushed them out in 1989.

After Soviet withdrawal, the Afghan government continued to fight internal forces, but after the Soviet Union fell apart, Afghanistan collapsed in 1992. A protracted civil war followed, in which anti-communist groups then fought with one another for control of the state. They fought, in other words, *to monopolize the right to use violence* by claiming legitimate control of the state. One such group, the Taliban, successfully fought its way to power in the 1990s the same way many states were formed historically: by crushing the

opposition. From 1996, the Taliban-controlled Afghan government imposed its strict interpretation of Islamic law, in which women were barred from working or going to school, or even from being in public without a male relative. Movies, music, and television were outlawed. Despite their brutal forms of rule, the Taliban brought some stability after so much fighting.

The Taliban were originally Islamic scholars (*Taliban* means "students") from the largest ethnic group, the Pashtuns. They were opposed by an alliance of northern Afghan groups, and by 2001, the Taliban government controlled most of the territory but was recognized by only three countries. Although the Taliban and the terrorist organization al-Qaeda were not one and the same, al-Qaeda leader Osama bin-Laden's forces joined with the Taliban in fighting northern groups that continued to oppose the government. Immediately after the September 11, 2001, attacks on the United States, attention turned to Afghanistan as a place where al-Qaeda had thrived in the absence of an effective state. A new president, Hamid Karzai, was elected in 2001 as the Afghan people voted in large numbers to reject the Taliban. But soon members of the former hardline Islamic movement began to regroup and began fighting the central government in a battle lasting over a decade.

The ongoing struggles to form a stable state in Afghanistan illustrate the interactions that characterize our global age. First, 90% of the world's opium, from which heroin is made, comes from Afghanistan. Heroin consumers in wealthy countries make this possible, as do the modern forms of transport infrastructure. The Taliban is said to earn over $100 million per year from the trade.[22] Second, the state is reliant on U.S. funding for much of its operations, but in Britain and the United States, support for the war has declined steadily, and international attempts to build an effective Afghan state

(Continued)

(Continued)

appear mixed at best. The government has consistently struggled to extend its authority in the south and east. In 2010 and 2011, reports emerged that the Taliban were once again issuing court judgments, collecting taxes, and running schools; in other words, they were governing.[23]

Third, Afghanistan's neighboring states have interests of their own. Pakistan has been an American ally throughout, but its own intelligence agency (Inter-Services Intelligence, or ISI) is known to have helped the Taliban. The long, mountainous borders between the two countries have enabled members of the Taliban to escape into ISI protection over the border. Most Pakistanis reject the Taliban's extremist interpretation of Islam, but others are infuriated by U.S. drone strikes in which Muslim civilians are killed by a "Christian country." By 2016, over 2,300 U.S. military have died and 20,000 have been wounded, and over 3,500 U.S.

military contractors have been killed.[24] The number of Afghan civilians dead is thought to be around 31,000[25] with 3,500 civilians killed in 2016 alone.[26]

Note the recurring themes in the history of the state. First, the government is unable to centralize power in the territory. Second, at every point in history, international actors (Iran, Pakistan, Soviet Union, United States) fought in and over the country and tried to shape it in ways that suited them. Moreover, the international movement of ideas in the form of radical Islam, or of commodities in the form of opium, facilitate the violence we have seen.

Read detailed reports from the International Crisis Group (ICG) on weak and failed states at crisisgroup.org.

Reflect

Is Afghanistan a state?

Stateness: The State as an Idea. Another explanation for the varied strength of states is the degree of cohesiveness or unity of the society in the state. People in Oregon probably think they have something in common with people from Arkansas, even if they've never been there. But why? Because they are both "American." One part of their identity is their "American-ness," which means they *think* they have common interests with other people in the vast U.S. territory, even if they've never met them. This is what Benedict Anderson meant when he said nations are "imagined communities."[27] Most stable, wealthy countries have a strong sense of their common identity. Countries that lack this have the problem of **stateness**, which Juan Linz and Alfred Stepan said occurs "when there are profound differences about the territorial boundaries of the political community's state and profound differences as to who has the right of citizenship in that state."[28]

stateness:
fundamental (dis)agreements on citizenship and what/who a state covers.

Many Igbos in Nigeria, for example, think of themselves as Igbos first and Nigerians second. Some scholars think this is a major problem. It becomes difficult for people to think in terms of their common goals when they do not identify with one another, and it becomes easier for politicians to politicize differences between groups. Much of this is rooted in colonialism—again, in historical international interactions—in which colonial powers mashed together different societies. They became "states" even though they were not nations.

Read "'Stateness' First" by Francis Fukuyama.[29]

But perhaps it is not surprising that two people that have never met would not identify with one another—say, an Igbo and a Yoruba in Nigeria. Maybe the more surprising thing is that two people who have never met would think *they* have something in common—an Oregonian and an Arkansan. The international nature of our lives again plays a role here. It reinforces the idea that the world is "naturally" divided into states and that our national identities are things that really exist.

Consider the example of global sport. Why do people participate in the Olympics or the World Cup as representatives of their states? We think it is natural for a Canadian to compete against an American even if he or she were born one mile either side of the U.S.–Canada border. But why is the nation-state the natural or logical way to organize international sport? The category is as arbitrary as making the Olympics a competition between people of different hair colors or religions. The point is that even *nonpolitical* things like sports reinforce our belief that states are a natural and inevitable way to organize our world. The Oregonian and the Arkansan thus compete as Americans against the Igbo and the Yoruba who compete as Nigerians at the World Cup. This reinforces in our imagination the idea that the nation-state is the natural way to order the world.

IS THE STATE FIT FOR PURPOSE? MODERN CHALLENGES TO STATES

Many of the challenges the world faces, from handling climate change to stopping potential pandemics like Ebola, require coordinated action above the level of the state. The principle of sovereignty, however, allows individual states to block global action. Moreover, many states struggle to function even within their own borders, with weak provision of security, sanitation, or education. Since goods, information, and money now flow so easily across borders, even strong states worry about keeping their wages low to stay globally competitive. This has led observers to question whether the state is "fit for purpose" in the 21st century. That is, are states—including even the most powerful among them—capable of effectively addressing those challenges, given their constraints and limitations? To answer that question, let's first look more closely at the three main sources of the challenges faced by states: actors, ideas, and technology.

The first challenge to states comes from *actors*. Multinational corporations (MNCs), international governmental organizations (IGOs), and NGOs represent some of the most difficult forces with which states have to contend. State-owned media have been replaced by private, global media companies like Facebook and Disney that are largely outside of state control. IGOs may be created by states, but UN and WTO bureaucrats do their best to expand their power over states. And MNCs are now so large that they can swing the fortunes of even wealthy states by pulling out investment and jobs: Wal-Mart's revenue in 2014 was $476 billion, larger than the GDP of 92 countries *combined*. David Rothkopf worries about a world in which the public institutions required to elevate people's living standards and prevent monopolies will be eroded because the power of states cannot compete with the power of **supercitizens**: "Whom would you pick in a one-on-one contest to influence, say, global climate talks—ExxonMobil or Morocco? Who has more clout in an effort to impact global financial markets—JPMorgan Chase or the Central Bank of Thailand?"[30]

supercitizens: small number of individuals and companies with extraordinary wealth and influence far exceeding most people and even some countries.

The second challenge to states comes from *ideas*, in particular the idea of neoliberalism discussed in Chapter 1. Some argue that MNCs and NGOs are powerful in part because advocates of neoliberalism have intentionally constructed a world in which states and governments are weak in relation to the power of private for-profit and nonprofit actors. Critics of the present form of globalization, in which global capital often trumps national power, claim that today's state is powerless because of the transnational nature of money and because of the neoliberal leanings of major intergovernmental organizations like the IMF and WTO.[31] State leaders say their hands are tied; they cannot strengthen workers' rights or environmental protections because employers will move elsewhere.[32]

The third challenge to states comes from *technologies*, in particular global telecommunications, which enable global markets to react faster than any government, and make it ever harder for governments to repress or control their own population. National laws on media, the press, and freedom of information make little sense in a world with Twitter.

These challenges to the power of states have led many to ask what the future of states will be. Let's look at three major arguments.

The Modern State Is in Decline

Some point to the declining ability of states to control borders, currencies, information, and populations. This affects wealthy and poor countries alike but in different ways. Some say globalization threatens the basis of the welfare states of western Europe and North America. In the welfare states of western Europe and North America, citizens pay higher taxes in return for more publicly funded benefits, like unemployment assistance, subsidized healthcare, or pensions. Weak economic growth has combined with rising costs of healthcare (United States) or pensions (Europe, Japan), so the ability of welfare states to afford their level of public services is a matter of real debate.

In the United States, the debate has centered on the long-term trend of deindustrialization since the 1970s. Observers see economic globalization as chipping away at the power of these welfare states, which can no longer pursue the socioeconomic policies that raised living standards over the past century. This is because globalization has reduced the policy space of states, meaning states' options to set taxes and laws that benefit the nation as a whole. Many agree that "it hardly matters whether the left or the right wins elections; the constraints of the internationalized economy will oblige either party to follow the same monetary and fiscal policies or else face a loss of national competitiveness and investment."[33]

Read "Will the Nation-State Survive Globalization?" by Martin Wolf. Foreign Affairs, *Jan/Feb 2001.*

The international economy affects policy space in developing countries as well, although in a different way. Many formerly poor states developed through the use of a developmental state, in which the state played an active role in growing the economy by using industrial policy to make domestic businesses more globally or regionally competitive. But the ability of poor states to become developmental states today is constrained in two ways.[34] First, free trade laws that enable a poor country to sell its goods abroad also hinder its ability to develop its own domestic industries. States are not allowed to protect their infant industries as much as they could even a few decades ago, and they are certainly not allowed to protect them as much as wealthy countries did over a century ago. The second constraint is that many poor countries are still reliant on the IMF and World Bank for loans, and getting these loans means they have to agree to a *reduced* role in the economy. As we discussed, the post–Washington Consensus allows states to invest in their people (like healthcare) and economies (like roads), but it is much less keen on states playing active roles in their economies.

The Modern State Will Endure

Other observers agree that states must contend with globally powerful actors, but they say the power of states in centuries past is easily overstated. States had competitors then just as they do now. To the pessimists who say the state is declining in importance, they remind us how states played a key role in the emergence of globalization itself. Economically, states created the international systems that enabled trade to flow in the eras of the Gold Standard and the Bretton Woods System, and more recently with the WTO. Politically, states have created international systems like the UN to facilitate decision making, resolve disputes, and punish states considered to be law breakers. Culturally, states have laid the physical infrastructure of telephone and Internet networks in the seabeds and in space that have made it possible for people in Vietnam to enjoy a video of a piano-playing cat produced in Madrid. Whichever way you think of globalization, the hand of the state can always be found.

The argument that states will endure has an economic and a cultural version. In the economic version, as citizens of wealthy countries have been exposed to several decades of ever freer trade, the demands they place on their governments to shield them from globalization have increased. This means, for example, that a factory worker in Detroit who loses her job is now reliant on the state for retraining in the long run and unemployment assistance in the short run, all while the state itself is taking in less in taxes because of the unemployment. This is why wealthy countries have seen growth in demands for social expenditure rise rapidly, and taxes have had to rise thereafter to pay for it.[35]

The idea that states will endure because they are indispensable to the modern economy is at the heart of the optimists' view. The 2008 financial crisis is an example. The interconnected banking systems of the world's wealthiest countries all suffered when some banks went bust while others froze and refused to lend money. It was action by states that was required to first contain the crisis, bail out private banks, and then try to jump-start economies. For critics of the "state decline" thesis, this is evidence that the world still needs states. As economist Dani Rodrik argued: "The hype that surrounds the decline of the nation state is just that: hype."[36]

Read "The Nation-State Reborn" by Dani Rodrik at https://www.project-syndicate.org/ commentary/the-nation-state-reborn.

The optimists also make a cultural argument. Voters in Western democracies are pushing back against globalization and are trying to reinforce the power of nation-states. We see the growth of far-right anti-immigrant political movements in western Europe and North America, which emphasize the cultural "losses" associated with globalization. Here it shares a concern with leftists that globalization really means **McDonaldization**—the growth of corporate capitalism and the ethic of materialism and self-interested pursuit of wealth. But on the right, the concern has been a more conservative one: to preserve the "culture" of a people against a tide of immigration and cultural displacement. In 2007, for example, 73% of Italians surveyed thought immigrants had a bad influence compared with 29% of Swedes.[37] Very often these anti-immigrant voices come from white, Christian men who trace their economic woes to the influx of immigrants, many of whom are nonwhite or non-Christian. Sovereignty for these people means an ability to control who gets to be called Japanese, English, or Italian. Globalization threatens their ability to maintain their community. When citizens want action, they turn to states, and grant states greater powers over them, just as Americans did with the Patriot Act after 9/11. This was seen in the aftermath of the 2016 U.S. presidential election with observers debating whether Donald Trump supporters were

McDonaldization: idea that global capitalism driven by Western companies will homogenize global culture, with values of profit, individualism, and consumption triumphant, especially at the expense of non-Western cultures. Synonym *Disneyfication*.

blue-collar victims of globalization experiencing "economic anxiety" or instead upper income white people facing the prospect of losing their social power.[38]

The Modern State Will Adapt

In the third view, the state will neither vanish nor stay the same. Instead, it will adapt. If we compare states today with the roles they played 50 years ago, they will of course look diminished, when in fact they have *adapted*. The European Union (EU) is an example. In 1957, a small number of western European countries signed an economic deal that, over time, would enhance all of their welfare. Their economies became intertwined and interdependent. Their agreement was so successful that more countries wanted to join in, and this expanding group sought to become more and more integrated over time. Europe went from being a place that had two major wars in the first half of the 20th century to the world's largest trading bloc in the second half. In an age where bananas, viruses, and drugs can easily cross borders, the EU has been more successful than any other corner of the world or any time in human history at being able to enhance peaceful cooperation between vast societies. The EU as an entity has made it possible for its member-states to enjoy the bounty of globalization by virtue of its size as a trading bloc, and to minimize many of the risks of globalization because member-states cooperate with one another on cross-border common concerns. Many people see the EU as a case of a successfully evolved state, a new type of organization that is better equipped than the nation-state to deal with the good and bad of today's world. Indeed, the EU persists despite predictions that it would not survive the global recession and the exit of the United Kingdom.

Other observers are not persuaded by government rhetoric about being forced to keep taxes low and regulations slack in the face of global competition. In *The Myth of the Powerless State*, Linda Weiss called this "the political construction of helplessness" . . . "political leaders—especially in the English-speaking world dominated by neoliberal economic philosophy—have themselves played a large part in contributing to this view of government helplessness in the face of global trends.[39] In canvassing support for policies lacking popular appeal, many OECD governments have sought to 'sell' their policies of retrenchment to the electorate as being somehow 'forced' on them by 'global economic trends' over which they have no control" (p. 193). She doesn't doubt that governments are constrained in their ability to control their own economies, but she is critical of the idea that, just because a state can no longer do what states did in the 1950s and 1960s, they can no longer do *anything*. She argues instead that states can adapt, and states can use their power to help their economies be globally competitive. Germany is an example of a 21st-century industrial and exporting powerhouse with strong unions and a welfare state. Moreover, Weiss argues that politicians who say there is no place in the global economy for economically activist states are simply ideologues who want states to have minimal roles in their economies. She doesn't see states as weakened by globalization. She says states have been the handmaidens (the enablers) of globalization since they are the ones who set up the global institutions to make our current globalization possible. This helps us make sense of the slogan around which much of the global leftist movement has rallied: "[A]another world is possible."[40]

Thus, there are different ideas about the ability of states as we know them to persist in this current global age. Although we might not settle the debate, we can note the importance of the interactions, tensions, and global forces we have seen throughout the book (see Figure 2.8).

GLOBAL FORCES	INTERACTIONS	TENSIONS
• Global markets: Multinational corporations are wealthier than many countries and neoliberalism is a pro-market, anti-state ideology. • ICT: States find it harder to control information in the internet age. • Shifting centers of power: No longer a unipolar world. • Global governance: IGOs are state actors, but the likes of WTO and IMF are more powerful than many states. Moreover, states may fail to cooperate to govern global challenges.	• States vie with nonstate actors to dominate the global stage. • States may fail to cooperate to govern global challenges such as climate change and global health.	• Crisis of welfare state in rich countries. • Constricted development policy space in poorer countries. • Nationalist backlash against forces threatening to weaken nation-states.

SUMMARY

We live in an age of states. The major features of the states are bureaucracy, control of people's lives, and the concept of sovereignty. States emerged when political systems influenced each other through interactions over many centuries. This continues today. States look to other states for ideas about how to attract investment, whether to decentralize, or how large their armies should be. States shape, and are shaped by, other states, as much today as they have been over the past several hundred years. It is not possible to understand what states are or what they do without thinking of them through the lens of *interactions*.

But we also know that interactions create tensions. Although the rise of states has its roots in rulers who centralized power and in communities who began to think of themselves as nations, it is not clear whether states today are capable of really controlling their populations, or whether their populations still identify primarily with their nation. States are not the only main actors on the international scene. Multinational corporations and civil society organizations try to shape global agendas and global governance in ways that suit them, and observers now debate whether states are the dominant actors at all today.

KEY TERMS

absolutist state 60
collapsed states 67
compulsory membership 54
failed states 67
free rider (or public goods)
  problem 59
government 54
hard power 65
legitimacy 53
McDonaldization 73

monopoly 53
nation 55
nation-state 55
nonstate actors 55
politically constrained 68
quasi-states 68
quasi-voluntary compliance 68
regime 54
rule of law 58
soft power 65

sovereignty 54
state 52
state actors 55
state capacity 64
stateness 70
strong states 67
supercitizens 71
territory 54
violence (or coercion) 53
weak states 67

QUESTIONS FOR REVIEW

1. How could you build a state? That is, how could you build an organization that centralizes power and controls people across a vast territory? What could you accomplish before making concessions to your people?

2. To what extent is colonialism important for understanding the strengths and weaknesses of states today?

3. Scholars debate whether global forces will see states as organizations decline, endure, or adapt. Rank the evidence that the United States of America ("the state") is declining, enduring, or adapting in recent decades.

4. Soft power is one dimension of a state's external power. How might information and communications technology (ICT), our second global force, affect the soft power of the United States?

5. Look at one of the world's major conflicts. Who is interacting? Are they state actors? Nonstate? Are they primarily international actors, or primarily national? Don't just focus on who is fighting. Also look at who is trying to stop the fighting.

LEARN MORE

Crisis States Research Network, London School of Economics, http://www.crisisstates.com

Governance and Social Development Resource Centre, University of Birmingham, http://www.gsdrc.org

Centre for the Future State, University of Sussex, http://www2.ids.ac.uk/futurestate/

Data on strong and weak states:

Worldwide Governance Indicators, World Bank, http://info.worldbank.org/governance/wgi/index.aspx#reports

Fragile States Index, Fund for Peace, http://ffp.statesindex.org/

NOTES

1. Max Weber, *Politics as a Vocation* (New York, NY: Oxford University Press, 1946), 78–79. Emphasis added.

2. Only Eritrea and the United States oblige their citizens to pay taxes no matter where they are in the world.

3. James C. Scott, *The Art of Not Being Governed: An Anarchist History of Upland Southeast Asia* (New Haven, CT: Yale University Press, 2009).

4. J. R. Hiltermann and Maria Fantappie, "Twilight of the Kurds," *Foreign Policy* (blog), January 16, 2018, https://foreignpolicy.com/2018/01/16/twilight-of-the-kurds-iraq-syria-kurdistan/.

5. The first reporting of the Declaration of Independence came on July 5, 1776, in *Der Pennsylvanische Staatsbote.*

6. David Rothkopf, *Power, Inc.: The Epic Rivalry between Big Business and Government—and the Reckoning That Lies Ahead*, 1st ed. (New York, NY: Farrar, Straus and Giroux, 2012).

7. Also known as the public goods problem.

8. Charles Tilly, "War Making and State Making as Organized Crime," in *Bringing the State Back In*, ed. Peter Evans, Dietrich Rueschemeyer, and T. Skocpol (Cambridge, U.K.: Cambridge University Press, 1985), 169–187.

9. Perry Anderson, *Lineages of the Absolutist State* (New York, NY: Verso, 1979).

10. Thomas Ertman, "Birth of the Leviathan: Building states and regimes in medieval and early modern Europe." *Comparative Political Studies* 30 (1997): 752; North, D. C., J. J. Wallis, and B. R. Weingast, *Violence and Social Orders: A Conceptual Framework for Interpreting Recorded Human History* (Cambridge, U.K.: Cambridge University Press, 2009); H. Spruyt, *The Sovereign State and Its Competitors: An Analysis of Systems Change* (Princeton, NJ: Princeton University Press, 1996).

11. Russia is included as part of Europe here. Japan, Korea, Thailand, and Liberia are usually considered the only countries never to be colonized by Europe, though Liberia was effectively a U.S. colony.

12. http://whynationsfail.com/blog/2013/1/9/political-dynasties-in-the-philippines.html. Pablo Querubin, "Family and politics: Dynastic persistence in the Philippines," *Quarterly Journal of Political Science* 11 (2016): 151–181. http://dx.doi.org/10.1561/100.00014182.

13. Joel Samuel Migdal, *Strong Societies and Weak States: State-Society Relations and State Capabilities in the Third World* (Princeton, NJ: Princeton University Press, 1988).

14. Stephen A. Wurm et al., *Atlas of Languages of Intercultural Communication in the Pacific, Asia, and the Americas: Vol I: Maps. Vol II: Texts* (Boston, MA: Walter de Gruyter, 1996), 272.

15. John T. Sidel, *Capital, Coercion, and Crime: Bossism in the Philippines* (Stanford, CA: Stanford University Press, 1999).

16. C. Cruz et al., "Politician Family Networks and Electoral Outcomes: Evidence from the Philippines," *American Economic Review* Forthcoming (n.d.), https://www.aeaweb.org/articles? id=10.1257/aer.20150343.

17. Crawford Young, *The African Colonial State in Comparative Perspective* (New Haven, CT: Yale University Press, 1994).

18. Daniel Kaufmann, Aart Kraay, and Massimo Mastruzzi, "Governance Matters VIII: Aggregate and Individual Governance Indicators, 1996–2008," *SSRN ELibrary*, June 29, 2009.

19. Joseph S. Nye, Jr., *Soft Power: The Means to Success in World Politics* (New York, NY: PublicAffairs, 2004).

20. Robert I. Rotberg, *When States Fail: Causes and Consequences* (Princeton, NJ: Princeton University Press, 2004).

21. UNODC, *Afghanistan Opium Survey 2016: Cultivation and Production* (New York, NY: United Nations Office for Drugs and Crime, 2016).

22. "In Eastern Afghanistan, at War With the Taliban's Shadowy Rule," *New York Times*, February 6, 2011.

23. Neta C. Crawford, "Update on the Human Costs of War for Afghanistan and Pakistan, 2001 to Mid-2016," in *Costs of War* (Watson Institute, Brown University, August 2016), http://watson.brown.edu/costsofwar/files/cow/imce/papers/2016/War%20in%20Afghanistan%20and%20Pakistan%20UPDATE_FINAL_corrected%20date.pdf.

24. The Guardian, "Afghan Civilian Death Toll 'Much Higher than the Official Estimate,'" *The Guardian*, May 7, 2016, sec. World news, https://www.theguardian.com/world/2016/may/07/afghanistan-civilian-death-toll.

25. Al-Jazeera, "Afghan Civilian Casualties at Record High in 2016: UN," *Al-Jazeera*, February 6, 2017, http://www.aljazeera.com/news/2017/02/afghan-civilian-casualties-2016-170206062807210.html.

26. Margaret Levi, *Of Rule and Revenue* (Berkeley: University of California Press, 1988).

27. Benedict Anderson, *Imagined Communities: Reflections on the Origin and Spread of Nationalism* (New York, NY: Verso, 1996).

28. Juan J. Linz and Alfred Stepan, *Problems of Democratic Transition and Consolidation: Southern Europe, South America, and Post-Communist Europe*, illustrated ed. (Baltimore, MD: The Johns Hopkins University Press, 1996), 16.

29. "'Stateness' First," *Journal of Democracy* 16, no. 1 (2005): 84–88, https://doi.org/10.1353/jod.2005.0006.

30. Rothkopf, *Power, Inc.*, 21.

31. Joseph Eugene Stiglitz, *Making Globalization Work* (New York, NY: W.W. Norton, 2007).

32. Philip G. Cerny, "Paradoxes of the Competition State: The Dynamics of Political Globalization," *Government and Opposition* 32, no. 2 (April 1, 1997): 251–274, https://doi.org/10.1111/j.1477-7053.1997.tb00161.x.

33. Suzanne Berger, "Globalization and Politics," *Annual Review of Political Science* 3, no. 1 (2000): 15.

34. Robert Hunter Wade, "What Strategies Are Viable for LDCs Today? The World Trade Organization and the Shrinking of 'Development Space,'" in *International Political Economy: A Reader*, ed. Axel Hulsemeyer (Oxford, U.K.: Oxford University Press, 2010), 490–502. Ha-Joon Chang, *Bad Samaritans: The Myth of Free Trade and the Secret History of Capitalism* (London, U.K.: Bloomsbury Publishing USA, 2008); Ha-Joon Chang, *23 Things They Don't Tell You About Capitalism* (London, U.K.: Bloomsbury Publishing USA, 2012).

35. Paul Pierson, *New Politics of the Welfare State* (Oxford, U.K.: Oxford University Press, 2001), http://www.oxfordscholarship.com/view/10.1093/0198297564.001.0001/acprof-9780198297567.

36. Dani Rodrik, *The Globalization Paradox: Why Global Markets, States, and Democracy Can't Coexist* (Oxford, U.K.: Oxford University Press, 2011), 28.

37. Pew Research Center, *Widespread Anti-Immigrant Sentiment in Italy | Pew Research Center's Global Attitudes Project* (Washington, DC: Pew Global Research, January 12, 2010).

38. Emma Green, "It Was Cultural Anxiety That Drove White, Working-Class Voters to Trump," *The Atlantic*, May 9, 2017, https://www.theatlantic.com/politics/archive/2017/05/white-working-class-trump-cultural-anxiety/525771/; Ben Casselman, "Stop Saying Trump's Win Had Nothing to Do With Economics," *FiveThirtyEight* (blog), January 9, 2017, https://fivethirtyeight.com/features/stop-saying-trumps-win-had-nothing-to-do-with-economics/.

39. Linda Weiss, *The Myth of the Powerless State* (Ithaca, NY: Cornell University Press, 1998).

40. David McNally, *Another World Is Possible: Globalization and Anti-Capitalism* (Winnipeg, Manitoba, Canada: Arbeiter Ring, 2006).

Intergovernmental Organizations

SITES OF GLOBAL GOVERNANCE

3

iStock/shaunl

LEARNING OBJECTIVES

After finishing this chapter, you should be able to:

- Place intergovernmental organizations in context with other international actors.

- Apply the ideas of realism, liberalism, and constructivism to real-world events.

- Describe the origins and functions of the United Nations.

- Distinguish between intergovernmental organizations (IGOs) and non-IGOs in later chapters.

GETTING ALONG IN THE WORLD

Backstabbing and treachery are common in *Game of Thrones*. Rulers engage in shifting alliances against common enemies, within their societies and between them. But as they fight among each other, a larger danger casts a shadow over them all. An unforgiving winter lasting 10 years or more is on its way and promises to devastate these preindustrial societies. Worse, from the frozen wasteland in the north will come "white walkers," demonic terrors with no interest in the factional politics of the humans to the south. Although the humans fight among themselves, they face a common foe that cannot be defeated by any one ruler. It is a problem of collective action on a global scale.

Like the rulers in *Game of Thrones,* states face challenges on a global scale that no state alone can address. When the Zika virus spread through the Americas and the Pacific in 2015, leaving in its wake newborns with severe brain defects, states worked within the World Health Organization for a solution. When the Islamic State of Iraq and Syria (ISIS, aka "the Islamic State") and its affiliates began spreading across Syria, Libya, and Iraq in 2016, and undertook terrorist operations in ten more countries, states worked within the United Nations (UN) Security Council to stop their spread. When in 2003 it emerged that Iran had begun to enrich uranium that could be used in a nuclear bomb, attention turned to the International Atomic Energy Agency to independently investigate. These organizations are called intergovernmental organizations (IGOs), and they are created by states to do collectively what no one state can do alone.

In this chapter, we will learn how IGOs differ from other international actors and how (and whether) they matter. IGOs are at the heart of one of our four *global forces*: global governance, although the term includes more than just IGOs. IGOs are also center stage when we study *interactions* (the language of international studies) as well as *tensions* (the challenges of international studies). We will see how IGOs are the place where many international actors interact, and how the tensions that result from interactions are often played out within IGOs. We will learn about three perspectives—**realism**, **liberalism**, and **constructivism**—that can help us think about what role IGOs play in the world. Each offers different interpretations of life in *Game of Thrones*, as you will see in this chapter. We will also learn about the United Nations, although this chapter is focused more on the concept of IGOs than on examples of IGOs. You will find discussion of other IGOs throughout the book, such as the World Bank (Ch. 9), World Trade Organization (Ch. 6), International Criminal Court (Ch. 8), or the Intergovernmental Panel on Climate Change (Ch. 13).

Realism Focuses on Power

Realists think states are focused on their security and self-preservation; because there is no global police to guarantee their existence, interactions between states are full of conflict, and cooperation is rare. States will create or join an IGO if doing so makes them more secure. Smaller states may join for protection while powerful states will use IGOs to bully lesser powers and suppress rising powers.

At first glance, *Game of Thrones* certainly seems to work in the way realists describe. With no single ruler able to guarantee their protection, the Stark, Greyjoy, and Lannister families constantly fear being dominated or destroyed. They make shaky alliances with other rulers, but they are just as often coerced into being junior partners. International agreements between rulers (such as creating an IGO) help strong states preserve their power, but it is the powerful states rather than the agreement itself (i.e., the IGO) that holds the power. Ultimately, a realist would say, the world works according to the will of the powerful, and in *Game of Thrones*, only one ruler possesses dragons, the nuclear weapons of the day.

Liberalism Focuses on Cooperation

Liberals would understand *Game of Thrones* differently since they see many more cooperative interactions among states than realists do.[1] They think states will create or join IGOs because IGOs help them engage in mutually beneficial interaction with other states. Liberals see states joining IGOs as an act of free choice rather than as an act of coercion, and in general, they see cooperation between rulers as commonplace despite occasional failures. Yes, rulers are focused on their security, but they understand they would all be better off if they could cooperate. In *Game of Thrones*, rulers contribute to maintaining a 300-mile-long, 700-foot-high, solid ice wall that keeps the rulers protected from the wild and demonic beings to the north. But the wall is severely

realism: theory of international relations that says because states are self-interested and cannot rely on others for their security, cooperation between states is the exception, and mutual distrust and conflict is the norm.

liberalism: theory of international relations that says states are self-interested but realize that mutually beneficial relations with other states are possible, and that democracy, capitalism, and IGOs can help states cooperate with each other.

constructivism: approach to international relations that sees states as social actors and norms as shaping the identities and wants of states.

understaffed and underresourced because rulers have not kept up their contributions. Liberals would point to the wall as a joint act by independent rulers to manage a common problem, but they would acknowledge that joint acts can suffer if participants are not forced to contribute.

Constructivism Focuses on Identity and Norms

Last, constructivists play down the importance of material things like weapons or money and emphasize instead nonmaterial forces in life such as identity and norms (expectations about appropriate behavior). Just like people, states behave according to how they think they are *supposed to* behave. Norms exist in our lives and in world affairs even in the absence of formal laws or police. We see them most clearly when they are violated. In *Game of Thrones*, one such norm is "guest right," meaning the right of visitors not to be harmed. In the infamous "Red Wedding," a powerful family is massacred during a wedding celebration. This is a gross violation of the guest right, and it does enormous damage to the reputation of the attackers. Other examples include the breaking of gender norms. Female characters challenge gender norms that define their roles in a world of extraordinary patriarchy. One ruler, Daenerys, clearly and repeatedly asserts her right to rule over men and women.[2] Constructivists are interested in where these norms come from. As we will see, IGOs matter because they can shape global norms and thus shape people's (and states') *perceptions* of their own interests.

IGOS: THE BASICS

An **intergovernmental organization** is an organization that is created and managed by states. Their key characteristic is that only sovereign states are members.[3] IGOs are not merely groups or clubs of states. An IGO is a legal entity that is recognized in international law. There are approximately 400 IGOs in the world today, which is more than a fivefold increase since World War II (WWII; Figure 3.1). Alongside states, civil society, and multinational corporations, IGOs are major actors in our world. They are part of *global forces* because they are part of the reason why states are not the only important global actors in the 21st century.

There is a lot of diversity within this group (see Table 3.1). Some IGOs are small in membership, such as the 14-member Organization of Petroleum Exporting Countries (OPEC), which is the prime global energy cartel. Some are regional in membership, such as the African Union, or subregional, such as the Southern Africa Development Community (SADC). Other IGOs are truly global in membership, such as the Universal Postal Union.

intergovernmental organization (IGO): organization created and controlled by sovereign states in which the members are states.

WHAT DO IGOS DO?

Some IGOs have very broad functions and mandates, such as the European Union (EU). The EU is like a national government in that it includes a variety of agencies including agriculture, space exploration, and defense. Other IGOs are narrowly focused on one issue or problem, such as the International Telecommunication Union (ITU), which helps to establish technical standards for things like satellites. What most IGOs have in common is that they provide some of the following five functions: promote the interests of member states, find solutions to common problems, increase efficiency with economies of scale, provide expertise on special issues, and produce and disseminate knowledge.

FIGURE 3.1

Growth in Intergovernmental Organizations

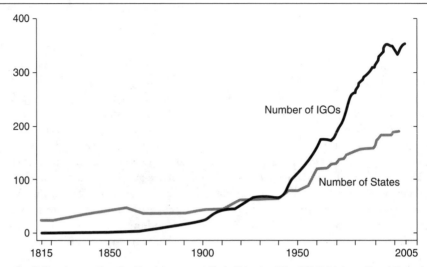

Source: Jon C. Pevehouse, Timothy Nordstrom, and Kevin Warnke, "The COW-2 International Organizations Dataset Version 2.0," Conflict Management and Peace Science (2004) 21:101–119. Data available at http://www .correlatesofwar.org/data-sets/IGOs.

TABLE 3.1

Examples of Intergovernmental Organizations

	Global	**Regional**	**Club**
Membership is usually...	Universal	Regional	Like-minded states
Example (size of membership)	United Nations (193) World Bank (189) International Monetary Fund (189) Universal Postal Union (192) International Labor Organization (187) International Bureau of Weights and Measures (98)	European Union (27) African Union (54) Association of Southeast Asian Nations (10) Arab League (22)	North Atlantic Treaty Organization (28) The Commonwealth of Nations (53) G20 (20) Organisation for Economic Co-operation and Development (34)

Promote the Interests of Member States

The staff of an IGO is ultimately accountable to a higher authority composed of member-states. For example, the World Intellectual Property Organization (WIPO) is an autonomous UN agency.

It has 188 member-states who oversee the work of a Director-General who runs the organization on a daily basis. The role of state officials is to promote the states' interests in the work of the WIPO.

Find Solutions to Common Problems

IGOs exist because states know they have a problem in common, yet they are unable or unwilling to be the one to fix it. An IGO can simply provide a meeting space for discussion, it can monitor compliance with an agreement, or if the parties agree, it can even impose a solution. This is the purpose of IGOs such as the International Seabed Authority (ISA), which was created by states that signed on to the United Nations Convention on the Law of the Sea (1982). ISA has the authority to regulate exploration and mining in the deep-sea bed. Thus, signatories gave up their right to mine the deep-sea bed and, in doing so, said, "I won't do it if you don't."[4] This IGO helps coordinate and monitor compliance with the Convention.

Increase Efficiency With Economies of Scale

Some IGOs are useful simply because they provide meeting spaces, expertise on technical issues, or administrative staff so governments can focus on making deals. Much of the collating and publication of material happens online. For example, the UN Statistics Division houses material on statistical offices from all over the world, including legal documents and organizational models, and they have published a *Handbook of Statistical Organization* that can be freely used by countries wishing to strengthen their agencies.

Provide Expertise on Special Issues

When the World Health Organization was grappling with an Ebola outbreak in West Africa in 2013, it brought in people with expertise in the disease and the region. These experts sometimes form **epistemic communities**, which means informal communities of experts with similar professional training, values, and ideas. Examples are climate scientists or international human rights lawyers. The theory of **functionalism** says that epistemic communities working in IGOs sometimes develop greater expertise on issues than do the states themselves. As an IGO builds its knowledge and expertise, it may develop a global reputation and thus a power of its own autonomous from states. For example, the WHO Secretary-General commands the attention of global media, and its health information is widely respected. The WHO is ultimately run by states, but on a daily basis, it is run by civil servants. In this way, IGOs and epistemic communities can invert the relationship between IGOs and the states that create them. IGOs can become global actors in their own right, not just pawns of states.

epistemic communities: informal communities of experts with similar training, values, and ideas.

functionalism: when interaction generates its own dynamic and leads to deeper interaction. Example: growth of the European Union.

Produce and Disseminate Knowledge

Member-states of the World Trade Organization (WTO) benefit when they have access to fine-grained data on global trade, tariffs, or economic conditions. The WTO provides this service, so every member does not have to collect the same data on its own. This information gathering and sharing work of IGOs also includes monitoring state behavior where trust is low. For example, the International Atomic Energy Agency (IAEA) was created in 1950 as a neutral third party to monitor the nuclear activity of non-nuclear states. In the 1990s, IAEA inspectors carried out surprise inspections of nuclear facilities throughout Iraq and, on some occasions, even destroyed banned materials.

THE UNITED NATIONS: MEDIATING GLOBAL TENSIONS

The United Nations is the world's most visible IGO. Although it is not a state or a government as a social scientist would use the term, it is nonetheless a preeminent IGO. It has a budget in the billions, thousands of employees, and offices in every country. It feeds tens of millions of people every year. It keeps peace in dozens of countries. It brings states together in neutral venues and gives civil society actors a platform to speak. As the "conscience of the world," the UN is one of the main places where the tensions that result from global interactions get mediated.

In this section, we will learn about why it was created and by whom. We will learn about its major parts, how it is run, and the challenges it faces in the 21st century.

Origins

The United Nations is an IGO of 193 member-states (see Figure 3.2).[5] Its foundational document is the UN Charter, signed by 51 states in 1945. Under the Charter, all states are equal under international law, all are sovereign over their domestic affairs, and all must fulfill their international obligations, such as respecting diplomatic activities and placing UN obligations above any other treaty. In reality, the UN cannot enforce its wishes on a state unless that state has explicitly allowed the UN to do so. For example, the 2008 *Convention on Cluster Munitions* bans the use of cluster bombs, but it does not apply to Russia and the United States since they did not ratify it.

The UN was created after several years of planning among the Allied powers (United States, United Kingdom, France, China, Union of Soviet Socialist Republics [USSR]). Its purpose was to enhance economic cooperation and provide a more robust security arrangement than the failed

FIGURE 3.2

Growth in UN Membership

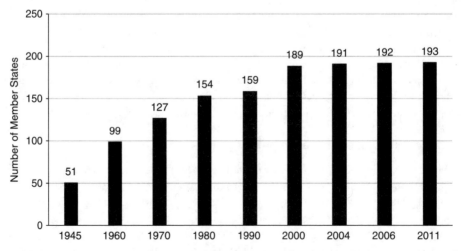

Source: The United Nations, http://www.un.org/en/sections/member-states/growth-united-nations-membership-1945-present/index.html.

League of Nations. Thus, the winners of WWII created an IGO in which they became the most important members. All "peace loving" states were eligible to join, a clear statement that Axis powers (especially Germany and Japan) were to be excluded. Therefore, the UN Charter was not an idealistic or humanitarian act, but "a meticulously crafted, power-oriented document carefully molded by hard-nosed drafters to conform to the global realities of 1945."[6]

Less powerful and non-Western states, however, influenced the development of the UN in ways that are often overlooked, so we should be wary of a Great-Powers–centric explanation of the organization's origins. Sixty-five percent of countries present at the creation of the UN Charter were from what is called the "Global South," so it is hard to argue that the UN was a Western or imperial imposition on non-nuclear, nonindustrialized countries. For example, Latin American participants were influential in the Charter's emphasis on regional arrangements and gender equality, and people from recently decolonized states influenced articles relating to territories that were not self-governing.[7]

The 1948 Universal Declaration of Human Rights (UDHR) was also the product of multiregional collaboration. Latin American states had adopted a human rights declaration one decade before.[8] Eleanor Roosevelt is well known for chairing the commission that drafted the declaration, but its vice-chair was Peng Chung Chang from China and the rapporteur Charles Mailk from Lebanon.[9]

More recently, in the sphere of poverty and development, Pakistani scholar Mahbub ul Haq and Indian economist Amartya Sen have dramatically shifted how the UN—and indeed the world— thinks of economic development as secondary to *human* development. Sen developed ideas that ul Haq shepherded into existence as creator of the Human Development Index in 1990, which today is the standard global measure of poverty worldwide.

The General Assembly also played a very important part in shaping global ideas over several decades as it provided a respected public platform for newly independent states to critique colonialism. By the 1960s, most UN members were nonindustrial, recently colonized, and offered counternarratives about global power.

Organization

The UN is not a highly centralized organization. It has something akin to legislative, executive, and judicial branches, but the analogy with national-level government organization is shaky. The key parts are as follows (see Figure 3.3: Organization of the UN System):

UN General Assembly (UNGA). The UN General Assembly is a body where every UN member-state has one seat, and each seat carries one vote (i.e., China and Comoros have one vote each). It meets every year for several months. Since resolutions passed in the UNGA are nonbinding (i.e., are not law), it is not really a legislature. But it does have some power. It controls budgets for UN agencies and peacekeeping

The UN General Assembly

Wikipedia user Basil D Soufi, https://commons.wikimedia.org/wiki/File:United_Nations_General_Assembly_Hall_(3).jpg. Licensed under CC BY-SA 3.0, https://creativecommons.org/licenses/by-sa/3.0/deed.en.

operations, and it has the power to admit states to UN membership, appoint judges to the International Court of Justice (ICJ), and nonpermanent members to the Security Council.

FIGURE 3.3

Organization of the UN System

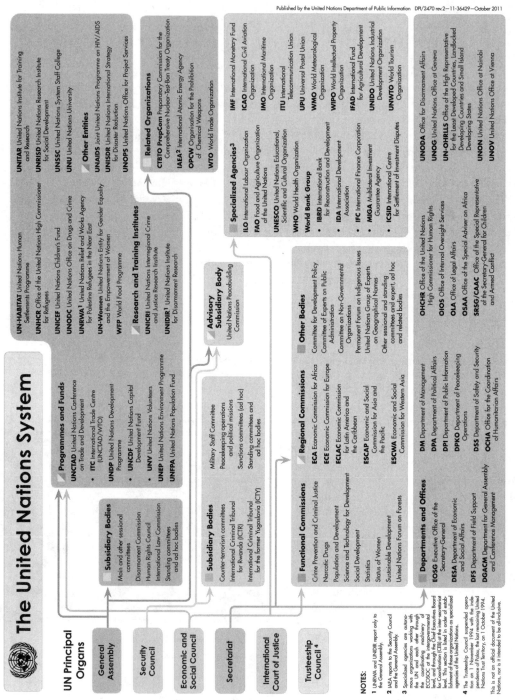

The United Nations System

Published by the United Nations Department of Public Information DPI/2470 rev.2—11-36429—October 2011

UN Principal Organs

General Assembly

Security Council

Economic and Social Council

Secretariat

International Court of Justice

Trusteeship Council [4]

Programmes and Funds

UNCTAD United Nations Conference on Trade and Development
 • ITC International Trade Centre (UNCTAD/WTO)
UNDP United Nations Development Programme
 • UNCDF United Nations Capital Development Fund
 • UNV United Nations Volunteers
UNEP United Nations Environment Programme
UNFPA United Nations Population Fund

UN-HABITAT United Nations Human Settlements Programme
UNHCR Office of the United Nations High Commissioner for Refugees
UNICEF United Nations Children's Fund
UNODC United Nations Office on Drugs and Crime
UNRWA[1] United Nations Relief and Works Agency for Palestine Refugees in the Near East
UN-Women United Nations Entity for Gender Equality and the Empowerment of Women
WFP World Food Programme

Research and Training Institutes

UNICRI United Nations Interregional Crime and Justice Research Institute
UNIDIR[1] United Nations Institute for Disarmament Research

UNITAR United Nations Institute for Training and Research
UNRISD United Nations Research Institute for Social Development
UNSSC United Nations System Staff College
UNU United Nations University

Other Entities

UNAIDS Joint United Nations Programme on HIV/AIDS
UNISDR United Nations International Strategy for Disaster Reduction
UNOPS United Nations Office for Project Services

Related Organizations

CTBTO PrepCom Preparatory Commission for the Comprehensive Nuclear-Test-Ban Treaty Organization
IAEA[2] International Atomic Energy Agency
OPCW Organization for the Prohibition of Chemical Weapons
WTO World Trade Organization

Specialized Agencies[3]

ILO International Labour Organization
FAO Food and Agriculture Organization of the United Nations
UNESCO United Nations Educational, Scientific and Cultural Organization
WHO World Health Organization
World Bank Group
 • IBRD International Bank for Reconstruction and Development
 • IDA International Development Association
 • IFC International Finance Corporation
 • MIGA Multilateral Investment Guarantee Agency
 • ICSID International Centre for Settlement of Investment Disputes

IMF International Monetary Fund
ICAO International Civil Aviation Organization
IMO International Maritime Organization
ITU International Telecommunication Union
UPU Universal Postal Union
WMO World Meteorological Organization
WIPO World Intellectual Property Organization
IFAD International Fund for Agricultural Development
UNIDO United Nations Industrial Development Organization
UNWTO World Tourism Organization

Subsidiary Bodies

Main and other sessional committees
Disarmament Commission
Human Rights Council
International Law Commission
Standing committees and ad hoc bodies

Subsidiary Bodies

Military Staff Committee
Peacekeeping operations and political missions
Sanctions committees (ad hoc)
Standing committees and ad hoc bodies

Counter-terrorism committees
International Criminal Tribunal for Rwanda (ICTR)
International Criminal Tribunal for the former Yugoslavia (ICTY)

Advisory Subsidiary Body

United Nations Peacebuilding Commission

Functional Commissions

Crime Prevention and Criminal Justice
Narcotic Drugs
Population and Development
Science and Technology for Development
Social Development
Statistics
Status of Women
Sustainable Development
United Nations Forum on Forests

Regional Commissions

ECA Economic Commission for Africa
ECE Economic Commission for Europe
ECLAC Economic Commission for Latin America and the Caribbean
ESCAP Economic and Social Commission for Asia and the Pacific
ESCWA Economic and Social Commission for Western Asia

Other Bodies

Committee for Development Policy
Committee of Experts on Public Administration
Committee on Non-Governmental Organizations
Permanent Forum on Indigenous Issues
United Nations Group of Experts on Geographical Names
Other sessional and standing committees and expert, ad hoc and related bodies

Departments and Offices

EOSG Executive Office of the Secretary-General
DESA Department of Economic and Social Affairs
DFS Department of Field Support
DGACM Department for General Assembly and Conference Management

DM Department of Management
DPA Department of Political Affairs
DPI Department of Public Information
DPKO Department of Peacekeeping Operations
DSS Department of Safety and Security
OCHA Office for the Coordination of Humanitarian Affairs

OHCHR Office of the United Nations High Commissioner for Human Rights
OIOS Office of Internal Oversight Services
OLA Office of Legal Affairs
OSAA Office of the Special Adviser on Africa
SRSG/CAAC Office of the Special Representative of the Secretary-General for Children and Armed Conflict

UNODA Office for Disarmament Affairs
UNOG United Nations Office at Geneva
UN-OHRLLS Office of the High Representative for the Least Developed Countries, Landlocked Developing Countries and Small Island Developing States
UNON United Nations Office at Nairobi
UNOV United Nations Office at Vienna

NOTES:

1 UNRWA and UNIDIR report only to the General Assembly.

2 IAEA reports to the Security Council and the General Assembly.

3 Specialized agencies are autonomous organizations working with the UN and each other through the coordinating machinery of the ECOSOC at the intergovernmental level, and through the Chief Executives Board for Coordination (CEB) at the inter-secretariat level. This section is listed in order of establishment of these organizations as specialized agencies of the United Nations.

4 The Trusteeship Council suspended operation on 1 November 1994 with the independence of Palau, the last remaining United Nations Trust Territory, on 1 October 1994.

This is not an official document of the United Nations, nor is it intended to be all-inclusive.

Source: UN Procurement Practitioner's Handbook, https://www.ungm.org/Areas/Public/pph/apa.html.

Within UNGA, the Economic and Social Council (ECOSOC) coordinates many UN agencies, such as the UN Population Fund and the UN Development Programme. This is in fact where the bulk of UN activity occurs. ECOSOC oversees the most programs and spends more money than any other part of the UN.

Within ECOSOC there are also many important IGOs known as "specialized agencies" that were established under the UN but are considered autonomous, such as the International Labor Organization or the Food and Agriculture Organization. These IGOs are legally within the purview of the General Assembly via ECOSOC, but their budgets, staffing, and policies are not. This part of the UN's structure is confusing since these autonomous ("specialized") agencies engage in activities that clearly overlap with IGOs controlled by ECOSOC. For example, in the area of poverty alleviation, the World Bank is a specialized agency and thus run autonomously, while the World Food Programme is accountable to ECOSOC and the General Assembly.

See the data: Map seven decades of votes in the UN General Assembly at https:// erikvoeten.shinyapps.io/UNVoting/.

UN Security Council (UNSC). Probably the most powerful and important part of the UN, the UN Security Council has five permanent members, the United States, the United Kingdom, France, Russia, and China. Each has veto power over any UNSC business. Ten nonpermanent states rotate on and off the Council, but they do not have a veto. UNSC decisions are binding on *all* 193 UN member-states. It meets on an occasional basis to deal with security issues, and it can authorize the use of force. Any and all military action authorized by the UNSC is legal simply because they are the authority that says so. For example, in 2011, the UNSC passed a resolution authorizing the bombing of parts of Libya to stop attacks against civilians and to enforce a no-fly zone. The UNSC has also become much more actively engaged in the "real world" in recent years. From 1945 until 1990, the UNSC passed only 22 resolutions to authorize the use of military force. Since 1990, however, it has done so hundreds of times.

UN Secretariat. The Secretariat is a bureaucracy led by the UN Secretary General (UNSG), who is an administrator rather than a person with executive power. The UNSG is nominated by the Security Council and must be approved by the General Assembly. The Secretariat has over 10,000 staff, most of whom work in over 100 UN offices rather than at UN headquarters.[10]

International Court of Justice (ICJ). States use the ICJ (also known as the World Court) to settle disputes among themselves. It is purely a court to settle disputes between or among states, not between or among

The UN Security Council

White House (Pete Souza)

The International Court of Justice (World Court) at The Hague, Netherlands

individuals or companies, nor is it a criminal court that issues arrest warrants. States can sue or be sued at the ICJ, which is based in The Hague, the Netherlands.[11] Its decisions are binding only if the parties have agreed so in advance. It is not a court as we usually think of them: It cannot summon a state leader to the Court, and it cannot jail any individual. States that go before the ICJ do so having agreed in advance that the ICJ's decision will be binding. This is how the ICJ helps facilitate global interactions and resolves tensions. Its rulings have successfully settled several border disputes, such as a 2002 ruling in which Nigeria peacefully transferred the contested peninsula of Bakassi to Cameroon.

Size

The UN is the world's largest IGO in terms of the number of employees but also in terms of its global presence on the ground. It provides food to over 90 million people in 75 countries. It vaccinates 58% of the world's children. It manages conflicts across multiple continents with 120,000 peacekeepers. It assists about 50 countries per year in holding elections.[12] Excluding peacekeepers, the total number of people working directly in the UN, or in autonomous entities that are legally part of the UN, is about 80,000. By contrast, the U.S. Department of Agriculture alone has over 100,000 employees.[13]

The UN's regular budget is usually about $5 billion, which is paid directly by member-states.[14] This $5 billion pays for the main administration, the UN Secretariat under the Secretary General, which employs about 10,000 people. The regular budget does not include money spent on autonomous UN agencies, nor on peacekeeping operations, which in 2015 was approximately $7 billion. These are huge numbers but less so in the global context. The entire UN peacekeeping budget is equivalent to one month U.S. military expenditure in Afghanistan at the height of its conflict, or less than 2% of the U.S. military budget.[15] The largest contributors to the budget are shown in Figure 3.4. The UN has frequently had trouble getting member-states to pay their dues. In the late 1990s, the UN was owed over $2.5 billion by the member-states.[16]

Most UN agencies that the public hears a lot about, such as the World Food Program or UNICEF, depend on states to make voluntary contributions. This means the bulk of their work is not funded by the UN's regular budget. UN agencies compete with one another for such voluntary contributions. This fact promotes some healthy competition between agencies, but it naturally means a lot of programs go unfunded. For example, when the World Food Program gets $4 billion of the $5 billion it says it needs, that is $1 billion worth of food that does not go to feed starving people.

FIGURE 3.4

Largest Contributors to the UN Budget

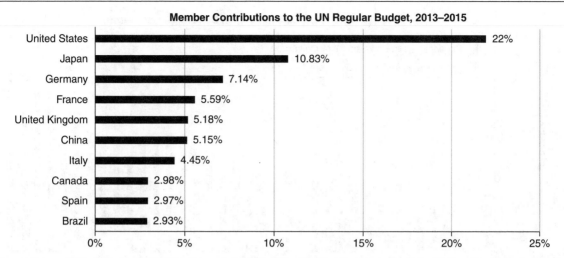

Source: Data available at The United Nations, "Assessment of Member-state Contributions to the United Nations Regular Budget for the Year 2015," http://www.un.org/ga/search/view_doc.asp? symbol=ST/ADM/SER.B/910.

All told, the total amount of money flowing through the UN varies significantly from year to year, but typically, it amounts to $30 billion when one includes peacekeeping, the "regular" UN budget, and voluntary funding of UN programs.[17] To put that in perspective, in 2015 the world spent $1.7 *trillion* on military expenditures, more than 50 times the UN expenditures.[18] In 2013, ExxonMobil's profits were $32 billion, the same as total UN expenditures.[19] In 2015, Americans spent $60 billion on pets, about double total UN expenditures.[20]

Changes over time in the regular budget expenditures are shown in Figure 3.5.[21] The graph shows that the UN's budget has grown but not as dramatically as one might think. The [black] bars show expenditures in current dollars, meaning the actual dollar amount that year. More relevant are the [gray] bars, which show expenditures after controlling for inflation. This is important because $1 in 1970 bought a lot more than $1 does today. Using this better data, we see that the growth in the UN's budget has been modest.

Challenges for a 21st-Century UN

The world has changed a lot since WWII when the UN was established, and many have questioned whether the UN is ready for the 21st century. For example, the UN did little while mass atrocities unfolded in Rwanda, Syria, Sudan, and Myanmar.[22] It was powerless to stop a U.S. invasion of Iraq that even the UN Secretary General called illegal.[23] Calls to make the UN fit for purpose in the 21st century have even come from within the UN itself, where debates have taken place for almost two decades. The UN's own top bureaucrat—Secretary General António Guterres—was equally scathing:

FIGURE 3.5
UN Expenditures: Current Versus Real Dollars

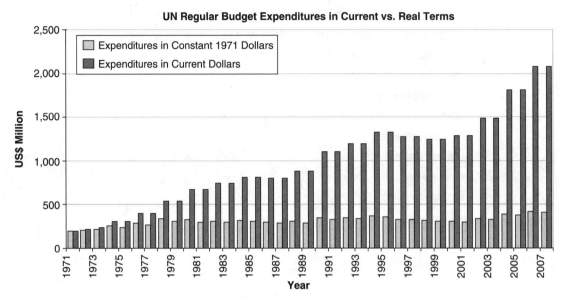

Source: Global Policy Forum, UN Regular Budget Expenditures, 1971–2007. https://www.globalpolicy.org/un-finance/tables-and-charts-on-un-finance/the-un-regular-budget/27466.html.

Someone recently asked what keeps me up at night. My answer was simple: bureaucracy. Fragmented structures. Byzantine procedures. Endless red tape. Someone out to undermine the UN could not have come up with a better way to do it than by imposing some of the rules we have created ourselves. I even sometimes ask myself whether there was a conspiracy to make our rules exactly what they need to be for us not to be effective.[24]

Critics have accused the UN of being too big, too weak (i.e., too small), or simply ineffective. U.S. president Donald Trump complained that the U.S. share of the world body's budget is unfair, pushed to slash funding, and described it as a "club for people to get together, talk and have a good time."[25] It is worth noting, however, that if it is a bloated organization, it is because states have made it so. If it is underresourced, it is because states have failed to resource it. As U.S. diplomat Richard Holbrooke said, to blame the UN for something is like blaming Madison Square Garden when the NY Knicks play badly. The UN is merely the place; the states are the players.

Two of our *global forces* are particularly important in understanding challenges for the UN (see Figure 3.6). First, there are *shifting centers of power* in the world with the rise of emerging market states. This means an expanded number of states is weighing in on global challenges. Global affairs cannot simply be managed by nuclear powers.

Read Mearsheimer's realist account of how China's rise will inevitably cause conflict: "The Gathering Storm: China's Challenge to US Power in Asia" at http://mearsheimer .uchicago.edu/pdfs/A0056.pdf.

Second, the *patchwork of global governance* is itself a force. Some voices call for a greater role for global IGOs in managing problems of global scale, while others instead call for regionalism when global institutions move too slowly. Indeed, while we tend to think of IGOs as large global organizations, many social scientists think regional organizations are having an even greater impact on the world. Regional IGOs such as the North American Free Trade Agreement (NAFTA) are especially strong drivers of economic integration. They tend to be more effective since they are smaller in number and are often like-minded, so it is not as hard to get agreement as it would be in a global organization. Moreover, states engaging in global governance now contend with major multinational corporations and NGOs. The arenas in which issues of global concern are governed have become more crowded, and states and state-run IGOs are not as able to shape global agendas.

Much of the debate concerns reforming UN institutions to make them more representative and effective centers on the UN Security Council (UNSC). Questions of reform have been made more pressing because the UNSC has been much more active since the end of the Cold War. It has not only significantly increased its use of sanctions and peacekeeping missions but also broadened the scope of what it can do, including using force to remove regimes.[26] But reform of the UNSC has not progressed. Its only significant change came in 1965 when membership expanded from 11 to 15. Recall that the UNSC is the only entity with the legal power to authorize violence in every country in the world.[27] It has five permanent members, known as the P5, each of which has the power to veto any UNSC action. There are also 10 nonpermanent members who rotate in and out and have no veto power.

Follow the debate about UN reform at https://www.globalpolicy.org/un-reform/un-reform-topics.html.

Since it is unlikely that any UNSC permanent member would voluntarily give up its seat at the world's most powerful table so that another country could join, discussion of UNSC reform usually focuses on expanding membership. The usual candidates are Brazil, India, South Africa, Japan, Nigeria, and Germany. Germany, India, Brazil, and Japan (the G4) have collaborated in an effort to

FIGURE 3.6

Global Forces, Interactions, and Tensions in the 21st-Century UN

GLOBAL FORCES	INTERACTIONS	TENSIONS
• Shifting centers of power: BRICS and Rise of the Rest. • Global governance: UN contends with a greater variety of actors, such as MNCs, as well as new IGOs.	• Emerging states seek greater say in UN Security Council. • Complex humanitarian emergencies lead to calls for expanded UN involvement. • States create UN rules but complain about slow UN processes, while some global challenges are not addressed at all, such as global financial stability.	• Frustration with UN prompts states to tackle global issues outside of the organization, further damaging the UN's legitimacy. • Global challenges such as migration lack global responses.

press their case for permanent membership. They proposed six more permanent UNSC members, their four plus two African, as well as four nonpermanent seats. Their UNSC membership would seem as legitimate as that of current members. India is as populous as China, represents about one seventh of humanity, and is the world's largest democracy. Germany and Japan are two of the world's largest economies and alone contribute about one quarter of the UN budget. Latin America currently has no UNSC representation at all.[28]

But even outside of P5 resistance there are geopolitical rivalries that hinder reform. For example, India might oppose the membership of Pakistan, South Korea might oppose Japan, and Mexico might oppose Brazil. In addition, a larger UNSC with more veto power-wielding members might make the body even less effective. As it is, there are already many security issues that UNSC members keep off the table. The United States has done so with regard to the conflict between Palestinians and its ally Israel; Russia has made sure the UNSC has not acted against its ally, Syria. China has blocked the UN from censuring its neighbor Burma for violence against its Muslim population.

No reform of the UNSC is in sight. The UNSC may be prompted into action if it fears becoming irrelevant, perhaps by the emergence of a military alliance among the excluded powers. This situation might happen if some other military alliance, such as NATO, simply asserts its right to use force without consulting the UN. This is one way of understanding the emergence of new IGOs such as the BRICS-led New Development Bank (NBD). Some have interpreted the NBD as emerging because the World Bank has failed to give more power to emerging powers.

DO IGOS ACTUALLY MATTER? THREE VIEWS

Recall that the several hundred IGOs that exist vary tremendously in the size of their membership, the scope of their mandates (the variety of things they are tasked with doing), and the powers states have given them. Many IGOs are like the UN Environment Programme (UNEP), in that their primary purpose is to disseminate knowledge and set global agendas, but they cannot force states to do anything. In this section, we will discuss answers to two questions: Do IGOs have an effect on the world? If so, how?

supranational authorities: supra means "above," so a supranational actor is above nations. These are IGOs to whom states have delegated authority to make decisions that are binding on member-states. Example: EU.

A small number of IGOs called **supranational authorities** have been granted authority to make decisions that are binding on members, even if the member disagrees with the decision. The European Union is the best example. Member-states have ceded some sovereignty to the EU, meaning they have legally empowered the EU to make laws in some areas and even override domestic laws. For example, a case brought to the European Court of Human Rights in 1988 ruled that Irish laws that criminalized certain homosexual acts were in breach of the European Convention on Human Rights. This decision changed Irish law. Of course, there are limits to the power of even the strongest IGO, since member-states can simply leave. The United Kingdom did exactly this when it voted to leave the EU in 2016, known as "Brexit." But in general, states rarely leave IGOs. In the Irish example, the government and citizens chose to remain in the EU because, on balance, they felt they get more from being in than out.

But very few IGOs are supranational. Most have little-to-no ability to force states to change their behavior. In this section, we discuss three perspectives (summarized in Table 3.2) that aim to describe how IGOs matter in the world. They are descriptive rather than normative, meaning they do not describe how IGOs *ought to* work but simply how they *do* work.

TABLE 3.2

Three Theories of IGOs

Variable	Realism	Liberalism	Constructivism
Key actors	States	States, MNCs, IGOs	States, MNCs, IGOs, NGOs
What states want	Security/power	Wealth and security	Goals influenced by culture
When states interact	Conflicting interests & coercion	Common interests & cooperation	Common or conflicting based on state identity. Interactions socialize actors
IGOs	Just reflect power of powerful states	Good for cooperation between states	Shape norms
Domestic politics	Unimportant	Important	Important
Global cooperation	Difficult and rare	Possible and common	No predictions
Theorists	Thucydides Machiavelli Hobbes Morgenthau Kissinger Waltz	Locke Kant Smith Ricardo Keohane Nye	Katzenstein Ruggie Wendt Keck Sikkink Finnemore

Realism Discounts the Role of IGOs Relative to States

Realism is a conflictual view of international relations. Realists say states are selfish actors who care first and foremost about their own survival. The theory is traced back 3,500 years to the Greek historian Thucydides. His *History of the Peloponnesian War* gives a history of conflict between Athens and Sparta. One of the most famous parts of his book is called the "Melian Dialogue," which realists think illustrates how the world really works.

The small island of Melos lies between Greece and Turkey, and in ancient Greece, it was strategically important to Athens and Sparta. Athens asserted its right to control over the islanders, and told the Melians to submit or be exterminated. The Melians pleaded their neutrality, they invoked God, and they spoke of ideals of justice. When the diplomacy ended, the Melians chose to fight Athens rather than submit to it. Thucydides concludes with a now famous sentence: "The strong do what they can and the weak suffer what they must." This is how realists think the world really works, as composed of those with innate strengths and those with innate weakness, those destined to lead and those destined to follow.

Realist thinkers like Thucydides and Machiavelli are referred to as classical realists since they viewed the way the world worked in terms of human nature. The behavior of states was seen as reflecting the nature and culture of the people within the state. Modern realism is called "neorealism" or "structural realism."[29] What is neo (new) is that the struggles between states are *not* interpreted in terms of human nature.

Neorealism is about how the international system of states affects relations between states. It makes two main assumptions. First, states are the dominant actors in the world. There may be influential IGOs such as the UN or powerful multinational corporations like Wal-Mart and Samsung, but states are the main political actors. Domestically, states make and enforce laws. Internationally, states create and control IGOs, and only states may legally wage war. To neorealists, states are "unitary actors," single entities that pursue their own interests in the global arena. It does not matter if a state's regime is democratic, its economy is socialist, or its society religious. Neorealists say all states can be counted on to do what they think is best for themselves in responding to international events, no matter what kind of state it is domestically.

Second, there is anarchy internationally. With no central authority to enforce rules, states live in constant fear of one another. States have to look out for themselves, so all states have an interest in self-preservation. This also means states have an interest in acquiring the means to protect themselves, so they build up military capabilities and generate arms races. States worry that if one state gets a good deal, it will use that to build up its strength later on, and ultimately threaten others. So realists say that states constantly forgo mutually beneficial exchanges, and thus cooperation is difficult and rare.

The realist view can seem bleak. It assumes states are the key actors and that anarchy shapes how states behave. The outcomes are poor relations between states, war is common, and IGOs can't do much to change any of this. Realists would agree that IGOs perform many of the functions listed in the previous section, but they would simply insist that IGOs have no *independent effect* on the world. For example, a realist would say that the World Bank protects the power of its founders, as reflected in their voting share. The United States, United Kingdom, France, and Germany alone have 29% of all votes. This contrasts with China and India, accounting for about one third of the human population, who together have only 8% of the votes.[30] A similar picture holds in the International Monetary Fund (IMF), where skewed voting is visualized in Figure 3.7. A realist would see this map as evidence that his or her theory is correct: Powerful states created the IMF to serve themselves, and we see their global power reflected in their disproportionate voting power within the IMF. For example, the United Kingdom has only one third the population of Nigeria, yet it has eight times the voting power.

Liberalism Views the Role of IGOs as Contributing to Increased Cooperation

Liberalism is a more cooperative view of international relations. Liberals acknowledge that states fight a lot, but they say states do realize that peace and trade are good things and that most of the time states do cooperate with one another. Just as classical realism was rooted in old ideas about human nature, so too was classical liberalism, this time that humans are fundamentally good, or at least capable of being good under the right conditions. Classical liberals like Immanuel Kant (1724–1804) said the world could be governed according to reason, morality, and law, and they saw a role for entities like IGOs in making this happen (realists thought it was naive to think the League of Nations could stop someone like Hitler, so they dismissed liberals as idealists).

Today's liberalism is different. Like modern realism, it is not based on ideas about human nature, but on an understanding of how political systems work. One important part of liberal thought harks back to Kant and what was called the "democratic peace theory." Kant thought if the decision to go to war was taken by the people rather than the Prince, war would be less likely. It turns out that the idea of the democratic peace is supported by a great deal of evidence, showing that democracies

FIGURE 3.7

(Dis)proportionate Voting Power in the IMF

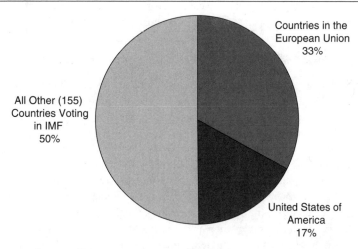

Countries in the
European Union
33%

All Other (155)
Countries Voting
in IMF
50%

United States of
America
17%

Source: Data from Worldmapper Dataset 365: International Monetary Fund. SASI, University of Sheffield, http://www.sheffield.ac.uk/sasi.

almost never fight each other. Kant thought this was partly because people in democracies would internalize peace-loving attitudes. Liberal thinkers also said states that traded with one another could learn to trust one another since they will start to learn about each other, and all the while they will become so interlinked that they would never want to fight one another.

Read an alternative explanation for the Democratic Peace.[31]

While realists say states want security and power, liberals say what states want is mostly a reflection of what is going on within their state. This is the second important assumption of liberalism: Domestic politics—what is happening within a state—is important for understanding international politics. Whereas realists would say the reaction of state leaders to external threats would be basically the same for democratic or authoritarian leaders, liberals say it absolutely matters who is in charge, and it matters whether the governing regime is a democracy. This liberal worldview is close to the way many people talk about international studies: The major players are states, but how states behave internationally is a function of what is happening socially, politically, and economically within those states.

Read Susan Shirk explain China's foreign policy in terms of Chinese domestic politics.[32]

On IGOs, liberals are much more optimistic than the realists about the possibilities for cooperation. Realists think all states are out to get the best possible deal for themselves, but liberals say this is not how states behave. States understand that they have many interests in common and they try to cooperate to achieve those goals. For example, states know that war is very costly even for the victor, so they try to avoid it. They also know they can gain from trading with one another, so they try to lower barriers to trade between one another. States also have a common interest in clean air, so they do things like sign treaties with one another. Whether or not states can reach deals on these things depends on domestic and international institutions. Domestically, liberals think democracy makes societies more peaceful and more in favor of being connected globally. Internationally, they see IGOs as playing a role in helping states to cooperate. They say the remarkable growth in IGOs seen in Figure 3.1 is evidence of this because it shows that states have found it useful to create many IGOs over time.

Read a liberal view of the role of the United States in creating IGOs by Lisa Martin.[33-35]

So, liberals are not idealists; they don't think the world is perfect. But they think progress is possible. They think war could be made less likely if more countries were democratic. They think the world could be wealthier if trade was further liberalized. And they think global challenges could be tackled if we strengthened IGOs.

complex interdependence: in liberal theory, the concept that states do not pursue just one policy. Government officials and nonstate actors within a country engage in international activity in the pursuit of diverse (often conflicting) policy goals.

A classic statement of this liberal view came with Keohane and Nye's idea of **complex interdependence**.[36] While realists said security concerns always dominate other issues for a state, even affecting nonmilitary issues, complex interdependence says there will be a variety of state goals being pursued at any point, with each bureaucracy pursuing its own goals. Military issues are not consistently on top of the agenda, as there are struggles within states to place different issues higher on the agenda (for example, when a new party comes to power and it wishes to emphasize women's rights, the environment, or migration in international affairs). Societies are connected to one another by their governments but also through informal gatherings and socializing among state elites and through transnational nonstate actors such as nongovernmental organizations (NGOs) or multinational corporations (MNCs). Therefore, liberals do not assume states act "in their own interest" since it is not clear what "own" means. There are just too many different actors.

While realists do not take IGOs very seriously, liberals do. They say that weaker states get more out of their IGO memberships than one might expect given their weakness in military or economic terms. They do this, the liberals say, by engaging in "linkage politics." For example, a small state might use its voting power in one IGO to get a favorable deal in another IGO. Small states began participating in IGOs not because they were coerced into doing so or because they were going along with whatever their protector wished. Rather, they participated in IGOs because it was simply in their interest to do so. For example, it is significant that even though Iraq suffered under UN sanctions during the 1990s, it never withdrew from the UN. The point for liberals is that IGOs exist because even smaller states find them helpful.

Liberals say IGOs exist because they increase the efficiency of international relations for states. Though there is anarchy internationally, states choose to cooperate with each other today because they will have to cooperate with each other tomorrow. Moreover, over time, membership in an IGO can actually affect a state's behavior. For example, while an IGO does not affect what states want (liberals say that is about domestic politics), an IGO can affect a state's concern about the likelihood of conflict. If a state feels secure because of the IGO, it may spend less on its military and more on universities. The perception of threat, which is directly influenced by the IGO, can thus affect how a state behaves within its own borders.[37]

Constructivism Sees IGOs as Having the Power to Influence State Behavior

While realism and liberalism have long philosophical traditions, constructivism is a fairly new approach. Constructivists are like liberals in thinking that an array of actors matter in the world, not just states. But they differ from the liberals in *de*-emphasizing the material basis of people's interest. Constructivists think it is too narrow to assume states only want money and security. They focus instead on the nonmaterial sources of interests that come from ideas, norms, and culture. What actors want is not fixed but is instead a function of their culture, global culture, and their identity. Constructivists say we can't assume what states will always want since that depends on their identity. Instead of making predictions about what states will do internationally, constructivist scholars try to describe why states are doing what they are doing.

In the constructivist view, states are like people. They interact with one another, and they have a sense of who they are—they have identities—and they have ideas about how they are supposed to behave. An important component of constructivism is an emphasis on norms, which are unwritten rules about appropriate behavior. This important part of constructivism is called the **logic of appropriateness**. While realists and liberals think states are governed by the **logic of consequences**—their behavior is all about getting or avoiding something—constructivism says a lot of the time states simply do what they think they *ought to* do. Why would a government like Brazil that engages in extra-judicial killings sign on to human rights treaties? Because they want to be seen as a modern state that protects human rights. They have ideas about what it means to be "modern," and they act accordingly. This is why some people call constructivism a "social theory of international relations" since states are social actors just like you and me. Sometimes a desire to conform will trump interests.

One prominent account of the importance of norms comes from Nina Tannenwald, who wrote about the taboo (strong norm) against the use of nuclear weapons.[38] Her book explains how and why it came to be that today the use of nuclear weapons is so unthinkable. Shortly after 1945, people thought of nuclear weapons as just another weapon that could be used, but activists in anti-war and anti-nuclear weapons movements started to shift popular opinion. Before leaders began to change their positions on nukes, these campaigns sought to reframe nuclear weapons as a moral rather than as a security issue. In the next phase, the movement went from an emergent taboo to an internalized norm as major powers agreed that nukes should only exist for deterrence.

Nina Tannenwald talks about her book Nuclear Taboo *at http://www.sgi.org/content/ files/resources/sgi-quarterly-magazine/1010_62.pdf.*

Constructivists give us optimism that the world is not condemned to anarchy as realists would have us believe. State behavior can be changed by the conscious efforts of activists to promote new norms. Indeed, constructivists say that what society considers a threat changes over time. Consider the following thought experiment: What comes to mind when you read the following? Nonstate actors that invade, kidnap, pillage, murder, and flaunt governing authority. Not terrorists, but pirates! Two hundred years ago, pirates were the scourge of the high seas and major powers including the United States used their navies to combat them. But today, even though there is still piracy around the world, we have incorporated the image of the pirate into our culture, and we now glorify them in movies. Imagine in 200 years' time your great, great grandchildren watching *Terrorists of the Persian Gulf*.[39] Constructivists point out that what societies consider terrifying is not universal or timeless. It is specific to every time and place.

logic of appropriateness: people respond to nonmaterial things, such as norms, values, and identities. Thus, how people act reflects their understanding of appropriate behavior. Constructivists say the behavior of people and states is shaped by socially shared understandings of appropriateness.

logic of consequences: people respond to material things, such as money or threats of violence. Thus, how people act reflects the consequences they expect. Constructivists say liberal and realist theories emphasize a logic of consequences in the behavior of states.

Carnival in Valletta

Wikipedia user Ronny Siegel, https://commons.wikimedia.org/wiki/ File:Carnival_in_Valletta_-_Pirate_Costume.jpg. Licensed under CC BY 3.0, https://creativecommons.org/licenses/by/3.0/legalcode.

IS From the Outside-In

GOVERNING THE DARK SIDE OF GLOBALIZATION

The growth of global markets has brought people together as buyers and sellers thanks to free flowing capital, advanced communications and transport technology, and a legal infrastructure favoring open borders and private banking. But this market integration—bringing markets closer together so as to create one larger market—also facilitates exchange between buyers and sellers of illicit (illegal) goods. For example, in 2012, Slovak officials discovered a 700-meter tunnel with its own train had been secretly moving millions of cigarettes from Ukraine to the European Union, where it is estimated that about 10% of all cigarettes are contraband.[40] This trade in illicit goods—children, sex workers, weapons, drugs, contraband—is often referred to as the dark side of globalization.

This is not merely a case of a criminal underworld versus the world of legal corporations and government officials because in many cases illicit networks consist of career criminals, businesses, and government officials. There is no neat division between a world of "clean global affairs" and a filthy underworld. For example, the United States has participated in some historic thefts, such as slavery and land grabs from Native Americans, while Israel is accused of stealing Palestinian land to build settlements for Israelis. And, yes, the global illicit economy even includes you if you have ever bought knock-off designer clothes, watched an illegal movie stream, or used tax havens to illegally avoid taxes at home.

Slovak Customs

Underground railroad bringing contraband goods into the EU.

TASR / Criminal Administration Office of the Slovak Republic

Governments like to target the supply of illicit goods rather than the demand since the supply usually means foreigners, while demand is their fellow citizens. Accusing the Chinese of not taking media piracy seriously, or accusing Mexico of not aggressively tackling drug traffickers, are both politically easier than confronting the demand for entertainment and drugs in the United States. Thus, the 2011 Global Commission on Drug Policy called for an end to the so-called "war on drugs," but in the case of the United States, anti-drug rhetoric remains a useful electoral tool for politicians. And if governments do take action, the result may be a profit paradox described by Eva Bertram: Constricting the supply of illicit goods only pushes up their prices, thus incentivizing more actors to enter the illicit economy.[41]

See the Financial Secrecy Index at https://www .financialsecrecyindex.com/.

Tax havens use their sovereignty to make this possible. Tax havens, as Nicholas Shaxson argues, are not fundamentally about taxes: They are about hiding, such as hiding money from a spouse in a costly divorce, hiding from anti-corruption officials, hiding money from police, and of course hiding from tax collectors. And tax havens are not all tiny Caribbean islands. The United States offers tax havens in states such as Delaware, where shell companies provide cover for foreign cash, while the British government retains a say in the legal affairs of Bermuda and the Cayman Islands.

Read what happened when sociologist Brooke Harrington became a wealth manager to the ultra-rich.[42]

Our global age has presented new opportunities for actors in illicit economies, and inevitably there have been calls for concerted global action. One result is the United Nations Office of Drugs and Crime (UNODC), created in 1997 to assist UN member-states in fights against illicit drugs, crime, and terrorism. As an IGO, they also engage in knowledge dissemination, such as the widely read annual World Drug Report. Ultimately, however, a core feature of the international system—state sovereignty—limits the potential contribution IGOs can make to governing this dark side of globalization.

For example, the Cook Islands—a self-governing entity associated with New Zealand—is a lesser known player in the illicit global economy. Patrons of Cook Islands include James Naples, the Texas doctor who allegedly treated cancer patients with pesticides and then billed Medicare. Placing his assets in the Cook Islands meant they could not be touched even after he pleaded guilty to obstructing justice.[43] The Cook Islands typically do not recognize U.S. court orders, so the Cook Islands would not compel people like James Naples to declare their assets on behalf of the United States.

The principle of sovereignty allows the Cook Islands to occupy this position in the global economy, and IGOs such as UNODC are powerless to stop them. Compounding the powerlessness of IGOs is that powerful states have rarely made tax havens such as the Cook Islands a plank of their foreign policy. One reason for this, as we saw with the leaked *Panama Papers*, is that many powerful government leaders are active customers of tax havens.[44] Another reason is that major states put the issue in the context of their broader foreign policies. For example, in 2012, Secretary of State Hillary Clinton visited the Cook Islands. She had earlier testified that China had "brought all of the leaders of the South Pacific to Beijing, and wined and dined them."

"Let's just put aside all the moral, humanitarian, do-good side of what we believe in, and let's just talk, you know, realpolitik," she said. "We are in a competition with China."[45] Clinton never discussed the Cook Islands' role in illicit global flows. In this context, it is perhaps no surprise that an IGO such as UNODC has not solved the global challenge of illicit financial flows.

Reflect

What tensions are created by the dark side of globalization?

Majdi Fathi/NurPhoto/Getty Images

While realists see IGOs as having no independent effect on the world, and liberals see IGOs as helping states to solve problems together, constructivists see IGOs as affecting the world because they can transform identities.[46] The classic example of how IGOs can shape identities is the European Union. Despite its current problems, the EU is widely regarded as one of the most successful IGOs in history. It took countries that had engaged in two devastating wars and made them peaceful partners—indeed pillars—in what is now the world's largest trading bloc. In the constructivist view, the IGO that became the EU began with modest goals, but due to its success, it showed Europeans that there was much to gain if they could see what they had in common. The growth of the EU from its birth as the European Coal and Steel Community (ECSC) was not simply about reflecting the power of major states, as realists would suggest, or just about helping states cooperate, as liberals would suggest. Instead, constructivists would say the EU had an effect on states' identities: This IGO managed to change what states wanted.

FIGURE 3.8

Global Forces, Interactions, Tensions, and the Relevance of IGOs

GLOBAL FORCES	INTERACTIONS	TENSIONS
• Global governance: Realists say IGOs have little power independent of the powerful states who control them, while liberals and constructivists think IGOs can influence global interactions. Liberals see global governance as increasingly crowded due to MNCs, while constructivists point to CSOs.	• Realists: IGOs are used by powerful states to govern internationally. • Liberals: IGOs are used by all states, not just the powerful, to govern common challenges. CSOs and MNCs also seek to engage IGOs. • Constructivists: States may create IGOs for selfish purposes, but once created the IGOs are managed by international civil servants. Along with civil society, these civil servants try to influence international norms and culture. Thus, IGOs are actors in their own right, and they interact with states.	• Realists: IGOs may be powerless if major powers do not want them to be effective. • Liberals: IGOs may be ineffective if even smaller powers do not want to cooperate. • Constructivists: Whether states wish it or not, IGOs may shift global cultures and identities.

SUMMARY

In international studies, we care about the *interactions* that characterize the 21st century, the *global forces* that drive change, and the *tensions* that can result. IGOs matter in all these ways. IGOs are the *product* of interactions among states: They are created by states. They are also the *sites* of interactions: They are where states interact on a daily basis. They are a global force because they are one of the actors that share the global stage along with states, corporations, and civil society. The global stage is no longer the sole preserve of states. Finally, IGOs provide a forum for the mediating of international tensions. IGO conferences, summits, and negotiations can provide states with a neutral and trusted venue for dialogue. Moreover, IGOs can give us—the mass public—a focal point for observing global interactions.

How IGOs such as the UN respond to 21st-century challenges remains to be seen. (Figure 3.8 sets the issue in our framework.) If the realists are right, what the UN does is not hugely important, since IGOs just do the bidding of the powerful states that control them. If the liberals are right, states, IGOs may receive even greater resources and responsibility to manage global problems, since IGOs exist to help states do together what they cannot do alone. And if the constructivists are right, IGOs will continue to shape the global social norms that affect the behavior of the very states that once created the IGOs.

KEY TERMS

complex interdependence 96
constructivism 80
epistemic communities 83
functionalism 83

intergovernmental organization (IGO) 81
liberalism 80
logic of appropriateness 97

logic of consequences 97
realism 80
supranational authorities 92

QUESTIONS FOR REVIEW

1. IGOs sometimes fail to stop countries from going to war. How would realists and liberals explain this?

2. The UN Security Council meets to discuss security emergencies. Using a recent conflict discussed at the Security Council, which actors are interacting in the attempt to end the conflict? Are they domestic or international? Are they state or nonstate actors?

3. IGOs often attempt to manage the tensions that come from international interactions. Which IGOs are involved in managing tensions related to global refugees, disease, and banking? What caused the tensions in each area?

4. Constructivists say states and state leaders have identities and that these identities shape state foreign policies. Using the most recent State of the Union address, what is the identity of the United States and how (if at all) does it matter for U.S. foreign policy?

5. IGOs sometimes try to shape global norms. Using only this month's news, can you find evidence of this?

LEARN MORE

The *Correlates of War Project* hosts the most comprehensive dataset on IGOs: http://www.correlatesofwar.org/data-sets/IGOs

The *Global Policy Forum* maintains comprehensive data on UN finance: https://www.globalpolicy.org/un-finance.html

Map seven decades of votes in the UN General Assembly

Who votes with the United States at the UN?

https://plot.ly/~evoeten/20/#plot

NOTES

1. There are similarities between the liberal theory of international relations discussed in this chapter and the (neo)liberal economic theories discussed in Chapter 6. But it is useful to keep them separate in your mind. While both are inspired by the promise of free trade, the liberal theory of international relations is not an ideology. It is an attempt to explain how the world actually works, but it is not trying to describe how it ought to work. By contrast, liberal theories of the economy or democracy are closer to an ideology because they contain a theory of how the world works and a vision of how it *ought to* work. Moreover, while ideologies typically involve discussions about human nature, such discussions are of much less interest to the liberal theory of international relations.

2. For more on the *Game of Thrones* analogy, see the following: Charli Carpenter, "Game of Thrones as Theory," *Foreign Affairs*, March 29, 2012, https://www.foreignaffairs.com/articles/2012-03-29/game-thrones-theory; Stephen Benedict Dyson, *Otherworldly Politics: The International Relations of Star Trek, Game of Thrones, and Battlestar Galactica* (Baltimore, MD: Johns Hopkins University Press, 2015); Alyssa Rosenberg, "Realpolitik in a Fantasy World," *Foreign Policy*, July 18, 2011, https://foreignpolicy.com/2011/07/18/realpolitik-in-a-fantasy-world/; Stephen Saideman, "The Game of Thrones and Popular Understandings of International Relations," *E-International Relations* (blog), March 22, 2013, http://www.e-ir.info/2013/03/22/the-game-of-thrones-and-popular-understandings-of-international-relations/.

3. An international organization in which membership is limited to states would be considered an IGO if it has at least three members.

4. Technically, only member-states are subject to the Convention. The United States has not ratified it.

5. The Holy See (Vatican City) and the State of Palestine hold observer status as nonmembers.

6. Schlesinger, 1997, p. 48.

7. Weiss and Roy, 2016.

8. *Declaration in Defense of Human Rights* (1938), adopted by participants at the 1938 Inter-American Conference in Peru. Glendon, 2003; Sikkink, 2014.

9. Acharya, 2016.

10. http://www.un.org/en/hq/dm/hr.shtml.

11. Not to be confused with the International Criminal Court (ICC).

12. Data from http://www.un.org/en/about-un/.

13. Government Accountability Office, 2014.

14. http://www.un.org/pga/70/2015/12/23/general-assembly-adopts-un-budget-for-2016-17/.

15. Clarke, 2016.

16. Karns and Mingst, 2010, p. 135.

17. https://www.globalpolicy.org/un-finance.html.

18. https://www.sipri.org/media/press-release/2016/world-military-spending-resumes-upward-course-says-sipri.

19. http://money.cnn.com/2016/04/29/investing/exxon-earnings-17-year-low-oil-crash-1999/.

20. Data from the American Pet Products Association. http://www.americanpetproducts.org/press_industrytrends.asp. Accessed 7/7/16.

21. It does not include peacekeeping operations, or the budgets of the autonomous "specialized agencies" like the World Bank.

22. Samantha Power, *"A Problem from Hell": America and the Age of Genocide*, Reprint edition (Basic Books, 2013).

23. Ewen MacAskill and Julian Borger, "Iraq War Was Illegal and Breached UN Charter, Says Annan," *The Guardian*, September 16, 2004, sec. World news, http://www.theguardian.com/world/2004/sep/16/iraq.iraq.

24. United Nations, "Secretary-General's Remarks at UN Reform Event," *Un.Org*, September 18, 2017, https://www.un.org/sg/en/content/sg/statement/2017-09-18/secretary-generals-remarks-un-reform-event-delivered. See also Thomas G. Weiss et al., *The United Nations and Changing World Politics* (Boulder, CO: Westview Press, 2017); Thomas George Weiss, *What's Wrong with the United Nations and How to Fix It*, 2016.

25. Reuters, "Trump to Host Sept. 18 Meeting of World Leaders on U.N. Reform," *Reuters*, September 1, 2017, https://www.reuters.com/article/us-un-reform-trump/trump-to-host-sept-18-meeting-of-world-leaders-on-u-n-reform-idUSKCN1BC5SP.

26. Voeten, 2007.

27. Technically, any UN member-state.

28. Burns, 2009.

29. We leave aside neo-classical realism, which is the theory's 21st-century face.

30. China has 5%, and India has 3%. http://siteresources.worldbank.org/BODINT/Resources/278027-1215524804501/IBRDCountryVotingTable.pdf.

31. Bandow, 2005.

32. Susan Shirk, "Trump and China: Getting to Yes With Beijing," *Foreign Affairs*, February 13, 2017, https://www.foreignaffairs.com/articles/2017-02-13/trump-and-china.

33. "Self-Binding," *Harvard Magazine* 107, no. 1 (2004): 33–36.

34. *Power and Interdependence: World Politics in Transition* (Boston, MA: Little, Brown, 1977), http://repository.tufs.ac.jp/handle/10108/17258.

35. *The Nuclear Taboo: The United States and the Non-use of Nuclear Weapons Since 1945*, Cambridge Studies in International Relations 87 (Cambridge, U.K.: Cambridge University Press, 2007).

36. Keohane and Nye, *Power and Interdependence*.

37. Karns and Mingst, 2010.

38. The Economist, "Tunnel Vision," *The Economist*, July 24, 2012, https://www.economist.com/blogs/easternapproaches/2012/07/slovakias-borders.

39. Eva Bertram et al., *Drug War Politics: The Price of Denial* (Berkeley: University of California Press, 1996).

40. Brooke Harrington, "Inside the Secretive World of Tax-Avoidance Experts," *The Atlantic*, October 26, 2015, https://www.theatlantic.com/business/archive/2015/10/elite-wealth-management/410842/.

41. Leslie Wayne, "Cook Islands, a Paradise of Untouchable Assets," *The New York Times*, December 14, 2013, sec. International Business, https://www.nytimes.com/2013/12/15/business/international/paradise-of-untouchable-assets.html.

42. https://www.theguardian.com/news/series/panama-papers.

43. Paul Richter, "Hillary Clinton's Visit Underscores New Value of Cook Islands," *Los Angeles Times*, August 29, 2012, http://articles.latimes.com/2012/aug/29/world/la-fg-south-pacific-20120829.

44. Nina Tannenwald, *The Nuclear Taboo*.

45. Goldstein and Pevehouse, 2014, p. 98.

46. This is the theory of neofunctionalism.

Civil Society

AGENTS OF CHANGE IN GLOBAL INTERACTIONS

LEARNING OBJECTIVES

After finishing this chapter, you should be able to:

- Distinguish a nongovernmental organization from a government.

- Articulate the Tocquevillian and Gramscian theories of civil society.

- Describe civil society's sources of power.

- Identify a transnational advocacy network in the news.

- Understand the historical origins of global civil society.

- Challenge the supposed benefits of civil society using major critiques.

Adam Bettcher/Getty Images

WHO CARES ABOUT CECIL THE LION?

Shipments of lion, leopard, elephant, rhino, buffalo trophies banned.

In July 2015, an American big-game hunter on safari in Hwange National Park, Zimbabwe, illegally killed and beheaded a protected lion named Cecil. That killing sparked international outrage, and within a month of the killing, several hundred thousand people had signed petitions protesting the killing, and thousands more, acting within civil society groups, joined forces to act on the issue. The African Elephant Conservation Coordinating Group was one of the organizing forces. The Group was established in 1990 when international nongovernmental organizations (INGOs) like the World Wildlife Fund and The World Conservation Union formed a coalition to conduct research, raise funds, and educate the public.[1] The Group accumulated considerable experience working with national government bodies like the U.S. Fish and Wildlife Service and intergovernmental organizations like the United Nations (UN) Environment Programme, as well as with civil servants staffing the secretariat of CITES, the main global agreement to ban trade in ivory.[2] The Coordinating Group also developed conservation strategies with governments in southern African countries, as well as with governments in ivory-consumer countries in East Asia.

When news emerged that a dentist from Minnesota had killed Cecil, coalitions such as the Group swung into action, and began pressuring companies and governments to act. Other responses followed. The U.S. Fish and Wildlife Service announced an investigation into the incident, and the Obama administration announced a near-total ban on commercial trade of African elephant ivory in the United States.[3] The UN General Assembly adopted a resolution on July 30th against trafficking in wildlife, with officials specifically citing Cecil's killing.[4] The next day, airlines including British Airways and Lufthansa announced bans on transporting animal trophies. The press statement shown at the beginning of this chapter was quickly released by Delta Airlines.[5] These actions by some of the world's most powerful companies and governments were in response to a public outcry, but this outcry did not emerge spontaneously.

The international outcry was energized by people known as global civil society actors, such as the Coordinating Group. For example, consider the people responsible for the online petition at SumOfUs.org, which received several hundred thousand signatures.[6] The biographies of those involved show a wealth of experience in animal and environmental rights movements, including Alliance for Climate Protection, Youth Climate Network, and Greenpeace. These nonprofit, non-government organizations were ready to provide journalists with accessible information on global poaching and trafficking. In their coverage of Cecil, journalists cited studies by the International Union for the Conservation of Nature, the University of Oxford's Wildlife Conservation Research Unit, the Zimbabwe Conservation Task Force, and the Wildlife Conservation Society. All are considered civil society actors.

A different part of the #CeciltheLion campaign involved loosely coordinated animal rights and preservation organizations, such as Greenpeace or the Humane Society. They focused mainly on publicity campaigns aimed at influencing the public. This was a much less centralized, and less well funded, campaign with no central leadership. There was much less direct engagement and partnering with states and IGOs. But their activism was important in shaping public perception of what it meant to be modern and humane.

So, why do we care about Cecil the Lion? Because the story introduces us to one of the most important types of actors in today's world: civil society actors, those individuals, organizations, and networks engaged in advocacy for change. Civil society actors are nongovernmental actors because they do not seek control of any government. Although civil society actors have no political or economic power, they nonetheless have an effect on our world. International activity in the form of treaties or changes in the behavior of billion-dollar companies does not come from nowhere. In the case of Cecil the Lion, the international outcry was intentionally and consciously engineered by a small number of organized individuals. This type of actor is the subject of this chapter.

First, we will define what civil society is, what it is not, and who is considered a civil society actor. We will then ask, "What is civil society good for?" Many people see civil society groups as agents for positive change on issues such as climate change and women's rights. But others are more critical, and they ask to whom these civil society groups are responsible. It was notable, for example,

GLOBAL FORCES	INTERACTIONS	TENSIONS
• Global markets: A U.S. hunter participates in global tourism trade. • ICT: Global outrage spreads with incredible speed online. The outrage is expressed almost entirely in nonphysical spaces. • Shifting global powers: Rise of East Asia means growing demand for ivory. • Global governance: International forums are increasingly crowded with states and nonstate actors. Civil society actors are especially important actors in global environmental governance, such as the global ban on trade in endangered species.	• Civil society actors such as the Coordinating Group bring together communities from Zimbabwe, the U.S., and others in a global protest. Civil society mobilizes, gathers and provides information, advocates for change, frames hunting as a moral rather than an economic issue. • International airlines find themselves forced to take sides. • Civil society actors find allies in the U.S. government and United Nations.	• Cultural clash between the values of Western-based animal rights activists and hunting enthusiasts as well as Zimbabweans employed in tourism. • Civil society is a dynamic force, pushing states, intergovernmental organizations, and multinational corporations to take stances.

that much of the civil society activism around Cecil the Lion came from outside of Africa. Finally, we will examine how it is that nonprofit organizations and people working outside of government and corporations can have any effect on the world. We will trace the growth in international civil society and relate it to our four *global forces*. We will see that the power of civil society comes from mobilizing and pressuring people by changing people's values and perceptions. We will also see how civil society actors are a primary agent of the *interactions* and *tensions* that interest us in international studies. Many civil society actors are engaged in confronting powerful governments and companies. Civil society actors can be a dynamic force driving rapid change in the world (see Figure 4.1).

WHAT IS CIVIL SOCIETY?

civil society: voluntary association of people outside of families, firms (companies), and states (governments). Includes nongovern-mental organizations (NGOs), social movements, and transnational advocacy networks (TANs).

In its simplest form, **civil society** is voluntary association outside the family, the firm, and the state. It is all of the organizations, networks, and movements formed by citizens to help define and pursue their own interests. It does not include political organizations. Rather, it is the web of nonpolitical organizations, like clubs, unions, environmental groups, churches, or sports teams. At a basic level, we label civil society any activity by people outside their family that is not for political power or profit. We say "voluntary" because membership in some associations is not voluntary in some societies, such as compulsory membership in a religion or a trade union. **Global civil society**, then, is simply civil society on a transnational or global scale. A widely used definition that is more technical but explicit in its international focus says global civil society is

> a supranational sphere of social and political participation in which citizen groups, social movements and individuals engage in dialogue, debate, confrontation, and negotiation with each other, with governments, international and regional governmental organizations and with multinational corporations.[7]

global civil society: civil society actors working to influence global society.

To understand the importance of this definition, think of the difference between acting globally and acting transnationally (across borders). Some people think of global civil society as acting transnationally. For example, Amnesty International operates multicountry campaigns to raise awareness of the torture of political prisoners in Saudi Arabia. Their efforts in that campaign are meant to affect change within Saudi Arabia specifically, to solve a specific problem. But others think of global civil society as acting globally, meaning the object or purpose of the action is the globe itself. It is not that this action is "merely" across borders. Rather, global civil society is activity directed at global issues and global centers of power. For example, Amnesty International is a member in a coalition of human rights organizations to strengthen the UN's human rights work. This is an important departure from the first vision of global civil society since now we are saying that civil society actors like Amnesty International *think* globally. They behave *as though* there is an international society they are trying to shape. Thus, the claim that there is *a* global civil society or there are global civil societ*ies* is a larger claim than simply talking about cross-border interaction. It means people think of themselves as global citizens or as invested in a global civic culture.

Digging deeper, we find two competing theories of what civil society is and what it does in the world: the Tocquevillian and the Gramscian. Distinguishing between the two will help us understand some of the arguments, concepts, and issues presented later in the chapter.

Tocqueville's Civil Society: Nonpolitical Actions Lead to Political Effects

One of the most important people associated with the idea of civil society is Frenchman Alexis de Tocqueville (1805–1859). He wrote *Democracy in America*, which was published in two volumes in 1835 and 1840. "Americans of all ages," he said, "all stations of life and all types of disposition are forever forming associations." These associations were "of a thousand types—religious, moral, serious, futile, very general and very limited, immensely large and very minute." He said America had a culture of civic activism, of people always joining associations, both for political purposes as well as for nonpolitical purposes. The important part of his observation is that even seemingly nonpolitical organizations—churches, bowling leagues, bird-watching groups—have an effect on politics. When people interact with one another in nonpolitical settings, they start to trust other people and to think of them as sharing common interests, and in this way, participation in civil society is said to produce better citizens and better democratic politics. So people often talk of civil society as a sort of training ground for the democratization of whole societies.[8]

This is why many people are excited about the possibilities of a stronger civil society and social capital locally, nationally, and globally. Some people see in civil society a means to a better world. Hence, in 2013, President Obama launched a program called *Stand with Civil Society*, which was a global call to action to support civil society around the world. The White House proudly proclaimed: "The United States is the largest supporter of civil society in the world, with more than $2.7 billion invested to strengthen civil society since 2010."[9] The "strengthening" referred to projects to support civil society actors in developing and authoritarian countries.

In the Tocquevillian view, global civil society can make the existing world order of powerful states and multinationals more representative and accountable to the global population. It will shine light on illicit flows of diamonds, cash, and humans. It will shame nuclear powers into never using chemical warfare. Thus, global civil society addresses all the failures of a world run by states and corporations. Global civil society actors are the conscience of the world. They raise alarms and advance humanitarian agendas.

Gramsci's Civil Society: Contests for Political Power

A competing view of civil society comes from Italian Antonio Gramsci (1891–1937). He wrote about the concept of hegemony (domination) and ruling class ideology. He said the voluntary organizations that make up civil society are not so benign. He also said civil society is the place "where ruling 'hegemony' was reproduced in cultural life through the media, universities and religious institutions to 'manufacture consent' and legitimacy."[10] Where the state (police, prisons, army) often rule through force, civil society rules through consent. Although Tocqueville saw civil society as a free arena, Gramsci saw it as a space in which hegemonic forces (i.e., the state) conflict with counter-hegemonic forces (i.e., social movements). Thus, rather than an apolitical space, civil society is all about power.

We can see Gramsci's ideas in a competing definition of civil society that comes from Scholte: Civil society is "a political arena where associations of citizens seek, from outside political parties, to shape societal rules."[11] What Scholte has in mind is that even seemingly nonpolitical activities such as parent–teacher associations have at least some effect on how a society works. Thus, the Gramscian view is that civil society is about power, even if it is defined in terms of actors that do not seek political office or profit.

Critics say global civil society helps the status quo by depoliticizing issues. For example, imagine the U.S. State Department wanted to commission a comparative study on prisons in Central Asia. Two U.S.-based INGOs have the capacity to write such a report. But one INGO has written op-eds in prominent newspapers critiquing the U.S. prison system. The other INGO uses U.S. prisons as the benchmark by which prisons in other countries are judged. Who gets the contract? The less critical INGO, of course. And months later, its press release will appear in newspapers describing how bad prisons are in "other countries." This is how power gets reproduced. In this view, civil society is not an autonomous or neutral actor. Civil society actively does the bidding of the powerful or is allowed to operate so long as the powerful are not challenged.

nongovern-mental organizations (NGOs): voluntary associations, operating at local, national, or regional levels, organized in pursuit of shared interests, but not seeking profit or public office. Example: Doctors Without Borders.

civil society organizations (CSOs): often used interchangeably with nongovern-mental organizations (NGOs), but they can also mean NGOs as well as community-based organizations (CBOs).

WHO IS CIVIL SOCIETY?

The activities of civil society take place inside of formal organizations with staff and headquarters, referred to interchangeably as **nongovernmental organizations (NGOs)** or as **civil society organizations (CSOs)**. There are several different kinds of civil society organizations.

International Nongovernmental Organizations (INGOs)

An **international nongovernmental organization (INGO)** is simply an NGO that has members in more than one country. There are just over 60,000 international NGOs.[12] Civil society also includes **social movements** and networks, which are groupings of individual and organizations that work for social change. Thus, "civil society" is a large umbrella, beneath which there are thousands of INGOs, networks, and social movements. These civil society actors are most visible to us when they engage in public campaigns, often led by individual philanthropists, artists, and prominent personalities (like the Pope, Dalai Lama, or Banksy). Recent examples might include #PantsuitNation, #JeSuisCharlie, #SendeAnlat, #YaMeCanse, and #icantbreathe.

There is great variety in what civil society actors do (see Table 4.1). Some try to shape global agendas, such as the 2015 Sustainable Development Goals (SDGs). At international negotiations, some lobby state delegations, while others serve as experts on technical matters. Some try to verify that states and companies comply with international law on things like fishing or chemical weapons. And a great many deliver actual services in countries, like vaccinating children, training nurses, or building wells. Indeed, civil society actors have become so professional at delivering health and education services that wealthy governments channel billions of dollars in development aid through them. For example, the U.S. Agency for International Development (USAID) reported that its program in Cambodia managed 62,000 births in 2011. But USAID staff did not run these health offices. Instead, USAID contracted with a Cambodian NGO called Reproductive Health Association of Cambodia to provide the actual services.[13] So, the actors we will learn about engage in a huge variety of activities.

How big is civil society? No one knows because it depends how granular we want to be. For example, if civil society includes "voluntary association outside the family, firm and the state," this means we could count anyone engaging in a religious association as participating in civil society. Add to this professional associations including labor unions and sporting associations, and one can see that the number of civil society organizations, and the number of civil society participants, is hard to count. What if we looked only at the part of civil society that exists in formal organizations in countries? Results would vary, but a "typical" country likely has tens of thousands of such organizations (i.e., entities with offices, staff, etc.).

Internationally, there is huge variety in the size and purposes of INGOs. Some INGOs are business associations, like the World Economic Forum, which is funded by over 1,000 of the world's largest companies. Some INGOs are almost entirely funded with money from governments usually because they carry out projects on the government's behalf. An example in the United States is the National Democratic Institute (NDI). It is a private INGO (not related to the Democratic Party) that supports democratization projects in over 60 countries. Almost all of NDI's funding comes from the U.S. State Department or U.S.

Protester

Wikipedia user Tim Pierce, https://commons.wikimedia.org/ wiki/File:-ICantBreathe_(15947352856).jpg. Licensed under CC BY 2.0, https:// creativecommons.org/licenses/by/2.0/deed.en.

international nongovernmental organization (INGO): nongovernmental organization (NGO) that has members in more than one country, typically meaning a physical office with employees.

social movements: collective action for social change involving very loosely organized individuals, networks, and nongovernmental organizations (NGOs). Example: Black Lives Matter.

TABLE 4.1

Issue Areas and INGOs

Issue area	Examples of INGOs
Poverty and Development	Oxfam Save the Children
Conflict	Search for Common Ground International Crisis Group
Human rights	Amnesty International Human Rights Watch
Environment	Greenpeace World Wildlife Fund
Women's rights	International Alliance for Women Madre
Humanitarian	Red Cross Action Against Hunger
Health	Gates Foundation Partners in Health
Democratic Governance	Carter Center Article19

Congress because most of NDI's activities involve carrying out U.S. democratization projects. NDI does not see itself as a mere contractor, however. It is an independent, nonprofit, nongovernmental organization of people committed to strengthening democracies around the world. It sees itself as partnering with like-minded actors, in this case, the U.S. government. Within global civil society, there are also religiously based INGOs such as the International Association of Engaged Buddhists. Many INGOs without an explicitly religious motivation nonetheless have roots in religious activism. For example, CARE, an INGO engaged in humanitarian activities around the world, was founded by U.S. Quakers.

Many INGOs began as national NGOs, but many were global from the outset. For example, Bangladesh-based BRAC is perhaps the largest NGO in the world with over 100,000 employees and revenue of almost $1 billion. It began working as a small-scale organization focusing on helping refugees from the Bangladesh Liberation War of 1971. It went global in the 2000s and can now be found in most of the world's poorest countries. By contrast, Global Witness began in 1993 as an explicitly INGO. It goes undercover to expose environmental and human rights abuses, such as the illegal timber trade that funded the genocidal Khmer Rouge in Cambodia. In 2014, Global Witness received the TED Prize for its campaign for transparency in the ownership of international companies. These are the two ways INGOs are born: as outgrowths from national-level activities and as globally oriented from the outset.

Transnational Advocacy Networks (TANs)

Global civil society actors often gather into **transnational advocacy networks (TANs),** which are "networks of activists, distinguishable largely by the centrality of principled ideas or values in motivating their formation."[14] "Transnational" means they are multicountry and usually multiregion. "Advocacy"

transnational advocacy network (TAN): coalition or network of people—but not a formal organization— working for change, typically narrowly focused on a specific issue. Example: Jubilee Debt Campaign.

When civil society actors form a transnational advocacy network, they juggle the desire to impact the global stage with the challenge of uniting actors from diverse origins in different countries and cultural contexts. Let's look at an example from activists advocating for lesbian, gay, bisexual, and transgender (LGBT) rights.

The International Gay and Lesbian Human Rights Commission (IGLHRC) is a U.S.-based LGBT rights NGO (now called OutRight Action International). Its staff documents rights abuses, trains activists, and lobbies national and international governments. Anthropologist Ryan Thoreson studied how IGLHRC engaged with worldwide partners.[15] These transnational partnerships were especially important in a pre-Internet age, Thoreson explains: "In 1992, brokers [staff] at IGLHRC provided documentation for a gay man from Argentina seeking asylum in Canada, who became the first person known to be granted asylum on the basis of sexual orientation" (p. 32). A decade later, IGLHRC had grown to be a truly international actor: "In 2004 alone, IGLHRC organized trainings in India, Uganda, Hungary, Thailand, Canada, Paraguay, Brazil, Mexico, Macedonia, the Netherlands, and Peru. In 2005, staff held a first-of-its-kind Activist Institute with transgender and intersex activists in the LAC region; co-hosted trainings and strategy sessions with HRW in Porto Alegre, Brazil, and Colombo, Sri Lanka; and hosted trainings or workshops for activists in the Balkans and China. In 2006, IGLHRC organized trainings on human rights documentation and a discussion on Pride in Eastern Europe with ILGA-Europe. In 2007, it held its second Activist Institute on lesbian and bisexual women's issues in the LAC region" (p. 46).

These sorts of international connections also provide an illustration of the boomerang model (see Figure 4.4 later in this chapter), as explained by Hildebrandt: "a Romanian NGO in the mid-1990s linked with other European gay groups and received

OutRight
ACTION INTERNATIONAL

Human Rights for LGBTIQ People Everywhere

Source: https://www.outrightinternational.org/.

funding from the Dutch government in its effort to repeal antigay criminal laws. The TAN compelled European countries, and the EU, to pressure Romania by making its admission into the Council of Europe contingent upon shedding these laws. This case might provide reason to be hopeful that LGBT activists in China can use international linkages and throw a boomerang of their own to affect policy change" (p. 848).[16]

But tensions arise when well-meaning civil society actors from different contexts interact. In Thoreson's study of IGLHRC, staff members were aware of the power differential between themselves and their counterparts in the "global South." In one example, staff debated whether to publish a study into rights violations in Senegal. IGLHRC engaged Senegalese partners while weighing the potential harm to Senegalese activists were a Western NGO seen to interfere in Senegalese society. Others worried that bringing international attention to Senegal's persecution of HIV/AIDS activists might slow the flow of donor funds for HIV/AIDS (p. 136).

(Continued)

Global civil society actors can also find themselves in powerful positions relative to Westerners because of the global and local expertise they develop. Thoreson recalls a phone call from a filmmaker who wanted to make a documentary on "the ways that the Christian Right in the United States was exporting homophobia to Africa. . . . As the call went on, it became increasingly clear that the producer knew which countries he considered homophobic—Malawi and Senegal—and wanted me to affirm that they should send film crews to both and provide contacts to make this possible. . . . I was adamant, however, that it was not a good idea to send a crew to Senegal, where the mere mention of homosexuality had set off mob violence and IGLHRC had tactically restricted its advocacy to working with groups behind the scenes. More prosaically, Senegal is 95 percent Muslim, with few known links to evangelicals in the United States; instead, there are strong indications that homophobia has escalated amid pressure from Saudi Arabia, the politicization of religious leadership, and a series of publicized, escalating sex panics in 2008 and 2009. My response did not seem to be what the producer was looking for, and the call grew almost hostile as I tried to dissuade him from sending a film crew to ask about homosexuality in Senegal" (pp. 174–175). Here the NGO acts as gatekeeper because of its control of information about which countries were experiencing the most homophobia, and who the key actors were in these countries.

Finally, the case of IGLHRC is also illuminating because it shows that individual NGOs—who are of course nonprofit—compete against each other for scarce funding and control of the agenda. This manifested itself in factionalism and tension within the LGBT transnational advocacy network (p. 177). Some NGOs within the TAN sought to publish reports before competitor NGOs, such was the need to be seen as reputable and leading and, thus, to be worthy of funding. Others disagreed on basic strategy. Should the LGBT NGO community seek sensationalist coverage of hate crimes to capture public attention? Or should it instead be cautious and forensic in its investigations to protect its credibility (p. 179)?

Reflect

In international studies, tensions are the unintended result of interactions. What tensions are shown in this example?

---

means the purpose of the activity is to advocate for some issue. It is not to make money or win office, but it is simply to advocate for some specific cause. "Network" means they are loose networks of activists all over the world who come together on issues that matter to them, like human rights, women's health, child labor, or land mines. But TANs can include state actors as well as the multinational corporations (MNCs) within them. TANs could include think tanks, which are research organizations, often composed of academics, who publish highly specific policy research that is intended to inform (or sway) opinion on an international issue. Examples include the Institute of Strategic Studies, a Pakistan-based NGO (although state-funded) that engages in research on regional and global security. It may also include foundations, which are NGOs dedicated to funding activities of others, such as the Ford Foundation or Bill and Melinda Gates Foundation in the United States or the Robert Bosch Foundation in Germany. These foundations control billions of dollars earmarked for things like research and services in health and education. Intergovernmental organizations (IGOs) like UN Women try to shape what the world thinks about women's issues and tries to keep them high on the global agenda.

Social Movements

Another important form of civil society comprises social movements: ongoing, organized, collective action oriented toward social change. Social movements are informal networks of people who share an identity. A recent example is the Tea Party movement in the United States. It is a loosely organized movement without one leader, organized by what it sees as opposition to the status quo in politics and society, with members that perceive themselves as outsiders, and which makes demands for fundamental change.

Although social movements are autonomous from states, they are typically political because they involve the pursuit of political goals that occurs *outside* of formal politics. This includes peaceful protests, but it can also include violent protest in the form of civil wars, insurgency, or terrorism. The second part is that social movements take place when citizens are organized over time. A spontaneous riot or a strike would not count, but ongoing pro-life or pro-choice efforts are social movements because they have remained organized over years.[17]

Social movements are similar to TANs because they are not centralized. Their major difference is simply the breadth of their ambition. Although TANs tend to focus on narrow issues, such as fair trade food or coral reef conservation, social movements focus on broader themes such as North–South inequality or climate change. Therefore, a civil society actor might consider that a TAN of which he or she is a member is also part of a bigger global social movement.

Actors within social movements share values, they interact, and they share information, but there is no hierarchy or set leadership. There might be one organization or individual that is the symbol of the movement, as Martin Luther King Jr. was for the civil rights movement, but social movements are not reducible to individuals or individual organizations. They also differ from interest groups, which tend to be small groups that are narrowly focused. Social movements tend to be much broader— involving more people—and tend to focus more on transforming society and spend a lot of their efforts outside of politics, not just lobbying politicians. It is difficult to count their number, but one scholar counts an increase in international social movement organizations from 183 in 1973 to 959 in 2000, most of which were active in human rights and the environment.[18]

RECENT HISTORY OF GLOBAL CIVIL SOCIETY: RISE OF A NEW GLOBAL FORCE

Global civil society is not new. In the late 1700s, groups dedicated to the ending of slavery formed in England, France, and the United States. In the mid-1800s, groups dedicated to finding peaceful means to resolve international disputes sprung up around Europe, with 425 by 1900.[19] Internationally minded civil society actors were instrumental in the movement for women's liberation after World War I. In 1920, a meeting of 132 associations led to the formation of the Union of International Associations, which remains a prime source of information on global organizations. The League of Nations invited NGOs to contribute to meetings in the 1920s and 1930s. Eglantyne Jebb, founder of NGO Save the Children, drafted the Declaration of the Rights of the Child, which was approved by the league assembly in 1924. A total of 1,200 representatives of voluntary organizations were later present at the creation of the UN in 1945. Activists in the peace and internationalist movements were also contributors to the Universal Declaration of Human Rights in 1948.

Many of these actors thought of themselves as engaged in more than simply doing things across borders. Intellectuals like Immanuel Kant (1724–1804) and Emmerich de Vattel (1714–1767) wrote about an international order that was civil and social. An international civil society would be an arena without government but very much with order. States were part of their imagined international order, even though it was not an order *of states*. Civility and enlightenment thinking would take the place of violent nationalism and imperialism. The idea that global civil society is a place of

Two girls wearing banners in English and Yiddish, reading "Abolish Child Slavery." Probably taken during May 1, 1909, labor parade in New York City.

Source: Unknown, "Photo: Protest against Child Labor in a Labor Parade" (Bain Collection, 1909), https://www.loc.gov/item/97519062/, Library of Congress.

civility remains, but today people also see global civil society as a site of political activism.[20]

What is new about global civil society, and of particular interest to us, is the rapid growth in the number and variety of global civil society actors in recent decades, especially since the 1990s. The International Campaign to Ban Landmines (ICBL) was an important step. The Campaign grew from the 1980s with the work of the International Committee of the Red Cross on the devastating effects of landmines, which littered communities decades after conflict. But in the 1990s, a range of actors joined to form the ICBL, including development NGOs, humanitarian NGOs, religious groups, medical organizations, and most famously Diana, Princess of Wales. Eventually the ICBL counted over 10,000 organizations across 60 countries as its members. The network and its founder, Jody Williams, received the Nobel Peace Prize in 1997 for their work in bringing about the Ottawa Treaty banning landmines. The work of the ICBL continues in monitoring state compliance with the ban, as well as in advocating for more states (including the United States) to sign up. ICBL's experience showed to many what was possible in the post–Cold War world. It was possible for grand coalitions of different but like-minded actors from all over the world—doctors, lawyers, organizers, priests, farmers, journalists, academics—to join forces on issues of concern. And it was possible for these forces to find allies in sympathetic states and IGOs. Global action on many issues seemed possible. One did not have to merely wait and hope that powerful states would act. Citizens could act.

The rise of global civil society has much to do with several of our *global forces*.

Global Markets

Global markets have increased the impact that societies make on one another, but they have also increased people's ability to see this impact and to do something about it. The globalization of production means our consumer choices and labor policies affect a larger number of people. Plummeting transportation costs boost global trade and intensify this interaction, and they make it easier for civil society actors to simply meet together. For example, since 2001, tens of thousands of civil society actors have attended the annual World Social Forum meetings, which is one of the major sites of dissenting opinion on current forms of globalization. This is not a meeting of the world's most powerful or well resourced. It is significant that civil society actors without significant resources can attend annual global meetings.

Information and Communications Technology

Technology has also been a major factor in the rise of global civil society. Even as recently as the 1990s, a human rights NGO in Paris would struggle to receive, let alone broadcast, reports of abuse from Cameroon in a timely or detailed manner. It was simply too hard and too slow to transport—physically transport—leaked documents, photographs of prisons, or statements from the abused.

Today, this can be done in seconds. We have seen national movements spread globally. For example, in 2011–2012, the Occupy movement had spread from the United States to almost 100 countries. On September 17, 2011, Occupy Wall Street set down in New York City's Zuccotti Park. Three weeks later, Occupy Mexico began with a hunger strike in front of the Mexican Stock Exchange to protest higher education opportunities. One week later, protestors started "Occupy Copenhagen" in Denmark. Three months later, Occupy Nigeria began to protest dramatic increases in the price of fuel.

Global Governance

Global governance is a patchwork arrangement: Some global issues have a multiplicity of actors and rules, while others are barely governed at all. The range of activity of global civil society reflects this patchwork. There are some areas with a lot of global civil society activity, such as deforestation, but much less in areas like security and international finance. In some cases, attempts by states to more actively govern global issues have seen them promote the growth of INGOs. This is especially the case in INGOs engaged in humanitarian or development work. For example, when Oxfam writes of their response to the massive earthquake in Haiti that they "helped more than half a million survivors with a range of support that included clean water and sanitation services, shelter, and income-generating opportunities," this leaves out the fact that most of their funding comes from states and state-run IGOs, for whom Oxfam performs a service.[21] The point is not to critique Oxfam. The point is that in the effort by states to govern global issues—to build global governance—they often create the conditions and the resources for global civil society to grow (see Figure 4.2).

FIGURE 4.2

Global Forces, Interactions, and Tensions in the Rise of Global Civil Society

GLOBAL FORCES	INTERACTIONS	TENSIONS
• Global markets: Global markets bring societies into closer contact. Societies impact each other, and they are also able to witness that impact. This increases people's awareness of global issues. • ICT: Instrumental in helping civil society actors—typically poorly resourced—to communicate with one another and to have media impact. • Global governance: Some intergovernmental organizations create a platform for global civil society actors, who in turn contribute to the "crowding" of actors on the global stage.	• Civil society actors may gain prominence by exposing the behavior of governments and corporations. Others become prominent by receiving government funding to carry out international development projects. • The presence of civil society is highly uneven: Areas such as deforestation have significant civil society presence, in contrast to areas such as security or finance.	• Civil society actors with the resources to act transnationally are predominately Western-based, which means the agendas of global civil society actors may be biased as a result. • Scrutiny and pressure from the growing number and variety of civil society actors may complicate the ability of states to govern global issues.

CIVIL SOCIETY ON THE GLOBAL STAGE

One of the most visible achievements of global civil society in recent decades has been its presence on the global stage. Where IGOs such as the UN once had to justify the inclusion of INGOs in their work, today it is civil society's *exclusion* that requires justification. The UN allows NGOs that meet certain criteria to attend meetings, access official documents, and contribute to discussions. From less than 100 in 1950, over 4,000 of these NGOs today enjoy "consultative status" with ECOSOC, the part of the UN devoted to social and economic policies and programs. Figure 4.3 shows the growth in the number of NGOs accredited with ECOSOC. Note the gradual increase from the birth of the UN and then a rapid increase since the 1990s. Research suggests that about one third of all intergovernmental organizations—not just the UN—grant consultative status to NGOs.[22]

How did this come to be? IGO engagement with INGOs developed over the course of three waves. The first was a small wave at the birth of the United Nations, which was one of the first IGOs to offer NGOs access to its organization. This was followed by a larger wave in the 1970s, when international cooperation was helped by the détente (easing of tensions) between the United States and the Union of Soviet Socialist Republics (USSR, aka the "Soviet Union" or "Russia"). Engagement spread to other UN agencies like the FAO, UNICEF, UNESCO, and UNHCR. Still, engagement in this period was largely confined to UN bodies rather than to IGOs more generally.[23]

FIGURE 4.3

Number of UN-Recognized NGOs Is Growing

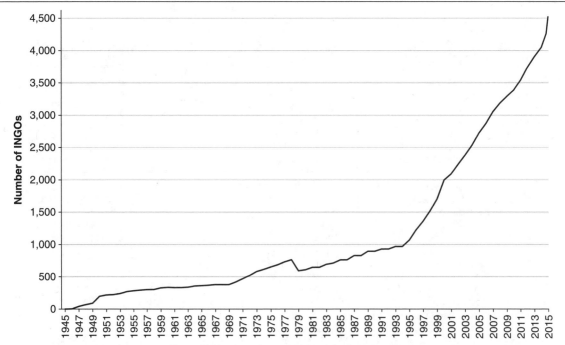

Source: © Peter Willetts, May 2015. http://www.staff.city.ac.uk/p.willetts/NGOS/NGO-GRPH.HTM.

The third, and biggest, wave began in the 1990s, and international actors are still experiencing it today. One of the first large-scale campaigns was *50 Years Is Enough*, which tried to shame the World Bank and International Monetary Fund (IMF) into opening up to civil society, and indeed the Bank began to engage with NGOs as a means, some argued, of turning around its much maligned image.[24] The percentage of World Bank–funded projects involving civil society participation went from 21% in 1990 to 72% in 2006. This means the World Bank involved some NGOs during the planning, consultation, or monitoring stages. NGOs could also critically engage with Bank officials through the World Bank-NGO Committee.[25] At the UN, ECOSOC reforms in 1996 expanded the right to consultative status to national and local NGOs, where before it was restricted to just international NGOs.[26] By the 2000s, the question within the UN was not whether to engage NGOs but how to institutionalize engagement.

Civil society's access to IGOs varies in terms of its *depth*.[27] For instance, the UN's ECOSOC has allowed the General Assembly of the Fund for the Development of the Indigenous Peoples of Latin America to make presentations at meetings and has provided it with full membership. Yet for some organizations access is not deep at all. The Pan-African Parliament of the African Union, for example, only allows for observing meetings for experts and special guests.

IGO-NGO engagement is also highly variable in the *range* of access, which is how selective the IGO is in its engagement with NGOs. For example, at the World Bank Inspection Panel, anyone can contribute statements in preliminary reviews, whereas the Scientific Council of the Northwest Atlantic Fishery Organization only invites guest experts. So, although we can talk about a tidal wave of IGO-NGO engagement over the past 20 to 30 years, it is also clear that this is a very uneven wave. IGOs vary tremendously in how *deeply* they engage with NGOs and in how *selective* they are in their engagement.

But why would states, and the intergovernmental organizations they control, have allowed NGOs to have any influence or involvement in the first place? It is not obvious that they should have. After all, by definition, civil society actors have no legal (i.e., governmental) authority. There are three prominent theories that try to explain why IGOs have opened up to NGOs in highly uneven ways: legitimacy, norms, and functionalism.

Legitimacy

The legitimacy explanation says IGOs open up to NGOs to appear more legitimate. This theory thinks of IGO-NGO engagement as a kind of public relations exercise, in which under-fire IGOs make themselves more legitimate by opening to NGO input. This theory has support among civil society activists themselves, who see the IGOs' need for legitimacy as a mean for NGOs to get greater access.[28]

Norms

The norms explanation says IGOs open up because a global norm has spread to legitimize or even require such opening. This theory says that there is a norm of openness and participation in global governance and that any IGO that wishes to be seen as modern will open up to at least some NGO input.[29] This is related to the idea of constructivism explained in Chapter 3.

Functionalism

The functionalist explanation says IGOs need NGOs to help them do their job. There are two versions of this theory. The first is somewhat benevolent, in that IGOs engage NGOs because it "lowers the costs" for the IGO, while the NGO itself benefits from the access. The second version is more cynical and thinks NGOs matter little in power politics and that IGOs will only engage with like-minded NGOs, which ultimately does nothing to change outcomes. In both of these versions, the NGO appears as a kind of handmaiden for the IGO and, ultimately, for states themselves. So NGOs help IGOs to solve problems and function effectively in a world that is increasingly complex with the mandates of IGOs growing all the time.[30] The latest research provides support for this explanation, as IGOs tend to engage with NGOs when the IGO's work is complex, or when its work involves monitoring or enforcement functions that an NGO could undertake on its behalf.[31]

These three theories may help us understand why civil society actors have become more accepted internationally over time. Yet, it is still not clear how nongovernmental actors have an effect on anything. We turn to this question next.

HOW DOES CIVIL SOCIETY HAVE AN IMPACT?

norm entrepreneurs: any actor that tries to create or change a norm. Many civil society actors are, or aim to be, norm entrepreneurs.

The major way civil society has an impact on the world is by working as **norm entrepreneurs**. Norms are unwritten but widely understood rules that define appropriate behavior. They are internalized and taken for granted, like personal hygiene standards or the practice of tipping servers in a restaurant. International political norms include things like not using nuclear weapons or not engaging in torture. Norm entrepreneurs are thus *individuals or groups that advance a principled standard of behavior for states and other actors.* Much of what civil society actors try to do is shape what we all think is appropriate. They do this by engaging in four types of action:[32]

Information Politics

Civil society actors are everywhere collecting their own data. They are live tweeting street protests. They are at UN meetings. They are watching whaling expeditions. They are visiting prisons. The data they produce tend to be seen as "neutral" because they are not disseminated in search of wealth or political office. Thus, in addition to serving as watchdogs of governments and corporations, the information they provide is a global public good.

Sometimes a government or IGO will ask civil society actors to gather data. For example, the Organization of Security and Co-operation in Europe has asked NGOs to report on hate crimes against LGBTQ people.[33] Sometimes civil society actors use their informational power to publicly endorse a new treaty or international agreement, as many civil society actors did upon global agreement on the SDGs. States and IGOs may also seek out civil society actors to partner with them on an ongoing basis because of civil society's expertise. For example, UN Women has a 25-member Civil Society Advisory Group, consisting of civil society actors from around the world, such as the Egyptian Center for Women's Rights. Finally, civil society actors may use their information to persuade audiences rather than simply educate them. That is, many (perhaps most) civil society actors are *advocates* on an issue. They will naturally present data in a way that furthers their cause.

Read the latest CIVICUS State of Civil Society Report at https://www.civicus.org/index .php/state-of-civil-society-report-2018.

Symbolic Politics

Civil society groups frame issues to get our attention, and they do it by creating symbols in our minds. For example, civil society actors have forged a connection in our minds between climate change and a lonely polar bear adrift on a melting icecap. This message operates on an emotional level. Sometimes framing is less visual than it is perceptual. In global social movements for human rights, actors have changed the way people think about sovereignty. Over the past few hundred years, governments have used the notion of sovereignty to insist that other states stay out of their business. But groups and individuals active in the global human rights community have gradually changed this idea. Today the "responsibility to protect" means countries have the responsibility, not merely the right, to intervene if gross violations of human rights are taking place in another country. The fact that we have concepts like humanitarian intervention or even human rights is a result of the work of international civil society actors. The global movement on human rights has succeeded in changing norms and ideas about what is acceptable behavior.

Leverage Politics

To have an effect on states, companies, or IGOs, civil society actors look for points of leverage. One way to do this is to link issues. For example, imagine an environmental INGO wants to influence the policies of the government of Nigeria. The INGO knows that the government is looking for a World Bank loan to build a highway. The INGO might lobby the World Bank directly, or it may lobby a powerful World Bank member-state to make the World Bank's loan to Nigeria contingent on the government's environmental policies.

Civil society actors use their connections with actors in other countries and intergovernmental organizations. These connections can include state officials, IGOs, and even companies. Civil society actors, in particular TANs, leverage their global connections to lobby a particular set of policy makers or IGOs. One of the ways they do this is through what is known as the "boomerang model," shown in Figure 4.4. The purpose of the boomerang model is to illustrate how globally connected civil society actors use their relationships with one another in order to affect change in government behavior.

Accountability Politics

Civil society actors try to hold powerful actors accountable for their promises and their actions. This often involves publicly "naming and shaming" governments to force them to act. For example, one of Amnesty International's most important activities involves its "urgent action" alerts concerning prisoners of conscience, human rights defenders, and others whose human rights are being abused. Here is how Amnesty describes it:

> Amnesty International USA receives Urgent Action alerts from all over the world. Once the Urgent Action Network responds with letters, emails, calls, faxes and texts, relevant authorities quickly realize that their actions are witnessed by an international audience deeply concerned about the case's outcome.
>
> Each Urgent Action has multiple targets including names, email addresses, phone numbers, postal addresses, and other important contact information. Each of the targets is tactically chosen to have [the] greatest impact on the individual or community at risk.[34]

Note the use of "international audience" and "tactical" choice of targets of its urgent action. In its public notices, Amnesty is clear to link a case with the offending state's obligations under international laws on human rights. Although many of its urgent actions are targeted at

FIGURE 4.4

The Boomerang Model

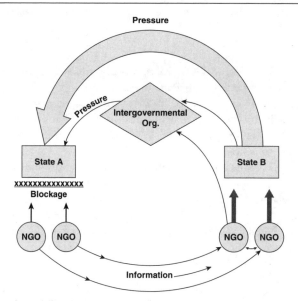

The Boomerang Model shows how civil society actors can influence governments.

Source: Adapted from Keck and Sikkink, *Activists Beyond Borders: Advocacy Networks in International Politics* (Ithaca, NY: Cornell University Press, 1998), p. 13.

It works like this:

- NGOs in State A (on the left) want a list of all political prisoners currently in jail. But State A is a dictatorship, so there is a blockage: The state will not engage with its own NGOs and may actively repress civil society.

- NGOs in State A relay the problem to NGOs in State B (on the right). They do it online or at conferences or social gatherings.

- State B is a democracy. The government and media are receptive to NGOs in State B, who use this openness to lobby and voice concerns about what is happening in State A.

- State B can then apply pressure on State A in two ways. State B can take up the issue in IGOs, such as the UN General Assembly. It can also address State A directly through one-on-one diplomatic channels.

- The boomerang effect is complete: NGOs sent the problem away, and a solution came back to them. NGOs in State A are able to affect change in their own countries, despite their governments' repressive regimes, thanks to their transnational linkages.

Reflect

Which of our four global forces are evident in the boomerang model?

FIGURE 4.5

Source: SOFII, Amnesty International: The Shame Shell Campaign, 2010. Retrieved August 16, 2017, from http://sofii.org/case-study/the-amnesty-international-shame-shell-campaign.[37, 38]

countries known for human rights abuses, such as the Sudan and China, the plurality concerns abuses in the United States.[35] Their campaigns extend to the naming and shaming of private corporations for broken promises, as in their campaign to change the oil and gas company Shell's activities in Nigeria's Niger Delta (see Figure 4.5).

We should also note that some social scientists think global civil society does not have a major impact on the world. It should be easy to see why as civil society actors have no money (nonprofit), no weapons (nonstate actors), and no legal authority. In our chapter on IGOs (Chapter 3), we read that the realist view of international politics is that the world generally works according to the wishes of the most powerful states. Things like multinational corporations, IGOs, or global civil society campaigns are not the fundamental forces in the world. In fact, in the 44-chapter, 732-page *Oxford Handbook of International Relations*, only three paragraphs discuss civil society at any length.[36] This means we must look for evidence that civil society impacts the world, rather than simply asserting it.

CRITICISMS OF GLOBAL CIVIL SOCIETY

Although civil society actors seem to be a force for good in the world, they are often accused of not being representative, accountable, or transparent.

Global Civil Society Is Not Representative

In 2015, UN Secretary-General Ban Ki-moon told an audience of civil society organizations that "now, more than ever, the world needs your advocacy, expertise, and ingenuity. . . . You are the voice of the people."[39] But is this true? Critics take issue with the assertion that those gathered in the room represent "the voice of the people." Indeed, criticisms of NGOs claiming to be the voice of the people began as early as the 1990s. In an influential article titled "The False Dawn of Civil Society," David Rieff asked, "So who elected the NGOs?"[40] Indeed, the global social movements described earlier may span many countries, but they are often led informally by a small number of professional INGOs, and those INGOs in turn are managed by a small number of people. The result is global social movements that are not at all mass based.[41]

Consider where most INGOs are located. Figure 4.6 ranks the number of INGO headquarters by country. The dominance of Western and Northern hemisphere countries is clear. On the far right column, we see the number of headquartered INGOs per 100,000 people, and the picture is even more dramatic. Belgium has about 3,500 headquartered INGOs per 100,000 inhabitants, compared with 4 in India. Of course, INGOs would naturally locate themselves near headquarters of major IGOs, which explains such high numbers of INGO headquarters in the United States (NY and DC), Belgium (Brussels), the United Kingdom (London), and France (Paris). But even still China is not in the top 15, and India just makes it.

Global Civil Society Is Not Accountable

Although NGOs may not be representative of humanity, it is possible for an individual NGO to be accountable to the group it purports to represent. For example, is a European NGO that represents the interests of Roma/Gypsy populations being accountable to Roma/Gypsy people? Are representatives from those communities on the Board? How do they know what Roma/Gypsy communities want? To whom is the NGO accountable if it does a bad job?

FIGURE 4.6

Headquarter Size of INGOs, Per Capita

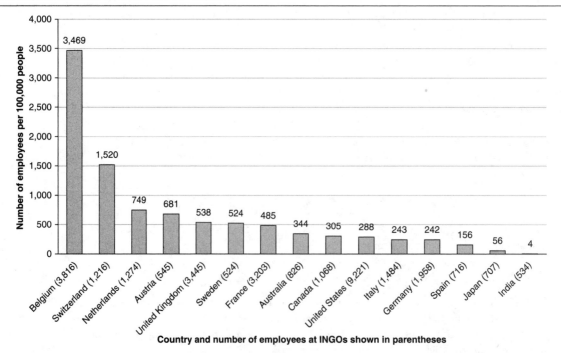

Source: Data from the Union of International Associations, *Yearbook of International Organizations*, Edition 52.

Civil society actors are also critiqued for not being accountable. This is especially the case for development and human rights organizations, whose stated purpose often involves working on behalf of some marginalized groups. In a widely read article titled "NGOs: Fighting Poverty, Hurting the Poor," Sebastian Mallaby wrote about international NGOs that actively opposed the construction of a dam in Uganda, which was intended to reduce the number of people living in poverty.[42] The INGOs' opposition was to dams in general, but they did not speak for the communities whose lives the dam was supposed to improve.

Read "NGOs: Fighting Poverty, Hurting the Poor" by Mallaby at http://foreignpolicy .com/2009/10/26/ngos-fighting-poverty-hurting-the-poor/, and a response to Mallaby at https://www.internationalrivers.org/resources/jim-macneil-s-response-to-mallaby-s-ngos-fighting-poverty-hurting-the-poor-3286.

Critics often accuse NGOs of being mostly accountable to their donors in wealthy countries. Remember that when the world's largest NGOs carry out projects in developing countries, most of their funding comes directly from governments in wealthy countries, or indirectly from those governments via the budgets of IGOs. It is not a coincidence, the critics suggest, that there are so many international development NGOs currently working in Afghanistan, a country of strategic interest to the United States. Afghanistan is poor, but is its need greater than that in Yemen or the Democratic Republic of Congo? INGOs are responsive to the interests of their own donors.

Global Civil Society Is Not Transparent

NGOs are private organizations, and they are under no obligation to reveal who funds them or what their activities are. Civil society actors are accused of hiding behind their private status while they critique states, corporations, and IGOs for their lack of transparency. This can fuel suspicion that civil society actors have hidden agendas, especially in cases where they receive most of their funding from one or two governments.

Read the debate "Do Nongovernmental Organizations Wield Too Much Power?" between Kenneth Anderson and Marlies Glasius.[43]

How do civil society actors respond to these criticisms? The first response is that there are a lot of internal checks on the behavior of INGOs. These internal checks come in several forms: Some INGOs have governing boards comprising people with no commercial interest in the INGO; INGO self-publication of activity reports and financial audits; INGO interaction with other INGOs, many of whom are critical of Northern Hemisphere INGOs and their claims to represent the Global South; and faith that INGOs seek no power or money, and as such have a genuine interest in doing good.

The second response to criticisms asks, "INGOs are not accountable compared with what?" Powerful actors who reveal little about their behavior run the world. Whether or not global civil society fails to meet some democratic ideal is beside the point, in this view.[44] It is simply better than nothing. Moreover, civil society actors are the only force pushing states, IGOs, and MNCs to be more transparent. Thus, asking whether global civil society is democratic is the wrong question. Perhaps it is better to ask, do global civil society actors make global governance more democratic? Do they increase the number and type of actors involved globally? Do they increase the variety of voices heard globally? Supporters of global civil society would say "yes" to these questions. It is easily forgotten, they would add, how much of international affairs were off-limits to the public only a few decades ago.

SUMMARY

In this chapter, we have learned about an important type of actor in our global age. Civil society actors may lack the legal and military power of states and intergovernmental organizations, or the economic power of multinational corporations, but we cannot understand the *interactions* that drive our world, and the *tensions* that result, without understanding civil society. Unlike states, IGOs, and MNCs, however, civil society refers to a category of actor that is incredibly diverse. The label "civil society actor" can apply to your local Girl Scout troop, to the global network of the Catholic Church, to a human rights NGO operating in Central America, or to a network of religious scholars from around the world meeting online to discuss 21st-century Islam.

The lesson for us is not that civil society actors are everywhere internationally but that civil society actors *could* be present on any issue. When we read about global food production, nuclear weapons, or global inequality, we must have our eyes open for civil society actors. On issues such as fair trade, we will find civil society actors, while on issues such as weapons sales, we will not see so significant a presence.

Where we do find civil society actors, we will see them using the tools of information, leverage, and accountability. We may see them endeavoring to be norms entrepreneurs, trying to shift perceptions and alter values. And when we find civil society actors, we may ask whether Tocqueville or Gramsci best describes their behavior, and whether any of the criticisms made of civil society actors have merit.

KEY TERMS

civil society 106
civil society organizations
   (CSOs) 108
global civil society 107

international nongovernmental
   organization (INGO) 109
nongovernmental organizations
   (NGOs) 108

norm entrepreneurs 118
social movements 109
transnational advocacy networks
   (TANs) 110

QUESTIONS FOR REVIEW

1. How would a Tocquevillian and a Gramscian interpret the example of Cecil the Lion?

2. What is the difference between a TAN and a social movement?

3. Read about the sex scandal that engulfed the charity Oxfam in 2018. Rank the most important interactions and tensions in Haiti's decision to suspend Oxfam.

4. Could an activist celebrity be considered a civil society actor?

5. Pick a story appearing in this week's international news in which global civil society actors appear. Which of the four types of action described in this chapter can you identify?

LEARN MORE

Transnational Access to International Organizations 1950–2010:

Data on the access of civil society and multinational corporations to intergovernmental organizations.[45]

Database of NGOs with UN consultative status:

Scholte, J. A. (2011). *Building Global Democracy? Civil Society and Accountable Global Governance*. Cambridge, U.K.: Cambridge University Press. Case study material on civil society engagement with specific intergovernmental organizations

Urgent Action database, Amnesty International, http://www.amnestyusa.org/get-involved/take-action-now?campaign=83.

Edwards, M., & Gaventa, J. (2013). *Global Citizen Action.* Oxon, U.K.: Earthscan.

Case studies of international campaigns:

Centre for Civil Society, London School of Economics, http://www.lse.ac.uk/CCS/home.aspx.

Policy documents and case studies:

Civil Society and Governance Programme, Institute for Development Studies, http://www.ids.ac.uk/project/civil-society-and-governance-programme

NOTES

1. This section draws on Margaret P. Karns and Karen A. Mingst, *International Organizations: The Politics and Processes of Global Governance* (Boulder, CO: Lynne Rienner, 2010), 217.

2. Convention on International Trade in Endangered Species of Wild Fauna and Flora (1973).

3. Peter Baker and Jada F. Smith, "Obama Administration Targets Trade in African Elephant Ivory," *The New York Times,* July 25, 2015, sec. Africa, https://www.nytimes.com/2015/07/26/world/africa/obama-administration-targets-trade-in-african-elephant-ivory.html.

4. dw.com, "UN Adopts Resolution to Battle Wildlife Trafficking | News | DW | 30.07.2015," DW.COM, July 30, 2015, http://www.dw.com/en/un-adopts-resolution-to-battle-wildlife-trafficking/a-18619091.

5. Delta Airlines, "Shipments of Lion, Leopard, Elephant, Rhino, Buffalo Trophies Banned," Delta News Hub, August 3, 2015, http://news.delta.com/shipments-lion-leopard-elephant-rhino-buffalo-trophies-banned.

6. https://www.sumofus.org/about/.

7. Helmut Anheier, Marlies Glasius, and Mary Kaldor, eds., *Global Civil Society 2001* (Oxford, U.K.: Oxford University Press, 2001), 4, http://www.lse.ac.uk/internationalDevelopment/research/CSHS/civilSociety/yearBook/contentsPages/2001.aspx.

8. Francis Fukuyama, "Governance: What Do We Know, and How Do We Know It?," *Annual Review of Political Science* 19, no. 1 (2016): 89–105, https://doi.org/10.1146/annurev-polisci-042214-044240; Marc Lynch, ed., *The Arab Uprisings Explained: New Contentious Politics in the Middle East* (New York, NY: Columbia University Press, 2014); Ebenezer Obadare, ed., *The Handbook of Civil Society in Africa* (New York, NY: Springer, 2013); Robert D. Putnam, *Making Democracy Work: Civic Traditions in Modern Italy* (Princeton, NJ: Princeton University Press, 1993); Robert D. Putnam, *Bowling Alone: The Collapse and Revival of American Community* (New York, NY: Simon & Schuster Paperbacks, 2000).

9. The White House, "FACT SHEET: U.S. Support for Civil Society," whitehouse.gov, September 23, 2014, https://obamawhitehouse.archives.gov/the-press-office/2014/09/23/fact-sheet-us-support-civil-society.

10. Andrew Heywood, *Political Ideas and Concepts: An Introduction* (New York, NY: St. Martin's Press, 1994), 100.

11. Jan Aart Scholte, *Building Global Democracy? Civil Society and Accountable Global Governance* (Cambridge, U.K.: Cambridge University Press, 2011), 8.

12. For 2015/16, they record 60,262 INGOs in Yearbook of International Organizations, Edition 52, Figure 2.8. They record 29,322 of these as inactive.

13. Frontlines, "Caring for Cambodia's Mothers," *Frontlines*, 2012, https://2012-2017.usaid.gov/news-information/frontlines/child-survival-ethiopia-edition/caring-cambodia%E2%80%99s-mothers.

14. Margaret E. Keck, *Activists Beyond Borders: Advocacy Networks in International Politics* (Ithaca, NY: Cornell University Press, 1998), 1.

15. Ryan Thoreson, *Transnational LGBT Activism* (Minneapolis: University of Minnesota Press, 2014), https://www.upress.umn.edu/book-division/books/transnational-lgbt-activism.

16. Timothy Hildebrandt, "Development and Division: The Effect of Transnational Linkages and Local Politics on LGBT Activism in China," *Journal of Contemporary China* 21, no. 77 (September 1, 2012): 845–862.

17. A social movement might use a riot or a strike as part of their strategy. What makes a public demonstration a social movement is thus the coordination that underlies it.

18. Jackie Smith, "Exploring Connections Between Global Integration and Political Mobilization," *Journal of World-Systems Research* 10, no. 1 (2004): 266, https://doi.org/10.5195/jwsr.2004.312.

19. Karns and Mingst, *International Organizations*, 224.

20. John S. Dryzek, "Global Civil Society: The Progress of Post-Westphalian Politics," *Annual Review of Political Science* 15, no. 1 (2012): 101–119, https://doi.org/10.1146/annurev-polisci-042010-164946.

21. Oxfam, "Haiti Earthquake - Our Response | Oxfam International," oxfam.org, ND, https://www.oxfam.org/en/haiti-earthquake-our-response; Oxfam, "Oxfam Annual Report 2014-2015," Annual Report, 2015.

22. Vabulas, "Consultative and Observer Status of NGOs in Intergovernmental Organizations," in *Routledge Handbook of International Organization*, ed. Bob Reinalda (New York, NY: Routledge, 2013), 189; uses the Correlates of War (COW) International Governmental Organizations Data Set, which is widely used by international relations scholars.

23. The following section draws on Tallberg et al., *The Opening Up of International Organizations: Transnational Access in Global Governance* (Cambridge, U.K.: Cambridge University Press, 2013) and Willets, "From Stockholm to Rio and Beyond: The Impact of the Environmental Movement on the United Nations Consultative Arrangements for NGOs," *Review of International Studies* 22 (1996): 57–80.

24. This section draws on Wade, "Greening the Bank: The Struggle Over the Environment, 1970–1995," *The World Bank: Its First Half Century* 2 (1997): 611–734.

25. Tallberg, Sommerer, and Squatrito, *The Opening Up of International Organizations*.

26. ECOSOC Resolution 1996/31.

27. This section draws on Tallberg et al. (2013).

28. Jens Steffek and Ulrike Ehrling, "Civil Society Participation at the Margins: The Case of the WTO," in *Civil Society Participation in European and Global Governance*, ed. Jens Steffek, Claudia Kissling, and Patrizia Nanz, 2008.

29. Martha Finnemore and Kathryn Sikkink, "International Norm Dynamics and Political Change," *International Organization* 52, no. 04 (1998): 887–917, https://doi.org/10.1162/002081898550789.

30. Kal Raustiala, "States, NGOs, and International Environmental Institutions," *International Studies Quarterly* 41, no. 4 (1997): 719–740, https://doi.org/10.1111/1468-2478.00064; Matthias Staisch, "Reaching Out or Not: Accounting for the Relative Openness of International Governmental Organizations Towards NGOs," in *Presentation at the Fifth Pan-European International Relations Conference, The Hague*, 2004.

31. Clayton, "Whitewash or Renovation: An Examination of Why Inter-Governmental Organizations Institutionalize Relations with Non-Governmental Organizations" (Annual Conference

of the American Political Science Association, Chicago, IL, September 1, 2013); Tallberg et al., *The Opening Up of International Organizations*; Vabulas, "Consultative and Observer Status of NGOs in Intergovernmental Organizations."

32. The following draws on Keck and Sikkink, "Transnational Advocacy Networks in International and Regional Politics," *International Social Science Journal* 51, no. 159 (March 1, 1999): 89–101, https://doi.org/10.1111/1468-2451.00179.

33. http://seta.fi/were-you-a-victim-of-a-hate-crime-tell-us-by-april-27th/.

34. Grand Bahama Human Rights Association, "GBHRA: Justilien Must Be Released Immediately," TheBahamasWeekly.com, December 4, 2015, http://www.thebahamasweekly.com/publish/local/GBHRA_Justilien_must_be_released_immediately_printer.shtml.

35. "The Oxford Handbook of International Relations," 2008, http://espace.library.uq.edu.au/view/UQ:314455.

36. "NGOs: Fighting Poverty, Hurting the Poor," 2004, http://foreignpolicy.com/2009/10/26/ngos-fighting-poverty-hurting-the-poor/.

37. James Meernik et al., "The Impact of Human Rights Organizations on Naming and Shaming Campaigns," *Journal of Conflict Resolution* 56, no. 2 (2012): 233–256.

38. This section draws on material in Dryzek, "Global Civil Society."

39. UN News Service, "UN Chief Hails Key Role of Civil Society in Financing Future Development Agenda," *UN News Service Section*, July 12, 2015, http://www.un.org/apps/news/story.asp?NewsID=51390#.WZSGWHd962x.

40. David Rieff, "The False Dawn of Civil Society," *The Nation*, February 4, 1999, https://www.thenation.com/article/false-dawn-civil-society/. See also Sabine Lang, *NGOs, Civil Society, and the Public Sphere* (Cambridge, U.K.: Cambridge University Press, 2013), http://www.books24x7.com/marc.asp?bookid=50210.

41. Lisa Jordan, "Global Civil Society," in *The Oxford Handbook of Civil Society*, ed. Michael Edwards (Cambridge, U.K.: Cambridge University Press, 2011), 93–105.

42. Sebastian Mallaby, "NGOs."

43. Kenneth Anderson and Marlies Glasius, "Do Nongovernmental Organizations Wield Too Much Power?," in *Controversies in Globalization: Contending Approaches to International Relations*, ed. Peter M. Haas and John A. Hird (Los Angeles, CA: SAGE/CQ Press, 2013), 461–485.

44. Dryzek, "Global Civil Society."

45. Thomas Sommerer, Jonas Tallberg, and Theresa Squatrito, "Transnational Access to International Organizations 1950–2010," *Dataset*, October 8, 2015, https://doi.org/10.7910/DVN/DDE1HE.

5

Social Identities and Culture

SHAPING INTERACTIONS AT THE INDIVIDUAL AND SOCIETAL LEVELS

LEARNING OBJECTIVES

After finishing this chapter, you should be able to:

- Define culture and social identity.

- Provide examples of how culture and social identities work across and within borders, i.e., from the outside-in and from the inside-out.

- Describe the social identities that matter for international studies.

- Articulate contrasting perspectives on culture and social identity.

- Explain how global forces shape culture and social identities and create tensions that are manifest in culture and social identities.

iStock/helovi

Kolkata is a bustling city of some 14 million people in northeast India. Kolkata was formerly known to much of the world as "Calcutta," which is the name British colonialists bestowed on the city. Although India gained its independence from Britain in 1947, the city's name officially did not return to "Kolkata" until 2001. Kolkata was always how the city was pronounced in Bengali, the main language in that part of India, but the British had Anglicized the name. Other Indian cities restored their names too. Bombay became "Mumbai," and Madras became "Chennai," both in the 1990s.

One way to view these name changes is as a reclaiming of Indian national identity and as an assertion of Indian nationalism. As India has risen globally, Indian government leaders have relabeled street names, national holidays, public monuments, and currencies according to the indigenous languages of the country as a way to reflect cultural and political heritage.

Another way to view such changes is as a source of tension and conflict. In recent years, for example, cities across the southern United States have found themselves embroiled in controversy around decisions to remove public monuments linked to the Civil War and slavery. For some, a monument honoring a Confederate hero, such as Robert E. Lee or a Ku Klux Klan leader, inherently paints slavery in a positive light and honors white supremacy. For others, a figure such as General Lee is an important part of southern history.

Such controversies exist all over the world; they represent contests over memory, history, identity, and politics. Returning to Mumbai, the party in charge of the local government that ordered the name change was a Hindu nationalist party, the Shiv Sena, which promoted India's Hindu culture and religion as the centerpiece of Indian society. On the one hand, promoting Hindu culture and the Hindi language is a testament to efforts to assert national pride, in particular, in a formerly colonized country. On the other hand, India is an exceptionally diverse country, in terms of religion, language, and ethnicity. By promoting and recognizing one group's language and history as the official one, other groups feel excluded and alienated; they also may reject the name change as a politically motivated one.

In India, although the largest religion is Hinduism—about four in five Indians are Hindu—there are significant religious minorities, of Muslims, Sikhs, Christians, and Buddhists. In a country with some 1.2 billion people, that means there are some 170 million Muslims and 27 million Christians. The language diversity is also extraordinary. Officially, India has 15 languages. The largest is Hindi, which along with the former colonial language of English, serves as a lingua franca, but there are 14 other official languages as well.

Although assertions of ethnic and national identity in a multireligious and multiethnic nation sometimes generate tension, diversity also is a source of creativity. Kolkata is a "foodie city." Indeed, food is a major part of Indian culture. Food is central to family life, to celebrations like weddings, and to religious and national holidays; food is meant to be shared, which fosters a communal, social dimension to meals. Indian food operates on a global scale too. Restaurants specializing in Indian food are plentiful across Europe, Africa, and the United States. In Kolkata, the diversity of foods is especially pronounced. Not only does Kolkata offer traditional Bengali recipes, but because the city has been a magnet for domestic and international migration, both during British occupation (when it was the capital) and afterward, Kolkata now hosts food from around India, but also Armenian, Jewish, Ajmeri, Chinese, and many other types of food. The food industry is also booming, in part, because India has generated so much growth, which has meant more people in the middle classes have more time and resources to devote to leisure and eating out for dinner.

These examples point to two of the most interesting and rich areas in international studies, namely, culture and social identities. Our world bristles with daily global cultural *interactions*. From sport to fashion, to music and art, to food and film, culture is pervasive. Global interactions constantly shape and are shaped by culture. You name an interest, be it food, sport, film, art, or YouTube surfing, and you will quickly see how deeply embedded it is in "outside-in" global interactions. In sport, for example, players are international, as are most television markets and sports audiences. Culture is also "inside-out." Culture shapes how people make meaning in their world, and culture is embedded in people's customs, habits, and values. Those meanings, habits, customs, and values in turn shape sport, food, film, music, fashion, and the like. The study of culture and its influences is a fascinating and rich terrain for international studies, one that shows the many ways that global interactions are at work in our world.

Social identities are also fundamental forces in people's lives. Social identities are "inside-out." They are about how people identify in relation to groups. Those identifications are personal and familial; they are micro-decisions. Yet social identities are also rooted in society, politics, and history. How people think about themselves is a product of ideas in the moment, and those ideas are in turn subject to influence. Here is where "outside-in" global interactions shape social identities. Information flows, politics in neighboring countries and around the world, and globalized culture from the outside push and pull how people think about themselves and define who they are.

This chapter explores these foundational concepts and roots them in our international studies framework. Culture and social identities are core concepts that remain fundamental for understanding our world—its myriad interactions as well as the *tensions* that result. This chapter will define these core concepts, provide some examples, and help you develop new ways to think about and analyze culture and identities.

WHAT ARE SOCIAL IDENTITIES AND CULTURE?

culture:
traditions, customs, and meanings that shape behavior and understanding

When they talk about **culture**, social scientists typically mean the shared meanings, expected behaviors, ways of doing things, and customs in a particular society. For example, when we say that most Americans value the importance of personal liberty, we are making a statement about a shared meaning of what binds us together as a national community, about what defines who we are. Americans' cultural disposition toward personal liberty shapes attitudes toward gun control, free speech, personal travel and movement, and all kinds of behavior that we might identify as distinctly American in flavor.

To emphasize culture in how we look at the world is to recognize that ideas, norms, and expectations influence how people experience the world and how they behave. Looking at culture helps us to understand the sometimes invisible forces that drive people to make the decisions that they make. In short, culture is one of the key influences on people's lives, and that is why we highlight it in this book as a foundational concept for international studies.

More formally, "Cultures are traditions and customs, transmitted through learning, that govern the beliefs and behavior of the people exposed to them."[1] Let's unpack that definition. First, cultures are "traditions and customs." They are, in other words, shared understandings about how to act. Second, they are "transmitted through learning." Communication is thus important for culture, which is often expressed and learned through language, education, families, and various media. Last, culture "governs beliefs and behavior." Culture influences how people think and how they act.

In international studies, we use culture to understand how people understand the world around them. Imagine, for example, a farmer in rural Peru. A naive approach is to assume that she thinks and understands her world just as you do. That *could* be true, but most likely her expectations about family, religion, gender roles, marriage, money, and community are different in important ways from your views. Culture shapes her worldview, just as it does yours, and culture is therefore a key concept in understanding how she thinks and behaves (as it is in understanding how you think and behave).

One way to make generalizations about culture is at the *national* level, as we did in the example of Americans valuing personal liberty. We might also say that *Peruvians* share common traditions and understandings. Indeed, if you have spent time abroad (and are a U.S. citizen), you will have likely remarked to yourself how people in that other country think and act, which is very different from how Americans think and act.

Culture also operates at a *subnational* level. In Peru, for example, those in the highlands might share a different culture from those in Lima, the capital. In the United States, southern culture is different from northern culture; West Texas is different from East Texas.

Region is just one way to think about subnational cultural differences. Norms and expectations often vary by religion, ethnicity, social class, and gender—social identities that we discuss in this chapter. Paying attention to these different ways of thinking and understanding—across countries and within them—provides insight into understanding the world around us.

In international studies, culture also covers a broader set of issues that are more visible and material than shared meanings. Here culture refers to common forms of practice and leisure, ones that often reflect shared understandings but that manifest as activities. In this context, culture includes visual entertainment (like film and television), music, food, fashion, and sports.

Again, there is extraordinary variation in these practices across the world. Food is probably most obvious (and tasty). Consider the variety of national foods in your home or college town; you likely have access to Chinese, Indian, Italian (pizza), Japanese, Mexican, and perhaps Korean, to name a few. Extend that to music, fashion, painting, and sport, and you are likely to see an exceptionally rich and diverse world unfold before your very eyes. Culture is one way think about these many areas in an international studies context.

Social identity is related but a little different. Social identities are about who we are, about how we define our primary communities of belonging, and about defining who we are not. In other words, social identity is about understanding one's self in relation to a group. Social identity is the concept we use to describe how people answer the question "who am I?" in relation to "to what group do I belong?"

social identity: understanding one's self in relation to a group.

The following definition captures these ideas: "Social identity is any social category in which an individual is eligible to be a member."[2] A social category is a collection of people who share some kind of characteristic. We might think of college students as a social category or of men and women as social categories. Social identity is a way of talking about how a given social category defines, in part, that person's identity. What is the social category to which a person belongs? Hence, the social identity would be "a college student" or "a woman."

Social identities are not just about answering the question "who *we* are" but also about answering the question "who *they* are." Social categories are almost inevitably about distinguishing one group from another. To be Peruvian is not to be Ecuadoran. To be sure, some scholars break down these binary distinctions in favor of fluid boundaries. But in practice social identities are often set off in contrast to different, other social identities. Hence, scholars of social identity often refer to the notion of **in-groups** (people of the same group) or of **out-groups** (people of a different group).

in-groups: people of the same group.

A common example of a social identity is an ethnic group. To return to Peru for a moment, a woman in the Peruvian highlands may hail from one of the indigenous ethnic groups in that country. She might be a Quechua (an indigenous ethnic group in the Peruvian and other highland parts of South America). When she asks herself, "who am I," a key part of her answer would be, "I am Quechua," which implies she is part of that social category but not some other one. Another common example of a social identity is a religious group. In India, someone might identify as Hindu. Being Hindu is likely to be central to that person's values and family. Being Hindu also implies that person is not Muslim or Sikh, which are two other major religions in India. Other examples include a gender group, such as being male or female, or a regional group, such as being southern or Appalachian.

out-groups: people of a different group.

GLOBAL INTERACTIONS AND FORCES IMPACT IDENTITY AND CULTURE

Social identities and culture shape, and are shaped by, global interactions in myriad ways. On the one hand, social identity and culture embody many inside-out dimensions. Look at the lives of millions and millions of people, and you will see that religion and ethnicity shape their lives, their worldviews, their food, their value systems, their family choices, and many aspects of their lives. At the same time, the global spread of information; the availability of television, cinema, and social media from around the world; the flood of cheap food; and global sports shape the ideas of people around the world, especially young people who want to expose themselves to new things. Those ideas can challenge more traditional ways of being. On the one hand, that can be very exciting and instill a sense of possibility and freedom. On the other hand, families can feel as though they are losing their customary ways of behaving, dressing, easting, and thinking; that in turn can create tension.

Our global forces play a role as well. The global markets that structure our world mean that entertainment is big business. The basketball great LeBron James is a household name in many parts of the globe. Consider soccer (or "football" to many), which is played all over the world. The World Cup is a massive international sporting event that brings together tens, if not thousands, of millions of fans every year. Like the Olympics, it is clearly a sporting event happening on a world stage. Look too at who plays in sports. The Premier League in the United Kingdom is one of the most storied of all football leagues. But the players who play in the league are not primarily British. Nearly 70% of the players are not British citizens; some 10% are from Sub-Saharan Africa.[3] Who watches and follows the Premier League is also not only a British phenomenon. Travel to India, Nigeria, or Canada, and you are likely to find many who follow the ins and outs of the league.

Consider music. The music business does $15 billion in sales globally.[4] Taylor Swift, Adele, and Justin Bieber are big not only in the United States but also in England and France. By the same token, African greats like Youssou Ndour and Selif Keita now have the opportunities to sell their music to millions of listeners around the world; half of all music sales are digital, which collapses time and space to make a song recorded in Senegal or Mali available to listeners in Australia and Japan instantaneously. Dance styles are not national; the same is true with dress styles. What we watch, what we listen to, and what we wear are part of a global network of cultural exchange. That world of possibility is exhilarating, but for some, it can be disorienting and threatening as they feel "their" values and better ways of life are being undermined.

Power is shifting globally. Many of the rising powerhouses are investing in cultural production. Consider the film industry. On the one hand, the U.S. film industry operates on a global scale; film distribution now happens in many national markets at the same time. But other countries are investing hugely in film. India has the largest film production globally. As many as 2,000 movies in 20 languages are now produced annually in the country, and the government, through its "Make in India" program, continues to invest in the industry.[5] Although its primary market is national, some Indian-made movies also are released elsewhere. *Baahubali 2*, an epic adventure dubbed the "Star Wars of India," was a major commercial success in the United States in 2017, becoming the number three grossing film at one point.[6]

With growing power, many states will look to insert their voices and their values onto the world stage. That will occur through entertainment, sports, and literature. What remains unclear is whether that process could lead to conflict and clash as nationals assert themselves in contrast to other values.

FIGURE 5.1

Inside-out and Outside-in Influences on Social Identity and Culture

Inside-out influence of individual and group identity and culture

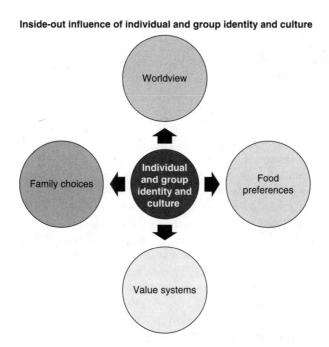

Outside-in influences of individual and group identity and culture

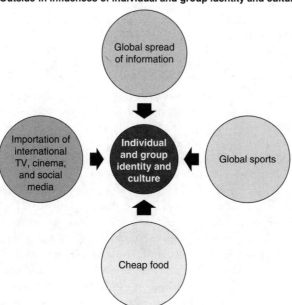

As culture operates globally, so do questions of rule making and regulation. Who shall judge and determine whether athletes take illicit drugs, and what should be the punishment for doing so? In football, the Zurich-based FIFA (Fédération International de Football Association) is a giant in that sport. FIFA determines where the World Cup will be played, how the tournament will be regulated, and the laws of the game. The United Nations Educational, Scientific, and Cultural Council (UNESCO) is an important world body that aims to shape and promote culture globally. Less a regulator per se, UNESCO tries to set agendas on culture globally. One example is the idea of World Heritage sites, which UNESCO designates. The concept of a World Heritage site emerged from the 1972 United Nations World Heritages Convention. A process within UNESCO has designated and promoted more than 1,000 sites worldwide.

Last, a major impact on culture will come from information and communications technology (ICT). ICT is a giant conduit for information, and culture and information are intricately linked. Culture is shared and transmitted, and that communication process is deeply connected to the dissemination of information. Because of advances in ICT, people all over the world can access information, ideas, songs, television shows, YouTube clips, and books at their fingertips. That intensifies cultural interactions in all kinds of ways whose effects are hard to foresee.

Culture and social identities are rich concepts through which to explore in an international studies context. They provide us with insights into how people perceive their world and how they act. The concepts also allow us to see the international studies framework in action. We can see interactions, both outside-in and inside-out, on many levels, and we can see how the global forces we identify are at play in these domains (see Figure 5.1).

In the remainder of the chapter, we further unpack the concepts of social identities and culture. In particular, we deepen the analysis of the concepts so you can develop a richer understanding of these core terms. We also provide some ways of thinking about these concepts in an international studies framework.

WHICH SOCIAL IDENTITIES MATTER?

Earlier we defined social identity as "any social category in which an individual is eligible to be a member." Social identity therefore covers a broad array of hypothetical groups. For example, you might belong to a group called "international studies majors" or a group associated with your university. One of us teaches at a school with a large athletics program and tons of school pride; many students at the University of Wisconsin identify as "Badgers," which is the sports mascot for the university. Badgers are often set in contrast to their rivals, in our case, the "Gophers" (University of Minnesota) or the "Wolverines" (University of Michigan). Indeed, sports teams claim a strong pull on people's social identities around the world. Undoubtedly, in your hometown there are teams with which many people fiercely identify and that are set in contrast to some despised "other" team.

Such a broad understanding, however, gives us limited insight into which identities are most consequential for social and political action around the world. The economist Amartya Sen provides a thought experiment of thinking about a group that could be formed around shoe size. He estimates there are some 100 million women in the world who wear a size 8 women's shoe. Women who wear size 8 shoes could constitute a group with a fairly well-defined boundary; you could determine who was in the group and who was out of the group. Moreover, their numbers are sizable (100 million at least!). They could organize across borders. Just imagine—a global group of women who wear size 8 shoes.

But the thought experiment shows how absurd the idea is. It is difficult to imagine a political movement on the basis of size 8 shoes. Just think: Women with size 8 shoes unite! That is probably true for international studies majors, and even probably for most sports teams. In fact, many social identities are fairly inconsequential for social and political action.[7]

That leaves us with a question: Which identities matter most in an international studies context and why? For international studies, the most salient identities are national, ethnic, religious, gender, and class. Undoubtedly, other social identities are significant. Sexuality is one. We will next discuss some of the most powerful identities when thinking about how identity matters for social and political action.

National Identity

A nation is a large community of people who, believing they hold a common bond, make a claim to have a sovereign state of their own. The Thai, for example, are the national community of Thailand; Kenyans are the national community of Kenya. Most nations have states but not all do, as we discussed in Chapter 2.

National identity is often very important to people and in particular when they are in a situation where they contrast their situation to that of another national group. Many students discover their national identity when they travel abroad. For example, if you are from China and studying in the United States, or vice versa, your national identity will be salient. You are likely to feel "Chinese" more on a daily basis than you might at home; you might spend time with your compatriots deliberately; you might seek out food or entertainment from your home country.

In international politics, national identity is also consequential. National governments act on behalf of the interests of the people in their states; they act in the national interest. That comes to the fore when thinking about international security (when thinking about protecting their state from another state) or economic interests (when thinking about bargaining in an international trade deal), or in other international contexts, such as the United Nations, when representatives act on behalf of their state.

Nationalism is a term that captures some of these ideas. Nationalism has two main meanings. Nationalism refers to the attitudes and emotions that individuals experience in reference to their national identity. When a woman speaks as a Senegalese and experiences pride and patriotism as someone from Senegal, for example, that is a form of nationalist sentiment.

Nationalist sentiment can lead to conflict and tension. One of the defining contemporary political issues in Europe today is the question of national identity. Because of immigration of nonwhites and often non-Christians, in many European countries, there is a sentiment among some of the electorate of a loss of their national identity. They feel that they are losing their country, losing their values, losing who they are and what defines their national community. That in turn fuels the rise of political parties who claim to defend a certain notion of national community in the face of immigration and globalization. That is the case in France, where the National Party campaigned on exactly these issues and won its largest share of votes ever in the national elections of 2017. A phrase such as "France is for the French" is an expression of nationalist identity based on a certain notion of what being French is. The same is true in the Netherlands, where the Party for Freedom cut a similar profile to the National Party and made steady gains in elections of the 2010s. Similarly, in Denmark, Norway, Sweden, and Italy, among other places, nationalist parties that campaign on cutting back immigration and promoting national values are rising in stature. The concept of social

national identity: social identity constituted by membership in a national group.

nationalism: attitudes and emotions that individuals experience in reference to their national identity, or the desire for self-determination, the desire for a state of one's own.

iStock/feradz

identity—in this case specifically national identity—is crucially important for understanding these political developments.

At the same time, people in France, the Netherlands, or other European countries could claim they have an idea of national identity that embraces ethnic and religious pluralism. To be French is not to be white and Christian but to be open, tolerant, and diverse. Their understanding of national identity would be different. We see some similar divisions in the United States, where some see the country as a land of immigrants and therefore the national community as a mixture of people from around the world. Others see the American national identity as fundamentally rooted in European heritage. The discussion demonstrates one aspect of social identity, which is that the content is often *contested*. People often disagree about what it is that makes them American, French, or Kenyan.

Nationalism also refers to the desire for self-determination, the desire for a state of one's own. For example, the newest country in the world is South Sudan. In 2010, the people of South Sudan voted overwhelmingly to form their own country, that is, to secede from Sudan. Their vote to create their own country was an expression of nationalism.

Nationalist movements are not limited to Africa. In Spain today, there are several movements to establish new states. The most powerful is an effort to create the country of Catalonia, with the city of Barcelona as its capital. Catalonia has its own language, Catalan. Many people in Catalonia believe that they share a distinctive identity, which is informed by a distinctive culture and language, that makes them different from the rest of Spain. The region is also one of the wealthiest in Spain, and some Catalans argue that they give more to Spain than they receive. These sentiments have fueled a pro-independence, nationalist movement in the region, but it is deeply contested by other Spaniards, including the party in control of the central government.

Nationalism has been central to the history of the modern world, as discussed in Chapter 1. Many internationally recognized countries came into existence in the past 100 years because of nationalist movements, like in South Sudan. Look at the map of Southeast and South Asia, the Middle East, and Sub-Saharan Africa. Almost all of these nations are the product of nationalism that followed European colonial rule. Nationalist sentiment can give rise to freedom, but also, it can give rise to armed conflict. Some countries might resist self-determination, as Sudan did for South Sudan for more than 50 years, which contributed to a long and nasty set of wars. Nationalism can also be a source of interstate war when one government fights another to safeguard its national interests.

Ethnic Identity

Ethnicity is one of the most significant social categories within countries. John Hutchinson and Anthony Smith define an ethnic group as a "named human population with myths of common ancestry, shared historical memories, one or more elements of common culture, a link with a homeland and a sense of solidarity among at least some of its members."[8]

Let's unpack that definition. The idea of a myth of common descent is that those in an ethnic group believe that they are connected through blood; an ethnic group is akin to a very large, extended family. But this is a myth: Most ethnic groups are not blood related. Rather, they *think* they are a large family even if in a biological sense that is not true. The idea of a shared historical memory is that the group claims some common events in the past. That could be a historic victory or defeat or some other major set of happenings that fundamentally affected the evolution of that group. The idea may be less familiar to you, but if you identify, for example, as Irish American, you are likely to remember the Irish potato famine as central to your group's history. These common memories are part of what makes a group into a group. Last, according to the authors, the idea of "elements of a common culture" could be language, religion, genetic attributes, tribal affiliations and practices, or any combination of these. Again, what defines a group might be the shared culture; they might have, for example, a dietary restriction around the consumption of pork.

In general, social scientists prefer the term "ethnicity" to the term "race." The concept of race, applied to human groupings, implies that there is in fact a biological foundation to different groups. Yet, as the definition given implies, such ideas of different biological races are myths; they are social constructions. Even if some people believe in a society that different groups do in fact have a common biological heritage, or even use the term "race," most social scientists prefer the term "ethnicity" to indicate that the construction of groups is rooted in society and history, not in biology.

Ethnic groups are enormously important groupings in most societies around the world. Many social scientists believe that trust and cooperation are essential for well-functioning states and societies. Trust facilitates everyday social, commercial, and political interactions—to conduct business, to put money in a bank, to send children to school, to report problems to the police, and to pay taxes. If ordinary citizens worry that their neighbors are plotting to kill them, that the police are utterly corrupt, and that there is no recourse to the law if someone steals their money, then society, business, and government would be paralyzed. Indeed, trust is fundamental to the concept of quasi-voluntary compliance that we introduced in Chapter 1, or the idea that states function in part because people comply with the rules.

Where does trust come from? Political institutions and performance are part of the story. If your government behaves well—is not corrupt or overly coercive, follows the law, and is fair—trust will ensue. But shared identities play a part too. Citizens are more likely to experience trust if they believe they are part of a common group, with shared heritage and a shared destiny. If they imagine that they share a national community, as represented by the state, then they will be willing to cooperate.

The challenge is that most countries around the world are multiethnic and multireligious, and in many instances, that creates distrust among citizens. The lack of a sense of commonality in turn weakens the ability of states to function, which in turn weakens the sense among citizens of a shared

ethnicity: named human population with myths of common ancestry, shared historical memories, one or more elements of common culture, a link with a homeland, and a sense of solidarity among at least some of its members.

national identity. Citizens' primary attachments remain to their ethnic group or their religious group, not to the national group. That has very important consequences for social and political action in their societies.

Consider Belgium. The country has a deep cleavage between French speakers, or Walloons, and the Flemish, who speak Dutch. The cleavage is so severe that Belgium's government often teeters at the point of collapse because of a lack of cooperation and apparent shared interests between the two populations. Belgium is just one example of a common issue that faces most multiethnic societies.

Religious Identity

Religious identity is also highly consequential. Just as many societies are multiethnic, many are also multiconfessional: Citizens of the same country identify with several different religions. In some societies, religious cleavages are extremely salient. In Northern Ireland, the divide between Protestants and Catholics has been one of the most important fractures in the country's history; the same is true for Shi'a and Sunni populations in Iraq or for Hindus and Muslims in India. In some societies, different branches of a main religion may matter tremendously. In Israel, which is officially a Jewish state, differences between Orthodox, Conservative, and Reform Jews shape where people live, with whom they socialize, and how they vote in many circumstances. In the United States, the lines between Evangelical Christians and mainline Protestant or Catholic Christians can be quite important.

Politicians and citizens alike can work to foster a sense of common bonds and common identity, even where existing divisions occur. That in turn can have real consequences on the development indicators in a society.

There is considerable overlap between these identities. An ethnic group that seeks an independent state is a nation. The Yugoslavia example is a good one. When Yugoslavia existed, Slovenes, Serbs, and Croats were generally considered ethnic groups. But as the country transitioned away from socialism in the 1980s and 1990s, many political leaders of those groups sought to form their own nations; they championed secessionist movements to become their own states. Religion is sometimes an attribute of ethnicity. Many ethnic groups claim to have specific religious practices; indeed, in some cases, the line between what is an "ethnic group" and what is a "religious group" can be blurry. The Northern Ireland case is again a good example. Are Catholics best thought of as an ethnic group with myths of common descent, shared historical memories, and the like, or as a religious group? The answer is probably not that important; the key is to recognize that these different types of identities—national, ethnic, and religious—shape behavior powerfully even if in some cases the dividing line between these categories is not rigid.

Gender Identity

gender identity:
social identity in which belonging is determined by gender difference.

Gender identity plays a critical role in international affairs. Norms around gender structure the ways many people experience their daily lives and their life choices. If you are born a woman in a society in which women are not expected to work, own property, or be educated beyond basic levels, gender identity might be one of the most determining factors for how your life is lived. Gender often shapes perception. Women might perceive a business or classroom environment very differently from men, and vice versa. Men and women might experience risk and security very differently. In many places, fear of sexual violence and harassment affect how and when women leave the home and go into public, as well as what they feel comfortable wearing. Gender also shapes preferences. Women sometimes choose candidates in elections differently from men; different issues are more salient.

On a global scale, gender is often a source for organizing and social movements. Nongovernmental organizations exist to promote women's rights, and women sometimes protest and make claims against their governments or to intergovernmental organizations on the basis of gender interests. In sum, as a source of identity, gender is crucial.

Class Identity

Last, socio-economic, is a critical category for action. **Socio-economic class** refers to a grouping based primarily on economic status. **Class identity** helps locate individuals on the basis of how they would situate themselves, or how they could be objectively situated, in relationship to the economic system. A common way to refer to people is as "lower" class or as "upper" class, referring to the professions that they have and their overall wealth. What constitutes higher and lower classes within a society varies; in some, being a schoolteacher and having a wealth of $75,000 could be considered an elite, upper class position, while in more industrialized, higher income societies, that profession and income level would be considered middle or lower class. There is no set rule on how many socio-economic classes analysts see in a society, but the basic insight is that socio-economic class is an important foundation for how people act—for their life experiences, for their voting choices, for their relationship to the international system, and for their leisure activities.

socio-economic class: grouping based on economic status.

class identity: social identity in which belonging is determined by social class.

WHY DO SOME SOCIAL IDENTITIES MATTER MORE THAN OTHERS?

The following question is important to ask: *Why* do some social identities matter more than others? Why are these the social identities that are most consequential for social and political action? The scholarship on this subject tends to point in three main directions. First, those identities that are "sticky" matter. Some identities are more difficult to change than others. You may change your major, your hometown, your hair color, and your favorite sports team.

But changing your ethnicity or race, your gender, and even your religion, nationality, or social class are difficult. Modern technology makes gender change possible, but the process is not easy and few people in a society typically do it. With enough education, intelligence, and luck, people change social class, but class mobility in many societies is difficult. The same is true for religion and nationality; people convert, but often the religion of one's birth is the religion of one's death. These "sticky" or "stable" identities are those that provide a basis for collective action, for identifying with others in a society and determining collective interests.

Second, identities that are visible are particularly powerful. Again, gender is usually quite visible, as are ethnicity and religion. Language often is an indicator of ethnicity, and sometimes of nationality; language is often visible and discoverable. In many societies, skin color shapes the perception of ethnicity, and phenotype is indeed quite visible. Religion shapes how people dress and where they worship, and that in turn makes that aspect of their social identity more visible. Social class can be difficult to read but often shapes where people live, what transportation they use, what they wear, what they eat, and other aspects of their daily lives that allow others to locate them within an economic hierarchy.

Third, those identities that have symbolic and emotional power are the ones that exercise the strongest pull on people. Some identities draw on the notion of being part of an extended family. The sense of being part of a family, being connected by blood, is often emotionally powerful, even if that notion is something of a myth. Americans are not all part of a single extended family, but the feeling of being connected to other Americans is often precisely that. The same is true for ethnic groups and even for religions. By contrast, there is little emotional power to having a particular shoe size or to having a major or to riding a certain brand of bicycle.

These arguments should be treated as a hypothesis. The questions to ask are as follows: Which social identities matter the most, and why?

SOCIAL IDENTITIES AND GLOBAL CHALLENGES

Social identities are enormously consequential for how people act in the world and for how they see the world. Social identities shape how people imagine community; how they imagine community in turn shapes how they see their interests; and how they see their interests in turn shapes how people act in several important social and political ways. As a result, social identities are often critical for understanding the global challenges that this book underlines.

Earlier we discussed how social identities shape political trust. But also consider democracy and voting, which we explore in Chapter 7. How people vote is often shaped by their social identity. In the United States, a voter's identity—whether he or she is African American, white, Latino, man, or woman—influences which party he or she supports. Older white men, for example, vote quite differently on average than their younger African American female counterparts. Around the world, social identities like religion and ethnicity weigh heavily on which party a voter will support. That is particularly true in new democracies where ethnic and religious cleavages run deep. New democracies with an overabundance of ethnic voting can in turn sow the seeds of conflict.

Think too about migration, which we cover in Chapter 11. Migration of people from one part of the world to another often creates *tensions* that are expressed in terms of national identity. In Europe

FIGURE 5.2

Global Forces, Interactions, Tensions, and the Rise of Nationalism

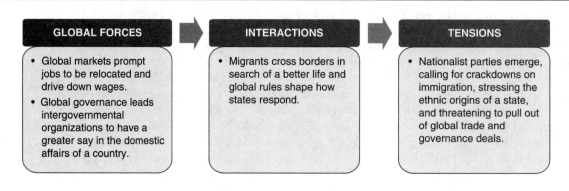

and North America, as the earlier example shows, immigration is a hot topic; this debate has given rise, in part, to a surge of populist, right-wing parties. National identity is at the core of those debates. The nationalist parties strive to protect and promote a certain version of a national identity that they see as threated from too much immigration (see Figure 5.2).

Poverty is another example, as we discuss in Chapter 9. Social identities are crucial for understanding social cooperation or social distrust in a society. If people find commonalities with others in their society, then the ability to share goods and cooperate is much easier. By contrast, if they see their primary community as being at odds with those of other groups in that society, then the chances for tension and conflict arise. Greater levels of diversity, on average, lead to less public goods provision.[9] By contrast, where political elites invest in creating a common identity and shared sense of solidarity among residents, the development impacts can be quite large. In India, one study showed how solidarity led to substantial improvements in health and education. Fostering solidarity paid off in terms of development.[10]

Last, think about civil war, which we cover in Chapter 10. Reflect on any case you know. In Iraq, for example, one of the key fault lines in the war has been among Shi'a, Sunnis, and Kurds—all social identities. As that country has experienced a devastating civil war, those social identities have often shaped how Iraqis define their interests and how they seek safety. The social identities are crucial in understanding how that civil war has unfolded.

UNDERSTANDING CULTURE

In this section, just as we did in the section on social identities, we introduce some key ways that social scientists think about culture.

Culture as a Worldview

Broadly speaking, culture encompasses two main ideas in an international studies context. The first is an analytical concept that denotes, in general, a "worldview" within a society, organization, or social category. One of the most influential definitions in this tradition is from the anthropologist Clifford Geertz. Geertz wrote that culture is "an historically transmitted pattern of meaning embodied in symbols, a system of inherited conceptions expressed in symbolic forms by means of which men communicate, perpetuate, and develop their knowledge about and attitudes toward life."[11]

For Geertz, as for many others, culture connotes the idea of a *system of meaning* by which people make sense of their world. Culture shapes how people communicate, perpetuate, and develop knowledge and attitudes. In short, culture is like a prism, or mental map, that filters how people see and understand the world around them.

Seen in this way, culture provides insight into what individuals consider appropriate, and that in turn sheds light on many dimensions of everyday life and broader social patterns. Consider gender roles. In some societies, ethnic groups, or businesses, there might be expectations about what men and women should and should not do that are very specific to the values in those communities. Think about attire. In the United States, the expectation that women should cover their skin in public is uncommon. But in other countries, to wear a short skirt or to expose a shoulder is considered offensive. Consider expression. In some businesses, the culture of an organization would expect young women to assert themselves in ways that are identical to men. In other organizations, however, the expectation would be for women to be deferential. Whether about attire, expression, marriage, sexual relations, worship, income, property, education, household chores, or many other aspects, culture shapes expectations about how men and women should behave.

Culture and Stereotypes

People's values and opinions vary considerably in every society, and they change: That is to say, culture is neither deterministic nor static, nor does it operate only at a national level. Where people live does not determine how they think, even if engrained ways of seeing the world shape how they understand their world. Think of your country. If you are American, you know that your friends, your family members, and your colleagues on a team or at work hold a variety of views. At the same time, there might be qualities about you as Americans that would become more visible when you travel to another country.

Indeed, the concept of culture can lend itself to overly broad generalizations and stereotypes, even ones that border on racism. Not everyone who belongs to a social category will necessarily share the same values, beliefs, and norms as others within that social category. Think about Asian Americans. One common image of Asian American families is that they push their children to excel in school and in extracurriculars. The term "Tiger mom" is one that captures this intrafamily drive for success. But in reality the idea of a "Tiger mom" reproduces ethnic stereotypes. Not all Asian Americans push their children to perform academically, and the idea of a "tiger" invokes Asia in a way that is off-putting. The same applies to a national culture of those in an ethnic group in an another country. Not all French love cheese. Not all Quechuas live in the highlands. In short, although the idea of a national culture or one that is specific to an ethnic group is often valuable, care should be taken not to generalize too greatly or to invoke stereotypes that will be offensive.

Culture is also not just a tool to understand "them." Culture also allows for a window into understanding "us"; it allows us to be self-reflective, to see how our often unstated expectations about what is right and wrong shape how we make decisions and how we respond to other people. Many current students might have ideas about gender equality, about child-rearing practices like spanking, about freedom of expression, about time, and about religion that are different from those with whom we spend time abroad. Indeed, for many students, navigating cultural difference is a central experience when living abroad.

Culture as the Product of Human Intellectual and Artistic Activity

The second broad concept of culture treats it as a catchall category to describe the intellectual and artistic activity in a society; this usage is arguably the most common.[12] Culture here is less about inherited ideas, customs, beliefs, systems of thought, and traditions and more about human creative production and creativity. Culture here refers to that which humans make—that which distinguishes humans from other animals. Under this broad rubric, "culture" encompasses film, theater, dance, music, fashion, literature, visual arts, and food. Some locate sport under an umbrella of culture. Sport is a human creation, a set of games with distinctive rules and where performance depends on learning and study. Indeed, many countries around the world combine sports and culture in a single ministry. In Kenya, for example, there is a Ministry of Sports, Culture, and the Arts, while in Japan there is a Ministry of Education, Culture, Sports, Science, and Technology.

Culture and Global Challenges

Culture helps us to understand all kinds of global challenges that are critical for international studies. For example, culture is critical for understanding global health, which we cover in Chapter 12. Questions of health often touch on sensitive issues that pertain to people's bodies and behavior. If, for example, a public health campaign wished to focus on promoting condom use as a way to prevent the spread of certain infectious diseases such as HIV, that campaign would have to consider sex and sexuality in that society. In a society where public discussion of sex was taboo, a public media campaign for condom use would likely fail. To be successful in that intervention, health officials would need to understand the culture.

Another example is menstrual hygiene, which is an area of critical importance for the health of young women, especially those going to school. Yet cultural taboos in many societies prevent a frank, open discussion of women's health and menstruation in particular. Again, understanding culture is critical to any kind of health intervention.

Culture is central to food. In Chapter 14, we look at food in a global context primarily through the prism of hunger. But consider the ways that different food cultures have globalized. Chances are everyone who reads this book has sampled foods from around the world: Chinese food, Italian food, Mexican food, American food, Indian food, French food, and Japanese food are some of the most common types of cuisine available in the United States. Consuming foods and flavors from around the world is one of the most pleasurable forms of international interactions! As with social identity, context shapes how these foods are labeled. In China, "Chinese food" is not an appropriate or common moniker: Food would likely be described according to region, such as "Sichuan" or "Cantonese." The point about regionalism applies to Italian food as well: Pizza is primarily a product of Rome and Naples, risotto is a product of northern Italy, Bolognese sauce is a product of Bologna, and so forth.

Food is also globalized in the sense of fusion. Many distinctive recipes have developed that combine flavors from different countries. "Asian fusion" is a common term, where the flavors of Korea, Japan, China, Thailand, and Vietnam might be combined. But cross-continental influences are also frequent. At a local market for one us, a "sushi burrito" is a favorite lunch: Salmon, avocado, wasabi, and sticky rice are the Japanese flavors, but the whole package is wrapped in a burrito and spiced with seasoning from Mexico. High-end restaurants around the world similarly bring flavors together. Chefs study and cook in other countries and then bring their knowledge back home. An Australian chef, Lennox Hastie, for example, learned roasting techniques in Basque country (Spain). Astushi Tenaka fuses Japanese and French in Paris. Paul Carmichael, from Barbados, is the executive chef at Momofuku restaurant in Sydney;[13] Momofuku is the creation of David Chang, a Korean American man who pioneered a Korean-inflected cuisine that incorporated flavors from around the world.

IS From the Inside-Out

HOW CAN A LOCAL NONGOVERNMENTAL ORGANIZATION IMPROVE GIRLS' HEALTH AND EDUCATION?

Copper Rose Zambia is a nongovernmental organization based in the southern African country of Zambia. The focus of the organization is to improve the lives of women and girls, in particular, in the areas of health and education. Those goals are consistent with many civil society organizations around the world. Yet one of the distinctive aspects of Copper Rose is its focus on culture, as culture pertains to health and education.

The motto of the organization is, "We believe in a society that appreciates beauty, value, and empowerment." The motto itself already indicates a focus on culture. The organization focuses on changing expectations about girls and women, about how to appreciate them in particular. Changing expectations about gender is fundamentally a cultural endeavor.

One of the innovative emphases of the organization is to focus on the values and information that hinder girls from attaining education and sexual and reproductive health. In the face of ignorance or silence around reproductive health, many girls around the world experience embarrassment and encounter discrimination when they menstruate. In some cases, girls who lack access to sanitary materials similarly worry about leaving the house. In both cases, their education might be compromised—they may not want to go to school.

One project that Cooper Rose began in 2015 is "Candid Pride." The campaign is designed both to combat silences and misunderstandings around menstruation and to provide sanitary materials to girls who attend school. The program also engages in educational programming about healthy menstrual hygiene practices.

The program's name is indicative of its priorities. "Candid" suggests an open, honest discussion about girls' and women's bodies, an effort that might run counter to cultural taboos in Zambian society. "Pride" indicates a sense of empowerment and positivity around a topic that girls may have experienced or learned to experience as shameful.

Copper Rose is a domestic organization, focusing on gender identity and cultural norms about gender, reproductive health, and education to improve the lives of girls and women. Yet the ideas that animate the organization are rooted in a broader set of discussions and interactions operating on a global level.

In recent years, many intergovernmental organizations focused on girls, women, health, and even human rights have promoted menstrual hygiene health and management as the key to better outcomes for girls and women. A Germany-based organization, WASH United, helped to create May 28 as a global Menstrual Hygiene Day to "help to break the silence and build awareness about the fundamental role that good menstrual hygiene management (MHM) plays in enabling women and girls to reach their full potential." Human Rights Watch, a major international human rights organization, frames menstrual hygiene as a human rights issue, in particular for women's rights.

The example is one of many about how culture is linked to education, health, and equality. Culture is the focus of domestic and international activism. Even if many of the most successful efforts to address harmful aspects of culture are initiated from within societies, the ideas are embedded in a global circulation of information, norms, and priorities.

Reflect

How do attitudes and expectations rooted in culture shape health outcomes? In your life, can you think of one cultural practice, understanding, or tradition that negatively impacts health?

Learn more about Copper Rose and other menstrual hygiene efforts here:

http://copperrosezambia.org/

http://menstrualhygieneday.org/

https://www.hrw.org/news/2017/08/27/menstrual-hygiene-human-rights-issue.

Culture and the Challenge of Globalization:
Clash, Convergence, or Localization?

As cultural products and activities have increasingly "gone global," and as people from different cultures themselves have increasingly moved from place to place, researchers have given thought to what happens when cultures interact internationally. Earlier we talked about how food cultures can be blended into a delicious fusion. But what about instances where cultures are in conflict? Or when one culture dominates another? Dutch sociologist Jan Nederveen Pieterse puts forward three main frameworks for thinking about culture and globalization.[14]

Clash of Cultures. The first is the idea of a "clash" of civilizations or cultures. In this model, cultures are somewhat static; they represent distinctive blocs of values and beliefs that are, or potentially are, in conflict with each other. In an era of intensified global interactions, one prediction is that as different cultures come together more frequently, so too will the collisions and confrontations be greater.[15]

People who see cultures as "clashing" in an international context tend to think of cultures as somewhat closed, and remaining so. Some cultures may coexist peacefully, but they also might be incompatible, and hence in conflict. Contemporary debates about immigration often frame cultures in this way. Segments of the population in Europe and the United States feel that there is a certain "way of life" in their countries. When immigrants from Asia, the Middle East, or Africa arrive, from this point of view, there is a cultural clash unless immigrants adopt the culture of their home country. Populist political movements in Europe and the United States similarly frame Islam and Muslims as representing a set of values that are incompatible with their own national cultures.

The Islamic State and other extreme Islamist organizations frame their struggle as a clash with "the West." For leaders of the Islamic State, the West represents an amoral culture that seeks domination and should be resisted. Boko Haram is an Islamic State affiliate that operates in and around northern Nigeria; the name roughly translates to the idea that Western education and Western influence more generally is a sin.[16]

Culture clashes are routine in the world. Zumba is a type of dance that was developed in Colombia; it spread to many countries in the world as part of a general upsurge in fitness in the 1990s and 2000s. But in 2017, Iranian officials declared the rhythmic exercise out of line with its Islamic principles and prohibited it.[17] Yoga is a Hindu-inspired form of stretching and breathing that also has become popular worldwide. In the United States, some parents and fitness enthusiasts object to having yoga in public schools or at their sports club because they consider yoga in conflict with Christian values.[18]

Convergence or Homogenization. A second model of culture and international interactions is the idea of convergence or homogenization. The concept here is that globalization will flatten difference; one culture will dominate. In most applications of this model, the idea is that the most powerful cultures of the world will export their values, beliefs, and practices through their power in the media, business, and politics, and will extinguish other cultures in their path.

The United States and the West in general is the culprit in convergence, with mega multinational food companies that span the globe, such as McDonald's, Coca-Cola, and Kentucky Fried Chicken as well as clothing companies like The Gap, Nike, and Under Armour. More powerful still is the global entertainment business, such as Hollywood movies, American television programs, the

National Basketball Association, and music studios based in the United States. In various ways, the cuisine, fashion, and entertainment industries model a certain way of living and acting that some worry will replace their cultures around the world.

A synonym for this notion of cultural domination is the "McDonaldization" or "Coca-colization" or "Disneyfication" of global culture, as we discussed in Chapter 2. McDonald's has franchises in more than 100 countries around the world (see Figure 5.3). Coca-Cola sells its beverages in more than 200 countries. Walt Disney operates theme parks in France, China, and Japan, as well as in the United States, but its movies and characters have worldwide appeal. In short, the idea here is something close to cultural imperialism: One culture will come to extirpate others, and the one that will dominate will come from the most powerful economy of the world. American technology will fuel this change: Microsoft programs, IBM and Apple computers, Uber, Facebook, and Google subtly promote a lifestyle that is American but that is projected onto a worldwide stage.

Localization. Is American culture steamrolling other cultures? Are cultures converging to a global ideal that conforms to Western values? The question is an empirical one: you should answer it based on your own observations of the world around you. Many scholars who study the issue argue against the idea. Instead of finding the powerful economies of the world dominating, they observe a much more nuanced process of cultural interaction and "localization," the idea of adapting to local conditions and tastes. This is the third model of culture and international interactions.

For example, McDonald's—the quintessential fast-food American restaurant—does not look or mean the same in every country. In Brazil, rice and beans are on the menu.[19] McDonald's caters not only to local diets but also to the demands of customers who may not want fast, cheap food. The same is true for Starbucks, which puts items on the menu that appeal to local consumers. Scholars who observed the restaurants found them to be spaces for young, middle class people to meet and even for women to find a space that was not male dominated. Moreover, the restaurants are franchises, in which local owners typically own about 50% of the company, and many aim to source their food locally. That structure prompted the president of McDonalds' International to call the company a "multilocal" one.[20]

If you look around, you are likely to see evidence of global cultural mixing in many places. The examples of a "Sushi Burrito" or a "Korean taco" illustrate the point, as does the Barbadian chef who cooks in a high-end pan-Asian restaurant in Sydney, Australia. Think of medicine, which often includes ingredients that originate from the tropical countries, or think about crops that were imported from one country that thrive in another, such as an orange, which likely originated in China and India. Consider wikis, which allow people from all over the world to contribute to a posting, or to open source software. In hip-hop, rappers sample recordings from around the world, as do DJs. In dance, artists copy moves from around the world. In Iran, surfboarding is a craze.

Scholars have developed numerous concepts to capture this process of global and local cultural *interaction*. One is the concept of "glocalization," which suggests that globalized processes become localized. The idea is that international cultural interactions produce all kinds of splicing and mixing. There is great creativity here, even unpredictability, in how ideas, practices, and beliefs from one place will adapt and be reshaped with ideas, practices, and beliefs from another place.

Watch Planet B-Boy, *a documentary about the evolution of breakdancing globally at https://www.youtube.com/watch? v=AmXWmGT1I-M.*

FIGURE 5.3
Global Reach of McDonald's

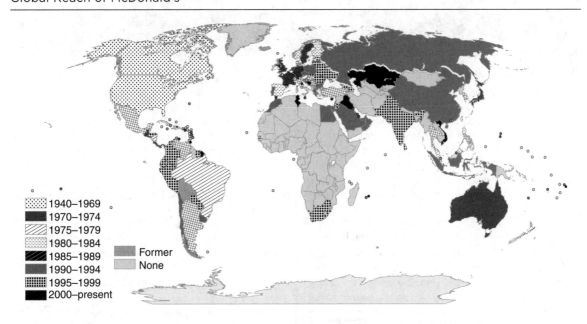

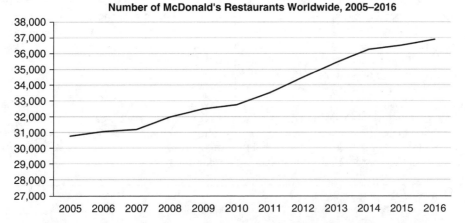

1940–1969
1970–1974
1975–1979
1980–1984
1985–1989
1990–1994
1995–1999
2000–present

Former
None

Number of McDonald's Restaurants Worldwide, 2005–2016

Source: Map is from Wikimedia Commons, https://commons.wikimedia.org/wiki/File: McDonaldsWorldLocations.svg. Data on number of McDonald's restaurants is from Statista, https://www.statista.com/statistics/219454/mcdonalds-restaurants-worldwide/.

The idea of glocalization highlights the fluidity of international interactions as it brings together "outside-in" influences such as McDonald's and Starbucks (global brands) and "inside-out" influences, such as local tastes, ownership, and adaptation. Rather than seeing globalization as a one-way conveyor belt of influence from the outside, global interactions produce dynamic and often unforeseeable mixtures of domestic and international forces.

IS From the Outside-In and the Inside-Out

HOW DOES MODERN B-BOY BREAKDANCING EVOLVE?

B-Boy breakdancing is an exciting, if perhaps unexpected, arena in which to consider the ways in which culture is shaped through inside-out and outside-in forces. Breakdancing is generally thought to have developed first and foremost among African Americans in the United States. The initial breakdancing, done by B-Boys (B stands for dancing to a "beat"), synthesized moves from famous African American performers, like James Brown, but also from gymnastics and Asian martial arts movies.

The remarkable documentary "Planet B-Boy" tells the story of the evolution of B-Boy dancing. From its earliest incarnations in music and film, B-Boy protagonists from Germany, France, Japan, and elsewhere describe how the electrifying dance moves that first originated in the United States spread. They describe how these extraordinary motions and dances mesmerized people around the world, leading people all over the world to adopt this new form of dance.

Some breakdancing enthusiasts in Germany began promoting breakdancing and eventually started a competition called "Battle of the Year." That idea then took off, with Battle of the Year qualifying competitions taking place in France, Japan, Korea, South Africa, Israel, Brazil, and elsewhere.

One way of seeing these developments is as a form of outside-in cultural homogenization. A new dance form originated in the United States, with its own specific "inside-out" history of African American

music and experience informing it. From the United States, it spread elsewhere, just as McDonald's, Kentucky Fried Chicken, and Hollywood have.

A closer look reveals a different story, however. As the dance spread to different countries, dancers in those countries developed their own styles, integrating their own histories of dance and choreography into their B-Boy performances. As different styles developed in other places, those styles influenced how other people danced.

B-Boy may be a particularly easy case in which to observe global cultural synthesis, or "glocalization." The origins of the dance themselves are about meshing different influences to create something new. The dance is more porous than something like classical ballet. Yet as a case study, B-Boy shows how culture can emanate across borders, but then be shaped in other spaces, and then refracted back. We see here an evolving set of global interactions in a distinctive cultural and entertaining space!

To learn more: https://www.youtube.com/watch? v=AmXWmGT1I-M.

Reflect

How do local cultural influences shape global ones? Beyond dance styles, can you think of a cultural sphere—music, food, sports, the arts—in which local influences shaped and reshaped cultural influences from the outside?

SUMMARY

Culture and social identities are core concepts for international studies. The concepts provide a lens through which to analyze how people make sense of their surroundings and how they act. Culture and social identity open up a huge range of global interactions, from entertainment to the most intimate decisions in a family. Culture and social identities are

sites for cooperation and creativity but also for tension. Some of the most visible global struggles in the world today point back to fundamental questions around identity. Social identity and culture are therefore key conceptual tools for understanding the global challenges that we cover in the second half of the book and that are central to international studies.

KEY TERMS

class identity 139
culture 130
ethnicity 137
gender identity 138

in-groups 131
national identity 135
nationalism 135
out-groups 131

social identity 131
socio-economic class 139

QUESTIONS FOR REVIEW

1. Identify examples of cultural products that are, or that have become, global. What makes them global?

2. What are your social identities? Which ones do you think matter the most in your life? Which influences—inside-out or outside-in—have shaped your social identities?

3. Do you think that culture around the world is clashing, becoming homogenized, or becoming a mixture of influences? Can you think of an example for each way of seeing global culture?

LEARN MORE

Rawi Abdelal, Yoshiko Herrera, Alastair Johnston, and Rose McDermott, eds. 2009. *Measuring Identity: A Guide for Social Scientists*. New York: Cambridge University Press.

Jan Nederveen Pieterse. 2004. *Globalization and Culture: Global Mélange*. Lanham, MD: Rowman and Littlefield.

Amartya Sen. 2006. *Identity and Violence: The Illusion of Destiny*. New York: W. W. Norton.

NOTES

1. Conrad Phillip Kottak, *Anthropology: Appreciating Human Diversity*, 16th ed. (New York, NY: McGraw Hill Education, 2015), 5.

2. Kanchan Chandra, "What Is Ethnic Identity and Does It Matter," *Annual Review of Political Science*, 9 (2006): 397–424, quote from p. 400; see also Henri Taffel, *Human Groups and Social Categories: Studies in Social Psychology* (New York: Cambridge University Press, 1981).

3. UEFA, The European Club Footballing Landscape: Financial Year 2015, http://telegraph.digidip .net/visit? url=http%3A%2F%2Fwww.uefa .org%2FMultimediaFiles%2FDownload %2FTech%2Fuefaorg%2FGeneral %2F02%2F42%2F27%2F91%2F2422791_ DOWNLOAD.pdf&pref=https%3A%2F%2Fwww .google.com%2F

4. http://www.ifpi.org/global-statistics.php.

5. Deloitte, Indywood, The Film Industry in India, 2016: https://www2.deloitte.com/in/en/pages/ technology-media-and-telecommunications/articles/ indywood-indian-film-industry.html.

6. https://www.wsj.com/articles/how-an-indian-superhero-film-beat-hollywood-competitors-at-the-box-office-1494260710.

7. Amartya Sen, *Identity and Violence: The Illusion of Destiny* (New York, NY: W.W. Norton, 2006).

8. John Hutchinson and Anthony Smith, eds., *Ethnicity* (Oxford, U.K.: Oxford University Press, 1996), 6.

9. James Habyarimana, Macartan Humphreys, Daniel Posner, and Jeremy Weinstein, *Coethnicity: Diversity and the Dilemmas of Collective Action* (New York, NY: Russell Sage Foundation, 2009).

10. Prerna Singh, *How Solidarity Works for Welfare: Subnationalism and Social Development in India* (New York, NY: Cambridge University Press, 2016).

11. Clifford Geertz, *The Interpretation of Cultures: Selected Essays* (New York, NY: Basic Books, 1973[SVV2]).

12. Raymond Williams, *Keywords: A Vocabulary of Culture and Society*, Rev. ed. (New York, NY: Oxford University Press, 1983), 90.

13. Pete Wells, "Global, With Local Flavor," https://www.nytimes.com/2017/06/14/insider/global-with-local-flavor-restaurant-critic-pete-wells-in-sydney.html?_r=0.

14. Jan Nederveen Pieterse, *Globalization and Culture: Global Mélange* (Lanham, MD: Rowman and Littlefield, 2004).

15. See also Samuel P. Huntington, *The Clash of Civilizations and the Remaking of World Order* (New York, NY: Simon & Schuster, 1996).

16. http://www.bbc.com/news/blogs-magazine-monitor-27390954.

17. http://www.independent.co.uk/news/world/middle-east/iran-zumba-ban-unislamic-tehran-ali-majdara-general-sports-federation-women-sports-a7796861.html.

18. http://www.nbcnews.com/id/16859368/ns/health-childrens_health/t/yoga-causes-controversy-public-schools/#.WU0Z6ytJlpl; http://newsfeed.time.com/2010/09/22/is-yoga-an-anti-christian-practice/.

19. https://www.ft.com/content/f8ac22fc-a7c1-11e4-8e78-00144feab7de? mhq5j=e2.

20. James Watson, *Golden Arches East: McDonalds in East Asia*, Rev. ed. (Stanford, CA: Stanford University Press, 2006), 12.

Money

PROPELLING GLOBAL INTERACTIONS

6

Bill Clark/CQ Roll Call

LEARNING OBJECTIVES

After finishing this chapter, you should be able to:

- Describe the liberal, mercantilist, and structuralist views on trade.

- Identify the major international actors in global markets.

- Distinguish between foreign direct investment and portfolio investment.

- Analyze the international components in major financial crises.

- Understand global currency systems.

WHY GLOBAL MONEY MATTERS

How much have you borrowed for college? If you are in Pennsylvania or Connecticut, the average student debt is $36,000. Even on the "low end" in places such as Florida or Arizona, the average is still $23,000 to $24,000.[1] The high cost of a college education is partly due to reduced support from states to their public colleges. But the reason you had to borrow so much for college, and the reason you *could* borrow at all, must be understood in light of the international economy. It turns out that the international economy is partly why college costs so much and why you could borrow so much to pay for it. As the U.S. economy has become increasingly oriented toward service-related jobs and less focused on industry, many manufacturing jobs have moved to developing countries. That has hurt some people's ability to pay for college and has made others less willing to have their taxes go toward subsidizing public education.

There is less money available domestically to fund education in the United States—but there are international sources of money. In this chapter, we will learn why the world's willingness to loan the United States money has made it possible for you to borrow so much.

Global money refers to three things:

- **Trade**: the global movement of goods and services

- **Finance**: the global movement of capital (money)

- **Currency**: the systems of money exchange that enable different economies to interact

As we will explore, trade, finance, and currencies each comes with its own controversies. For instance, among economists, there is much debate about whether the ability of capital to move freely around the world is a good thing. Likewise, China and the United States have ongoing struggles over their currencies. Before we look at 21st-century global money, however, let's get some historical perspective by looking at what capitalism is, where it came from, and how it works today.

WHAT IS CAPITALISM?

capitalism:
socioeconomic system of production characterized by market-based transaction, private property, and wage labor.

At its most basic, **capitalism** refers to an economic and social system of free markets, private property, and wage labor. It is possible to have one of these but not be capitalist, so capitalism is not interchangeable with a free market, despite how the words are popularly used. For example, communities rather than individuals might own a farm and freely sell their goods. This would be a free market without private property. Today, almost every state has a capitalist economy, but they vary according to how capitalist they are. Let's look at its core features.

First, in capitalist socioeconomic systems, markets rather than governments coordinate economic transactions. For example, the delivery of this textbook to you was not coordinated by a government but by the *interactions* of profit-seeking individuals. To paraphrase Adam Smith, we don't expect the baker to make bread because she is benevolent but because it is in her own self-interest. Thus, markets work because everyone is pursuing their own best interest. But self-interest does not mean anarchy because capitalism also involves competition between individuals. This ensures that the baker will produce good bread for fear of losing customers.

Second, private property means an individual person or firm has the legal right to own land (farms, mines, etc.) or capital (machinery, software patents). Capital is something that can be owned that generates an income. Think of it as money but also as the physical things that go into producing a good, such machinery or office equipment. The profits that come from owning capital are also the property of the capitalist, even if she did not do the work. For example, if you spend $1 million on a factory, and your employees produce things for sale, the profit on those sales (after wages and other expenses) goes to you even though you did not engage in wage labor. In capitalist systems it is considered legitimate to profit from the work of others. The private ownership of capital is also where class distinction comes from, since some people own the businesses while others do not. A class is a socioeconomic group that gets its identity from its place in the economic system. Thus, if I am a wage earning laborer rather than a business owner, my class will be defined by the power of labor in relation to capitalists.

Third, things are commodified in capitalist socioeconomic systems, which means they have a price and can be bought and sold. The most important are land, labor, and goods. It was not always the case that all land could be bought and sold (i.e., commodified). Even today in places such as Ghana, land does not exist to be bought and sold. Chiefs manage land for the benefit of the community. This is even true for U.S. national parks, which are not simply a commodity to be bought and sold. In capitalist systems things become commodified: Before things like labor or goods can be traded in a market, people have to consider something to be a commodity. For example, humans were once commodities as slaves, but this is generally seen as unacceptable now.

Commodification also goes hand in hand with freedom of enterprise, meaning I have the right to use my capital however I please in the pursuit of profit. Labor is also said to enjoy freedom of enterprise as I am not forced to work with one employer. Critics such as Joan Robinson say this is really a choice between hunger and exploitation: "The misery of being exploited by capitalists is nothing compared to the misery of not being exploited at all."[2]

commodification: assessing something's worth in terms of its value in an economic or trading transaction.

Where Did Capitalism Come From?

The origins of capitalism are typically located in northwestern Europe in the 15th through the 17th centuries, but capitalism was not invented in one big bang. Societies had been trading for millennia beforehand. Rather, the 15th to 17th centuries are usually highlighted because the major elements we recognize as capitalism—market exchange, private property, wage labor—expanded rapidly in some places.

Scholars debate why capitalism emerged when and where it did. Those in the liberal tradition have tended to see capitalism as emerging naturally because it reflected people's innate willingness to trade with one another and to protect their own property. Once restrictions on labor and businesses were removed, people's natural tendency to maximize their wealth shone through. For example, the 1688 Glorious Revolution was a period of significant reform in Britain. It began as a Dutch/Protestant attack on the Catholic monarchy and was significant for some scholars of capitalism because it led to greater protections for private property.[3] The British Parliament—and its economic elite—gained greater power over the economy, and they set about limiting arbitrary taxation, protecting private property rights, and abolishing monopolies. Their behavior was self-interested, but it was good for the emerging capitalist system, and Britain began centuries of extraordinary economic growth thereafter.

By contrast, scholars in the Marxist tradition have tended to see capitalism as something that was actively produced by powerful forces rather than by simply emerging organically and inevitably. Karl Polanyi said capitalism emerged in 17th century Britain as farmland was privatized, people were pushed off the land and into small factories, and money was generated through trade. In what Polanyi called "market society," people began to relate to one another in an individualistic and transactional way. Thus, capitalism did not simply emerge out of people's natural tendencies; it had to be created and had to change how people behaved.

Capitalism also grew in tandem with states, which were also emerging in 15th to 17th century Europe (see Chapter 2). This makes sense since capitalist economies need court systems to enforce contracts, for example, so the idea of a completely "free market" without states is mostly fantasy. Indeed, one of the earliest forms of capitalism was mercantilist (or merchant) capitalism of the 16th through 18th centuries, in which companies were seen as valuable because they could enrich the state (see Chapter 1). States, in turn, protected their national companies. This was a form of capitalism

Marxism: ideas of Karl Marx, that capitalism exploits labor and inequality is rooted in unequal control of means of production.

Fordism: form of capitalism characterized by mass production for mass consumption, as introduced by Henry Ford, with repetitive, semiskilled factory work in production for mass consumer markets

Post-Fordism: late 20th century form of capitalism characterized by product quality rather than by price, with global production, flexible labor markets, and weak worker bargaining strength.

with private property and wages but only partially free markets, in which the purpose of companies was to make nations rather than individuals wealthy.

The industrial revolution around the 18th century marked the beginning of industrial capitalism. Factory workers received wages but had no ownership of the tools they used, nor a claim to the profits they produced. Their tasks were highly routinized on the factory floor, such that a worker was a substitutable piece of a production machine and no longer a skilled artisan. States, meanwhile, engaged in protectionism to benefit their national companies, and they produced education systems to meet the needs of employers. **Marxism** then arose as a scientific critique of capitalist industrial society. Karl Marx argued that capitalists rely for profit on their power to pay workers less than their fair share. Internationally, industrializing states colonized most nonwhite societies and often introduced capitalism to places where private property or wage labor had not existed. Marxism also offered an explanation for this, in which industrialized countries were subjugating distant peoples in a relentless pursuit of new markets and new raw materials.

Capitalism around 1900 is often known as the age of Fordism. **Fordism** refers to the way Henry Ford organized production at his Ford Motor Company factory. At the heart of the Fordist model of production was the assembly line. Rather than one person making one car, it was better to have one person specialize in seat belts, another in pedals, and so on, and have them jointly produce the car. This innovation led to vehicles produced with greater efficiency and thus reduced cost.

Again states played a role in facilitating capitalism by reducing opposition to it. Karl Polanyi argued that welfare states arose because of popular opposition to the harmful effects of capitalism, such as unemployment and inequality.[4] Thus, modern working conditions such as a minimum wage and an 8-hour workday are the result of protests by workers organized in unions.

Few non-Western countries were industrialized by the mid-20th century, yet some observers still saw the footprint of global capitalism. This is where dependency theory comes from (see Chapter 9). Scholars such as Andre Gunder Frank, Samir Amin, and Walter Rodney argued that rich countries were rich *because* poor countries were poor. To speak of global capitalism, therefore, does not simply mean "capitalism in every country" but how capitalism ties countries together in relations of exploitation.

21st-Century Global Capitalism

Twenty-first century capitalism is characterized by **post-Fordism** and global financial capitalism. Industrialized economies are increasingly postindustrial, with a growing share of workers employed not on a factory floor but in service positions, whether as accountants or as baristas. In this version of capitalism, capital moves around the globe in search of returns (see the definition of capital controls later in this chapter).[5]

The shift from Fordism to post-Fordism was not just about how firms organized themselves. During the Fordist period, governments were heavily involved in their economies. They provided social welfare and mediation between labor unions and business, and companies relied on their own workers to purchase their products. Henry Ford, for example, wanted his workers to be able to afford the cars they made. This is not so today. Under post-Fordism, states have largely liberalized their economies and have scaled back the social welfare programs like unemployment and childcare; labor unions have declined in strength; and major companies now seek global, not national, customers. Workers under post-Fordism are supposed to provide flexible labor that is easy to hire and fire, and they are not expected to be able to consume the goods they produce.

Watch the TED Talk by Thomas Piketty on 21st-century capitalism at https://www .youtube.com/watch?v=JKsHhXwqDqM.

Rather than globalization gradually forcing all countries to look the same, the **Varieties of Capitalism** theory says globalization will deepen the differences between countries. For example, in a liberal market economy such as that in the United Kingdom or United States, firms interact with each other and secure finance through market-based transactions. That is, they compete or trade with each other. Their ability to access finance is determined by their stock price, which leads them to pursue short-term profits. The relationship between firms and workers is also competitive and short term, with employers allowed to fire workers with ease. The role of the state in these capitalist economies is to ensure that no one actor is able to monopolize, whether it be a union or a firm. Education systems provide a broad-based education because workers need to be able to move across different industries.

By contrast, in a coordinated market economy (similar to a social market economy), such as that in Germany or the Netherlands, there is coordination between firms, workers, and government. Firms often hold stock in other firms and sit on their boards, as do union representatives. Because firms see what is happening in other firms, it is possible for them to engage in trusting long-term coordinated activities, such as industry-wide investments in new technologies. This explains why Germany has more advanced manufacturing compared with the United States. Education systems in these places provide a narrowly focused skill set because workers are expected to stay with a firm or industry for their careers (see Figure 6.1).[6]

Varieties of Capitalism: theory that different capitalist economies have entire institutional setups designed to work for specific needs of the local variety of capitalism. Major types are liberal market economy (firms compete with each other; labor relations are poor) and coordinated market economy (firms, labor, and government cooperate).

FIGURE 6.1

Global Forces, Interactions, Tensions, and 21st-Century Capitalism

GLOBAL FORCES	INTERACTIONS	TENSIONS
• Global markets: The hallmark of 21st-century capitalism is that it is global. • ICT: Logistics communications enable the mass movement of goods as well as the instantaneous buying and selling of foreign financial assets. • Shifting centers of power: 21st-century capitalism is intimately tied with the rise of emerging markets, not only as a factory but increasingly as a market itself. • Global governance: Weak global governance on trade and finance. Multinational corporations are the key nonstate actors.	• Relationship between workers and bosses in industrialized economies has changed in some places. Western factory workers have become accountants, nurses, and baristas in the service economy. • Interaction of markets and states varies. In Liberal Market Economy, states play a minimal role. In Coordinated Market Economy, states facilitate cooperation between businesses and unions.	• In Liberal Market Economies, service sector jobs replaced factory shops, but the pay and working conditions are worse. Leads to income inequality and resentment. • As businesses move easily around the globe, some states find it hard to tax at a level needed to pay for public programs.

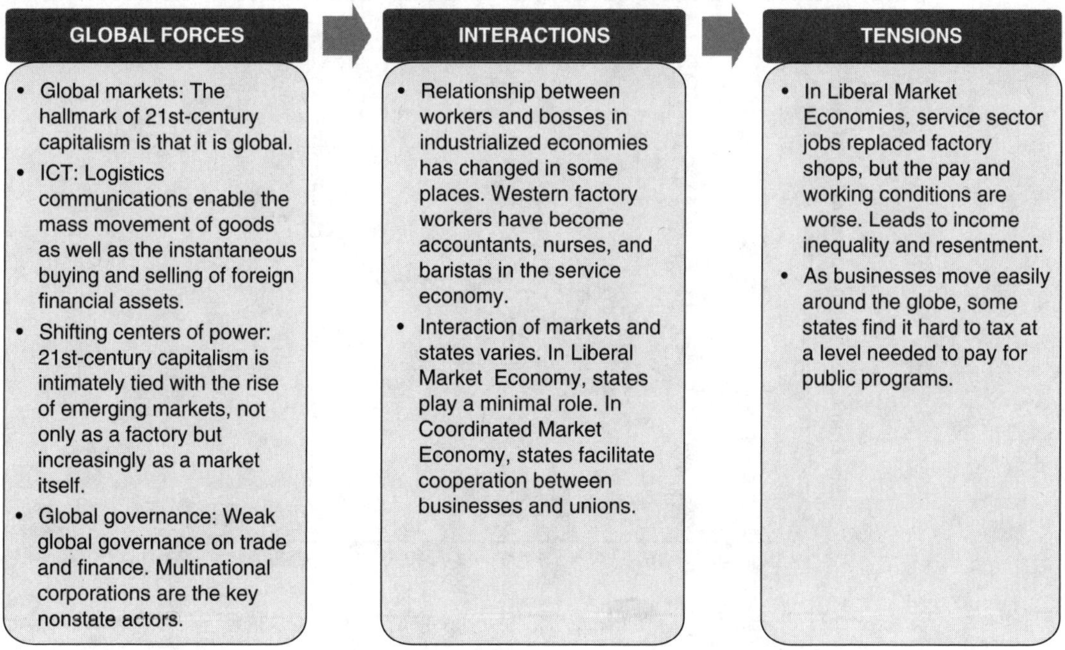

WHAT IS TRADE?

Trade involves the import and export of goods and services. For an example of an import, consider what you are wearing right now or the device in your pocket. For an example of an export, consider the international students in your class. From a financial perspective, international students purchase a U.S. service, in this case, a college degree. Money comes into the United States in the form of tuition, and we export the service the foreigner has purchased (leave aside for now the student who comes here to consume the service). Thus, U.S. higher education is like an export sector. When visas issued to foreign students declined under U.S. President Donald Trump, many observers of higher education decried the loss of income for colleges (and the U.S. students who were subsidized by foreign students), while Canadian colleges were glad to see a boost in their "exports."[7]

The incredible growth in global trade is so important that many consider it the defining feature of globalization and of the modern era. Figure 6.2 shows how important trade has become in the past half-century. The line shows the percentage of global gross domestic product (GDP) that comes from trade in merchandise. Note both the ups and downs as well as the strong upward trend over time. These trends are controversial. Some associate trade with sending middle class jobs abroad, while others say it leads to economic growth and that a rising tide lifts all boats. We want to know, though, is free trade good? Let's begin by looking at trade in theory and then at trade in practice.

See visualizations of global trade at http://wits.worldbank.org/trade-visualization.aspx and http://viz.ged-project.de/.

FIGURE 6.2

Growth in Global Trade, 1960–Present

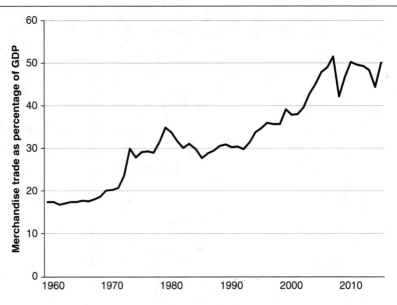

Source: Data are from the World Bank Development Indicators. https://data.worldbank.org/indicator/TG.VAL.TOTL .GD.ZS.

Trade in Theory

Should a country make it easy for its consumers to import goods cheaply by removing taxes on imports? Doing so would help consumers, but would it help the country's own export businesses? Views on whether a country should embrace free trade come in three broad schools. Liberals favor **free trade**. Mercantilists are economic nationalists who fear trade might make other countries wealthy at their expense. Structuralists think the global economy is organized in a way that hurts poor countries. Let's look at each.

Liberalism

Liberals favor free trade, and their view is probably the globally dominant one today. Liberal economic theory says that global welfare is enhanced when there are few barriers to trade. It is associated with people such as Adam Smith and Jagdish Bhagwati, with organizations such as the International Monetary Fund (IMF) and the World Trade Organization (WTO), and with policy ideas such as the Washington Consensus (see Chapter 9 on poverty and development). Some use liberalism interchangeably with neoliberalism. Where classical economic liberalism emphasized markets and free trade, neoliberalism is an ideology that sees all of life (government, healthcare, schooling) as a market that benefits from competition. Neoliberals follow economist Friedrich Hayek in seeing capitalism as not just economically efficient but as a morally correct way to order a society.[8]

Watch a LIVE map of cargo ships sailing everywhere in the world at https://www .marinetraffic.com/.

At the core of the classical liberal view of trade is the theory of **comparative advantage** associated with David Ricardo.[9] The idea of comparative advantage simply says that countries should specialize in what they do best, where "best" means most efficiently. It does not mean what one can produce most abundantly!

But how do we know what a country's comparative advantage is? According to the Heckscher–Ohlin Theorem, a country's comparative advantage will be in industries that make intensive use of the country's "abundant factors." There are three factors of production, meaning things that go into making a product: land (size and quality), labor (size and skill), and capital (money, machinery, etc.). So, if a country is abundant in high-quality land, its comparative advantage may be in exporting high-quality agricultural produce.

A country is abundant or scarce in a particular factor *relative* to or *compared* with the world average. For example, Bangladesh has an abundance of low-skill labor, so its comparative advantage is in low-tech industries like textiles. Sweden is abundant in high-skill labor, so its comparative advantage is in industries that make intensive use of high-skilled labor, such as software development. The liberal theory of trade holds that when countries specialize in their comparative advantages, all are better off from free trade: Bangladesh should not waste resources trying to invent the touchscreen phone, while Sweden should not make T-shirts. If all countries likewise specialize in their comparative advantages, liberals say that world output will be maximized and all resources will be used efficiently.

Importantly, every country has a comparative advantage in something even if it does not have an absolute advantage in any one thing. (An absolute advantage means that a country has the ability to produce a greater quantity of something, using the same amount of resources, than its competitors.)

free trade: reduction or removal of barriers to buying and selling across borders. Common barriers include tariffs or quotas on imported goods.

comparative advantage: economic principle that countries should specialize in what they do best, where "best" means most efficiently.

Even if Sweden could produce more T-shirts per year than Bangladesh (that is, if Sweden had an *absolute* advantage), Bangladesh could still have the comparative advantage in textiles.

Read about the Balassa Index, which attempts to figure out a country's comparative advantage at http://www2.econ.uu.nl/users/marrewijk/research/balassa.htm.

Mercantilism

Advocates of **mercantilism** are in favor of trade, but they think it should serve to strengthen the state or nation. Thus, mercantilists are often called "economic nationalists." In an economic downturn, mercantilists turn to policies that shield their country's industries from foreign competition and reduce their vulnerability to trading partners. Notable mercantilist and one of the framers of the U.S. Constitution Alexander Hamilton once argued that protection from global markets was necessary because trading freely with Europe would destroy America's infant industries before they had a chance to grow.

Few economists today would identify as mercantilists, but mercantilism still finds its way into policy debates even if the label is not used. It can be seen in debates over who "wins" from trade between countries even though economic theory says both trading partners gain. Mercantilism can also be seen in China's focus on exports, and on the United States's attempt to emulate them. In the United States, Republicans and Democrats in power have both tended to favor free trade, yet one hears constant talk of being "tough on China," which reflects a mercantilist way of seeing trade as making one vulnerable to other countries. In President Donald Trump's inaugural address, he told the world, "We must protect our borders from the ravages of other countries making our products, stealing our companies, and destroying our jobs. Protection will lead to great prosperity and strength." What's mercantilist here is the idea that a country that imports what it needs ("other countries making our products") is somehow vulnerable or poorer because of it, as well as the idea that economic prosperity and national strength go hand in hand.

Read "The New Mercantilist Challenge" by Dani Rodrik.[10]

Structuralism

Structuralist economic thought is more popular in developing countries and among civil society and academics in developed countries. **Structuralism** sees the international economic order as *structurally* unfair because it was set up by powerful countries to serve their own interests. Like mercantilists, structuralists do not see the international economy as a value-neutral free market but as something that can be very harmful for countries. They see wealthy and poor countries existing in an exploitative relationship since wealthy countries grew on the backs of today's poorer countries. Thus, the Global North and Global South are *structurally* connected. They are connected in history through colonialism, and they remain connected through many neo-colonial global organizations like the WTO. Famous structuralists—sometimes called "dependency theorists"—include Andre Gunder Frank, Fernando Cardoso, Immanuel Wallerstein, Ha-Joon Chang, and Robert Wade.

Many structuralists are not opposed to trade in theory, but they simply think the global system of trade is unfair to developing countries, and some are critical of mainstream economic concepts like comparative advantage. They say that countries have no "natural" advantage, but they *create* their

mercantilism: belief that trade is only good if it strengthens a state's power as well as its economy.

Structuralism: belief that global trade rules have been created by rich countries to protect their wealth. Hence, the global economy is "structurally" unfair to poor countries.

advantages through investment. They point to East Asian countries that actively invested in their own companies, which only over time became globally competitive.

Read an expert debate "Should Industrial Policy in Developing Countries Conform to Comparative Advantage or Defy It?."[11]

Trade in Practice

Although the global economy is liberalized (few barriers to trade), *all* states protect their domestic markets to some extent. Indeed, **protectionism** is the norm and pure free trade the exception (see Figure 6.3).

Countries make use of three common barriers to trade to protect their markets. First, countries use **tariffs**, which are taxes on imports. Tariffs make imported goods more expensive for the consumer, and thereby protect domestic producers from foreign competition. Second, countries apply **quotas** to limit imports. That policy can sometimes backfire on the consumer. In the 1980s, the U.S. government capped the number of Japanese cars that could be imported, hoping to spur sales of domestically made cars within the United States. But in the absence of that competition—without the ability to buy cheaper and more efficient Japanese cars—U.S. consumers in effect paid more for their cars than they would have done without the quota.

protectionism: government policies to favor domestic producers and discriminate against imported goods.

tariff: tax on imported goods.

quota: cap on the amount of imported goods.

FIGURE 6.3

Recent Increase in Global Protectionism

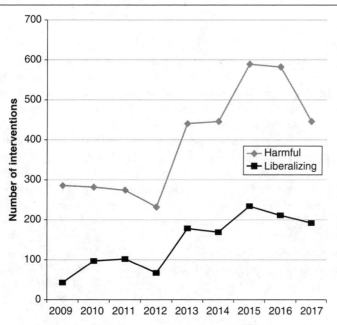

Source: Data are from Global Trader Alert, http://www.globaltradealert.org/global_dynamics/day-to_1028.

Are "ethical farming" standards a nontariff barrier?

iStock/tanukiphoto

Third, some states use nontariff barriers, which are any regulation that has the effect of discriminating against imports. For example, requiring that tuna must be farmed to certain ethical standards might seem like a well-meaning regulation. But if the regulation requires that the tuna farmer meet standards of safety or humane treatment of fish, then inevitably tuna farmers in poorer countries will be discriminated against. Thus, health and safety regulations are often labeled "nontariff barriers." Nontariff barriers are especially difficult issues to resolve: It seems legitimate that a democratic society can decide that tuna must be farmed ethically, but so, too, does it seem legitimate that poorer countries see this as a smoke screen designed to protect producers in wealthy countries.

Free Trade Agreements

Trade has been internationally institutionalized in the form of international governmental organizations (IGOs) such as the WTO and in hundreds of trade agreements signed between countries, like the North American Free Trade Agreement (NAFTA), the Association of Southeast Asian Nations (ASEAN), the European Union (EU), and Mercosur (see Figure 6.4 and Table 6.1). Although the WTO is small, with about one tenth the staff and operating budget of the World Bank, it is the most important international actor in global trade. In this section, we will learn about how it works and how it is viewed. The WTO's most important features are reciprocity, nondiscrimination, dispute settlement, and trade negotiation. Although its supporters see it as facilitating the incredible growth in global trade in recent decades, critics say it enforces trade deals that hurt poorer, smaller countries. Let's begin with its four main features.

First, the WTO encourages international trade. It is often mistakenly said that it enforces free trade. It does not. It enforces *reciprocal* trade, which means that when one state agrees to allow imports of a good, its trading partner reciprocates by allowing imports of its partner's goods. The form this takes in the WTO is the Most Favored Nation (MFN) status. Here's how it works: If Belgium agrees with Cameroon that it will reduce tariffs on the import of Cameroonian musical instruments, Belgium must offer that same reduced tariff to every other WTO member. There are some general exceptions: One rule allows wealthier countries to put lower tariffs on imports from developing countries, and countries can ignore MFN status if they have joined a regional trade agreement.

Second, WTO members agree not to discriminate in favor of their own companies. Governments are not allowed to give preferential treatment to their companies over things like taxes and regulations. This is controversial because many multinational corporations like Samsung were grown with the help of their government. Third, there is a system for settling disputes among member-states. A member-state may take another to the WTO's own dispute resolution body where outcomes are binding. A country found to be in violation of WTO rules must change its behavior or face a penalty. For example, in 2016, the WTO ruled that India's requirement that some solar power producers use solar cells made in India violated WTO rules because they effectively discriminated against non-Indian companies.[12] The country brought before the dispute resolution body most often is the United States, which has lost the majority of complaints made against it, although it has won most cases where it brought the complaint.

FIGURE 6.4

Map of Major Regional Trade Agreements

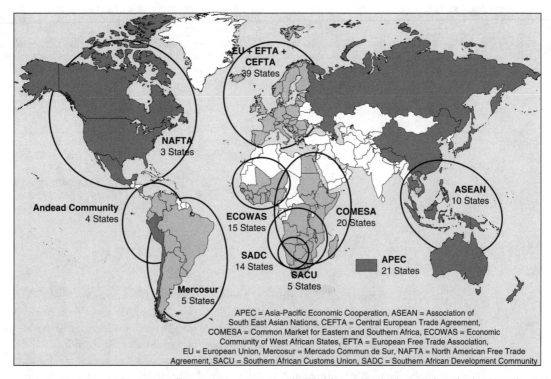

APEC = Asia-Pacific Economic Cooperation, ASEAN = Association of South East Asian Nations, CEFTA = Central European Trade Agreement, COMESA = Common Market for Eastern and Southern Africa, ECOWAS = Economic Community of West African States, EFTA = European Free Trade Association, EU = European Union, Mercosur = Mercado Commun de Sur, NAFTA = North American Free Trade Agreement, SACU = Southern African Customs Union, SADC = Southern African Development Community

Source: Adapted from map located at http://s3-ap-southeast-1.amazonaws.com/wpcd-uploads/uploads/2016/02/14080516/img26.jpg.

The WTO is also a forum for states to negotiate global trade agreements. Governments participate in discussions about what the WTO will govern in series of dialogues called "rounds." These negotiations are protracted because the number of states is large, the issues are politically sensitive, and the subject is complex. The current WTO agreement is a document over 20,000 pages long with detailed listings of tariffs countries have agreed on highly specific products such as dictionaries, maps, and postcards, all of which have their own tariff agreement. The most recent was the Uruguay Round, which concluded in 1994 with the creation of the WTO, succeeding the GATT. The current round of negotiations began in 2001 as the Doha Round. The negotiations were dominated by complaints from developing countries that wealthy countries would not open their agricultural markets, which would have a tremendously positive effect on poverty, but agricultural groups in wealthy countries remain powerful actors. Wealthier countries wanted concessions on intellectual property to protect against counterfeit goods like drugs, technology, and media in places like China. In the past decade or so, talks have progressed very slowly on the next round. Although the negotiations are technically still ongoing, optimism about their future was low even before the election of Donald Trump as president and the departure of the United Kingdom from the EU.

TABLE 6.1

How Integrated Are Two Economies? Balassa's Regional Integration

	Free trade area	Customs union	Common market	Economic union	Complete economic integration
What is it?	Tariffs and quotas removed between members of the free trade area	Common external tariff	Free movement of workers, services, and goods	Harmonization of some national policies, such as trade and agriculture	Single currency and single central bank
Example	North American Free Trade Agreement	Southern African Customs Union	European Union pre-1992	EU	None apart from states themselves, which internally are completely economically integrated

Source: Bela Balassa, *The Theory of Economic Integration* (Homewood, IL: R.D. Irwin, 1961).

The WTO is subject to some criticism. Many developing states experience the WTO as an entity created by powerful states to serve powerful states. Unlike the IMF and World Bank, within the WTO, every member has an equal vote regardless of size. Nevertheless, despite this equality, the largest trading powers effectively set the agenda in negotiations. In addition, wealthy countries can afford legal teams to petition the WTO's dispute settlement body, which is why the poorest countries rarely initiate disputes.[13] Transnational advocacy networks that are active on issues of trade also critique trade deals more broadly, and they don't just focus on the WTO. A major criticism is that free trade agreements give too much power to corporations. For example, the proposed Canada-EU free trade agreement (CETA) allowed investors to sue EU states for health or environmental laws that damage their businesses.[14] This would allow Canadian companies (as well as U.S. companies with Canadian subsidiaries) to sue EU states. Critics say this is an example of how free trade agreements erode national sovereignty and put profits before people.

Read about the Trade Justice Network, a transnational advocacy network on trade.[15]

Is Free Trade Good for Countries?

Is free trade good for countries? Is free trade good for people? Part of the difficulty in answering these questions is that the success of trade can be measured in different ways. Success is measured by liberals in terms of economic indicators like economic growth, and trade usually grows economies by moving resources into more efficient production. Mercantilists measure the success of trade in terms of growth in the power of a country, which can be understood in terms of vulnerability to or dependence on other economies. Structuralists tend to measure success in terms of trade's effect on sustainable development.

If the "experts" don't agree on free trade, it should not surprise us that voters are similarly torn. The *tension* arises because voters are workers *and* consumers and because, at a very general level, free trade is good for consumers but bad for workers in the industry concerned.[16] For example, if tariffs (taxes) on Vietnamese tires were lifted, millions of Italian consumers would save money on their tires, which they would either save or spend elsewhere in the economy. But the result would be joblessness for the few thousand workers in Italian tire factories. It makes sense, therefore, that the opinions on free trade are mixed when it means cheaper imports for most but job loss for some. Because some win and some lose with free trade, we say that trade has **redistributive effects**, which means that it affects who gets what in society.

An additional complicating factor is that trade is not merely an issue of economics: It also affects people's sense of national identity. A lively academic debate occurred following Donald Trump's 2016 presidential election victory about whether Trump voters were experiencing "economic anxiety" or "cultural anxiety." One side argued that Trump voters were people hurt by imports of manufactured goods from China and Mexico, while others argued that Trump voters were motivated more by identity politics than by their exposure to the global economy (see Chapter 5 on identity). Because most white voters supported Trump, the "cultural anxiety" theory held that many Trump voters had biases—however consciously held—against nonwhites and non-Americans. These biases were created or reinforced as decent working-class jobs many white communities depended on were lost to automation or outsourcing or were "taken" by immigrants. As the historically privileged position of some whites was threatened (think "War on Christmas"), the backlash came in the form of a rejection of liberal trade. Thus, Anatole Kaletsky's headline declared, "Trump's rise and Brexit vote are more an outcome of culture than economics," while Jed Kolko's headline stated, "Trump was stronger where the economy is weaker."[17]

Follow the debate:

Yes: Mireya Solis, Brookings Institution[18]

No: Jeronim Capaldo et al., Tufts University[19]

The ability of groups to insulate themselves from the redistributive effects of trade affects all of our lives. Consider the example of sugar. Why are U.S. soft drinks sweetened with corn syrup, while the rest of the world uses real sugar?[20] It's partly because sugar produced in the United States is 24 cents a pound compared with 15 cents a pound on the world market, so soft drink makers use corn syrup rather than real sugar to make their drinks. But why the difference? The U.S. government offers loans to U.S. sugar producers that are subsidized by the public, and it protects domestic sugar producers by taxing imports of sugar. The goal is to protect sugar producers from major volatility in prices, but the effect is that U.S. consumers pay almost twice what the rest of the world pays for sugar.

Although the sugar program increases the profits of some U.S. farms, the U.S. economy as a whole spends far more on sugar than it would if it paid the global price. This illustrates a key point about protectionism and the redistributive effects of trade: Those who suffer are small in number and find it easier to self-organize. Sugar beet and sugarcane farms account for less than 1% of U.S. farms, and only 1% of total farm production. But the sugar sector accounts for 33% of all campaign donations from crop industries![21] In contrast, it's not hard to see why 350 million Americans are not about to come together for a grand conference on sugar.[22]

redistributive effects: when trade policies affect who gets what in society.

The Trans-Pacific Partnership (TPP) was a free trade agreement signed in 2016 by 12 countries that border the Pacific Ocean. These countries represented about 40% of the entire global economy and almost one billion people. The agreement would have reduced or eliminated some 18,000 tariffs among members and would have boosted cooperation on issues such as business regulation. Ultimately, some members hoped it would lead to a single market similar to the European Union, in which goods, services, and labor could move freely as part of one large economy.

The Obama administration was an energetic force behind the agreement. In addition to the economic opportunities the TPP represented, the Obama administration also thought it had geo-strategic value by checking the rising power of China since so many members were in its neighborhood.

Although the TPP was a priority during the Obama administration, the deal was vilified (and ultimately killed) by presidential candidate Donald Trump, who called it "a rape of our country."[23] Upon declaring the TPP dead on his first day, President Donald Trump told a gathering of applauding union workers: "We're going to stop the ridiculous trade deals that have taken everybody out of our country and taken companies out of our country, and it's going to be reversed . . . I think you're going to have a lot of companies come back to our country."[24]

But the TPP made unusual bedfellows in U.S. politics. The anti-trade economic agenda of Trump supporters was new for the Republican Party, while trade skepticism had a longer heritage among progressives in the Democratic Party. During the 2016 presidential campaign, Democratic candidate Bernie Sanders criticized fellow Democrat Hillary Clinton for once referring to the TPP as the "gold standard in trade agreements." Thus, the campaign saw both Republican and Democratic candidates joined in a common criticism of trade deals.

Reflect

Should the United States have joined the TPP?

TPP members: Vietnam, Australia, Canada, Mexico, Peru, Chile, Malaysia, Singapore, Brunei.

Don't confuse the TPP with the TTIP (Transatlantic Trade and Investment Partnership), which is a trade agreement between the United States and the EU.

---

fair trade: voluntary agreement between producers of raw materials and manufacturers of consumer products to return a larger share of a final price back to the original producer, usually in a developing country.

Liberals do not deny that there are winners and losers from trade. But rather than change the nature of trade, they prefer to compensate people for their losses and retrain them for different industries. Critics say this is insufficient, and that even though there may be gains from trade, the social costs (not just the individual costs) are also very large, when one considers the problems associated with unemployment, such as poverty and crime. Worse, they contend that growing inequality in developed countries will lead to more support for protectionism and protection from global markets.[25] Again, scholars point to the election of Donald Trump as evidence of what happens when a country's economic elite pursues free trade while ignoring the economic suffering of the losers from trade.[26]

Read "Trade Adjustment Assistance Works!" by Howard Rosen at http://blogs.piie.com/realtime/?p=2376.

Others critique trade from the perspective of poorer countries. Civil society organizations call for **fair trade** over free trade, by which they mean a trading relationship in which the poor farmer or fisherman is the real beneficiary of selling goods to developed countries. The most famous example of this is probably coffee, but one can buy a variety of fair trade goods including soccer balls, chocolate, or shea butter.

Read about Fairtrade International (FLO), an international nongovermental organization that sets fair trade standards at http://www.fairtrade.net/.

The balance of evidence suggests fair trade improves the lives of producers, but the results are somewhat mixed.[27] Recent research has ignited a debate about whether fair trade does improve lives. Development economists studied fair trade certified coffee, tea, and flowers in Ethiopia and Uganda and found no evidence that the lives of those employed in production were any better than those employed in non–fair trade certified production, in terms of either wages or living conditions.[28] Two main problems seem to be at issue. First, it is possible that better farmers may decide to become fair trade certified, so it is not surprising that they have higher incomes. Second, large plantations consist of farmers and their laborers, and some research suggests laborers do not get much benefit from fair trade.[29]

iStock/ranplett

Read the debate on Fair Trade: Amrita Narlikar and Dan Kim write about Unfair Trade at http://www .foreignaffairs.com/articles/139127/amrita-narlikar-and-dan-kim/unfair-trade and Harriet Lamb responds with Fairtrade Is Fair at http://www.foreignaffairs.com/ articles/139837/harriet-lamb/fairtrade-is-fair.

FINANCE: BORROWERS, LENDERS, AND DEBT

Although liberal economic theory has held that specializing and trading in one's comparative advantage makes both trading partners better off, a related belief has been that capital (money, machines, buildings) must be free to invest in productive activities. Finance is what makes it possible to expand an economy. Countries, corporations, and households need to be able to borrow to invest in their future. The free movement of capital means that money is moved around the world 24 hours a day. It goes *to* actors who need money, such as banks who want to provide loans, governments who need to pay their civil servants, or businesses that need to buy new equipment. It comes *from* actors with money to lend or invest: global banks like HSBC or ICBC, private investors like Goldman Sachs, and other financial actors who send their money outside of their own country in search for an investment. It includes states with **sovereign wealth funds** looking to reinvest their national wealth elsewhere, such as Norway's *Government Pension Fund of Norway* with almost $1 trillion that it invests around the world.

The main actor in international finance is the IMF. It is known as the "lender of last resort," meaning the organization that will lend to an indebted government when no one else will. This recognition of a shared fate is a core reason for its existence: It is bad for the whole world, not just the country concerned, if an economy collapses. The IMF was created in 1944 as a Bretton Woods institution with the purpose of serving a role in monetary (i.e., currency) relations, but gradually it has expanded its role to help countries deal with debt and currency crises. The IMF is not a private bank. It is an IGO with 188 member-states, and as such, it is operated by, is resourced by, and works for states first and foremost.

sovereign wealth fund: country's investment fund. Usually money from sale of energy exports, and used to invest elsewhere in the world.

Like the World Bank, the power that any one member has in the IMF is proportional to that country's contribution. Together the United States and EU countries contribute about half of IMF resources, meaning they have a veto over the Fund's activities since all decisions require an 85% supermajority. Because the purpose of the IMF is to bail out countries in crisis, it needs to have an extraordinary amount of money on hand. At any given time, it holds about half a trillion U.S. dollars from member-states, and it can call on another half. Although the IMF has traditionally—and controversially—been associated with developing countries, its purpose is not expressly developmental. In the recent global financial crisis, it loaned billions to Ireland, Greece, Spain, and Portugal.

See how much power each state has in the IMF at https://www.imf.org/external/np/sec/memdir/members.aspx.

Finance Is the Engine of Growth

portfolio investment: ownership of "paper" assets such as stocks and bonds. Does not involve managing the asset.

The main forms of cross-border investment are **portfolio investment** and foreign direct investment (FDI). Think of portfolio investment as the purchase of paper, like stocks, which can be sold as quickly as it was bought. Think of FDI as money that gets sunk into a country in the form of building factories. Under portfolio investment, the investor does not manage the asset. For example, when a Chilean company lends money to the Nicaraguan government, the Chilean lender does not directly manage the Nicaraguan government, but it still hopes to receive interest and eventual repayment. Most portfolio investment into developing countries is a government borrowing from a financial institution in a developed country, which is called a "sovereign loan." Because a portfolio investment can be the purchase of a stock or currency for short-term gain that can be sold very quickly, this form of finance is often referred to as "hot money," and it is associated with speculative capitalism and with market instability (see the discussion on financial hyperglobalization later in this chapter).

FDI involves active management of the asset. It typically comes in the form of a multinational company building a factory in a developing country, where it manages production. This is called the internationalization of production. The 100 largest multinational corporations each have an average of over 500 foreign affiliates across 50 countries.[30] For example, General Electric operates over 200 plants in 26 countries. Most of what is produced in each plant is just one part of an overall product. Thus, GE engages in international trade with *itself* (known as "intrafirm trade") whenever it sends, say, dishwasher parts built in Turkey and water heaters produced in Malaysia to an assembly plant in Tennessee (see the Introduction for discussion of Fordism).

FDI presents huge opportunities for companies. Since GE manages its own factory, its ability to maximize its profits and its return on its investment is greatest since it can make all the decisions. The downside of FDI is that, unlike portfolio investment, FDI cannot be quickly withdrawn. If there is a government coup or a revolution, portfolio investors can sell shares in an instant, but it would take GE weeks or months to sell off or ship out its entire factory.

We see global trends in FDI in Figure 6.5. First, note the size of FDI in 1995; it is much lower than it is today. Second, note the three peaks followed by dips (or crashes) around 1999–2000, 2007, and 2011–2012. Third, see how most FDI is money going to developed countries (Figure 6.6). This is an important fact of FDI: It is mostly investment *between* wealthy countries. But fourth, note that the amount of FDI that is going to developing economies has grown steadily in the past decade.

In Figure 6.7, we see how money going into emerging markets began to increase in the 1990s, and then again in the late 2000s. The extraordinary growth in investment into developing countries since the 1990s is partly because of financial liberalization, meaning the ease with which money has been able to move around the world. One way capital is liberalized is when a country removes capital controls. Capital controls enabled government to retain some control over their economy. For example, if a government worried that foreign money was fueling a property bubble, they could prevent the buying and selling of their currency or limit how much money a person could take out of the country, which would make their country less attractive to foreigners. With less capital coming in, the economy will slow down and the property bubble will quietly deflate rather than burst into a full-blown recession. Capital controls were a way for countries in the Bretton Woods System (1945–1971) to retain some control over their economy, but they were gradually removed in industrialized countries in the 1970s and 1980s. By the 1990s, controls were mostly gone and capital (money) was free to go most places in the world. Money to developing countries grew astronomically. Money flew into emerging markets everywhere, and asset bubbles were often the result.

Watch a short explanation of capital controls at https://www.cnbc.com/video/2014/12/17/ cnbc-explains-what-are-capital-controls-anyway.html.

Financial *Hyper*globalization

By removing capital controls, the world has entered a period some call **financial *hyper*globalization**. Neoliberals had encouraged the removal of capital controls. Development economists thought removing restrictions on capital would mean more investment in developing countries, while banks were

FIGURE 6.5

Trends in Foreign Direct Investment (FDI)

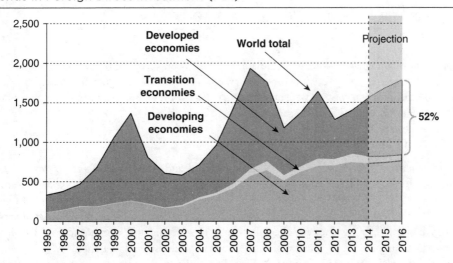

Source: United Nations Conference on Trade and Development, *World Investment Report 2014*, p. xiii. http:// unctad.org/en/PublicationChapters/wir2014ch0_en.pdf.

financial *hyper*globalization: idea that since the 1990s, allowing finance—the buying and selling of financial assets such as stocks, bonds, insurance, mortgages, or currencies—to move freely around the world has become the point of globalization rather than a means to an end. Under financial *hyper*globalization, global political and economic systems serve the interests of finance, rather than finance serving the interests of the global population.

Asian Financial Crisis: in 1997, investors worried that some Southeast Asian countries might not be able to repay international loans. Panic led to massive withdrawals of investment from Thailand, South Korea, Indonesia, and Malaysia. Because some countries had fixed the value of their currency, the financial panic also led to currency crises.

FIGURE 6.6

Top Spenders and Recipients of FDI, 2014-2015

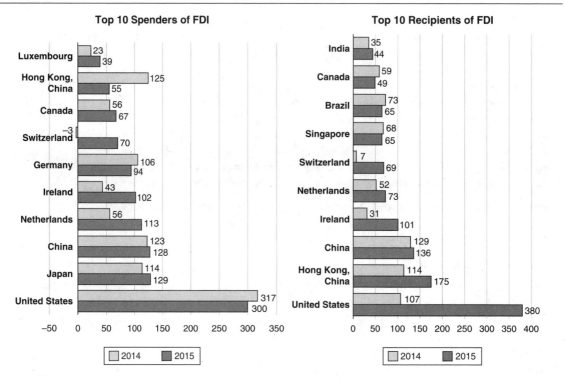

Top 10 Spenders of FDI

Luxembourg	23 / 39
Hong Kong, China	125 / 55
Canada	56 / 67
Switzerland	-3 / 70
Germany	106 / 94
Ireland	43 / 102
Netherlands	56 / 113
China	123 / 128
Japan	114 / 129
United States	317 / 300

Top 10 Recipients of FDI

India	35 / 44
Canada	59 / 49
Brazil	73 / 65
Singapore	68 / 65
Switzerland	7 / 69
Netherlands	52 / 73
Ireland	31 / 101
China	129 / 136
Hong Kong, China	114 / 175
United States	107 / 380

☐ 2014 ■ 2015

Source: UNCTAD, "World Investment Report 2016," pp. 5-6, http://unctad.org/en/PublicationsLibrary/wir2016_en.pdf.

happy to move into markets with great growth potential. They were both right, as huge sums flowed into developing countries. The downside, however, has been financial instability and crises. It now seems as though capital controls were one of the few defenses developing countries had against flows of "hot money" in and out of their economies.

The Asian Financial Crisis

capital controls: policies used to control the amount of money coming in and out of a country.

To understand how financial *hyper*globalization, crises, and **capital controls** are related, let's look at the **Asian Financial Crisis** that began in 1997 with the collapse of Thailand's currency.[31] To attract investors in the early 1990s, Thailand had offered good savings rates for investors to deposit money in Thai banks. When an investor moved money into the country, they usually brought dollars to exchange for the Thai currency, and the dollars sat in the government's currency reserve. Thai banks then loaned this money from international depositors to businesses and households. Money flooding into the country led to overinvestment in things like property, with more and more money driving up values. When it emerged that many Thai banks had made bad loans, people worried about the

FIGURE 6.7

Portfolio Investment in Emerging Markets

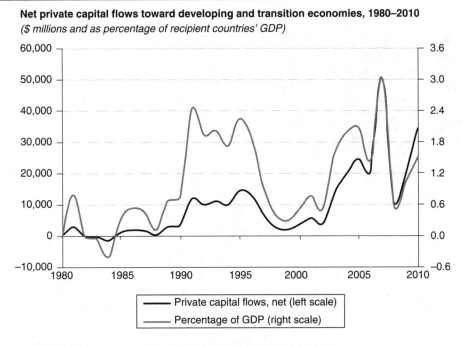

Net private capital flows toward developing and transition economies, 1980–2010
($ millions and as percentage of recipient countries' GDP)

Private capital flows, net (left scale)
Percentage of GDP (right scale)

Source: UNCTAD, "Development and Globalization: Facts and Figures," 2012, 15.

ability of Thai borrowers to pay their debts, and thus of Thai banks to pay back their foreign lenders. International investors began to withdraw their money. Since Thailand had to allow people to withdraw in U.S. dollars, they began to run low on the currency. The problem was that the Thai baht was fixed to the U.S. dollar. If their exchange rate wasn't fixed, the withdrawals would have devalued the Thai currency and Thailand would have had to pay out in fewer dollars. As it was, however, Thailand quickly ran out of U.S. dollars. Investors then worried that if they withdrew too slowly there would be no more dollars left for them, so the scramble began to get out of the country.

Watch the documentary "Commanding Heights," which shows the unfolding of the Asian Financial Crisis at https://www.youtube.com/watch?v=9jH7iQTSHK8.

Thus, the currency speculation began. To maintain the credibility of a fix to the U.S. dollar, the Thai central bank had to use its reserve of U.S. dollars to buy up its own currency whenever it was sold in international currency markets. But as its dollar reserves ran low, speculators doubted whether the Thai central bank was prepared to keep spending dollars to buy all the Thai baht being sold off. In the end, Thailand had to abandon its fixed exchange rate midcrisis, and it would no longer use its reserve of U.S. dollars to buy back its own currency on international markets.

No longer fixed, the baht plummeted. The effects were devastating. For Thai households, a plummeting currency meant their money bought little in global markets, such that imports of food, clothing, and medication become much more expensive. Thais became much poorer almost overnight. Thai businesses that had international loans denominated in dollars went bankrupt because now far more baht were required to pay back loans. These households and businesses had little to do with the asset bubbles and speculative currency attacks that brought down the economy, but they paid the price nonetheless. And because of the interconnectedness of the global economy, the panic spread to neighboring Taiwan, Indonesia, and Malaysia, causing Malaysian Prime Minister Mahathir bin Mohamad to complain of the "rape of our share market" and for society to be "protected from unscrupulous profiteers."[32]

Office of the Vice President, The Republic of Indonesia

The response of the IMF in all of this drew criticism. In return for helping these countries in crisis, the IMF, known as the "lender of last resort," required that they make changes to their economic policies, including lower government spending and liberalized financial markets. These were Washington Consensus policies (which we explain in more detail in Chapter 9). Many said these prescriptions missed the mark entirely: The problem was not economies that were poorly run but economies that could not stand up to the weight of highly mobile capital that could move in and out of a country with extraordinary speed, causing bubbles, panics, and currency collapses along the way. These were otherwise sound economies.

Because of crises like the one in Asia, people began to suggest that capital controls could have helped these emerging markets control their economies and avoid collapse. In fact, major figures in the world of liberal economics, such as Brad DeLong, *The Economist*, and the IMF are sympathetic to capital controls and point out that free trade and free capital are not the same thing.[33] The problem with the free movement of money is that countries—often developing countries—find themselves trying to convince international investors not to suddenly withdraw all of their money from their country when some minor crisis happens. To placate international investors, a developing country might raise its interest rates to entice international capital to deposit in its bank. The problem with this is that the interest rates paid by its own businesses to borrow also go up, hurting the economy. Thus, emerging markets are highly vulnerable to the whims of highly mobile global capital.

Is the IMF Helpful or Harmful to Countries in Crisis?

IMF supporters point out that it is willing to lend to countries the world has abandoned. As the lender of last resort, it is the difference between crisis and chaos. Not only does the IMF provide loans to pay public salaries when private markets will not, but it also brings expertise in dealing with financial crises to governments for whom economic calamities may be new. And recall, they say, that countries go *voluntarily* to the IMF.

Critics counter with two points. First, they criticize it for being undemocratic and nontransparent. Critics say it is structurally biased against developing countries because the wealthiest countries get the largest vote share. It has been one of the slowest intergovernmental organizations to become

The financial crisis that began in 2007 had many of the components of financial crises of the past: Foreign capital stimulated the U.S. economy while encouraging risky lending and too much consumption, ultimately ending in a crash. What made it remarkable was its sheer enormity. In late 2008, the U.S. housing market was revealed to rest on a mountain of bad investments by consumers and by financial institutions including banks. There was so much borrowing between major companies that, by mid-2009 when banks stopped lending to businesses, many large companies went out of business or were nationalized (bought) by governments. Employers found that banks were unwilling to lend, so they stopped hiring. Reduced economic activity meant lower taxes and higher unemployment expenditures for governments, so public debt soared.

The crisis quickly had global ramifications, as credit that was once easy to borrow in the United States and invest in emerging markets quickly dried up. The crisis became strongly identified with the United States and then Europe, such that Brazil's President Lula said: "It is a crisis caused and encouraged by the irrational behaviour of white people with blue eyes . . . who before the crisis appeared to know everything, but are now showing that they know nothing."[34]

The U.S. mortgage crisis soon became a European debt crisis, with European countries suffering from a mixture of bad loans, overborrowing, and wasteful spending by governments, businesses, and households.[35] What made the problems in Europe drag on for so many years has to do with the common currency, the euro, used by 19 of the 28 EU member-states. When a country is in a financial crisis, it can manipulate the value of its currency and interest rate. This is called "monetary policy." For example, if an economy is growing slowly, a central bank could lower its core interest rate, which is the rate at which all banks borrow from the central bank. Doing this would make borrowing cheaper and lead to more borrowing and more economic activity. Alternatively, a country could print more of its own currency, knowing that an increase in supply would cause the currency to be devalued since it is now oversupplied, and a cheaper currency would boost the country's exports.

This is important for understanding the Eurozone crisis: If the Greek or Spanish governments want to boost their economies, they cannot alter the value of their currency because in joining the euro, they gave up control. The euro floats in global currency markets, so its value is not set by any bank or country. This means that a major instrument governments use to get out of financial problems is not available to them if they use a common currency. This is a major part of the Eurozone's problem.[36]

Reflect

One of the tensions during the Global Financial Crisis is who would pay for public education. How has the Global Financial Crisis affected your college tuition? Should the cost of higher education mostly come from taxpayers, or from individual students? Use this data visualization to see how your state has changed its reliance on individual students versus state taxpayers to pay for public college. Click on the "Student Share" tab at the top, and then select your state.

Source: https://public.tableau.com/profile/sheeo#!/vizhome/SHEFInteractiveStateData_1/About

more transparent. Over the past two decades or so, organizations like the World Bank have made it easier for civil society watchdogs to monitor their decisions and meetings, but the IMF has been criticized for remaining insular.[37]

Read about civil society attempts to open up the IMF: 50 Years Is Enough campaign at http://www.50years.org/.

Second, they criticize how it handles financial crises. The austerity measures it requires in return for help "force" countries to cut back on spending on healthcare, education, or childcare, which can be socially destabilizing in addition to plunging people into poverty. Requiring austerity is also problematic when in many cases government spending was not the initial problem. In Spain, for example, economic troubles were rooted in risky lending by private banks.

In addition, although it is an intergovernmental organization that facilitates *interactions* between states, some say it serves the interests of private creditors over debtors. For example, if the Greek government turns to the IMF for help because it and Greek consumers have borrowed too much from German banks, the IMF's rescue package will require German banks to be repaid. Critics say that if German banks made bad loans, they should pay the price for it, something known as taking a "haircut." But the German government will support its banks since the savings of German pensioners are at risk should Greece default. Thus, Germany will use its influence within the IMF to force Greece to repay the German banks. This is why critics say the IMF does not serve the interests of the debtor (here, Greece) but that of the creditor (here, German banks).

Debate: Has the IMF outlived its usefulness? Read the debate at http://www.debate.org/opinions/has-the-imf-and-world-bank-outlived-their-usefulness.

CURRENCIES

In the previous section, we read about how borrowing and investment move in and out of countries. But another global market sits below the surface of global trade and investment. This is the global currency market. Although we take it for granted today, it is not inevitable that Ethiopian coffee farmers can sell to Dutch consumers since Ethiopia uses the birr while the Dutch use the euro. What makes the trade possible is that both governments agree that birr can be exchanged for euros and vice versa. Currency exchange thus makes it possible for people, goods, and services to move between different economies. Beyond that, currencies also matter—and are the source of much international tension—because the price at which one currency is exchanged for another can have powerful effects on prices within both countries, such as the price of a mortgage, food, transport, or workers' salaries. In this section, we will learn about the international agreements that (sometimes) make it possible for currencies to be exchanged with one another, as well as about the tensions that can emerge.

The value of a currency is affected by how much demand there is for it: If the rest of the world needs U.S. dollars, it increases the demand for dollars and the "price" (i.e., the value) of the dollar goes up relative to other currencies. On Monday, your $1 might buy you 1 euro's worth of goods on a Spanish website. But if the dollar went "up" in relation to the euro, on Tuesday, your $1 buys you 2 euros' worth of stuff. Your wealth hasn't changed, but as an importer of Spanish goods, you now seem wealthier. Conversely, Spanish consumers now pay more to import the same good from the United States: $1's worth of goods used to cost them 1 euro but now costs them 2 euros. Generally, therefore, consumers like currencies to be strong and exporters like them to be weak.

Currencies can be "hard" or "soft." Hard currencies are used in everyday international exchange. These are the currencies of major, reliable economies like the United States, Eurozone, Switzerland, United Kingdom, Canada, and Japan. Soft currencies are just used in their country or region, and they are not used in international business. Developing countries with soft currencies have to buy hard currencies to do international business or to pay their international loans that are denominated in a hard currency. They generally do this by borrowing it, or by earning it through exports, which are paid for in a hard currency. Importantly, this also reveals that currencies are not naturally or inevitably convertible into one another. Countries have to agree to allow their currencies to be converted. This means countries must cooperate if economic activity is to take place across their borders.

Exchange Rate Systems

Currencies are of interest to international studies for three reasons. First, they affect the prosperity of people and nations. Second, states are engaged in fights over currency. Every recent U.S. presidential election has involved tough-talking candidates decrying China's currency manipulation, and global economic actors worry about the possibility of currency wars. The problem is that some countries are accused of keeping the value of their currencies artificially low, which helps their exporters but hurts exporters in other countries.[38] Third, there is no global governance on the issue. In this section, we will see how countries have tried with varying success to cooperate with one another on currencies.

Gold Standard

The Gold Standard was an international system that lasted from the 1870s until World War I. Different currencies were pegged to a set price of gold, and countries had to have enough gold to match the amount of their currency in supply. A country with a negative balance-of-payments (it spent more money on trade and other things than it earned) would sell some of its gold to earn enough currency to pay its bills. The idea underpinning the Gold Standard was that holders of currency (shopkeepers, bankers, miners) had to believe that the currency was backed by *something*, that it was not just paper. Under the Gold Standard, one could in theory exchange bank notes for actual gold. The Gold Standard was hugely beneficial for global economic activity. It enabled long-distance, high-value trade because businesses could trust that their trading partners' currency would be worth something many years into their trading relationship. The Gold Standard began to fall apart in the 1930s, however, as many countries faced social pressure to spend more money on services than they could match with their gold supplies.

Bretton Woods Monetary System

The **Bretton Woods Monetary System** was created by the United States and its allies after World War II.[39] One of its aims was to avoid **competitive devaluations**, in which a country tries to boosts its exports by setting the value of its currency artificially low. Every country has an incentive to devalue this way, but if all countries did, no one would benefit. In the Bretton Woods Monetary System, one ounce of gold was set at US$35, while other countries had "adjustable pegs," meaning currency values were fixed for long periods but governments were allowed to adjust them occasionally. Thus, the Bretton Woods monetary regime was a compromise: By reducing the volatility of exchange rates, it enhanced global economic exchange, but by allowing occasional readjustment, it allowed states to manage their domestic situation when necessary. This system worked because the United States had the largest amount of gold backing its currency.

Because the dollar was set to a specific value of gold, the U.S. government could print dollars without worrying about weakening its value, which it did for the Vietnam War. This led to European

Bretton Woods Monetary System: agreement on currency exchange among mostly Western nations after World War II. Non-U.S. members set their currencies to certain values of US$, and the United States set the rate at $35 for an ounce of gold (also see Chapter 1).

competitive devaluations: when a country tries to boost its exports by reducing the value of its own currency.

complaints that the dollar was being cheapened by the U.S. government printing it so heavily. European countries had to buy U.S. dollars to keep their currencies in line with the dollar, but this restricted their economic policy freedom because they could have put their purchasing power to other ends. In 1971, Nixon was worried that European countries might try to convert the dollars in their bank of actual gold, so without notice, he declared that dollars were no longer convertible to gold. This effectively ended the exchange rate system.[40]

floating currency regime: price of a currency is not formally set by a government but by global supply and demand.

FLOATING

Most currencies today "float." Their value is not backed by any commodity like silver or gold, and they are not pegged to the value of another currency. Instead, their value is set by global demand (read about global currency trading in Chapter 1). The system is referred to as a **floating currency regime** that is a flexible or a managed float exchange rate system. Under a managed float, states buy and sell currencies, including their own, in an intentional effort to affect their currency's value. This is one function of China buying huge amounts of U.S. private-sector and government debt (i.e., loaning you money for college): by creating demand for the debt in U.S. dollars, it elevates demand for dollars themselves, thus keeping the value of the U.S. dollar high relative to the Chinese yuan, which is good for Chinese exports and bad for U.S. exports. In the Introduction, we learned how China's currency policy created unemployment in Zambia. Officially, the yuan is pegged to a basket of currencies and the Chinese government allows its value to change. Unofficially, however, the government intervenes to ensure that the currency is kept below that of the United States to give its exporters a competitive edge. This is why many accuse China of being a "currency manipulator" even though China has not kept its currency artificially low for several years now.[41]

Currency Politics

balance of payments: accounting record of an economy's transactions with the rest of the world.

At the center of the disputes are **balance of payments** and what some call the problem of "**surplus**" **economies**. Every country has a balance of payments that registers all monetary transactions between it and the rest of the world. All money coming into a country is registered as an inflow. This includes money from the export of goods and services, money sent in or out by migrants, or foreign aid. Imports represent money spent on the rest of the world, and the amount is calculated as an outflow.[42] This has nothing to do with government revenue or budgets; it refers to the entire economy.

surplus economy: economy that exports more goods and services than it imports, which mathematically requires that the country also import more financial assets than it exports. China, Japan, and Germany are major surplus economies.

The United States has a large deficit mostly because it imports more goods and services than it exports (see Figure 6.8). Again, here we are talking about the entire U.S. economy, of which the budget of the federal government is only one part. When we import goods, foreigners end up with dollar bills, which they receive when we buy/import their goods. To get more dollar bills to import more, we need to get some dollar bills back. Since foreigners aren't interested in importing from the United States, and thus won't give dollar bills back to the United States, we can attract dollar bills back by selling financial assets to foreigners. This is how a country can pay for its imports when the rest of the world isn't interested in the country's exports. The United States is a "deficit country" because it has had a trade deficit for decades, but the rest of the world buys huge sums of U.S. financial assets, such as U.S. government bonds or shares in Apple. Therefore, the United States has a trade deficit but a "capital account" surplus; that is, we export more financial assets to foreigners than we import from them.

Figure 6.8 shows three broad periods in U.S. economic history. In the first, from 1790 until the late 1800s, the United States generally imported more than it exported. It had high tariffs during this period, while it also imported goods for growing cities and factories. In the second period, until after World War II, the United States exported more than it imported. Infrastructure in the United States was not harmed during the world wars, so the United States was in a position to export machinery and consumer goods to countries trying to recover from war. But since the 1970s, the United States has had very large trade deficits. These ballooned in the 1980s and 2000s. The United States was able to import more goods than it exported because foreigners were happy to buy a different kind of U.S. export: financial assets, such as stocks and bonds.

In recent history, the United States has sold its own bonds (government debt) to the rest of the world. Saudi, Russian, and German purchases of U.S. property help the U.S. economy to balance its accounts, effectively providing the economy the money it needs for consumers' imports and government spending. China and Germany do the opposite: Money earned from exports does not go into workers' pockets but gets recycled into their export industries. Many countries say this is unfair, and that one of the big problems in the international economy today are these surplus economies.

FIGURE 6.8

Trade Balance in the United States Since 1790

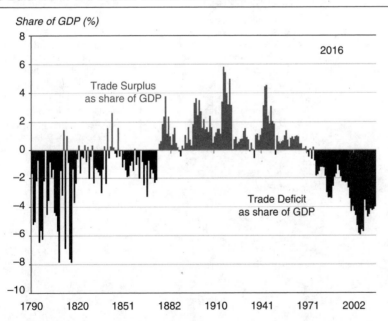

Source: The White House, "Economic Report of the President: Together with The Annual Report of the Council of Economic Advisers" (Washington, D.C., 2018). p. 231.

https://www.whitehouse.gov/wp-content/uploads/2018/02/ERP_2018_Final-FINAL.pdf.

Their surpluses should result in appreciation of their own currencies or increases in their citizens' consumption. But instead of allowing this, they send their surplus out again into the world, which means other countries must, by definition, be deficit countries.

When China receives the dollars the United States sends over for purchases, it can (a) use them to buy goods and services from the United States (i.e., import from the United States), (b) leave the dollars in its central bank vault, or (c) buy financial assets like property in the United States. It turns out that it does mostly b and c. China builds up very large reserves of dollars, while some money comes in to buy U.S. assets. This contributes to inflation in the United States because when a foreigner buys a house, it increases values without increasing productivity. This is why critics complain that surplus countries like China "export inflation." Many countries would like Germany and China to "rebalance" by exporting less and by allowing their consumers to import more, but they are under no obligation to do so. Whereas in trade we have the WTO, and in security we have the United Nations Security Council, there is no international organization or arena dedicated to helping countries cooperate for mutual gain on the issue of balancing their payments (see Figure 6.9).

FIGURE 6.9

Global Forces, Interactions, Tensions, and Currency Politics

GLOBAL FORCES	INTERACTIONS	TENSIONS
• Global markets: Currencies enable global markets, but one country might manage its currency in a way that hurts another country. • ICT: Instantaneous communication enables the buying and selling of currencies to the tune of *billions* per day. • Shifting power centers: China in particular has been reluctant to allow its currency to rise, making the exports of all other countries less competitive. • Governance: Very little cooperation between states on currency tensions, and a proliferation of nonstate actors add to the complexity: Merchants (importers/exporters), currency traders, and multinational corporations.	• Saudia Arabia, Germany and Russia buy U.S. property, which is considered an export of a financial asset. • China receives dollars when Americans import Chinese products. China uses some of those dollars to buy U.S. government debt, effectively lending money to the U.S. government so the government can spend more than it collects in taxes.	• By buying America's financial assets such as mortgages, property values in the U.S. go up but productivity (and thus wages) do not. • Exporters in the U.S. might like China to import more, but there is no international body to make China and the U.S. cooperate on this.

SUMMARY

To conclude, let's consider how our theme of interactions has mattered for global money. It is impossible to talk about global money without talking about interactions. In fact, so central is global money to contemporary globalization that many define it in terms of money. The complex economic interaction of states and nonstate actors is one of the defining features of our time. Interactions can be enormously beneficial when they involve mutual cooperation. We saw this during the Gold Standard and the Bretton Woods Monetary System, in which the agreements made between states allowed for shared prosperity. But interactions can cause problems when they are conflictual. We see this in the inability of developing countries to control flows of hot money in and out of their countries, as well as in the conflict between China and the United States over currency manipulation.

Let's also reflect on our four cross-cutting global forces. The first is global markets, which is the subject of the chapter. The second is information and communications technology. Its effects can be seen in computerized trading, which is the hallmark of global exchange of things like stocks and currencies. Computerized trading is one of the things that enables portfolio investment and capital in general to be so mobile because a trader in Hong Kong can sell shares in a Latin American company only seconds after a news flash online. Information and communications technology is also what enables would-be borrowers in developing countries to market themselves and to reach those with capital to invest.

The third global force is shifting centers of power. An important part of this is the rise of the rest. Emerging markets have been recipients of extraordinary amounts of investment that has made it possible for them to expand, as has their ability to sell goods to wealthy countries. Perhaps more than other issues in this textbook, global civil society is less visible in the arena of global money in part because there are few opportunities for institutional representation since so much of global money (trade, finance, and currencies) is not governed in any way. But global civil society is not absent, of course: Actors are present on issues like fair trade and in pressing the IMF to be more open in its operations. Transnational actors are not just civil society actors, of course, and the story of global money cannot be told without reference to global corporations that move billions on a daily basis.

The final global force is global governance. Here the picture is quite mixed. In trade, there is the WTO, which is an effective organization in the sense that countries want to participate in it, and in doing so, the WTO rules require them to change how they run their countries. In finance, there is the IMF, the lender of last resort. It is a well-resourced and experienced institution that continues to play a prominent role in global finance. Many criticize how it handles crises, however, and it is critiqued for failing to put the welfare of poor countries and poor people above that of the creditors who make bad loans. In the area of currency, there is essentially no global governance at all, and countries have not been successful in cooperating on how to manage their currencies.

KEY TERMS

Asian Financial Crisis 168

balance of payments 174

Bretton Woods Monetary
   System 173

capital controls 168

capitalism 152

commodification 153

comparative advantage 157

competitive devaluations 173

fair trade 164

financial *hyper*globalization 167

floating currency regime 174

Fordism 154

free trade 157

Marxism 154

QUESTIONS FOR REVIEW

1. How has the interaction of states on currency issues changed in the past century?

2. Most FDI has traditionally gone from one wealthy country to another, but in recent decades, this trend has been changing. What global forces might contribute to this change?

3. Is the United States a "surplus economy"? Why or why not? What are the tensions that result from this?

4. Identify a tariff on a product you recently used. Who might be harmed, and who might be helped, by the tariff?

LEARN MORE

United Nations Conference on Trade and Development (UNCTAD) reports: http://unctad.org/en/pages/publications.aspx

World Bank's data on global finance: http://data.worldbank.org/data-catalog/global-financial-development

NOTES

1. The Institute for College Access & Success, "Student Debt and the Class of 2016," Annual Report (Oakland, CA: TICAS, September 2017), https://ticas.org/sites/default/files/pub_files/classof2016.pdf.

2. Joan Robinson, *Economic Philosophy*, 1st ed. (New Brunswick, NJ: Routledge, 2006), 45.

3. Daron Acemoglu and James A. Robinson, *Why Nations Fail: The Origins of Power, Prosperity and Poverty*, 1st ed. (New York, NY: Crown Publishers, 2012), 102; D. C. North and B. Weingast, "Constitutions and credible commitments: The evolution of the institutions of public choice in 17th century England," *Journal of Economic History* 49, no. 4 (1989): 803–832; for a critique, see Francis Fukuyama, *The Origins of Political Order: From Prehuman Times to the French Revolution*, Reprint ed. (New York, NY: Farrar, Straus and Giroux, 2012), 418.

4. Karl Polanyi, *The Great Transformation: The Political and Economic Origins of Our Time* (Boston, MA: Beacon Press, 2014).

5. David Harvey, *The Enigma of Capital: And the Crises of Capitalism* (New York, NY: Oxford University Press, 2010).

6. Peter A. Hall and Daniel W. Gingerich, "Varieties of capitalism and institutional complementarities in the political economy: An empirical analysis," *British Journal of Political Science* 39, no. 3 (July 2009): 449–482, https://doi.org/10.1017/S0007123409000672; Bruno Amable and Karim Azizi, *Varieties of Capitalism and Varieties of Macroeconomic Policy: Are Some Economies More Procyclical than Others?* (Köln, Germany: Max-Planck-Inst. für Gesellschaftsforschung, 2011); Nancy Gina Bermeo and Jonas Pontusson, *Coping With Crisis: Government Reactions to the Great Recession* (New York, NY: Russell Sage Foundation, 2012).

7. Simona Chiose, "Canadian universities see surge of international students," *The Globe and Mail*, May 14, 2017, https://www.theglobeandmail.com/news/national/education/international-admissions-to-canadian-universities-see-significant-increase/article34984977/; Laura Meckler and Melissa Korn, "Visas issued to foreign students fall, partly due to Trump immigration policy," *Wall Street Journal*, March 11, 2018, sec. US, https://www.wsj.com/articles/visas-issued-to-foreign-students-fall-partly-due-to-trump-immigration-policy-1520766000..

8. Friedrich Hayek, *The Road to Serfdom*, 1944, http://jim.com/hayek.htm.

9. David Ricardo, *The Principles of Political Economy and Taxation* (Mineola, NY: Dover Publications, 1821).

10. Dani Rodrik, "The new mercantilist challenge," *Project Syndicate* (blog), January 9, 2013, https://www.economics.utoronto.ca/gindart/2013-01-09%20-%20The%20new%20mercantilist%20challenge.pdf. Also Salman Ahmed and Alexander Bick, "Trump's national security strategy: A new brand of mercantilism?" (Carnegie Endowment for International Peace, August 17, 2017), http://carnegieendowment.org/2017/08/17/trump-s-national-security-strategy-new-brand-of-mercantilism-pub-72816.

11. Justin Lin and Ha-Joon Chang, "Should industrial policy in developing countries conform to comparative advantage or defy it? A debate between Justin Lin and Ha-Joon Chang," *Development Policy Review* 27, no. 5 (September 1, 2009): 483–502.

12. Tom Miles, "India loses WTO appeal in U.S. solar dispute," *Reuters*, September 16, 2016, https://www.reuters.com/article/us-india-usa-solar/india-loses-wto-appeal-in-u-s-solar-dispute-idUSKCN11M1MQ.

13. Aurelie Walker, "The WTO has failed developing nations | Aurelie Walker," *The Guardian*, accessed February 20, 2015, http://www.theguardian.com/global-development/poverty-matters/2011/nov/14/wto-fails-developing-countries.

14. "Signed, not sealed," *The Economist*, September 28, 2014, http://www.economist.com/blogs/americasview/2014/09/canada-eu-trade-deal.

15. http://tradejustice.ca/.

16. A more sophisticated version of this idea in economics is called the Stolper-Samuelson theorem.

17. Anatole Kaletsky, "Trump's rise and Brexit vote are more an outcome of culture than economics," *The Guardian*, October 28, 2016, sec. Business, http://www.theguardian.com/business/2016/oct/28/trumps-rise-and-brexit-vote-are-more-an-outcome-of-culture-than-economics; Jed Kolko, "Trump was stronger where the economy is weaker," *FiveThirtyEight* (blog), November 10, 2016, https://fivethirtyeight.com/features/trump-was-stronger-where-the-economy-is-weaker/. See also Erica Owen and Noel P. Johnston, "Occupation and the political economy of trade: Job routineness, offshorability, and protectionist sentiment," *International Organization*, September 2017: 1–35, https://doi.org/10.1017/S0020818317000339.

18. Adam Behsudi, "Trump's trade pullout roils rural America," *POLITICO Magazine*, August 7, 2017, https://www.politico.com/magazine/story/2017/08/07/trump-tpp-deal-withdrawal-trade-effects-215459.

19. Peter Baker, "Trump abandons Trans-Pacific Partnership, Obama's signature trade deal," *The New York Times*, January 23, 2017, sec. Politics, https://www.nytimes.com/2017/01/23/us/politics/tpp-trump-trade-nafta.html.

20. Mireya Solís, "The case for trade and the Trans-Pacific Partnership," October 4, 2016, https://www.brookings.edu/research/the-trans-pacific-partnership-the-politics-of-openness-and-leadership-in-the-asia-pacific/.

21. Jeronim Capaldo, Alex Izurieta, and Jomo Kwame Sundaram, "Unemployment, inequality and other risks of the Trans-Pacific Partnership Agreement," Working Paper, GDAE (Tufts University, 2016), http://www.ase.tufts.edu/gdae/policy_research/TPP_simulations.html.

22. As of 12/7/2014.

23. http://www.heritage.org/research/reports/2014/06/us-trade-policy-gouges-american-sugar-consumers.

24. This is known in social science as the problem of "collective action."

25. Kenneth F. Scheve and Matthew J. Slaughter, "A new deal for globalization," *Foreign Affairs*, August 2007, http://www.foreignaffairs.com/articles/62641/kenneth-f-scheve-and-matthew-j-slaughter/a-new-deal-for-globalization.

26. Mariana Mazzucato and Michael Jacobs|14 Comments, "The Brexit-Trump Syndrome: It's the economics, stupid," *British Politics and Policy at LSE* (blog), November 21, 2016, http://blogs.lse.ac.uk/politicsandpolicy/the-brexit-trump-syndrome/.

27. Raluca Dragusanu, Danile Giovannucci, and Nathan Nunn, "The economics of fair trade," *Journal of Economic Perspectives* 28 (Summer 2014): 11.

28. FTEPR, "Fairtrade, employment and poverty reduction in Ethiopia and Uganda," 2014, http://ftepr.org/wp-content/uploads/FTEPR-Final-Report-19-May-2014-FINAL.pdf.

29. Daniel Jaffee, "'Better, but not great': The social and environmental benefits and limitations of fair trade for indigenous coffee producers in Oaxaca, Mexico," in *The Impact of Fair Trade*, ed. Ruerd Ruben (Wageningen, the Netherlands: Wageningen Academic, 2008), 195–222.

30. UNCTAD, "Increasingly complex ownership structures of multinational enterprises poses new challenges for investment policymakers," June 21, 2016, http://unctad.org/en/pages/PressRelease.aspx?OriginalVersionID=303.

31. A financial crisis can be any number of specific types of crises, such as a currency crisis, banking crisis, or a market bubble and crash. Prominent examples include Mexico in 1994, East Asian countries in 1997, Russia in 1998 and 2014, Argentina in 1999, and of course the global financial crisis in 2007.

32. Manila Standard, 9/22/1997.

33. Ilene Grabel and Ha-Joon Chang, "Why capital controls are not all bad," *FT.Com*, October 25, 2010. Brad DeLong, "Should we still support untrammelled international capital mobility? Or are capital controls less evil than we once believed?," *The Economists' Voice* 1, no. 1 (2004). "A place for capital controls," *The Economist*, May 1, 2003, http://www.economist.com/node/1748890. Alan Rappeport, "IMF reconsiders capital controls opposition," *FT.Com*, February 22, 2010, http://search.proquest.com.ezproxy.library.wisc.edu/docview/229280418/6BFD6E2C79B24E34PQ/5?accountid=465. See also Carmen M. Reinhart and Kenneth Rogoff, *This Time Is Different: Eight Centuries of Financial Folly* (Princeton, NJ: Princeton University Press, 2009); Kristin J. Forbes, "The microeconomic evidence on capital controls: No free lunch," *NBER*, May 16, 2007, 171–202. Jagdish N. Bhagwati, "The capital myth: The difference between trade in widgets and dollars," *Foreign Affairs*, June 1998, http://www.foreignaffairs.com/articles/54010/jagdish-n-bhagwati/the-capital-myth-the-difference-between-trade-in-widgets-and-dol.

34. BBC, "Brazil's Lula raps 'white' Crisis," *BBC*, March 27, 2009, sec. Business, http://news.bbc.co.uk/1/hi/business/7967546.stm.

35. Do not confuse the Eurozone crisis with an EU crisis since not all EU members use the euro.

36. For more on the Eurozone crisis, see Pettis, "Syriza and the French Indemnity of 1871–73," *Financial Sense*, February 4, 2015, https://www.financialsense.com/contributors/michael-pettis/syriza-french-indemnity-1871-73/.

37. Jan Aart Scholte, *Building Global Democracy? Civil Society and Accountable Global Governance* (Cambridge, U.K.: Cambridge University Press, 2011).

38. By "artificially low," we mean a currency that is not valued as highly as it would be if it floated freely in international markets.

39. This is referred to as the Bretton Woods era, but keep in mind that the Bretton Woods Institutions (BWIs) refers specifically to the IMF, World Bank, and GATT/WTO, which still exist. Therefore, while the Bretton Woods System and the Bretton Woods era have ended, the three BWIs still exist.

40. Barry J. Eichengreen, "Hall of mirrors: The Great Depression, the Great Recession, and the uses—and misuses—of history," *Business History Review* 89 (2016): 557–569; Barry J. Eichengreen, *Exorbitant Privilege: The Rise and Fall of the Dollar* (Oxford, U.K.: Oxford University Press, 2013); J. A. Frieden, *Global Capitalism: Its Fall and Rise in the Twentieth Century* (New York, NY: W.W. Norton, 2006).

41. Michelle Fox, "Trump is wrong—China is not manipulating currency downward, says Dennis Gartman," cnbc.com, April 6, 2017, https://www.cnbc.com/2017/04/06/trump-is-wrong--china-is-not-manipulating-currency-downward-says-dennis-gartman.html.

42. National accounts are composed of the current account and the capital (aka "financial") account. Capital accounts keep track of changes in ownership of assets, such as real estate. When balancing national accounts, we usually think of the current account as more important than the capital account. A current account deficit (sending out more money than is being taken in) requires balancing somehow. Sometimes a country's national account can be balanced because it has a capital account surplus; for example, if it is a creditor country, then it loans to other countries. The surplus in the capital account meets the need for payment arising from the current account deficit.

7 Democracy and Representation

STRUGGLES FOR FREEDOM AND EFFORTS TO RESTRICT IT

LEARNING OBJECTIVES

After finishing this chapter, you should be able to:

- Distinguish the core features that make a regime democratic or authoritarian.

- Define terms like "democratization" and "competitive authoritarianism."

- Identify major historical trends in the development of democracy.

- Understand what the state of democracy is today in the world.

- Make arguments about why some countries are democratic while others are not.

- Pinpoint the ways in which the global forces of international studies are shaping democracy.

iStock/MOHPhoto

Freedom is a universal aspiration. People all over the world want to live their lives without undue restrictions. They want to be free to make choices, pursue their ideas, worship their religion, buy the products they want, associate with whom they want, go to school or work without interference, and express themselves as they wish.

At the same time, many with power want to limit freedom. States inherently exercise control over populations; they make and enforce rules; and they exercise a monopoly on the legitimate use of violence. In some states, governments exercise extensive control over citizens' choices, limiting their ability to express themselves and select whom they want to represent them. In those states, citizens who actively seek a change in government likely face repression. By contrast, in other states, citizens have a wide swath of freedoms—to worship, to participate in politics, to express themselves, to choose whom they want as their politicians, and to move.

Struggles for freedom and efforts to limit it define politics around the world. How open a country is to ideas, expression, competition, and participation fundamentally shapes how citizens engage government, how change occurs, and how ideas circulate. Around the world, many citizens want to live their lives without undue restrictions, and yet many states and some civil society actors want to restrict people's political behavior to stay in power or to impose their vision of social order.

Questions of **representation** also define politics. In most states, citizens do not govern directly. They are *represented* through politicians, and the politicians are the ones who make policy decisions based on their understanding of citizen preferences. In some states, citizen preferences play a central role; politicians are responsive to their constituents. In other states, citizen voices are heavily marginalized.

Consider Egypt. For 30 years, Egyptians lived under a military dictatorship. In 2011, as part of a movement for greater political freedom in the Arab world known as the "Arab Uprisings," Egyptians poured onto the streets to demand an end to dictatorship. Day in, day out for weeks, Egyptians faced down the police and rallied for change. Eventually, Egypt's leader stepped down. The protests in Egypt were a potent example of the thirst for freedom; the success of the protesters demonstrated the power of the people when they act collectively to resist oppression.

Unfortunately, the gains for freedom were short-lived. Elections led to a new party coming to power that based its policies on a narrow vision of Islam. That party in turn implemented a religiously conservative agenda that alienated many Egyptians. Many citizens felt that the new party did not *represent* them and that the revolution's gains were being betrayed. That prompted new protests in Egypt, which in turn led the military to intervene again. Today, Egypt is again under a military dictatorship. What the future holds for Egypt remains uncertain, but the struggle for freedom, the questions of representation, and the eventual repression point to the central political dynamics that are in play in this chapter.

representation: idea that citizens delegate the authority to convey their preferences to elected or appointed officials who in turn act on the citizens' behalf. In democratic politics, elected representatives are supposed to advocate and legislate in a way that accurately reflects the wishes of citizens.

WHAT MAKES SOME COUNTRIES FREER THAN OTHERS?

The degree to which people in some countries are free and fully represented by their leaders has to do with the political rules that govern the political systems they live in. Different sets of rules create different types of political regimes. At either end of the political spectrum of freedom and repression are democracy and dictatorship, two different types of regimes.

Democracy is a system of government that systematically allows ordinary citizens to have a say in who represents and governs them: democracy formally means "rule by the people." Democracy is also a system of government that allows citizens to be free to express themselves, associate with whom they choose, and participate in politics. By contrast, **dictatorship (or authoritarianism)** is a system of government in which states severely restrict political participation, expression, and association.

Even hardcore advocates recognize that democracy is an imperfect form of government, subject to many forms of manipulation and corruption. Democracy also comes in many variants. But as a system of government that promotes freedom and participation, democracy is unrivaled. In that, democracy is somewhat revolutionary, and many citizens and elites around the world push for it—just as much as other leaders with entrenched interests resist it, as we saw from the Egypt example.

democracy: system of government that means rule by the people in which citizens are allowed to associate, express, and participate in politics freely.

dictatorship (or authoritarianism): system of government that severely restricts association, expression, and participation in politics.

The world has witnessed a remarkable historical trend toward democracy during the last 240 years. What began in the United States and France gradually spread across the globe, and accelerated after the Cold War. That trend has not been linear, and in many instances, countries that started as democracies or fashioned themselves as democracies acted in highly undemocratic ways. But at the end of the Cold War, democracy emerged as the world's leading political system, just as capitalism emerged as the leading economic system. The Soviet model of authoritarianism failed, and with it many of the rationales for authoritarianism died too. Indeed, many considered the end of the Cold War a "triumph" of democracy, and some even called the period the "end of history" because the liberal ideas behind democracy and capitalism were so dominant that they appeared unassailable.[1]

Citizens today, on a global scale, have considerably more say in policy debates and considerably more freedom to move, express themselves, and participate in public discourse compared with the past two centuries. This change is one of the major and most significant global accomplishments in the history of the last 200 years, alongside economic growth, industrialization, and rising standards in global health.

**democrati-
zation:** process
of transitioning
from an
authoritarian
political system
to a democratic
one.

The central concept that scholars employ to mark the transition from a nondemocratic political system to a democratic one is **democratization**. The concept captures the idea of change, or of a process of change, that leads from one regime type (a nondemocratic one, such as a dictatorship) to another (a democratic one). How long that process takes, whether that process is linear, and how violent that process may be all depend on the country and the circumstances.

Recently, however, the broad trend toward democracy has stalled and even reversed. Many countries that eliminated the most obvious forms of authoritarianism refused to embrace democracy completely. Others found democracy untenable and reimposed restrictions that previously had been lifted. Still other countries, like China, which some hoped would gradually democratize, have become increasingly authoritarian. Moreover, many countries settled into a kind of compromise between democracy and dictatorship in what political scientists call **competitive authoritarianism (or hybrid regimes)**.

**competitive
authoritari-
anism (or hybrid
regimes):** system
of government
that combines
elements of a
democracy and
authoritarianism.

This chapter is the first in our series of global challenges. The push for deeper and more responsive democracy around the world is a burning priority for many. Yet movements for change, whether inspired from inside or outside a country, often spark fierce resistance and tension; sometimes they can lead to violence. The chapter provides an overview of some of the key concepts, trends, and arguments in this field. The next section focuses on the core components of democracy and dictatorship, followed by a section on trends in and processes of democratization, including a debate about how to count a democracy. We illustrate the chapter through case studies, including ones on Mexico, the Arab Uprisings, and a pro-democracy movement in Hong Kong. The chapter closes with discussions about the factors that make a country likely to remain democratic, or not, and about how democracy intersects with the global forces at the heart of this book.

WHAT DO DEMOCRACIES CONSIST OF?

**popular
sovereignty:**
authority to
rule is vested
in the general
population.

A core notion in democracies is **popular sovereignty**, or the idea that the people grant leaders the right to rule. In practice, that means that people choose their own leaders, and the main mechanism for doing so is elections. To be democratic, however, elections must be competitive, meaning there must be an actual opposition. Furthermore, the opposition must be able to operate freely, and the election process itself must be fair. Thus, perhaps the simplest distinction we make between democracies and dictatorships—and indeed one of the most common—is that democracy is a type of political regime in which citizens choose government leaders through free, fair, and competitive elections.[2] By contrast, a dictatorship is a political system in which leaders are not elected through competitive, free, or fair elections.

Elections

What makes an election free, fair, and competitive? There must be an opposition; that opposition must be able to campaign actively, to voice its views, and to raise funds without harassment or intimidation. Furthermore, there must be some marketplace of ideas. Civil society needs to operate, including the media, and citizens need to be able to articulate their views and support whomever they want without fear of retribution. In addition, the institutions that govern elections, such as Electoral Commissions, must operate without bias or undue interference from those competing in an election. Absent any of these civil and political liberties, democracy is compromised.

Quality of Democracy

But democracy is more than just elections. Many people care about the *quality* of the democracy. Rule by the people means that citizens should have some say and influence in how the government is run and about what policies are implemented. Political scientist Robert Dahl argues that democracy entails the "continuing responsiveness of the government to the preferences of its citizens, considered as political equals."[3] *Continuing responsiveness*, he notes, requires that all citizens have the following opportunities:

- To form their own preferences
- To communicate their preferences individually or collectively
- To have their preferences weighed equally by government[4]

Consider voting as central to the democratic process. Through voting, citizens *communicate preferences*. If the votes are counted properly and respected, the *government weighs the preferences* of voters. Dahl's proposition is consistent with an emphasis on elections, but Dahl's ideas go well beyond elections and voting. Citizens also must be able to form their own preferences. That means having access to information, being able to express oneself freely, being able to organize associations, and being able to run for office, among other qualities.

For Dahl, these various principles coalesce around two concepts: contestation and participation. **Contestation** is the idea that there is competition—of ideas, parties, politicians—and the idea that citizens choose among the alternatives. Having a viable, legal opposition is a *sine qua non* of democratic contestation; so too is having the ability to voice dissent without punishment or repression.

Participation is the idea that ordinary people take part in the political process—voicing opinions, voting, and standing for office. If there is neither contestation nor participation—if there is single party rule, no freedom of expression, major restrictions on who can vote, and the absence of freedom of expression—then there is not a democracy. To be sure, each of these qualities exists in different quantities. Freedom of expression is rarely absolute, even in democracies. Countries may limit speech that they consider dangerous or overly offensive, such as denying the existence of the Holocaust.

contestation: processes of political competition and dispute.

participation: act of taking part in the political process, through voting, supporting organizations, and voicing concerns and preferences.

WHAT DO DICTATORSHIPS CONSIST OF?

Dictatorships and authoritarian political systems are alternatives to democracy. For most scholars and policy makers, the terms are synonymous. They refer to political systems in which there are severe restrictions on contestation and participation. In these systems, citizens' freedom of expression is curtailed; typically, if citizens express dissent, they will face negative consequences, such as arrest. Similarly, in such systems, the ability to oppose the government is often highly restricted. Either the ruling party does not allow an opposition at all or it does not allow an opposition to operate freely. Opponents to a government are imprisoned, harassed, or even assassinated.

Forms of Authoritarianism

monarchy:
system of government in which sovereignty is vested in a single person, typically a king or queen whose entitlement to rule is assigned through hereditary traits, such as a royal lineage.

Dictatorships and authoritarian systems come in many forms. One example is a **monarchy**, or rule by a king or queen. Monarchies are systems of government in which the right to rule is hereditary. There is no popular sovereignty, no contestation, and little participation. Citizens do not have the right to vote, or if they do, their vote is not responsible for selecting the political executive. There are also significant restrictions on eligibility for public office—only members of the royal family can serve as the executive. In sum, there is very little contestation or participation.

Saudi Arabia is a contemporary example. Formally, the country is called the "Kingdom of Saudi Arabia." The head of state is limited only to sons of King Abdul Aziz bin Abdurrahman Al Faisal Al Saud, who is the country's founding father. The monarch chooses members of the cabinet, which is often composed of other royal family members, as well as of the Shura council, which is a legislative body.

Saudi Arabia is an "absolute" monarchy; the king effectively has all the power as head of state and head of government. In the contemporary world, there are also some "constitutional monarchies," in which a monarch is head of state but where his or her political power is substantially limited by the country's constitution. The United Kingdom is an example. The Queen is the Head of State in the United *Kingdom*, but her power is largely ceremonial. The authority of government is vested in the parliament, which is democratically elected. The United Kingdom is indeed a democratic political system, unlike Saudi Arabia.

Monarchies are uncommon in the contemporary world. More common forms of authoritarian political systems are where a ruling party effectively monopolizes power—by significantly restricting the opposition or by significantly restricting participation of citizens in the political process.

Office of the President of Russia

China is an example. China has elections. Citizens may vote to elect representatives at various levels of municipal and local government. Those representatives in turn elect representatives at the National People's Congress, which in turn elects the president and premier in the country. So there is participation through voting—in both direct and indirect ways.

China is effectively a single-party state, however. The Communist Party of China is the only main party that exists; real opposition in the form of an alternative political party is forbidden. For decades, China rotated the presidency after two five-year terms, but in 2018, the Party removed that requirement, allowing the current leader, Xi Jinping, to rule indefinitely. Furthermore, active political dissent is restricted, and the state plays a heavy hand in controlling the flow of information—in print and electronically. A study by Freedom House, a leading organization that measures levels of democracy, found that China had the least free Internet space of the 65 countries it surveyed (Iceland had the best).[5] Similarly, China ranked in the bottom 15 of 202 surveyed countries in terms of press freedom.[6]

Contemporary Russia is similarly a dictatorship. Russia is a powerful example of how processes of democratization are not linear. At the end of the 1980s, the Soviet Union (which was a dictatorship) underwent a process of political and economic liberalization, which in turn saw a breakup of the union into a number of independent states—of which Russia is the most powerful. In the early 1990s, Russia experienced a gradual opening of the political space, with new opportunities for political opposition and press freedom. Starting around the turn of the millennium, however, Russia proceeded to become increasingly authoritarian with crackdowns on opposition figures and civil society organizations, including the media. Unlike China, opposition parties are allowed, but their ability to operate freely is severely constrained by intimidation and other restrictions. In 2015, a leading opposition figure was assassinated near the Kremlin. President Vladimir Putin, who was elected for eight years between 2000 and 2008, and then again starting in 2012, has championed the concentration of power in the presidency's hands and openly railed against Western-style democracy. In 2017, Freedom House ranked the country as having a total score of 20 out of 100, in terms of overall freedom, making Russia one of the least free upper middle income countries in the world.[7]

Several countries in the world are "competitive authoritarian" or "hybrid" states, meaning that they combine elements of democratic and authoritarian political systems. In these countries, typically, opposition parties nominally exist, as does an independent press and other types of independent civil society. There are also regular elections in which citizens have the right to choose between parties. These are not classic one-party dictatorships or monarchies; the regimes have formal democratic institutions. But in reality, the ruling party uses the government to harass the opposition, manipulate elections, and intimidate the press. In the words of two scholars who wrote a book on the subject, competition is "real but unfair."[8] The playing field is heavily stacked in favor of those who are in power. Freedom House designates a similar label, namely, that of "partly free" countries. In 2017, the organization found that 30% of the world's political systems were "partly free," compared with 45% that it labeled as "free" (democratic) and 26% as "unfree" (authoritarian) (see Figure 7.1).

In recent years, Turkey has served as an example. Turkey has a multiparty political system. Besides the ruling party, the country has three main opposition groups who contest elections and hold seats in parliament. The country also has an independent press. Government forces, however, frequently harass and arrest journalists. Some opposition figures have been arrested. In general, under President Recep Tayyip Erdogan, there has been a climate of intimidation and increasing centralization of power in the presidency. In the aftermath of a failed coup in 2016, Turkey imposed a state of emergency; arrested scores in the military, civil service, and education; and purged people suspected of being loyal to an opposition figure based in the United States (and who was said to be behind the coup). Turkey is thus not a one-party state; it is a place with a degree of contestation and participation, but both are significantly constrained. The playing field is competitive, but the competition is highly constrained. For all of the 2000s and 2010s until 2018, Freedom House considered Turkey a partly free country, but in 2018, the organization downgraded Turkey to "Not Free" because of increasing crackdowns on the opposition and because of increasing centralization of power.

"Partly free" or "competitive authoritarian" regimes are important for several reasons. One is that many exist: As we mentioned earlier, nearly a third of all countries in the world are considered

FIGURE 7.1

Free, Partly Free, and Not Free Countries

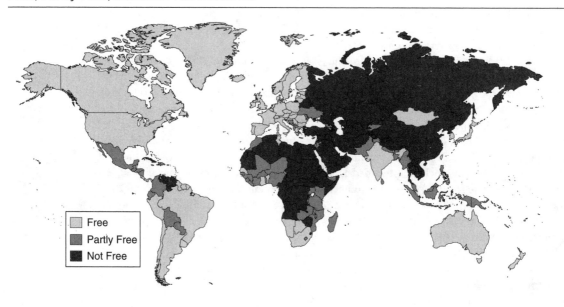

Source: Freedom House, "Freedom in the World 2018," https://freedomhouse.org/report/freedom-world/freedom-world-2018.

TABLE 7.1

Forms of Authoritarianism

Type of regime	Absolute monarchy	Constitutional monarchy	Single-party authoritarian system/ dictatorship	Competitive authoritarian/hybrid systems
Characteristics	Right to rule is inherited; no popular sovereignty; no contestation; little participation	Monarch is head of state but political power is mostly ceremonial and limited by the country's constitution	Political power monopolized by one political party; political opposition, participation significantly restricted	Elements of democracy combined with authoritarianism; some opposition ("real but unfair"), some civil society
Example	Saudi Arabia	United Kingdom	China, Russia	Turkey until 2018

"partly free." Another is that the existence of "partly free" countries suggests that the process of democratization moves in complicated directions. Around the end of the Cold War when democracy looked like the future of regimes all over the world, many scholars conceptualized the process of democratization in linear terms. Once a county began to liberalize, the expectation was that the process of democratization would continue. Perhaps the speed would be different across countries and regions, but the direction would be similar. In fact, that has not been the case, as we will explore in the next section. Some countries liberalized but then reversed course and became increasingly authoritarian—such as in Russia and Turkey. Other countries liberalized, but the process of liberalization became stuck; the "partly free" zone became the new status quo in places like Pakistan and Uganda. Indeed, the competitive authoritarian space looks here to stay (see Table 7.1).

TRENDS IN DEMOCRATIZATION

All that raises the question of the history of democratization: Over time, what has been the direction of countries on a global scale? What is the most recent trend? As a general statement, the world over time has become increasingly democratic, measured by the terms introduced in the previous sections. Compare the world today with 250 years ago, or even 50 years ago, and there is considerably more contestation and participation today—considerably more competitive elections, political freedom, and capacity to oppose rulers—than there has been. In the early 19th century, democracy was exceedingly rare and highly constrained. Monarchies, colonial rule, and other forms of dictatorship were the norm. Even in those countries with competitive elections and commitments to democracy, who could participate was much more limited than in the contemporary scene. In particular, women could not vote. Today, politics is much more competitive, inclusive, and freer. Many consider that change to be one of humanity's great accomplishments. But even if that is the case, there remains some distance to travel.

How to *depict* the process of democratization is subject to debate but an informative one. A highly influential characterization comes from the late political scientist Samuel Huntington, who famously coined the idea of **"three waves of democratization."**[9] He argues that transitions toward democracy take place in time-bound clusters, or waves, followed by reversals. Writing in the early 1990s, he argued that such waves had taken place three times since the 19th century. His depiction provides a snapshot of the global spread of democracy.

Is Democratization Wavy or Flat?

According to Huntington, the first "long" wave took place from 1828 through 1926. The wave was rooted in the American and French revolutions of the late 18th century. Huntington, marks the beginning of the wave to when the United States extended the right to vote to a large portion of the white male population. In this long wave, Huntington also counts Finland, Iceland, Switzerland, France, the United Kingdom, Australia, Canada, and eventually several Latin American countries. Many of these countries are high and middle income countries today.

The reversal started after World War I. He dates the turn back to the period between 1922 and 1942. After the world war, several countries turned to fascism and Communism. Both of these political systems are inherently anti-democratic. They believe in single-party rule and, in the case of fascism, near total subservience to a leader. In each of these arenas, states rolled back democratic freedoms. The state shrunk the space for public criticism, whether through the press, civil society, or potential opposition parties. The state also limited public protests and freedom of movement, among many other changes. Fascism took hold in this period in high income countries, such as Italy and Germany. Communism took hold most notably in Russia. In other locations, in particular in Latin America,

three waves of democratization: phrase coined by political scientist Samuel Huntington; clusters of countries that democratize around the same time period; in particular, the world has witnessed three big waves of change.

military leaders replaced democratic governments through coups and went on to rule. Military rule typically limited open political competition; it was anti-democratic.

The second wave of democratization, between 1943 and 1962, took place primarily after World War II, with several formerly fascist states turning democratic as well as several Latin American countries reasserting their democratic credentials. In addition, numerous countries became independent after decolonization. Several started as democracies—such as in Malaysia, Nigeria, Kenya, and elsewhere. Others, such as India, started and stayed democratic. But beginning in the early 1960s a number of newly independent countries restricted their political space by becoming one-party states or by introducing military rule. This happened across Sub-Saharan Africa and in Latin America, especially, but also in Southeast Asia. This period—when newly independent states created single-party systems—marks the period of retrenchment after the second wave of democratization.

The third wave started in the mid-1970s. The trigger was the end of dictatorships in southern Europe, notably in Spain, Portugal, and Greece. Within a decade, several Latin American countries that had been previously under military rule started to return to civilian, multiparty rule. That took place in big, important countries such as Brazil, Argentina, Chile, and Uruguay, to name a few. But perhaps the biggest shift took place after the end of the Cold War when numerous eastern European countries democratized, throwing off a Communist yoke and often introducing competitive rule. Finally, following the end of the Cold War, in Africa, the continent shifted from having one-party rule as the mainstay to having competitive, multiparty environments. The most famous shift took place in South Africa, where a system of racial hierarchy that had excluded people of color (who were the outright majority) shifted to multiracial, multiparty rule in the early 1990s.

Figure 7.2 depicts the broad changes that Huntington describes.[10] The figure shows a first long period of growth for democratization, followed by a retrenchment after World War I, following by a

FIGURE 7.2

Huntington's Waves of Democratization

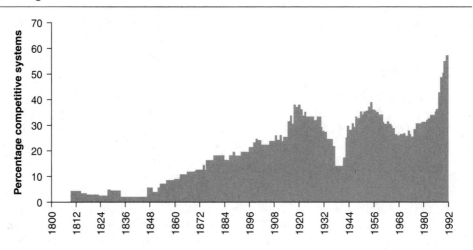

Source: Renske Doorenspleet, "Reassessing the Three Waves of Democratization," *World Politics* 52 (2000): 393. Reproduced with permission.

FIGURE 7.3

Democratization from the Perspective of Competitive Elections and Universal Suffrage

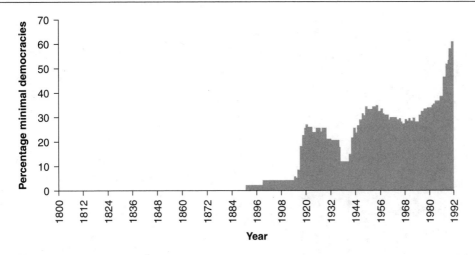

Source: Renske Doorenspleet, "Reassessing the Three Waves of Democratization," *World Politics* 52 (2000): 393. Reproduced with permission.

growth after World War II, followed by a retrenchment in the early 1960s, followed by an increase in the mid-1970s. Whether one labels these changes as "waves," or clusters, or something else, is subject to dispute, but the historical patterns hold.

But is this an accurate picture of the history of democratization during the past 200 years? Huntington employed a somewhat minimal measure for democracy. He measured waves based primarily on whether the political opposition existed and could contest elections. As we saw from earlier in the chapter, however, competition is not the whole story. Participation is another crucial element, and if one focuses on participation using an indicator such as universal suffrage—that is, the idea that democracy exists only when every adult may vote—then the history of democratization looks fairly different. This is the case because many of the "first wave" early democratizers, such as the United States and the United Kingdom, had very limited suffrage and noticeably excluded women and certain ethnic groups. Participation in voting and politics was highly constrained. Thus, looking at a measure of democracy in which a country is counted as democratic only if there are competitive elections *and* universal suffrage, the picture is quite different, as Figure 7.3 shows.[11]

Universal suffrage begins with New Zealand and Australia, moves to the Scandinavian countries, and spreads from there. Should we count a country as democratic if women and ethnic groups could not vote? If the answer is no, Figure 7.3 is a more accurate representation of the history of democratization. If the answer is yes, then Figure 7.2 suffices.

That brings us to the contemporary period. Huntington was writing in the early 1990s. If his theory was correct, we should have experienced a steady rise in the number of democracies, followed by a retrenchment, or a period of retrenchment after the mid-1990s. But neither picture is exactly right; the 1990s and 2000s have not been "wavy"; they have been rather flat.

FIGURE 7.4

Democratization from the Perspective of a Multifaceted Measure

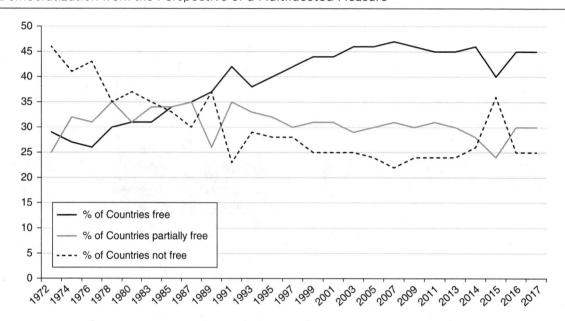

Source: Data from Freedom House/Freedom in the World, https://freedomhouse.org/report-types/freedom-world.

To examine the contemporary period, we turn again to Freedom House, which has one of the most influential measures of democracy. Using an algorithm that indexes political rights and civil liberties, Freedom House labels countries into three main categories—free, partly free, and not free. Political liberties include the ability to participate in politics freely, the right to vote freely, the presence of distinct alternatives in legitimate elections, and the right to join parties and compete for political office. Civil liberties include freedom of expression and belief, associational rights, and personal autonomy.

Freedom House began collecting data in the early 1970s, or around the start of Huntington's third wave. Indeed, from the early 1970s to the late 1990s, there is a gradual increase of countries that become democratic, or "free," in Freedom House's parlance. From the start of the century, however, the number of countries that fit into these categories stabilizes. That is, for the first 15 years of the 21st century, we do not really see a democratic reversal or a growing trend toward democratization. We appear to have an equilibrium, as Figure 7.4 shows.

Regime Stability

The data from the contemporary period bring us to one of the clearest lessons of the contemporary period: Semi-authoritarian, or competitive authoritarian, states are stable, as are authoritarian ones. Starting in 2000, the number of "free" or democratic countries stabilized—such that Freedom

House categorized about 45% of the world's states in that way. But so did the number of "partly free" (competitive or semi-authoritarian states) and the number of "not free" states. Indeed, the number of not free states seems to be on the increase. Indeed, summing those two categories suggests that 54% of states, according to Freedom House, are not democracies.

One can quibble with the coding that Freedom House employs, but the organization remains one of the most well respected and influential in the study of democracy. In any case, the trend lines defy some expectations. Following Huntington, and in particular after the Cold War and the end of Communism, many observers expected that democratization would march on. In other words, many observers expected that authoritarian political systems would not be stable. They expected that, with the apparent death of the Communist model and the triumph of democracy, most countries would become democratic. Indeed, many donor countries in the world—notably the United States but also many European countries—explicitly pressured states to adopt democratic political systems. Following Huntington, one could have also expected a reversal, followed by a fourth wave.

The continuing trend toward democratization has not been the case, however. Nor has there been a dramatic reversal, although the increasing authoritarianism of some major powers like Russia, China, and Turkey prompt some observers to worry about an eventual reversal. But on the whole, many countries have learned how to be partially democratic and to remain in that space. Bowing to international pressure, they might hold multiparty elections, but in reality, the countries prevent any real opposition from taking hold. They continue to thwart civil society, including human rights groups, labor groups, and other associations that lobby for change. They continue to restrict the press, or they might not be responsive to citizens. In short, they have a veneer of democracy but in reality stop short of allowing their countries to become fully democratic.

Consider Mexico, a country of nearly 130 million people to the south of the United States. Mexico has a remarkable political history. Between 1929 and 2000, a single party dominated Mexican politics; that party was the PRI (Institutional Revolutionary Party), and its tenure in power was one of the longest running in the world. During much of that period, Mexico did not face a strong challenger to the PRI; when it did face stronger opposition and political threats, the party responded with patronage, policy changes, or sometimes repression. It also allegedly stole elections.

That began to change in the late 1980s and 1990s when Mexico introduced reforms that allowed for more open competition; opposition parties received public financing and stronger representation on public media. Economic crises also diminished the resources that the party could use to buy off voters and win over local elites. In 2000, after more than 70 years in power, the PRI lost the presidential election to opposition leader Vincente Fox; that process was repeated again in 2006 when Felipe Calderón won the presidency. The PRI won back the presidency in 2012, but lost it again in 2018.

Between 2000 and 2010, Freedom House ranked Mexico as free, given the freedoms that the country introduced and protected. Starting in 2011 and continuing to this day, however, the country ranks as "partly free." (See Figure 7.5.) Although Freedom House ranks the country fairly highly on its electoral process, political pluralism and participation, freedom of expression, and personal liberty, the country performs poorly on the functioning of government and the rule of law. Freedom House reports high levels of corruption across the political system, impunity in the judicial system, and high homicide rates from organized crime. All of those aspects—plus the disappearance of many Mexicans, including 43 students whose charred remains were found in a municipal dump after engaging in political protests—have undermined Mexican democracy. Mexico thus has fluctuated between a dictatorship, a democracy, and a "hybrid" or "partly free" state in recent decades. Rather

FIGURE 7.5

Freedom in Mexico, From 1972 to Today

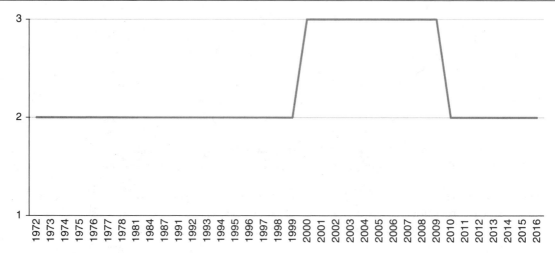

1 = Not free, 2 = Partly free, 3 = Free

Source: Data from Freedom House/Freedom in the World, https://freedomhouse.org/report-types/freedom-world.

than exhibiting linear progress, the quality of the democracy declined, a fate that many countries shared across the globe.[12]

democratic initiation:
initial process that leads a country to end authoritarianism.

democratic consolidation:
process by which democracy takes root and stabilizes in a country.

democracy promotion:
in their foreign policy, governments encourage, and often finance, other governments to become more democratic.

THE PROCESS OF DEMOCRATIZATION

Democratization is a transition process that has two major parts—the initiation of change and the sustainability of change. The first issue scholars call **democratic initiation.** How does a previously authoritarian political system change and become more democratic? What forces lead a society to change the political regime? The second issue scholars call **democratic consolidation**. What are the ingredients that allow a country to stay democratic once it has started to liberalize? What are the conditions that allow a democratization process to be successful? Why do some countries that transition away from authoritarianism complete that transition, and why do others fail?

Two schools of thought exist on democratic initiation. One emphasizes *outside-in* forces, while another emphasizes *inside-out* processes. The two sets of forces can and often do intersect and reinforce each other, but the two approaches emphasize different factors.

Democratic Initiation From the Outside-In: Promotion and Diffusion

A key source of outside-in pressure is **democracy promotion** on the part of wealthier, democratic countries in the world. Since the end of the Cold War, several states in the Global North that provide development, financial, and military assistance to countries in the Global South have tied such assistance to the promise of democratic reforms. That is the idea of **aid conditionality**—or making the provision of aid dependent on whether a country meets certain conditions, in this case, that they initiate a democratic process. Donors also provide assistance to civil society organizations that in turn lobby for democratic change.

From the donors' perspective, democracy promotion has several advantages, even if such moves create backlash from some leaders who resist democracy and argue that such action amounts to infringements on their sovereignty. Many donors argue that democratic systems are inherently more stable and will make the world more peaceful. Such an argument is debatable but harkens back to the idea of a **democratic peace**, or the idea that democracies typically do not fight each other. In addition, wealthier democracies face domestic pressure not to support dictatorships—in the sense that taxpayers do not want to supply autocrats with funds, thereby indirectly supporting and contributing to repression. In the 1990s, democracy promotion had its heyday. The period marked the end of the Cold War, in which there was considerable and arguably naive optimism about the triumph of democracy and global markets.

Democracy promotion has fallen out of favor, to a degree. For one, wealthier states often practiced double standards. Key strategic allies often did not face negative repercussions if they failed to enact democratic reforms. That was the case for countries, such as Saudi Arabia, that were critical partners of the United States in the world economy and in the fight against terrorist organizations. Despite Saudi Arabia being an absolute monarchy in which women face systematic discrimination, the United States remains a key supporter of the country. Another major thorn in the side of democracy promoters is that the efforts often failed. Leaders of states around the world learned how to enact incomplete reforms, ones that led to multiparty elections and that often relaxed restrictions on speech and assembly but nonetheless essentially preserved an incumbent's tenure in power. Indeed, as we have seen, these "partly free" or competitive authoritarian regimes have proven stable. Many of these "partly free" countries are not transitioning—either toward fully democratic states or fully authoritarian ones. Rulers have learned to live with the opposition without granting the opposition the full freedoms necessary to contest as effectively as possible. Last, many citizens in developing countries have found democracy promotion disappointing. Partial democracies do not necessarily yield development gains. Even when there is democratic turnover—voters remove one party from power and the losers accept defeat—new leaders fail to deliver better lives. They practice favoritism; they are as corrupt as the old leaders; and unemployment remains rampant, to name a few concerns. Although this is not the case in every country where a democratic turnover takes place, such disappointments exist and create headwinds to the push toward democracy.

Not all outside-in pressure flows from the Global North to the Global South. Several regional organizations strongly promote democratic practices in member states. In Africa, both the African Union and the Economic Community of West African States (ECOWAS) have consistently taken a stand against unconstitutional changes in government, notably through coups. In Latin America, regional human rights institutions, such as the Inter-American Commission on Human Rights (discussed in more detail in the next chapter), similarly have leveraged pressure on states to conform to standards that protect freedom. And some states in the Global North, notably Russia, have been powerful voices against democracy promotion, seeing it as undo interference, and Russia has, partly in response, taken aggressive measures to meddle in the elections of countries in the Global North, notably in the United States and in some European countries, such as France (see the feature box later in this chapter). In sum, outside-in pressure is one key source of democratic initiation; that pressure comes in several forms; and that pressure can spur significant backlash.

aid conditionality: donor governments require governments that receive foreign aid to take steps to become more democratic.

democratic peace: democratic states do not fight wars against each other.

**demonstra-
tion effect
(or diffusion):**
process by
which actors
in one country
watch and
initiate political
processes in the
other country.
Applied to
democrati-
zation, the idea
is that actors
in one country
are inspired
by, learn from,
and initiate
challenges to
authoritari-
anism that they
observe in other
countries.

A different outside-in force is what some social scientists call a **demonstration effect (or diffusion)**. The idea here is that citizens in one society learn from, and ultimately copy, actions that are taken in another society. Such actions often arrive in clusters or waves, as per Huntington, in the sense that citizens watch and learn from movements for democratic change in one country. Such demonstration effects often occur in regional clusters, as was the case across eastern Europe at the end of the Cold War when many states took measures to end the authoritarian system of rule under Communism. Such was also the case in Sub-Saharan Africa in the early 1990s when most states ended one-party political monopolies and introduced multiparty electoral competition.

More recent is what many refer to as the "Arab Uprisings" in North Africa and the Middle East, as the opening example from Egypt shows and as we discuss later in this chapter. In each of these cases, democratic ideas *diffuse* across borders; citizens in one society *demonstrate* to citizens in another how people power can work. Advances in information and communications technology (ICT) likely accelerate and shape that process. Through social media and transborder television channels, people in one society see, learn, and are inspired by people in another society.

Democratic Initiation From the Inside-Out: Social Movements

**social
movements:**
collective
action for
social change
involving
very loosely
organized
individuals,
networks, and
nongovernmen-
tal organizations
(NGOs).
Example: Black
Lives Matter.

A bottom-up, or inside-out, approach locates democratic initiation to domestic forces. An important way that scholars conceptualize such processes is as social movements, which are sustained campaigns of pressure and claim-making that involve multiple actors working together to generate change (as introduced in Chapter 4).[13] **Social movements** take many forms. They can amount to protests against the prices of food or gas; they can take the form of demonstrations for recognition of the rights of an ethnic or religious minority; and they can amount to claims for fair housing or against economic globalization. Recent student protests in favor of gun control and increased protection in schools is another example. One key manifestation includes efforts to make countries more democratic. In these cases, a coordinated group of actors in a society comes together to demand an end to dictatorship or to protest fraud in an election or some other action that would make a country more democratic.

Cases in Democratic Pressure: Inside-Out and Outside-In Dynamics

Two contemporary examples show how inside-out and outside-in forces work to create pressure for democratic change. They also highlight the ways that one of our global forces, ICTs, are intimately a part of these processes in the contemporary world—both in terms of facilitating protests and in terms of providing states with opportunities to practice surveillance on their citizens.

The Arab Uprisings. The Arab Uprisings, sometimes called the "Arab Spring," were the most important political movement in the North Africa and Middle East region in recent decades. The process started in Tunisia in December 2010 when a market trader committed suicide, through self-immolation, following government restrictions on his business. Witnesses filmed the burning, and the video spread across social media and television rapidly. His suicide inspired protests in the capital city in Tunisia, and those protests primarily called for greater democracy and for the ouster of President Ben Ali and his family. Within weeks, Ali and his family had fled Tunis, paving the way for a new government and ultimately the adoption of democratic reforms in that country.

The movement for democracy in the region did not stop there. In neighboring Egypt, the events in Tunisia inspired citizens who were fed up with decades of authoritarian military rule under Hosni Mubarak. Protesters converged in Tahrir Square in central Cairo, demanding Mubarak's ouster and the opening of the political system. In a remarkable turn of events, the Egyptian security forces refused to fire on the protesters or to break up the movement. Eventually, the armed forces took control, arrested Mubarak, and set the process in motion to hold multiparty democratic elections. In Egypt, the winner of the eventual election was the Muslim Brotherhood, an Islamist political party long repressed in the country. After two years of rule, however, the military again intervened, arguing that the Muslim Brotherhood was undermining the integrity of the country. As of this writing, the military remains in control.

Events in Tunisia and Egypt inspired further protests. In Morocco, Kuwait, Bahrain, and Jordan, citizens took to the streets to demand democratic change. In none of these countries did the protest movements lead to regime change; authorities made some democratic concessions or, in the case of Bahrain, repressed the movement. In Libya and Syria, as well as in Yemen, the Arab Spring gained traction, but events in those countries turned violent, quickly spiraling into civil war. In Libya, regional organizations in the Middle East and Europe eventually moved to prevent the forces loyal to President Muammar al-Qaddafi from massacring citizens. That action led rebels to take power, but the rebel coalition itself soon fragmented and led to significant disorder in the aftermath of Qaddafi's ouster. In Syria, the security forces loyal to President Bashar al-Assad cracked down on the pro-democracy protesters, in turn ushering in a long civil war that lasts to this day (and is discussed in greater detail in Chapter 10). In Yemen, the president eventually fled, but that country also remains mired in civil war.

The protests were remarkable. They brought in millions of people from across a wide array of ethnic, class, and gender backgrounds. There were huge upheavals in the politics of the region. In several countries, they led to changes in leadership; in others, they led to changes in the regimes, in the rules of the game—making the countries more democratic. In some countries, the results were violent and disastrous; in others, a process of democratic opening and dialogue started.

What prompted the democratic initiation in the region? Why did the protests take place then and there? There is no consensus, as of yet. Clearly many citizens were frustrated with authoritarian rule, which had persisted for decades in most of the states in question. But the authoritarian order had been famously stable for decades; the Middle East and North Africa were outliers to the democratic trends in Sub-Saharan Africa and eastern Europe. Some scholars point to food prices and other globalization forces, which prompted protests. But major studies point to media and sharing of information across borders. Scholar Marc Lynch argues that the new media environment had three major effects. First, it ruptured one of the key dimensions of authoritarianism—it loosened the control of ideas and information. Second, the new media environment shaped the skills and expectations of a younger generation of activists. Finally, the new media created a shared, virtual space across borders in which citizens and activists could communicate, share stories, and relate to each other.[14] A key part of the media space was the Qatar-based television station, Al-Jazeera, which provided a common narrative and sense of a shared fate within much of the Arab World.[15]

Another key question is why the outcomes varied so much. Why did Tunisia's uprising result in the ouster of the president and the start of a contentious but largely nonviolent democratic process? Why did Bahrain succeed in repressing the protests and in keeping the regime intact? Why did

Egypt temporarily democratize but then revert back to the status quo ante of military dictatorship? Why did Syria and Libya's uprisings end in devastating civil war and anarchy? Social scientists will answer these questions in time. The answers are likely to point to external factors—such as whether foreign countries rallied to the defense of the state or the opposition—as well as to domestic factors, such as whether a regime's economy depended on oil and whether the country's executive was hereditarily selected (such as in a monarchy).[16]

In sum, the Arab Uprisings show the ways in which both outside-in and inside-out factors shaped the process of change and the variations in what happened afterward. Clearly, events in one country affected events in another country, what scholars call "demonstration" or "diffusion" effects. Satellite television, social media, and the general availability of information and ideas through new information and communications technology shaped the regional process. But also important were domestic actors who took action as well as the structure of the regimes prior to the onset of the uprisings.

The Umbrella Movement in Hong Kong. Another social movement took place in Hong Kong in 2014. The protest was primarily about democracy in China-administered Hong Kong. Britain transferred sovereignty of Hong Kong to China in 1997. At that time, the agreement between the countries held that in 2017, Hong Kong would experience "universal suffrage." In the run-up to that date, a key question became who would choose the territory's chief executive, and how. Pro-democracy Hong Kongers wanted to pick the executive without interference from mainland China, but the Chinese government stipulated that all candidates would be selected by Beijing and they had to be "patriotic," which was interpreted as loyal to China.

Upon hearing this news, pro-democracy activists adopted terms that had been used in the United States and elsewhere to "occupy" space; in this case, they termed the protest "Occupy Central," which would occupy the government and financial district in Hong Kong to pressure the Hong Kong authorities for a more open electoral process. Protesters established barricades and tents as well as the means to support the occupiers, including food distribution, shelter, and reading spaces. The police sought to break up the occupation, and the term "Umbrella Movement" took shape as protestors lifted umbrellas to shield themselves from pepper spray and tear gas. The protests grew rapidly in strength. Of Hong Kong's 7.2 million residents, tens of thousands took part before the protests ended peacefully 2.5 months after they started. In the end, the movement seems to have had little effect in persuading Chinese authorities to allow for a more open process of selecting the territory's chief executive.

As in the case of the Arab Uprisings, social media played an important role in galvanizing protest and mobilizing citizens and civil society. Protestors established the webpage HKGolden.com as a forum to spread news, encourage protest, organize, and share information. Protestors also used social media platforms to share information, images, and messages. The government, however, forced the organizers to release IP addresses from the website, which triggered the arrest of a leader, and they

Hong Kong Umbrella Revolution

Wikipedia user Pasu Au Yeung, https://commons.wikimedia.org/wiki/File:Hong_Kong_Umbrella_Revolution_-umbrellarevolution_-UmbrellaMovement_ (15292823874).jpg. Licensed under CC BY 2.0, https://creativecommons.org/licenses/by/2.0/legalcode.

eventually blocked Instagram from showing images of protests and blocked the words "Occupy Central" from Weibo, China's microblogging platform.

In addition to the importance of ICT, the Hong Kong example shows both the importance of external and internal factors and how protests do not always lead to change. Local actors were the primary drivers of protest, but they drew inspiration from movements around the world, notably the Occupy Wall Street movement that took place in the fall of 2011 in the United States as well as other movements.

DEMOCRATIC CONSOLIDATION

Both the Arab Uprisings and Umbrella Movement cases return us to the question of democratic consolidation, or why some democratic transitions succeed while others fail. There is a wide range of thinking on this topic, again with no consensus.

One of the most robust findings is the correlation between a certain level of income and democratization. Broadly speaking, richer countries tend to be democratic and poorer countries less democratic. It is not that democratization does not take place in poor countries. Rather, the claim is that for democratic *consolidation* to occur—that is, for a country to deepen or sustain democracy once the democratization process has started—a certain level of economic development is needed. One influential study by a team of political scientists found that almost all countries with an average per capita income of $4,000 where there had been a transition remained a democracy.[17]

Another major argument in the literature is that a middle class or a bourgeoisie is essential for democracy. Paraphrasing a famous social scientist, Barrington Moore: "No bourgeoisie, no democracy." Middle classes, he argues, have economic and political interests that are independent of landed elites; they also require and benefit from greater education among the workforce. They thus see a benefit to the distribution of political power.[18]

A third major argument about consolidation concerns inequality. The argument is that in societies with high degrees of inequality, the elites at the top worry about the costs of democratization. In this theory, should a country democratize and stay democratic, nonelite citizens would be empowered and they would have an interest in redistributing wealth in the country. That prospect is so concerning to elites with much to lose that they prefer to repress and maintain dictatorship, rather than give up their hold. By contrast, in other locations with less severe forms of inequality, elites who face the prospect of revolution and losing everything prefer democratization that would lead to some redistribution but not complete disenfranchisement. At the same time, the relationship to inequality is "U shaped" in the sense that with high degrees of equality, the incentives for democratization are fewer—citizens who are not in government are less concerned with the need for democracy and therefore do not threaten major unrest to achieve it.[19]

A different theory stresses the importance of civil society, which acts as a buffer between states and citizens. Inherently those who control states might be inclined to restrict the political space, which over time would squeeze out democratic processes. If a society has a strong civil society—independent media, social organizations such as mutual benefit societies or even sports clubs, independent religious organizations, and other forms of associational life—however, then those organizations can serve to mediate the power of the state. Journalists might call out state repression and corruption; religious authorities might invoke their moral authority to condemn elite violations of the public trust. In these cases, civil society softens the raw power of the state and can push back on that power. Civil society also aggregates and organizes interests. A chamber of commerce, for example, might assemble the views of businessmen and women and then channel those views onto state practice. Similarly, human rights organizations or women's organizations have a voice in challenging the state. In short, civil society can play a key role in mediating the power of the state and in directing the interests of citizens.

Last is a question of multiethnic and multireligious societies. Ethnic and religious diversity is not inherently fracturing; indeed, in countries with a strong sense of civic national identity, in which race, ethnicity, or religion is not the primary social and political identity, diversity may create interests and perspectives but does not fundamentally inhibit political cooperation. In other societies, however, people define themselves as belonging to different principal communities; they do not believe in or have faith in a national political system. They view politics as a zero-sum game in which one group's gain is another's loss. In that situation, a stable, competitive, free political system is a challenge to sustain. Democracy requires some faith that states can rule in the common good and that institutions will adjudicate competition fairly. If there is no fundamental trust between social groups in a society, the leaders of those groups are less likely to trust the institutions of the state and are less likely to participate over time in a democratic process.

These are some leading theories of how and why countries sustain democracy, or do not. None of them is definitive. Each society is likely to have its own set of circumstances. In the case of the Arab Uprisings, the importance of mineral wealth appears to be the key. To be sure, oil wealth is associated with higher levels of inequality. In the Hong Kong case, the state successfully beat back an effort at democratization despite the existence of a society with low levels of ethnic and religious heterogeneity, high levels of income, a prominent civil society, and a sizable middle class. That said, inequality is significant in Hong Kong. According to one report, the top 10% earns 29 times the bottom 10%, and one in three elderly citizens lives in poverty—despite exceptional wealth and opulence in Hong Kong.[20] Whether inequality was key to China's decision is an open question. More likely is that China is against political liberalization for a variety of reasons, and it saw danger in providing an opening in Hong Kong that could diffuse to the mainland. China remains a strong, powerful state that has the capacity to repress pro-democracy movements and sustain the political status quo. In short, the theory here provides insight and food for thought, but why states democratize and consolidate democracy remains a subject of vital debate.

DEMOCRACY AND INTERNATIONAL STUDIES THEMES

Democracy is a story about global interactions. Democracy is about political liberalization, about the flow of ideas. Although democracy primarily refers to a domestic regime type, the more open a society is politically, the greater the exposure of ideas will be. But more than that, democracy is an ideal that has come to appeal to people around the world. The idea of democracy spreads across borders and inspires citizens who live under dictatorship (see Figure 7.6).

Global Markets and Democratization

Several of our global forces are changing the nature of democracy worldwide. First consider the importance of global markets. There was once a time when governments routinely controlled the prices of key commodities, such as sugar, wheat, rice, and corn; there was once a time when governments routinely used steep tariffs to protect domestic industries from competition;

FIGURE 7.6

Global Forces, Interactions, and Tensions: Markets and Global Governance Create Backlash at the Polls

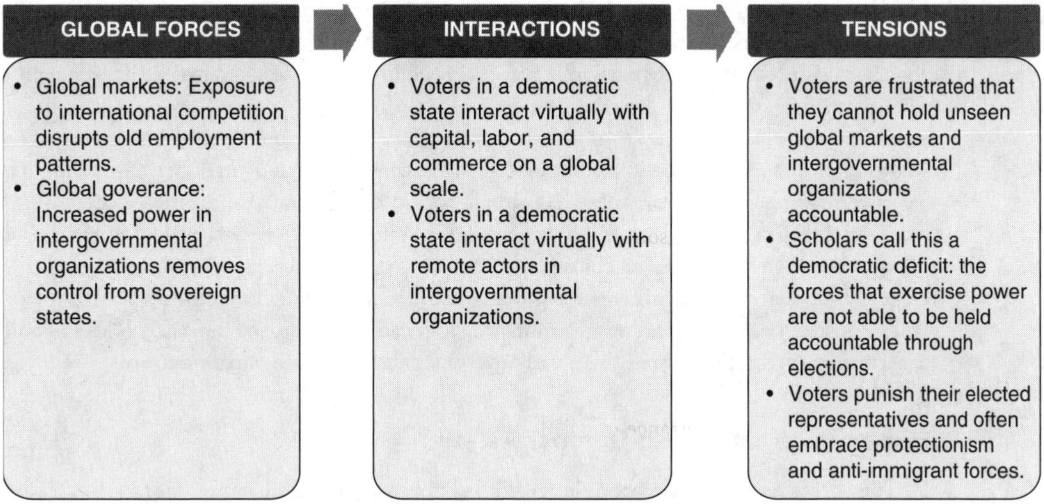

GLOBAL FORCES	INTERACTIONS	TENSIONS
• Global markets: Exposure to international competition disrupts old employment patterns. • Global goverance: Increased power in intergovernmental organizations removes control from sovereign states.	• Voters in a democratic state interact virtually with capital, labor, and commerce on a global scale. • Voters in a democratic state interact virtually with remote actors in intergovernmental organizations.	• Voters are frustrated that they cannot hold unseen global markets and intergovernmental organizations accountable. • Scholars call this a democratic deficit: the forces that exercise power are not able to be held accountable through elections. • Voters punish their elected representatives and often embrace protectionism and anti-immigrant forces.

and there was once a time when governments set the price of their currencies. With the rise of economic liberalization, however, economic markets have become global. Although governments still regulate, the broad trend in the contemporary world has been to open domestic economies to global competition—for labor, finance, goods, and services. Global competition in turn means more exposure to the market and less government interference to protect citizens from it.

Global markets create winners and losers. On the winning side, if a particular industry or firm has lower labor costs and can make a product for cheaper at roughly the same quality, then that sector will benefit from exposure to global markets. Those companies will sell more goods, which means more profit for the executives and shareholders and more jobs. For consumers, global competition generally means cheaper prices, which also translates into more spending money. But many sectors will be losers. In particular, in a country that has high labor costs—which is often the case in the Global North—companies from the Global South will compete with cheaper products. Alternatively, companies based in the Global North will relocate to the Global South in a process called "outsourcing." When they do so, they will move employment to the place where labor costs are cheaper, resulting in huge job losses in their home countries. Other losers are consumers whose governments previously had subsidized key livelihood items, whether foodstuffs, petroleum products, or even electricity. Opened to the market, the prices for such basic goods can increase significantly, which can have a major impact on households in the affected countries.

In both cases, losers would look to their governments to express dissatisfaction. In a democratic system, they might vote against incumbents because the latter represent the status quo. Those in government face a dilemma, however, which is that the globalized system that underpins most economies is not in their control. Their power to lower prices and keep jobs on their soil is diminished—unless they were to unwind the liberal economic order.

These issues were in play during the 2016 presidential elections in the United States. Although the ultimate outcome of the vote had many determinants, a factor was the support that candidate Donald Trump received from working-class families, especially men, whose wages had stagnated and who had experienced job losses in numerous sectors, particularly in manufacturing. Their resentment helped to fuel a victory for Trump, who made "America First" and keeping jobs on U.S. soil a major part of his campaign. Once in office, though, the question that he faced was whether he *could* reverse globalization trends and bring back jobs that had been lost to overseas industries. That remains an open question.

The point is that as the power of global markets grows, power is more concentrated in the hands of large multinational corporations who are driven by economic fundamentals. As result, the control that governments and people exercise has diminished. What determines the purchasing power of a poor or middle income farmer throughout the world? Who decides where factories (and hence jobs) will be located? In many cases, the answer points back to global markets, over which many farmers, workers, *and their governments* have little power. Here lies another paradox at the center of our world: Although democracy as a form of government has spread over time, the increased power of global markets undermines the power of national governments to influence outcomes.

Global Governance and Democratization

Consider a second cross-cutting force: global governance. In the contemporary world, many states have chosen to cooperate by establishing intergovernmental organizations that regulate and monitor interaction. In most cases, leaders find cooperation in their state's interest, and hence, they establish organizations to facilitate that cooperation. That is the case for cross-border environmental challenges, such as climate change; for cross-border security threats, such as nuclear weapon proliferation; and of course for economic issues, such as trade. The most extensive form of interstate cooperation is the European Union (EU), which establishes a common currency (the euro), a common migration policy (the Schengen system), and the right for anyone from one country in the EU to work in another.

But ceding power to intergovernmental organizations reduces government's control, which in turn can fuel citizen resentment, which in turn can lead governments to try to reassert control. As we discuss in Chapter 13, a major breakthrough took place in 2015 when states came together to sign an accord to combat climate change. Shortly after being elected, however, Donald Trump—riding a wave of support to put America first—indicated that the United States would withdraw from the agreement. Moreover, in recent years, a backlash against the EU has grown in established democracies in that region. From the Netherlands, to France, to Spain, support for populist movements has grown dramatically. In each of these countries, dissatisfaction with the EU has been central to the populist movements.

One major shift took place in Britain in 2016 when voters unexpectedly chose in a referendum to leave the European Union—a move that was dubbed "Brexit." Democratic control was a major theme of the "leave" campaign. For example, one of the key voices in favor of leaving the EU was former London mayor Boris Johnson. He likened "Brexit" to Independence Day. Regaining control was one of his refrains: "The ideal position for us is to take back control . . . of huge amounts of money, so we can spend it on our priorities. Take back control of our immigration system, take back control—fundamentally—of our democracy."[21] In the end, his arguments carried the day in the United Kingdom.

In short, global markets and global governance create a **democratic deficit**, or the sense that national leaders who are elected no longer have control over the destiny of their citizens. The increasing power and influence of intergovernmental organizations have generated feelings of a loss of democracy. That deficit combined with dissatisfaction has fueled a growing backlash against globalization in some states that were the earliest and most avid champions of it. Global interactions in this case generated new resentment, new turmoil, and new tensions around the world. The sense that faceless, unaccountable, unelected officials now make key decisions in a world with greater global governance makes many citizens feel as if their democratic voice is undermined—and that has given rise to a major backlash against established political parties in Europe and a major boost to populist parties. Democracy is again now center stage in the politics of the United States and Europe but driven by concerns about how global governance and global markets undermine it.

democratic deficit: when elected officials no longer have control over the destiny of citizens. In this case, democratic voting is not able to hold representatives accountable because the elected officials are not making the crucial decisions.

Information and Communications Technology and Democratization

The impact of ICT on regimes is mixed. On the one hand, the efficiency and low cost of information and communications are inherently democratic. They allow more people to express themselves and to have access to new ideas, on a global scale. In some cases, information and communications technology has been central to democratic social movements. We saw that with the Arab Uprisings and the Hong Kong pro-democracy movement; in both cases, social media were accelerators of protests.

On the other hand, advances in technology have given governments profound powers of surveillance, and the threats of terrorism we describe in Chapter 10 have prompted many governments to impinge on privacy and other democratic rights in the name of security. Government contractor Edward Snowden revealed how intelligence agencies can track and listen to citizens through devices that are ubiquitous in our lives, such as our cell phones and televisions. The private sector also has massive new surveillance powers. Popular companies like Alphabet (Google) and Amazon track our searching and spending histories to target us with new products.

In addition, savvy authoritarian rulers have learned how to use and manipulate ICT in sophisticated ways. New forms of information and communications technology have become woven into the fabric of dictatorship. Putin of Russia is a master of call-in televisions shows. Other leaders seek to disconnect social media or cell phone networks as a way to curtail protest and organizations. Terrorist groups too traffic in information. Both to recruit and publicize their exploits, terrorist organizations have become sophisticated users of cutting-edge communications technology.

In short, the communication technology cuts both ways in terms of how much it contributes, or not, to political freedom. Optimists hail it as a revolutionary tool that will unlock potential and sink dictatorship, but in practice, the technology has shown itself also to be a powerful tool in the hands of nondemocratic forces.

Shifting Centers of Power and Democratization

Like ICT, the rise of newly powerful countries is having a mixed effect on democratization. On the one hand, some of the great rising powers—notably, China and Russia—are fiercely resistant to democracy and to civil and political rights. Their examples and their leadership on the world stage are powerful counterweights to the secular trend toward democracy.

Voting in Indonesia
iStock/ajriya

On the other hand, other rising giants are fiercely democratic, notably Brazil and India, which is the world's largest democracy. Other rising powers, such as Indonesia and South Africa, have recent, strong democratic credentials—even if internal forces in both cases want to impose illiberal policies. The global force here cuts both ways.

How these issues will play out in coming decades is unclear. But the struggle for freedom and representation, and the ways in which the contemporary global forces foster and undercut those struggles, make this area particularly fascinating to study in an international studies context.

IS From the Outside-In and the Inside-Out

ELECTORAL INTERFERENCE AND RESPONSES TO IT

Voters electing representatives would seem to be a quintessentially domestic process. Yet the 2016 elections in the United States revealed the ways in which external powers can harness the power of social media to manipulate and disrupt electoral processes.

Although the extent of the electoral interference is still being uncovered, U.S. law enforcement has now documented an elaborate scheme by which Russian operatives created profiles online and promoted false, often inflammatory, news stories. Those stories often were designed to fire up angry voters who presumably vote against the status quo. They were also meant to sow divisions in the American public.

Russian hackers also infiltrated the electronic records of the Democratic National Committee in the United States. They in turn released the hacked e-mails to influence the 2016 presidential vote in the United States.

Both actions have spurred elaborate investigations by the U.S. Justice Department. Announcing indictments in 2018, a high ranking official called

the Russian interference an attempt to "promote discord . . . and undermine public confidence in democracy."

Russia's use of social media and other forms of electronic technology to influence democratic processes is not unique to the United States. Russian operatives are suspected of trying to manipulate electoral processes in the Ukraine, France, and the United Kingdom.

A U.S.-based democracy promotion organization, the National Democratic Institute, calls disinformation in politics a "critical threat" to democracy itself. In response, the organization has offered some of its most prestigious honors to organizations that seek to counter disinformation and manipulation. One is "StopFake.org" in the Ukraine, which aims to monitor and uncover such disinformation. Another is "Rappler" in the Philippines that also seeks to expose social media "bots" that peddle false information.

This example illustrates many dimensions of an international studies approach. On the one hand, we have here a powerful state, Russia, asserting its influence on the global stage, in particular by trying to undermine democratic processes in the United States and elsewhere. Russia is one of the key states in the current shifting center of power globally. Moreover, Russia is using ICT to accomplish its goals. In both cases, these outside-in forces are sowing divisions, creating tensions, prompting investigations, and undermining trust in democracy. At the same time, we can see the effects of domestic, inside-out responses, including judicial investigations but also organizations committed to countering disinformation and electoral interference.

Reflect

Does modern information and communications technology strengthen or weaken democracy?

Sources: https://www.ndi.org/our-stories/disinformation-vs-democracy-fighting-facts https://www.nytimes.com/2018/02/16/us/politics/russians-indicted-mueller-election-interference.html? rref=collection%2Fnewseventcollection%2Frussian-election-hacking&action=click&contentCollection=politics&region=stream&module=stream_unit&version=latest&contentPlacement=38&pgtype=collection

SUMMARY

One of us once lived under a dictatorship in a country in eastern Africa. The sense of fear and paranoia was palpable and constant. At every turn, one wondered: Am I being watched? Will what I say land me in jail or force me to be expelled? The experience was humbling and at times terrifying; it made the appreciation for democracy run incredibly deep. Many people around the world long to throw off the yoke of repression. Yet democracies around the world are in crisis today, in part, because of the global forces we underline in this book. The sense of a loss of democratic power and the sense that national communities are under threat from immigration have given rise to populist parties, ones that promise to undo the status quo. How that will play out in the coming years is an open question.

This chapter covered a broad introduction to the subject. The chapter defined the key terms in the field, notably, democracy and authoritarianism. The chapter then moved to questions of democratization, or the process of becoming more democratic, and discussed how often states do not move in a linear fashion from dictatorship to democracy. Many get stuck in a "hybrid" space. The chapter further documented historical trends in democratization and outlined arguments for why states initiate and consolidate democratic processes. Finally, the chapter showed how democracy is connected to the four major global forces in focus in this book—global markets, global governance, information and communications technology, and shifting centers of power.

KEY TERMS

aid conditionality 195
competitive authoritarianism
   (or hybrid regimes) 184
contestation 185
democracy 183
democracy promotion 194
democratic consolidation 194
democratic deficit 203

democratic initiation 194
democratic peace 195
democratization 184
demonstration effect
   (or diffusion) 196
dictatorship
   (or authoritarianism) 183
monarchy 186

participation 185
popular sovereignty 184
representation 183
social movements 196
three waves of democratization 189

QUESTIONS FOR REVIEW

1. How would you distinguish a democracy from a dictatorship?

2. Do you think the world will become increasingly democratic over time, or will there be a growing reversal? Why or why not?

3. What do you think is the most important condition that sustains democracy?

LEARN MORE

Daron Acemoglu and James Robinson, *The Economic Origins of Dictatorship and Democracy* (New York, NY: Cambridge University Press, 2006).

Erica Chenoweth and Maria Stephan, *Why Civil Disobedience Works: The Strategic Logic of Nonviolent Conflict* (New York, NY: Columbia University Press, 2011).

Steven Levitsky and Daniel Ziblatt, *How Democracies Die: What History Reveals About Our Future* (New York, NY: Random House, 2018).

Marc Lynch, *The New Arab Wars: Uprisings and Anarchy in the Middle East* (New York, NY: Public Affairs, 2016).

Explore the Freedom House website and country reports: https://freedomhouse.org/

NOTES

1. Francis Fukuyama, *The End of History and the Last Man* (New York, NY: Free Press, 1992).

2. See Adam Przeworski, Michael Alvarez, José Antonio Cheibub, and Fernando Limongi, *Democracy and Development: Political Institutions and Well-Being in the World, 1950-1990* (New York, NY: Cambridge University Press, 2000), 19 and Michael Bratton and Nicolas van de Walle, *Democratic Experiments in Africa: Regime Transitions in Comparative Perspective* (New York, NY: Cambridge University Press, 1997), 13.

3. Robert Dahl, *Polyarchy: Participation and Opposition* (New Haven, CT: Yale University Press, 1971), 1–2.

4. Dahl, 1971, p. 2.

5. https://freedomhouse.org/report/freedom-net/freedom-net-2015.

6. https://freedomhouse.org/report/freedom-press-2016/table-country-scores-fotp-2016.

7. https://freedomhouse.org/report/freedom-world-2018-table-country-scores.

8. Steven Levitsky and Lucan Way, *Competitive Authoritarianism: Hybrid Regimes After the Cold War* (New York, NY: Cambridge University Press, 2010), 3.

9. Samuel Huntington, *The Third Wave: Democratization in the Late Twentieth Century* (Norman: University of Oklahoma Press, 1991).

10. The data used to calculate the figure are slightly different from those used in Huntington; hence, the dates of the waves are slightly different. But the broad pattern of three waves, followed by reversals, holds; see Renske Doorenspleet. "Reassessing the three waves of democratization," *World Politics* 52 (2000): 384–406.

11. Doorenspleet, 2000.

12. Summary based on Kenneth Greene, *Why Dominant Parties Lose: Mexico's Democratization in Comparative Perspective* (New York, NY: Cambridge University Press, 2007). Freedom House Mexico Reports available here: https://freedomhouse.org/report/freedom-world/2017/mexico.

13. Charles Tilly and Sidney Tarrow, *Contentious Politics* (Boulder, CO: Paradigm, 2007).

14. Marc Lynch, *The Arab Uprisings: The Unfinished Revolutions of the New Middle East* (New York, NY: PublicAffairs, 2012).

15. Lynch, 2016.

16. In addition to Lynch, 2016, see Jason Brownlee, Tarek Masoud, and Andrew Reynolds, *The Arab Spring: Pathways of Repression and Reform* (Oxford, U.K.: Oxford University Press, 2014).

17. Adam Przeworski et al., 2000.

18. Barrington Moore, *The Social Origins of Dictatorship and Democracy: Lord and Peasant in the Making of the Modern World* (Boston, MA: Beacon Press, 1966).

19. Daron Acemoglu and James Robinson, *The Economic Origins of Dictatorship and Democracy* (New York, NY: Cambridge University Press, 2006).

20. http://www.oxfam.org.hk/en/news_5160.aspx.

21. http://www.bbc.com/news/uk-politics-eu-referendum-36582567.

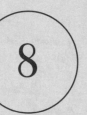

8 Human Rights

THE CHALLENGE OF SETTING AND ENFORCING GLOBAL NORMS

LEARNING OBJECTIVES

After finishing this chapter, you should be able to:

- Articulate the scope of human rights on an international scale.

- Identify some of the major human rights instruments, like the UDHR, ICCPR, and ICESCR.

- Understand some of the strengths and weaknesses of the international human rights treaty system.

- Locate the main regional human rights system, and understand some of the trade-offs of a regional approach compared with an international one.

- Identify the ways in which nonstate actors play a crucial role in human rights promotion.

- Present different arguments for whether and how human rights have power on a global scale.

- Analyze how global forces shape the human rights field.

iStock/Joel Carillet

The Rohingya are a minority ethnic group in western Myanmar. As Muslims with a distinctive language, Rohingya have faced persecution since the country was founded in 1947. The government does not recognize the group as a legitimate ethnic minority; the Rohingya lack citizenship rights and are considered foreigners in their own land.[1] In the mid-2010s, militants escalated the violence against the Rohingya, leading hundreds of thousands of Rohingya to flee the country. With thousands of Rohingya killed, villages torched, many raped, and half a million living precariously as refugees, the Rohingya crisis became one of the world's defining human rights crises.

Human rights groups documented and condemned the violence. The United Nations (UN) High Commissioner for Human Rights, who is one of the key human rights actors in the UN system, deplored the violence as a "textbook example of ethnic cleaning."[2] In a collaborative report with the Asia-based human rights organization Fortify Rights, the U.S. Holocaust Memorial Museum issued a detailed report that pointed to "mounting evidence of genocide."[3] And through satellite imagery, Human Rights Watch, an international human rights organization, recorded before and after pictures, clearly and powerfully showing the razing of Rohingya villages.[4]

The documentation and condemnation of the atrocities brought new attention and visibility to the Rohingya crisis. Leaders at the UN, in global civil society, and in several governments around the world called the violence "unacceptable." In doing so, they drew on human rights norms and law. Various human rights instruments were the benchmark against which various international actors assailed the mass human destruction—even though the violence happened at the hands of a foreign country. At the same time, the documentation and condemnation did not stop the violence or magically improve the lives of the hundreds of thousands of Rohingya refugees who fled the violence.

The Myanmar example shows both the promise and the limits of human rights. Human rights capture many of the loftiest ideals in the contemporary world. **Human rights** cover a broad range of issues, including mass violence, as in Myanmar, repression, and torture. Human rights also include commitments to a decent life, through education, health, and even access to clean water. Underlying these diverse areas is the core concept that every person anywhere in the world, irrespective of citizenship, has some basic, **inalienable rights**. That they are "inalienable" means that people anywhere in the world, no matter their country, their age, their gender, their ethnicity, their income level, their religion, or their profession, are born with rights that are necessary for a life with human dignity. By virtue of being human, people have such rights. Governments like those in Myanmar cannot wish them away, even if they would like to.

Human rights are meant to apply globally. Human rights activists seek to ensure that rights apply in practice to all people everywhere. In condemning the violence in Myanmar, Human Rights Watch drew on international standards of how governments must treat their citizens. On those grounds, the organization called on the United Nations to take various actions, including the imposition of economic penalties.

In these and other ways, human rights are fundamentally about international interactions. As the Myanmar case shows, they involve violations in one country, documentation by organizations in other countries, and condemnations by the United Nations and other organizations. More generally, human rights have been spread through a global circulation of ideas, standards, and laws. Human rights norms, initially promulgated at the global level, in turn shape how people think and act at the local level; human rights frame what is considered acceptable and unacceptable behavior. In that way, human rights operate from the outside-in.

By the same token, people in all countries—whether leaders, activists, or ordinary citizens—draw on the language of human rights to name their oppression and press for change and remedy. In this way, human rights operate from the inside-out; they provide local level tools. In much the same way, domestic courts draw on global human rights standards and judgments in other countries to adjudicate cases in the countries where the court cases are heard. Diplomats furthermore intervene routinely on human rights grounds, leveraging global standards and norms against states that commit human rights abuses. All of this constitutes a complex web of interaction between ideas and people, between different governments, and between the international and the local.

Human rights are also the source of tensions. Human rights inspire contestation and disillusionment. There are many who believe that human rights mark a false promise. Human rights aspire to protect all people from abuse and to guarantee a minimum standard of living. But the reality is that

human rights: set of rights afforded to individuals on the basis of being human, i.e., irrespective of national citizenship, gender, ethnicity, or other traits.

inalienable rights: human rights are inalienable in that they cannot be removed; human rights adhere to persons by virtue of being alive.

human rights are not a firewall against tyranny or deprivation. Human rights offer a language and tools to challenge oppression, but they do not guarantee such freedom or protection. How much difference did the global outcry over the violence in Myanmar make? The human rights work shamed the government; they made the international community uncomfortable. But as of this writing, the violence continues and the refugees number in the hundreds of thousands.

Moreover, many around the world claim that human rights represent the core values of the Global North and the wealthy. Such people dispute the idea that human rights are, in fact, truly universal. They view the imposition of a global value system as an exercise of power that runs contrary to their own values and culture. They argue that human rights norms should not take precedence over their norms and values, which they say run contrary to those represented in the major treaties. Human rights in this way are a source of global tension. Most people in Myanmar appear to resent the defense of the Rohingya as unwanted interference. Indeed, a government commission dismissed the UN's allegations, calling them untrue and an effort to "tarnish the image" of Myanmar.[5]

This chapter provides an introduction to international human rights. The chapter begins with a discussion of the foundations of human rights and then explores how human rights ideals were translated into formal documents, treaties, and institutions. The chapter in turn examines how human rights systems work at a regional level and the centrality of nongovernmental organizations, like Human Rights Watch, to the function of human rights. The chapter closes with a discussion of different arguments about the relative power of human rights, and last, it shows how human rights intersect with the global forces that are central to this book.

WHAT IS THE HUMAN RIGHTS REGIME?

Many argue that the world's major religions form the foundation for human rights. Human rights are, after all, the idea that all people are endowed with dignity and worth. That idea is similar to the idea that all people are created in the likeness of God, which is common in most world religions. Major world religions also codify the spirit of help to strangers and charity, ideas that resonate with the human rights mandate to advocate on behalf of people around the world. Human rights are also grounded in core philosophical traditions that espoused an ideal "state of nature" in which rights exist, notably the ideas of John Locke, Jean-Jacques Rousseau, and Hugo Grotius. These ideas inspired the American and French revolutions of the 19th century, which later became models for the human rights movement. In these ways, the idea of human rights is old.

human rights regime: modern system of human rights declarations, treaties, and institutions designed to define and promote human rights on a global scale.

The specific, modern **human rights regime** that encompasses a set of declarations, laws, and dedicated institutions, however, is a fairly recent development in world history. Prior to World War II, the idea that all people were invested with certain basic rights was primarily a national concern. That is, states determined citizenship, and through citizenship, individuals were eligible to have certain rights. That was the core innovation in the American and French revolutions, even if in the United States and France the revolutions did not immediately translate into voting or other rights for women, people of color, non-landowners, and others. But the concept was that states protected and guaranteed people's rights. States, in short, were sovereign with respect to the governance and rights of citizens.

The idea of human rights is different. In human rights, people do not access rights through states but by virtue of being human. That idea formally took shape in the aftermath of World War II. Until that point in history, the idea of international relations and international law was primarily about the regulation and management of *interstate* behavior, of protecting one state's rights against another state's rights.

FIGURE 8.1

Global Force, Interactions, and Tensions in the Aftermath of World War II

GLOBAL FORCES	INTERACTIONS	TENSIONS
• The major Allied powers in World War II promised to promote freedom and human rights if victorious.	• The wartime promises created expectations among people around the world and less powerful governments that the post-war order would include strong commitments to human rights.	• The major powers did not want to diminish sovereignty greatly or to create human rights standards that would have strong enforcement powers. The resulting UN Charter "promotes" human rights but does not "guarantee" them.

World War II was a turning point for two main reasons. First, in combating fascism in the war, the United States and Britain in particular used the language of rights and freedom as an ideological tool; they claimed that the fight against fascism was fundamentally about rights and freedom. Those claims created expectations, and once the war ended, states and citizens pressured the dominant powers to make rights and freedom central to the postwar order. Second, the specific experience of the Holocaust during World War II—the systematic destruction of six million Jews, hundreds of thousands of Roma and Sinti, and millions of Polish citizens, among other victim groups—showed the dangers of deferring to state sovereignty. In that case, deference to state sovereignty meant that outside powers did not have a strong rationale to intervene to protect civilian populations under Nazi control. In other words, the Holocaust played a very important role in making it clear that human rights did belong, at some level, beyond the sovereignty of states.

At the same time, the powerful players in the international arena still believed in sovereignty and still insisted on sovereignty. Britain maintained a network of colonies. The United States had entrenched practices of racism. Neither country wanted to invest an outside body with the power to force change in their domestic space (see Figure 8.1).

HUMAN RIGHTS AT THE UN LEVEL: ROOTS OF THE TENSION BETWEEN UNIVERSAL RIGHTS AND STATE SOVEREIGNTY

These tensions are embedded in the **Charter of the United Nations,** which as discussed in Chapter 3 lays the foundation for order in the world since World War II. The Charter itself is not a human rights document but a wide-ranging treaty that establishes the architecture for peace and shared governance. The Charter, however, does recognize human rights as a central principle of the new international order. The Charter links human rights to international peace and security, and the Charter pledges all member states to achieve "universal respect for, and observance of human rights and fundamental freedoms without distinction as to race, sex, language, and religion." These are significant statements that structure human rights into the postwar global order.

Charter of the United Nations: United Nations treaty that establishes the architecture for peace and shared governance, pledging all members to achieve "universal respect for, and observance of human rights and fundamental freedoms without distinction as to race, sex, language, and religion."

But the Charter also clearly recognizes the importance of state sovereignty. Article 2, for example, states, "Nothing contained in the present Charter shall authorize the United Nations to intervene in matters which are essentially within the domestic jurisdiction of any state."

This tension between a commitment to universal human rights and deference to state sovereignty is baked into the architecture of the international system. That tension both inspires and weakens human rights action. On the one hand, the United Nations stands to "promote" and "encourage" human rights, which is the language of Article I of the Charter. Indeed, human rights is central to the organization, and the United Nations (from the Secretary-General through to many specialized agencies) remains one of the most central actors in the human rights domain. We saw, for example, how UN officials were at the forefront of the condemnation of Myanmar's treatment of the Rohingya. On the other hand, the UN Charter does not "guarantee" human rights, and the specific concrete action that the United Nations can take to enforce human rights is limited. With some exceptions (discussed later in this chapter), the United Nations does not have the authority to interfere directly to protect people from human rights abuse or to punish human rights offenders. In the human rights world, this is known as the **enforcement problem**—the structural obstacles to enforcing human rights rules and norms. This too is amply evident in the Myanmar example, where the ability of the United Nations did not directly change the situation or stop the violence.

Despite the inherent weakness of human rights protections, the UN Charter did create a mandate to promote human rights. But what exactly are human rights? To what was the UN committing itself? To answer those questions, in 1946, the United Nations established a Commission on Human Rights that was tasked with drafting a substantive declaration on human rights. That Commission was chaired by Eleanor Roosevelt, the widow of President Franklin Delano Roosevelt, and a major proponent of human rights. The resulting document was the **Universal Declaration of Human Rights (UDHR)**, which is a statement that defines what human rights are. Today, even though the document is not law, the UDHR towers over a crowded field; the UDHR is widely recognized as the touchstone, the foundation, for defining human rights.

enforcement problem: idea that human rights treaties and institutions have a weak ability to force violators to comply with human rights standards and laws.

Universal Declaration of Human Rights (UDHR): 1948 document that remains a touchstone for codifying human rights on a global scale; the document is a declaration, or statement of principles, not a binding legal treaty.

Fotosearch/Getty Images

The Universal Declaration of Human Rights

To create the UDHR, Eleanor Roosevelt assembled a team of lawyers, philosophers, and jurists from around the world, who in turn collected petitions from other scholars around the world. That consultation is important. One of the persistent critiques of human rights is that they represent a "Western" or Global North perspective on political and social values. Yet in the drafting of the document, Roosevelt and her team explicitly solicited the views of scholars, jurists, competing political ideologies, and religious authorities from around the world. In the end, the UN General Assembly approved the document in December 1948, and Roosevelt called the UDHR the "international magna carta of all men everywhere."

The UDHR contains 30 articles as well as a preamble, which calls the declaration a "common standard of achievement for all peoples and all nations." Broadly speaking, the UDHR brings together five major categories of rights:

1. Protection of individuals' physical integrity, as in provisions on torture, arbitrary arrest, slavery, and life.

2. Procedural fairness when government deprives an individual of liberty, as in provisions on arrest, trial procedure, and conditions of imprisonment.

3. Equal protection norms defined in racial, religious, gender, and other terms.

4. Freedoms of belief, speech, and association, such as provisions on political advocacy, the practice of religion, press freedom, and the right to hold an assembly, form associations, own property, or participate in politics.

5. Economic and social rights, such as provisions on a decent standard of living, food, education, leisure, health, social services, culture, and the development of personality.

The rights set forth in this document remain highly influential; they concisely carve out a human rights space, defining what human rights are and shaping the agenda on human rights. For these reasons, the UDHR is a major achievement and speaks to the ways in which intergovernmental organizations shape and diffuse norms and values, which is the key to the constructivist account of intergovernmental organizations, as discussed in Chapter 3.

United Nations Human Rights Treaties

The UDHR is a statement of principles, not a legally binding instrument. It defines human rights. In its wake, creating binding **international treaties** became the primary way that the UN and member-states advanced human rights. Over time, the effort has yielded dozens of treaties. A treaty is different from a declaration. A treaty is a binding formal agreement that establishes obligations between two or more subjects of international law. In this way, treaties are core tools in the global governance structures described throughout the book. They establish rules, create mechanisms to monitor enforcement, and empower institutions to issue guidelines on compliance.

In the human rights field, the two most important treaties are the **International Covenant on Civil and Political Rights (ICCPR)** and the **International Covenant on Economic, Social, and Cultural Rights (ICESCR)**. Together with the UDHR, these three documents constitute what

international treaties: binding formal agreement that establishes obligations between two or more subjects of international law, usually states.

International Covenant on Civil and Political Rights (ICCPR): main international human rights treaty that covers civil and political rights.

International Covenant on Economic, Social, and Cultural Rights (ICESCR): main international human rights treaty that covers economic, social, and cultural rights.

some call the "International Bill of Rights." The two treaties represent different versions of rights. The first, the ICCPR, concerns core civil and political rights issues, such as freedom of worship, speech, and assembly; protection against gender or race discrimination; and freedom from torture. The ICCPR represents a classic liberal view of human rights, represented in documents like the U.S. Constitution and the Bill of Rights. Many label such rights **negative rights** in that they protect individuals *from* harm, violation, and interference. In essence, they encapsulate the first four categories of rights described earlier. By contrast, the ICESCR represents a more developmentalist approach to rights, one that comes primarily out of socialist political thought. Many label such rights **positive rights** in that they represent rights *to* things. These include the rights to decent living conditions, food, basic healthcare, social security, and education—those rights included in the fifth category described earlier.

Although the ICCPR and the ICESCR are the most important and comprehensive human rights treaties, there are several other core treaties. These include but are not limited to the International Convention on the Elimination of All Forms of Racial Discrimination (ICERD); the Convention on the Elimination of All Forms of Discrimination Against Women (CEDAW); the Convention against Torture and Other Cruel, Inhuman or Degrading Treatment of Punishment (CAT); the Convention on the Rights of the Child (CRC); and the International Convention on the Protection of the Rights of All Migrant Workers and Members of their Families (ICPRMW).

In each issue domain—racism, women's issues, the rights of children, torture, and migrant workers—these treaties are essential instruments. They are definitive in terms of identifying the problem (i.e., how do you define discrimination against women), they delimit the scope of the issue (i.e., in what issue areas do children's rights surface), and they establish a space for action on the part of human rights institutions and organizations (i.e., in creating the authority to call attention to a particular problem and to hold states accountable for their action). In these ways, the human rights treaties are major components of global governance.

How Human Rights Treaties Come Into Being

Human rights treaties are the product of a complex process. The first step is drafting and negotiating the language of a treaty. The second step is that the executive branch of a state signs a treaty; in so doing, a state indicates its general agreement with the treaty's principles. The third step is that a country's legislative body ratifies the treaty. In most states, ratification is the crucial step; ratification makes the treaty legally binding within those states. Finally, human rights treaties establish a UN treaty committee, which monitors the implementation record of compliance of a particular country. In so doing, the committee enters into dialogue with a country, whereby the country reports on its record and the committee issues a response, followed by the state's response. For example, there is a Committee on the Elimination of Discrimination against Women, which monitors whether countries around the world are doing what they said they would do when they ratified the CEDAW treaty.

Each of these steps represents different examples of *interaction*. The clearest case is the interaction between state representatives and the treaty committees. Here states directly engage with an intergovernmental organization; states review their record of action in their domestic space, which they then summarize for the international body. The latter in turn scrutinizes the report and makes recommendations on how the state may improve its domestic record. In addition, individuals and nongovernmental organizations (NGOs) have the right to petition a treaty committee to register a complaint about human rights violations in a particular country. In these different ways, we see how information, rules, ideas, and specific instances of human rights abuse circulate between local, domestic, and international spaces.

The human rights treaty system is indeed *global*. Most states have ratified most core human rights treaties, and some treaties enjoy near-universal ratification, as shown in Figure 8.2.

FIGURE 8.2

Ratification of Key Rights Treaties

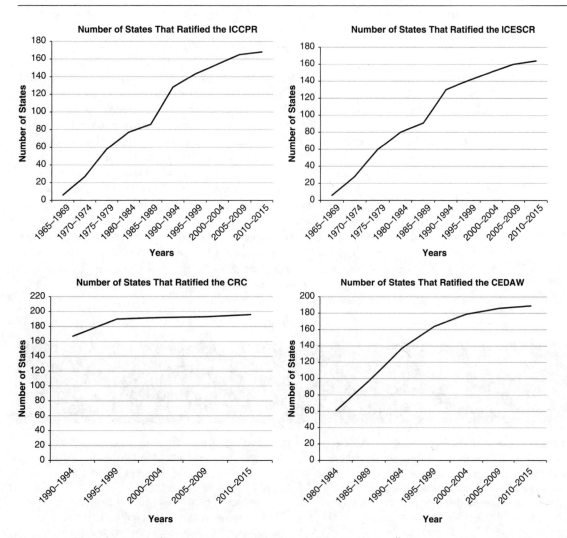

Source: Data from the Database of the United Nations Office of Legal Affairs (OLA) https://treaties.un.org United Nations Human Rights, Office of the High Commissioner, http://indicators.ohchr.org/.

There are a couple of points to underline in these figures. First, the number of countries that ratified major human rights treaties sharply increased after the end of the Cold War in the early 1990s. This is part of a general trend. During the Cold War, the United Nations and even the idea of global governance remained a hostage to the superpower rivalry between the United States and the Soviet Union. With the end of the Cold War, more countries invested hope in the United Nations to manage international problems, and the overall prominence of international issues that were not strictly about national security and economic interests gained prominence. Indeed, the greater visibility of global governance and nontraditional international issues—whether for human rights, global health, the environment, food, water, and other topics—is part of the reason why international studies took off as an area of study. International studies is designed to bring these issues to the fore and to take a multidisciplinary approach to such topics.

The other point to note is that the United States is not party to some major human rights treaties. Of the four graphed, the United States has ratified only the ICCPR. Such behavior is puzzling to many students. On the one hand, the United States is a beacon for human rights in the world; since its beginning, the United States has stood to promote freedom within its own boundaries and the world—even if at different points in history, the United States legalized slavery, prevented women from voting and holding office, and otherwise undermined the idea of equality and freedom. On the other hand, the United States has a complex relationship with global governance that scholars often refer to as **American exceptionalism**. As a general statement, the United States has promoted global governance institutions that support U.S. interests and values, whether in areas of trade, security, or human rights. But the United States has been wary to subject itself to those same global governance institutions. In the realm of human rights, with regard to specific treaties, different U.S. governments have advanced a variety of reasons. But typically the arguments boil down to the claim that the United States believes its own record on human rights issues is exemplary, that U.S. legal institutions are so powerful that the country should not ratify treaties with loose language, and that the United States does not want foreign oversight of its governance practices. To some, such exceptionalism undermines the whole global human rights project; to others who are wary of global governance, such behavior is not only warranted but wise.

American exceptionalism: idea that the United States is special and distinct and should not subject itself to human rights global governance, even as it promotes human rights for other countries.

IS From the Outside-In and the Inside-Out

HUMAN RIGHTS AND ABORTION IN IRELAND

A good example of the complex interactions in the human rights system comes from a case in Ireland. In November 2013, Amanda Jane Mellet, an Irish national who was represented by an Irish NGO, the Center for Reproductive Rights, submitted a complaint to the Human Rights Committee in regard to Ireland's alleged violations of the International Covenant on Civil and Political Rights (ICCPR). Ireland has ratified the ICCPR and is therefore party to the treaty. The Human Rights Committee is the treaty committee of the ICCPR.

In November 2011, Mellet was 21 weeks pregnant when her doctor informed her that the fetus had congenital heart defects and that the fetus "would die in utero or shortly after birth." Irish law criminalized abortion, even in instances when the fetus was likely to die of natural causes. Given the circumstances, the doctor informed Mellet that she could continue her pregnancy until the fetus died of natural causes, or "travel." By "travel," the doctor implied that Mellet could terminate her pregnancy in a foreign country where abortion in her situation was legal. Due to the complexity of Irish abortion law, the doctor did not provide any other information. Mellet decided to travel to England to receive the necessary medical procedures to terminate the pregnancy. Deprived of financial assistance, the process was financially draining, prompting her to travel alone and to leave the hospital early. The trauma was furthered by denied access to psychological counseling and the social stigma attached to her situation.

Mellet claimed Ireland's abortion law had violated her rights as protected under the ICCPR. Specifically, she argued that it violated article 7 by subjecting her to "cruel, inhuman and degrading treatment and encroached on her dignity and physical and mental integrity"; article 17 by infringing on her right to privacy; and article 19 by hindering the availability of vital information; articles 2(1), 3 and 26 on equality and nondiscrimination by rejecting services unique to women's health. The State rejected all of Mellet's claims.

In June 2016, the UN Human Rights Committee issued a comment in favor of Mellet. The committee concluded that the State should financially compensate Mellet and provide her with psychological treatment. Furthermore, it urged the Irish government to "prevent similar violations occurring in the future . . . [by] amend[ing] its law on voluntary termination of pregnancy, including if necessary its Constitution, to ensure compliance with the Covenant, including ensuring effective, timely and accessible procedures for pregnancy termination in Ireland, and take measures to ensure that health-care providers are in a position to supply full information on safe abortion services without fearing being subjected to criminal sanctions."

The comment was controversial in Ireland, but it renewed calls in Ireland to change the Constitution and to relax the laws on abortion. In the wake of the UN treaty comment, some domestic NGOs, political figures, and media reiterated that the government should hold a referendum to amend the constitution and provide greater abortion rights. Those voices grew louder after a second UN human rights committee comment in 2017 similarly found Ireland's restrictions on abortion to be at odds with human rights.[6]

In May 2018, Ireland held a referendum on whether to repeal the 8th Amendment of its constitution. The amendment conferred "equal right to life" on the fetus and the mother; it effectively criminalized abortion in almost all circumstances. With the amendment repealed, the Irish government took steps to make abortion legal in the country in the first 12 weeks of pregnancy.

The Ireland example illustrates the way in which human rights interactions work and the power that human rights may have, even in the absence of strong enforcement. In this case, we see outside-in global governance at work: A UN committee issued a comment, based on an international human rights standard, which in turn strengthened domestic (inside-out) forces to push forward an agenda that faced significant opposition in a heavily Catholic country. We see here a set of complex interactions between individuals, NGOs, other parts of civil society such as the Catholic Church, states, international law, and a monitoring committee. In addition, we also see how a comment may contribute to change in a country even if that comment is not legally binding; in other words, the enforcement power of the treaty committee is weak, but its normative claim to what is right and wrong, based on international human rights standards, proved influential.[7]

Reflect

Through what mechanisms do international human rights treaties and institutions, such as the Human Rights Committee, influence outcomes in states around the world?

United Nations Human Rights Institutions

Treaties anchor the global human rights regime, but international law is only one dimension of the human rights regime. Indeed, there are numerous intergovernmental organizations that specialize in human rights, at both the international and regional levels. In addition, nongovernmental organizations and principled actors more generally play very important roles in the human rights field.

Internationally, within the United Nations system, there are several dedicated intergovernmental organizations. One is the **Human Rights Council**, which is based in Geneva, Switzerland, and has 47 representatives from UN member-states. The mandate for the institution is broad: to address any human rights issue in any country in the world. The Council hears complaints brought by NGOs and by individuals; usually thousands are filed every year. In so doing, the Council essentially serves as a forum for human rights concerns to come to light. In a similar vein, the Council also conducts periodic reviews of all states, which serve as a point of dialogue between an international organization and a government. Finally, the Council also has a special procedure by which it appoints independent experts or working groups to address particular themes or countries. The most common are **Special Rapporteurs** who conduct country visits, consult with states, provide expert opinion, and publicize human rights issues around the world. There are also **Commissions of Inquiry**, which are investigative bodies designed to collect evidence and report on a specific human rights situation. A Commission of Inquiry exists for human rights crimes in Syria (see below). A similar, fact-finding mission exists for Myanmar. Pick almost any human rights issue, and there is likely to be a Special Rapporteur or some other special procedure on it. In the mid-2010s, there were more than 40 thematic ones—on everything from people with albinism, to persons with disabilities, to the right to food, to human trafficking, to the right to safe drinking water. Country-specific Special Rapporteurs exist for countries from Syria and Myanmar to Somalia and Haiti.

A related United Nations institution is the **High Commissioner for Human Rights**, which we saw from the Myanmar example. The High Commissioner is a particular person who travels the world to promote human rights, to draw attention to particular problems, to provide expert information, and to consult with governments. High Commissioners are generally accomplished human rights advocates, lawyers, or diplomats. In recent years, they have come from Jordan, Canada, South Africa, Brazil, and Ireland. Like the work of the Human Rights Council and its special procedures, the High Commissioner and the office attached to the High Commissioner primarily engage in establishing and promoting norms. They are doing the nuts and bolts of global governance—of setting standards, monitoring, and providing authoritative evidence. At the same time, the enforcement power of the institutions is weak. As with the Human Rights Council, the High Commission can issue statements or reports—thereby drawing attention to an issue—and consult with governments. But these bodies lack any real power to impose direct costs on governments or other actors that violate human rights, even on a systematic and large-scale basis.

At the international level, one intergovernmental institution with stronger enforcement power is the **International Criminal Court (ICC)**. The ICC is a permanent standing court that focuses on international criminal justice. That is, the court holds individuals responsible for human rights crimes that they have committed; those individuals are not shielded or protected from the court's jurisdiction by virtue of serving in an official capacity. Indeed, of the cases that the ICC has investigated, several defendants are former or sitting heads of state. The ICC is a treaty-based court. As with other human rights treaties, states may sign and ratify the **Rome Statute**, which is the treaty that establishes the court; the Rome Statute became available for signing in 1998, and the court, which is based in The Hague in the Netherlands, was established in 2002. Although the UN helped establish the ICC, the court is independent of the UN.

The ICC has jurisdiction over only a limited range of the most heinous, human rights crimes: genocide, crimes against humanity, and war crimes, each of which is defined in the Rome Statute. Furthermore, the court practices a principle of **complementarity**, which means that the court is one of last resort—domestic remedies must be exhausted (or nonexistent) for the court to claim jurisdiction. In reality, that means the court handles fairly few cases. Since its existence, the court has completed only a handful of trials, and there have been less than a dozen situations under active investigation. The majority of those have been in Africa, including cases in Sudan, Kenya, Mali, Côte d'Ivoire, Uganda, and the Democratic Republic of Congo. The Africa focus of the court has prompted some strongly negative reactions to the court from some African leaders and opinion-makers, who accuse the court of acting in a neocolonial fashion. Indeed, that the court at one time had indicted two sitting heads of state—in Sudan and Kenya—smacked of a Europe-based institution infringing on the sovereignty of African countries. At the same time, it should be noted that in the majority of ICC cases, African leaders are the ones who recommended that the court investigate through what is known as a "referral process" (see Figure 8.3). Time will tell how effective and powerful the court will be. For now, it is an institution that embodies many of the international studies themes underlined in this book—varieties of interactions that sometimes inspire conflict and that are part of an increasingly interconnected globe.

The Example of the Commission of Inquiry for Syria. In recent years, the conflict in Syria (which we discuss in more detail in Chapter 10) has ripped that country apart and has created one of the world's worst humanitarian disasters. Human rights violations have been a constant in the conflict—and on all sides. One of the chief sources for information about those abuses is the Independent Commission of Inquiry for Syria, which was established by the United Nations Human Rights Council. The Commission of Inquiry has released several reports documenting the human rights abuses on all sides of the conflict. In 2016, the Commission issued a report claiming that the Islamic State of Iraq and Syria (ISIS, aka "the Islamic State"), a militant jihadist organization, had committed genocide, crimes against humanity, and war crimes against the Yazidi population. The Yazidis are a religious minority in Iraq and Syria. The report detailed killing, sexual slavery, enslavement, torture, inhumane and degrading treatment, forcible transfer, birth prevention, dangerous living conditions, forced conversion of adults, mental trauma, and forcible transfer of children. The report concluded that ISIS is acting to destroy the Yazidi population, constituting genocide.

The Commission and its reports are a good example of how human rights work, and of how human rights interactions operate. The Commission is doing the stock and trade of human rights work: documentation. It grounds the work, however, on the existence of established human rights treaties—in this case, the United Nations Genocide Convention, as well as on a host of the core human rights treaties discussed earlier in this chapter. With regard to the genocide claim, the Commission also recommended that the United Nations Security Council refer the case to the ICC for investigation. The case again shows how the human rights regime is a system of interlocking treaties and institutions, which involve complex interactions between states and intergovernmental organizations like the United Nations. In this case, those interactions are about global governance in the human rights space.[8]

International Criminal Court (ICC): permanent standing international court that is designed to prosecute individuals for exceptionally severe crimes, including genocide, crimes against humanity, and war crimes. The court is based in The Hague (the Netherlands).

Rome Statute: international treaty that establishes the international criminal court (ICC).

complementarity: principle that an international court gains jurisdiction only after domestic remedies have been exhausted or are nonexistent; the international body does not substitute for domestic judicial processes but complements them.

FIGURE 8.3

Global Forces, Interactions, and Tensions: The ICC and Human Rights Cases in Africa

GLOBAL FORCES	INTERACTIONS	TENSIONS
• Global governance: States ratify the Rome Statute that establishes the International Criminal Court, based in the Hague, Netherlands.	• The ICC office of the prosecutor investigates select cases of massive human rights violations in states that have ratified the treaty or in situations refered to the court by the UN Security Council. • Most investigations and cases to date have been in Africa.	• Despite having ratified the Rome Statute and in some cases intitated cases, African states resist the court. They claim it intrudes on their sovereignty and smacks of colonialism. • Some African states are pressing for a withdrawal from the court.

REGIONAL APPROACHES TO HUMAN RIGHTS

The human rights institutions within the United Nations system represent an international approach to redressing violations. Another influential approach is a regional one. Indeed, some human rights advocates and policy makers consider a regional approach to human rights to be more effective than an international one. The main advantages of a regional system are that states within a single region tend to be more like-minded than all states in the world are. In addition, a regional approach provides states with greater control and voice in the direction of human rights policy. In that way, leaders of states usually feel more comfortable committing to the human rights standards outlined in regional systems. Moreover, a couple regional human rights systems have stronger enforcement mechanisms than are found at the international level.

By the same token, however, a regional approach has two main disadvantages. One is that by definition the human rights system is not universal (but regional), which runs contrary to the founding idea of human rights. Two is that the greater control that a regional system provides also could serve as a shield from international criticism. That is, human-rights–violating states can better manipulate a regional system than they can an international one.

The two most developed regional human rights systems are in Europe and in Latin America. A third human rights system exists in Africa. A fourth is in Southeast Asia. As Figure 8.4 shows, there is an inverse relationship between higher risks for human rights and stronger regional human rights systems.

The European Human Rights System

The anchor of the European human rights system is the **European Court of Human Rights**, which is based in Strasbourg, France. The human rights treaty from which the court derives its jurisdiction is the European Convention on Human Rights, which was signed in 1950 and

European Court of Human Rights: regional human rights court based in Strasbourg, France; the court hears petitions from individuals and states who are citizens within the Council of Europe.

FIGURE 8.4

Human Rights Risk Worldwide

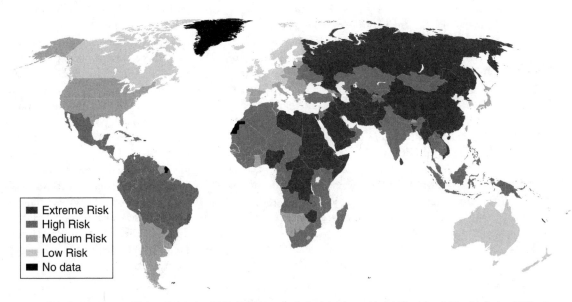

Extreme Risk
High Risk
Medium Risk
Low Risk
No data

Source: Relief Web, Human Rights Risk Index 2016, Q4, https://reliefweb.int/report/world/human-rights-risk-index-2016-q4.

Note: In regions where regional human rights organizations are weakest, the risk of human rights violations is greatest.

incorporates the main civil and political rights outlined in the Universal Declaration of Human Rights. Both the European court and convention operate through the **Council of Europe (CoE)**, which is distinct but related to the **European Union (EU)**. Although the EU's main function is to harmonize markets, currency, immigration, security, and foreign policy, the CoE's main function is to promote human rights, democracy, and the rule of law. While the EU has 28 members, the CoE has 47 members, including Turkey and Russia, who have all ratified the European Convention of Human Rights and are subject to the jurisdiction of the European Court of Human Rights.

Any of the roughly 800 million European citizens who live in a Council of Europe country may bring a case to the European Court of Human Rights. The European institution is a court of last resort in the sense that plaintiffs must have exhausted their domestic remedies first. Indeed, in the past decade, the average number of cases brought to the court per year is more than 40,000. Not every one of those petitions is admissible, but the court is indeed quite busy. The court has issued landmark rulings on torture, freedom of expression, gender equality, and LGBTQ rights, among other issues. In recent years, the overwhelming bulk of cases brought to the court concern Russia, Turkey, and Ukraine. Although the European Court and Convention are the main instruments, they are not the only ones in Europe—the EU has some provisions to promote human rights, for example—the Court and Convention are unusual in terms of an advanced machinery for enforcement and the degree of activity.

Council of Europe (CoE): regional organization composed of 47 European member-states; the Council promotes common values for the continent, including democracy, human rights, and the rule of law.

The Latin American Human Rights System

Within Latin America, the two main human rights institutions are the **Inter-American Commission on Human Rights** and the **Inter-American Court of Human Rights**. Both institutions are within the **Organization of American States (OAS),** which is the main regional organization for the Americas. The Inter-American human rights system is different from the European one. The Inter-American Commission, which is based in Washington, DC, conducts investigations and on-site visits, similar to the way that a UN Commission of Inquiry operates. The Inter-American Court, which is based in San José, Costa Rica, gains jurisdiction if states ratify the **American Convention on Human Rights**. The court only hears cases brought by states against other states or brought by individuals in those countries that have accepted the jurisdiction of the court. For an individual petition to reach the court, however, the Inter-American Commission must deem the complaint admissible.

By and large, the Inter-American system was quiet and ineffective during the periods of military dictatorship in Latin American (in the 1970s and 1980s). The activity and influence of the regional human rights system, however, in particular the court, have grown in the past two decades. Although still less active than the European equivalent, the court has handed down several important decisions for numerous Latin American countries—Honduras, Peru, Brazil, El Salvador, Guatemala, and Chile, among others. Neither the United States nor Canada accepts the jurisdiction of the court by virtue of not having ratified the American Convention on Human Rights.

The African Human Rights System

The next most developed regional human rights system is in Africa. The main regional human rights document is the 1981 **African Charter on Human and People's Rights**, which later established a human rights Commission. A subsequent protocol created an **African Court on Human and People's Rights**, which came into force in the mid-2000s. The court is based in Arusha, Tanzania. About half of the 54 African countries have accepted the jurisdiction of the court, but less than 10 African states have accepted a protocol that allows nongovernmental organizations and individuals to bring cases directly to the court. That means that for most countries that accept the court, one state party would need to bring a human rights complaint against another state, which has been rare in practice.

The Southeast Asian Human Rights System

The three main regional human rights systems are not the only ones. In Southeast Asia, the heads of state in the **Association of Southeast Asian Nations (ASEAN)** launched the **ASEAN Intergovernmental Commission on Human Rights (AICHR)**, which coordinates thematic areas of human rights focus for the region and the drafting of a human rights declaration for Southeast Asia.

In short, alongside the international layer of human rights institutions is a complex network of regional institutions and documents, all of which are part of the complex system of human rights *interaction* around the globe. The regional bodies influence the United Nations ones, and vice versa. States shape and respond to regional and international bodies, and vice versa. In addition, those who suffer human rights abuse or those who wish to advocate on behalf of human rights victims often work through all of these different institutions—they contact NGOs and media in their own country, they petition domestic courts, and in some cases, they file complaints with regional and international bodies. As in many other international areas, we are dealing here with intersecting networks of institutions and declarations that interact and reinforce each other.

WHAT ROLES DO NONSTATE HUMAN RIGHTS ACTORS PLAY?

Nonstate actors are a major force in human rights. Organized citizens and nongovernmental organizations play several different and important roles. They matter for creating human rights standards and laws; that is, they pressure states and international bodies to adopt measures. Examine almost any major human rights law, and behind that process you will find activists and civil society groups that organized, pressured, and contributed to the process of creating the law. Indeed, the human rights field is one of the most visible and active areas for the global civil society actors described in Chapter 4.

Nonstate actors play a critical role in **naming and shaming**. Because in general human rights enforcement mechanisms are weak, human rights work through the politics of reputation and advocacy. Human rights activists play a critical role in that process. They document abuses, they publicize abuses, they call out specific governments or people for responsibility, and they pressure for change. In effect, they traffic in information and use that information to "name" abuses and abusers and "shame" abusers into change, often drawing on international and regional human rights standards. If the international and regional bodies create a common language and common standards by which to hold governments accountable, it falls to the nonstate actors often to use that common language and those common standards to pressure for change.

Domestic Human Rights Organizations

The range of human rights organizations is broad. Some organizations are domestic. Some are general human rights organizations; they focus on all and every human rights issue in that country. Pick a country, and you are likely to find several domestic human rights organizations. Consider, for example, the Association for Human Rights in Peru (APRODEH in Spanish); the organization investigates human rights violations, publishes reports, and advocates on behalf of victims in that country. APRODEH is a central voice for human rights in that country. Other domestic human rights organizations focus on a specific issue, such as torture, women's rights, or press freedom. Take, for example, the Egyptian Center for Women's Rights, which advocates on behalf of women in that country. Many of these domestic organizations play a critical role not only in documenting violations and advocating for victims but also in holding governments accountable. The organizations are often the ones that claim that a government ratified a particular treaty. They in turn leverage those government commitments to pressure for change; in effect, the organizations breathe life into the treaties that governments sign. Given the weak enforcement powers of the human rights system at the international level, these domestic organizations play a central role in pressuring governments to adhere to the rules and standards in the treaties.

Organization of American States (OAS): regional organization to promote cooperation within North and South America.

American Convention on Human Rights: regional human rights treaty for the countries that are a part of the Organization of American States.

African Charter on Human and People's Rights: regional human rights treaty for African states.

African Court on Human and People's Rights: regional human rights court for those countries that have ratified the African Charter of Human and People's Rights; the court is based in Arusha, Tanzania, and it hears cases brought by other states or by individuals if those individuals live in states that have ratified a special protocol allowing citizens and nongovernmental organizations to petition the court directly.

International Human Rights Organizations

The same is true for international human rights organizations. Like domestic human rights NGOs, international human rights organizations can be general or specific. The largest general ones are Amnesty International and Human Rights Watch. These are organizations that essentially have a global reach. They are organizations that are well funded, whose staff size rivals and exceeds some United Nations agencies on human rights. There are also more single-issue organizations, such as Article 19 that focuses on press freedom, Anti-slavery International (which caters to issues of slavery), or the Enough! Project, which focuses on atrocity prevention. As with domestic organizations, the international human rights organizations play a central role in shaping public discourse on human rights. They investigate, document, and publicize human rights abuses; they advocate on behalf of victims; and they pressure governments to abide by their commitments. Some human rights organizations also influence the legislative process, offering expertise or leading the charge for a new human rights treaty.

Transnational Advocacy Networks

A central concept for theorists of human rights advocacy is that of a transnational advocacy network (TAN; introduced in Chapter 4).[9] The idea of a "network" is that several different organizations and individuals participate in a shared project. Networks are open; they are places for exchange and interaction. Generally, these networks are voluntary, meaning that people and organizations choose to participate in them. In the human rights realm (or in other areas, such as in healthcare or the environment), the networks are about change. People and organizations come together to raise awareness, spread information, and pressure for change. The networks are also "transnational" in the sense that they bring together people and organizations in different parts of the world; at least, they have that potential. In practice, they often bring together NGOs, foundations, bloggers, editorialists, religious leaders, citizens, academics, unions, and sometimes members of intergovernmental organizations or governments.

The Example of "Save Darfur". A good example is the "Save Darfur" movement, which was a force on college campuses in the mid-to-late 2000s. The issue in question was the large-scale, state-led violence against non-Arab civilian populations in Darfur (Sudan). The violence ultimately claimed upward of 200,000 civilian lives. During that period, an unusual coalition of forces formed to advocate for policy change. That coalition often organized under the umbrella name of "Save Darfur," which included student groups, Jewish groups, African American groups, human rights advocates, the U.S. Holocaust Memorial Museum, and dozens of other organizations. The network that focused on Darfur also included celebrities, such as Mia Farrow and George Clooney. In practice, the network sought to raise awareness about the mass atrocities in Darfur; they also pressured governments, elected officials, and intergovernmental organizations to intervene more forcefully in Darfur to stop the violence. They also encouraged a divestment campaign. Save Darfur was clearly a network, in which there was a great deal of interaction between people in different locations and organizations. Save Darfur was also about advocacy: The network existed to raise awareness and pressure for a stronger response to the atrocities. It was also transnational, although more minimally. While Save Darfur was open to international actors, and while it sought to integrate local information from victims and their advocates in Sudan, in practice the coalition was primarily based in the United States.

The point about U.S. dominance of Save Darfur speaks to some common criticisms about human rights NGOs and advocacy networks more generally. One is the question of representation: Whom do these activists and advocates represent? Many of the most influential international human rights NGOs are headquartered in the Global North, and their funding comes primarily from individuals and foundations in the Global North. Even for those domestic NGOs, the heads of organizations are often city-based elites in that society who have extensive connections outside the country. Most domestic human rights organizations are not membership-driven but funded by donors, foundations, or external governments. Do these organizations represent the values and norms of the societies where they operate, or do they represent the values and norms of a global elite, generally rooted in the North? Human rights advocates respond by arguing that human rights are universal; they gain their legitimacy and authority from the treaties and standards to which many nations have agreed. They claim to speak on behalf of those with less power and fewer connections. This is an enduring tension, one that these kinds of global interactions foster.

Another, related concern is about accountability. To whom are these organizations accountable? NGO officials are not elected. If they present information inaccurately, or if citizens do not like how they are represented, what are the consequences for these organizations? The criticism is fair, but in reality, because human rights NGOs traffic in information, they rely on credibility. If the information they supply is false, if they are perceived as overly partisan to one side, or if they are seen to offer poorly thought out solutions and positions, then their influence diminishes. In other words, their power depends on credibility and impartiality. Without those qualities, officials in governments and intergovernmental organizations, which often have the most power to create change, do not take such organizations and advocacy networks seriously (see Figure 8.5).

The Example of "Kony 2012." A good illustration of these concerns is the phenomenon known as "Kony 2012." The title refers to a short documentary film that three young men made about the devastation that an insurgent organization, called The Lord's Resistance Army (LRA), wreaked on East and Central Africa. Indeed, the LRA is a devastating rebel group that kidnaps children and forces them into soldiering, sexual slavery, or both. They invade and lay waste to vil-

FIGURE 8.5

Global Forces, Interactions, and Tensions: Accountability and Human Rights Activists

GLOBAL FORCES	INTERACTIONS	TENSIONS
• Global goverance: Rooted in international human rights norms and treaties, networks of human rights activists form around a particular issue, such as mass atrocities.	• Network activists, including citizens, oragnizations, and celebries, interact as part of their campaign. • Activists pressure governments and international organizations to do more on the issue.	• Activists based in one place often speak on behalf of people elsewhere, but should they? Are activists accountable for the actions they take? • Activists sometimes promote ill-thought-out policy recommendations or regurgitate stereotypes in their work.

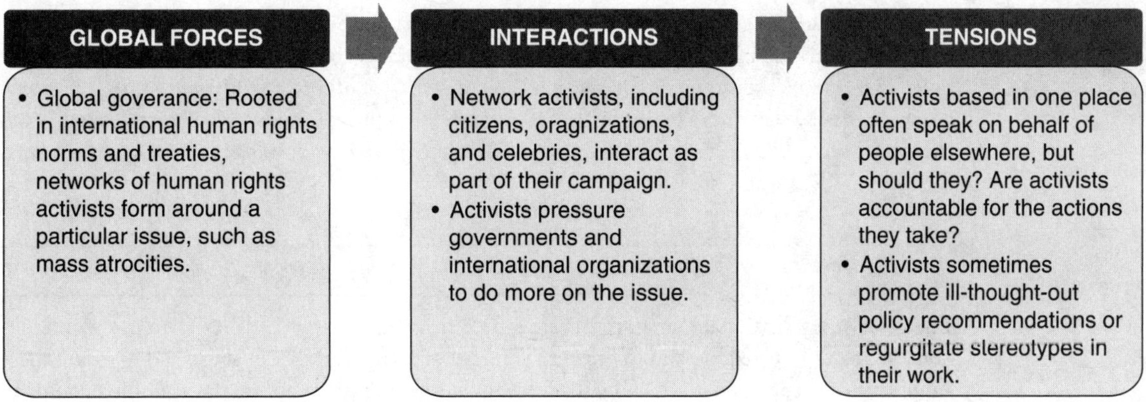

lages. Kony 2012 was part of an NGO called "Invisible Children." The film is powerful; using the language of universal human rights, and skillfully tugging on the viewers' heartstrings that implicitly tied the comfortable lives of children in the United States to the devastated lives of children in northern Uganda, the film claims its purpose is to stop the LRA, whose leader is Joseph Kony. The policy approach the film championed was for U.S. military assistance to the Ugandan military to capture Kony and transfer him to the ICC, where he faced an arrest warrant. Their tool was to "shine a light" on the situation of the LRA, to "make Kony famous."

The film is powerful. It is also simple. One of the narrative plots is for the film's narrator to explain the problem in northern Uganda to his young son. Indeed, the film went viral, garnering more than 100 million views by 2016 on YouTube alone. The film itself is a good example of the potential power of new media in the hands of human rights NGOs.

The film, however, also quickly attracted significant criticism. Some challenged the naivety of championing the Ugandan military, which has a poor human rights record; others pointed to the local resistance to the ICC arrest warrant, which some Ugandans claimed was the wrong solution to the problem; others raised questions about the film's finances, arguing that too much money went to the organization rather than to helping Ugandans; and many others raised concerns about the accuracy of the information in the film and the narrative tactics.[10] In particular, Africans were often presented in simplistic, stereotypical terms—as singularly evil, as helpless victims, or as dependents who were grateful for external assistance. In contrast were the filmmakers and their supporters, who were presented as heroes. These concerns echo those about representation and credibility. Although no one can dispute the extraordinary attention to the LRA that the film garnered, many countered that the attention was in the end not helpful and even reinforced prejudices. Indeed, a few years after the film, the organization disbanded.

Human Rights Actors Engage Global Forces to Bring About Change

Human rights organizations—both domestic and international—are a good place to observe some of the key global forces highlighted in the book at work. First, human rights organizations have nongovernmental authority. They trade on credibility and reputation; what they bring to a discussion is their reputation, acumen, and expertise. They are key actors in *global governance*; they shape the rules and then they monitor them, and those are rules that are meant to apply to all states across the globe. Through their efforts to create rules and to enforce rules through pressure, human rights organizations are prime examples of global governance and how such governance is not located only in intergovernmental organization.

Second, human rights organizations also are communication outfits. They "name and shame." They document and publicize; as such, new media are often critical to the success of such organizations. The Internet, social media sites, e-mail, and a variety of other new *information and communications technology* allow human rights NGOs to reach thousands of thousands of people quickly and cheaply. The communications technology amplifies and gives new power to these organizations, as the Kony 2012 example shows.

DO HUMAN RIGHTS WORK?

The goals of international human rights are lofty. The rules and standards set forth in the international human rights regime aim to protect people all over the world from abuse and to assure them a minimally decent standard of living. In these ways, human rights capture the aspirations of many.

They represent a global set of ideals and provide the backbone for global governance around issues of human welfare. Human rights are hard to ignore, and the web of human rights instruments create levers that intergovernmental organizations, NGOs, and citizens can pull to create change. All this represents remarkable progress in the human rights field since World War II. What constituted a vague, but essential, idea in the 1940s has blossomed into an elaborate set of treaties, institutions, declarations, and regional systems. Most countries in the world have ratified the most important human rights treaties. None of these developments was a fait accompli; they are the product of deliberate organization and pressure, often from NGOs and transnational advocacy networks.

Issues of Enforcement

But skeptics have many good points to make. The reality of the human rights regime is that the enforcement mechanisms are weak. There is no human rights police force to arrest abusers. Although the ICC exists to punish the offenders of the worst crimes—genocide, crimes against humanity, and war crimes—there is no international human rights court as such that deals with the 30 rights outlined in the Universal Declaration of Human Rights. Moreover, even the ICC depends on states to cooperate with its orders; if a state refuses to cooperate with the ICC—say, for example, in handing over a sitting president—the ICC lacks the power to enforce its order. Even though there are effective regional human rights courts in Latin America and Europe (and a burgeoning court in Africa), those courts only cover those regions. For the most part, European states already are committed to human rights (with some countries, such as Russia, as exceptions). So although the court adds value in pushing countries toward greater human rights protections, the court does not in effect create human rights commitments where none existed beforehand, as Figure 8.4 suggests. In Latin America, the court's power and prominence accelerated only after Latin American countries emerged from dictatorship; in other words, even this court has gained traction only after the countries committed to democratic rule.

The reality is that the power of human rights law and institutions is limited. That is indeed the reality of much international law and global governance; the rules that states create, and the norms that spread, serve as common reference points and shared commitments. The laws clarify what the obligations are. But when states violate international law, the punishment is weak. There is no global body that arrests the violators. There are international arbitration bodies to solve trade disputes, and those bodies can impose fines (as discussed in Chapter 6). In the extreme, the United Nations may impose general or targeted sanctions on a country that systematically abuses its citizens, but such abuse must be construed as a threat to international peace and security. In reality, such moves—international sanctions premised on human rights grounds—are rare.

Issues of Compliance

Human rights are also weak in the sense that the incentives for compliance differ from other international issues.[11] In many areas of global governance and international law, states have stronger reasons to act on their commitments because they perceive doing so as in their interests. Scholars point to a mechanism of **mutual benefit**. Two states or more gain if everyone cooperates with an agreement. In many areas of international cooperation—trade, security, even the environment—the actions of one state affect the actions of another state. Consider the case of agreements to nuclear nonproliferation. If one state violates the terms of the agreement by building nuclear weapons, that action puts the other states at risk. They all have an incentive to abide by the commitment and to

mutual benefit: idea that states will gain jointly if each complies with the terms of an international agreement; mutual benefit creates an incentive to comply with treaties. In human rights, the mutual benefit that would come from compliance is weak because those that suffer from human rights violations are typically not other states.

empower an intergovernmental organization to monitor the agreement. That is the theory, at least. But human rights are different because, if a state violates the agreement, those who typically suffer are the state's own citizens. Torturing a political dissident in one country does not create a security or financial risk, or some other direct harm, in another country that has ratified the United Nations Convention against Torture. In other words, human rights treaties lack a strong mutual benefit mechanism that would incentivize compliance even in the absence of powerful external enforcement mechanisms.

Skeptics emphasize these arguments. They dismiss human rights as "cheap talk" in the sense that countries face limited obstacles to opt into the human rights regime and they pay few costs for not complying with its rules. That many countries have ratified the core human rights treaties does not in fact mean much. Countries can sign and ratify the treaties, but they face few penalties if they fail to abide by the treaties' terms. Indeed, scholars who measure human rights records in general find that treaty ratification does not improve, and sometimes worsens, the ratifying state's human rights record.[12] For those that take this position, the human rights regime is deeply flawed; it is weak; it does not serve the purpose of protecting human rights. The human rights regime, in short, is powerless—by design.

The Differential and Indirect Powers of Human Rights Systems

There is an essential truth to this, but some human rights scholars and many advocates would point to the ways in which the human rights system does have power and influence. Its power is differential and indirect. Its power is differential (or conditional) in the sense that the international human rights system has an impact under certain conditions but not others. Its power is indirect in the sense that human rights gain power through intermediaries and over time.

Countries vary in terms of their domestic political and civil society institutions. In some countries, there is a degree of political competition; opposition parties can exist, make noise, and campaign for votes, as we saw in Chapter 7. In other countries, the political space is closed; they are authoritarian systems. Scholars who make claims about the differential effects of human rights point to the ways in which the political opposition can use human rights commitments against a government that violates the human rights of its citizens. If a government has ratified a treaty, and then breaks that commitment, the opposition can use the treaty commitment to mobilize and criticize the sitting government. Here the treaties provide a standard by which to "name oppression" and by which to hold a government accountable. Where an opposition party exists to make that case, the treaty can have an impact. By contrast, in a country where no political opposition exists or is so repressed as to be unable to mobilize and criticize, the human rights treaty has no one to champion and use it.[13] In this example, the power of the human rights treaty system is conditional upon the domestic political environment—here again showing another example of an international–domestic interaction.

The same type of argument applies to the domestic civil society space. In some countries, there might exist a somewhat independent media, a somewhat independent judiciary, and several independent NGOs. These different institutions and actors are key players in a domestic civil society. In the same way that the political opposition may mobilize around human rights issues, using the international standards that the treaty system creates, so too may a judge in a court or an editorialist at a newspaper or a domestic human rights organization. Here again the effects are conditional and entail an interaction. They are conditional on the fact that a space for domestic civil society exists;

those actors can, in effect, make noise in the public domain. They can "name" the violation, and they can "shame" the government by drawing attention to the violation. But the ability to make a normative argument rests on the prior existence of an international standard, one to which a government has committed, and that is where the international human rights regime comes into play. Without those shared norms, the domestic civil society actors have a weaker argument to make. So the power derives from the interaction between these two sets of actors.[14]

Some scholars also make the argument in reference to international human rights NGOs. They argue that where international NGOs have a stronger presence and actively draw attention to human rights issues in a country, governments will improve their human rights record. The international NGOs in effect shine a light on abuse, and they derive their arguments and criticisms from the normative and legal foundation that the treaty system creates.[15]

The Power of Socialization

Last, some scholars argue that human rights have power through a process of socialization. By creating normative standards about what is right and wrong, human rights treaties shape people's values and expectations. They also create the foundations for public debate and political mobilization. Over time, citizens in countries around the world will come to think differently about human rights issues—torture, the right to food, children's rights, women's rights, LGBTQ rights, and so forth. By setting and promulgating standards, human rights treaties trigger and shape that socialization process that ultimately leads to people holding different opinions and values about what is right and wrong. That socialization process gives human rights power.[16]

These arguments are not mutually exclusive. They are more subtle claims about how the power of human rights systems work internationally. The reality is that dictatorships and even some democratic governments continue to violate human rights, sometimes on a widespread and systematic basis. The immediate consequences of such violations are usually negligible because the power to enforce human rights is weak on an international level. But that does not mean that the human rights regime has no power, and these latter arguments provide some useful ways to think about how human rights gain power in indirect and conditional ways.

Human Rights and International Studies Themes

Human rights are one arena in which to observe the interactions that structure the world today. States and intergovernmental organizations have created both international and regional human rights systems. Those were the products, in many cases, of pressure from below, from citizens and nongovernmental organizations. Once established, the international standards and institutions become reference points, sites of mobilization, and instruments for citizens, domestic civil society organizations, and international NGOs. We saw that unfold in the Rohingya crisis. Over time, at least according to some theories, the global standards shape, and in some cases are shaped by, people's values around the world.

Human rights are also a source of contestation and conflict. There are many people, civil society leaders, and government officials who claim that the human rights system does not represent their values. They argue that human rights are fundamentally Western and reflect the values of the wealthy. In some cases, they argue that human rights are a form of imperialistic power; they represent the values of the West, and through claims to universality, the West is essentially imposing its values and its priorities on the rest of the world. Human rights claims are also by their nature conflictual. When a human rights body issues a report condemning the practices and policies in another country, those are often fighting words. The named government often resists. In these various ways, human rights seed conflict and contestation, even while they purport to improve human welfare.

The chapter also references different global forces. The international and regional human rights regimes are fundamentally about global governance; the regimes create standards and laws, and they set up institutions to monitor compliance with them. When the High Commissioner for Human Rights condemns the violence in Myanmar or the Human Rights Committee ruled against Ireland's laws on abortion, those are examples of global governance at work, as is the work of transnational advocacy networks.

Information and Communication technology increases the capacity of citizens and NGOs to communicate quickly and cheaply. Such technology creates risks—sometimes the message and the information are of poor quality. Sometimes people engage in "slactivism," clicking a "like" button on Facebook instead of engaging in deeper political activism to create change. But information technology clearly shapes the current human rights field. Kony 2012 is an example. With more than 100 million YouTube hits, the video was viral. An issue that had no visibility suddenly had tons. At the same time, the engagement with the crisis was thin and the proposed solutions simplistic.

A third global force represents a critical issue going forward: Will the rising powers embrace human rights? Broadly speaking, China champions a foreign policy that does not interfere in the domestic political affairs of other countries. As such, China is often skeptical of human rights, especially civil and political rights, and moreover some officials argue that human rights reflect Western values. China is the most important supporter of Myanmar, and indeed China has been reluctant to allow the United Nations to take strong action against Myanmar. At the same time, China is an advocate of social and economic rights, and indeed China's record on poverty alleviation is extraordinary. As you will see in the next chapter, probably no country in the history of the world has brought so many people out of poverty so quickly. Is that a human rights victory?

India is the world's largest democracy. India also has been a champion of human rights, and India's Supreme Court has been especially proactive in defending a broad vision of social and economic rights. At the same time, Russia has a very tense relationship with much of the international human rights system. A member of the Council of Europe, Russia has had the European Court of Human Rights issue many rulings against it. Indeed, Russia has threatened and continues to threaten to withdraw from the European human rights system. For their part, Brazil, Indonesia, Mexico, Vietnam, Turkey, South Africa, and the other rising states each has a complicated relationship to human rights doctrine. Their positions across the long 21st century are likely to determine whether human rights become weaker and more marginalized or whether they strengthen and become truly universal.

SUMMARY

In providing an overview to human rights, this chapter should give you the foundations to understand how human rights work in our world. The chapter has underlined the various norms, treaties, and institutions that breathe life into human rights. At the same time, the chapter has not shied away from the many shortcomings and problems associated with human rights. Ultimately, you will have to decide for yourself whether you think human rights are a mere paper tiger or represent a real force for bettering the world.

KEY TERMS

QUESTIONS FOR REVIEW

1. What are the two broad visions of human rights that are represented in the ICCPR and the ICESCR?

2. What are the main differences between a regional and an international human rights system?

3. What are some of the key strengths and weaknesses of human rights activism?

4. What are the main mechanisms by which human rights have power?

LEARN MORE

Mary Ann Glendon, *A World Made New: Eleanor Roosevelt and the Universal Declaration of Human Rights* (New York, NY: Penguin, 2002).

Eric Posner, *The Twilight of Human Rights Law* (Oxford, U.K.: Oxford University Press, 2014).

Kathryn Sikkink, *Evidence for Hope: Making Human Rights in the 21st Century* (Princeton, NJ: Princeton University Press, 2017).

Explore the website of the United Nations High Commissioner for Human Rights: http://www.ohchr.org/EN/AboutUs/Pages/HighCommissioner.aspx.

Explore the websites of the European Court of Human Rights and the Inter-American Court of Human Rights: https://www.echr.coe.int/Pages/home.aspx?p=home and http://www.oas.org/en/iachr/.

Explore the websites of Human Rights Watch and Amnesty International: https://www.hrw.org/ and https://www.amnesty.org/en/.

NOTES

1. Azeem Ibrahim, *The Rohingyas: Inside Myanmar's Hidden Genocide* (London, U.K.: Hurst, 2016).

2. United Nations, "UN Human Rights Chief Points to 'Textbook Example of Ethnic Cleansing' in Myanmar," *UN News*, September 11, 2017, http://www.un.org/apps/news/story.asp? NewsID=57490#.WlkZoEtG3uQ.

3. "They Tried to Kill Us All," Atrocity Crimes Against Rohingya Muslims in Rakhine State, Myanmar, 2017, United States Holocaust Memorial Museum and Fortify Rights, https://www.ushmm.org/confront-genocide/cases/burma/introduction/the-plight-of-the-rohingya.

4. Human Rights Watch, "Burma: Satellite Imagery Shows Mass Destruction," *HumanRightsWatch.org*, September 19, 2017, https://www.hrw.org/news/2017/09/19/burma-satellite-imagery-shows-mass-destruction.

5. See Myanmar News Agency, "No Evidence of Crimes Against Humanity, Ethnic Cleansing," *The Global New Light of Myanmar*, August 7, 2017, http://www.globalnewlightofmyanmar.com/no-evidence-of-crimes-against-humanity-ethnic-cleansing/ and Human Rights Watch, "Burma: National Commission Denies Atrocities," *HumanRightsWatch.org*, August 7, 2017, https://www.hrw.org/news/2017/08/07/burma-national-commission-denies-atrocities.

6. See https://www.reproductiverights.org/press-room/un-committee-criminalization-of-abortion-in-ireland-violates-womans-human-rights-0.

7. Drawn from The United Nations, Human Rights Office of the High Commissioner, http://tbinternet.ohchr.org/_layouts/treatybodyexternal/Download.aspx? symbolno=CCPR/C/116/D/2324/2013&.

8. Human Rights Council, "'They Came to Destroy': ISIS Crimes Against the Yazidis," http://www.ohchr.org/Documents/HRBodies/HRCouncil/CoISyria/A_HRC_32_CRP.2_en.pdf.

9. Keck and Sikkink, 1998.

10. Amanda Taub, *Beyond Kony2012: Atrocity, Awareness, & Activism in the Internet Age* (Vancouver, BC, Canada: Lean, 2012).

11. Eric Posner, *The Twilight of Human Rights Law* (Oxford, U.K.: Oxford University Press, 2014).

12. Emilie Hafner-Burton and Kiyoteru Tsutsui, "Human rights in a globalizing world: The paradox of empty promises," *American Journal of Sociology* 110 (2005): 1373–1411; Posner, 2014.

13. Oona Hathaway, "Do Human Rights Treaties Make a Difference?" *Yale Law Journal* 111 (2002): 1935–2042; Beth Simmons, *Mobilizing for Rights: International Law in Domestic Politics* (Cambridge, U.K.: Cambridge University Press, 2009).

14. Hathaway, 2002.

15. Hafner-Burton and Tsutsui, 2005; Dongwook Kim, "International non-governmental organizations and the abolition of the death penalty." *European Journal of International Relations* 22 (2016): 596–621.

16. Thomas Risse, Stephen C. Ropp, and Kathryn Sikkink (eds.), *The Power of Human Rights: International Norms and Domestic Change* (New York, NY: Cambridge University Press, 1999).

Development

THE CHALLENGE OF GLOBAL POVERTY

Pixabay/billycm

LEARNING OBJECTIVES

After finishing this chapter, you should be able to:

- Distinguish between measures of poverty such as GDP, PPP, HDI, SDGs, and GINI.

- Contrast competing explanations for why some countries are poor.

- Describe different theories of what poor countries should do.

- Adjudicate between opposing arguments on foreign aid.

- Understand recent innovations in the study of poverty, including cash transfers and the use of experiments to study development interventions.

By the time you finish this sentence, one more child will have died before reaching the age of five.[1] Many of these children will look like the boy shown in this picture. What killed them may have been war, famine, or natural disaster, but in most cases, they will die from much more mundane causes, such as diarrhea. A child dies from diarrhea approximately every 60 seconds.[2] Because they lack clean water, immunizations, or sources of nutrition, these children die needlessly. But this image of poverty is merely a symptom. These children die, not because their families lack medication or safe water, but because their families lack the *power* to get medication or safe water. The difference is subtle but important. What is distinctive about poor people in poor countries is not that they lack "stuff," but that they lack the power to get "stuff." Families that lose children to preventable illness may lack vaccinations because they lack the political connections to get vaccinations, they lack access to markets to earn money for vaccinations, or they may not be able save money for vaccinations because their country is at war.

In this chapter, we will ask one of the biggest questions in all of social science and the humanities: Why are some countries so poor? We will start by learning about how poverty and development are defined and measured, and thereafter we will read prominent explanations for why some countries are poor. We will then be in a position to turn to another big question: What should a poor country do? As students of international studies, we especially want to know: Is globalization good for poor countries? We will see that different explanations for development have very different answers to that question. Some see global forces like global markets as permitting the unchecked exploitation of poor countries. Others see the poverty of poor countries as lying precisely in their failure to embrace globalization. We will conclude by reflecting on the forces, interactions, and tensions in evidence throughout the chapter.

Let's begin with a look at poverty and wealth around the world. The map in Figure 9.1 shows the percentage of the population living in extreme poverty in 2013, defined as living on less than $1.90 per day.[3] We see that the most severe poverty is in South Asia and much of Africa. These are also places with the worst younger than age 5 mortality rates.[4] This is the probability that a child will die before reaching the age of 5. The rate is generally about 10 times higher in developing countries (60%, on average) than it is in developed countries (7%, on average). In Sierra Leone, for example, the rate is 182 deaths per 1,000 births. Read that closely: It means almost every fifth baby born in Sierra Leone will be dead by the age of 5.[5] Globally, about half of all deaths occur in the first month of life. For children dying between the ages of 1 and 5, almost half are due to preventable and treatable illnesses like pneumonia, malaria, and even diarrhea.[6] Global poverty is also gendered: Women are more than 50% of the global population but own only 1% of the world's wealth.[7]

The difference between the poorest and the wealthiest societies is not just money. In the wealthiest societies, the poorest can generally rely on some publicly funded safety net to keep them from falling into dire poverty. In many developing countries, however, small misfortune can turn into massive calamity, as the state does not offer retraining, welfare subsistence payments, or housing support. More than one billion people in poor and middle income countries have some sort of social safety net, but almost another billion have none. In the poorest countries, a social safety net may cover only 10% to 15% of the population. This is usually because in the poorest countries, these programs are quite small, or they are not designed to target the extreme poor within the country.[8]

Watch what it means to be poor in "The Name of the Disease" at https://www.youtube .com/watch?v=rOenEucIS30&feature=youtu.be.

multidimensional poverty: recognition that poverty is more than income. Poverty can be experienced as poor health, education, quality of work, or violence.

The poorest people in the poorest countries are exposed to the vicious winds of life in ways that we in the wealthy world can barely understand. This is why poverty is described as **multidimensional**: To be poor is to be vulnerable on all sides—your children drink unsafe water, teachers do not show up to work, government does nothing about it, and police confiscate your meager income just because they can. To understand how poverty works, think of it not in terms of material deprivation—no shoes, malnutrition—but in terms of powerlessness. *What poor people lack is not things, but the power to get things.*

The difference between the poorest people in Sweden and the poorest people is Sierra Leone is not just income. It is that poor Sierra Leoneans are significantly more constrained in their

FIGURE 9.1

Income Poverty Worldwide

Poverty

Share of population living on less than 2011 PPP $1.90 a day, 2013 (%)

Less than 2.0

2.0–9.9

10.0–24.9

25.0–49.9

50.0 or higher

No data

Source: The World Bank, "WDI 2017 Maps," https://data.worldbank.org/products/wdi-maps.

ability to do anything about their situation. They lack power over their own governments. They lack power over climate-change–induced droughts and floods caused by industrial nations. They lack power over even their own land and homes, which can be taken from them. This is why Nobel-Prize–winning economist Amartya Sen talked about "development as freedom."[9] Poverty, he said, generally occurs when people lack one of three major freedoms: political freedom, such as civil rights and transparent governance; freedom of economic opportunity, such as access to credit and free markets; and freedom from want, such as opportunities to advance through health or education services, or in the form of social safety nets. He said freedom is both the goal of development *and* the means to achieve it.

To get the most from this chapter, browse your notes from the chapters on history (Chapter 1) and money (Chapter 6). Those chapters will help you understand how wealth around the world has changed over time, and how global economic factors like trade, debt, and currencies affect poor countries. Knowing these things will help us weigh the merits and logic of different explanations for wealth and poverty.

WHAT IS DEVELOPMENT, AND HOW IS IT MEASURED?

development: variously defined as economic growth, improving living standards, or enhancing people's control over their own lives.

Although we use the terms "developing" and "developed" when talking about the wealth of countries, these terms are not technically accurate. In fact, they are not technical terms at all. They refer to general differences between poor countries and rich, but scholars of **development**—that is, scholars of the poverty and wealth of humans—need precise definitions to measure and compare poverty in countries across the world and over time. The two main ways in which people discuss development are in terms of the wealth of *places* or the welfare of *people*. As we will see, there are several ways to measure both types of wealth.

Development as the Wealth of Places

gross domestic product (GDP): value of all goods and services in an economy, including everything produced by all people and all companies, including people's salaries.

The most common measure of the wealth of a country is **gross domestic product (GDP)**, which is the value of all economic activity in an economy—everything produced by all people and all companies, including people's salaries—as measured by government statistics offices. When we talk about a country's growth rate, we are usually talking about annual changes in a country's GDP.[10] We can compare the wealth of nations by dividing the size of the whole economy (its GDP) by the size of the population to get GDP per capita. If we do this, we see Luxembourg has the highest GDP per capita in the world at $102,000, and Burundi has the lowest at $304 (the United States is 8th).[11]

purchasing power parity (PPP): method for adjusting exchange rates to account for differences in living costs.

But since things are cheaper in poorer countries, we know that $285 goes a lot further in Burundi than it would in the United States. This means we will be misled if we compare GDP per capita across the world. This is where **purchasing power parity (PPP)** comes in. PPP is an adjustment to wealth data that takes the cost of living into account by factoring exchange rates into GDP per capita calculations. Rather than compare countries by their GDP per capita, we instead compare them by their GDP (PPP) per capita. When we compare countries this way, Burundi is now second to last at $778, with the Central African Republic last at $699, and Luxembourg is second at $106,000 with Qatar first at $128,000 (the United States is 11th).[12] PPP makes poorer countries seem less poor than before since their living costs are low. Conversely, PPP makes wealthy countries seem less wealthy than before since the cost of living is higher in wealthy countries.

Development as the Welfare of People

GDP is a measure of *economic* development, rather than a measure of *human* development. It tells us about the country's overall wealth but nothing about people's well-being, such as their life expectancy, the probability that a child will reach the age of 5, or basic literacy.[13] To understand the difference, think of Equatorial Guinea. This small country has so much oil that it is one of the top 50 wealthiest countries in the world. But that wealth is controlled by the family and friends of the dictator Omar Teodoro Obiang. The country is wealthy; the people are not. Figure 9.2 shows life expectancy and wealth across the world. The colors indicate the region, and the size of the dot indicates the size of the population. In the bottom right, we see Equatorial Guinea. Its income per person is about the same as Israel's, but its health outcomes are at the level of Eritrea.

To address this difference between economic development and the actual experience of humans, the United Nations (UN) publishes an annual Human Development Index (HDI), which takes into account economic development, life expectancy, and education.[14] When we

FIGURE 9.2

Wealth and Life Expectancy

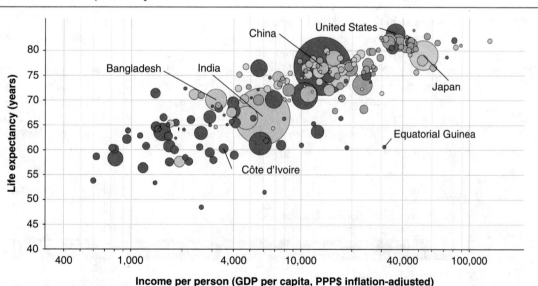

Source: Data are from the World Bank.

compare a country's human development with its GDP, we notice countries with higher HDI than we would expect given their wealth. We also notice countries with lower HDI than we would expect. This shows us that economic development and human welfare are highly correlated but actually distinct.

Table 9.1 compares economic development and human development in Georgia and Equatorial Guinea. Although Equatorial Guinea's GDP (PPP) per capita is about 2.5 times that of Georgia's, Equatorial Guinea's HDI score is similar to that of much poorer Congo or Bangladesh. Georgia's HDI score is closer to that of oil-rich Kuwait. Georgia is a poor country, but Equatorial Guinea has poorer people.

The United Nations takes human development into account when it groups countries by their wealth. For example, the world's poorest countries are referred to as **least developed countries (LDCs).** A total of 47 countries are currently designated LDCs, and over several decades, only a few countries have graduated from this status. Most inhabitants in these LDCs live in **extreme poverty,** which is an international poverty line set at $1.90 a day.[15] About 787 million people—1 in 11 humans—live in extreme poverty. Extreme poverty has roughly halved in the past two decades, from 36% of the world population in 1990 to 11% in 2013. Rapid economic growth in East Asia and South Asia (and in China, Indonesia, and India in particular) accounts for much of this decline. Most LDCs are in Africa, with a few in Southeast Asia. Together, the 880 million people living in LDCs represent 12% of the global population but only 2% of global GDP.[16]

Watch American college students try to live in Guatemala on $1 a day at https://www .youtube.com/channel/UCYTwCNZG6IChfNO252Vyl3A.

In 2016, all UN member-states agreed upon a set of development goals called the **Sustainable Development Goals (SDGs).** The 17 goals set ambitious targets to be met by 2030, and they follow from the eight goals targeted from 2000 to 2015 known as the **Millennium Development Goals (MDGs).** The SDGs are not laws, and there is no punishment if a country fails to meet any or all of the goals. Instead, the goals are a kind of device to focus international attention on national-level progress and international-level assistance. For example, SDG number 3 is Good Health and Well-Being, which is broken down into 13 specific targets such as reducing "under-5 mortality to at least as low as 25 per 1,000 live births" by 2030. We see in Figure 9.3 that although under-5 mortality has declined significantly since 1990, it remains stubbornly high globally as well as in Sub-Saharan Africa, South Asia, and Oceania especially.

least developed countries (LDCs): countries with gross national income (GNI) per capita below approximately $1,000.

extreme poverty: also known as the "Poverty Headcount Ratio," it is the share of a country's population living on less than $1.90 a day.

Sustainable Development Goals (SDGs): also known as "Global Goals," the successor to Millennium Development Goals. A total of 17 goals agreed upon by United Nations member-states in 2016 to be reached by 2030.

Millennium Development Goals (MDGs): eight goals agreed upon by UN member-states in 2000 to be reached by 2015.

TABLE 9.1

Economic and Human Development Compared

Country	GDP (PPP) per capita	Human Development Index
Eq. Guinea	$25,535	0.59
Georgia	$9,997	0.77

Use GapMinder to watch how GDP and HDI change over time at http://www.bit .ly/1nQegpw.

FIGURE 9.3

Global Decline in Under-5 Mortality: 1990–2015

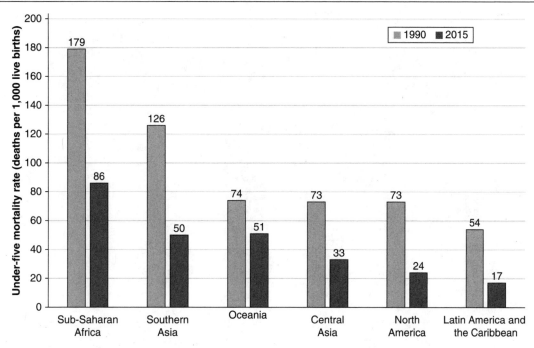

Source: United Nations, Millennium Development Report 2015. http://www.undp.org/content/undp/en/home/librarypage/mdg/the-millennium-development-goals-report-2015.html.

Read more about the SDGs.[17]

Another way to measure poverty and wealth is by taking inequality into account with the **Gini Index of Inequality**, named after its inventor, Corrado Gini. This is important because a Human Development score is an average for an entire population, and even a country with a high score for most people could still be a place with extreme poverty. The Gini Index looks at the percentage of national income earned by each percentage of the population: If 10% of the population had 10% of the wealth, we would say this is a situation of relative equality. If, however, 10% of the population had 90% of the wealth, we would say this is a highly *unequal* distribution of wealth.

Figure 9.4 shows income inequality around the world using the Gini Index. Note how Africa has less inequality than many countries in the Americas. This is partly because Latin America and the United States are very unequal, especially compared with Europe, but also because in the world's poorest countries, what little wealth exists is held by a tiny fraction of the population but not by the top 5% or 10%.

Now that we understand how poverty and development are defined and measured, we can turn to the deeper question: Why are some countries poor?

Gini Index of Inequality: share of national income earned by each percentage of the population.

FIGURE 9.4

Income Inequality Within Countries (Gini Index)

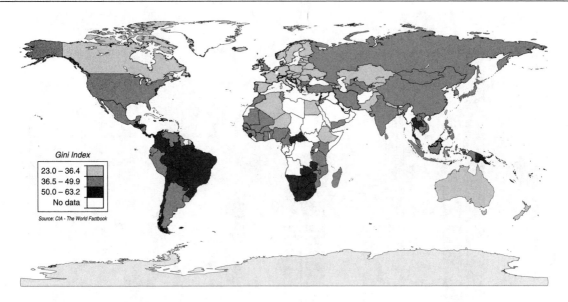

Source: Data from the CIA World Factbook.

WHY ARE SOME COUNTRIES POOR?

At a very basic level, the cause of poverty is low productivity: The hard labor poor people put into their farms and small businesses does not provide enough for them to feed their family, let alone reinvest in their farm or business. It is not that they are inefficient: Given their meager resources, for example, farmers in Africa get a lot out of their land. But they lack the things that could help them be more productive, such as loans, property rights, or the power to change their government. Poor countries (not poor *people*) have low productivity, in turn, because they do not have the right policies to grow their economies and raise living standards. But this tells us very little: What are the "right" policies, and how much freedom does a poor country have to choose policies anyway? In fact, we may be asking the wrong question to begin with. The reality is that for most of human history, societies had much lower living standards than we have today. Rather than asking "why are some countries poor," it might be more useful to ask, "how did some countries get so rich?"

How Did Some Countries Get So Rich?

Although different corners of the globe enjoyed periods of innovation and prosperity throughout history, it is only in the last 300 years or so that living standards began to radically improve in some parts of the world, even if this process was highly uneven across the world. Countries that are wealthy today are typically those that developed strong political *and* economic systems. Even though most wealthy countries today are free market democracies, many developed without free markets and without being very democratic. Some were democratic, whereas others were authoritarian monarchies or dictatorships. More recently, we have seen in just one generation in China the largest number of people lifted out of extreme poverty in a generation in human history. And China, of course, is not synonymous with capitalism or democracy. What such places have in common was a government that was able and willing to provide services like police, courts, and schools, but was also interested in ruling on behalf of more than just itself or a small religious, ethnic, or economic elite. Political systems that are *able* and *willing* to govern this way are historically rare. Societies with strong political systems were able to develop strong economic systems, which is a system with continuous investment and innovation. Investment and innovation are two of the most important things that wealthy countries have but poor countries lack. Let's take each in turn.

Investments are expenditures that are made with the expectation of future gains. There is an endless list of investments wealthy countries make that we rarely stop to consider. We know roads and electricity services are investments that are good for the economy, and that governments play a key role in providing them because they are a **public good**: People want the service, but no one wants to be the one to provide it. But governments also provide other services that are essential to an economy, like a court system to help individuals and firms avail themselves of the law; intellectual property laws to protect and incentivize investments; anti-discrimination laws, so minorities have an incentive to participate in the economy; or trusted statistics on the economy itself, which helps farmers and businesses know where and when to buy or sell. These services are good for economic growth because they reduce **transaction costs**, the cost of doing business. Instead of worrying that your invention will be stolen, your patent protects you and you feel comfortable investing your time and money, and society may ultimately benefit from your innovation.

Second, we normally think of **innovation** as the technology that comes from research and development wings of major corporations, like medical MRI machines and touchscreen tablets. Some innovations require such massive funding that often the government is the only one willing to take on the risk. Many pharmaceuticals, for instance, are developed in publicly funded universities. It is often only after a promising drug emerges that it is tested on a large population by a private company, but few companies want to do the early work in innovating something that might completely fail. This is why higher education systems have played such a crucial role in the development of wealthy countries like Germany, Ireland, and the United States.[18]

Another way political systems matter for innovation is **creative destruction**, which means allowing for the destruction of older technologies, even if it hurts a small group in society. Every innovation creates losers: When the automobile was created, the makers of horse-drawn carriages suffered badly. When cell phones were invented, makers of home telephones also suffered. But if those whose livelihoods will suffer because of the innovation are also politically powerful, they will work to stop the innovation. If MySpace had been politically powerful, it could have blocked the growth of Facebook by requiring that all laptops come with MySpace pre-installed. This would have been good for MySpace but bad for consumers. Companies, just like citizens, use the state to block innovations that threaten them. In many poor countries, bad policies persist because they serve the interests of some powerful group.

Watch a video on why Internet in the United States is slow at http://vimeo.com/ 59236702.

investments: wealthy countries continuously invest in integral parts of their economy, such as physical infrastructure, healthcare, security, and childhood as well as third-level education.

public good: anything that a person can use even if he or she did not contribute to it. Example: national security.

transaction costs: cost of doing something, above the good or service itself, such as lawyers' fees when buying a house, or the time it takes to walk to a store.

Innovation: one way to create wealth is to make or do something new that makes more efficient use of resources.

creative destruction: destruction of old technologies to make way for new, including destroying the sociopolitical power of the owners of the older technology. Countries that cannot do this will stagnate.

There is one more thing we should add to understand why some countries are wealthier than others today. This is a country's good fortune in being able to take advantage of economic growth happening elsewhere. Imagine you owned a restaurant near a rail line in the late 1800s, and your sister owned one near a river only a few miles away. For reasons completely out of your control, someone invented cars, and soon the government is building highways across the country. Because they are worried that the ground is too soft near the water, they build a highway near your hotel, but far from your sister's. Naturally, your hotel benefits from the huge increase in travelers, and your sister's business suffers because, through no fault of her own, her hotel is in the "wrong" place. Who was the better businessperson? Well, neither. Sometimes certain industries, or certain countries, benefit from what's happening regionally or globally. They just happen to be in the right place at the right time, and some are able to take advantage of this. Ireland has the good fortune of sitting between the United States and the European Union (EU), two of the world's major economic centers, whereas Ghana has the unstable Ivory Coast, poor Burkina Faso, and authoritarian Togo as its neighbors. Some countries have the good luck to be in the *right* time. Today, for example, a developing country can borrow huge sums of money from banks in developed countries, but this is a recent innovation. Estonia did not invent the Internet, but its well-educated workforce was able to take advantage of the growing Internet economy, and Skype, an Estonian company, was sold to Microsoft in 2011 for $8.5 *billion*. Many countries that have "made it" are those with strong political and economic systems, as well as a good dose of good luck.

Let's now turn to the explanations for poverty. We can organize them into three groups: Poverty trap explanations say there are things that keep poor countries stuck in their condition but are out of the countries' control; ideas explanations say the way people in poor countries think is the problem; and institutional explanations say poverty persists because powerful groups in the poor country have no incentive to change it and the poorest are powerless to do anything about it.

Poor Countries Are Stuck in Poverty Traps

This set of explanations holds that poor countries are simply unable to develop their economies and raise their living standards for reasons that are largely out of their control; that is, poor countries are stuck in a **poverty trap**, endlessly repeating a cycle of poverty from which a country cannot escape without external help.

Imagine a poor country with 10 million people, 1 million of which are children. All of the children need to go to school to become literate and to develop what economists call "human capital." But by definition, the poor country is poor and cannot afford the necessary teachers and school buildings. They might have enough to send 15% of children to school right now and hope that when they leave university, they will grow the economy through innovation and productivity. They may expand the economy by enough to send 25% of children to school, but that would take a generation. Do you see the poverty trap? To break out of this cycle, the country needs to *immediately* have 80% to 90% of children in school. Any other investment will be too small to have much of an impact. In a poverty trap, poverty causes poverty. This is the problem faced by the poorest countries: They are so poor, they can never invest the massive amounts—the one-off investments—they need to jump-start their economies.

Advocates of the poverty trap model are in favor of using aid to help poor countries. One example of this is the Millennium Villages Project (MVP). Rather than running a small health program in one town, building some schools in another, and improving electricity in yet another,

poverty trap: idea that poverty is cyclical, such that my poverty today is caused by my poverty yesterday. The solution is once-off jolts to the system in the form of rapid change or investment.

the MVP tries to end extreme poverty by doing all of these at once in a small set of communities. A few villages across ten African countries were selected to receive huge and simultaneous investments in things like water, sanitation, healthcare, and education. The MVP is less concerned with changing the power structures of the community. Instead, it thinks massive simultaneous investments can help villagers overcome their basic development challenges. Whether the MVP has been successful is hotly debated. Those running the program point to greater agricultural yields and improved health. Critics say that because of Western consultants and program managers, the true cost of the MVP is about $10,000 per villager per year, rather than the $160 publicized by the MVP, and that its successes may be overstated anyway.[19]

Photo of girls at Dertu Primary School in Kenya by Flickr user Millennium Promise, http://www.millenniumpromise.org/.

Read about the MVP at millenniumvillages.org.

Advocates of the poverty trap model also point to the curse of bad geography. Look again at Figure 9.1. Notice how many of the world's poorest countries tend to be along the equator (running through the middle of the map). Countries very near to the equator have climates that are good for malaria-carrying mosquitoes but not so good for humans. A little bit either side of the equator tends to be quite dry, with many deserts. Maybe some countries just have so few natural resources that we should have an honest conversation about their viability. Some countries have the misfortune of being in the wrong place. As Ricardo Hausmann argues: "Economic-development experts promise that with the correct mix of pro-market policies, poor countries will eventually prosper. But policy isn't the problem—geography is. Tropical, landlocked nations may never enjoy access to the markets and new technologies they need to flourish in the global economy."[20]

Jared Diamond argued that several hundred years ago, some parts of the world like the Fertile Crescent in the Middle East had lots of species that could be domesticated, and this incentivized people to move from hunter gathering to farming.[21] The growth of farming economies then led to population growth, and increasingly specialization within society, which further enhanced economic growth. In other parts of the world, however, there were few species that could be easily domesticated, and as a result, people took a very long time to embrace farming. For Diamond, this is a major reason why certain regions of the world became much wealthier than others over time. Those that began with the most favorable ecological conditions then got a head start on the rest of the world, culminating in the technologically advanced societies conquering the backward societies over the past few hundred years.

Life is surely harder when soil is not fertile, when the natural environment carries more diseases that affect humans, and when a country lacks an easy means of importing and exporting goods. But critics say these theories put too much weight on geography as an explanation for poverty around the world. Botswana, for example, is both landlocked and close to the equator, yet it has been politically stable and prospering for several decades. South Korea is one of the world's wealthiest countries, while neighboring North Korea is one of the poorest. It is political systems, not geography, that have made the difference between them. And although the inhabitants of modern Canada and the United States had mostly primitive technologies about 500 years ago, to the south the Incas and Aztecs were significantly more technologically developed, with roads, money, and writing, despite living in otherwise unsuitable climatic conditions.

Poor Countries Have Bad Ideas

ideology: theory of how the world works, how it could work, and how to get there. Examples: conservatism, communism, anarchism.

The second set of explanations believes the problem lies in the ideologies or cultures of poor countries. Let's begin with ideology. An **ideology** is a powerful set of ideas that shape how people think the world works and what they ought to do in it. Ideas have been hugely important in human history. Communism is a good example. We know from history that governments do a bad job of directly managing and controlling an entire economy. In the early 1970s, North and South Korea had similar levels of wealth, but today South Korea is almost 20 times as wealthy as its neighbor. If North Korea's state-run economy has failed, why does it stick with it? As growth slowed in the Soviet Union from the 1970s onward, why did it take two decades to reform the system? The theory of ideology would say that the North Koreans and the Soviets did not believe they were wrong. Instead, they attributed their failures to what the rest of the world was doing to them, or to how "traitors" in their own country were standing in the way of their revolutionary reforms. But critics would argue that ideologies can serve to legitimize behavior after the fact. Centrally planned economies, for example, were not unique to communism. The ideology of communism was used to legitimize Stalin's total control: It was the effect, not the cause, of the Soviet economic model.

There is also a popular idea that poor countries are essentially backward in their thinking. This was an especially popular idea in the Western world from the 1700s to the 1900s during the high point of colonialism and imperialism. A famous version of this came from the German sociologist Max Weber. He said the Protestant Reformation in Europe led to the "Protestant work ethic," which valued hard work and individualism, values he argued were at the root of Europe's economic advances in the Industrial Age.[22] Many people still support this idea. Harvard historian Niall Ferguson recently wrote, "the experience of Western Europe in the past quarter-century offers an unexpected confirmation of the Protestant ethic. To put it bluntly, we are witnessing the decline and fall of the Protestant work ethic in Europe."[23] Haiti provides a good example of how cultural explanations pervade journalistic explanations of the world. Shortly after an earthquake killed tens of thousands, the *New York Times* columnist David Brooks wrote, "Haiti, like most of the world's poorest nations, suffers from a complex web of progress-resistant cultural influences. There is the influence of the voodoo religion, which spreads the message that life is capricious and planning futile. There are high levels of social mistrust. Responsibility is often not internalized."[24] In this view, the problem with Haiti is the Haitian mentality.

Critics say cultural explanations treat societies as if they are unified blocks and values as unchanging over time. Thus, there is such a thing as an African culture, or as an Asian culture. It is then easy to explain major differences between these supposed coherent groups in terms of some cultural traits. So it was that people once claimed that Catholics were incapable of sustaining a democracy because in the mid-20th century, most Catholic-dominated countries were not very democratic. And so it was that Asian governments once claimed there was something called "Asian values" that held that Asians did not desire democracy. This also worked in reverse: Prosperous societies convinced themselves that their success was due to the superiority of their culture, so Germans congratulate themselves on their austere character, Japanese for their intense corporate culture, or Americans for their love of "freedom." But it turned out that Catholic countries could democratize and that Asian people had no inherent love for authoritarianism, and that Germany, Japan, and the United States were not immune to stagnant economies. The lesson is not that a society's values do not matter but that cultures change. People's ideas of their own self-worth, and their willingness to demand a share in their society, also change. Cultural perspectives, on the other hand, treat the values of different groups as set in stone and as extremely slow moving and difficult to change.

One other recurring theme in popular ideas about development also relates to ideas and information. This is encapsulated in the familiar parable that asks, why give a man a fish when you can teach him to fish? In this view, poor people lack the education and skills to develop. But many find this parable highly problematic because it erroneously assumes that poor people in poor countries are poor because they don't know how to *not be* poor. But the reality is much different. Is a fisherman in Vietnam poor because he has inferior fishing techniques, or because the corrupt police constantly take his profits, so he has little incentive to invest in better nets; or telecommunications are so weak that he is not able to react when the capital city is offering good prices for fish; or the constant electricity outages in the area mean he can never refrigerate his fish, and it spoils before it makes it to the city? The root of his poverty is not his ignorance. It is that his wider context does not allow him to thrive.

Poor Countries Have Bad Institutions

The third explanation emphasizes politics, and it is strongly associated with the theories of Daron Acemoglu and James Robinson. They say differences in wealth across history and between nations are about politics pure and simple, and that any country can prosper—no matter its religion, climate, region, or culture. What's required, they say, is for a country to have the right political institutions in order for the right economic institutions to emerge. The countries that make it are those with **inclusive institutions** rather than with **extractive institutions**.[25] Institutions are the formal or informal rules that govern a society. Some rules are formal, like a country's constitution or its laws, or the organization of a corporation. But rules can be informal, which is a rule that is widely understood but just happens to not be formally written down on a legal document. An example of an informal institution is marriage. It has a lot of unwritten rules, like the socially acceptable age for marriage, the permissibility of interracial marriage, or what constitutes grounds for divorce. What makes a difference to the wealth of countries is when rules (institutions) favor narrow elite groups (and so become extractive institutions) rather than society as a whole (i.e., inclusive institutions).

In the view of Acemoglu and Robinson, to ask "why are some countries poor?" is really to ask "why do some countries have inclusive institutions while others do not?" Their research points to the long-run effects of colonialism, one of the earliest faces of global interactions and tensions in recent centuries. Acemoglu and Robinson's "reversal of fortunes" theory begins with the observation that societies that were wealthier around the year 1500 are poorer today, whereas societies that were poorer in the year 1500 are wealthier today.[26] For example, around 1700, the United States was poorer than India, Indonesia, Brazil, and Mexico, but now the opposite is true.[27] Why? Their answer

inclusive institutions: inclusive political institutions are pluralistic (many forces may compete for power) and centralized (there is a coherent public authority, as in the modern state). Inclusive economic institutions are rules that reward investment and innovation.

extractive institutions: political institutions are extractive if they fail to be pluralistic or centralized; economic institutions are extractive when designed to allow elites to extract resources from the rest of society.

is colonialism, but it is more specific than that. They argue that colonialism operated differently depending on local context.

Native societies with large populations offered colonials the opportunity to use native (slave) labor to work mines and fields. In such places, Europeans did not need to settle in large numbers because there was no labor scarcity. Instead, they set up very extractive institutions. These were places with highly abusive labor practices, in which people were forced into wage labor because they had to pay a tax to the colonial government. Colonizers built highly repressive systems of rule, purely to extract resources. This describes the colonial experience of much of Latin America and Africa today. The exploitative economic and political institutions established by colonials to control these economies persisted throughout history, such as landlessness and authoritarianism. So, although colonials may have had advantages in terms of their weapons and medicine, colonialism was not simply a case of advanced economies taking over backward economies.

Thus, the places that were wealthy around 1500 also had densely populated settlements (since people were attracted to the economic activity), which meant they were *least* likely to attract a major colonial (white) settlement and, thus, least likely to have enjoyed institutions that would be good for long-run economic growth. By contrast, where colonial destinations were sparsely populated, colonials settled in significant numbers because their immigrant labor was needed to take advantage of the "discovered" land. When they did so, they created institutions (courts, laws, rules) that would protect property and incentivize investment because it was in their own economic interest to do so. These institutions tended to be good for economic growth over decades and even centuries. Think of the United States, Australia, Canada, South Africa, and New Zealand today. By 1619, the British colony of Virginia had a representative assembly elected by men regardless of property ownership.[28]

Political explanations for seemingly irrational economic behavior are often called "political economy analyses" because they treat politics and economics as inseparable. Political economists think that in most cases a poor country's bad policies *are* on purpose. A classic example of this comes from Robert Bates's *Markets and States in Tropical Africa*.[29] At the time, African governments bought produce from their farmers at a very low price, and they sold it for profit in global markets. Bates wanted to know, if so many of the world's poor are farmers, why do African countries have policies that hurt farmers? He found that governments kept food prices low by paying farmers poorly to keep urban workers happy with cheap food. What looked like a bad policy from the outside—punishing the poor farmers to help the less-poor urbanites—had a political logic behind it. The policies may have kept rural people poor, but they kept the more politically organized urban population from threatening the government.

We see something similar today with petrol subsidies in poor countries. Globally, hundreds of billions of dollars are spent annually on energy subsidies.[30] It happens in poorer countries, like Indonesia, but also in wealthier countries, like Argentina, as well as in energy exporters, like Nigeria, and energy importers, such as Turkey.[31] Fuel subsidies are very wasteful because they benefit those who use the most energy, which in a poor country is wealthier people (they drive more and have more household appliances). If fuel subsidies are economically wasteful, why are they so widespread? In 2011, Nigeria spent $13.6 *billion* subsidizing the fuel that ordinary Nigerians use to power their cars and other machines—about one quarter of the government's entire budget. The subsidies disproportionately benefit wealthier Nigerians. Development economist Paul Collier called petrol subsidies a "scam" perpetuated on the poor and the young. But this is not how many Nigerians see the issue. When Nigeria cut subsidies in 2012 under pressure from the International Monetary Fund (IMF), the price of petrol immediately doubled, and the government faced mass street protests. Similar protests, often violent, forced governments in Bolivia, Jordan, and Indonesia to back away from planned cuts to subsidies.[32] Faced with a corrupt government, many Nigerians see fuel subsidies as one of the few benefits they get from living above tremendous amounts of oil. Politicians were nervous about reducing these subsidies because they knew that ordinary Nigerians viewed cheap fuel as one of the few benefits they received. So why did Nigeria have economically harmful fuel subsidies? Because it kept Nigerians from protesting in the streets: Subsidies were bad economically but good politically.

Another prominent theory in this institutional, political economy perspective concerns the strange finding that some of the most resource-rich countries have some of the world's worst poverty. This "paradox of plenty" is known as the resource curse. An **economic resource curse (or Dutch Disease)** can occur when the natural resource industry crowds out other industries in a country, thereby harming the overall economy. Imagine a poor country with small industries involved in the export of flowers and fruits to wealthy countries suddenly discovers oil. Billions of dollars of investment comes in to develop the infrastructure to extract and transport the oil. An influx of money creates a demand for the currency, making the currency more expensive, and thus hurting exporters like the flower and fruit growers. To develop the oil industry, therefore, the global competitiveness of nonoil industries has been hit. This is often called the "Dutch Disease" because Dutch gas exports in the 1970s led to their currency appreciating (becoming expensive) and their nongas exporters suffered.

A **political resource curse** occurs when a government becomes unresponsive to its people because it does not rely on their taxes. The Nigerian dictator Sani Abacha was famous for this. This soldier-turned-politician ruled Nigeria for much of the 1990s, a country that had enjoyed significant amounts of oil revenues for decades without significantly improving the welfare of its own citizens. Abacha used money from oil exports as his personal credit card. He and his family are said to have stolen over $1 *billion* from the public purse. The percentage of Nigerians living in extreme poverty actually *increased* in the decades after oil was discovered. Leaders like Abacha, as well as Obiang in Equatorial Guinea or Muammar Gadafi in Libya, are the face of the political resource curse.

Jeffrey Sachs and Andrew Warner used the logic of the Dutch Disease to explain why so many resource-rich countries remained poor.[33] More recently, however, scholars have cast doubt on the supposed negative relationship between natural resource abundance and economic growth, pointing instead to things such as the quality of a country's institutions. They say proponents of Dutch Disease theories failed to look at resource-rich countries that *did* manage to grow. The country with the third largest amount of oil beneath its ground is not Nigeria or Venezuela but Canada. The third largest oil producer in the world is the United States. The top five exporters of natural gas include Canada, Norway, and the Netherlands.[34] Australia's most valuable export is not high-tech machinery or software but iron ore. So, many poor countries have extraordinary amounts of natural resources, but natural resources are not destiny (see Figure 9.5).[35]

economic resource curse (or Dutch Disease): when investment in the energy sector drives up the exchange rate, thus hurting a country's nonenergy exporters.

political resource curse: when a government does not need to rely on citizens for revenue, it may become less accountable and may allow public institutions to deteriorate.

FIGURE 9.5
Global Forces, Interactions, and Tensions and the Resource Curse

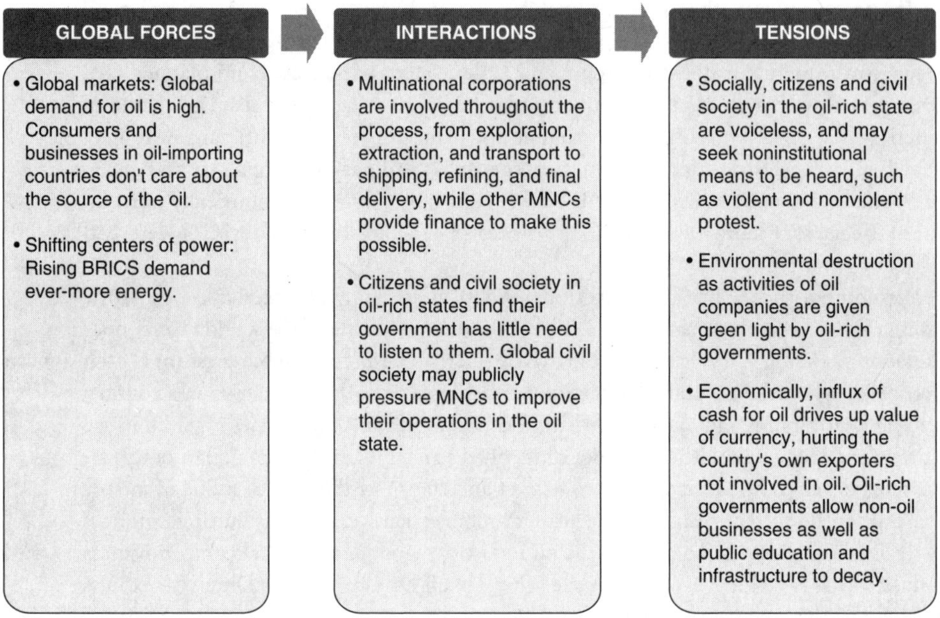

GLOBAL FORCES	INTERACTIONS	TENSIONS
• Global markets: Global demand for oil is high. Consumers and businesses in oil-importing countries don't care about the source of the oil. • Shifting centers of power: Rising BRICS demand ever-more energy.	• Multinational corporations are involved throughout the process, from exploration, extraction, and transport to shipping, refining, and final delivery, while other MNCs provide finance to make this possible. • Citizens and civil society in oil-rich states find their government has little need to listen to them. Global civil society may publicly pressure MNCs to improve their operations in the oil state.	• Socially, citizens and civil society in the oil-rich state are voiceless, and may seek noninstitutional means to be heard, such as violent and nonviolent protest. • Environmental destruction as activities of oil companies are given green light by oil-rich governments. • Economically, influx of cash for oil drives up value of currency, hurting the country's own exporters not involved in oil. Oil-rich governments allow non-oil businesses as well as public education and infrastructure to decay.

HOW CAN DEVELOPING COUNTRIES GROW THEIR ECONOMIES? FIVE THEORIES

Since the formal emergence of development studies and development economics around 1950, there have been five major answers to the question of how to grow an economy. What differed in each were the emphases placed on the role of state intervention in the economy to stimulate growth, and on whether poor countries should embrace global markets. On the question of the global economy, recall from Chapters 1 and 6 that in the latter half of the 20th century, global trade was increasing tremendously. Developing countries that took advantage of this were able to grow their economies. And in the past 20 years or so, financial globalization has made it possible for developing countries to borrow huge sums for investment. The debate continues over whether a developing economy should plug in to the global economy and take advantage of it, or instead plug out, and avoid being exploited by it.

Modernization Theory: To Get Rich, Copy the Rich!

modernization theory: idea attributed to Walt Rostow that there are stages of growth for each society, and that poor countries should copy what rich countries do.

From the 1950s to the 1970s, a widely accepted theory of development called **modernization theory** held that countries wishing to develop economically should simply do what wealthy countries had once done. Modernization theory is mostly associated with Walt Rostow's 1960 book *The Stages of Economic Growth*.[36] He said that societies could develop through a series of stages of economic development, beginning with a "traditional society" and ultimately (hopefully) culminating in "mass consumption society." The key, Rostow said, was for a society to reinvest in its economy (increase the savings rate, as an economist would say). A poor country could be helped along by massive investment, which is similar to arguments made today in favor of foreign aid. Rostow is often incorrectly criticized for suggesting this would be an inevitable path: In fact, he said societies could stall at any stage. But in the 1960s, it seemed as though developing countries were not making significant strides in closing the wealth gap between them and wealthy countries, despite heavy investments of the sort called for by modernization theory.

Dependency Theory: Plug *Out* of Global Markets

Around the 1960s, the rich-poor gap in the world appeared stubbornly persistent, and in a context of radical, leftist, liberationist ideologies in the developed and developing world, people turned to an alternative explanation. Raul Prebisch argued that the international economic order was essentially exploitative. It consisted, he said, of a wealthy core and a poor periphery, and the rules of international trade only served to reinforce the domination of the poor by wealthy countries. Rather than embrace free trade, Prebisch said wealthy countries like the United States, Germany, and Japan had all used protectionism at one stage of their economic development, and that developing countries should do the same.

Prebisch became a central figure in **dependency theory**, which held that wealthy countries were wealthy *because* poor countries were poor. Global markets would entrap poor countries in dependent relations. While modernization theory thought of poor countries as essentially blank slates upon which one could easily build progress, dependency theorists saw the world in a more political way: Poor countries are intentionally oppressed by wealthy countries. Dependency theorists were thus often anti-capitalist, although they varied on how far left on the political spectrum they were.

The idea that the world was composed of a core and a periphery became very attractive. Many poor countries at the time were emerging from under the yoke of colonialism. Their experience of global markets was that it was an exploitative thing, in which poor countries sold raw materials to wealthy countries. Countries like Brazil saw only danger in embracing global markets, and instead, they turned inward in an effort to become largely self-sufficient. They relied on their domestic markets to fuel their growth, and they did this by substituting imports for locally produced goods: hence the name **import substitution industrialization (ISI)**. ISI became popular from the 1930s onward, and it was practiced by countries in Latin America, the Middle East, Asia, and Africa. Governments kept out foreign competitors and subsidized industries in an attempt to become self-sufficient. By the 1970s, many ISI countries had growth rates that were better than any in their history.

In the long run, however, ISI countries did a bad job of understanding markets, and because of heavy state involvement, many failing industries persisted at great cost to the public. Despite their failures, the long-term effect of investing in manufacturing, however inefficient, was to create a pool of citizens who were skilled in manufacturing. In countries like India, experience with manufacturing and developed universities positioned them well to make Bangalore a center of IT in the 1990s.[37]

Developmental States Theory: Plug *In* to Global Markets

While ISI countries plugged out of global markets they saw as exploitative, a small group of countries plugged in. The **East Asian miracle** referred to the incredible economic growth and improvements in living standards seen in eight East and Southeast Asian countries in the second half of the 20th century: South Korea, Thailand, Malaysia, Hong Kong, Taiwan, Indonesia, Singapore, and Japan. Living standards rose by about 50% over the course of the Industrial Revolution in Britain, roughly the late 1700s to the mid-1800s, but 10,000% over half the number of years in

dependency theory: Theory that rich countries got rich at the expense of poor countries, and that the international economy has been designed to structurally favor rich countries. Raul Prebisch was central figure.

import substitution industrialization (ISI): attempt to industrialize by producing domestically what was formerly imported. Used in many developing countries from the 1940s to the 1980s.

East Asian miracle: rapid and unprecedented growth in economies and living standards seen in several East Asian countries in the 21st century.

FIGURE 9.6

Exponential Growth of East Asian Tigers

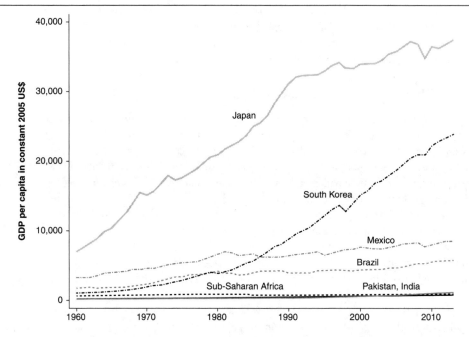

Source: Data from the World Bank's Development Indicators, https://data.worldbank.org/indicator/NY.GDP.PCAP .KD?end=2005&locations=JP-KR-MX-PK-IN-ZG&start=1960&view=chart, licensed under CC BY-4.0 https://creativecommons.org/ licenses/by/4.0/.

Asia, a 100-fold increase.[38] Figure 9.6 compares economic growth in Japan and South Korea with growth in other major regions and countries. Although South Korea started poorer than Mexico and Brazil, by the mid-1980s, it surpassed their wealth, while wealth in India, Pakistan, and an average for Sub-Saharan African countries has grown only slightly in recent years.

Like the growth of Britain in the 18th and 19th centuries, the success of East Asian states owed less to free markets and more to a combination of states and markets working together. Like ISI countries, these states kept foreign competitors out of their markets and subsidized domestic industries. But, unlike the ISI countries, export-oriented countries used the state to create globally competitive industries. They plugged in to global markets with their **export-oriented industrial-ization (EOI)**. They were called **developmental states**, where the state actively tries to grow the economy by incentivizing industrialization. This is not socialism or communism: A developmental state is not necessarily one in which the state owns, say, a shoe factory, but one in which the state provides subsidies and export targets to private shoe factories to make them globally competitive.

In the late 1950s, Taiwan was not much richer than most Sub-Saharan African countries. As an agricultural country, it was dependent on exports of rice and sugar. But it began to transform in the 1960s. The Taiwanese government invested heavily in the private sector and cut taxes, red tape, and infla-tion.[39] Tax incentives were provided for businesses to invest in sectors the government had prioritized. This was the state intervening in the market, but it was not taking over the market: It was incubating, cultivating, and developing the market. They did not allow foreign competition into the country until

export-oriented industrialization (EOI): state-led economic development model that emphasizes growing an economy by exporting ever-more sophisticated manufactured goods.

the 1980s, which was enough time for their own industries to develop. Although they were protected domestically, businesses understood they would be supported by the state only if they were competitive globally. The state would help to absorb any short-term losses, and incentives were provided for businesses to become more productive in their manufacturing. So it was that countries like Taiwan moved up the value-added ladder, over time moving from producing rice to bigger ticket items like laptops.

Watch a video on economic growth in Asia at https://www.youtube.com/watch?v=fiK5-oAaeUs.

Neoliberalism and the Washington Consensus: Shrink the State, Embrace the Market

The 1980s marked the rise of neoliberalism as an economic philosophy. While the EOI and ISI models emphasized the importance of state involvement in the economy (although they went about it in entirely opposing ways), neoliberals thought countries that develop through free markets and governments should largely stay out of the way.[40] Liberalism here does not mean leftist or progressive, as in American political discourse. In fact, it is closer to the opposite: It emphasizes the free movement of capital (money), goods (free trade), and labor (people). In the early 1980s, neoliberalism (introduced in Chapter 1) was strongly associated with conservative governments under U.S. president Ronald Reagan and British prime minister Margaret Thatcher. As ISI countries and communist economies faltered, conservatives said the world was witnessing the failure of leftist economics, and that governments should stop interfering with markets.

The importance of neoliberalism cannot be overstated. For many people, *globalization is neoliberalism.* Conservative and neoliberal ideas began to gain popularity in wealthy countries in the mid-1980s, just as many poor countries were crumbling under the debt crises. Neoliberalism became the narrative to explain the sorry state of poor countries: All forms of leftist economics, from moderate Keynesianism to extreme communism, were seen as the core reason for the continued economic stagnation in developing countries. Poor countries' problems were not seen as cultural: Asian economies had shown that non-Western countries could develop. Rather, the problem with poor countries according to neoliberals was the politics they practiced.

In the late 1980s, major international financial institutions like the World Bank and the IMF embraced the idea that poor countries had too much state intervention in their economies. What emerged became known as the **Washington Consensus**. At its most basic level, the Washington Consensus was a set of ideas about what is wrong with poor countries and what ought to happen in them. John Williamson created the term to describe the assumptions and ideas that appeared to be held in common by powerful international actors based in Washington, DC, where both the World Bank and IMF are headquartered.[41] These organizations are pillars of global governance on the issue of poverty, not because they "govern" the issue, but because it is in their halls and offices that rich and poor countries alike interact.

The Washington Consensus is not a treaty or a law or an agreement of any kind. It is just a set of ideas about poor countries that lots of powerful actors seemed to agree on (hence, "Consensus"). At its core were ideas of macroeconomic discipline (not overspending), freeing markets from state intervention, and opening up to globalization.[42] It is summarized as recommending that poor countries should *privatize, liberalize, and deregulate.* Williamson listed ten reforms that people in Washington thought most Latin American countries should be doing in the late 1980s:

1. Fiscal discipline: Government should not overspend or borrow heavily.

2. Reorder public expenditure priorities: Use targeted pro-poor policies rather than indiscriminate subsidies.

developmental states: where the state plays an active role in investing in the economy, including through the use of subsidies, credit, or limits on imports, to build the global competitiveness of national industries.

Washington Consensus: set of neoliberal assumptions shared by Western policy makers from the 1980s about what is wrong with poor countries and what ought to happen in them.

3. Tax reform: Cut taxes, raising just enough to provide essential public services.

4. Liberalize interest rates: Let the market determine rates.

5. Competitive exchange rate: Do not fix or manipulate exchange rates.

6. Trade liberalization: Free trade is good. The only question is how quickly a country should embrace it.

7. Liberalization of investment: Welcome foreign investment.

8. Privatization: Sell off state-owned assets. The private sector will run them more efficiently.

9. Deregulation: Make it easier to start businesses.

10. Property rights: Help people in the "informal sector" gain property rights.

Read John Williamson's famous essay on the Washington Consensus at http://www .petersoninstitute.org/publications/papers/paper.cfm?ResearchID=486.

structural adjustment programs (SAPs): set of neoliberal reforms developing countries had to agree to in order to receive assistance from the World Bank or International Monetary Fund in the 1980s and 1990s.

conditionality: what an aid recipient country must do to receive aid.

In the late 1980s, poor countries were crippled by debts, and the global organizations to whom they turned were increasingly accepting ideas at the core of neoliberalism and the Washington Consensus that, above all, the problem in poor countries was too much state and not enough market. This was the scene at the beginning of the era of **structural adjustment programs (SAPs)**. When the government of a poor country could not afford to pay its workers, let alone pay its international loans, it turned for help to the World Bank and the IMF. Rather than simply hand over huge loans at low interest rates, the Bank and IMF required countries to meet certain conditions, known as **conditionality**. These conditions entailed changing how the country managed its economy, and eventually the Bank and IMF started to demand that countries change their political systems, too. The term "structural adjustment programs (SAPs)" arose from the fact that poor countries were being asked to adjust the very structures of their economic and political systems. A SAP was an agreement—a document—signed by poor countries with the Bank and IMF that detailed exactly what changes the government would make and how much it would receive from the Bank and IMF in return.

SAPs were highly controversial right from the beginning. Bankrupt governments were forced to undertake extremely unpopular changes to access loans. When water was privatized, prices shot up, and poverty worsened. Austerity measures meant cutting government spending, but when health spending was cut, maternal and child health declined, and poverty worsened. When agricultural subsidies were cut, crop prices rose, and poverty worsened. When protections for domestic industry were removed, unemployment soared, and poverty worsened. Worse, some economists argued for "shock therapy": making all dramatic changes at the same time so as to not delay reform. The result was high inflation, unemployment, and deepening poverty. This was a period in which a multitude of actors (poor people and government officials in poor countries, officials with IGOs and rich states) interacted, and in which the unintended consequence was new tensions in the form of social instability in countries undergoing "shock therapy."

Read a debate on "shock therapy" in the 1990s at http://www-tc.pbs.org/wgbh/ commandingheights/shared/pdf/ufd_shocktherapy_full.pdf.

The overall effect of SAPs was either neutral or downright negative. The number of people in extreme poverty in Latin America and Africa *increased* over this period. People disagreed on why

IS From the Inside-Out

WHO DOES THE WORLD BANK WORK FOR?

The World Bank was created at a 1944 UN conference in Bretton Woods, New Hampshire, by 44 countries, mostly victors of World War II. The meetings also led to the creation of the IMF and the General Agreement on Tariffs and Trade (GATT; the precursor to the World Trade Organization [WTO]). Hence, the Bank, IMF, and GATT/WTO are often collectively referred to as the "Bretton Woods Institutions (BWIs)." Each organization was to have a specific purpose in the postwar global economy. GATT/WTO was created to enable countries to trade. The IMF was to ensure global financial stability. The World Bank was supposed to grow (mostly European) economies devastated by war. Gradually its mission expanded, and today its purpose is to help its member countries to alleviate poverty by growing their economies.

The World Bank is the most important development agency in the world. It is an enormous organization, with almost 10,000 staff and an operating budget of about $1 billion. It has loaned hundreds of billions of dollars to poor and middle-income countries. Because of its size, it also shapes global development discourse, which means it affects what conversations people have on global issues. This power is hard to quantify, but it can be seen in how widely its annual *World Development Reports* are covered by media and used by researchers (including in this textbook). Annual reports are thematic, so what the Bank chooses to discuss can set the agenda for global debate.[43]

When people talk about "the Bank," they usually have in mind the International Bank for Reconstruction and Development (IBRD), which is just one of the five organizations within the World Bank Group. The Bank is legally part of the United Nations General Assembly, but it operates independently. The highest decision-making body is the Bank's Board of Governors, which consists of the representatives from each member country. They set the direction for the Bank's daily operations, which are in turn carried out by the 24-member Executive Board. Voting power at both levels is based on a country's financial contribution to the Bank. Naturally this means that the poorest countries—who logically need the most help—have the least say in how the Bank works. For example, India has a 3% vote share while EU countries collectively have over 25% and the United States alone has 16%, giving it enough weight to veto any action. This power imbalance has long been a contentious issue in global diplomacy.

By tradition, major European states have nominated the head of the IMF while the United States nominates the head of the World Bank. This has long been controversial, and especially so when U.S. president George H.W. Bush nominated Paul Wolfowitz to be World Bank president in 2005. Wolfowitz had no experience in development and at the time was best known for pushing the United States to invade Iraq. U.S. president Barack Obama then brought international opinion back on the U.S. side in 2012 when he appointed a globally respected health expert—Dr. Jim Yong Kim—to be president. Yet, Kim's nomination was not universally welcomed. Many developing countries decried the practice of having a U.S. citizen run the Bank, and for the first time, there was more than one candidate as Ngozi Okonjo-Iweala, Nigeria's Finance Minister, was also nominated.

Despite its name, it is not really a bank as you and I use the term. Individuals cannot become members, and the Bank's purpose is not to make a profit. Only states may become members, which then entitles them to Bank assistance. The Bank's main activity is to provide loans to developing countries at cheaper (sometimes zero) interest rates than the country could get from private/commercial banks. The Bank gets this money by borrowing from private lenders. World Bank borrowing is guaranteed by governments of the countries in which

(Continued)

(Continued)

they are borrowing. This means the Bank borrows at very low interest rates, which it can then pass on to poor countries.

Another way the Bank differs from conventional banks is that it usually attaches economic and political conditions to their loans. These conditions (aka "conditionality") typically emphasize a neoliberal approach to development. Some observers see conditionality as poor countries being forced to liberalize their economies by Western-controlled intergovernmental organizations (IGOs).[44] Criticism of the Bank as too focused on free markets even came from some its own former senior economists such as Paul Collier, William Easterly, and Joseph Stiglitz. Even World Bank president Jim Yong Kim was critical in his *Dying for Growth*.[45] Criticism of the Bank was most vociferous in the 1980s and 1990s, after which the Bank moderated its emphasis on free markets and began to acknowledge that social safety nets and effective state institutions also play important roles in development. The Bank is not as market fundamentalist as it was in the 1980s, but it nonetheless believes that functioning (and fairly free) markets are part of the solution.[46] Moreover, the Bank no longer tells poor countries what to do. At least in theory, poor countries design their own aid program, known as a Poverty Reduction Strategy, and they do so in consultation with civil society groups in their own country.

In its early years, Bank lending focused on large infrastructure projects, such as dams. Around the 1970s, it leaned more toward "basic needs" projects, such as building schools and hospitals. In the 1980s and 1990s, it focused more on the private sector, which meant getting the state out of the economy (see "Washington Consensus"). Today Bank lending is broad, spanning infrastructure and basic needs, but also environmental programs and "governance reform" such as training civil servants. Its environmental activities are relatively new. In a leaked 1991 memo signed by then chief economist (and since U.S. treasury secretary and president of Harvard University) Larry Summers, "the economic logic behind dumping a load of toxic waste" in poor countries was described as being "impeccable."[47] For the Bank's critics, the memo revealed how obsessed the Bank was with economic efficiency no matter the environmental cost. In response the Bank might point to the Global Environmental Facility (GEF), which is housed at the Bank. GEF specifically funds environmental activities in poor countries.

Reflect

Which of our global forces are reflected in the management of the World Bank? Consider also global forces in the tensions surrounding the Bank's management.

SAPs were not more successful. Some said that the flaw was inherent in the market fundamentalism of neoliberalism that was at the heart of SAPs. If poor countries need investments in human capital and infrastructure, they argued, then neoliberalism would clearly never succeed in bringing prosperity to poor countries. Some called it **kicking away the ladder**: The wealthy countries that control the World Bank and IMF had once subsidized and protected their own industries when they were trying to develop, but now they were telling poorer countries that they could not do the same.[48] Others said the problem was instead that corrupt leaders signed their SAP, took the loans, but did not do any of the reforms, while others objected to the one-size-fits-all nature of conditionality and SAPS, which assumed that all poor countries faced the same problems.

kicking away the ladder: argument by Ha-Joon Chang that wealthy countries prevent poorer countries from using policies that once helped the wealthy countries industrialize.

A Post-Washington Consensus? The Role of Good Governance

What some people now call the **post-Washington Consensus** has emerged to supplement, but not replace, the Washington Consensus. Much of the neoliberal economics remains: Prosperity generally comes with private sector growth, free trade is good, and embracing global markets is the way to go. But it adds other dimensions. First, in the post-Washington Consensus, the government has a role in investing in society. This is a recognition that markets underprovide public goods like schools, roads, and police. Today, the World Bank would not require a poor country to reduce spending on health and education. Second, there is no one-size-fits-all policy. Different countries have different problems. Contrary to modernization theory, they should not simply copy wealthy countries. The post-Washington Consensus places greater emphasis on having a functioning state compared with its predecessor. Under the label of **good governance**, Western countries pushed developing countries to improve the quality of their governance. Good governance, however, means different things to different people, even though there are roughly three categories good governance advocates focus on: rule of law, property rights, and democratization.

Read about the Post-Washington Consensus at http://www.foreignaffairs.com/articles/ 67456/nancy-birdsall-and-francis-fukuyama/the-post-washington-consensus.

iStock/Bene_A

First, rule-of-law advocates say that in many developing countries laws are not evenly applied. In a monarchy like Saudi Arabia, King Abdullah bin Abdulaziz is above the law. But in a democracy like India, even the powerful Prime Minister Narendra Modi serves under the Constitution. The rule of law is fundamentally about making a society governable by making everyone—including the state—constrained by law. It is not necessarily about making the state democratic.

Second, property rights advocates like Peruvian economist Hernando de Soto argue instead that poor people are stuck because their governments do a poor job of protecting their property.[49] This makes it hard to buy and sell property, and it reduces incentives to invest in a piece of land or a building that could be taken away at any time. Property rights advocates think that political liberalism would be good to have, but it is really economic liberalism in the form of property rights, private enterprise, and free trade that matters.

Watch a documentary on property rights in the Amazon at http://indigenouspeoplesissues .com/index.php?option=com_content&view=article&id=1919:the-mystery-of-capital- among-the-indigenous-peoples-of-the-amazon-video-documentary&catid=68:videos-and- movies&Itemid=96.

The third group of good governance advocates are explicitly political. They point to the fact that the world's wealthiest countries tend to be democratic, while the poorest are frequently authoritarian. Democracy might be good for economic development in one of three ways. First, elected governments might be more responsive to the population and so might be less likely to experience civil wars. Merely avoiding mass conflict would be an achievement for many poor countries. Second, democracy could be good for growth indirectly when governments invest more in health and education. These might not have immediate impacts, but over the long run, these investments in human capital will be good for a country. It is not that nondemocracies are incapable of investing in human capital but

post-Washington Consensus: updated version of the Washington Consensus, with greater emphasis on "good governance" and slightly reduced enthusiasm for free markets.

good governance: ideological belief in core features of a well-governed society, including private property, effective and impartial judiciary, low corruption, and government transparency. Good governance is not necessarily democratic governance.

that they are less likely to do so. Third, democracy might make it hard for vested interests to stand in the way of innovation (i.e., creative destruction).

Good governance, in its various forms, is now an important part of the post-Washington Consensus. But the softening of the Washington Consensus should also be seen from the perspective of poor countries wanting to develop, and in the context of another of our global forces—shifting centers of power and the Rise of the Rest. Looking to the West, a developing country sees industrialized states with very weak growth despite their free market economies, and it was Western countries that caused the 2008 Global Recession. Looking to the East, however, they see China, which is neither economically nor politically liberal, yet has grown tremendously despite ignoring the Washington Consensus. The model of development many poor countries try emulate thus looks less like what happens in the United States or western Europe, and much more like China. The **Beijing Consensus**, therefore, is the growing popularity of an alternative model for growth. It has the added attraction for many governments of not requiring any political reform, unlike Western aid packages with their demands for political liberalization.

THE ROLE OF FOREIGN AID

Our image of poor countries and the aid they receive mostly comes from advertisements from charities like Oxfam and CARE. Pictures of sickly babies with swollen bellies appeal to our better selves, and this is how many think money goes from wealthier to poorer countries. In fact, charitable donations by citizens in wealthy countries are a tiny and mostly insignificant fraction of development aid. This is also true of philanthropy, for which the Bill and Melinda Gates Foundation is probably the most public face. In 2013, the Foundation gave out over $3 billion. That makes it easily the largest private aid organization, but this is still small compared with the approximately $140 billion spent in aid globally that same year. So, when we talk about actors in the aid world, we are usually talking about government and intergovernmental organizations.

What Is Foreign Aid?

Development aid goes by many names—**official development assistance (ODA)**, foreign aid, or just aid—but they all mean the same thing. ODA is resources given by one government to another for economic development. Aid can be money or things, known as "in-kind aid." In-kind aid is when a poor country receives physical materials, like rice or flour, or technical assistance, such as sending an economist to work in a finance ministry. Aid in the form of money usually goes to a government to help pay for part of its budget. Sometimes aid is a grant, and sometimes it is a loan given at a concessional (cheap) interest rate.

Aid is sent bilaterally or multilaterally. Bilateral aid is from one government to another. Multilateral aid is channeled indirectly through an international (hence, multilateral) organization like the World Bank or a UN agency, which uses the funds for development programs in a country. Bilateral aid is usually a grant, while multilateral aid is often, although not always, a loan. In the United States, aid usually flows through the U.S. Agency for International Development (USAID) or from U.S. embassies if given bilaterally. All donor countries have similar aid or development agencies.

Aid is supposed to help poor countries in one of three major ways. First, aid is given in an emergency such as a natural disaster or a war. This is often when food aid is given. Second, aid is given to boost economic growth. This is often when aid comes in the form of loans to build highways and bridges. Third, aid is given to directly improve people's lives and to indirectly strengthen a country's economy, by spending on health and education services.

FIGURE 9.7

Global Foreign Aid (ODA) Over Time

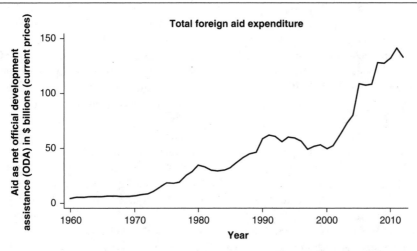

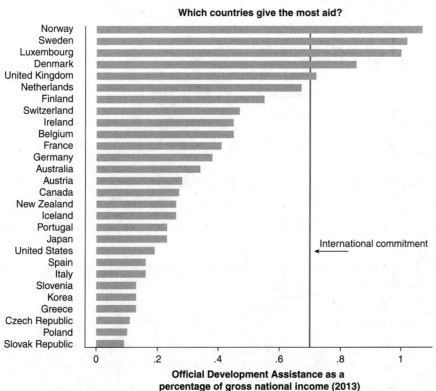

Source: OECD 2017, International Development Statistics, Aid (ODA) disbursements to countries and regions [DAC2a] accessed on 4/12/2018.

In 2005, global aid passed $100 billion for the first time. In Figure 9.7, you can see a gradual increase in aid in the 1980s, which was largely due to the large number of highly indebted poor countries borrowing from the World Bank and IMF. The spike in the 2000s was heavily driven by U.S. spending in Iraq and Afghanistan. The graph makes it seem as though aid has ballooned over time. It has, but remember that economies have also grown. In fact, aid as a share of an aid recipient's overall economy has *not* increased over time. In 1970, countries agreed to commit 0.7% of their gross national product (GNP), similar to GNI, to ODA.[50] Only Scandinavian countries typically meet the target. The 0.7% commitment is a much smaller figure than is popularly understood. In opinion polls asking people to estimate how much of the U.S. federal budget is spent on foreign aid, the median estimate is 25%, while the real figure was less than 1%.[51]

We might imagine that the world's poorest countries are the main recipients of aid, but this is not the case. A big reason for this is that military aid is included in aid data. In 2010, the top five recipients of U.S. ODA were Afghanistan ($4.1 billion), Israel ($2.2 billion), Pakistan ($1.8 billion), Egypt ($1.3 billion), and Haiti ($1.3 billion).[52] Israel is not a poor country, and Egypt is not one of the poorest. Afghanistan, Pakistan, and Haiti are certainly among the poorest in the world, but what they really have in common is that they are strategically important to the United States. This gets to one of the main reasons countries give ODA, which is they think it is in their own best interest to do so. This is why the major recipients of ODA tend to be politically connected to a donor country, whether through military occupation (Iraq), because they are a client of the major donor (Afghanistan), because they are allies (Israel), or because of colonial ties (French assistance to former colonies in West Africa).

So, does aid improve living standards and grow economies? One view says no, another says yes, and a third is somewhere in the middle. The aid debate concerns whether ODA brings prosperity. It is *not* a debate about humanitarian aid: Even though some debate how efficiently it is delivered, few criticize giving aid to victims of tsunamis or earthquakes. Humanitarian (or disaster) aid is usually about 10% of global money spent on aid. In the debate about aid we are about to read, note that humanitarian aid is *not* being debated.

Say No to Aid

For people such as William Easterly and Dambisa Moyo, aid not only fails to improve human welfare, but it also may even make it worse.[53] They make strong arguments:

1. Sub-Saharan Africa has little to show for the more than $1 *trillion* given to it in the past 50 years or so.

2. East Asian countries received little aid in the past few decades, yet brought more people out of poverty.

3. In the Cold War, aid was used to prop up friendly dictators like Zaire's Mobutu Sese Seko, who was estimated to have stolen over $5 *billion* in his three decades in power.

4. Aid packages are often designed by foreigners with little understanding of a poor country's needs, and this leads to poorly targeted projects and cookie-cutter approaches.

5. Donors do a very poor job of tracking the effectiveness of their work, yet are rarely punished for poor performance.

Critics say aid perverts the relationship of accountability between a government and its citizens. If the government in a developing country gets all of its money from European states, why would it be responsive to what its people want? They also argue that markets will often do a better job than donors of figuring out what people need. Moyo tells the following story:

> There's a mosquito net maker in Africa. He manufactures around 500 nets a week. He employs ten people, who (as with many African countries) each have to support upward of fifteen relatives. However hard they work, they can't make enough nets to combat the malaria-carrying mosquito. Enter vociferous Hollywood movie star who rallies the masses, and goads Western governments to collect and send 100,000 mosquito nets to the afflicted region, at a cost of a million dollars. The nets arrive, the nets are distributed, and a "good" deed is done. With the market flooded with foreign nets, however, our mosquito net maker is promptly out of business. His ten workers can no longer support their 150 dependents . . . [and] in a maximum of giver years the majority of the imported nets will be torn, damaged and of no further use.[54]

In this hypothetical scenario, Moyo describes how aid can be wasted when it is not given in a sustainable manner, and worse, aid may crush local entrepreneurs and thereby deepen poverty.

Read "The Aid Debate Is Over" by William Easterly at http://reason.com/archives/ 2013/12/26/the-aid-debate-is-over.

Say Yes to Aid

On the other side are people who say aid does work. This group is really split into two: those who believe massive injections of funds can get countries out of poverty traps, and those who think aid can be used to improve the quality of a country's political system, and thereby improve its people's welfare. Let's take each in turn.

Jeffrey Sachs does not buy the argument of Easterly and Moyo. Together with Bill Gates, Sachs is a major proponent of the poverty trap model: the idea that what poor countries fundamentally lack is money, and that large injections of it can push poor countries out of their trap. Sachs *does* think good governance matters, but he thinks a lot can be achieved with nonpolitical aid interventions. Take the bed nets example again. Free bed nets is now an official UN policy. Hundreds of millions of bed nets have been passed out for free around the world in the past few years. From 2000 to 2012, the number of children younger than 5 dying from malaria was cut *in half*, a remarkable achievement. This means over 3 million deaths were avoided. In 2013, about one half of households in Africa's malarial areas had at least one bed net. Similar results have been seen in tuberculosis, where deaths have halved since 1990, with HIV/AIDS, where millions of victims have received life-saving drugs, and with polio, which has been almost totally eradicated.

Read "The Case for Aid" by Jeffrey Sachs.[55]

The other group in the pro-aid camp is not as enthusiastic about aid as Sachs. They think Easterly and Moyo are right a lot of the time, but that aid can be used intelligently to force the kinds of deeper changes in poor countries that Sachs and the poverty trap do not think are essential. This group is associated with the democratic governance work of major organizations like the United Nations Development Programme (UNDP), the UN's main body for poverty alleviation. Even though it is unusual for a UN agency to be politically active, UNDP is explicit in emphasizing the importance of power for human development, and one of its major departments is even called the "Democratic Governance Group." UNDP believes that when citizens do not have a voice in their society, when they do not enjoy freedoms of speech or assembly, and when they do not have the power to participate in their own development, then they will never be able to hold the powerful to account. UNDP typically spends $5 billion on thousands of projects in poor and middle-income countries. They brought political parties in Lesotho together to agree to incorporate MDGs in their manifestos.[56] In Laos they provided free legal aid clinics and a legal aid hotline for the public. They also help countries run elections, they train civil servants how to use software, and much more. Their work is not only in democratic governance—they also work in the areas of HIV/AIDS, environment and energy, women's empowerment, poverty reduction, and crisis prevention—but what is significant is that this major organization understands the importance of politics in development.

See how and where UNDP works in interactive map an at http://open.undp.org/#2014.

The best studies suggest aid has a positive effect on economic growth, but the effect is not very large.[57] Clemens et al. point out that not all types of ODA are targeted at economic growth.[58] They analyzed all ODA and separated it into aid that is not expected to boost growth (like humanitarian aid), aid that should boost growth in 1 to 3 years (like funding the government budget or building roads), and aid that should boost growth in a generation (like educating children). When they did this, they found evidence that aid for short-term growth does help. They did not find evidence that aid for long-term growth works, even though they clearly point out that in statistics, not finding an effect is not the same as evidence of no effect. They also find that the effects on growth are positive but modest, which suggests that the intense aid debates may be a distraction. This is the conclusion reached by other scholars, who say that aid can do some good—even if some funds are stolen, a school with a new roof is still an improvement—but that aid often will not change the underlying structures or institutions that keep people poor, whether they be monopolists who dominate the economy, political exclusion in dictatorships, or social exclusion in ethnically or racially divided societies.

Watch experts debate the effect of aid in Africa at http://intelligencesquaredus.org/ debates/past-debates/item/547-aid-to-africa-is-doing-more-harm-than-good.

A Middle Ground on Aid

Despondence with the endless debates on whether aid was working or not has recently led to the emergence of a middle ground. These approaches are often aid based, but they take seriously measuring the effectiveness of interventions. Abhijit Banerjee and Esther Duflo say that the question of human welfare is so huge that we should ask small rather than large questions. Instead of asking "how can our country be as wealthy as Norway," we should ask "if we give out bed nets for free, will we reduce malaria?" These scholars use the method of randomized controlled trials (RCTs) used in pharmaceutical research to answer narrow but important development questions.

Watch Esther Duflo talk about her work at http://www.ted.com/talks/esther_duflo_ social_experiments_to_fight_poverty.

In one study, Banerjee and Duflo wanted to improve the quality of education in poor countries. Children in poor countries may simply lack resources like textbooks. Or maybe teacher-to-pupil ratios are too high. Or maybe students are just too malnourished to develop intellectually. These all sound like worthy interventions, but which should a poor country or a donor prioritize? They compared the effectiveness of better textbooks, more teachers, and healthier students by giving some students the "treatment" of better textbooks, others more teachers, and others treatment for intestinal worms across several studies. These randomly selected treatment schools were then compared with randomly selected "control" schools that did not receive the treatment. What did they find? Schools with extra textbooks did not do better in tests than schools in the control group, and neither did adding more teachers have an effect. When Kenyan children were treated for intestinal worms, however, absenteeism was reduced by about 25%. Children who took deworming pills for two years went to school for longer, and as adults, they earned 20% more than children who took the pills for one year. What's more, treatment cost $0.49 per child per year, roughly 1/20th the cost of hiring an additional teacher.[59]

This reluctance to embrace catch-all theories of development is not confined to randomistas. Development economists like Dani Rodrik are critical of one-size-fits-all approaches to development. Developing countries, he argues, are not the same. The key to helping them is to identify their **bottlenecks**, which are the problems specific to particular countries. One country might have a bad credit market, for example, which means small businesses pay extremely high interest rates on loans. Liberalizing the banking sector or using microcredit schemes could help. Another country might have frequent power outages, so businesses have to pay for expensive generators and fuel, which is a drag on the economy. This country does not need microcredit. It just needs better infrastructure. This is an important argument because **microcredit**—also known as "microfinance"—has grown in popularity. Microfinance provides loans to groups of small business owners, usually women, who ensure that other members of the group stay on top of their loan repayments. The number of very poor families with a microloan went from 8 million in 1997 to 138 million in 2010.[60]

But the evidence for the effectiveness of microfinance is not strong. In 2005, an Indian NGO called "Spandana" made loans of around $250 to hundreds of women at low interest rates. The program used an RCT method: Microfinance offices were opened in a randomly chosen half of Hyderabad's slums but not in the other half. Three years later, however, there was no evidence that the beneficiaries had better education or health outcomes, and the women did not seem to be any more empowered.[61] People used the money in entirely rational ways: to cope with crises. Rather than invest in their small business, they used it to repair storm-damaged roofs or pay medical bills for infants.

Watch Nobel Peace Prize Winner Muhammad Yunus explain micro-finance at http:// video.mit.edu/watch/muhammad-yunus-ending-global-poverty-9957/.

The newest approach to development involves **conditional cash transfer (CCT) programs**. These programs are usually known as "conditional transfer programs" or as "conditional cash transfer programs" because they involve a direct payment from a government to a citizen. Of the billion or so people in low- and middle-income countries, about half of these are covered in just five huge programs: China's *Di Bao*, India's *School Feeding Program* and *National Rural Employment Guarantee Scheme*, and Brazil's *Bolsa Familia* and *Programa de Alimentacao Escolar*.

Brazil is famously one of the most unequal places in the world, where slums butt up against leafy suburbs. Its *Bolsa Familia* program aimed to change that through CCTs. The program realized that poor children are poor not out of parental neglect but because their long-term need to become healthy and educated was outweighed by their short-term need to eat and survive. The program tackles this by giving a grant to mothers so long as they keep their children in school and get frequent medical checkups. Over 10 million households participate, which is about one quarter of the entire country. The program only costs about half of 1% of Brazil's GDP—a minuscule amount to invest in the next generation—and payments are typically about $12 per month per child. Its

bottlenecks:
idea that development interventions should focus on the specific local challenges in poor countries, such as corruption, weak credit, or poor communications, rather than assuming that all poor countries have the same long list of problems.

microcredit:
very small loans given to group of small business owners to expand their business.

conditional cash transfer (CCT) programs:
programs that come with conditions, such as enrolling a child in school. An unconditional program has no strings attached.

effect on poverty—and thus inequality—has been extraordinary. The proportion of people living in extreme poverty went from 9% to 4% in just 10 years, which is an incredible change in the context of human history. These gains are not all due to *Bolsa Familia*—the economy has grown strongly, and a minimum wage has been introduced—but experts are clear that the program played a huge rule.

Read about Bolsa Familia at http://www.economist.com/node/16690887.

Cash transfers have been so successful that some have tried unconditional cash transfers. Rather than creating a development project, donors just give money to poor people. Recipients are not told how to spend it. Cash transfers take advantage of two things. First, no one knows better than the poor what they really want. Maybe a poor farmer wants a better hoe, stronger plastic for the roof, or a bicycle. Only she knows what she needs. Second, one of our global forces—information and communications technology—enables us to instantly send money, even in remote areas, through mobile phone banking. Although it has been slow to take off in the United States, two thirds of Kenyans use mobile banking, which allows employers to pay employees, households to pay bills, and friends to pay friends. GiveDirectly is an NGO working in Uganda and Kenya that sends money via SMS to the poorest households, which the recipient is free to use however he or she pleases.[62] Recipients tend to use the money to expand businesses or even to manage crises of health or employment. Another project gave $200 to drug addicts and petty criminals in the slums of Liberia. The money was not squandered: recipients spent most money on basic necessities or in starting their own business.

Listen to a podcast on GiveDirectly and cash transfers at http://www.thisamericanlife .org/radio-archives/episode/503/i-was-just-trying-to-help?act=1.

FIGURE 9.8

Global Forces, Interactions, and Tensions in Foreign Aid

GLOBAL FORCES	INTERACTIONS	TENSIONS
• Global markets: Some poor countries find it expensive to borrow from private actors, but the World Bank borrows on their behalf and thus poor countries take advantage of abundant global finance. • Shifting centers of power: Rise of China in particular creates new sources of financing for poor countries who may wish to avoid the reformist demands of Western donor countries. • Global governance: Multilateral aid is channeled from donor countries through IGOs, such as UNDP and World Bank.	• In wealthier countries, civil society groups, for-profit contractors, and government agencies lobby to affect the size of foreign aid budgets. • In poorer countries, local and international NGOs, as well as government agencies, vie to receive the aid. • Internationally, more powerful countries seek to build alliances by providing aid to poorer, smaller countries. • Poorer countries try to unite in order to increase their voting power within the World Bank and IMF.	• International NGOs compete to deliver aid programs on behalf of donor governments, with some incentivized to overstate aid effectiveness in order to receive further funding. • Resentment when aid-recipient governments cater to the wishes of donor countries rather than to their own people. • Powerless groups in poor countries may be ignored if their need is not a priority for donor countries. Example: migrant labor.

Unconditional cash transfers already exist closer to home than you might know: Every year, the state government of oil-rich Alaska sends a check of about $1,000 to all of its residents. The check is their share of the state's oil wealth. Some people think that this oil-for-cash model can help countries avoid the resource curse, by giving money from oil and gas directly to citizens rather than stashing it all in the hands of corrupt governments. But there are some things a society needs that cash transfers will not help: public goods. These are things like roads and police that will be underprovided by individuals, so conventional aid may still have a role to play (see Figure 9.8).

Watch a video on how Oil-to-Cash works at https://www.youtube.com/watch?v=b8f7MSOLMRk.

SUMMARY

The theme of *interactions* is at the heart of our approach to international studies, and interactions have run through this chapter: Colonialism was important in shaping the long-term fortunes of poor countries; different views on global markets shaped whether countries embraced ISI or EOI, with significant consequences for long-term development; neoliberalism and the Washington Consensus emerged in wealthy countries but were experienced by many poor countries as a period of decline at the hands of intergovernmental organizations in which they had little power.

Our four global forces have also appeared throughout the chapter. Countries that made the most rapid development gains in the past 50 years were ones that embraced global markets. But they did not throw open their doors to global competitors. Rather, they protected their own industries in ways that would not be allowed under current free trade agreements, so it is not clear how easy it is for countries today to copy the East Asian export-driven model. Indeed, as we saw in the global markets chapter, poor countries have often found that embracing globalization means opening up to the instability of global finance.

Second, information and communications technology makes it easier for farmers to get information on market prices. Satellite imagery can help a poor country identify untapped resources beneath the ground. Mobile banking can speed up everyday business for rural communities. But we also know that mobile phones and the Internet are not a panacea: They are a tool but not a substitute for ensuring that governments are working in the interests of the majority, or that the world's most powerful states are not exploiting the weakest.

Third, shifting centers of power: The idea that we are experiencing a post-Washington Consensus may miss the mark entirely. The rapid growth of Brazil and China was not a simple matter of limiting the government's role in economic development. Thus, the "rise of the rest" may chip away at the legitimacy of the Western model of economic development.

Fourth, global governance: Many poor countries stagnated under structural adjustment, and it took a generation for the World Bank and IMF to accept that social spending in particular was a good thing for a poor country. Poor countries experience themselves as powerless at the World Bank and IMF, which are controlled by the wealthiest countries, and changes to the SAP system were slow in coming. The ability of poor countries to develop and keep developing may depend on their ability to better represent themselves in the halls of global governance, and it should come as no surprise that BRICS have set up the New Development Bank, intended as an alternative to the U.S.-dominated World Bank.

KEY TERMS

Beijing Consensus 256
bottlenecks 261
conditional cash transfer (CCT)
 programs 261

conditionality 252
creative destruction 241
dependency theory 249
development 236

developmental states 250
East Asian miracle 249
economic resource curse
 (or Dutch Disease) 247

QUESTIONS FOR REVIEW

1. "Why give a man a fish when you can teach him to fish?" How would a dependency theorist respond to this parable?

2. Which of the five theories of development would most agree with the statement "Global markets are a great opportunity for poor countries"?

3. Tensions are the unintended consequence of international interactions. What does creative destruction have to do with tensions?

4. How would Acemoglu and Robinson differentiate between the colonialism once practiced in the United States with the colonialism once practiced in Argentina?

5. Which term is associated with the idea that poor countries are victims of bad government rather than victims of globalization?

   Washington Consensus

   Dependency Theory

   Import Substitution Industrialization

   Poverty Trap

   Microcredit

6. Which side of the foreign aid debate would believe in the existence of poverty traps?

LEARN MORE

Gapminder, http://www.gapminder.com – watch countries develop throughout history

Human Development Index, http://hdr.undp.org/en/data – data on countries' HDI

World Bank Data, https://data.worldbank.org – a wealth of economic and social data

Worldwide Governance Indicators, http://info.worldbank.org/governance/wgi/index.aspx#home – data on the quality of governance

STATCompiler, https://www.statcompiler.com/en/ – detailed health data

Our World in Data, https://ourworldindata.org – online visualizations of global development

NOTES

1. Per the UN's Sustainable Development Goals, over six million children die each year before the age of five, or roughly one every ten seconds. http://www.un.org/sustainabledevelopment/health/.

2. Source: https://data.unicef.org/topic/child-health/diarrhoeal-disease/.

3. The extreme poverty rate is also known as the poverty headcount ratio. It is the share of the population living on less than $1.90 a day, measured in 2011 purchasing power parity terms. The $1.90 a day poverty line reflects the value of national poverty lines of some of the poorest countries in the world. The World Bank constructs these estimates using household surveys in which people report their income as well as their consumption, i.e., their spending. In total, over two million households are randomly sampled across 138 countries. The research does not take place in high income countries.

4. The International Monetary Fund, http://www.imf.org/external/pubs/ft/fandd/2010/09/images/pict_map.gif.

5. Data from 2012. World Bank Indicators.

6. World Health Organization. http://www.who.int/gho/child_health/mortality/mortality_causes_region_text/en/.

7. Data from UNDP's Gender and Poverty Reduction website. Accessed 9/15/14.

8. World Bank, "The State of Social Safety Nets 2014," 2014.

9. Amartya Sen, *Development as Freedom* (New York, NY: Knopf, 1999).

10. Gross National Income (GNI) is also widely used. For most countries, GNI and GDP are very similar. Imagine a Belgian company operating in Thailand. When we calculate Thailand's GDP, the output of that Belgian company would be included, but we know that some of that wealth will be sent back to Belgium. These inflows and outflows of wealth are precisely what GNI takes into account. Thailand's GNI would thus be lower than its GDP, while Belgium's GNI would be higher than its GDP. We can also express a country's GNI per capita in Purchasing Power Parity (PPP) terms. In 2012, the country with the highest GNI (PPP) per capita was Singapore at $71,900, followed by Norway. The United States was 7th. The World Bank, http://data.worldbank.org/indicator/NY.GNP.PCAP.PP.CD? order=wbapi_data_value_2012+wbapi_data_value+wbapi_data_value-last&sort=desc.

11. Data from World Bank Indicators. Figures are GDP per capita in current US$.

12. Data for 2016 from World Bank Indicators.

13. UNDP, Human Development Reports, http://hdr.undp.org/en/statistics/hdi.

14. Also check out the UN's Inequality-Adjusted Human Development Index at http://hdr.undp.org/en/content/inequality-adjusted-human-development-index-ihdi and the Gender Inequality Index at http://hdr.undp.org/en/content/gender-inequality-index-gii.

15. This is equivalent to $1 a day in 1996 prices, which was the original line.

16. UN-OHRLLS, http://unohrlls.org/about-ldcs/.

17. UNDP, http://www.undp.org/content/undp/en/home/sustainable-development-goals.html.

18. Mariana Mazzucato, *The Entrepreneurial State: Debunking Public Vs. Private Sector Myths* (London, U.K.: Anthem Press, 2015).

19. Michael Clemens, "Millennium Villages Project Needs Proper Evaluation," *The Guardian*, October 19, 2011, http://www.theguardian.com/global-development/poverty-matters/2011/oct/19/millennium-villages-project-proper-evaluation.

Although Jeffrey Sachs and Bill Gates are generally in favor of the use of development aid to tackle extreme poverty, they have been divided on the benefits of the MVP. See Sachs, "Why Bill Gates Gets It Wrong," *Project Syndicate*, May 23, 2014, http://www.project-syndicate.org/commentary/jeffrey-d-sachs-defends-the-track-record-of-the-millennium-villages-project.

20. Ricardo Hausmann, "Prisoners of Geography," *Foreign Policy*, January 2001, http://www.hks.harvard.edu/fs/rhausma/editorial/fp01_prisoners_geog.htm.

21. Jared Diamond, *Guns, Germs and Steel: The Fates of Human Societies* (New York, NY: W.W. Norton, 1999).

22. Max Weber, *The Protestant Ethic and the Spirit of Capitalism* (New York, NY: Routledge, 2013).

23. Niall Ferguson, "The World; Why America Outpaces Europe (Clue: The God Factor)," *New York Times*, June 8, 2003, http://www.nytimes.com/2003/06/08/weekinreview/the-world-why-america-outpaces-europe-clue-the-god-factor.html.

24. David Brooks, "The Underlying Tragedy," *New York Times*, January 14, 2010, http://www.nytimes.com/2010/01/15/opinion/15brooks.html?_r=0.

25. Daron Acemoglu and James A. Robinson, *Why Nations Fail: The Origins of Power, Prosperity and Poverty*, 1st ed. (New York, NY: Crown, 2012), 81.

26. Because they cannot measure economic wealth around 1500, they study the population density of societies. Their justification is that there must have been robust economic activity for populations to have been densely settled.

27. Acemoglu et al., "Reversal of Fortune: Geography and Institutions in the Making of the Modern World Income Distribution," *Quarterly Journal of Economics* 117, no. 4 (2002): 1231–1294.

28. This excluded women, natives, indentured servants, and slaves, though there were few slaves at the time.

29. Robert H. Bates, *Markets and States in Tropical Africa: The Political Basis of Agricultural Policies* (Berkeley: University of California Press, 1981).

30. David Victor, "The Politics of Fossil-Fuel Subsidies" (Global Subsidies Initiative, 2009).

31. Maria Vagliasindi, "Implementing Energy Subsidy Reforms: An Overview of the Key Issues," Policy Research Working Paper (New York, NY: World Bank, 2012).

32. *New York Times*, "Under Pressure, Nigerian Leader Relents on Gas Price," January 16, 2012.

33. Jeffrey D. Sachs and Andrew M. Warner, "Sources of Slow Growth in African Economies," *Journal of African Economies* 6, no. 3 (1997): 335.

34. Data from International Energy Agency. http://www.iea.org/statistics/.

35. Read more about the resource curse. http://www.foreignpolicy.com/articles/2010/12/06/what_resource_curse.

36. W.W. Rostow, *The Stages of Economic Growth: A Non-Communist Manifesto* (Cambridge, U.K.: Cambridge University Press, 1990).

37. Dani Rodrik, *The Globalization Paradox: Why Global Markets, States, and Democracy Can't Coexist* (Oxford, U.K.: Oxford University Press, 2011), 70. Atul Kohli, *State-Directed Development: Political Power and Industrialization in the Global Periphery* (Cambridge, U.K.: Cambridge University Press, 2004). Kohli argues that some countries presented as ISI failures, such as Nigeria, never even tried ISI.

38. Damien Kingsbury et al., *International Development: Issues and Challenges* (New York, NY: Palgrave Macmillan, 2012), 67.

39. Dani Rodrik, *The Globalization Paradox: Why Global Markets, States, and Democracy Can't Coexist*, 147.

40. "Neo" means "new," so neoliberalism means "new liberalism." What is new about it can be hard to pin down, but many would say that the classical liberalism of Adam Smith's era (1700s) was mostly

interested in freeing markets, that is, in liberal economics. But neoliberals want to change how government and public institutions work.

41. John Williamson, "What Washington Means by Policy Reform," in *Latin American Adjustment: How Much Has Happened?*, ed. John Williamson (Peterson Inst for Intl Economics, 1990).

42. But it is important to note that the Washington Consensus, and Williamson himself, are often associated with the neoliberal ideas that the state should not provide welfare services or income redistribution. Neoliberals thought that, but that was not an explicit part of the Washington Consensus. John Williamson, "Did the Washington Consensus Fail?" (Center for Strategic & International Studies, November 6, 2002).

43. Robin Broad, "Research, Knowledge, and the Art of 'Paradigm Maintenance': The World Bank's Development Economics Vice-Presidency (DEC)," *Review of International Political Economy* 13, no. 3 (August 1, 2006): 387–419.

44. For an alternative argument, see Patrick Sharma, "Bureaucratic Imperatives and Policy Outcomes: The Origins of World Bank Structural Adjustment Lending," *Review of International Political Economy* 20, no. 4 (August 1, 2013): 667–686, https://doi.org/10.1080/09692290.2012.689618.

45. Jim Yong Kim et al., eds., *Dying for Growth: Global Inequality and the Health of the Poor*, 1st edition (Monroe, ME: Common Courage Press, 2002).

46. Adrian Robert Bazbauers, "The Wolfensohn, Wolfowitz, and Zoellick Presidencies: Revitalising the Neoliberal Agenda of the World Bank," *Forum for Development Studies* 41, no. 1 (January 2, 2014): 91–114, https://doi.org/10.1080/08039410.2013.868821.

47. "Summers Memo," *Wikipedia*, December 1, 2017, https://en.wikipedia.org/w/index.php?title=Summers_memo&oldid=813081156. The response and partial denial can be found at *Harvard Magazine*, "Toxic Memo," May 1, 2001, https://www.harvardmagazine.com/2001/05/toxic-memo.html.

48. H.-J. Chang, *Kicking Away the Ladder: Development Strategy in Historical Perspective* (London, U.K.: Anthem Press, 2002); "Should Industrial Policy in Developing Countries Conform to Comparative Advantage or Defy It? A Debate Between Justin Lin and Ha-Joon Chang," *Development Policy Review* 27, no. 5 (September 1, 2009): 483–502.

49. Hernando De Soto, *Mystery of Capital: Why Capitalism Triumphs in the West and Fails Everywhere Else* (New York, NY: Basic Books, 2003).

50. This international aid "commitment" is often misunderstood. The commitment is not binding on states that have agreed to it, and the United States is often shamed for failing to meet it, yet the U.S. government has never formally agreed to the target.

51. *World Public Opinion*, "American Public Vastly Overestimates Amount of U.S. Foreign Aid," *World Public Opinion* (blog), November 29, 2010, http://www.worldpublicopinion.org/pipa/articles/brunitedstatescanadara/670.php.

52. Congressional Research Service, "Foreign Aid: An Introduction to U.S. Programs and Policy," 2011, 13.

53. William Easterly, "The Aid Debate Is Over," *Reason.Com*, 2014, https://reason.com/archives/2013/12/26/the-aid-debate-is-over; Moyo, *Dead Aid: Why Aid Is Not Working and How There Is a Better Way for Africa* (New York, NY: Farrar, Straus & Giroux, 2009).

54. Moyo, *Dead Aid*, 44.

55. Sachs, "The Case for Aid," *Foreign Policy*, January 21, 2014.

56. UNDP, http://www.undp.org.ls/democratic/MDGs%20&%20Political%20Parties%20Prodoc%201%20of%202.pdf.

57. Channing Arndt et al., "Assessing Foreign Aid's Long Run Contribution to Growth and Development," *World Development*, 2014, https://doi.org/10.1016/j.worlddev.2013.12.016.

58. Michael A. Clemens et al., "Counting Chickens When They Hatch: Timing and the Effects of Aid on Growth," *The Economic Journal* 122, no. 561 (June 1, 2012): 590–617, https://doi.org/10.1111/j.1468-0297.2011.02482.x.

59. Abhijit Banerjee and Esther Duflo, "The Experimental Approach to Development Economics," *Annual Review of Economics* 1, no. 1 (2009): 151–178, https://doi.org/10.1146/annurev.economics.050708.143235.

60. Abhiji Banerjee et al., "The Miracle of Microfinance? Evidence From a Randomized Evaluation," SSRN Scholarly Paper (Rochester, NY: Social Science Research Network, April 10, 2013), 2, http://papers.ssrn.com.ezproxy.library.wisc.edu/abstract=2250500.Banerjee et al., 2.

61. Banerjee et al., "The Miracle of Microfinance?"

62. Not everyone is impressed by GiveDirectly: https://ssir.org/articles/entry/givedirectly_not_so_fast.

Civil Wars and Terrorism

NEW GLOBAL SECURITY CHALLENGES AND EFFORTS TO MANAGE THEM

iStock/bwb-studio

T he dynamics of global security have changed considerably in recent decades. During the Cold War, the dominant security concern was interstate armed conflict. Grand strategy revolved around the super-power rivalry between the United States and the Soviet Union, and all the major conflicts or conflict risks that involved the United States were wars where the battle for communist or capitalist ascendancy was at stake—in Korea, Vietnam, Cuba, and elsewhere. Before the Cold War, interstate war dominated security debates as well, notably during World War I and World War II. Indeed, one of the central purposes of the United Nations (UN), which was created to safeguard world order after World War II, is to prevent wars between states.

To be sure, interstate war remains a major concern today. The rise of China, India, Brazil, and other large developing countries creates new security risks. Military planners worry about a war between China

LEARNING OBJECTIVES

After finishing this chapter, you should be able to:

- Define civil war and terrorism.

- Identify the causes and consequences of civil war.

- Examine civil war's causes and consequences in some recent cases.

- Understand how terrorist actors use information and communications technology.

- Identify some prominent explanations of terrorism.

- Articulate the ways in which international interactions shape, and are shaped by, civil war and terrorism.

- Discuss how international actors respond to civil war and terrorism, including through peacekeeping, peacebuilding, counterinsurgency, and counterterrorism.

- Consider the risks of cyberattacks and the ways in which information and communication technology may be harnessed to launch computer-based attacks.

and Japan, China and the United States, Russia and Ukraine, India and Pakistan, North Korea and Korea, and many other potential interstate conflicts. The global consequences of an interstate war between two or more major states or two states with nuclear weapons would be enormous.

At the same time, the end of the Cold War has brought a host of new global security challenges into focus. These new challenges now command considerable policy and academic attention, and they have emerged as key areas of interest for students of international studies as well. First is the issue of **civil war**, or armed conflict between a government and one or more rebel organizations within a domestic territory. Civil wars are not only prevalent in the world today, but they also cause tremendous human suffering, as we discuss in this chapter. Second is the issue of **terrorism**, which almost always includes actors who use violence against civilians. In addition, as we will discuss later in the chapter, there is transnational criminal violence, often organized through gangs or drug traffickers, and the prospect of cyberattacks. These various forms of insecurity typically involve nonstate actors: rebels in civil war, militant organizations in terrorism, gangs or traffickers in criminal violence, and hackers (sometimes connected to states) in the case of cyberattacks. As such, they represent new global challenges.

The rise in these new forms of violence and insecurity has generated a lot of new thinking among policy makers about how to respond and manage these threats. In particular, issues such as counterinsurgency, which is a strategy designed to manage and defeat rebellions in the context of civil war, has become a top priority. So has the issue of counterterrorism or coordinated efforts to combat terrorism. Within the United Nations and some regional organizations, the issue of international peacekeeping has received a great deal of attention as a mechanism to contain civil wars and prevent new outbreaks of them. Similarly is the issue of postconflict peacebuilding, which concerns how to rebuild societies after civil war so as to prevent another recurrence. Last is the issue of cybersecurity or ways to protect states, industry, and individuals from cyberattacks.

Each of these issues is fascinating. Each also touches on the international studies themes that this book develops. Civil wars and terrorism, as well as the management of them, involve complex webs of *interactions* across borders. The cross-cutting *global forces* discussed throughout the book shape the dynamics of violence discussed in this chapter too. *Information technology* is central to global terrorism, as well as to civil wars, and it is obviously essential to cyberattacks. *Global markets* shape the flow of weapons and the financing of rebellion. Peacekeeping, peacebuilding, and even counterterrorism have become *global governance* projects, subject to the rules, rulemaking, and general influence of intergovernmental organizations like the United Nations. Although the rise of the large developing countries has not yet sharply affected the dynamics of civil wars and terrorism, the change in polarity could. New powers could sponsor and fund insurgencies to undermine their rivals. In short, the global forces that structure democracy, human rights, poverty, migration, and the other global challenges discussed in this section of the book also shape civil wars and terrorism.

civil war: armed conflict between two or more organizations actively fighting for sovereign control over the same territory.

terrorism: use or threat of use of violence against civilians to sow fear and create political change.

WHAT ARE CIVIL WARS?

Civil war is the most common form of organized armed conflict in the world today (see Figure 10.1).[1] Civil wars are armed conflicts, within an internationally recognized state, between two or more military organizations that fight for sovereign control over the same territory. Civil wars can involve secession, in which an armed organization fights to break away from an existing state to form an independent one. Civil wars more commonly entail a rebel organization looking to oust and replace an existing government.[2]

Measuring Civil Wars

How to measure a civil war is the subject of some debate. The main idea is that there needs to be active fighting in a country between at least two armed organizations who seek to gain sovereign control of the same piece of territory. "Active fighting" is generally measured by the number of battle deaths annually (i.e., the number of deaths due to combatant on combatant fighting). Civil war and battle deaths are related but distinct from violence (as defined in Chapter 2), which typically refers to the infliction of deliberate harm against civilians. In any case, the standard social science measure of civil war is that there must be at least 1,000 battle deaths in a single year to count as an ongoing civil war.[3] Others put the threshold at 25 battle deaths per year.[4]

FIGURE 10.1

Armed Conflict by Type, 1946–2016

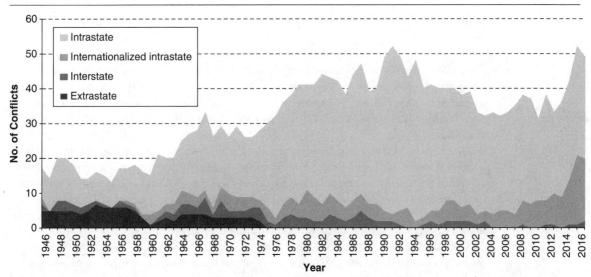

Source: Marie Allansson, Erik Melander, and Lotta Themnér, "Organized Violence, 1989–2016," *Journal of Peace Research*, 54(4):574–587 (2017). http://www.pcr.uu.se/research/ucdp/charts-graphs-and-maps/#tocjump_6799652384604542_0.

Civil wars thus involve most typically states (governments with armed forces) that fight rebellions (nonstate actors who form a military organization to unseat a government or to secede). Sometimes there can be multiple rebel organizations in the same territory. Those rebel organizations may fight the state, each other, or both each other and state forces. In recent years, the civil war in Syria is an example in which rebel forces fight each other and state forces in the same conflict, as discussed later in this chapter. In the contemporary world, civil wars rage on most continents, as Figure 10.2 shows.

In recent years in Asia, some of the most devastating wars have been in Syria, Iraq, Afghanistan, and Myanmar. The number of deaths in those cases rises well above 1,000 deaths per year, as Figure 10.2 shows. In Africa, some of the most devastating have been in the Democratic Republic of Congo, South Sudan, Somalia, Mali, Libya, and the Central African Republic. In Europe, civil wars have taken place recently in Ukraine, Russia, and Azerbaijan. In South America, a civil war in Colombia has lasted two generations, although it now appears to be ending. In North America, although it is not technically a civil war, the Mexico government's war with drug traffickers comes close to counting as a civil war. In this case, the traffickers do not aim to gain control of the government or to form their own sovereign state. In that way, the case usually falls under the heading of **criminal violence**, or organized violence to support an illicit activity, such as the drug trade, rather than to gain sovereign control of territory. But the Mexico example as well as the examples of other armed traffickers and gangs in Guatemala, Brazil, El Salvador, and elsewhere in Latin America show how these categories of organized violence blur together.

criminal violence: organized violence to support an illicit activity, such as the drug trade.

Characteristics of Contemporary Civil Wars

Civil wars are complex, but researchers find that they do share several defining, often interrelated, features.

Civil Wars Are Often Connected to Illegal Activities. Our discussion about criminal violence underlines one of the characteristics of contemporary civil wars, which is that they are connected to other forms of illicit activity and organized violence. As countries descend into war, black markets often arise.[5] Common forms of illegal trade in war include trafficking in drugs, weapons, and people.

Moreover, most major contemporary terrorist organizations take root in the midst of civil wars. Civil wars involve contested sovereignty in which an insurgent organization holds territory and looks to weaken a sitting government. As such, civil wars represent pockets of instability and disorder. Global terrorist organizations capitalize on those conditions. They typically make common cause with the insurgents, offering military assistance in weakening a sitting government or in strengthening a government against insurgents (as in the case of Afghanistan).

Consider some examples. The Islamic State of Iraq and Syria (ISIS, also known as the Islamic State of Iraq and the Levant or ISIL) is the preeminent terrorist organization at the time of writing this book. ISIS has launched or inspired some of the worst terrorist attacks in recent years—in more than a dozen countries, including the United States. The Islamic State took root initially in the civil war in Iraq that followed the ouster of Saddam Hussein in 2003. Thereafter the Islamic State found a foothold in the civil war in Syria and ultimately collapsed parts of a 100-year border that separated Iraq and Syria. Prior to the Islamic State, al-Qaeda was the preeminent terrorist organization (and now is a rival to the Islamic State). Civil war in Afghanistan was the breeding ground for al-Qaeda;

FIGURE 10.2

Organized Violence Worldwide (2016)

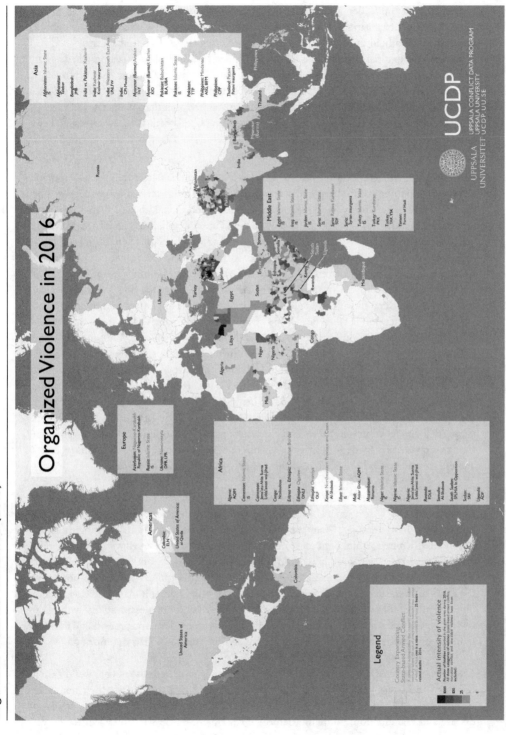

Organized Violence in 2016

Source: Marie Allansson, Erik Melander, and Lotta Themnér, "Organized Violence, 1989–2016," *Journal of Peace Research,* 54(4):574–587 (2017). http://www.pcr.uu.se/digitalAssets/667/c_667494-l_1-k_map16.png.

indeed, Osama Bin Laden and his advisers planned the 9/11 attacks on the United States from their field bases in Afghanistan. An al-Qaeda offshoot, al-Qaeda in the Maghreb, established a foothold in Mali because of a long-running civil war in that country.

Sometimes terrorist organizations morph into operating like rebel organizations; they seek to gain and hold territory, as well as to unseat a sitting government. The Islamic State again serves as an example. ISIS considers itself a *state*, and it seeks to establish a Caliphate across the Middle East. The tactics of the Islamic State are terrorist ones, but the organization operates like a rebel army seeking to overthrow established authority and replace it with their own. Indeed, ISIS shows how these categories of civil war, terrorism, and even global criminal violence often blur.[6]

Civil Wars Spill Across Borders. A second, related characteristic of contemporary civil wars is that they often have major regional and often international consequences. The number of refugees is one way to measure the regional and global impact: Wars force families to flee their homes, and the displaced often end up in neighboring countries. In recent years, there have been a record number of refugees and other persons who have been forcibly displaced from their homes. In 2015, the world hit a new record with more than 65 million people forcibly displaced (UNHCR, 2016). The overwhelming majority of global refugees originate from civil wars—in Syria, Afghanistan, Somalia, South Sudan, Sudan, the Democratic Republic of Congo, Myanmar, and Libya, among other countries.

Another dimension is cross-border interference. In other words, even though the main fighting in a civil war is domestic, rival states get involved. They sponsor, fund, and equip the fighting, and sometimes they intervene with their own troops. Consider Yemen, where Saudi Arabia supports the government while Iran and others support anti-state rebels. The same is true in Syria, where Turkey, Saudi Arabia, and other states have lined up behind rebels while Iran, Lebanon, and other states have lined up behind government forces. Even more broadly, the United States and Russia have found themselves at odds in Syria, with the United States supporting anti-government forces and Russia supporting government ones. In sum, even though a civil war is by definition a war within one country, such wars have consequences and effects well beyond the borders of the country where it is taking place.

Laws of War: humanitarian rules designed to regulate the conduct of armed conflict, in particular how civilians, prisoners of war, and other noncombatants are treated in wartime.

Civil Wars Are Fought by People Who Aren't Professional Soldiers. Third, contemporary civil wars often involve nonprofessional nonstate actors. Many rebels today have minimal and hasty training. Many are quickly recruited and pushed into fighting. In some wars, well-structured armies fight each other. But most contemporary civil wars involve a mixture of armed combatants: militias, child soldiers, mercenaries, and other militarized actors who have limited experience in fighting. Often, these hastily trained soldiers do not know the **Laws of War,** such as the Geneva Conventions, or other humanitarian rules designed to limit the impacts of war on civilians. The result is that civil wars are messier affairs, with often significant victimization of civilians. Many armed actors do not have the professional training that happens in established militaries, a gap that is connected to civilian victimization.

Civil Wars Affect Civilians Most. Last, civilians suffer the most in civil wars. When fighting breaks out, civilians often flee for their lives. When they do so, their ability to secure adequate food, medical assistance, and shelter declines, making them vulnerable to disease and malnutrition. Humanitarian organizations often do what they can to protect and care for refugees and other displaced persons, but still many civilians die from these effects of civil war. Armed groups also directly target civilians in some cases. Sexual violence often occurs in civil wars.[7]

The Effects of Civil Wars

Civil wars have many negative consequences. They create pockets of instability where terrorist organizations and traffickers can thrive, as noted. They generate refugees and other cross-border sources of instability, also as noted. In addition, civil wars devastate societies and affect the global community in direct and indirect ways.

Significant Human Costs. Civilians suffer disproportionately in civil war. They are often scarred emotionally and psychologically for decades. Trust is a casualty in civil war. People in the same society often find themselves on different sides of an armed conflict, and wars often exacerbate ethnic and religious cleavages. Deep distrust is the legacy. During civil wars, educational systems collapse or are severely disrupted. Children are displaced. Teachers cannot get to work. In addition, national health systems also suffer. Civil wars destroy infrastructure. There are also opportunity costs in civil wars. Instead of putting their energy toward economic growth and wealth creation, people devote their lives to survival. In short, the basic functioning of a society severely declines—in education, physical and mental health, the social fabric of society, and economic development.

Clear Economic Impacts. The World Bank has studied these impacts. The Bank found that countries that experience civil wars lag behind countries that do not in terms of poverty reduction and other basic development indicators. One stark illustration is a comparison between Burkina Faso and Burundi, two lower income countries in Africa (see Figure 10.3). The countries had broadly similar development trajectories from 1960 to 1990, but in the early 1990s, Burundi fell into an intense civil war. From that point forward, the development paths of the two countries diverged. Fifteen years after the Burundian armed conflict began, Burkina Faso's per capita income was more than double that of Burundi's, while in 1990 the difference was only about 15%.

International Costs in Peacekeeping and Peacebuilding. Although civilians in societies where civil wars rage bear the brunt of civil wars, civil wars cost the international community as well. These are some of the indirect effects of civil wars—the ways in which international actors respond to civil wars. To settle wars or lock in ceasefires, the United Nations and regional organizations often deploy peacekeepers. International peacekeeping entails the deployment of military and police personnel from several countries to a country that has had or is experiencing conflict. These missions have become increasingly large and complex over time; they sometimes last for a decade or more. Peacekeeping is expensive. Missions in some countries, such as the Democratic Republic of Congo, involve close to 20,000 peacekeepers and more than a billion dollars per year.

Peacekeeping is a form of *global governance*. In effect, member-states in an international or regional organization task that organization with trying to contain the spread of armed conflict. They seek to govern security matters through peacekeeping. United Nations

peacekeeping: international deployment of soldiers and police to guarantee a ceasefire or peace agreement.

FIGURE 10.3

Costs of Civil War: Examples of Burkina Faso Versus Burundi

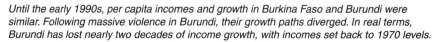

Until the early 1990s, per capita incomes and growth in Burkina Faso and Burundi were similar. Following massive violence in Burundi, their growth paths diverged. In real terms, Burundi has lost nearly two decades of income growth, with incomes set back to 1970 levels.

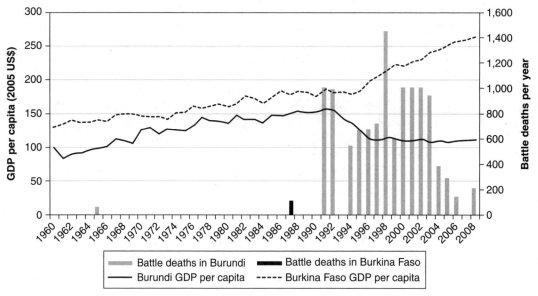

Source: World Bank. 2011. World Development Report 2011: Conflict, Security, and Development. World Bank. © World Bank. https://openknowledge.worldbank.org/handle/10986/4389 License: CC BY 3.0 IGO.

peacekeeping has undergone a great deal of development in recent decades. Since the end of the Cold War, the number of peacekeepers has increased 10-fold, and the missions themselves have become more complex and elaborate. Whereas peacekeeping before the end of the Cold War was principally about monitoring borders and ceasefires, peacekeeping in the 21st century involves civilian protection, training of armies and police forces, assisting countries in the holding of elections, and other state building matters that would allow a country to operate independently of the peacekeepers (see Table 10.1).

The United Nations does not have a standing army. When the Security Council wishes to deploy a peacekeeping unit, the Department of Peacekeeping Operations, which is a specialized agency within the United Nations, must assemble a force. They do this by asking member-states to contribute personnel and funds. In practice, the countries that contribute personnel are usually middle- and low-income nations, such as Morocco, Pakistan, Bangladesh, and Senegal. Such countries have large and somewhat professional armies; for them, international peacekeeping provides steady income to soldiers as well as international experience and professionalization. By contrast, the countries that pay for peacekeeping tend to be the wealthiest states in the world, such as the United States, Japan, Germany, and France, among other countries. Rarely does the United States contribute soldiers to UN-commanded

TABLE 10.1

Top 5 Largest Current UN Peacekeeping Operations as of May 2016

	Name of mission	Location of mission	Start date	# of troops	2014–2015 budget
1	MONUSCO	Democratic Republic of the Congo	July 2010	16,978	$1,332,178,600
2	UNAMID	Darfur	July 2007	13,760	$1,102,164,700
3	UNMISS	Republic of South Sudan	July 2011	12,110	$1,085,769,200
4	UNIFIL	Lebanon	March 1978	10,750	$506,346,400
5	MINUSMA	Mali	March 2013	10,601	$923,305,800

Source: Data are from United Nations Peacekeeping, http://www.un.org/en/peacekeeping/resources/statistics/factsheet.shtml.

TABLE 10.2

Top 10 Peacekeeping Troop Contributing Countries, and Top 10 Funding Countries

	Top contributors of military and police peacekeeping forces	Top funders
1	Ethiopia	United States
2	India	Japan
3	Pakistan	France
4	Bangladesh	Germany
5	Rwanda	United Kingdom
6	Nepal	China
7	Senegal	Italy
8	China	Russian Federation
9	Burkina Faso	Canada
10	Ghana	Spain
	As of April 30, 2016	For 2013–2015 Budget

Sources: Data are from United Nations Peacekeeping, http://www.un.org/en/peacekeeping/contributors/2016/apr16_2.pdf and http://www.un.org/en/peacekeeping/operations/financing.shtml.

peacekeeping missions. To observe the inverse relationship between peacekeeping personnel contributions and financial contributions, compare Columns 1 and 2 in Table 10.2.

Peacekeeping prevents wars from recurring.[8] Large peacekeeping missions with strong mandates to protect civilians reduce levels of violence against them.[9] In these ways, peacekeeping can establish the security and stability essential for a broader range of peacebuilding activities.

peacebuilding:
multidimensional
efforts to
rebuild states
and societies
after civil war to
prevent a future
armed conflict.

The basic concept of **peacebuilding** is to undertake a multidimensional approach to rebuilding institutions and repairing social relations in a country so as to reduce the risk of future violent conflict. The peacebuilding agenda includes everything from holding elections, constitutional reform, rebuilding infrastructure, security sector reform, and developing the economy. After war, governments often introduce some kind of accountability mechanism, through trials, truth commissions, and memorials. These forms of accounting for the past are an integral part of the peacebuilding agenda; they are designed to acknowledge and account for past atrocities so that they do not recur.

Security is a critical ingredient for various peacebuilding operations to take hold. Peacekeeping contributes to security after war, and thus, peacekeeping is often a core element of peacebuilding. Yet peacekeeping is hardly a panacea. Peacekeepers often remain aloof from the societies where they operate, misdiagnosing problems, and contributing to inequalities between international officers and locals.[10] Peacekeeping suffers from problems of interoperability—of troops with different languages, weapons systems, and chains of command working together in a single military mission. In other words, peacekeeping falls prey to bureaucratic inefficiencies and pathologies, not unlike other intergovernmental organizations (see Chapter 4).

Causes of Civil Wars

How and why civil wars start and persist is the subject of lively research. After the Cold War, as the prevalence of civil wars came into view for many policy makers and scholars, the primary prism by which to explain them was social identity. In essence, the argument was that civil wars take place in multiethnic and multireligious societies marked by persistent divisions between the identity groups. During the wars in the Balkans in the 1990s—in Bosnia-Herzegovina, Croatia, and Serbia—ethnic hatred was the main explanatory lens. Similarly in Rwanda, where civil war and genocide took place in the mid-1990s, scholars and policy makers sought to explain the violence by referencing deep and long-standing identity differences in the country.

**relative
deprivation:**
type of
grievance when
individuals
believe they
have less than
they should
have.

Another common argument was that grievances cause insurgencies. People rebel because of discrimination, political repression, or some other source of dissatisfaction with the government, such as corruption or unemployment. One famous theory points to the concept of **relative deprivation**.[11] The idea here is that absolute deprivation (for instance, abject poverty) does not drive rebellion but that people rebel when they feel that their situation should be better than it is. That gap between expectation and reality is the root cause of rebellion.

In recent years, scholars have challenged these traditional explanations. Rather than focus on the factors that push citizens to rebel, scholars have underlined the conditions that make rebellions feasible. Two major arguments have proven influential. One centers on the economic conditions that facilitate civil war. In effect, rebels need to finance civil wars—to purchase weapons and communications equipment as well as to pay recruits. Some rebels in fact operate more like bandits, looking to get rich from capturing lucrative minerals and metals. The research pointed to how civil wars concentrated in countries with high-value commodities—diamonds, gold, oil, cobalt, expensive timber, and the like.[12] The academic research spawned social movements to curtail **conflict minerals**, or those commodities that facilitated civil wars. Campaigners focused on banning conflict minerals or pressuring companies to source their minerals from non-conflict zones.

**conflict
minerals:**
presence of
minerals that
are considered
to motivate
and sustain
civil war.

Another stream of scholarship emphasizes that civil wars concentrate in low-income countries. One claim is that states in low-income countries are weak. Their militaries do not have the capacity to find and root out rebellions. By the same token, rebellions thrive in geographies where rebels can hide and evade government forces. Rebels need mountains or lagoons, places that are inaccessible to armies and air forces.[13] Others argue that weapons trade in small arms facilitate warfare, in particular, in low-income countries with weak states. If rebels can cheaply and easily get their hands on AK-47s, mortars, rocket-propelled grenades, and other cheap mobile firearms, then they can wage war.

The academic debate over the causes for civil war is far from settled. Indeed, the range of explanations is large, and some new research now challenges the second wave of research. For example, some new research finds that identity-based grievances do matter. When inequality exists and is structured around ethnic groups, then civil war is more likely. **Horizontal inequalities**—or inequalities between groups—facilitates rebellions.[14]

horizontal inequalities: inequities between groups that are considered to cause grievances that drive civil war.

Civil Wars and Forces, Interactions, and Tensions

At first glance, the idea of a civil war—an armed conflict within a country—would seem to cut against the notion of inside-out and outside-in *interactions*. But the reality is more complicated. Consider the idea that high-value minerals make financing civil wars possible. In essence, rebel leaders are like a set of nodes within much broader markets. For example, some rebels in a civil war might seize a diamond mine. Through a network of traders and merchants, the rebels sell their diamonds into a market for precious minerals that would end up in a jewelry store in East Asia or the United States. Alternatively, the rebels might tax local miners a hefty fee, and then the miners would sell their product into a global marketplace. Another example is coltan, a thick sludge that when boiled down conducts energy at low heat. Coltan was for years an essential ingredient in handheld electronics, such as gaming devices and smartphones. The device in your hands might in fact have components that were sourced from war zones. In the eastern part of the Democratic Republic of Congo, rebels harvested large amounts of coltan, or taxed miners who did, and that in turn provided them revenue and incentive to keep fighting. In both of these examples—diamonds and coltan sourced from rebel-held territory—we can see how the micro, domestic dynamics of civil war in fact play out across borders. Large multinational companies source these materials from these conflict areas, and countries such as the United States formulate legislation to regulate their import.

Civil wars extend beyond the borders where they are fought in many other ways. Terrorist organizations with global ambitions and global media campaigns often base themselves in countries in the midst of a civil war. Recall the examples from earlier in the chapter, in which we showed how the Islamic State and al-Qaeda made civil war spaces their main theater of operations (in Iraq, Syria, Libya, and Afghanistan). From there they planned attacks on a global stage. In addition, as noted, civil wars produce millions of refugees—that is, people fleeing across borders to gain safety. Refugees cross borders. In sum, although civil wars by definition are primarily fought within a single sovereign territory, they often extend well beyond those borders.

Responses to civil wars are also transnational. As noted, peacekeeping is a complex form of interaction, in which the United Nations or a regional organization such as the African Union authorizes multiple states to deploy military and police personnel to conflict zones around the world. Peacekeepers hail from many countries; while on a peacekeeping mission, they interact with each other and with the citizens in the countries where the mission takes place. In and of themselves, these are complex international interactions—multinational forces in another country. Indeed, peacekeeping should be understood as an exercise in *global governance*. In this case, an international organization mobilizes to manage security threats and conflict recurrence in various countries around the world. They are seeking to regulate and manage the conflict space.

International peacebuilding is another, related form of cross-national interaction that shapes civil war spaces after the wars have ended. Peacebuilding is a complex effort that entails some combination of rebuilding shredded infrastructure, stimulating a wrecked economy, rewriting constitutions, reforming the security sector, and some form of justice and accountability. Intergovernmental organizations, foreign states, and international nongovernmental organizations (INGOs) often play crucial roles in international peacebuilding. For example, various UN specialized agencies—from development, to women, to children— often contribute to the peacebuilding process, as do the World Bank and the International Monetary Fund. Donor governments, like the United States, Japan, Saudi Arabia, and various European states, often contribute to reconstruction efforts. In Iraq and Afghanistan, for example, the United States is estimated to have contributed billions of dollars to the rebuilding effort. These are all forms of international interaction and engagement with the postwar country. The intergovernmental organizations and their staff, the foreign governments and their staff, companies based in their countries and their staff, and many aid workers converge on a postwar country. They inject large amounts of money and seek to shape the policy and direction of the postwar state. Indeed, in the aftermath of war, multinational companies often look for opportunities. Countries that were previously closed become open to investment. In many cases, postwar states lack the technology and know-how to sustain large businesses. Postwar countries thus often enter into major deals with foreign companies, such as over mining, generating electricity, or starting supermarket chains (see Figure 10.4).

The dynamics, determinants, and consequences of civil war are visible through a couple contemporary examples, as are the ways in which outside-in and inside-out interactions shape civil war and its management.

The Example of the Democratic Republic of Congo. The Democratic Republic of Congo (the DRC) is the largest country in Sub-Saharan Africa. The contours of the DRC are the product of colonial competition and greed during the late 19th century, itself a form of outside-in interference. In its 19th century incarnation as the Congo, the country was initially the personal property of the Belgian king, Leopold II, who hired the explorer Henry Morton Stanley to make land deals with local African leaders. The result was a vast expanse of territory that stretches across the center of the continent.

The Congo was born in violence. Leopold imposed quotas, forcing Congolese to produce certain amounts of rubber and ivory or face whipping and torture. Leopold's system devastated the Congo, leading to widespread hardship, violence, and death.[15] In the early 20th century, given what became the notorious abuses under Leopold, the Belgian state took control of the Congo from Leopold and governed it until 1960 when Congo became an independent, postcolonial state.

Congo's early years of independence were also violent. In many ways, Belgium did not lay the groundwork for a successful transition. At the time, Congo had only a handful of college graduates. The administration was a pure colonial construction, designed to oppress rather than to facilitate participation.[16] Congo's most dynamic independence leader was Patrice Lumumba, a socialist, whose fiery speeches alarmed the United States and Belgium, who worried that the Soviet Union would establish a foothold in huge, mineral-rich Congo. In quick succession, a secessionist civil war broke out; Lumumba was assassinated, with Belgian and likely American complicity; and a military dictator took power, with American support. Mobutu Sese Seko, the new leader, would rule the country until 1997 when he was ousted. In that period, the country became home to endemic corruption and the hollowing out of the state.

The turning point for Mobutu was a set of developments along its eastern border, in particular, in the neighboring country of Rwanda. In 1994, the Rwandan government orchestrated a genocide against the minority Tutsi population; that genocide took place during a civil war, which the genocidal government subsequently lost. Upon defeat, the government uprooted itself, along with more than a million refugees, and fled across the Rwandan border into Congo. In rushed a variety of international humanitarian agencies, which established a string of refugee camps not far from Rwanda. Although the humanitarian need was great—the refugees lacked food, water, and shelter, and many fell victim to cholera and other diseases—the humanitarian response was problematic. The camps themselves were too close to the Rwandan border, and in turn, some were militarized. The rump ex-Rwandan government cynically used the camps to prepare a new attack on Rwanda. The international response was also uneven. During the genocide, the international community famously abandoned Rwanda, allowing the genocide to proceed quickly and reneging on the promises embodied in the United Nations Genocide

FIGURE 10.4

Global Forces, Interactions, and Tensions: Civil War Causes and Consequences

GLOBAL FORCES	INTERACTIONS	TENSIONS
• Market demand for minerals and other resources create incentives and resources for rebel groups to fight civil wars. • Markets in weapons provide rebels and states access to the equipment to prosecute civil war. • Intergovernmental and non-governmental organizations coordinate and fund efforts to keep and build peace as a complex form of global governance.	• Rebel groups and states exchange goods and support with actors inside and outside their borders. • Refugees fleeing war cross borders. • Civil war gives rise to criminal markets. • Armed actors predate on civilians during civil wars. • Peacekeepers from multiple countries, as well as non-governmental actors, seek to manage the negative effects of war.	• Fighting for control of resources causes widespread suffering. • Refugees destabilize or create environmental stress in neighboring countries. • Civil war in one country leads another country to intervene or become directly or indirectly involved. • Global terror groups take root in areas of civil war and instability. • Global governance actors become embroiled in complex conflicts. • Peacekeepers prove unable to keep the peace, leading to resentment.

Convention to "never again" allow genocide. Here the international community rushed to intervene to protect those allied with the government that had committed genocide. To be sure, some were innocent of the genocide crimes, but others were not and the old government manipulated the aid to their advantage. Here too we observe complex forms of cross-border interaction: how one war and mass atrocity (in Rwanda) unsettled a neighboring state (Congo), and how international humanitarian actors unwittingly exacerbated tensions.

Frustrated with the situation, the new Rwandan government invaded Congo to break up the refugee camps. In doing so, the Rwandans teamed up with long-standing Rwandan refugees political opposition figures, notably, Laurent Kabila. The Rwandan army succeeded in emptying the camps. Most refugees returned to Rwanda, but many former officials fled westward, as did hundreds of thousands of Congolese. The Rwandan army pursued them, killing tens of thousands.[17] Eventually, the Rwandan government forces and their Congolese counterparts marched into the capital, Kinshasa, unseated Mobutu, and installed Kabila as the new leader of Congo.[18]

That was the first Congo War. The second war started a year later when Kabila fell out with his Rwandan counterparts. There ensued an even more complex international war, in which several African states intervened to support Kabila while Rwanda partnered with Uganda and Burundi to prop up Congolese rebel groups in the east of the country. The second war lasted until 2004, when a comprehensive peace agreement was signed. The deal called for a complex peacebuilding program, which included a UN peacekeeping force, preparations for elections, and other peacebuilding projects. As of this writing, the peacekeeping force remains in place, and fighting is continuing in the east. Both the peacekeeping and peacebuilding projects are examples of global governance in the aftermath of civil war, a form of security governance.

The Congo wars are particularly complex. They are civil wars that spilled over and directly involved neighboring countries, a less common type of civil war noted in Figure 10.1. In this case, other countries intervened actively in the Congolese conflict vividly illustrating the regional dynamics. The start of the 1996 war also shows the regional effects of refugees: In this case, armed refugees from Rwanda prompted the Rwandan government to intervene militarily in Congo. The first and second Congo wars also show the extraordinary toll on civilian life. In the first war, rebel and Rwandan government forces hunted down and murdered tens of thousands of refugees. The second war and its aftermath were even more devastating. The state administration, the education system, the healthcare system, the road networks, and even food markets—while already weak—collapsed. Many Congolese died as a function of malnutrition and disease. One NGO estimated the civilian death toll to be greater than five million, which would have made the Congo wars the deadliest since World War II.[19] More than 95% of those deaths were civilians not involved in the fighting. Sexual violence also became widespread and systematic in the Congo wars. The UN Special Representative on Sexual Violence in Conflict at one point referred to Congo as the "rape capital of the world."[20] In the east, where the fighting lingered and where the devastation was greatest, there were multiple armed groups, many poorly trained and many who included child soldiers—indicating the presence of nonprofessional combatants.

The Congo wars illustrate the debates about the causes of civil war. Congo is indeed home to dozens and dozens of ethnic groups. Ethnic resentment was certainly a factor in the east, in particular, toward those populations aligned with the state in Rwanda. Moreover, given the history of dictatorship and corruption, many Congolese hold burning grievances toward the state. But equally important is that the Congo is home to a rich array of mineral resources—diamonds, gold, cobalt, copper, coltan, tungsten, and other high-value minerals. The capture and exploitation of the mineral resources also sustained and likely fueled the fighting, and the sale of them was facilitated by global markets. The Congo state was exceptionally weak, and the rebels could hide in some cases in thick jungle or the countryside. These dimensions concerning the feasibility of war and the opportunities that war afforded also played a role in the ongoing conflict.

The response to Congo also shows the complex interactions that structure our world. In response to the analysis that minerals fueled the war and sexual violence in it, human rights campaigners sought to ban "conflict minerals." They succeeded to the point of amending legislation in the United States, thereby requiring companies to source their minerals from nonconflict zones.[21] Critics, however, responded that the "conflict minerals" lens oversimplified the war in Congo and indeed risked putting legitimate Congolese miners out of work, thereby enhancing the risk of future conflict.[22] The issue is far from settled.

The Example of Syria. The war in Syria is very different from that in Congo. The proximate origins of the war in Syria were the Arab Uprisings, a protest movement against authoritarian regimes that took place in multiple countries in the Middle East and North Africa discussed in Chapter 7. The protests in Syria began in March 2011, primarily calling for democratic reforms to the government of Bashar al-Assad and for an end to corruption. Syria's security forces brutally repressed the demonstrations, action that in turn sparked even more protest. By July 2011, protests spread around the country, and demonstrators called for Assad's resignation. As the state increased the violence toward the protesters, they in turn began to arm themselves, both for protection and to liberate parts of the country from government control. In so doing, what began as a protest movement escalated into a civil war and continued to intensify as the anti-Assad forces won over defectors.

The civil war in Syria became even more complicated. Assad gained international support from Iran, Hezbollah in Lebanon, and eventually Russia, which maintained a military base in Syria. The opposition gained support from states in the Persian Gulf, notably Saudi Arabia and Qatar, as well as Turkey. The United States took the position that Assad had to step down. The international dimensions of the civil war made the conflict more complex and raised the geostrategic stakes of the civil war—in effect, two major world powers (the United States and Russia) have risked fighting each other, as have Middle East states (Iran against Gulf states, for example). In these ways, the Syrian civil war demonstrated the ways in which internal armed conflicts have implications well outside one state's borders.

In the first years of the war, neither side in the armed conflict was able to prevail against the other, leading to a military stalemate. That situation created an opportunity for *jihadist* movements, notably, the Islamic State (described in more detail later in this chapter) and an al-Qaeda group, to make inroads. The opposition to the government thus fractured. There were more traditional rebels fighting to overthrow the Assad states. But then there were jihadist groups that inserted themselves and became more powerful than the traditional rebels. There also appeared a Kurdish militia that gained control of the north. In short, armed groups fragmented the territory, with multiple groups controlling different amounts of territory. That makes the civil war exceptionally complex and difficult to resolve. Moreover, the intense involvement of the jihadist groups complicates the international effort. Although the United States, for example, initially took the position that President Assad had to step down, any military action that the United States takes against the Islamic State may benefit the Assad forces, and vice versa.

Consistent with other contemporary civil wars, civilians have suffered disproportionately in Syria. By the middle of 2015, the United Nations estimated that 250,000 Syrians had been killed, predominantly civilians, and some 12 million had been displaced, which is about two thirds of the country's total population.[23] Various reports from the UN Commission of Inquiry on Syria documented systematic violence against civilians, the use of chemical weapons, and other crimes against humanity and war crimes. In 2016, the Commission accused the Islamic State of committing "genocide" against the Yazidi religious minority, as we saw in Chapter 8.[24] All of these forms of violence point to systematic suffering by civilians in the civil war.

The Syrian civil war has international consequences. In addition to the diplomatic and regional consequences, Syria became a base for ISIS, which in turn recruited fighters from all over the world. The Islamic State recruits in turn fanned out into other parts of the world and were responsible for terrorist attacks in France, Belgium, Turkey, Libya, Bangladesh, and several other countries. The Syrian refugee crisis also had far-reaching effects. Syria produced millions of refugees, many of whom sought to resettle in Europe, the United States, and other developed countries. The refugee crisis became a central issue in European politics, where questions of immigration already roiled the continent (see Chapter 11).

In terms of causes, the traditional explanations for civil war hold for Syria. Grievances drove the initial protests and efforts to oust the Assad government. Ethnic identity also is a factor. Assad is from the Alawite ethnic minority in Syria, which has dominated the state since 1970 when Assad's father, Hafez al-Assad, took power in a coup. Many Sunni Arabs, who constitute a majority in the country, felt excluded, and indeed the opposition to Assad in the 2010s was concentrated in Sunni-dominated areas. By the same token, certain conditions in Syria facilitated the war. Although Syria is not a huge oil producer, oil is a factor in the war. Control of oil fields in the east has been central to the finances and operations of the Islamic State and other armed opposition groups during the war. This is consistent with a theory of civil war that stresses the natural resource foundation of such conflicts. A chain of mountains has also provided cover for rebels at different points in the conflict.

Syria also shows the complex outside-in and inside-out interactions that shape civil wars. Protests in one country sparked protests in Syria, but once protest turned to civil war, Syria became a magnet for a broad array of international groups. As in Congo, the war prompted interventions from other states, and various United Nations agencies have sought to document and contain the violence against civilians.

As of this writing, the war in Syria shows no sign of ending. The conflict remains one of the most intractable foreign policy problems and the source of the some of the greatest human suffering since World War II.

WHAT IS TERRORISM?

The situation in Syria brings into focus another major global security challenge: terrorism. Terrorism is a central concern not only in the United States but also in many other countries. The Global Terrorism Database, which tracks terrorist attacks on a worldwide scale, counts incidents per country per year. In the past 10 years, the countries with the most terrorist incidents include Iraq, Afghanistan, Pakistan, India, the Philippines, Thailand, Somalia, Nigeria, Yemen, Russia, and Colombia.[25] The United States does not typically enter the top ten (see Table 10.3).

In addition to these countries, terrorism is a major concern across western Europe, East Africa, West Africa, and Indonesia, among other places. In each of these locations, there have been major terrorist attacks in recent years. In France, attackers massacred people at nightclubs and restaurants in November 2015 (as we will discuss in more detail); in Belgium, a terrorist attack at the main international airport in Brussels and at a metro station maimed and murdered more than 30 in 2016; in Kenya, a stunning attack on an upscale shopping mall killed dozens in 2013; and in Indonesia and Mali, terrorist attacks on multiple occasions killed people at hotels and restaurants in recent years. By the time this book appears in print, there are likely to be new rounds of attacks that will have grabbed headlines. Terrorism is clearly an issue of global import.

Less obvious to some may be the ways in which terrorism only recently emerged as one of the most dominants global security challenges. During the Cold War, terrorist attacks were not uncommon—in particular, in and around Israel, in the United Kingdom (over

TABLE 10.3

Total Terrorist Attacks for the Decade Between 2005 and 2014

Country	Total # of attacks 2005–2014
Iraq	15,439
Pakistan	9,465
Afghanistan	7,387
India	5,123
Thailand	2,767
Philippines	2,503
Somalia	2,293
Nigeria	2,137
Yemen	1,790
Russia	1,272
Colombia	1,109
Libya	1,084
Ukraine	913
Syria	833
Israel	801

Source: Data are from the Global Terrorism Database, http://www.start.umd.edu/gtd/.

Notes: The Global Terrorism Database also collects information on level of fatalities. The countries with the largest numbers of attacks are typically the countries with the highest numbers of fatalities.

independence for Northern Ireland), and in Sri Lanka, where rebels frequently used suicide bombing as a tactic.[26] These different terrorist organizations, however, tended to have a more national orientation. They employed terrorist tactics to liberate territory or force some other type of reform. By contrast, a hallmark of contemporary terrorism is the ways in which some organizations are simultaneously local *and global*, as our feature box in this chapter on Boko Haram shows. Indeed, the two most influential organizations of the 21st century—al-Qaeda and the Islamic State—have a global reach. They recruit from around the world; they target locations around the world; and they capitalize on global banking and communications technology. They are part and parcel of the global fabric, representing for many a "dark side" of outside-in interactions.

Defining Terrorism

The familiarity with the term "terrorism" masks considerable confusion about how to define the term. What is the difference between terrorism and war fighting? How is terrorism different from gang violence or genocide? The United Nations has yet to agree on a standard definition.

One good place to start is the U.S. Department of State, which defines terrorism as "premeditated, politically motivated violence perpetrated against noncombatant targets by subnational groups or clandestine agents." In this definition, we have the concept of deliberate political violence in contrast to murder or other forms of criminal violence. The targets are noncombatants (i.e., civilians), which is different from the way that war is supposed to be conducted (pitting fighters against fighters). Moreover, the perpetrators are subnational groups or clandestine agents, which in this case suggests that states do not commit terrorism. The last part is probably the most contested and self-serving aspect of the U.S. definition; some argue that states also commit terrorism.

A second conceptualization comes from a renowned scholar of terrorism, Bruce Hoffman. Along with the State Department definition, he argues that terrorism has a political motivation; it involves violence, and it is committed by a nonstate entity. But embedded in his definition is the idea that terrorism is designed to have far-reaching psychological impacts beyond the immediate victim or target. This dimension cuts to the heart of what terrorism is. He writes that terrorism is "the deliberate creation and exploitation of fear through violence or the threat of violence in the pursuit of political change. . . . Terrorism is specifically designed to have far-reaching psychological effects beyond the immediate victim(s) or object of the terrorist attack. It is meant to instill fear within, and thereby intimidate, a wider 'target audience' that might include a rival ethnic or religious group, an entire country, a national government or political party, or public opinion in general."

The definition underscores the way in which terrorism is both political and communicative violence. Terrorism sends a message; it creates fear and intimidation—for a political purpose. Perpetrators choose targets not because eliminating them will weaken their enemy militarily but because killing them will create fear in a society and may lead governments to overreact in their response. That is why terrorist attacks are often theatrical or designed to garner publicity; the targets often have symbolic importance. Again, the purpose of the violence is to send a message, and the victims of the violence are not the primary targets. The primary targets are the societies and governments where the violence takes place.

Causes of Terrorism

There is no consensus on the causes of terrorism. There is also no consensus as to whether terrorism is best conceptualized as a *tactic*, which some militant organizations and armed actors use, or as a characteristic of an organization or a situation. If terrorism is primarily a tactic that insurgents use, that has implications for how scholars study the phenomenon. They would be studying why armed groups use one tactic over another. By contrast, if terrorism is primarily that by which scholars describe an entire organization or situation, then scholars may seek to understand what different terrorist organizations have in common. The U.S. government, for example, considers some organizations to be terrorist—if they consistently use terrorist tactics. Indeed, the United States maintains a list of foreign terrorist organizations.[27] But others conceptualize organizations as insurgents that seek to gain and control territory by unseating existing states; those insurgents sometimes employ terrorist tactics.[28] The distinction matters not only for thinking about causes but also for thinking about responses, as we will discuss.

Scholars generally agree that those who commit terror attacks are not, on average, insane or somehow uniquely predisposed to violence for mental health reasons.[29] One study of more than 300 persons charged with *jihadi* terrorism in the United States found that about 1 in 10 had mental health problems, less than the average for the population in the United States. They also did not have, on average, particularly criminal records. The study concluded that no single profile or mixture of factors predominated. Some were motived by militant Islamist ideology; some disapproved of American foreign policy in the Muslim world; and others had personal disappointments (such as family or career problems) that led them to look for a different kind of answer. For some, peer or family pressure mattered.[30]

Another, earlier study of suicide bombing found that on average terrorist perpetrators are not mad, fanatical, or religiously motivated. They come from all walks of life. Rather, the argument was that suicide terrorism follows a "strategic logic": Terrorist organizations promoted suicide bombing to coerce modern liberal democracies to make territorial concessions. In the 1990s, the leading organization that committed suicide terrorism was the Liberation Tigers of Tamil Elam (LTTE) in Sri Lanka. Their objective was to force the Sri Lankan government to withdraw from the northern Tamil areas of the country to pave the way for an independent state. Suicide bombing also took place in the Israel to force the Israeli government to withdraw from the Gaza Strip and the West Bank. In Turkey, Kurdish perpetrators employed suicide bombing to push Turkey to withdraw from Turkish parts of the country.

That said, since the year 2000, the most active organizations—those who have committed the most terrorist incidents, according to the Global Terrorism Database—are jihadist movements. Most are organizations committed to a **Salafism**, an extremist vision of Islam. Those organizations include the Islamic State (which operates primarily in Iraq, Syria, and Libya), al-Qaeda in the Arabian Peninsula (which principally operates in Yemen), Al-Shabaab (which principally operates in Somalia), the Taliban (which principally operates in Afghanistan), and Boko Haram (which principally operates in Nigeria). Other, nonjihadist organizations are also active—in the Philippines, India, Colombia, Sri Lanka, and Uganda.[31] These are organizations that use terrorist tactics but are not seeking to impose a strict version of Islam on the territories they conquer.

The Salafist organizations, such as the Islamic State, bring into focus the ideological origins of some terrorist organizations (or organizations that use terrorist tactics). Through violence and the capture of territory, the organizations aim to establish a new order, one based on a strict

Salafism: interpretation of Islam emphasizing a literalist reading of the Koran and setting an activist agenda to purify the religion of deviations and to shape the public sphere in the image of this interpretation of Islam.

foundationalist interpretation of Islam. Ideas and beliefs motivate the actors, especially the leaders, even if specific individuals may be recruited for more banal reasons, such as via a family member or a friend. Many scholars contest the idea that Islam per se is the foundation of these movements. The world is home to some 1.8 billion Muslims; more than 99.9% of them have nothing to do with an organization that employs terrorist tactics, and indeed historically, many non-Muslims and nonjihadi groups employ terrorist tactics, as was in the case in Sri Lanka. Modern terrorists are not all Salafists, as the Norwegian extremist Anders Breivik showed when he went on a killing rampage in Norway in 2011. On the other hand, for some Salafists, they believe they are acting in the name of Islam and they see themselves as pious and religious purists.[32] Again, the issue matters not only for thinking about causes but also for thinking about responses.

radicalization:
process of embracing extreme ideologies and violence as a form of political action.

One common concept that scholars and policy makers use to describe the process of embracing extreme ideologies and violence is **radicalization**. The concept refers to the idea of a process, whether short term or long term, by which the embrace of violence and extremism takes place. One recent study found that those who became radicalized experienced a three-part process: a sense of humiliation, victimization, and then connection to a new group. That new sense of belonging happens with a group that embraces a vision of action that justifies violence in the name of fighting historic oppression, in particular of Islam.[33] Media, and specifically information and communications technology, often play a key role in the process of radicalization, by which recruiters and propagandists share ideas and try to convert individuals to their cause.

Terrorism and Forces, Interactions, and Tensions

At the broadest level, terrorist action involves complex forms of *interaction*, often across borders. As noted, terrorist organizations recruit on a global basis, and the staffs of the organizations themselves involve complex mixtures of fighters and leaders from many organizations. Many organizations select targets on a global basis; they specifically choose symbolic targets that have international recognition, such as the Twin Towers in New York, an upscale shopping mall in Nairobi, or Brussels as the capital of the European Union. Global politics also motivate terrorists. For example, they often see themselves as fighting a world order that benefits the West and unfairly discriminates against Muslims. Some terrorist organizations specifically campaign against Western occupation of what they consider Muslim lands or seek to end Western support for a particular state. Overall some terrorist organizations aim to change the existing world order. In other words, the interactions that underpin the global order are at stake in much of contemporary terrorism. Al-Qaeda and the Islamic State want to change the configuration of power in the world and in the Middle East and North Africa, in particular. That includes changing governments, changing legal codes, changing foreign support, and even redrawing borders.

The global forces that shape contemporary challenges similarly impact terrorism. The clearest candidate is *information and communications technology*. Many contemporary terrorist organizations are masters of social media. They have strong presences in online chat rooms. They use YouTube and other sharable electronic media to share sermons that in turn play a role in radicalizing individuals. They produce glossy magazines, online and in print, for recruiting and propaganda. They use and develop complex encryption technology to encode messages and to communicate clandestinely. Above all, they produce, often in sophisticated ways, graphic videos about the violence the organization commits. The videos are often chilling. For example, ISIS in a variety of countries films and produces execution videos. These include videos of beheadings, as well as of other forms of execution. The victims are sometimes individuals accused of apostasy, of supporting a government that ISIS is fighting, of defecting, or of being foreigners, such as captured American journalist Steven Sotloff and James Foley. During its attack on the shopping mall in Nairobi, Kenya, in 2013, Al-Shabaab militants tweeted the attack and later produced a special edition of the organization's magazine about the attack.[34] In short, terrorism is communicative violence, and the organizations that employ terrorism often exploit advances in information and communications technology to propagate their message.

Markets are also fundamental to terrorist organizations. The Islamic State, for example, captures oil fields and sells oil into markets. ISIS and other organizations also raise revenue from contributions and taxation, and they have developed complex banking systems to transfer money to and from countries. One challenge for some of these organizations is that some states around the world actively look to intercept and seize the assets of terrorist organizations. Hence, the Islamic State and its operatives channel a considerable amount of money through parallel banking systems. The movement of money moves through countries, and often it is founded on trust. One person walks into a money exchange center in one country and hands over bank notes, and another person in another country can instantly remove it.

Two examples of well-known incidents illustrate the patterns and dynamics of contemporary terrorism. Attacks in the United States and western Europe are not the most frequent globally, as Table 10. 3 shows. Yet as incidents that are likely to be familiar to you, we select them to illustrate some of the main points in this section.

The Example of al-Qaeda and 9/11. The first example we will cover is 9/11, which was a multipronged attack on the United States in 2001 organized by al-Qaeda, which was then led by Osama bin Laden. Bin Laden was a wealthy Saudi national, an heir to his father's lucrative construction business. Osama bin Laden committed himself to *jihad* in the 1980s when he fought in Afghanistan. There he joined self-styled Islamic fighters called the *mujahedeen* to depose the secular, Soviet-backed state. He went on to found al-Qaeda in the 1980s, in part based on the preaching of the Egyptian scholar Sayeed Qutb, who railed against the decadence and immorality present in the West.

Bin Laden developed an intense hatred of the United States in the 1990s during the Gulf War when the United States based hundreds of thousands of personnel and large amounts of equipment in Saudi Arabia. Bin Laden considered Saudi Arabia to be a holy land. As a persona non grata in Saudi Arabia, bin Laden moved to Sudan and then back to Afghanistan. From Sudan, al-Qaeda planned the attacks on U.S. embassies in Kenya and Tanzania in 1998. From Sudan, bin Laden relocated to Afghanistan, from where he and other leading al-Qaeda officials planned the 9/11 attacks in 2001.

In essence, al-Qaeda dispatched four teams of recruits to the United States, where after pilot training, they hijacked four planes on the morning of September 11, 2001. Two planes that had departed from New York City were flown into the World Trade Center in downtown New York; a third plane that had departed from the Washington, DC, area was flown into the Pentagon; a fourth plane, which had departed from New Jersey, was hijacked and headed for

Washington, DC, before passengers sought to overcome the hijackers. The plane crashed in Pennsylvania. The coordinated attacks on 9/11 led to the death of some 3,000 people, injuring many more; they were the deadliest attacks on U.S. soil since Pearl Harbor. Reaction to them led the United States into wars in Afghanistan in 2001 and Iraq in 2003, interventions that reverberated in the United States and the Middle East for a decade thereafter.

Al-Qaeda was the preeminent terrorist organization during the 2000s. The group operated as a franchise and network that supplied finance, training, and inspiration to organizations around the world. That led to al-Qaeda groups forming or affiliating in the Sahelian region of Africa (al-Qaeda in the Maghreb), in Iraq (al-Qaeda in Mesopotamia), in Yemen (al-Qaeda in the Arabian Peninsula), and in Somalia (Al-Shabaab), among other locations. The United States eventually found bin Laden in Pakistan, where he was living with some members of his family. He was killed during a raid in 2012, and thereafter, al-Qaeda lost some prominence as the stature of the Islamic State rose.

Some dimensions of al-Qaeda provide vivid, if disturbing, examples of the characteristics of contemporary terrorism. First, the 9/11 target, the World Trade Center, had symbolic importance; the Trade Center represented the heart of global capitalism and U.S. leadership in the capitalist world. The Pentagon was the symbol and headquarters of military power. Moreover, the victims were civilians, at least most were. The attack was also theatrical: the hijacking of four planes and flying them into buildings in the United States itself. The attack captured tons of attention and publicity; it was aimed to inspire other *jihadists* and to show the vulnerability of the United States. In these various ways, the violence was both political and communicative.

Second, the rise of al-Qaeda and the aftermath of 9/11 were inherently about interactions across borders. Bin Laden was from Saudi Arabia but operated in multiple countries. Key leaders in his organization came from Egypt, Jordan, and Iraq, among other places. The 9/11 attackers themselves were from Saudi Arabia, Lebanon, Egypt, and the United Arab Emirates. The organization inspired franchises in multiple other countries. The training and financing of the operations happened through multiple countries, and indeed, the open migration of people facilitated the attack. Finally, the reaction to the attacks had profound implications for the United States in the world, as well as for the rest of the Middle East and North Africa.

Third, while social media was in its infancy in 2001, al-Qaeda mediatized the attacks. In their aftermath, Bin Laden became famous for videotaped lectures, which were broadcast on the Arab-language network Al-Jazeera. Here again we see how information and communications technology are central to terrorist operations.

The Example of the Islamic State and the November 2015 Attacks in Paris. The Islamic State came to rival al-Qaeda in the 2010s and had emerged by the middle of the decade as the most influential global terrorist organization. ISIS emerged first in Iraq. It was initially a splinter group of al-Qaeda in Mesopotamia (also called al-Qaeda in Iraq), which was the backbone of resistance to the U.S.-backed government in Iraq after the fall of Saddam Hussein. Formed in the late 2000s in Iraq by a Jordanian who was killed by an American airstrike, the group's most influential leader is an Iraqi named Abu Bakr al-Baghdadi, who heads the organization as of this writing. Baghdadi was born to a lower middle class family; he became a cleric with an advanced degree in Islamic studies. During the insurgency in Iraq, he was imprisoned at Camp Bucca, which became a focal point for recruitment for the Islamic State.[35]

ISIS grew over time in Iraq and eventually in Syria. The organization captured significant territory in both countries by the mid-2010s, including several large Iraqi cities. The organization in turn organized and inspired attacks in some 17 countries in 2014 and 2015 alone.[36] The organization heavily mediatized much of its violence, as described earlier. Although the organization primarily appeals to Sunni Arabs, and indeed the Islamic State has sought to sow divisions between Sunnis and Shia's, the organization has recruited fighters and converts from around the world.

Many of the Islamic State's attacks on civilians have been exceptionally brutal. One example is the attacks in Paris on November 13, 2015. On that day, a team of about 15 attackers targeted several civilian locations in Paris: bars, restaurants, a concert hall, and a soccer stadium. Traveling from Belgium, the attackers were in three teams. The first detonated suicide bombs at a soccer stadium where the president of France was present. The second arrived in a popular neighborhood and opened fire on a restaurant and bar, followed by a series of attacks on cafes and restaurants. The third team opened fire on a concert hall. All told, the attack claimed the lives of 136 people—primarily civilians—and injured many more. Killing dozens of people in one of the world's great cities was a devastating attack, designed to instill fear in the heart of the West. The attackers were a mixture of people, primarily from Belgium and France. Some were Syrian. Several had been involved in petty crime; a few had traveled to Syria, Greece, and Turkey before the attacks.[37]

Again, the Paris attacks illustrate key aspects of contemporary terrorism. The victims were not the main targets; those going to cafes and a music concert had nothing to do with the war in Syria. The main targets were France, and the West more generally. Through these attacks, the Islamic State aimed to instill fear, disrupt normal life, and otherwise goad France and the West into impulsive action. The violence garnered huge publicity. The network of attackers was, again, international, and they moved between borders fairly easily.[38]

These are but two examples in a much broader context of terrorism. Yet, although extreme in the number of casualties and somewhat unusual in that they took place in major cities in the United States and France, respectively, the examples reveal patterns that

FIGURE 10.5

Global Forces, Interactions, and Tensions: Patterns in Terrorist Organization Tactics, Recruitment, and Reaction

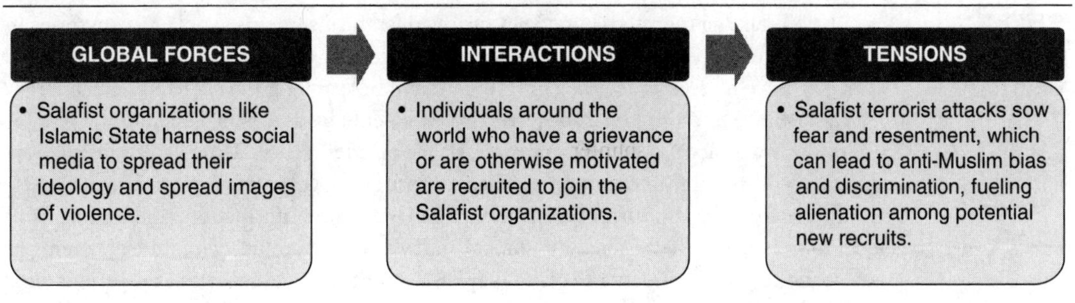

GLOBAL FORCES		INTERACTIONS		TENSIONS
• Salafist organizations like Islamic State harness social media to spread their ideology and spread images of violence.	→	• Individuals around the world who have a grievance or are otherwise motivated are recruited to join the Salafist organizations.	→	• Salafist terrorist attacks sow fear and resentment, which can lead to anti-Muslim bias and discrimination, fueling alienation among potential new recruits.

are not exceptional. If one examines recent attacks in Mali, Somalia, Turkey, Iraq, Libya, and elsewhere, frequently the attackers are plugged into international networks. They have traveled abroad, trained abroad, formed coalitions with other attackers, and received funding or equipment from abroad. Many key leaders have extensive international experience, again whether in Somalia, Mali, Libya, Turkey, or beyond (see Figure 10.5).

Confronting Terrorism

If contemporary terrorism is embedded in international networks, what is the best way to confront and contain it? What should counterterrorism entail? There are three approaches, which, although complementary, also stress very different strategies.

One approach is to fight a **war on terror**, in which fighting a direct armed conflict with terrorists via the armed forces is the central strategy. By and large, however, a direct military confrontation is an approach that many experts have come to shun. One concern is that, depending on the organization, organizations that use terrorism often operate clandestinely. They do not maintain standing armies; they operate under cover. That is not true of, say, some of the Islamic State fighters fighting Syrian or Iraqi government forces. But it would be true of Islamic State militants who sneak into hotels, airports, cafes, streets, office buildings, and clinics and then set off explosives or open fire on civilians. Is the military the best tool in these circumstances? If so, some Western states such as the United States have gravitated toward selective targeting, via drone attacks, as a better approach than large-scale troop deployments. But in the absence of a declaration of war, does a drone attack amount to an extra-judicial (i.e., illegal) killing and then constitute a human rights violation? A second concern is that achieving victory and closure are elusive. Terrorists generally do not surrender or sign peace agreements; splinter groups and new leaders fight on for long periods, even after a head leader is killed. That is the case for al-Qaeda and the Islamic State, as well as for other groups. Last, declaring war against a group can become a recruitment tool. Terrorists want to be considered soldiers. Organizations gain stature if great powers fight wars against them.

Another approach is **counterinsurgency**. The thrust of counterinsurgency is that the populations where the violence takes place are the key to turning the tide in an armed conflict. States try to win the "hearts and minds" of civilian populations—through interaction, development projects, finance, consultation, informants, and so forth—so that the civilians throw their support behind the state. The United States pioneered the approach in Afghanistan and Iraq when it confronted insurgents who sought to oust the U.S.-backed governments in those countries. Counterinsurgency can be expensive; sometimes policy makers prefer "sticks" (coercion) over "carrots" (incentives) to confront these armed actors; and sometimes civilian populations take all the goods but do not turn against the insurgents. Applying counterinsurgency to terrorism implies that terrorists operate like insurgents—that they are identifiable armed actors who seek to unseat a government and hide among the civilian population.

Last, some conceptualize **counterterrorism** essentially as a police operation. Here too interactions with local populations matter. Police or intelligence officers cultivate relationships with people in the communities where terrorists might hide and operate clandestinely. Counterterror police operations depend on intelligence and information. Rather than using force to stop an attack, the idea is to understand who in a community might be planning an attack and to prevent it. After 9/11, an emphasis on intelligence gathering drove an interest

war on terror: term that U.S. administrations have used to describe the fight against terrorism on a global scale; a war on terror implies a military fight against terrorism.

counterinsurgency: coordinated actions to defeat or contain insurgency.

counterterrorism: coordinated actions to anticipate, contain, and defeat terrorism, ones that often emphasize intelligence and police action and not only military action.

in electronic surveillance, through phone, Internet, and e-mail monitoring, which in turn prompted a backlash in many countries where such information was being collected. Did the surveillance techniques go too far? Did they impinge on privacy?

These are the concerns with which those who confront terror must contend. When does surveillance go too far? Will winning hearts and minds through counterinsurgency work? How can military force be best deployed against asymmetric, weaker armed threats? Moreover, in the context of international, globalized networks, states must cooperate with other states. Intelligence services, militaries, and even police must talk to their counterparts in other countries. In that way, counterterrorism becomes a form of *global governance*, of states working together to manage a common, inherently international threat.

Cyberattacks and State-Sponsored Terrorism

A growing global security challenge concerns the different ways in which state and non-state actors may use computing or other forms of information and communication technology to launch attacks on a variety of targets.

Cyberattack is a concept that refers to a broad range of computer- and information-based threats. Cyberattacks could include efforts to incapacitate computer-based infrastructure, such as launching an effort to knock out an electrical grid or water delivery system. Cyberattacks could similarly include efforts to infiltrate and paralyze a computing network, either in a government, military, or company. Cyberattacks also take the form of stealing data and sensitive information. Indeed, the realm of cyberattacks is quite broad.

Some examples include the actions that Russia took to interfere in the U.S. presidential elections in 2016, through hacking computers and disseminating false information. Cyberattacks also take the form of state agents attacking a private company, as North Korea did against Sony Pictures to interrupt the release of the film *The Interview* (that cast the North Korean leadership in an unflattering light). Similarly, such attacks take the form of raids on banking or stealing money, as North Korea did against Bangladesh's central bank and tried to do against the U.S. federal reserve.[39]

What to call these computer-based attacks is the subject of some debate. One common term is **cyberwarfare** or the idea that state or nonstate actors use computing technology to disrupt and damage a state or organization, often with a military or a strategic purpose. Cyberwar also implies some "kinetic" or physical consequence. An example would be attacks on infrastructure, such as an electrical grid, that could lead to widespread blackouts. Experts call these "denial-of-service" attacks. Other examples would be the dissemination of viruses to disrupt state or military operations. Are these acts of warfare? The concept of "warfare" implies the use of force, which can be murky as applied to computer-based attacks.[40]

A related concept is **cyberterrorism**, or using computer-based information technology to disrupt and spark fear among a population. The difference between cyberterrorism and cyberwarfare is primarily the idea that the former produces fear and intimidation, rather than the denial of service or breakdown of an information system per se. But that distinction can be blurry, and in practice, cyberterrorism often means cyberattacks that terrorist organizations employ. Thus, if the Islamic State were to launch an attack that would shut down a utility or some other system, that would be called "cyberterrorism." But would efforts by Russian operatives to spread false information in order to sow fear be considered cyberterrorism? The answer is less clear.

cyberwarfare: computer-based forms of disruption designed to disrupt or damage a state or organization, often with a military or strategic purpose.

cyberterrorism: computer-based forms of disruption and misinformation to cause fear and disorder.

IS From the Outside-In or the Inside-Out?

THE CASE OF BOKO HARAM IN NORTHERN NIGERIA

One of the most devastating insurgent organizations in the world is Boko Haram. Initially based in northeastern Nigeria, the organization recently has conducted attacks in Nigeria's neighboring countries, including Cameroon, Niger, and Chad. Over time, Boko Haram has increasingly embraced terrorist tactics to advance its insurgency. One of its most notorious tactics is to kidnap girls from schools. The most infamous example was a raid on a school in Chibok in 2014 when Boko Haram fighters captured 276 schoolgirls and brought them back to the insurgents' hideouts.

The Chibok schoolgirl kidnapping prompted the Nigerian government to increase its counterinsurgency activities, often in heavy-handed ways. The kidnapping action also prompted a large social media campaign to raise awareness and increase efforts to rescue the girls called #BringBackOurGirls. The social media campaign is a good example of how transnational advocacy networks harness information and communications technology to generate pressure, a tactic that we saw in Chapter 8 on human rights.

Is Boko Haram a product of international forces or local ones? On the one hand, Boko Haram has drawn inspiration from other jihadist organizations. For a period, the organization had close ties to al-Qaeda, and in 2015, Boko Haram's leaders pledged allegiance to the Islamic State. The group's origins also have an external heritage. The name "Boko Haram" is also a reference in the local language of Hausa to the idea that Western civilization and education are forbidden for Muslims. They see modern Nigerian education as a continuation of colonial practice and as at odds with the Salafist Islamic principles they espouse.

On the other hand, Boko Haram has a very local history. It is rooted in family lineages, politics, and religion in northern Nigeria, in particular, around the northern city of Maiduguri. Poverty and alienation in the northern part of the country created the raw material for recruits and receptivity for a radical movement to take off. Boko Haram emerged in part from a series of local religious figures and politicians. The movement also radicalized and increasingly embraced terrorist tactics in response to the heavy-handed counterinsurgent tactics of the Nigerian military.

Alongside the external influences, the movement thus has a very distinct set of inside-out forces that gave rise to it and continue to shape its evolution.

Reflect

In what way are contemporary terrorist organizations shaped by global forces, and in what way are they shaped by local ones?

Source: Alexander Thurston, *Boko Haram: The History of an African Jihadist Movement* (Princeton, NJ: Princeton University Press, 2018).

The Russian example points to the question of whether states may commit terrorism. Most definitions of terrorism consider the violence to be the work of nonstate actors. The definitions we supplied earlier in the chapter are consistent with that. But states sometimes sow fear through attacks or sponsor armed groups to advance their interests or destabilize their adversaries. If those armed groups embrace terrorism as a tactic, that is, if they use violence to sow fear to achieve a political aim, then scholars talk about how one state sponsors terrorism. Scholars have developed the concept of **state-sponsored terrorism** to capture this idea. Classically, the concept refers to a state that funds groups that use violence to instill fear and cause disruption. Iran is often cited as an example of a country that sponsors groups that use terrorism in the Middle East. With the onset of cyberattacks, states may hire technology specialists or otherwise sponsor computer-based attacks to sow disorder and fear; this too might be considered a form of "state-sponsored terrorism."

Whatever the proper definitions and terms, many scholars and security experts believe that outside-in, often state-sponsored, computer-based attacks are likely to become increasingly prominent in years to come. They are likely to be major new types of global security challenges, for which governments and citizens around the world will have to prepare.

state-sponsored terrorism: states that fund groups that use violence to instill fear for a political purpose.

SUMMARY

International security is a core theme in international studies. Whereas for years the dominant focus in this area was war between states, more recently, civil wars, terrorism, and increasingly cyberattacks are emerging as core areas of interest. This chapter provides an introduction to major ideas and arguments in this field. The chapter defines civil wars, discusses their global prevalence, and examines both the causes and consequences of civil wars. Examples from complex wars in Central Africa and the Middle East illustrated some of the key concepts and arguments. Terrorism is also an area of focus in the chapter. Although likely a familiar term to you, the concept is difficult to define precisely. The chapter nonetheless discusses some common definitions, followed by a discussion of its global prevalence and some leading causes. Examples from recent attacks in the United States and France illustrated some of the core ideas and arguments.

Civil wars and terrorism have been and are likely to remain major global challenges. They cause tremendous suffering, particularly to civilians, and sow fear among populations. Addressing the causes and consequences of these challenges is not easy. Each has generated responses from intergovernmental organizations, states working together, and often global civil society. Also true is that civil war and terrorism are connected to other global challenges. Civil war deepens poverty and makes economic development exceptionally difficult. Some of the worst human rights abuses occur during civil wars, as we have seen in the Democratic Republic of Congo, Syria, and Myanmar. Challenges such as migration (wars cause refugees), health (wars make regular healthcare delivery difficult and cause negative health outcomes themselves), and food security (war makes it hard to grow and harvest crops) are also affected by war. As with other themes in the book, the problems of civil war and terrorism must be seen in a broader context of other global challenges.

KEY TERMS

civil war 270
conflict minerals 278
counterinsurgency 292
counterterrorism 292
criminal violence 272
cyberterrorism 293

cyberwarfare 293
horizontal inequalities 279
Laws of War 274
peacebuilding 278
peacekeeping 275
radicalization 288

relative deprivation 278
Salafism 287
state-sponsored terrorism 295
terrorism 270
war on terror 292

QUESTIONS FOR REVIEW

1. What are some prominent explanations of why civil wars occur?

2. Could you identify three to five civil wars in the world and discuss some of the consequences of those wars?

3. How is terrorism different from civil war?

4. What are some prominent explanations of terrorism?

5. Besides the Islamic State, could you name two terrorist groups around the world?

LEARN MORE

Séverine Autesserre, *Peaceland: Conflict Resolution and the Everyday Politics of International Intervention* (New York, NY: Cambridge University Press, 2014).

Lars-Erik Cederman, Kristian Skrede Gleditsch, and Halvard Buhaug, *Inequality, Grievances, and Civil War* (New York, NY: Cambridge University Press, 2013).

Virginia Page Fortna, *Does Peacekeeping Work: Shaping Belligerents' Choices After Civil War* (Princeton, NJ: Princeton University Press, 2008).

Seth Jones, *Waging Insurgent Warfare: Lessons From the Vietcong to the Islamic State*

(New York, NY: Oxford University Press, 2017).

Farhad Khosrokhavar, *Radicalization: Why Some People Choose the Path of Violence*, trans. Jane Marie Todd (New York, NY: The New Press, 2017).

William McCants, *The ISIS Apocalypse: The History, Strategy, and Doomsday Vision of The Islamic State* (New York, NY: St. Martin's Press, 2015).

World Bank, Conflict, Security, and Development: World Development Report, 2011.

Explore the UCDP Conflict Database: http://ucdp.uu.se/.

NOTES

1. Marie Allansson, Erik Melander, and Lotta Themnér, "Organized violence, 1989–2016," *Journal of Peace Research* 54 (2017): 574–587. http://www.pcr.uu.se/research/ucdp/charts-graphs-and-maps/#tocjump_6799652384604542_0.

2. Nicholas Sambanis, "What Is Civil War? Conceptual and Empirical Complexities of an Operational Definition," *Journal of Conflict Resolution* 48 (2004): 814–858.

3. James Fearon and David Laitin, "Ethnicity, Insurgency, and Civil War," *American Political Science Review* 97 (2003): 75–90; Sambanis, 2004.

4. The most commonly cited international database that measures armed conflict uses the 25 battle death threshold. This is the PRIO/UCDP armed conflict database, which is the foundation for Figure 10.1. See link in footnote 1.

5. World Bank, *Conflict, Security, and Development: World Development Report, 2011*.

6. William McCants, *The ISIS Apocalypse: The History, Strategy, and Doomsday Vision of the Islamic State* (New York, NY: St. Martin's Press, 2015); Graeme Wood, "What ISIS Really Wants," *The Atlantic*. March 2015, http://www.theatlantic.com/magazine/archive/2015/03/what-isis-really-wants/384980/.

7. Dara Kay Cohen, *Rape in Civil War* (Ithaca, NY: Cornell University Press, 2016).

8. Virginia Page Fortna and Lise Morjé Howard, "Pitfalls and Prospects in the Peacekeeping Literature," *Annual Review of Political Science* 11, no. 1 (2008): 283–301.

9. Lisa Hultman, Jacob Kathman, and Megan Shannon, "United Nations Peacekeeping and Civilian Protection in Civil War," *American Journal Of Political Science* 57, no. 4 (2013): 875–891.

10. Séverine Autesserre, *Peaceland: Conflict Resolution and the Everyday Politics of International Intervention* (New York, NY: Cambridge University Press, 2014),

11. Ted Robert Gurr, *Why Men Rebel* (Princeton, NJ: Princeton University Press, 1970).

12. Paul Collier and Anke Hoeffler, "Greed and Grievance in Civil War," Oxford Economic Papers 56 (2004): 563–595.

13. Fearon and Laitin, 2003.

14. Lars-Erik Cederman, Kristian Skrede Gleditsch, and Halvard Buhaug, *Inequality, Grievances, and Civil War* (New York, NY: Cambridge University Press, 2013).

15. Hoschild, 1998.

16. Crawford Young and Thomas Turner, *The Rise and Decline of the Zairian State* (Madison: University of Wisconsin Press, 1985).

17. Jason Stearns, *Dancing in the Glory of Monsters: The Collapse of the Congo and the Great War of Africa* (New York, NY: PublicAffairs, 2012).

18. Philip Roessler and Harry Verhoeven, *Why Comrades Go to War* (Oxford, U.K.: Oxford University Press, 2016).

19. International Rescue Committee, "Legacy of Violence: Democratic Republic of Congo," http://www.rescue.org/news/irc-study-shows-congos-neglected-crisis-leaves-54-million-dead-peace-deal-n-kivu-increased-aid--4331.

20. *UN News*, "Tackling Sexual Violence Must Include Prevention, Ending Impunity—UN Official," April 27, 2010, http://www.un.org/apps/news/story.asp? NewsID=34502# .V2m5RK4z2T8.

21. The law is known as "Dodd-Frank" after the legislators who sponsored it; the law is a wide-ranging effort at financial reform but includes the provisions on conflict minerals.

22. Séverine Autesserre, "Dangerous Tales: Dominant Narratives on the Congo and Their Unintended Consequences," *African Affairs* 111, no. 443 (2012): 202–222; see also the "Open Letter" signed by more than 70 academics, https://christophvogel.net/mining/open-letter/.

23. United Nations Security Council, "Alarmed by Continuing Syria Crisis, Security Council Affirms Its Support for Special Envoy's Approach to Moving Political Solution Forward," August 17, 2015, http://www.un.org/press/en/2015/sc12008.doc.htm and http://www.ohchr.org/EN/NewsEvents/Pages/DisplayNews.aspx? NewsID=17078&LangID=E.

24. United Nations Human Rights Office of the High Commissioner, "UN Commission of Inquiry on Syria: ISIS Is Committing Genocide Against the Yazidis," June 16, 2016, http://www.ohchr.org/EN/NewsEvents/Pages/DisplayNews.aspx? NewsID=20113&LangID=E.

25. The Global Terrorism Database, https://www.start.umd.edu/gtd/globe/index.html.

26. Robert Pape, "The Strategic Logic of Suicide Bombing," *American Political Science Review* 97 (2003): 343–361.

27. U.S. Department of State, "Foreign Terrorist Organizations," http://www.state.gov/j/ct/rls/other/des/123085.htm.

28. David Kilcullen, *The Accidental Guerrilla: Fighting Small Wars in the Midst of a Big One* (New York, NY: Oxford University Press, 2009).

29. Louise Richardson, *What Terrorists Want: Understanding the Enemy, Containing the Threat* (New York, NY: Random House, 2006); Pape, 2003.

30. Peter Bergen, *United States of Jihad: Investigating America's Homegrown Terrorists* (New York, NY: Crown, 2016).

31. Data available at The Global Terrorism Database, https://www.start.umd.edu/gtd/.

32. Wood, 2015.

33. Farhad Khosrokhavar, *Radicalization: Why Some People Choose the Path of Violence*, trans. Jane Marie Todd (New York, NY: The New Press, 2017).

34. Seth Jones, *Waging Insurgent Warfare: Lessons From the Vietcong to the Islamic State* (New York, NY: Oxford University Press, 2017), 114–115.

35. Ian Fisher, "In Rise of ISIS, No Single Missed Key but Many Strands to Blame," *The New York Times,* November 18, 2015, http://www

.nytimes.com/2015/11/19/world/middleeast/in-rise-of-isis-no-single-missed-key-but-many-strands-of-blame.html?_r=0.

36. Ibid.

37. "Paris Attacks: Who Were the Attackers?" *The BBC News,* April 27, 2016, http://www.bbc.com/news/world-europe-34832512.

38. Katrin Bennhold, "Paris Attacks Highlight Jihadists' Easy Path Between Europe and ISIS Territory," *The New York Times,* November 18, 2015, http://www.nytimes.com/2015/11/19/world/europe/paris-attacks-islamic-state-jihadis.html.

39. David Sanger, David Kirkpatrick, and Nicole Perlroth, "The World Once Laughed at North Korean Cyberpower. No More," *The New York Times*, October 15, 2017, https://www.nytimes.com/2017/10/15/world/asia/north-korea-hacking-cyber-sony.html.

40. On how definitions in international law apply to cyberattacks, see Michael N. Schmitt, ed., *Tallinn Manual 2.0 on the International Law Application to Cyber Operations* (Cambridge, U.K.: Cambridge University Press, 2017).

Migration

CONFRONTING THE MYTHS OF HUMAN MOVEMENT

iStock/Michał Fiałkowski

LEARNING OBJECTIVES

After finishing this chapter, you should be able to:

- Distinguish between a refugee, a migrant, an asylum seeker, and a stateless person.

- Describe trends in global migration.

- Adjudicate between the brain drain and brain gain arguments.

- Analyze a country's migration in terms of push, pull, and policy factors.

- Evaluate popular claims about the effect of migration on host countries.

In September 2014, a fishing boat carrying 500 people, mostly Syrians, Palestinians, Egyptians, and Sudanese, left the port of Damietta, Egypt.[1] As it neared Malta, the smugglers running the operation ordered the migrants to move from the fishing boat to a smaller boat. The passengers saw that they could not possibly safely fit, and they protested. According to reports, the smugglers deliberately rammed the migrants' boat, and it sank in minutes. Two days later, when rescuers arrived, most were dead at sea. Twenty-three-year-old Mohammed Ali Amadalla was one of the few survivors. "We were treated like dogs all the way, but these Egyptian smugglers were the worst. Half the people on board died instantly because they went down with the boat," Mr. Amadalla said. Another survivor said, "After they hit our boat they waited to make sure it had sunk completely before leaving. They were laughing." Mamoun Dougmoush recounted the horrors: "I saw an entire Syrian family perish. First the father died, then the mother, then I was left to take care of their one-year-old boy . . . and he died in my arms."

FIGURE 11.1

Internal Migration is Most Common: Internal and External Migration Rates, 2000–2002

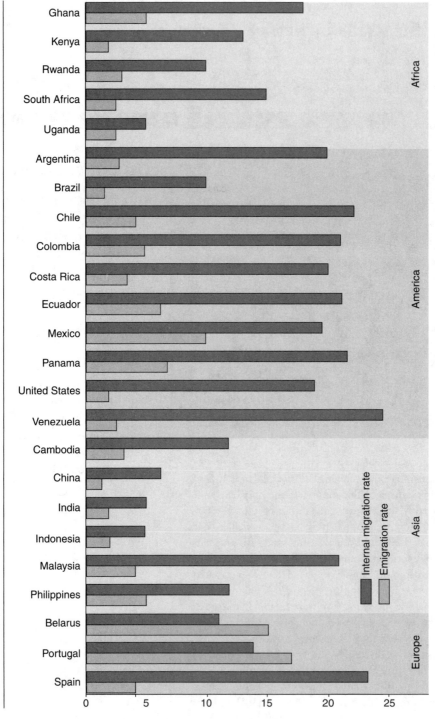

Source: UNDP, "Human Development Report 2009: Overcoming Barriers: Human Mobility and Development" (New York, NY: United Nations Development Programme, 2009), p. 22, http://hdr.undp.org/en/content/human-development-report-2009.

Notes: "Internal migration" is moving within a country. "Emigration" is moving away from a country. "Emigration rate" is the percentage of a home country's population that have emigrated. The percentage includes the total home population as well as the emigrant population.

Watch an interview with survivors of the attack at http://www.bbc.com/news/world-europe-29330821.

This scene of people on the move is synonymous with the image of our globalized world. Some observers have written about the "globalization of migration," meaning the "tendency for more and more countries to be crucially affected by migratory movements at the same time."[2] But on closer inspection, it turns out that migration is rife with myths and misinformation. For example, not only do most international migrants *not* move from poor to wealthy countries, but also migration between countries is not even the most common type. Internal migration—moving within countries—is the most globally common type of human movement (see Figure 11.1). There are about *four times* more internal than international migrants.[3]

Another myth is that migration is increasing. In fact, the percentage of the world population that are international migrants has remained stable over the past 50 years at about 3%.[4] This is because, although the absolute number of migrants has increased, so has the global population.

In this chapter, we will learn about the types of voluntary and nonvoluntary migration, the global trends, and the tensions and debates they produce. Let's begin with some basic concepts and terms and then with some basic facts.

WHAT IS MIGRATION?

"Migrant" is a general term. Simply put, a **migrant** is someone who has changed his or her usual place of residence. Some definitions of migrant make reference to how long a person has stayed, but the label "migrant" says nothing about whether a person is coming into a place (immigrant) or leaving a place (emigrant).[5] It does not tell us whether the purpose of migration is work (migrant worker) or to escape persecution (refugee/asylum seeker). It also says nothing about whether the migration is coerced (trafficking) or voluntary. It does not tell us anything about the person's intention to reside over a short (temporary) or long period (permanent). The European Union (EU), for example, says an immigrant is a person who resides (or expects to reside) for at least 12 months.[6]

If you left your city or state to study at your current college, you are a migrant. You probably intend to return home when done, and most international migrants are the same. They migrate with the aim to work for a period, return home, and repeat the cycle. This is called **circular migration**. It is different from the typical image of migration as the purpose is not permanent settlement. It is very common. In West Africa, tens of thousands of people move toward coastal areas to work on a seasonal basis and return home to harvest crops. Problems occur when the return route is blocked as often happens with strict immigration policies.

The routes migrants take tend to cluster into major **corridors** that connect the world's major population centers (see Figure 11.2). The largest migration corridor in the world is the Mexico–U.S. corridor, followed by Russia–Ukraine, Bangladesh–India, and Ukraine–Russia corridors.[7] Of the top 20 migration corridors globally, more than half involve people migrating south–south, and none of the top 20 run north–south.[8]

Voluntary Migration

Most of the world's migrants are considered "voluntary" because their movement is not due to some direct threat. Migrant farm laborers, international students studying abroad, and highly trained foreign-born tech employees are all examples of voluntary migrants. As you can see, many voluntary

migrant: person who has changed his or her usual place of residence.

circular migration: migrants moving back and forth between home and host countries. Common for migrant workers in seasonal sectors such as agriculture.

corridors: tendency for migrants to move along specific geographic routes.

voluntary migration: migrant moves without coercion.

FIGURE 11.2

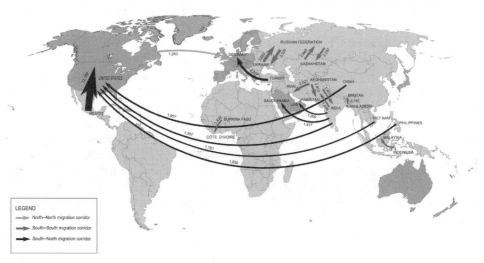

Source: World Migration Report 2013, p. 61, International Organization for Migration (IOM), 2013.

economic migrant:
not a legally recognized term. Preferred is "migrant worker." Scholars debate whether migrant workers move voluntarily to seek better jobs or involuntarily because their home country economy or government is dysfunctional.

migrants are what we call **economic migrants**; they emigrate primarily for economic reasons. But not all voluntary migration is concerned with economic activity. When a church opens in a new country, its members become voluntary migrants when they settle. When researchers move to the Antarctic for a long stay, they are voluntary migrants. And when an investigator with a human rights non-governmental organization (NGO) settles in a country with a dictatorial government, he or she is a voluntary migrant.

Within this group, some migrants are more vulnerable than others. Because migration is not always undertaken under duress, some voluntary migrants are portrayed as being simple opportunists and thus less worthy, while nonvoluntary migrants such as refugees are seen as deserving of respect and legal protection. Many economic migrants, however, are fleeing dysfunctional economies, broken healthcare systems, or failed political systems—situations that make finding work and earning a livelihood in their home countries practically impossible. In other words, it is not only refugees who are forced to leave their homes. What's more, even though the term "economic migrant" is widely used, it has no legal basis. International law uses the term "migrant worker."

Nonvoluntary Migration

refugee:
migrant who has been granted refugee status because the home country endangers the refugee's well-being.

Although the share of all migrants who are nonvoluntary is small, the category represents millions of people. Involuntary migrants include asylum seekers, refugees, internally displaced persons, and victims of trafficking (including slaves and child laborers). Asylum is "the grant, by a state, of protection on its territory to individuals or groups of people from another state fleeing persecution or serious danger."[9] A **refugee** is a person who has "fled their country of origin because of a well-founded fear of being persecuted for reasons of race, religion, nationality, political opinion or membership of a particular social group and who cannot or do not want to return."[10] An **asylum seeker** is one seeking recognition as a refugee. You can think of a refugee as a "successful" asylum seeker. Every refugee was at some point an asylum seeker.

asylum seeker: migrant fleeing persecution or war and seeking refugee status in another country.

In 2014, there were almost 900,000 asylum seekers worldwide.[11] Under the Geneva Convention Relating to the Status of Refugees (1951), states are obliged to extend asylum and protection for people fleeing persecution on grounds of nationality, race, religion, or political ideology. In practice, asylum seekers have the right to *seek* asylum, rather than the right to *receive* asylum. This is because states are sovereign, and they define for themselves who is a refugee and who is a "legitimate" asylum seeker. If they grant asylum, states commit to not send back a refugee to a country where he or she will likely face danger.

Figure 11.3 shows the number of asylum seekers in Europe over the past decade. Note that these are people *seeking* asylum. It does not mean their claims are accepted. Indeed, politics often plays a role in deciding whether an asylum seeker's application is approved. In the early 1980s, hundreds of thousands of migrants fled to the United States because of civil war, dictatorship, and poverty in Central America. The Reagan administration was reluctant to accept Salvadorans and Guatemalans as asylum seekers because to do so would be to acknowledge that America's Cold War allies were committing human rights abuses. The administration said that the asylum seekers were "economic migrants."[12] As a result, less than 3% of asylum cases for Salvadorans and Guatemalans were accepted in 1984, while applicants from Cold War enemies fared much better: the approval rate for Iranians was 60% and 40% for Afghans. The message was clear: People fleeing enemies were "victims" in need of asylum while people fleeing allies were opportunistic "economic migrants."

There are about 25 million refugees, which is about 10% of the world's migrants.[13] Palestinians are the world's largest refugee population, with 4.6 million registered with the United Nations (UN). Figure 11.4 shows how the number of refugees compares with the number of international migrants. Over half of the world's refugees come from just three countries: Somalia, Afghanistan, and Syria, with a combined

FIGURE 11.3

Asylum Seekers in Europe, 2006–2017

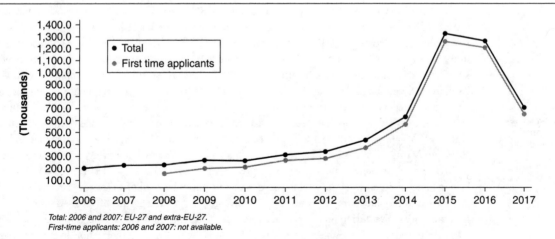

Total: 2006 and 2007: EU-27 and extra-EU-27.
First-time applicants: 2006 and 2007: not available.

Source: Phillip Connor, "Number of Refugees to Europe Surges to Record 1.3 Million in 2015," *Pew Research Center*, August 2, 2013. http://www.pewglobal.org/2016/08/02/number-of-refugees-to-europe-surges-to-record-1-3-million-in-2015/.

FIGURE 11.4

Global Stock of Refugees and International Migrants Since 1970

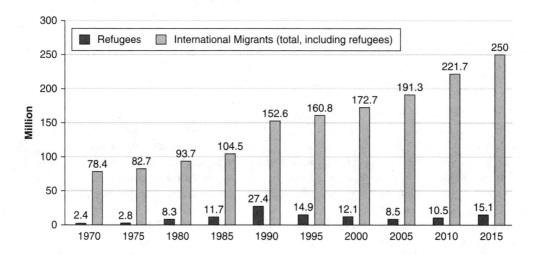

Source: World Bank "Migration and Remittances: Recent Developments and Outlook," *Migration and Development Brief* (World Bank: Washington, D.C., April 2016), http://pubdocs.worldbank.org/en/661301460400427908/MigrationandDevelopmentBrief26.pdf. Original report excludes 5.1 million Palestinian refugees.

8.6 million refugees.[14] Most refugees remain near their country, typically in refugee camps, hoping for the chance to return home or simply lacking the means to move further away. Only about half a million per year travel to developed countries to seek asylum.[15] Figure 11.5 shows the countries taking in Syrian refugees. Contrary to popular beliefs, most Syrians never leave the region. Thus, although Turkey welcomed approximately two million Syrians fleeing conflict, the United States welcomed just 1,500.[16]

The Geneva Convention Relating to the Status of Refugees (1951) defines a refugee in terms of the crossing of borders. This means a refugee who remains within his or her own borders is called an **internally displaced person (IDP)**.[17] It also means that IDPs do not have the same rights as refugees under international law, nor do states have the same legal responsibilities toward them. This is why IDPs are even more vulnerable than refugees.[18] In 2018, there were an estimated 40 million IDPs, with 7 million in Colombia, 2.8 million in Iraq, and 4.4 million in the Democratic Republic of Congo alone.

A final category is **stateless persons**, who are not considered citizens of any state. The UN Refugee Agency estimates that 10 million people are currently denied a nationality, over one third of whom are children.[19] Myanmar has the world's largest stateless population, denying citizenship to one million Rohingya Muslims. When a Rohingya militant group renewed its attacks on the Myanmar government in 2017, the government's brutal response led to over half a million Rohingya fleeing in terror to neighboring Bangladesh, creating the world's largest refugee camp composed of an already stateless people.[20]

Two examples illustrate how these populations are created. Thousands of West Africans moved into the Ivory Coast during French colonial rule, but upon independence in 1960, they did not receive citizenship. Today, there are an estimated 300,000 people who have lived their whole lives in the Ivory Coast, but they do not possess legal citizenship to a state. In 2013, the Constitutional Court in the Dominican Republic said children born in the country to foreign parents were not citizens. This meant

internally displaced person (IDP): refugee within one's own country.

stateless persons: person with citizenship in no country.

FIGURE 11.5

Countries Taking In Syrian Refugees

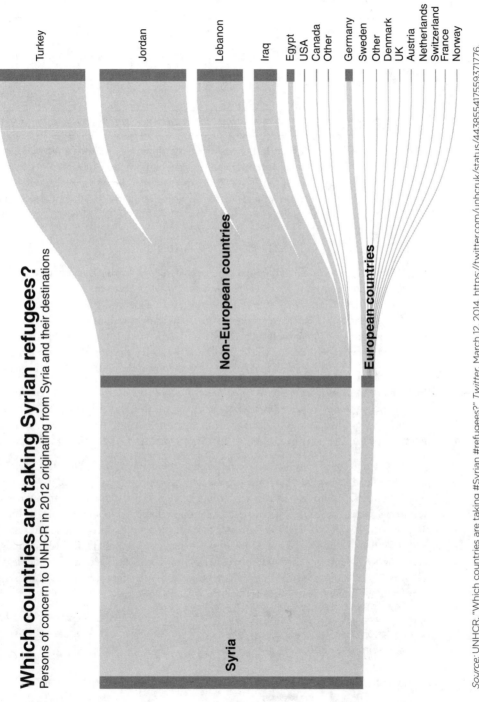

Which countries are taking Syrian refugees?

Persons of concern to UNHCR in 2012 originating from Syria and their destinations

Turkey
Jordan
Lebanon
Iraq
Egypt
USA
Canada
Other
Germany
Sweden
Other
Denmark
UK
Austria
Netherlands
Switzerland
France
Norway

Non-European countries

European countries

Syria

Source: UNHCR. "Which countries are taking #Syrian #refugees?" *Twitter,* March 12, 2014. https://twitter.com/unhcruk/status/443855417559371776.

200,000 Dominican citizens of Haitian descent were not citizens, nor could they become Haitian citizens, since a person needs one parent to be a natural-born Haitian citizen to get citizenship. Overnight, the Dominican Republic created one of the world's largest stateless populations.[21]

Read about #ibelong, the UN campaign to end statelessness at http://www.unhcr.org/ibelong/.

TRENDS IN GLOBAL MIGRATION: FACTS AND MYTHS

There are 954 million migrants in the world.[22] Seven hundred and forty million are internal, and 214 million are international. International migrants are roughly split 50/50 between men and women.[23] At the beginning of this chapter, we explained that the rate of global migration is not on the increase, and that most migration is within borders, not international. In this section, we will lay out five other big migration facts.

Fact 1: Migration Is Mostly an Urban Affair

Although discussion of migration often focuses on people leaving their country, the biggest trend is people moving from rural to urban areas, whether within or between countries. The current urban population of 3.9 billion (54%) is projected to reach 6.4 billion by 2050.[24] About 50% of all international migrants reside in just ten countries and overwhelmingly in cities.[25] Since 1990, the Asia-Pacific Region has added 1 billion people to its cities, with 120,000 people moving to urban areas *every day*.[26] Figure 11.6 shows the urbanizing world. On the left, we see less developed regions, with urban populations (orange line) soaring upward and projected to dominate the rural population in coming decades.

Watch migration expert Hein de Haas describe 7 myths about migration at https://www.youtube.com/watch?v=Z8x3HIh9Zpo.

Fact 2: Urbanization in Developing Populations Often Means Growing Slums

slums: urban settlements characterized by poor or absent public services, poor housing quality, and weak claims of ownership to land.

A challenge posed by this trend for developing countries in particular is that social services are already strained and weak. Thus, migrants are disproportionately represented in the **slums** of developing countries. A slum is an urban (nonfarming) community that has any of the following: insecure residential status, inadequate access to safe water or sanitation, or poor structural quality of housing and overcrowding.[27] UN-Habitat estimates there are 863 million people living in slums, and there will be 2 billion by 2030.[28] Migrants are especially likely to begin their city lives in slums, where the very roof over their heads can be destroyed at any time because the settlement is not legal. In one of Ghana's largest slums, Old Fadama, 92% of households are migrant families. They live in a settlement with no running water or toilet facilities.[29]

Watch Sheela Patel talk about the work of Slum Dwellers International at http://unhabitat.org/the-federation-model-of-community-organizing-sheela-patel-slum-dwellers-international/.

Fact 3: International Migration Is Reversing a Historical Trend

Although the *extent* of migration has not changed much in recent decades, the *nature* of migration has. Europe has become the world's number one destination. This is a reversal of a trend over

FIGURE 11.6

Urban and Rural Populations in Less Developed Regions, 1950–2050

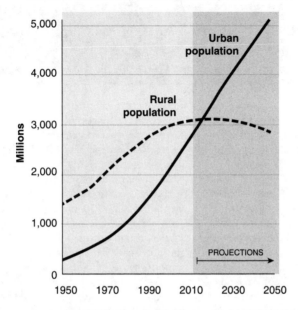

Less developed regions

Africa, Asia (excluding Japan), Latin America and the Caribbean, Melanesia, Micronesia, and Polynesia

Source: European Environment Agency (EEA). "Towards a More Urban World (GMT 2)," Briefing, February 18, 2015, http://www.eea.europa.eu/soer-2015/global/urban-world#tab-figures-used. Data from the UN World Urbanization Prospects: The 2012 Revision.

several centuries in which Europeans emigrated in huge numbers to colonize far corners of the world. This was one of the largest illegal migrations in history. Today, migrants from a wide array of non-European countries have concentrated in a small number of European destinations.[30] Increasing international migration is a European experience, not a global experience. Thus, the perception that migration is increasing is a Eurocentric one.

From a historical perspective, movement over great distances in large numbers is not new. Over one million British, Spanish, and Portuguese moved to the Americas during the colonial period, and 10 to 15 million Africans were forcibly moved to the Americas during the period of the Atlantic slave trade. Around the industrial revolution, millions of Europeans, Indians, and Chinese moved to North America but also to Southeast Asia and to Africa. Indeed, New World countries such as the United States had far more immigrants in 1900 than they do today: About 8% of their population was foreign-born.[31]

International migration in the 19th century was enormous by modern standards. In the 20 years from 1880 to 1900, 600,000 people left Europe for the New World *every year*. At the dawn of the 20th century, it was one million per year.[32] Fourteen percent of the Irish population emigrated, the equivalent of almost 50 million Americans leaving the country today. They moved to places where labor was in demand, and they were able to get better wages. But ironically, with labor increasingly scarce in high-emigration

European countries, wages went up. From the 1850s to World War I, wages in Ireland increased significantly.[33] Money sent home was also a contributor to living standards for those left behind, as well as a source of funding for more family members to emigrate. There was also considerable return migration. Estimates suggest 58% of Italians returned from the United States around the turn of the century.

IS From the Inside-Out

WHO PRODUCES THE DATA?

Readers in international studies must always be aware of the source of data, as well as of the politics involved in producing it. Human migration is hard to study. People involved in illicit migration, whether smuggling or trafficking, obviously try to avoid detection. An estimated 50 million people are living abroad with "irregular status," that is, without legal permission.[34] But even official government data on legal migration are not reliable or available for every country in the world. National statistical offices do not record migration data in a systematic way that would allow countries to be compared. Thus, in the study of migration, "what we know is dwarfed by what we don't know."[35] There has been more global coordination of migration data in recent years, but we are still unable to answer basic questions, such as how many Chileans moved to Brazil last year?

Moreover, the study of global slavery is beset by sensationalism. For example, the Global Slavery Index estimates there are 46 million slaves worldwide.[36] It derives this number based on estimates for 162 nations. But since data are so hard to come by, they use statistics from similar countries to make educated guesses about slavery in another. This is not a problem, so long as researchers possess data for most cases. But this exercise is done for 155 of the 162 countries in the Index. For example, the Index has no data for Iceland, so it used the numbers for the United Kingdom. All western European countries were given the average score for the United States and the United Kingdom.[37] Statistics produced by this INGO have even been used by the U.S. State Department. Global policies on slavery can thus be informed by bad informa-

tion, which results from a kind of mission creep "driven by activists interest in drawing greater attention to the problem."[38]

Media coverage of sex trafficking and sex work also tends toward the lurid and sensational. In 2001, Cambodian NGOs said there were 80,000 to 100,000 trafficked sex workers in the country, with almost 15,000 child prostitutes in Phnom Penh alone.[39] NGOs, journalists, and government officials repeated these numbers for many years, but later research showed just how highly these numbers were inflated. One reputable study visited every known prostitution venue in Cambodia in 2008. The researchers counted 1,058 trafficked women out of the population of 27,925 sex workers. In other words, the popular estimate by activists was about 100 times greater than the actual number. In a separate study of five eastern European countries thought to have major trafficking problems, researchers found about 2% of households reported having a family member who met the study's definition of a trafficked victim. About 0.4% were estimated to be victims of sex trafficking.[40]

Reflect

How do researchers count people who don't want to be counted? Read how researchers concluded there are 11 million undocumented immigrants in the United States.[41]

Source: Philip Bump, "Here's How We Can Be Confident That There Are 11 Million Undocumented Immigrants in the U.S.," *Washington Post*, September 21, 2016, sec. The Fix, https://www.washingtonpost.com/news/the-fix/wp/2016/09/02/heres-how-we-can-be-confident-that-there-are-11-million-undocumented-immigrants-in-the-u-s/.

FIGURE 11.7

International Migrants, 1960–2010 (Millions)

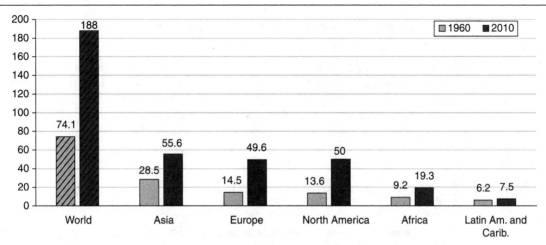

Source: UNDP, 30. Data for world excludes former Soviet Union and former Czechoslovakia.

The picture of global migration changed after World War II. We can see the change in Figure 11.7. We see that in 1960 there were 74 million international migrants, which was 2.7% of the world population. In 2010, there were 188 million international migrants, which was 2.8% of the world population. So, no change in the share of the global population that were international migrants.

Now look at the regions. The regions with the biggest increases in the share of the regional population that are international migrants are North America and Europe, which went from 6.7 and 3.5% to 14.2 and 9.7%, respectively, over the 50 years. This means these two regions had growing international migrant populations as a share of their overall populations. In contrast, we see international migrant shares in Africa, Latin America, and Asia have stayed about the same or declined. Thus, to conclude that the world has more international migration, or is becoming more diverse, would be incorrect and Western centric. This is the major change in global migration over the past 200 years: Previously, people from European countries moved outward, but in the past 50 years, people from developing countries have moved to Europe.

Mathias Czaika and Hein de Haas point to three groups of factors to explain these trends.[42] The first is the lifting of emigration controls on citizens, especially in communist countries, in the 1990s. This change added to the liberal migration policies in EU member-states to enable many Eastern Europeans to migrate to western Europe. The second is the development process itself. As countries become wealthier, it becomes easier to leave due to better financial systems, more disposable income that can be saved for travel, and better communication and transport infrastructure. A third factor relates to the declining importance of colonial ties. In the 1960s and 1970s, immigrants to western Europe tended to come from former colonies. But today this is less the case, and immigrants come from a greater variety of countries. On the receiving end, developed countries have generally removed criteria that favored emigrants on bases of race or ethnicity. For example, until the 1970s, a group of policies informally known as "White Australia" effectively restricted migration to Australia from majority white countries. Removal of such laws allowed for a greater diversity in the pool of potential immigrants.

Fact 4: Development Makes Migration More Likely

The famous words of New York poet Emma Lazarus are found at the bottom of the Statue of Liberty: "Give me your tired, your poor, your huddled masses yearning to breathe free." This vision of immigrants as poor, embattled, and suffering occupies the popular imagination. Whether it was ever historically accurate, however, it is certainly outdated today. People in the poorest countries are the *least* mobile. Emigration (leaving) becomes more likely as economies grow, so the world's poorest countries do not have the most emigration.[43] For example, fewer than 1% of all Africans live in Europe.[44] Figure 11.8 shows that the poorest do not migrate the most. The first graph shows the

FIGURE 11.8

Who Migrates? Not the Poorest

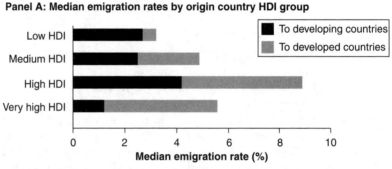

Panel A: Median emigration rates by origin country HDI group

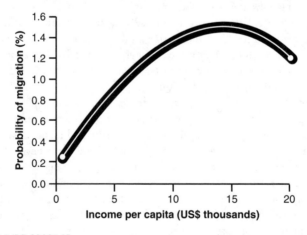

Panel B: Probability of emigration by income level in Mexican households

Source: UNDP, "HDR 2009," 25.

emigration rate for countries according to their level of development using the Human Development Index (HDI). Almost 10% of people in high HDI countries emigrate compared with less than 4% in the lowest HDI countries. Note the destination, shown in the lighter color: In medium and low HDI countries, the destination of migrants is overwhelmingly other developing countries. Indeed, 38% of all international migrants are south–south.[45]

This phenomenon is shown in another form in the second graph. This study from Mexico shows the probability that households migrate increases as the household gets wealthier but only up to a point. Migration becomes more likely as individuals and communities get wealthier, and only becomes less likely again when they are very wealthy. Other research has tested the idea that a little money helps people leave. For example, in a rural part of Bangladesh, a regular famine known as *Monga* occurs before the harvest.[46] Researchers randomly selected households to receive cash, some received information about the conditions at the destination, while others received nothing. The results were striking. Compared with the group receiving nothing, people provided with information were 2% more likely to migrate, while those provided with monetary incentives were 40% more likely. What these studies show is that if efforts to help a country develop are successful, migration from that country will *increase*, not decrease. So, when we see headlines such as "EU to use aid and trade to stop Africa migration," we should expect the policy to have the opposite effect.[47]

FIGURE 11.9

Immigration Policies Have Become Less Restrictive

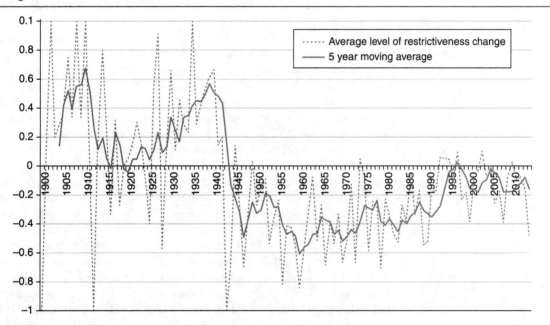

Source: Haas, Hein de, Katharina Natter, and Simona Vezzoli. "Growing Restrictiveness or Changing Selection? The Nature and Evolution of Migration Policies." *International Migration Institute, Oxford. OpenURL* 96 (2014). https://www.imi-n.org/publications/wp-96-14.

Fact 5: Over the Long Run, Migration Policies Have Become Less Restrictive

Despite talk by politicians of "getting tough" on immigration, migration policies have generally become *less* restrictive in recent decades. Figure 11.9 uses a dataset of 6,500 changes in migration policies for 45 countries for most of the 20th century.[48] The researchers coded every restrictive migration policy as 1, and any change toward less restriction was coded −1. Any move toward or below the line means less restrictive policies. We see two waves of restrictive policies, both around the world wars. But since the end of World War II, migration policies have become much less restrictive. In the last decade or so, there has been greater focus on migrant expulsion and border control, which explains the slight upturn in the graph. But such exclusionary policies tend to target specific groups rather than migrants in general. Developed countries tend to have immigration policies favoring high-skill and educated workers. Skilled workers are disproportionately represented among migrants to wealthy countries.[49] So, although some politicians talk of tightening borders, the longer term trend points in the opposite direction.

WHY DO PEOPLE MIGRATE?
PUSH, PULL, AND POLICY FACTORS

Thus far we have learned about the concepts and terms, facts and myths, surrounding migration. Now we ask a simple question: Why do people migrate? The simple version of migration is a story of "push and pull." Migrants are "pushed" from their home by forces such as political or social discrimination, poor health or education services, weak job prospects, or natural disasters. Migrants are "pulled" toward their destination by positive versions of these same factors. Of all these, research suggests the most important is demand for labor in the destination country.[50] But environmental factors are increasingly important in pushing people to move. Mass migrations due to natural disasters such as tsunamis, hurricanes, or floods shift unprecedentedly large numbers of people. Although natural disasters have always occurred, it is the ability of humans to live in dense settlements—cities—that makes natural disasters today so destructive. There is also a more gradual phenomenon, in which global climate change affects local soil and rainfall conditions and thus affects the size of the populations that can be locally sustained. As those resources grow scarcer, people migrate into the communities of others, creating more potential for conflict. Estimates of the number of people forced to migrate due to climate change fluctuate greatly.[51]

Although "push and pull" factors account for changes in *demands* for migration, government policies are the key to understanding changes in *actual amounts* of migration. For example, a major reason for the 19th century mass migration described earlier was government policies that actively encouraged people to migrate, on both the entrance and the exit side. In 1850, Brazilian law gave free land to migrants, and in the 1880s, about half of all migrants to Argentina received a travel subsidy from the Argentine government. In the United States, there was no visa requirement to settle permanently until 1924, and denial of entry was extremely rare.[52] This is not to say that the period was hospitable to non-natives. U.S. immigration policy welcomed millions of people, but specific laws were designed to keep out Chinese (1885); unaccompanied women (1892); polygamists (1903); "all idiots, imbeciles, feebleminded persons, epileptics, insane persons"; people "likely to become a public charge" (1907); and Asians (1917).

What Makes Some Countries Open to Migration and Others Not?

But why are some countries more open to migration at some times but not others? Research by Margaret Peters has shown was that over the past 200 years, countries tend to have open migration policies when they have restrictive trade policies, and restrictive migration policies when they have open trade policies.[53] Why? Decades ago, companies lobbied to allow immigrants to fill jobs in expanding low-skill sectors. But when trade liberalized and foreign goods were allowed in, low-skill sectors did not fare well. Companies in low-skill sectors closed, and there was less lobbying to allow low-skill immigrants. Without the pressure for migration from company lobbying, politicians could respond to demands for protection from foreign workers. Thus, the key was how global trade affected the size of some companies and, thus, their ability to lobby. Importantly, this means migration policy is *not* about prejudice against foreigners.[54] Anti-immigrant policies result from the absence of pro-immigration lobbies.

Another approach to thinking about why migration policies differ between countries and throughout history focuses more on ideas rather than on lobbying by economic interests. Liberals (including neoliberals) tend to see restrictions on migration as restrictions on the free market. Labor is a commodity, just like apples and computers, and it should be allowed to move wherever it can receive its highest price and where it can be used most productively. Allowing labor to move will mean more efficient allocation of resources and, thus, be best for the economy. Therefore, liberals tend to favor policies that make it easier for migrants to move. Some liberals focus on individual freedom, however, and favor intervention to protect the rights of migrants. They see a role for intergovernmental organizations in governing global migration along essentially liberal standards. The realist view, on the other hand, is a nationalist one that sees migration as a threat. Realists depict the "home nation" as threatened in several ways by "non-nationals" usually because non-nationals allegedly do not share the values of natives, or because they threaten their security, purity, or welfare. This is how one can make sense of Donald Trump's proposal for "ideological certification" of immigrants.[55]

The third view is a structural (or dependency) one that sees global migration patterns as reflecting and reproducing global inequalities. Some would point to brain drain arguments to show that migration can hurt developing countries (see Figure 11.10). Others would say global inequality is built into the economic structures of wealthy countries. Saskia Sassen has written extensively about how low-wage international migrants are not some peripheral phenomenon in the world but inseparable from the growth of high-skill industrialized economies. The role that many international migrants, especially women, play is in the service sector providing services to high-wage earners in wealthy countries. They are cleaners, gardeners, baristas, cooks, nannies, sex workers, and so on. For Sassen, "globalization relates to the extraction of services from the Third World to fulfill what was once the First World women's domestic role."[56] This means as women in wealthy countries become increasingly professionalized, family care that was once defined as a women's job increasingly becomes a service that can be commodified (paid for) and imported (i.e., performed by migrants). Thus, it may be the case that low-wage migrants have made it possible for women in wealthy countries to become high-wage earners.

What Happens When It Gets Harder to Migrate?

On September 2, 2015, the world was shocked by the image of 3-year-old Aylan Kurdi washed up on a beach in Turkey. Aylan's family members were ethnic Kurdish refugees fleeing war in Syria.

FIGURE 11.10
Global Forces, Interactions, and Tensions in Openness to Migrants

GLOBAL FORCES	INTERACTIONS	TENSIONS
• Global markets: Free trade affects the prosperity of a country's industries, and with it their political power. Growth of global cities with financial centers made possible by the migration of women for low-skill domestic work, such as childcare and cleaning. • Global governance: Liberals see a role for the global governance of migration, but actual governance is weak. Global oppenness to migration is mostly due to national-level factors.	• Businesses in low-skill industries will pressure their governments to welcome low-skill migrants, but if free trade weakens the low-skill industry, the lobbying for low-skill migrants will also weaken. Migrant women in low-skill domestic work are the unseen face of global cities. • Despite weak global governance of migration, there is a bias in favor of migration among many international and national policymakers.	• With few businesses lobbying for low-skill migration, governments become responsive to native-born low-skill workers. • A backlash against this elite bias in favor of migration is witnessed in the presidency of Donald Trump as well as Brexit, the withdrawal of the UK from the EU.

Aylan Kurdi, a young Kurdish boy, drowned off the coast of Turkey in September 2015 after the boat he was on sank. He is one of the thousands of migrants who die each year seeking refuge. Aylan's case highlighted the role of smuggling in the problem of migration.[58]

Nilufer Demir/AFP/Getty Images

After several failed attempts to gain asylum in Canada, the Kurdis paid smugglers $5,860 for four spaces on a boat. Twelve people boarded a small inflatable boat intended for eight. The trip to Greece should have taken 30 minutes, but the boat capsized just minutes after leaving. Had Aylan made it to Greece, he would have added one more to the one million people who arrived in Europe by sea in 2015, half of whom were from Syria.[57] Figure 11.11 documents the deaths of 6,142 migrants in 2017.

The image of Aylan dead on the beach was shocking, and it reignited debates about the ethics of migration, refuge, and the role of smugglers. Smugglers receive a lot of focus and anger. Yet many researchers argue that blaming smugglers for migration crises misses the point. Migration crises are created by restrictive policies in the host countries that are often counterproductive. Immigration restrictions limit the circular nature of migration. People desperate to emigrate seek increasingly dangerous and exploitative means if safe channels are closed to them.

Watch a TED Talk by Alex Betts, Director of the Refugee Studies Centre at the University of Oxford, at https://www.ted.com/ talks/alexander_betts_our_refugee_system_is_failing_here_s_how_we_can_fix_ it?language=en.

FIGURE 11.11

Migrant Deaths in 2017

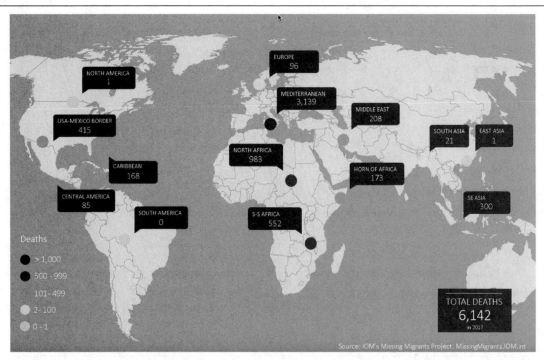

Source: IOM's Missing Migrants Project, https://missingmigrants.iom.int/sites/default/files/infographic/img/MMP%20world%20map%202017.png licensed under CC-BY 4.0, https://creativecommons.org/licenses/by/4.0/.

We can see the logic of this argument in the coverage of the boat migration crisis in southern Europe. The crisis is not new. Researchers trace it to a requirement introduced in the 1990s that migrants coming through North Africa needed visas. Before that, migrant workers moved back and forth from North Africa to southern Europe. They stayed for a few months or years, mostly working on farms and building sites, and returned home. But the new visa requirements made it harder to come to southern Europe. Yet the immigration of North Africans to Spain increased. Figure 11.12 shows that migration from Morocco skyrocketed in the 1990s *after* the border was tightened. Why?

Moroccans who were in Spain when the law changed simply stayed put. Their circular route was cut off. If they left for home, they might not be able to get back to Spain to work again. Meanwhile, those trying to enter for the first time had no safe and legal means, so they turned to smugglers. North Africans who were unable to get visas began to use *pateras* (small fishing boats) to cross the Mediterranean illegally. The smuggling was initially a small-scale operation, but it steadily grew in professionalism and profitability. Over time, the boats spread along the coast, no longer just from Morocco but also from Algeria, Tunisia, and Libya. In the 2000s, North Africans were joined by West African migrant workers and refugees. In recent years, the numbers have grown further with refugees fleeing Syria.

FIGURE 11.12

Moroccan Migration to Europe, 1967–2009

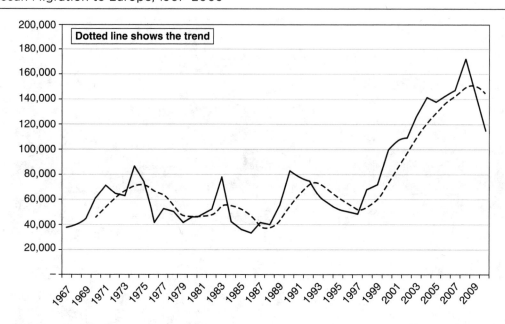

Source: Data from DEMIG (2015) DEMIG C2C, version 1.2, Limited Online Edition. Oxford: International Migration Institute, University of Oxford. www.migrationdeterminants.eu

What to do? Researchers tend to agree: "The more restrictive the barriers to cross-border migration, the greater the odds that the migrant will be victimized by third parties."[59] It is not that we should praise smugglers. Rather, we should understand them as actors in a larger system that has been created due to government policies. Although stories of the ruthlessness of smugglers abound and must not be downplayed, it is important to also note that most smugglers are businesspeople who care about their reputations as service providers. Recall that smugglers are not traffickers. They are not forcing people to migrate; they provide a service for which people (albeit desperate) are willing to pay. "Smugglers could be compared to those individuals who helped black people during slavery moving from the South to the North in the U.S. and today are considered heroes," said Eritrean refugee Yohannes. "Who knows? Maybe one day smugglers will be considered heroes too because they helped people find freedom."[60]

There is a dangerous cycle: Deaths of migrants lead to calls to combat the smugglers and increase border security, which in turn worsens security for the migrants and forces them into riskier migrant routes and into the hands of even more reckless smugglers. And yet expenditure on immigration and border enforcement has never been so high. In the United States, for example, the government spends more on its immigration enforcement agencies than on all its other principal criminal federal law enforcement agencies combined. In 2012, the U.S. federal government spent almost $18 billion on immigration, which was 24% higher than the *combined* budgets of the

FBI, Drug Enforcement Agency, Secret Service, U.S. Marshals, and Bureau of Alcohol, Tobacco, Firearms and Explosives.[61]

THE IMPACTS OF MIGRATION

Whether migration is good for the host country, the migrant, or the migrant's home country is an area in which opinions often scream louder than evidence. In this section, we will examine the impacts of migration on the host country and home countries separately. Within each category, we can think about the impacts on the economy, politics, culture, and society. Let's start with the host country, which is the country receiving a migrant.

How Do Migrants Affect the Host Country's Economy?

Research is clear that migrant workers boost economic output where they migrate, and they do so at little or no cost to locals.[62] New immigrants add to the supply of labor, but they also consume goods and services in their host countries and thus create demand for new jobs there as well.[63] Immigrants generally do work that locals will not do or are not equipped to do. Michael Clemens tells the story of farms in North Carolina that hire several thousand workers on a temporary basis every year:[64]

> When last year's growing season ended, there were 468,000 unemployed Americans in North Carolina. The farmers of the North Carolina Growers Association had over 7,000 manual agricultural jobs to offer to those unemployed North Carolinians in 2011. How many unemployed Americans in North Carolina applied to a manual agricultural job at the NCGA? The Association told me: 250.

> In accordance with federal regulations, the Association reports that it offered the job to all 250 U.S. citizen applicants. Of those, how many showed up for the first day of work? 70. Of those 70, how many chose to stay past the first few weeks of hard labor, to complete the season? The Association told me: Five.

> If you're keeping score at home, this means that 0.001% of all unemployed U.S. citizens in North Carolina last year were willing to spend a full season doing hard, manual field labor. Five out of 468,000.

Clemens's point is that a large share of America's Latino migrants do jobs that Americans are unwilling to do. His research showed that the 7,000 farm workers added $250 to $380 million to the local economy and created one additional American job for every 3 to 5 seasonal immigrant farm workers.[65] That finding directly contradicts the idea that immigrants take away jobs.

This idea that immigrants take away jobs is a version of the **lump of labor fallacy**: the incorrect belief that there is a fixed amount of work in the world, and so any worker that does more work automatically reduces the amount of work (and thus jobs) for someone else. Fears about automation in factories or free trade agreements are classic examples: Neither affects the overall number of jobs in the economy, however. Were the lump of labor fallacy correct, unemployment should go up every time someone graduates from school: Either the student will have a job, or someone else will. Debates about immigration suffer from this fallacy: "If that immigrant didn't have that job,

lump of labor fallacy: incorrect belief that there are a set amount of jobs in an economy, such that an entrant into the market must deprive someone else of a job.

someone born here would have it!" The statement seems logical, but it is wrong. A famous study by David Card showed why.[66] In 1980, mass migration of Cubans to the United States brought 45,000 working-age people to Miami. The lump of labor fallacy would predict unemployment in Miami, with more people competing for the same number of jobs. But after a few months, wages and employment in Miami had not changed even though the labor supply went *up* 7%.[67] Why did unemployment not go up with an influx of new job seekers? Because the immigrants provided labor while stimulating demand by spending money. Because the labor of migrants is put to more productive ends in host rather than home countries, the entire global economy gains from migration. This is why some economists estimate that by simply allowing everyone to move to where their labor can be more productively used would grow the global economy by *trillions* of dollars.[68]

A collection of anti-immigrant headlines from British newspapers. In many Western countries, the political left supports more open immigration policies while right-leaning parties push for closed borders.

AP Photo/Mike Fuentes

How Do Migrants Affect the Host Country's Workers?

The idea that immigrants "steal jobs" is not uniquely a nationalist idea. It was once the case that labor unions perceived migrants as a threat to working-class jobs. But today it is leftists critiquing those on the right for their anti-immigrant policies.

Economists agree that the effect of migration on the economy as a whole is positive, but there is more disagreement on the economic effect on particular groups within society. Well-respected economists disagree about how much low-skill immigrants affect the wages and employment of low-skill native-born U.S. workers. George J. Borjas, for example, argues that immigration of Mexicans is good for Mexicans, as well as for the overall U.S. economy, but bad for low-skilled Americans.[69] One difficulty in figuring this out is the idea of "substitutability": Low-skill immigrants do not compete with *all* U.S. low-skilled workers. For example, non–English-speaking immigrants do not compete for jobs where English is a necessary skill, such as a receptionist. Thus, policy makers need to focus on the effect of migration on low-skilled U.S. workers who are doing work for which a non-U.S. immigrant could easily be "substituted" in. When economists do this, they find low-skill immigrants compete with earlier immigrants much more than low-skill native-born people. Earlier immigrants do jobs for which new immigrants are competitive. Thus, the frequent "losers" from migration are existing migrants that get crowded out by new migrants.[70]

How Do Migrants Affect the Host Country's Public Services?

Another supposed impact immigrants have is on the public's ability to pay for social services, including schools, hospitals, pensions, and unemployment benefits. Former British Prime Minister David Cameron complained of "benefit tourism." A report by a conservative U.S. think tank, The Heritage Foundation, said in 2013, "The average unlawful immigrant household received around $24,721 in government benefits and services while paying some $10,334 in taxes."[71]

But evidence from across industrialized countries shows immigrant and native-born households are equally as likely to receive social benefits; that is, immigrants are not more likely than natives to receive benefits.[72] Research also shows that the fiscal impact (i.e., government expenditure) of the average native household and the average immigrant household are positive, meaning both contribute more than they receive. The average immigrant household contributes about $11,000 more in taxes than it receives in benefits.[73] These numbers make sense since most migrants are working-age people who are healthy, and thus, they need little schooling, healthcare, or retirement support. The impact of undocumented immigrants is likely larger. For example, illegal immigrant workers in the United States are not entitled to public services, but their employers pay federal payroll taxes from the workers' wages. Thus, on top of their economic productivity and consumer spending, illegal immigrants contribute about $7 billion to the U.S. federal government.[74]

How Do Migrants Affect the Host Country's Society and Culture?

Even if immigrants contribute, they may never belong. This is because identity and citizenship politics shape how native-born people think of non-natives. The United States is unusual in its practice of *jus soli* (birthright citizenship), which means any person born in a U.S. territory is a U.S. citizen, irrespective of the parents' status. In most countries, a child's citizenship is based on location at birth or his or her ethnicity, while most states allow people to become citizens (i.e., to be naturalized) through a process typically including many years of residence. Countries that confer citizenship based on birth are less common than citizenship based on ethnicity. For example, a child born in Germany to non-German citizen parents is not automatically a German citizen, while a child born in the United States to non-U.S. citizen parents is automatically a U.S. citizen.

The idea of **cultural citizenship** is that a person's sense of belonging is not just a matter of legal status. One can be a citizen and still feel like a foreigner. France has provided many recent examples, although similar cases can be found in almost every society. Many nonwhite French citizens simply do not feel French. In the 2014 World Cup, the French team was significantly nonwhite. Star striker Karim Benzema said, "Basically, if I score, I'm French. And if I don't score or there are problems, I'm Arab."[75] Benzema is not alone. Defender Benoit Assou-Ekotto was born in France to a French mother and Cameroonian father. Asked why he chose to play for Cameroon rather than France, he said, "The country does not want us to be part of this new France. . . . I have no feeling for the France national team; it just doesn't exist. When people ask of my generation in France, 'Where are you from?', they will reply Morocco, Algeria, Cameroon or wherever."[76]

Read New York Times, *"What Makes Someone French?," at http://www.nytimes .com/2005/11/11/world/europe/what-makes-someone-french.html?_r=0.'*

cultural citizenship: person's sense of belonging to, or being accepted by, a host community, beyond one's legal acceptance.

An anti-immigrant advertisement for right-wing political party SVP on the side of a bus in Switzerland speaks to the fear of some that immigrants (and nonwhites generally) take Swiss social benefits rightfully belonging to "real" Swiss citizens.

FABRICE COFFRINI/AFP/Getty Images

Standing opposite the descendants of immigrants like Benzema and Assou-Ekotto are anti-immigrant political movements that can be found in most countries. The Global Financial Crisis of 2007, jihadist terrorist attacks, and the Syrian refugee crisis in Europe's case have contributed to their recent electoral success. There are anti-immigrant, right-wing parties in every country, but their strength varies across countries and over time.

The popularity of these right-wing parties with working-class voters suggests a class dynamic, but other research suggests economic interests do not explain everything. Although voters are often concerned about the perceived adverse economic or social effects of migration, they are also influenced by the norms and values of **cosmopolitanism** and cultural respect. These views suggest assimilation (cultural integration) is possible. Yet, research also shows that some voters who are not threatened economically may still feel threatened by immigration. Many well-educated U.S. voters are just as opposed to immigration as low-skill voters.[77] This statistic is important because in theory and in practice high-skill workers do well from globalization, yet this research shows that some voters base their positions on considerations of identity. Thus, nativism may trump multiculturalism.

cosmopolitanism: view that cultural diversity, and thus immigration, is to be welcomed because all people share a common humanity and morality.

How Do Migrants Affect the Home Country's Economy?

remittances: money sent (i.e., remitted) by immigrants back to their home country.

In 2015, international migrants sent $600 *billion* back to their country of origin. This money is called **remittances**. This is an enormous transfer of wealth from developed to developing countries. Figure 11.13 shows that remittances are worth more than foreign aid. The largest recipients are large countries, and not all are the poorest: India, China, the Philippines, Mexico, and France.[78] But

FIGURE 11.13

Remittances Are Worth More Than Foreign Aid[79]

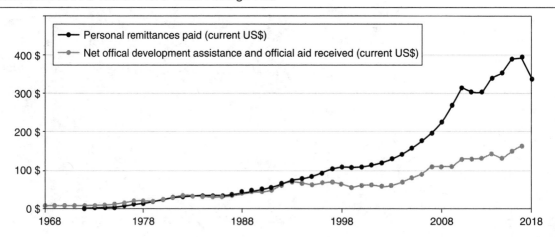

Source: Copyright (c) The World Bank, Data from World Health Organization, Global Health Observatory Data Repository, https://data.world bank.org/indicator/BM.TRF.PWKR.CD.DT?end=2016&start=1970&view=chart licensed under CC BY-4.0 https://creativecommons .org/licenses/by/4.0/.

as a share of their economy, smaller countries receive more. Remittances account for 42% of gross domestic product (GDP) in Tajikistan, 30% in Kyrgyz Republic, and 29% in Nepal.

Unlike foreign aid, remittances put cash in the hands of those who need it most and know how to spend it most effectively. Decisions about allocating resources are not left to corrupt politicians or distant bureaucrats. Rather, remittances allow people to survive bad harvests or health calamities or to invest in businesses or education. Remittances also contribute to public services. Many migrants send money back to what are called "hometown associations." These are community-based NGOs that channel remittances into investments in community projects. For example, people in Kerala, India, have used remittances to finance the building of private schools and hospitals.[80] In Mexico, remittances from migrant workers in the United States are associated with the provision of clean water and drainage systems.[81] Migrants also impact their homes when they return with skills and foreign connections, or when they provide networks from abroad to exporters at home.[82]

The impact of remittances is so significant that it has prompted a global campaign to reduce the cost of sending money. The average charge for sending $200 is 7.4%. The cost of south–south remittances can be very high: It costs a whopping 19% to send money from South Africa to Zambia.[83] Thus, the World Bank's Global Remittance Working Group is leading a campaign to reduce the cost of sending money to 5%. The target in the Sustainable Development Goals is 3%. A reduction in this fee would lead to billions of dollars more money in poor countries.

How Do Migrants Affect the Home Country's Politics?

Perhaps the most important effect immigration has on the home country is on the country's political institutions. Research suggests that students from poor countries return home with pro-democracy attitudes if they have studied in a democracy.[84] These attitudes are spread among neighbors and friends and throughout the political system as students enter elite professions. Research also suggests that immigrants affect their home country even if they don't return. The daily calls and messages influence the attitudes and knowledge of those at home. For example, emigrants from Moldova affected elections at home by influencing the pro-Western or pro-Russian views of friends and family.[85] Research from Mexico suggests remittances make local elections more competitive by making it more difficult for powerful politicians to use patronage networks.[86]

brain drain: idea that sending country has its resources drained when its best and brightest emigrate.

brain gain: contra the brain drain argument. Idea that sending country may benefit when some people emigrate, primarily due to remittances, personal investment in skills, and transmission of new sociopolitical values.

BRAIN DRAIN OR BRAIN GAIN?

Most migrants gain from migration. More than three quarters of international migrants go to countries with higher living standards than their country of origin. Migrants generally have higher incomes, better access to healthcare and education, improved prospects for their children, and greater self-reported happiness relative to those that did not migrate.[87] Movers from the poorest countries have the most to gain. International migrants from the poorest countries saw a 15-fold increase in income, a doubling of education enrollment, and a 16-fold decrease in child mortality.[88]

But what about the communities they leave behind? **Brain drain** is the idea that home communities are worse off when the best and brightest migrate. **Brain *gain*** is the counterargument, which posits that sending countries do better when some of their own emigrate. This section lays out arguments on both sides. It is important to understand that although the debate is polarized and intensely fought, it is really about the extent and speed of migration. While both sides raise ethical questions—some say a medical brain drain denies people their basic human right to health, whereas others say it is unethical to prevent people from leaving any community[89]—few seriously propose zero controls on migration or zero migration whatsoever.

Home Countries Lose Money

Brain Drain: Poor countries spend their meager government budgets on bare-bones universities and reap no reward whatsoever. The real winners are the receiving countries. The American Medical Association estimates that the savings for the United States of the annual arrival of thousands of immigrant health professionals are "equal to the output of 50 additional medical schools without any cost to the taxpayer."[90] Remittances do not come close to offsetting these large losses. Average remittances amount to only about $1,000 per year, which is less than a worker would produce for the economy (and themselves) had they stayed in the country.[91]

Brain Gain: Africa loses an estimated $2 billion when its health professionals move to wealthy countries, but wealthy countries give far more than that back to Africa in development aid: $206 billion from 2008 to 2013.[92] African-trained doctors in the United States send home money that eventually exceeds the cost of their medical training.[93]

Read "America Is Stealing the World's Doctors" at https://www.nytimes.com/2012/03/11/ magazine/america-is-stealing-foreign-doctors.html.

Home Countries Lose Talent

Brain Drain: Not only is third-level education expenditure wasted, but also the country now lacks trained engineers, nurses, and lawyers. Developing countries have critical shortages of skilled professionals. For example, Mozambique has just 548 doctors for 22 million people.[94] When Sierra Leone had its Ebola outbreak, it had 1 doctor per 100,000 people compared with 242 per 100,000 in the United States.[95] Africa, with 1 in 7 of all humans, has only 3% of global medical staff. The Americas, including Canada and the United States, have 37% of the world's health workers.[96] In 2011, there were about 10,000 doctors in the United States who were born or trained in Sub-Saharan Africa. Two thirds had been trained in Africa.[97] The worst affected are postconflict states, which are "hemorrhaging their scarce talents."[98] "Brain waste" can also occur if the migrant works in a job that is beneath his or her skill level. Picture the stereotype of the Uber driver who was a doctor in Syria. Both the migrant and the home country lose.

Brain Gain: The exit of educated people might hurt, but people getting extra education in the hope of emigrating compensate for the loss. If people thought they could not emigrate, they would not invest time and money in getting further skills. But emigration—*no matter if they emigrate or not*—has this incentive effect. For example, a simple change in educational requirements for some Nepalese to move to Britain led to large numbers of people increasing their education, even though only a few moved.[99] Thus, the prospect of migration can improve development. This fact implies that large countries where only a fraction of the population emigrate (i.e., India or China) will have a brain gain if people are extra-motivated to get skilled. But it also implies that small countries where a large fraction of the population emigrate (i.e., Haiti) will still have a brain drain. It is also the case that in the poorest countries with the highest levels of skill emigration, the stock of skilled workers is increasing, not decreasing. In other words, there is brain drain, but home countries are increasing their supply of skilled workers nonetheless.[100]

Watch "Why It's Time to Move Past the Brain Drain" at https://www.youtube.com/ watch?v=G9U1JwVjpuA.

HUMAN TRAFFICKING AND MODERN SLAVERY

Before petroleum was king, the major global oil was palm oil. Today it is one of the most-consumed vegetable oils in the world. You've used it this week if you ate Pop Tarts, Pringles, Oreos, or instant noodles, or if you used Dove soap, chapstick, Garnier Fructis, or Head and Shoulders. It is farmed in places like Jempol, Malaysia, by people like Bangladeshi Mohammad Rubel, 22 years old.[101] When journalists met him, Mohammad had been working seven days a week without pay since arriving from Bangladesh with the help of smugglers. He had spent three weeks on a crowded boat with inadequate food and water, followed by several weeks in a jungle camp while his parents back home were told to pay a ransom. Mohammad watched many fellow migrants die from exhaustion, disease, or beatings. "If I had known what was waiting, I would never have left home," he said.

Watch Mohammad and the immigrants harvesting palm oil at https://www.wsj.com/ articles/palm-oil-migrant-workers-tell-of-abuses-on-malaysian-plantations-1437933321.

Mohammad's story could be told a million times over by people trafficked to work in farms, brothels, and factories. **Trafficking** is migration without consent. It is different from smuggling, which is helping someone to migrate illegally, but the migration involves consent. In the absence of consent, traffickers use coercion or deception. Often smuggling and trafficking blur together, as a person seeks help getting smuggled across a border, but at some point becomes subject to the whims of the smuggler/trafficker. In U.S. and international law, a person does not technically need to have been moved to be trafficked. For example, simply recruiting a person, receiving a person, or harboring a person involved in trafficking is a violation of the law.

> **trafficking:** migration without consent.

In this section, we will learn about types of trafficking, including sex trafficking, slavery, and child labor. By far the most common form is trafficking for labor. But quality data on human trafficking are in very short supply. There are no accurate estimates of the number of people who have been trafficked.[102] This is partly because of difficulty distinguishing between forced and voluntary migration, as well as because trafficking is illegal and hidden. As a consequence, many publications rely on a small number of studies, which in turn rely on dubious data. For example, in a content analysis of 41 books on sex trafficking, three quarters used statistics from two sources that "have long been criticized for making grandiose claims about the magnitude of trafficking and slavery."[103]

Modern Slavery

Debt bondage is a common form of modern slavery. It is also known as debt slavery or bonded labor. It involves a person paying off a debt to a person by working directly for them. The U.S. government and the International Labor Organization both consider debt bondage to be forced labor. A problem with this definition is that bonded labor does not always involve coercion. Sometimes people willingly agree to provide labor in return for a loan, and thus, they work off their debts. For example, Filipino women working in Japanese "hostess clubs" are compelled to enter into bonded labor arrangements to pay off their debts to the brokers who arranged their travel. This is a common arrangement in global migrant labor, both for women (often in domestic, sex, or entertainment work) and for men (often in construction). The Filipino women are easily exploited. Their debts are arbitrarily inflated, their wages and passports are withheld, and they are overcharged for food and housing. Because victimization occurred at some point in their migration, they are considered victims of trafficking.[104]

> **debt bondage:** paying off a debt to a person by working for them.

Watch "Watch an Indian family make mud bricks to work off family debt" at http://www .aljazeera.com/programmes/slaverya21stcenturyevil/2011/10/2011101014441794232I.html.

Violence and the threat of violence occur, but they are not the main means of coercive control of migrants. For example, many Gulf states have temporary worker programs called *kafala*, meaning "guaranteeing and taking care of" in Arabic.[105] Migrant workers require a citizen to sponsor them, and the sponsor signs a document with the government guaranteeing the migrants' care. Human rights groups have extensively documented abuses in the program. The employers who sponsor the migrant workers, usually to work on construction sites or as domestic labor, take away passports and often charge a large fee to hand them back, denying migrants the ability to leave. When Bahrain declared its repeal of the system in 2009, its Labor Minister likened it to slavery.[106] Human Rights Watch recently estimated that there were 146,000 female migrant domestic workers in the United Arab Emirates alone, a country of just 4 million, with widespread reports of unpaid wages, extreme working conditions, and sexual and physical abuse.[107] The authors quote 23-year-old Farah, originally from Indonesia, but now working for a family in Dubai:

> The work wasn't what I expected it to be. It was totally different. I would wake up to start cooking, then cleaning, washing clothes, and then cooking again. No rest, there was just no rest. . . . Because she kept yelling, I cried and asked to go back to agency, but madam said, "I already bought you."

Watch The Workers Cup documentary about the experience of migrant workers building stadiums for the 2022 World Cup in Qatar.[108]

Sex Trafficking

The experience of sex workers is highly varied around the world. Some (mostly) women suffer the worst forms of abuse and can be thought of as sex slaves, while others are migrant workers rather than trafficked humans. Research on 4,600 trafficked sex workers in Europe and Central Asia found 40% were regularly prevented from using condoms. On average, they worked 13 hours per day and kept one sixth of their earnings.[109] Research on trafficked sex workers in Mexico City found 40% of women had unwanted pregnancies, and reports of violence were very high, including cigarette burns, druggings, rape, and threats of death.

But research with sex workers usually finds that trafficked victims are rare. A study in Tijuana, Mexico, found 12% of sex workers were forced or deceived into sex work, but 88% were not trafficked victims.[110] A study of 149 Chinese sex workers found that those who facilitated the women's travel around Asia were in fact other sex workers who had returned to China. This "chain migration" consists of networks of sex workers, and research shows that these networks are used to socialize and protect the sex workers.[111] None of the women interviewed reported any harassment, coercion, or deceit. Georji Petrunov interviewed 92 Bulgarian women who had returned from sex work in western Europe.[112] One quarter reported physical coercion, 4% were abducted, 7% were deceived, and 7% experienced debt bondage. Under Bulgarian law, all 92 were considered trafficked by virtue of the fact that they had been recruited and transported for sex. But the research showed that coercion was not the norm for the women. A study of 580 sex workers in India found two thirds were working voluntarily.[113] Belanger interviewed 646 Vietnamese labor migrants.[114] Two thirds reported no deception, exploitation, or abuse. A study of 826 Mexican migrant laborers to the United States found one third were victims of trafficking.

Chinese sex workers in Kuala Lumpur told researchers that the work is not only about the higher income but also about the personal freedom the women get from the income.[115] Research with Russian sex workers in Norway reported a similar finding: "The women distanced themselves from the stereotype of the passive victim. . . . They talked about their actions in terms of intentions, choices and desires."[116] A study of foreign sex workers in Britain found that many began the work simply because other job offerings were not appealing. This is consistent with other recent studies that contradict the notion that women are voiceless in migration decisions.[117]

Child Labor

Under international law, consent is irrelevant when people assist or employ migrant children. Children cannot consent. The International Labor Organization (ILO) considers any child younger than 15 engaged in labor to be a victim of child labor. The ILO uses the term to refer to work that "is mentally, physically, socially or morally dangerous and harmful to children" or interferes with their education. The ILO does not consider every working child to be a victim: "Children's or adolescents' participation in work that does not affect their health and personal development or interfere with their schooling, is generally regarded as being something positive."[118] There are approximately 170 million children engaged in what the ILO considers child labor.[119] This is about 1 out of every 10 children alive. Of these, 85 million are estimated to be engaged in especially hazardous work or work that directly endangers their lives. It is especially problematic in Sub-Saharan Africa and in Asia and the Pacific.

Ethnographic research has enriched our understanding of how different cultures understand child labor. Neil Howard conducted fieldwork with migrant workers in Benin.[120] He found that the young men sent from villages to work endured the worst forms of child labor. Yet migrants still saw the labor as an opportunity. Howard wrote, "In my case study villages, work, whether inside the home or for remuneration outside, is not seen as a damaging 'adult' sphere from which under 18s are to be sheltered, nor in fact as anything other than an eminently positive and necessary part of being young and growing up" (p. 463). Howard's conclusions are not unusual. Other research finds that young people that meet the definition of child labor frequently do not identify themselves as exploited.[121]

CAN MIGRATION BE GOVERNED GLOBALLY?

There is little-to-no global governance of voluntary migration. The International Labor Organization has conventions on the rights of migrant workers, but they are considered weak and not enforced. There is a long established convention on refugees, but most international migrants are not refugees. The main international law on migrants is the International Convention on the Protection of the Rights of All Migrant Workers and Members of Their Families (1990). Only 52 states have ratified the Convention, while 39 have signed the Convention but not ratified it, so it is not the law of their land. Moreover, signatories are generally the "sending" countries rather than the "receiving" countries. No North American or western European states have ratified it.

Several intergovernmental organizations (IGOs) matter in global migration. The International Organization for Migration (IOM) has expanded from its initial narrow focus on refugees to a broader focus on migrants. But it is outside the UN system and is more focused on providing services to migrants than on leading global rule-making. One hundred and fifty countries participate in the Global Forum on Migration and Development, which brings together states, as well as NGOs and

FIGURE 11.14

Global Forces, Interactions, and Tensions in the Governance of Migration

GLOBAL FORCES	INTERACTIONS	TENSIONS
• Shifting centers of power: Migration between emerging market economies is both cause and effect of their rise, and is enabled by regional agreements such as MERCOSUR and ECOWAS. • Global governance: Weak global governance of most migration challenges, with possible exception for refugees. Governance tends to be regional rather than global. Major agreements such as NAFTA and WTO mostly consider high-skill migrants only.	• Movement toward governance of migration often occurs outside UN bodies and involves NGOs, such as in the Global Forum on Migration and Development. • Millions of migrants have legally protected resident status where there are regional agreements, but millions more migrate with no legal protection. • Companies in wealthy countries introduce automation and outsourcing, leading to deindustrialization at home with declining living standards for industrial workforce.	• Frustration with UN prompts states to tackle global issues outside of the organization, further damaging the UN's legitimacy. • Declining living standards see rise of anti-immigrant sentiment in deindustrializing economies. • Failure of states to govern migration fuels abuse of migrants, such as smuggling, trafficking, and victimization for "illegal" populations. • Some poorer countries would like opportunities to migrate to wealthier countries, and for the rights of their emigrants to be protected, but wealthier countries have much less interest in the opposite direction.

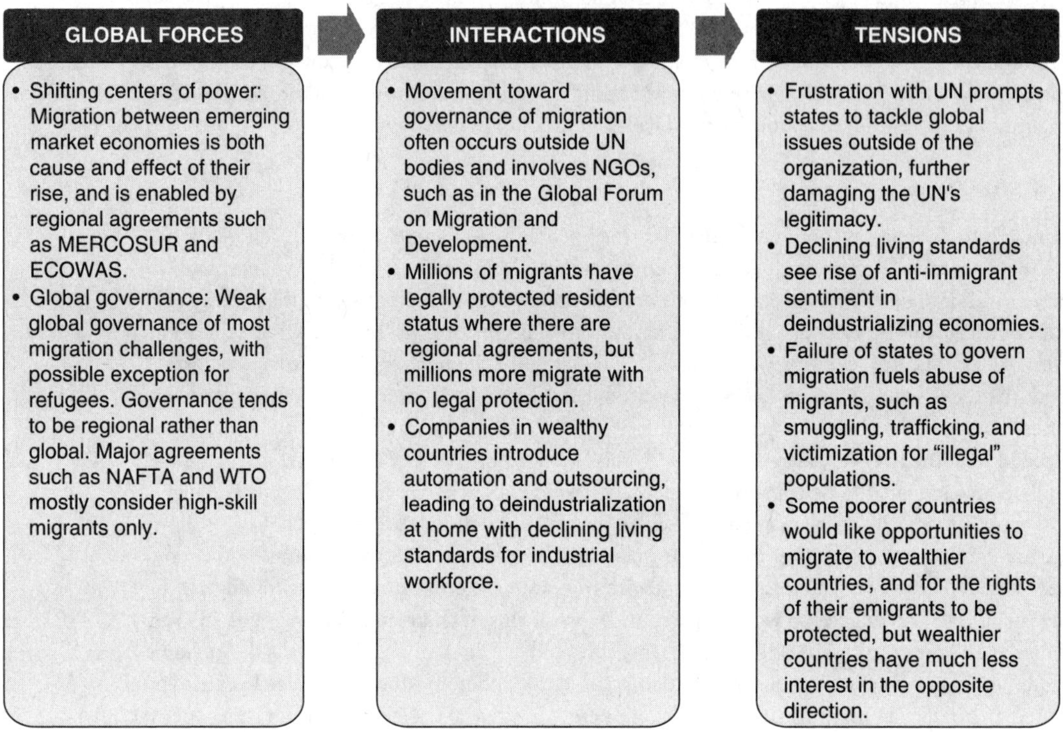

IGOs, to discuss challenges in governing migration especially as it relates to developing countries. But it is a non-UN forum, meaning a place for dialogue, which speaks to how far international governance of migration has to go. The World Trade Organization (WTO) is another global actor that impacts migration. Most WTO members have signed a treaty committing to allow temporary admission of migrant workers, but these are usually very short term and often help high-skill labor rather than the much more numerous low-skill labor.

The major international governance for migration is regional. Most are modeled on the European Union, with the unprecedented amount of freedom granted to its citizens to move. Citizens of the 28-member EU have the right to work, study, live, and retire in any other EU state by virtue of being a citizen of any EU state. Approximately 2.5% of EU citizens live in another EU state.[122] In South America, Mercado Común del Sur (MERCOSUR), a 1991 agreement between Argentina, Brazil, Paraguay, Uruguay, and Venezuela, promotes free trade among this group of almost 300 million people, and since 2002, it has allowed its citizens the right of residence in any of its countries. In West Africa, 15 member-states with 300 million people join together in the Economic Community of West African States (ECOWAS). The population of West Africa is highly mobile, with significant numbers of people moving from hinterland to coastal areas. Within ECOWAS, a citizen of, say, Mali could move to Benin without a visa for 90 days. With an ECOWAS residence permit, they can work and eventually establish businesses. The African Union, meanwhile, has long-term plans for the free movement of all Africans within the continent. New Zealand and Australia have an informal agreement known as the Trans-Tasman Travel Arrangement, which allows citizens to travel and work freely between the countries. Other agreements allow for movement by certain categories of people rather than all people. For example, NAFTA allows for the free movement of high-skilled workers.

Why so little global agreement on migration? One reason is the nature of migration itself. Although developing countries would like greater access to developed countries, the opposite is not usually true. Thus, one side wants a deal more than the other, and this imbalance makes it hard to progress. In addition, the massive loss of industrial jobs in developed countries is tied to rising anti-immigrant sentiments among the low-skilled workers in the now-deindustrialized countries.

SUMMARY

In this chapter, we have learned about one face of this global era: the movement of people. We learned, however, that cross-border migration in the 21st century is probably not much greater than it was in the 20th century. What is new is that Europe and North America are on the receiving end of more migration than was the case in the mid-to late 1900s. This fact shapes popular understanding of the importance of migration as an issue since the countries affected are disproportionately wealthy and powerful.

Migration is also an issue through which our global forces are intertwined (see Figure 11.14). Our first global force, markets, is both cause and effect of migration. Internationally, migrant workers move toward vibrant economies. In so doing, they also create further demand in their new country, which boosts economic growth even more, and they also send large sums of money home. Within countries, the effect that global markets can have on a country's agriculture can lead to people moving from the countryside to urban areas, and sometimes to slums.

Our second global force, information and communication, technology makes migration possible by helping migrants identify countries with available jobs or a high probability of granting refugee status. Technology also makes migration more tolerable for families who can now stay in touch, and it makes it possible to instantly and safely transfer money home.

Our third global force, shifting centers of power, can be seen in the proliferation of new and different actors that matter for migration. Multinational corporations drive demands for labor, whether it be inducing tens of millions of Chinese to move to cities to work in factories, or millions of Mexicans to move to the United States to work in growing agriculture and food services industries. International civil society organizations, such as Doctors Without Borders, Human Rights Watch, and Amnesty International, reported the atrocities committed against the Rohingya by Myanmar as well as their mass movement into Bangladesh. These nonstate actors simply did not exist in such volume, and such global spread, one century ago.

By contrast, migration is a topic in which our fourth global force, global governance, is notable for its relative absence. Because there is no global consensus on migrant workers, for example, different countries and regions pursue their own policies, some of which lead to tragedies such as the death of little Aylan Kurdi. The absence of global governance can also be seen in the millions of women who have been trafficked for sex work. But international migration is not without some rules. Although the World Trade Organization does not cover migration, regional free trade agreements typically do. In the European Union, any EU citizen can move to any EU country.

KEY TERMS

asylum seeker 302
brain drain 321
brain gain 321
circular migration 301
corridors 301
cosmopolitanism 320

cultural citizenship 319
debt bondage 323
economic migrant 302
internally displaced person
   (IDP) 304
lump of labor fallacy 317

migrant 301
remittances 320
slums 306
stateless persons 304
trafficking 323
voluntary migration 301

QUESTIONS FOR REVIEW

1. What is the relationship between an asylum seeker and a refugee?

2. How does the "lump of labor fallacy" relate to migration?

3. What is the difference between smuggling and trafficking?

4. What tensions are in evidence in the "brain drain" debate?

5. How does global cross-border migration in the 21st century compare with one century ago?

6. Search online: Does the United States have more international or internal migrants?

7. Which global forces are at play in human trafficking?

LEARN MORE

Datasets:

Data on remittances and migration, World Bank. http://www.worldbank.org/en/topic/migrationremittancesdiasporaissues/brief/migration-remittances-data.

Global Bilateral Migration, World Bank. http://databank.worldbank.org/data/reports.aspx? source=Global-Bilateral-Migration

UN Habitat Urban Data. http://urbandata.unhabitat.org.

Missing Migrants Project, International Organization for Migration. http://migration.iom.int/europe/.

Organizations:

Center on Migration, Policy and Society, Oxford University. http://www.compas.ox.ac.uk.

International Migration Institute, Oxford University. https://www.imi.ox.ac.uk.

Migration Research Group, PRIO. https://www.prio.org/Research/Group/? x=1.

Institute for the Study of International Migration, Georgetown University. https://isim.georgetown.edu.

International Organization for Migration. http://weblog.iom.int.

Centre for Research and Analysis of Migration, University College London. http://www.cream-migration.org.

UNDP. (2009). Human Development Report 2009: Overcoming Barriers: Human Mobility and Development. http://hdr.undp.org/en/content/human-development-report-2009.

NOTES

1. Herman Grech, "'Treated Like Dogs': Migrants Speak of Horror at Sea of Malta," *BBC News*, September 20, 2014, http://www.bbc.com/news/world-29279074.

2. Castles and Miller, 2009, 10, cited in Czaika and de Haas, "The Globalization of Migration: Has the World Become More Migratory?," *International Migration Review* 48, no. 2 (June 1, 2014): 286, https://doi.org/10.1111/imre.12095.

3. The 2009 Human Development Report estimated 214 million international migrants. UNDP, "Human Development Report 2009: Overcoming Barriers: Human Mobility and Development" (New York: United Nations Development Programme, 2009), 1, http://hdr.undp.org/en/content/human-development-report-2009.

4. UNDP, 2.

5. An emigrant is "an individual from a given country of origin (or birth) who has changed their usual country of residence to another country" (UNDP, 2009). An immigrant is "an individual residing in a given host country (country of destination) that is not their country of origin (or birth)."

6. Michal Cenker, "The Complexity of Migration," in *From the Global to the Local*, ed. Gerard McCann and Stephen McCloskey, 3rd ed. (London, U.K.: Pluto Press, 2015), 191–212.

7. World Bank, "Migration and Remittances Factbook 2016" (Washington, DC: World Bank, 2015).

8. International Organization for Migration, "World Migration Report 2013," Annual Report (Geneva, Switzerland: International Organization for Migration, 2013), 53.

9. UNDP, "HDR 2009."

10. UNDP, 2009.

11. UNHCR, "Aslyum Trends 2014: Levels and Trends in Industrialized Countries" (Geneva, Switzerland: United Nations High Commissioner for Refugees, 2015), http://www.unhcr.org/en-us/551128679.

12. Susan Gzesh, "Central Americans and Asylum Policy in the Reagan Era," *Migrationpolicy.Org* (blog), April 1, 2006, http://www.migrationpolicy.org/article/central-americans-and-asylum-policy-reagan-era.

13. UNHCR website. http://www.unhcr.org/en-us/figures-at-a-glance.html.

14. UNHCR website. http://www.unhcr.org/en-us/figures-at-a-glance.html.

15. UNDP, 2009, p. 2.

16. CNN, "Syrian Refugees: Which Countries Welcome Them," *CNN*, September 10, 2015, http://www.cnn.com/2015/09/09/world/welcome-syrian-refugees-countries/index.html.

17. A full definition is "individuals or groups of people who have been forced to leave their homes or places of usual residence, in particular as a result of or in order to avoid the effects of armed conflict, situations of generalized violence, violations of human rights or natural or human-made disasters, and who have not crossed an international border" (UNDP, 2009).

18. Cenker, "The Complexity of Migration," 193.

19. http://www.unhcr.org/en-us/stateless-people.html.

20. International Crisis Group, "Myanmar's Rohingya Crisis Enters a Dangerous New Phase" (International Crisis Group, December 7, 2017), https://www.crisisgroup.org/asia/south-east-asia/myanmar/292-myanmars-rohingya-crisis-enters-dangerous-new-phase; Gettleman, "Fate of Stateless Rohingya Muslims Is in Antagonistic Hands," *The New York Times*, November 3, 2017, sec. Asia Pacific, https://www.nytimes.com/2017/11/03/world/asia/rohingya-myanmar-bangladesh-stateless.html.

21. Georgetown Law, "Left Behind: How Statelessness in the Dominican Republic Limits Children's Access to Education" (Washington, DC: Georgetown Law

Human Rights Institute Fact-Finding Project, 2018); Mirna Adjami, "Statelessness and Nationality in Cote D'Ivoire" (UNHCR, 2016).

22. Using the 2009 Human Development Report's estimates in Chapter 2.

23. Women are 48% of all international migrants. UNDP, "HDR 2009," 25. Although this has not changed much over the past 50 years, it represents a significant change from the 19th century when most international migrants were men.

24. IOM, "World Migration Report 2015: Migrants and Cities: New Partnerships to Manage Mobility" (Geneva, Switzerland: International Organization for Migration, 2015), 1, http://publications.iom.int/system/files/wmr2015_en.pdf.

25. Australia, Canada, UKSA, France, Germany, Spain, UK, Russia, Saudi Arabia and UAE. Source: IOM, 2015, 2.

26. IOM, 2015b, 2.

27. UN Habitat, *Slums of the World* (UN Habitat, 2003), 8, http://unhabitat.org/books/slums-of-the-world-the-face-of-urban-poverty-in-the-new-millennium/.

28. https://www.cordaid.org/en/news/un-habitat-number-slum-dwellers-grows-863-million/; UNDP, "HDR 2009," 2.

29. IOM, 2015b, 4.

30. Czaika and de Haas, "The Globalization of Migration."

31. The stock of foreign-born migrants in 1910–1911 in northern Europe, North America, Australia and New Zealand, and Argentina and Brazil was 23 million people, or 8% of the population.

32. Barry R. Chiswick and Timothy J. Hatton, "International Migration and the Integration of Labor Markets," in *Globalization in Historical Perspective*, ed. Michael D. Bordo, Alan M. Taylor, and Jeffrey G. Williamson (Chicago, IL: University of Chicago Press, 2003).

33. UNDP, "HDR 2009," 2.

34. UNDP, 2.

35. UNDP, "HDR 2009."

36. http://www.globalslaveryindex.org/.

37. Weitzer, "Human Trafficking and Contemporary Slavery," 224.

38. Weitzer, "Human Trafficking and Contemporary Slavery," 224.

39. Thomas Steinfatt, "Sex Trafficking in Cambodia: Fabricated Numbers Versus Empirical Evidence," *Crime, Law and Social Change* 56, no. 5 (October 28, 2011): 443–462, https://doi.org/10.1007/s10611-011-9328-z.

40. Weitzer, "Human Trafficking and Contemporary Slavery," 224.

41. Philip Bump, "Here's How We Can Be Confident That There Are 11 Million Undocumented Immigrants in the U.S.," *Washington Post*, September 21, 2016, sec. The Fix, https://www.washingtonpost.com/news/the-fix/wp/2016/09/02/heres-how-we-can-be-confident-that-there-are-11-million-undocumented-immigrants-in-the-u-s/.

42. Czaika and de Haas, "The Globalization of Migration."

43. Czaika and de Haas, "The Globalization of Migration."

44. UNDP, "HDR 2009," 2.

45. "South" refers to all non–high-income countries. World Bank, "Migration and Remittances Factbook 2016."

46. Shyamal Chowdhury, Ahmed Mobarak, and Gharad Bryan, "Migrating Away From a Seasonal Famine: A Randomized Intervention in Bangladesh," *Human Development Research Paper 2009/41*, 2009.

47. Nikolaj Nielsen, "EU to Use Aid and Trade to Stop Africa Migration," *EU Observer*, June 28, 2016, https://euobserver.com/migration/134067.

48. DEMIG POLICY dataset.

49. Michael Clemens, "International Harvest: A Case Study of How Foreign Workers Help American Farms Grow Crops—and the Economy" (Partnership for a New American Economy and the Center for Global Development, 2013), http://www.cgdev.org/sites/default/files/international-harvest.pdf.

50. Czaika and de Haas, "The Globalization of Migration."

51. UNDP, "HDR 2009," 2.

52. UNDP, "HDR 2009," 2.

53. Peters, "Trade, Foreign Direct Investment, and Immigration Policy Making in the United States," *International Organization* 68, no. 4 (2014): 811–844; "Open Trade, Closed Borders: Immigration in the Era of Globalization," *World Politics* 67, no. 1 (2015): 114–154.

54. Judith Goldstein and Margaret E. Peters, "Nativism or Economic Threat: Attitudes Toward Immigrants During the Great Recession," *International Interactions* 40, no. 3 (2014): 376–401.

55. NBC News, "Trump Calls for New Immigration Screening Including 'Ideological Certification,'" *NBC News*, August 31, 2016, https://www.nbcnews.com/video/trump-calls-for-new-immigration-screening-including-ideological-certification-755544131788.

56. Saskia Sassen, "Global Cities and Survival Circuits," in *Global Woman: Nannies, Maids, and Sex Workers in the New Economy*, ed. Barbara Ehrenreich and Arlie Russell Hochschild (New York, NY: Macmillan, 2004), 273.

57. IOM, 2015b.

58. https://en.wikipedia.org/wiki/Death_of_Alan_Kurdi#/media/File: Alan_Kurdi_lifeless_body.jpg

59. Ronald Weitzer, "Human Trafficking and Contemporary Slavery," *Annual Review of Sociology* 41 (2015): 223–242.

60. http://america.aljazeera.com/articles/2014/11/30/human-smugglers-exploiters.html.

61. Doris Meissner, Donald Kerwin, Muzaffar Chishti, and Claire Bergeron, "Immigration Enforcement in the United States: The Rise of a Formidable Machinery" (Migration Policy Institute, January 2013), http://www.migrationpolicy.org/print/631#.V55t5JMrKV4.

62. UNDP, 2009, 3.

63. Heidi Shierholtz, "Immigration and Wages: Methodological Advancements Confirm Modest Gains for Native Workers," Briefing Paper (Economic Policy Institute, 2010), http://www.epi.org/publication/bp255/.

64. Michael Clemens, "Do Farm Workers From Developing Countries Take Jobs From Americans?," *Center For Global Development* (blog), February 28, 2012, http://www.cgdev.org/blog/do-farm-workers-developing-countries-take-jobs-americans.

65. Michael Clemens, "International Harvest: A Case Study of How Foreign Workers Help American Farms Grow Crops—and the Economy."

66. David Card, "The Impact of the Mariel Boatlift on the Miami Labor Market," *Industrial & Labor Relations Review* 43, no. 2 (1990): 245–257.

67. George J. Borjas, "The Wage Impact of the Marielitos: A Reappraisal," *Working Paper*, October 2015, https://web.archive.org/web/20151007165844/http://www.hks.harvard.edu/fs/gborjas/publications/working%20papers/Mariel2015.pdf. Presents a reevaluation of the data and contradicts Card's (1990) findings. But the debate goes on. Giovanni Peri and Vasil Yasenov, "The Labor Market Effects of a Refugee Wave: Applying the Synthetic Control Method to the Mariel Boatlift," Working Paper (National Bureau of Economic Research, December 2015), http://www.nber.org/papers/w21801.

68. Michael Clemens, "Economics and Emigration: Trillion-Dollar Bills on the Sidewalk?," *Journal of*

Economic Perspectives 25, no. 3 (September 2011): 83–106, https://doi.org/10.1257/jep.25.3.83.

69. George J. Borjas, "For a Few Dollars Less," *Wall Street Journal*, April 18, 2006, sec. Opinion, http://www.wsj.com/articles/SB114532411823528296.

70. Shierholtz, "Immigration and Wages."

71. Robert Rector and Jason Richwine, "The Fiscal Cost of Unlawful Immigrants and Amnesty to the U.S. Taxpayer," Special Report (The Heritage Foundation, May 6, 2013).

72. Immigrants are twice as likely to do so in Nordic countries and three times in Belgium, but the actual sums involved are small. All of these countries have sizable humanitarian populations, for whom unemployment is higher than the native-born population. OECD, "The Fiscal Impact of Immigration in OECD Countries," in *International Migration Outlook 2013*, by OECD (OECD, 2013), 155, http://www.oecd-ilibrary.org/social-issues-migration-health/international-migration-outlook-2013/the-fiscal-impact-of-immigration-in-oecd-countries_migr_outlook-2013-6-en.

73. Some caveats need to be added. First, this $11,000 figure also does not include the cost of schooling since education is an investment that benefits everyone rather than a consumption that benefits the individual consumer (i.e., the child). Second, countries where immigrants contribute less to the public purse do so not because they receive more in social benefits but because their wages are so low, meaning their taxes do not make a large contribution to the government's budget (OECD, 2013). Third, migrant households in Germany and France receive more than they contribute because immigrant populations are older and overrepresented among people receiving pensions (OECD, 2013, 147). Where the immigrant population is working age, they tend to put in more than they take out. Where the immigrant population is older, or nonworking, they tend to take out more than they put in (p. 161). But either way, the differences are small.

74. UNDP, "HDR 2009."

75. PRI, "At the World Cup, There Are More French-Born Players Playing Against France Than for It," *Public Radio International*, June 30, 2014, http://www.pri.org/stories/2014-06-30/frances-cosmopolitan-society-shines-world-cup-other-countries-too.

76. David Hytner, "Benoît Assou-Ekotto: 'I Play for the Money. Football's Not My Passion,'" *The Guardian*, April 30, 2010, sec. Football, https://www.theguardian.com/football/2010/may/01/benoit-assou-ekotto-tottenham-hotspur.

77. Jens Hainmueller and Michael J. Hiscox, "Attitudes Toward Highly Skilled and Low-Skilled Immigration: Evidence From a Survey Experiment," *American Political Science Review* 104, no. 1 (February 2010): 61–84, https://doi.org/10.1017/S0003055409990372.

78. World Bank, "Migration and Remittances Factbook 2016."

79. Data saved in folder.

80. Devesh Kapur, *Diaspora, Development, and Democracy: The Domestic Impact of International Migration From India* (Princeton, NJ: Princeton University Press, 2010).

81. Claire L. Adida and Desha M. Girod, "Do Migrants Improve Their Hometowns? Remittances and Access to Public Services in Mexico, 1995–2000," *Comparative Political Studies* 44, no. 1 (January 1, 2011): 3–27, https://doi.org/10.1177/0010414010381073.

82. Frederic Docquier and Hillel Rapoport, "Globalization, Brain Drain and Development," SSRN Scholarly Paper (Rochester, NY: Social Science Research Network, March 28, 2011), http://papers.ssrn.com/abstract=1796585.

83. World Bank, "Migration and Remittances Factbook 2016."

84. Devesh Kapur, "Political Effects of International Migration," *Annual Review of Political Science* 17 (2014): 479–502.

85. Hillel Rapoport, Andreas Steinmayr, Christoph Trebesch, and Toman Omar Mahmoud, "The

Effect of Labor Migration on the Diffusion of Democracy: Evidence From a Former Soviet Republic," CReAM Discussion Paper Series (Centre for Research and Analysis of Migration (CReAM), Department of Economics, University College London, 2013), https://ideas.repec.org/p/crm/wpaper/1320.html.

86. Tobias Pfutze, "Does Migration Promote Democratization? Evidence From the Mexican Transition," *Journal of Comparative Economics* 40, no. 2 (May 2012): 159–175, https://doi.org/10.1016/j.jce.2012.01.004.

87. UNDP, "HDR 2009," 2.

88. UNDP, "HDR 2009," 2.

89. The number of countries restricting individual internal mobility is increasing. UN, "World Population Policies 2013" (Department of Economic and Social Affairs, Population Division, 2013), 107, http://www.un.org/en/development/desa/population/publications/policy/world-population-policies-2013.shtml. A small number of countries representing a large number of people places restrictions on leaving the country, including Cuba, North Korea, China, Eritrea, Iran, Myanmar, and Uzbekistan. Other countries, including Saudi Arabia and Swaziland, restrict the ability of women to leave their country. UNDP, "HDR 2009," 40.

90. Cited in Eszter Kollar and Alena Buyx, "Ethics and Policy of Medical Brain Drain: A Review," *Swiss Medical Weekly*, October 25, 2013, https://doi.org/10.4414/smw.2013.13845.

91. Paul Collier, *Exodus: How Migration Is Changing Our World* (New York: Oxford University Press, 2013). Other economists have found evidence for this argument. See Faini, 2007; Niimu Ozden Schhiff, 2010.

92. Cenker, "The Complexity of Migration," 204; Michael Clemens, "What Do We Know About Skilled Migration and Development?," Policy Brief (Migration Policy Institute, September 1, 2013), http://www.migrationpolicy.org/research/what-do-we-know-about-skilled-migration-and-development; Clemens, "International Harvest: A Case Study of How Foreign Workers Help American Farms Grow Crops—and the Economy."

93. Clemens, "The Labor Mobility Agenda for Development," in *New Ideas on Development After the Financial Crisis*, ed. Nancy Birdsall and Francis Fukuyama (Baltimore, MD: The Johns Hopkins University Press, 2011), 260–287.

94. http://www.irinnews.org/report/89186/africa-ten-countries-desperately-seeking-doctors.

95. http://time.com/3543077/west-africa-doctor-ebola/.

96. WHO, "The World Health Report 2006: Working Together for Health," Annual Report (World Health Organization, 2006), 6.

97. Ahkenanten Benjamin Siankam Tankwanchi, Caglar Özden, and Sten H. Vermund, "Physician Emigration From Sub-Saharan Africa to the United States: Analysis of the 2011 AMA Physician Masterfile," *PLOS Med* 10, no. 9 (September 17, 2013): e1001513, https://doi.org/10.1371/journal.pmed.1001513.

98. Collier, *Exodus*.

99. Shlesh A. Shrestha, "No Man Left Behind: Effects of Emigration Prospects on Educational and Labour Outcomes of Non-Migrants," *The Economic Journal*, April 1, 2016, n/a-n/a, https://doi.org/10.1111/ecoj.12306.

100. Docquier and Rapoport, "Globalization, Brain Drain and Development," 9.

101. Syed Zain Al-Mahmood, "Palm-Oil Migrant Workers Tell of Abuses on Malaysian Plantations," *Wall Street Journal*, July 26, 2015, sec. World, http://www.wsj.com/articles/palm-oil-migrant-workers-tell-of-abuses-on-malaysian-plantations-1437933321.

102. UNDP, "HDR 2009," 26.

103. Weitzer, "Human Trafficking and Contemporary Slavery," 224.

104. Weitzer, "Human Trafficking and Contemporary Slavery," 224.

105. UNDP, "HDR 2009," 26.

106. Mohammed Harmassi, "Bahrain to End 'Slavery' System," *BBC*, May 6, 2009, sec. Middle East, http://news.bbc.co.uk/2/hi/middle_east/8035972.stm.

107. Human Rights Watch, "'I Already Bought You': Abuse and Exploitation of Female Migrant Domestic Workers in the United Arab Emirates" (Human Rights Watch, 2014).

108. Ken Early, "Shamefulness of the Qatar World Cup Laid Bare," *The Irish Times*, December 4, 2017, https://www.irishtimes.com/sport/soccer/international/ken-early-shamefulness-of-the-qatar-world-cup-laid-bare-1.3314428.

109. Weitzer, "Human Trafficking and Contemporary Slavery," 224.

110. Sheldon Zhang, "Sex Trafficking in a Border Community: A Field Study of Sex Trafficking in Tijuana," Final Report Submitted to United States Department of Justice, 2010, https://www.ncjrs.gov/pdffiles1/nij/grants/234472.pdf.

111. Ko-lin Chin and James Finckenauer, *Selling Sex Overseas: Chinese Women and the Realities of Prostitution and Global Sex Trafficking* (New York, NY: NYU Press, 2012).

112. Georji Petrunov, "Human Trafficking in Eastern Europe: The Case of Bulgaria," *The ANNALS of the American Academy of Political and Social Science* 653, no. 1 (2014): 162–182.

113. Sarkar.

114. Belanger, 2014.

115. Weitzer, "Human Trafficking and Contemporary Slavery," 224.

116. Jacobsen and Skilbrei, 2010, cited in Weitzer, "Human Trafficking and Contemporary Slavery."

117. UNDP, "HDR 2009," 26.

118. http://www.ilo.org/ipec/facts/lang--en/index.htm Accessed 7/30/16.

119. The following data come from ILO, "Marking Progress Against Child Labour: Global Estimates and Trends 2000–2012" (Geneva, Switzerland: International Labour Organization, 2013).

120. Howard, "Protecting Children From Trafficking in Benin: In Need of Politics and Participation," *Development in Practice* 22, no. 4 (2012): 460–472.

121. Weitzer, "Human Trafficking and Contemporary Slavery," 224.

122. Meghan Benton and Milica Petrovic, "How Free Is Free Movement? Dynamics and Drivers of Mobility Within the European Union" (Migration Policy Institute, March 2013), 3, http://www.migrationpolicy.org/research/how-free-free-movement-dynamics-and-drivers-mobility-within-european-union.

Global Health

ADDRESSING INEQUALITIES IN OUTCOMES

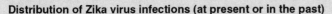

Distribution of Zika virus infections (at present or in the past)

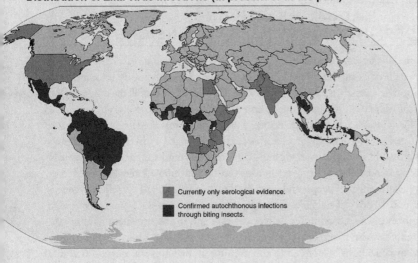

Currently only serological evidence.

Confirmed autochthonous infections through biting insects.

Map of Zika Virus Infections Worldwide

Wikipedia user Furfur, https://commons.wikimedia.org/wiki/File:Zika_virus_infections_worldwide .svg. Licensed under CC BY-SA 4.0, https://creativecommons.org/licenses/by-sa/4.0/legalcode.

LEARNING OBJECTIVES

After finishing this chapter, you should be able to:

- Understand the scope of the global health field.

- Describe the difference between a "global health security" and a "humanitarian biomedicine" approach to global health.

- Cite some specific global health outcomes in the world.

- Analyze how and why inequalities in health outcomes exist across countries.

- Discuss the ways in which inside-out and outside-in interactions shape global health.

- Consider how global forces, in particular global markets, governance, and information and communications technology (ICT), are shaping global health now and for the future.

- Understand the current state of the global HIV and AIDS pandemic.

- Articulate some specific improvements in HIV and AIDS access to treatment and care.

Health may seem like the ultimate local problem. You get sick after being infected by someone you know or from some infection that develops in your body. The reality, however, is that many health problems are global.

Consider the Ebola virus. Ebola is a nasty disease, a hemorrhagic fever. If you contract it, you are likely to bleed uncontrollably, develop an extremely high fever, and die if you do not receive proper treatment. People become infected by coming into contact with or eating infected animals or by coming into direct contact with the bodily fluids of someone who is infected, such as vomit, blood, or spit.

The world's worst outbreak to date started in 2014 in West Africa and lasted for about two years. From an initial case in Guinea, the disease spread to Liberia and Sierra Leone, and eventually to Nigeria, Mali, and the United States (where two healthcare workers were diagnosed with it).

In the end, the World Health Organization (WHO), a United Nations (UN) agency, reported more than 28,000 cases, of which more than 11,000 people died.[1]

The Ebola crisis sparked international alarm. The disease spread rapidly in West Africa. Because humans cross borders all the time, and human-to-human infection was quick, the risk that the disease could spread well beyond West Africa was real. Left unchecked, undetected, and untreated, the disease could have morphed into a global pandemic. That at least was the nightmare scenario. In the end, a concerted response from the Centers for Disease Control and Prevention (CDC), the WHO, some international nongovernmental organizations (INGOs), and the national governments of those most affected contained and controlled the disease. By 2016, the WHO declared it to be over.

GLOBAL HEALTH AND
FORCES, INTERACTIONS, AND TENSIONS

Ebola demonstrates some of the ways in which health is global. First, many diseases are inherently cross-national. One expression that captures this idea is "Bugs do not respect borders!" In other words, parasites in and on people, insects, vessels, food, and merchandise move across borders all the time in a globally interactive world, just as Ebola did. Or think about a parasite like malaria that stows away in a mosquito, which in turn lives in a border region. Mosquitos do not need passports to cross borders, and states have a hard time controlling the pesky bloodsuckers. Consider a parasite that is lodged into a crop or meat grown and raised in one part of the world, packaged in another, and consumed in a third. Left untreated, that parasite may well travel halfway around the world to infect someone very far away from its initial origins. Indeed, the increasing international exchanges of people and products that are the hallmark of global markets, in particular, create new forms of health vulnerabilities for people all around the world.

Second, health is global in the cross-border delivery of care and in the transnational humanitarian concern that often gives rise to cross-border healthcare delivery. The Ebola example shows how intergovernmental organizations responded to and monitored the outbreak. Beyond that kind of response to a potential pandemic, fundamental to global health is a concern with equity, or the idea that all people around the world should have access to adequate care. Global health frequently entails people with resources and knowledge seeking to improve health outcomes for people with limited access to care. In that sense, global health is about a transfer of assistance, care, medicines, and expertise across borders. Such a transfer is conditional upon the idea that people in one part of the world can and should care about the fate of people in other parts of the world. Inherent to global health then is a globalization of humanitarian values, similar to the field of human rights. The grounding idea is that people in one part of the world who *can* help people in other countries *should*.

Third, health is global in the ways that the cross-cutting *global forces* shape the field. For example, *global governance* is core to the health field. Intergovernmental organizations such as the WHO or the Global Fund for AIDS, Tuberculosis, and Malaria play a very large role in setting agendas, establishing rules and guidelines, creating standards, defining key concepts, monitoring diseases, and providing scientific, neutral information and disseminating it to the public. The United Nations has created goals for how to achieve health in different societies, such as the Sustainable Development Goals. National health agencies often operate on a global stage, interacting with partner governments. As Ebola showed, the CDC in Atlanta has a vibrant international profile. Nongovernmental organizations that operate transnationally, such as Partners in Health or Médecins sans Frontières, are often key players in the field, providing healthcare directly but also serving as advocates, messengers, and fundraisers. Foundations such as the Bill and Melinda Gates Foundation are major players in the field, also setting agendas, providing funding, and establishing priorities. Moreover, pharmaceutical companies, scientists, doctors, religious organizations, and ordinary citizens are very active in shaping the norms, debates, and practices in global health issues.

Markets are equally a big part of the story. *Global markets* increase the flow of goods and transportation, which increases the range and penetration of diseases. In other words, the global circulation of bugs is closely bound up with the global circulation of goods and people in today's world economy. A little more abstractly, the world economy is underpinned by neoliberal ideals, in which markets are preferred over states for solving problems. In the global health field, the dominance of neoliberal policies has shaped for decades public health services and systems around the world. Health is often privatized, and government clinics face a difficult funding landscape in an era of smaller government. Drug production is global; large pharmaceutical companies control much of the production, pricing, and distribution of life-saving drugs. The ingredients for many pharmaceuticals are sourced globally.

These are just some of the ways in which health is global. Indeed, global health is one of the most rapidly growing and energetic areas in international studies. Global health has emerged as a focal point for thousands of students, medical professionals, policy makers, academics, and nongovernmental organizations (NGOs), including both foundations and humanitarian agencies. One of the things that makes it so vibrant is that, similar to many other global challenges underlined in this book, global health is inherently interdisciplinary. On the one hand, global health involves many areas within the health sciences: physicians, nurses, health researchers, demographers, research scientists, and biostatisticians, among others. On the other hand, global health engages economists, political scientists, anthropologists, historians, and sociologists, among others, who seek to understand how health is embedded in society, politics, history, and the economy.

In this chapter, we explore these dimensions of global health. We discuss what global health is as well as some key themes in the field. From there, we discuss key health outcomes in the globe, ranging from maternal health to life expectancy. To illustrate some themes, we delve a little deeper into the global HIV and AIDS crisis. On the one hand, that crisis has been devastating. Millions have died, and tens of millions remain infected. On the other hand, the global response to the crisis has transformed its dynamics. Through sharp changes in funding and treatment, millions have access to life-saving care. The response to the crisis offers some hope that dedicated and concerted effort in global health can make a real difference. In closing, we return to how global health is interconnected with themes and topics in the book. We also underscore some problems for reflection. Global health has been a magnet for many students in recent years. Many are attracted to what seems like an apolitical, straightforward, and effective way of helping others. If the medicine exists to keep people alive, and certain practices could improve health outcomes, eager students have looked for ways to improve the lives of others in a concrete way. But global health as a field of practice and study is not as straightforward as it sometimes seems. Health outcomes are embedded in society, states, and politics, and international healthcare delivery is a short-term fix, rather than a long-term solution, in much the way that foreign aid is not a solution to global poverty. This chapter should help students understand not only the scope and field of global health but also develop some critical analysis of the field.

public health: wide range of activities that are concerned with health in a community; questions of prevention, the conditions that favor health, and equality of access are key for public health.

WHAT IS GLOBAL HEALTH?

At the broadest level, global health is about **public health**. In contrast to private medicine, "public" health indicates a wide range of activities that are community or population based in some fashion. Public health emphasizes not just treatment and cures but also prevention and the conditions for health. That includes publicly accessible services, such as clinics, hospitals, and access to medication, but also education and information about health and environmental issues such as clean water. Equity and justice are central to public health; healthcare for the poor and the idea of access to healthcare are central tenets in the public health field. By contrast, private medicine indicates more a concern with individuals and their ability to procure care.

Defining Global Health

Global health is public health on a global scale. In the same way that equity in health nationally is central to the public health field, equity on a global scale is central to global health. In the same way that public health embeds health in populations and societies, so too does global health examine how social processes shape health outcomes. In addition, global health conveys the idea of transnational processes; diseases, care, and research are all global.

Although there is no single agreed-upon definition, most definitions of global health stress these, as well as the collaborative foundations to global health. According to one influential definition, **"Global health** is an area for study, research, and practice that places a priority on improving health and achieving equity in health for all people worldwide. Global health emphasizes transnational health issues, determinants, and solutions; involves many disciplines within and beyond the health sciences and promotes interdisciplinary collaboration; and is a synthesis of population-based prevention with individual-level clinical care."[2]

The definition emphasizes the worldwide dimensions of global health, the importance of equity, and the broad scope of action and research. A more streamlined, also influential, definition gets at that idea: Global health is a "collaborative trans-national research and action for promoting health for all."[3] Again, here the notion is of a broad space for collective responses, for care and inquiry across borders, and crucially "health for all."

global health: wide range of transnational activities that promote public health for all people around the world.

What Does the Field Include?

Within the global health field, there are several typical areas of concern:

- Maternal and Reproductive Health—a broad field that includes prenatal care, maternal health, contraception and family planning, and gynecology.

- Pediatrics—essentially everything that affects the health of children.

- Immunization—the procurement, distribution, and safe application of vaccines for adults and children, ranging from measles, mumps, and yellow fever to polio.

- Infectious Diseases—another broad area that concerns diseases caused by dangerous microorganisms, such as bacteria, viruses, and parasites; infectious diseases include tuberculosis, malaria, HIV and AIDS, rabies, hepatitis, Dengue, cholera, Ebola, and a whole range of often very fatal diseases.

- Nutrition or the consumption of food in relationship to health.

- Chronic (noninfectious) Disease—this is an area that concerns heart disease, cancer, diabetes, respiratory problems, blood pressure, and a range of other noninfectious diseases.

- Injuries and Violence—people around the world suffer from injuries and violence, including broken bones, damaged joints, other health consequences of trauma.

- Mental Health—an area of research and practice that concerns psychological well-being.

- Environmental Health—an area that concerns how people interact with their environmental circumstances; access to clean water and sanitation are key parts of environmental health in a global health context, as are freedom from pollution in the air and in and around dwellings.

- Essential Medicines—the idea that certain medicines should be readily available, with proper dosages; the World Health Organization produces a report that lists 30 categories of essential medicines, which range from anesthetics and oxygen to medicines for pain and palliative care to medicines that affect the blood.

iStock/Spondylolithesis

Many of these domains are interactive. For example, immunization, nutrition, mental health, environmental health, and essential medicines all factor into pediatrics; the same could be said for maternal health.

Analytic Themes in Global Health

Global health outcomes are inseparable from some of the core themes in the book. For example, there is a strong correlation between the income level of a country and health outcomes. The richer a country is, the more that country may devote to a healthcare system. There is not a perfect correlation, as different governments can prioritize public health. The same is true for state capacity. Weak governmental institutions will have trouble monitoring health outcomes, as well as delivering needed services. As noted, global governance and intergovernmental organizations play a big role in this field, as do nongovernmental organizations. Culture is a critical issue as well. Health involves bodies, intimacy, and sometimes sexuality. Prevailing norms about gender, sex, and even common customs and understandings will shape how people in a country think about health and will respond to modern medicine. Those are some issues covered in the Foundations section of the book.

Global health also interacts with some of the global challenges we have covered in the second half of the book. Global health specialists often speak about "complex emergencies," by which they typically mean armed conflict, in particular, civil war. In wartime, populations face the direct health impacts of war. They may be hurt, they may be poisoned, and they may be traumatized or face other health concerns. Moreover, the displacement and disruption that typically accompany civil war also shape access to health; people who flee have a harder time gaining access to health. Health is a human right. Indeed, the right to health is listed in the Universal Declaration of Human Rights. Last, environmental issues such as climate change and access to clean water are also critical for global health. In particular, climate change is changing the range and geography of microorganisms, which in turn makes different people more vulnerable to certain infectious diseases.

Beyond these themes, there are also several analytic distinctions that are specific to the global health field. Examining them helps to understand the field.

IS From the Outside-In

CONTAGION AS AN EXAMPLE OF A GLOBAL HEALTH SECURITY CONCERN

The movie *Contagion* (2011) is rooted in a dooms-day story of how a deadly infectious disease, MEV-1, rapidly killed millions of people around the world, sowed a breakdown of social order, and nearly led to complete global collapse. Although fictional and dramatized, the film is a good example of a global health security approach to issues of global health. The film also illustrates some of the key global forces underlined in this book and how they inter-act with global health concerns.

The film depicts how a jet-setting business-woman (Gwyneth Paltrow) consumes pork in Hong Kong and unknowingly contracts a virus that involved a mutation from a bat whose habitat had been disturbed through economic development. The woman then traveled to Macao and Chicago, before returning to her home and company headquarters in Minneapolis. While in Macao, she infected a server at a casino, a Ukrainian model, and a Japanese busi-nessman. There begins an explosion of infection, which is transmitted through breathing and touch-ing, that killed tens of millions of people around the world. The film cites experts who suggest that the stunningly rapid infection rates could take the lives of 1 in 12 people around the world, or somewhere around 500 million people.

The epidemic engenders a set of responses. As society breaks down through looting and runs on food, governments establish quarantines and call out the military to patrol streets and maintain a semblance of order. The U.S. president moves to an undisclosed lockdown location. Meanwhile, health professionals from the World Health Organization in Geneva, Switzerland, go on a disease detective journey, while scientists at the Centers for Disease Control and Prevention work on a vaccine. The lat-ter eventually prevail, and after some months, the vaccine is produced in enough quantities to be dis-tributed around the world.

The film is a good example in which to see how a security approach underlies some work in the global health field. In this case, the disease is a highly lethal airborne disease contracted from ani-mals. With relative ease, the disease passed from continent to continent, and from people to people. That engenders a massive global threat, which in turn justifies a state-led militarized response. The explicit involvement of the WHO and the CDC point to two of the most important global governance institutions in the global health field.

Global markets are at the heart of the story. An economic deal between a China-based and a U.S.-based company, coupled with international execu-tive travel, are at the origin story of the film. From there, the film depicts an exponential number of human interactions, often rooted in markets and densely populated urban spaces, that ultimately fuel the disease's transmission. The film even has a side story of a health blogger (Jude Law) who transmits false conspiracy theories but whose real motive is to get rich through peddling a false cure.

Contagion is a fictional story, but the film rep-resents the fears of a global pandemic that might arise from a highly infectious and deadly disease. The kinds of concerns depicted in the film were in play during the recent Ebola crisis in West Africa, discussed in the introduction to the chapter. Another real-world example is the Swine influenza, also called H1N1, which similarly triggered concerns about a deadly infectious disease on a global scale. A telling moment comes in the film when repre-sentatives of the U.S. Department of Homeland Security and the Department of Defense explain their worries of a deliberate terrorist effort to wea-ponize and distribute a disease. A top official at the CDC (depicted by Laurence Fishburne) responds: "Someone does not have to weaponize the bird flu. The birds are doing that." That line shows vividly the security approach taken in the film.

Reflect

In what way do the four global forces of interna-tional studies inform the backdrop for the film *Contagion*?

Global Health Security vs. Humanitarian Biomedicine. One important distinction is between global health security and humanitarian biomedicine.[4] The concept of health security frames health problems as threats, and **global health security** in turns looks at health threats on a global scale.

For example, a global health security approach focuses on emerging infectious diseases that are highly communicable and dangerous, and that, by crossing borders, can represent a grave threat to people all over the world. Ebola is a good example. Other diseases of concern are the Zika virus, SARS, H1N1, H5N1, and other highly communicable and dangerous diseases.

The core preoccupations in this field are security—preventing outbreaks that might rapidly endanger the lives of many. In this area, the focus of work is often surveillance and monitoring of diseases but also preventing outbreaks through quarantines, quick interventions, developing vaccines, and other measures designed to contain and ideally inoculate against outbreaks. Fears of infectious diseases escaping the Global South into the Global North often drive this field, as well as funding for it.

Watch the trailer for Contagion *at https://www.youtube.com/watch? v=4sYSyuuLk5g.*

Diseases as weapons, or as bioweapons, are another type of global health security challenge. Biological weapons are one type of weapon of mass destruction (alongside nuclear and chemical weapons). Some states maintain active biological weapons programs, in which the idea is to take a highly contagious disease and spread it via bullets, bombs, and other projectiles. A major concern of counterterrorism experts is that terrorist organizations might procure or develop programs to use biological matter in terrorist attacks, and indeed security officials voice that fear in the film *Contagion*, as noted in the feature box. The concept of "bioterrorism" captures this idea. In the past, some individuals and organizations have sent anthrax, a deadly biological agent, through the mail as a mechanism of terror. But anthrax is only one example. The CDC in the United States maintains a list of dozens of bioterrorism agents.[5]

Global health security is a major challenge for some of the dedicated health intergovernmental organizations, such as WHO, again as the film shows. The WHO actively monitors outbreaks of such diseases and helps to coordinate interventions, if necessary. But a health security focus also includes the national security institutions of various states whose job it is to protect populations from intentional attack. The United States—like other states—has a developed strategy for countering biological threats or **biothreats**.[6] The United Nations also has developed a biological weapons convention, known formally as the "Convention on the Prohibition of the Development, Production and Stockpiling of Bacteriological (Biological) and Toxin Weapons and on their Destruction." The treaty has more than 175 state parties.

Humanitarian biomedicine is quite a different set of concerns. The main focus in this area is providing healthcare to those whose care and health resources are inadequate, primarily in the developing world. The main idea is to improve health outcomes by providing resources, expertise, and treatments to those who need it. A broad concern with global equity and humanitarianism, as opposed to security, underpins much of the motivation in this field. In this vein, global health involves the transfer of resources and knowledge from wealthier parts of the world to poorer parts.

Consider a basic health issue, such as maternal health. Many women around the world lack access to prenatal care or they lack access to clean water, or both. Some do not have access to vaccines for their children once they are born. The lack of healthcare for pregnant women, which broadly is fixable (as opposed to a highly infectious disease like Ebola), imperils their lives and those of their children. A core global health concern is thus improving access to healthcare for pregnant women.

global health security: framing global health concerns through a security lens, for example, as sources of threat that would endanger human populations.

biothreats: idea that biological matter, such as a disease, may be intentionally used as a weapon.

humanitarian biomedicine: efforts to improve health outcomes for people who have inadequate care or resources.

primary healthcare:
essential, nonspecialized, accessible healthcare.

Alma Ata Declaration:
1978 declaration that emerged from a global meeting convened by the World Health Organization; the Alma Ata declaration shaped the global health agenda, in particular through promulgating definitions, setting goals, and emphasizing primary healthcare as an anchor for global health.

ELEMENTS:
acronym emerging from the Alma Ata conference; ELEMENTS emphasizes eight core tenets of primary healthcare: education, local disease control, expanded immunization, maternal and child health, essential drugs, nutrition and food supply, treatment of disease and injury, and sanitation and safe water supply.

The focus on improving health outcomes that principally concentrate among the world's poor put humanitarian biomedicine in close conversation with poverty alleviation and foreign assistance debates (see Chapter 9). Indeed, the range of actors involved in poverty alleviation and foreign assistance—intergovernmental organizations, nongovernmental organizations, and states—also tend to be involved in global health. For the health-oriented programs and organizations, the focus is on helping the sick on their own terms (as opposed to containing diseases that could spread to the richer parts of the world).

As with any distinction, the opposition between health security and humanitarian biomedicine is not absolute. Basic health services and access to them will make any prevention and containment effort of a highly infectious disease much more successful. Yet the two approaches represent fairly different ways of thinking about and developing a global health agenda. For the most part, global health in an international studies context focuses on humanitarian biomedicine, and that agenda will be the primary concern in the subsequent sections of the chapter.

The Centrality of Primary Care. For those who focus on humanitarian biomedicine, the provision of primary healthcare is a focal point. **Primary healthcare** is essential, nonspecialized, and ideally accessible healthcare, which should anchor a healthcare system. In particular, in low-income countries with limited resources to health, primary healthcare is seen as the foundation for better health outcomes. In global health, in particular, in the humanitarian biomedicine tradition, primary health often also refers to a broad range of public health–related issues, such as education, sanitation, and community resources. Primary healthcare is not just about seeing doctors and nurses but about communicating information and creating a social and environmental context that fosters health.

An emphasis on primary health emerged in particular in the wake of the **Alma Ata Declaration** of 1978, a key reference point in global health. Alma Ata is where the World Health Organization organized one of its first major conferences.

The conference has had many lasting influences on global health. One has been to provide a central, broad definition of health as "a state of complete physical, mental and social well-being . . . [which] is a fundamental human right." Not only does this definition frame health as a human right, but the definition also conceptualizes health as "complete well-being" that involves various dimensions, including not just physical health but also mental and social well-being.

A second lasting impact has been that the conference emphasized equity. At the conference, the WHO concluded that "the existing gross inequality in the health status of the people, particularly between developed and developing countries as well as within countries, is politically, socially, and economically unacceptable and is, therefore, of common concern to all countries." In making this claim, the WHO was setting an agenda. The organization, through the Alma Ata conference, was declaring that massive levels of inequality in health outcomes should end. In so doing, Alma Ata committed the United Nations to improving health outcomes as a worldwide goal.

The third legacy, and another important way in which Alma Ata shaped the global health agenda, is its focus on primary health. At Alma Ata, the WHO strongly promoted the idea that primary healthcare should be the foundation for a global health approach. The vision for primary health again was broad. Rather than simply thinking about primary health as nonspecialist care, Alma Ata emphasized that primary health should be rooted in communities and should be connected to a broad range of development issues. That broad range is summarized in the acronym **ELEMENTS**, which refers to the broad conception of primary health that emerged from this meeting and which continues to shape the global health agenda. ELEMENTS refers to education, local disease control, expanded immunization, maternal and child health, essential drugs, nutrition and food supply, treatment of disease and injury, and sanitation and safe water supply. This is a very broad understanding of primary health, which includes not just first-level healthcare delivery but also aspects of society (education), environment (sanitation), and markets (food supply).

Alma Ata remains a central focal point for global health debates, especially with the emphasis on primary care and equity. Alma Ata is also an example of how an intergovernmental organization can help set the agenda for a field, of how global governance works.

Horizontal vs. Vertical Interventions. A third, related distinction focuses on the difference between healthcare interventions that are horizontal and those that are vertical. **Horizontal interventions** are those in which practitioners devote energy to improving the baseline conditions that underpin health outcomes. Horizontal interventions tend to be grassroots oriented and have multiple effects; they impact a wide range of health outcomes.

An example would be clean water, which is a contributor to child mortality, maternal health, overall mortality, and a host of diseases, such as dysentery and worms. Similarly, healthcare access through clinics but also education are types of horizontal intervention. If people lack access to a nurse, doctor, or other healthcare professional, they typically not only lack the information needed to prevent and respond to infections but also typically lack access to medication and treatment. Having clinics in place, as well as trained healthcare professionals, will have positive effects on multiple health outcomes, from maternal health to malaria to heart conditions.

By and large, those that emphasize horizontal interventions devote resources and energy to primary care. Indeed, investments in primary care for many in the global health field remain the top priority as the knock-on effects of primary care are large. They extend nearly to the entire range of health outcomes. In this way, humanitarian biomedicine with a focus on helping to improve health outcomes around the world is very consistent with a horizontal approach. Those motivated by health security are less engaged in these horizontal, more longer term and diffuse approaches to global health.

By contrast, **vertical interventions** tend to focus on eradicating or containing a single, specific disease. These interventions are vertical in the sense that they zero in on one problem rather than address the underlying health infrastructure or environmental condition that improves or detracts from health in a community; they are narrow. Although global health security approaches that focus on a single disease or outbreak are almost always vertical interventions, some humanitarian biomedicine efforts are also vertical interventions. In particular, great effort has gone into immunizations of preventable diseases, such as polio, smallpox, mumps, measles, and yellow fever. These are diseases that since World War II were primarily located in the Global South, and eradicating them was in the service of a humanitarian impulse. Yet the approach was vertical—vaccinations, primarily, which were oriented toward a single disease.

Understanding these different analytical themes is important to thinking through how global health works. Global health is a large umbrella, and through these distinctions, readers will be able to focus on some specific priorities and approaches in the field.

horizontal interventions: healthcare interventions that aim at improving baseline conditions, such as access to clean water, education, or clinics.

vertical interventions: healthcare interventions that focus on addressing one specific health issue, such as a vaccine.

GLOBAL HEALTH OUTCOMES HIGHLIGHT SYSTEMIC INEQUALITIES

The state of global health can be measured in multiple ways. In this section, we report on some common indicators of global health. One critical dimension, which is observable across these statistics, is the inequity of outcomes across countries.

Life Expectancy

How long people live, on average, is an important indicator of health. In 2015, the mean life expectancy for the entire globe was 71.4 years, according to the World Health Organization. That global average masks some key regional variation, however. In Europe, the mean life expectancy was 76.8 years compared with 60.0 years in Africa. In 2015, the lowest expectancy was Sierra Leone with 50.1 years compared with Japan with 83.7 years (in the United States, the average is 79.3 years; see Figure 12.1).[7]

See WHO's interactive map of life expectancy at http://gamapserver.who.int/gho/ interactive_charts/mbd/life_expectancy/atlas.html.

Although the data in Figure 12.1 show important inequity between regions, they also reveal a gradual improvement in life expectancy during a 15-year period. If the data were extended backward to 1950, 1900, and before, the positive trend would be even more dramatic. Even though global data are much less valid the further one travels back in time, Figure 12.2 effectively shows global trends and highlights a couple key countries.

Broadly speaking, improvements in global health outcomes during the 20th and early 21st century are important and significant, as Figure 12.2 shows. People in the United Kingdom live twice as long as they did, on average, 200 years ago. That long-term trend reflects major improvements in treatments and care, as well as improvements in basic sanitation. More recently, in higher income countries, the change is broadly a function of better care for noncommunicable diseases, such as heart disease and cancer. In low-income countries, better child survival and treatment of basic diseases matter. Moreover, better management of HIV and AIDS has been a big contributor to average longer life spans, as we will discuss shortly.

FIGURE 12.1

Life Expectancy at Birth, by WHO Region, 2000 and 2015

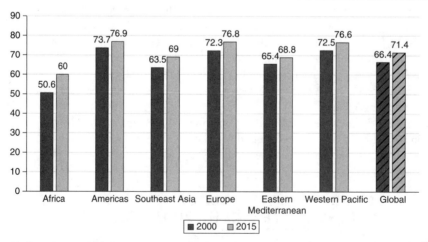

Source: World Health Organization, Global Health Observatory (GHO) Data, 2017. http://www.who.int/gho/en/.

FIGURE 12.2

Life Expectancy Has Increased Over Time

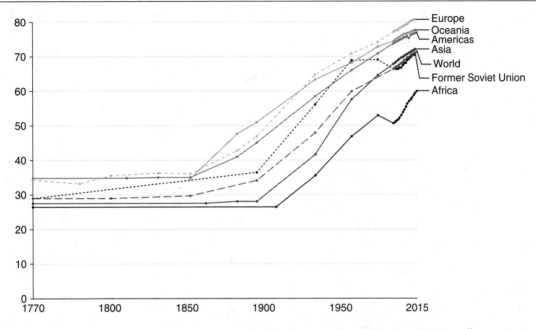

Source: "Life expectancy globally and by world regions since 1770," in Max Roser, Our World in Data, 2017. https://ourworldindata.org/slides/global-health/?linkId=29368678#/7, licensed under CC BY-SA 4.0 https://creativecommons.org/licenses/by-sa/4.0/deed.en_US.

Child Mortality and Maternal Health

Child mortality is another key indicator in the global heath field, as is maternal mortality. The former measures how many children die before a certain age, while the latter measures how many women die as a function of giving birth. Both are considered areas where simple interventions and basic medicines could save considerable lives. Deaths among children are often linked to malnutrition and lack of access to basic care, including not having access to vaccines.

Child mortality can be measured in different ways, including what percentage of newborns die as well as what percentage of infants reach their first or fifth birthday. Figure 12.3 shows both neonatal (newborn) and child (younger than 5) mortality rates from 1990 to 2015. There has been progress in both areas but in particular in the areas of child mortality rates younger than the age of 5. On that point, between 1990 and 2015, the under-5 child mortality rate decreased by more than half to 43 per 1,000 live births. That represents about four of every 100 births, or 5.9 million children younger than 5 who died in 2015.

Explore more UN SDG Goals data related to good health and well-being at https://unstats.un.org/sdgs/report/2016/goal-03/.

The global data mask considerable inequity among countries and regions in the world. According to the WHO, children in Africa are 14 times more likely to die before the age

FIGURE 12.3

Neonatal and Under-5 Mortality Rates Worldwide, 1990–2015

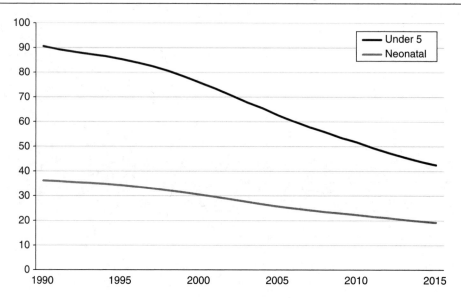

Source: "Neonatal and under-5 mortality rates worldwide, 1990–2015," in United Nations, "SDG Goal 3: Good Health and Well-Being," Statistics Division, 2017. https://unstats.un.org/sdgs/report/2016/goal-03/.

of 5 than are children in developed regions.[8] Through more education, access to basic care, and vaccines, many in the global health field see reducing child mortality as a key and achievable goal.

Care for women who are pregnant or who recently delivered a child are also core priorities in the global health field. Again, the data demonstrate considerable variation across world regions but also a generally positive trajectory (see Figures 12.4 and 12.6).

Another way to visualize the trend is by looking at some specific countries and over a longer period of time, as Figure 12.5 does.

Infectious Disease: The Example of Malaria

Infectious diseases that are preventable and curable afflict many people around the world. Some of the most common infectious diseases are tuberculosis, malaria, cholera, rabies, measles, mumps, yellow fever, hepatitis, and HIV and AIDS. Many of these diseases are preventable through immunization. Indeed, a simple shot can immunize someone from measles, mumps, rabies, and other infectious diseases. A core concern then in humanitarian biomedicine is increasing access to immunizations for people around the world.

Other diseases are not preventable through immunization but through prophylactic drugs or simple precautionary measures. One such disease that afflicts people throughout the Global South, in particular, in Sub-Saharan Africa, is malaria. Malaria is a mosquito-borne parasite that, when

FIGURE 12.4

Maternal Mortality Ratio (per 100,000 Live Births) by WHO Region, 2000 and 2015

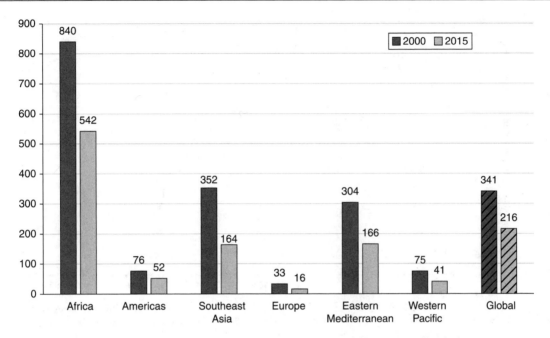

Source: World Health Organization, Global Health Observatory (GHO) Data, 2017. http://www.who.int/gho/en/.

infecting humans, can become quickly lethal if untreated. Malaria, like other diseases, is especially lethal among children and other vulnerable populations.

Through mosquito eradication efforts in parts of the Global North, there remain few places where malaria exists (although new mosquito-borne illnesses, such as West Nile Virus and Zika, are appearing). The story in the Global South, however, is quite different. Malaria remains a common danger, and infection rates remain high, as are deaths from malaria.

According to the World Health Organization, some 3.2 billion people are at risk of malaria infection globally, of which some 1.2 billion are at "high" risk, which is measured as a greater than 1 in 1,000 chance in a year. There were 214 million cases of malaria globally in 2015 and about 438,000 deaths. The infection and resulting deaths were overwhelmingly concentrated in Sub-Saharan Africa, as Figure 12.7 shows.

As these data show, there have been significant improvements in both the incidence and the mortality of malaria in recent years. In the period between 2000 and 2015, there was a 60% reduction in mortality from malaria and a 37% reduction in incidence.[9] Reducing malaria infections has been a priority in the field for years, as malaria is a preventable and treatable disease that takes a heavy toll in countries that are already low income. Through simple interventions like the provision of mosquito nets treated with insecticide or other low-cost measures to prevent bites or to detect malaria at an early stage, infection and mortality rates have declined.

FIGURE 12.5

Maternal Mortality Has Decreased Over Time

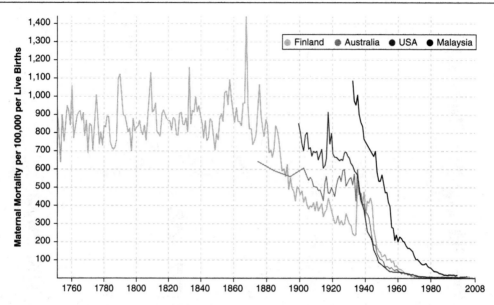

Source: "Maternal Mortality, 1751–2008," in Max Roser, Our World in Data, 2017. https://ourworldindata.org/slides/global-health/?linkId=29368678#/Maternal-Mortality, licensed under CC BY-SA, https://creativecommons.org/licenses/by-sa/4.0/deed.en_US.

Notes: Figure 12.5 powerfully shows the improvements in maternal mortality since the Industrial Revolution, in particular, in developed, high-income countries. At the same time, the figure shows significant inequities across countries. Similar disparities across regions exist for antenatal care. See Figure 12.6.

FIGURE 12.6

Antenatal Care Coverage by WHO Region, 2013

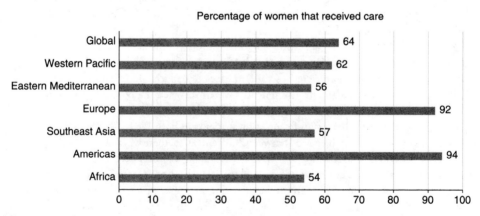

Source: World Health Organization, Global Health Observatory (GHO) Data, 2017. http://www.who.int/gho/en/.

FIGURE 12.7

Estimated Number of Malaria Deaths by WHO Region, 2000 and 2015

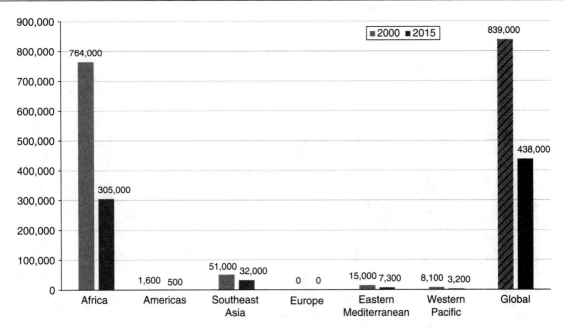

Source: "Global malaria deaths by world region, 2000–2015," in Max Roser, Our World in Data, 2017. https://ourworldindata.org/slides/
global-health/?linkId=29368678#/Malaria-Deaths licensed under CC BY-SA, https://creativecommons.org/licenses/by-sa/4.0/deed
.en_US.

Chronic Diseases

Another area of concern in the global health area is noninfectious chronic diseases. These include cardiovascular disease (CVD), cancer, diabetes, and chronic respiratory disease (CRD). The challenges for these types of diseases are different. Although some are preventable, not all are—such as several types of cancer. Similarly, some diseases are curable, but most are not. The treatment is therefore chronic and designed to mitigate the negative health consequences of the disease. As such, the inequities between world regions are a little less pronounced. For cases like maternal mortality and malaria, which are extremely rare events in the Global North but frequent in parts of the Global South, many chronic diseases are widespread, as Figure 12.8 shows.

Healthcare Access

Access to healthcare is a key determinant of health outcomes. The more that people can access health professionals, the better their health outcomes are likely to be. One of the likely determinants of access is how much a country spends on healthcare, which in turn is highly correlated with the income level of the country (see the last two columns of Figure 12.9).

FIGURE 12.8

Mortality from Cardiovascular Disease, Cancer, Diabetes, or Chronic Respiratory Disease, Ages 30–70, by World Bank Region, 2000 and 2015

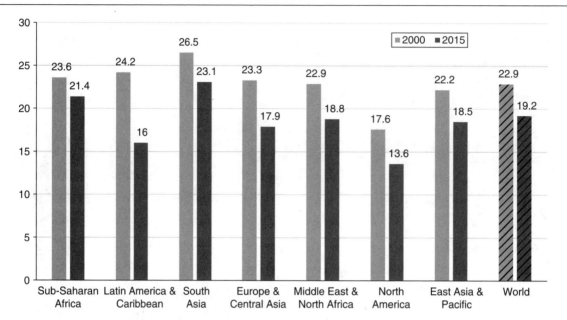

Source: Copyright (c) The World Bank, Data from World Health Organization, Global Health Observatory Data Repository, https://data.worldbank.org/indicator/SH.DYN.NCOM.ZS licensed under CC BY-4.0 https://creativecommons.org/licenses/by/4.0/.

Notes: Figure shows the percentage of people who die in the age bracket 30–70 from the named diseases in a given year. Although the data indicate some improvement during the last 15 years, the gains are not nearly as dramatic, on average, as they are for other types of diseases or health issues we have discussed.

As Figure 12.9 shows, healthcare spending has increased in all world regions. In percentage terms, nearly every world region doubled, or more, their spending in the years between 2000 and 2014. As this figure also illustrates, however, there are large discrepancies in per capita spending across world regions. The bars on the right compare high-income countries with low-income ones, and they show high-income countries spend 50 times as much as low-income ones, on average.

The same trends are visible in how many health professionals exist on a per capita basis. Figure 12.10 captures the number of physicians per person in a country in a world region. Again, the disparities are large.

These data and Figure 12.10 provide a snapshot of global health in the world today. They are certainly not the only diseases and outcomes of interest, but they are some of the most common areas of interest and concern. Through these data, we can see two general trends that are fundamental to the contemporary global health field. First is inequality. The health conditions and the vulnerability to disease are consistently, on average, worse in low-income parts of the world. Second is improvement over time, in particular, in the 20th century. For most major diseases, the trend is toward better

FIGURE 12.9

Per Capita Total Health Expenditure (Using Purchasing Power Parity $) by WHO Region, 2000 and 2014

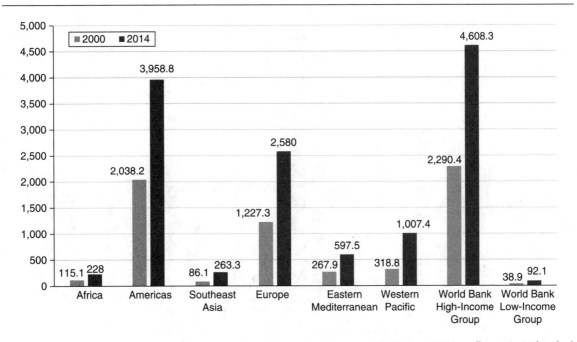

Source: Data available from the World Health Organization, Global Health Observatory (GHO) Data, 2017. http://www.who.int/gho/en/.

outcomes—a function of improvements in medicine, increasing attention and funding, and growing economies in most parts of the world. These same trends are very much apparent in the global HIV and AIDS crisis, which is the subject of the next section.

THE GLOBAL HIV AND AIDS PANDEMIC

To gain greater insights into global health, we focus in this section on the global HIV and AIDS pandemic. The pandemic has been one of the most significant crises in global health in recent decades. HIV and AIDS have claimed the lives of millions, and today more than 30 million people live with HIV in the world. At the same time, in recent years, there has been great progress in limiting new infections, and there have been major advances in treatment efficacy and treatment access. In other words, in the midst of enormous tragedy, there is also evidence of significant improvement.

By examining the HIV and AIDS crisis in greater detail, we can see some of the major analytical themes at work in global health. For one, the scale is huge and the disease is global, affecting nearly every world region. HIV knows no boundaries—its bugs do not respect borders—and tens

FIGURE 12.10

Physicians per 1,000 People, by World Bank Region, 2000 and 2012

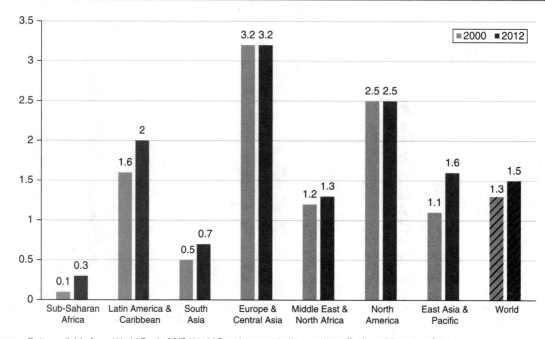

Source: Data available from World Bank. 2017. World Development Indicators, http://wdi.worldbank.org/tables.

of millions have the disease. Second, when the disease first spread, many governments and intergovernmental organizations framed it as a security issue: Left unchecked, the disease could spread and threaten countries. But over time, as medicine advanced and the disease turned into one that could be treated as a chronic disease (rather than a death sentence), the issue turned more to one of equity and humanitarianism. Would those in the Global South get access to the care that those in the Global North did? Third, the disease has generated a huge global response, one that involves government, intergovernmental organizations, philanthropic foundations, and nongovernmental organizations, usually working across borders. The response is thus a good case study of the kind of complex actors and interactions that we seek to underline in this book. Fourth, the response to the disease has been primarily vertical—education, treatment, and changing behavior oriented toward stemming the spread of the disease. Yet the focus on HIV and AIDS in that way has sometimes eclipsed other diseases and ultimately has shown that baseline, primary care is also critical for a holistic response. Last, the case shows how a concerted effort can really make a difference on a global scale.

Global Prevalence

According to UNAIDS, which is the principal international organization that tracks the spread of the crisis, about 36.7 million people in the world are living with HIV and about 35 million people have died from the disease worldwide. An estimated 19.5 million people received anti-retroviral

FIGURE 12.11
Percentage of 15- to 49-Year-Olds Living with HIV, 2016

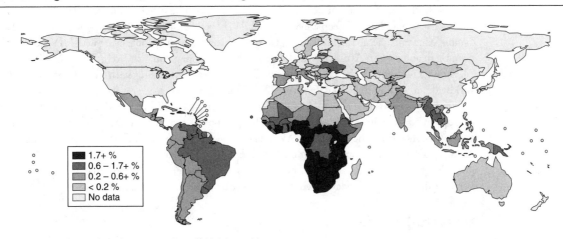

1.7+ %
0.6 – 1.7+ %
0.2 – 0.6+ %
< 0.2 %
No data

Source: UNAIDS, "HIV Prevalence," Map. http://aidsinfo.unaids.org.

FIGURE 12.12

New HIV Infections (All Ages)

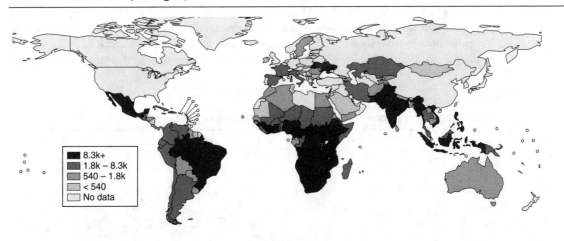

8.3k+
1.8k – 8.3k
540 – 1.8k
< 540
No data

Source: UNAIDS, "New HIV infections (all ages)," Graphs, 2017. http://aidsinfo.unaids.org.

therapy worldwide in 2016, and there were about 1.8 million new infections. In 2016, approximately 1 million people died from the disease. Anti-retroviral therapy is a type of treatment that attacks HIV, which is the virus that causes AIDS.

As with other health outcomes, the global data mask significant regional variation. The disease is concentrated in the Global South, and the epicenter is southern Africa. Indeed, the countries with the highest percentage of infected adult populations are in southern Africa—Lesotho, Swaziland, Botswana, and South Africa, in particular. In those countries, the percentages of 15- to 49-year-olds living with HIV average about 20% in those age brackets. The other countries in southern Africa also have very high rates of people living with HIV, hovering around 13% and 14% in countries like Zambia, Mozambique, and Zimbabwe. Indeed, more than half of all people living with HIV are located in southern and eastern Africa, of which nearly 60% are women and girls, according to UNAIDS.

Figure 12.11 shows the percentage of 15- to 49-year-olds living with HIV in each country worldwide, according to 2016 data from UNAIDS.

The good news is that new infection rates are beginning to fall. Despite the exceptional number of people who live with HIV, one of the key bright spots is that the number of new infections has steadily declined since the mid-1990s. Whereas in the mid-1990s, UNAIDS estimated the number of new infections to be more than 3 million, that figure dropped to 2.5 million in the mid-2000s, and now is less than 2 million. Although those are still very high numbers, the decline of new infections is significant, nearly half today of what it was 20 years ago—as Figure 12.12 shows.

Access to Treatment and Care

The other major change that has taken place in the life cycle of this disease concerns breakthroughs in treatment regimens and treatment access. When the HIV crisis first took off in the 1990s, contracting HIV was generally thought to be a slow death sentence. The virus would develop into AIDS (autoimmune deficiency syndrome), and people would die through commonplace opportunistic infections that healthy people could fight off without difficulty.

Medical scientists in the late 1990s, however, developed cocktails of anti-retroviral drugs that essentially turned HIV from a fatal disease into a manageable chronic one. Those medical discoveries did not immediately translate into improved outcomes for several reasons, including the fact that many people did not know of their status and many states did not want to acknowledge the

FIGURE 12.13

Coverage of People Receiving ART (All Ages)

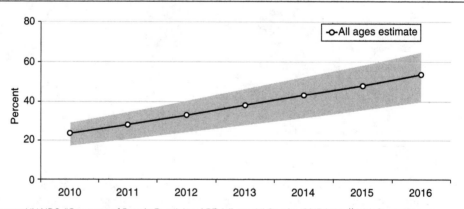

Source: UNAIDS, "Coverage of People Receiving ART (all ages)," Graphs, 2017. http://aidsinfo.unaids.org.

problem. The treatment was also extremely expensive and out of reach for many with HIV, and medical practitioners who could prescribe and administer the medications were not widespread in the Global South.

That is no longer the case, and today some 53% of people with HIV in the world have access to anti-retroviral therapy (ART). The change is staggering. According to UNAIDS, in 2000, the number of people with HIV who had access to ART was 685,000 people worldwide; in 2010, the number was 7.7 million, and in 2016, the number was 19.5 million people. The percentages of people with access to ART, and a steady increase in access even since 2010, can be seen in Figure 12.13.

The sharp increase in the number of people with access to ART has had two major benefits. The first is that fewer people with HIV now die from the disease. Since the mid-2000s, the number of AIDS-related deaths has declined by 43%, according to UNAIDS.[10] The second is that transmission rates from those who are infected to those who are not decline considerably if the infected person is being treated with anti-retrovirals.

Treatment Costs

There are several reasons why treatment access has improved so dramatically. One is cost. When ART first became publicly accessible, the cost per person per year was exceedingly expensive. In 2000, according to the United Nations Development Program, the cost was as much as $10,000 per year per person. Putting that figure in context, in most low- and middle-income countries, the treatment costs were unaffordable. In many cases, they were more than 10 times what the average annual income per person was in such a country. But fast forward to the mid-2010s and the costs of ART are now less than $100 per person. The change is primarily due to the rise of generic brand drug production, which itself is a function of lobbying and activist efforts to relax the international property rights protections and patents.[11] In addition, competition between drug manufacturers and international incentives for drug and cost innovation has also played a role.[12]

Increases in Funding

The second major reason for improved access is funding. National governments have dedicated increased resources to HIV and AIDS, but so too has there been a large increase in international bilateral assistance. For example, PEPFAR in the United States (President's Emergency Plan for AIDS Relief) is widely considered a game-changer in the field. Since President George W. Bush created the program in the 2000s, it has spent some $70 billion on HIV/AIDS and tuberculosis. Much of that money goes toward purchasing anti-retroviral therapy for people living with HIV. Indeed, in 2016 alone, PEPFAR accounted for more than 11 million people receiving ARTs.[13] But PEPFAR is not alone. Major foundations, such as the Bill and Melinda Gates Foundation and the Clinton Foundation, have prioritized global health. Innovations with the United Nations system, in particular, the emergence of a dedicated Global Fund to Fight AIDS, Tuberculosis, and Malaria, have contributed to greater funding for the HIV and AIDS crisis.

The global trends in funding for HIV and AIDS demonstrate significant progress in this area from the first days of the pandemic. In 2000, according to UNAIDS, the resources available to low- and middle-income countries for HIV and AIDS amounted to $4.8 billion. Today that number is $19 billion, of which more than half is from domestic sources. That is about a fourfold increase in a short period of time, which demonstrates significant progress.

Increases in funding for HIV and AIDS treatment and education are not the only areas in which there has been a significant increase in funding for global health. In general, global health has seen a large increase in funding during the past 20 years. Figure 12.14 shows increases in health assistance resources for several major issues in global health. The data reflect assistance that intergovernmental organizations, nongovernmental organizations, and governments give to other governments, mainly in low- and middle-income countries, for global health. The data show that the first transformative change in funding in global health was around the global HIV and AIDS pandemic. In recent years, however, the funding for that crisis has leveled off, while funding for more "horizontal" interventions, such as maternal and child health or strengthening health systems, has increased significantly.

FIGURE 12.14

Increases in Development Assistance for Health

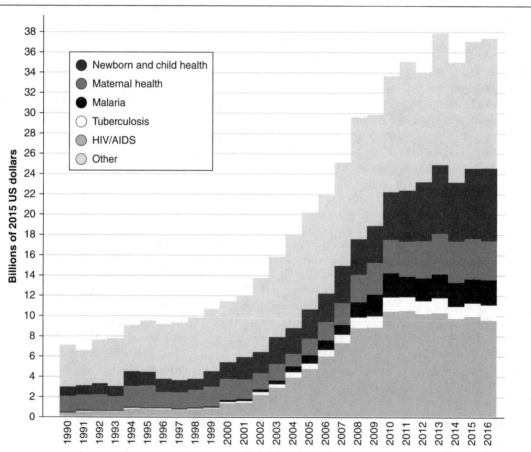

Source: Institute for Health Metrics and Evaluation (IHME). Financing Global Health 2017: Funding Universal Health Coverage and the Unfinished HIV/AIDS Agenda. Seattle, WA: IHME, 2018.

Figure 12.14 demonstrates a sharp spike in funding for HIV and AIDS beginning in the late 1990s. That was part of what some refer to as an "unprecedented rise" and "golden age" of global attention to and funding for the HIV and AIDS crisis.[14] Yet as funding for that heath priority leveled off in 2010, increases in funding for maternal heath as well as for newborn and child health increased, to the point where those two areas now receive the largest percentage of global health assistance.

In terms of who provides such funding, the funding landscape has changed dramatically since global health became a prominent issue. The changes in global funding patterns reflect a broader trend toward the importance of nongovernmental and intergovernmental bodies since the end of the Cold War. Bilateral government assistance remains a big part of the funding landscape—an effort that includes direct funding from one government to the health section; PEPFAR is a prominent example. Bilateral funding is now at around 29% of the overall funding for global health, with the United States being the largest contributor. In 1990, however, bilateral support was at 55% of the overall.

The biggest change has been in the form of nongovernmental organizations and private foundations. Whereas in 1990, those two entities provided some 5% of overall health assistance funding, they now constitute some 30% of overall funding. That reflects the increased prominence of organizations like the Bill and Melinda Gates Foundation, the Clinton Foundation, and the Bloomberg Philanthropies. Intergovernmental organizations, such as the Global Fund and Gavi—which did not exist until the early 2000s—now are also key players. Gavi, the Vaccine Alliance, is a public–private partnership devoted to research and provision of vaccines. Its governing board includes not only government representatives but also representatives from the World Health Organization, private foundations (like the Gates Foundation), and business executives from pharmaceutical companies that develop vaccines.[15] Changes in the funding composition for global health, including HIV and AIDS, is visible in Figure 12.15.

Normative and Legal Changes

In addition to the advances in funding and treatment access, there have also been major improvements in public awareness and education campaigns. Having once been shunned by many governments, particularly in socially conservative countries—and still today shunned by some—HIV/AIDS education has really increased. There are increasing numbers of anti-discrimination laws to protect people with HIV. But compared with when the outbreak first took off, the discussion of sex, sexuality, and transmission are much more commonplace.

The eastern African country of Uganda is often upheld as an example of how a concerted public education campaign can help to reverse trends in transmission. After HIV rates accelerated in the late 1980s, the government implemented a national action plan in the 1990s, with help from the World Health Organization. Part of the plan included the use of cleaner needles and better care in handling blood and medical equipment. But the more innovative aspects concerned the public messaging around sex. One public education campaign centered on the idea of "zero grazing," an analogy to animal husbandry (which is prominent in Uganda) but which translates into the idea of not having multiple sexual partners. Similar ideas were "Love Faithfully" and "Love Carefully." Uganda also developed the "ABC" program, which is an acronym for "Abstain, Be Faithful, and Condomize." Both public education campaigns were highly successful, and they helped to increase condom use, decrease multiple partners, and reduce transmission rates significantly.[16]

FIGURE 12.15

Development Assistance for Health by Channel

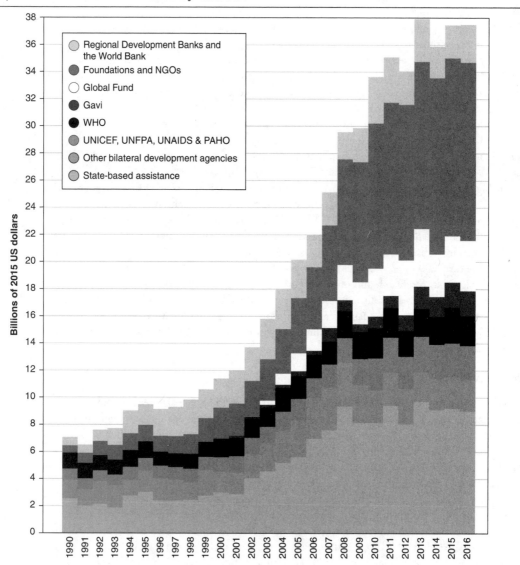

Source: Institute for Health Metrics and Evaluation (IHME). Financing Global Health 2017: Funding Universal Health Coverage and the Unfinished HIV/AIDS Agenda. Seattle, WA: IHME, 2018.

Indeed, the changes in Uganda reflect efforts in many countries to increase education about sex, condom use, and information about how the virus is transmitted. At one level, these campaigns have led to specific changes in sex and health practices, including greater condom use but also significant increases in male circumcision (which can reduce HIV transmission). Those changes speak to questions of culture and prevailing norms in a society. More broadly, attention to HIV and AIDS has implications for thinking about gender, women's empowerment, and women's health. There is growing recognition that HIV and AIDS transmission—like many global health issues—intersects with gender roles in society. Education for women and girls as well as empowerment within families and societies are crucial parts of the HIV and AIDS crisis.

A Long Way to Go

The progress should not negate the sheer size of the problem. Many challenges remain. Despite the progress on education, recent surveys of young people in heavily infected countries show that significant numbers of young people could not correctly answer questions about HIV transmission. HIV and AIDS remain stigmas in many countries. There are still more than a million new infections and deaths every year.

UNAIDS has set an ambitious "90-90-90" goal for coming years. The three goals are that by 2020, 90% of people with HIV will know their status; 90% of those with HIV will have access to anti-retroviral therapy; and 90% of those with ARTs will have viral suppression; that is, their drugs will be effective. Although there has been some progress toward these goals, much work remains, as Figure 12.17 shows.

FIGURE 12.16

Global Forces, Interactions, and Tensions in the Treatment of HIV and AIDS

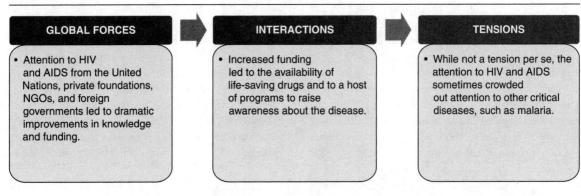

GLOBAL FORCES

- Attention to HIV and AIDS from the United Nations, private foundations, NGOs, and foreign governments led to dramatic improvements in knowledge and funding.

INTERACTIONS

- Increased funding led to the availability of life-saving drugs and to a host of programs to raise awareness about the disease.

TENSIONS

- While not a tension per se, the attention to HIV and AIDS sometimes crowded out attention to other critical diseases, such as malaria.

FIGURE 12.17

Progress Toward 90-90-90 Target

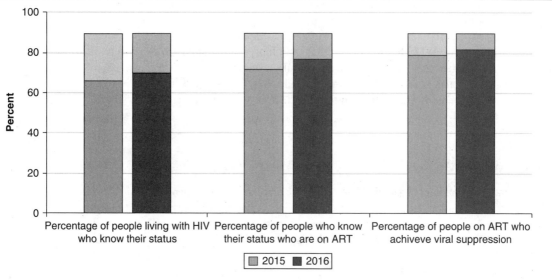

Source: UNAIDS, "Treatment cascade (90-90-90)," Graphs, 2017. http://aidsinfo.unaids.org.

SUMMARY

Global health remains one of the most exciting and dynamic areas within international studies. As the HIV and AIDS crisis shows, concerted efforts may have dramatic results in terms of tangible improvements in people's lives around the world. That people in one country care about the fate of others in different countries reflects a globalization of values that is very prevalent in international studies. That increased attention, increased funding, and dedication could have such a big impact is inspirational. The change also reflects how the composition of key global actors is evolving globally. Whereas once governments were the main players in the provision of assistance, nongovernmental actors, intergovernmental organizations, and private–public partnerships are increasingly important in the field. (See Figure 12.16.)

The HIV and AIDS interventions illustrate a couple key themes in the global health field. Although the ini-

tial concern among governments when HIV started to spread globally was one of security, over time the global response morphed into a prime example of humanitarian biomedicine. While HIV and AIDS are global pandemics initially thought to threaten the security of states in the Global North, the main impact of the disease has been on the economies and societies of states in the Global South, most devastatingly in Sub-Saharan Africa. The global response was primarily about health equity and improving health outcomes for the most vulnerable, and that reflects a humanitarian ethic that is core to global public health.

The evolution of funding also reflects a general appreciation for "horizontal" interventions that complement or even rival vertical ones. Many developments in the HIV crisis remain quite specific to that particular global health issue. The provision and increased access to anti-retroviral therapy is a good example, as is male circumcision. As funding for HIV and AIDS have leveled off, increased attention to other diseases, such as malaria and tuberculosis, have increased. But in addition, the global health community is increasingly investing in health issues that will have impacts for multiple health problems. Those areas for intervention include a focus on health systems, maternal and child health, and environmental factors, such as access to clean water through better sanitation systems.

The global health field also clearly intersects with many themes and chapters in this book. The roles of states, global civil society, and intergovernmental organizations are clear and significant. Less obvious are questions of culture, yet norms about gender, sexuality, marriage, and practices are crucial to health outcomes. Beliefs about multiple sexual partners, condom use, circumcision, the inheritance of brides, and other issues are fundamental to global health outcomes. So too are questions of poverty and even environmental issues. While not detailed in this chapter, climate change is affecting the range of different parasites, including mosquito-borne illnesses like malaria and West Nile virus. Similarly access to clean water, which is the key for a range of health outcomes, is also shaped by climate change. Issues such as civil war, which displace populations,

diminish access to healthcare, increase harm, and sometimes lead to greater sexual violence, also intersect with global health. In other words, the themes and topics within international studies are mutually constitutive.

Implicit here is the increasing recognition that global health is not simply making medicines available, training health professionals, and vaccinating. In other words, global health is not just delivering care. Some leaders in the global health field propose an interdisciplinary "biosocial" approach to global health, ones that recognizes how health outcomes are embedded in societies, cultures, governments, and economies.[17] Power and exclusion—who has privilege, who does not—are critically important for understanding health outcomes and dynamics. Many students and activists have had powerful impacts on health outcomes, and progress in particular in the area of HIV and AIDS is noticeable. But sometimes well-meaning interventions can have negative impacts. They can reinforce hierarchies between rich and poor, or they can create unsustainable relationships and dependencies that do not fundamentally change inequities in health on a global scale. Heeding the lessons from the rest of the international studies field has value for global health outcomes.

KEY TERMS

Alma Ata Declaration 342
biothreats 341
ELEMENTS 342
global health 338

global health security 341
horizontal interventions 343
humanitarian biomedicine 341
primary healthcare 342

public health 337
vertical interventions 343

QUESTIONS FOR REVIEW

1. What do you think are the most important global health priorities?

2. Why do you think such vast health disparities exist in the world, and what can be done about them?

3. What is the difference between a global health security and a humanitarian biomedicine approach?

4. What progress has been made in the HIV and AIDS field?

5. Why do you think such progress was made, and are there any unintentional negative consequences to the focus on HIV and AIDS?

LEARN MORE

Paul Farmer, Jim Yong Kim, Arthur Kleinman, and Matthew Basilico, eds., *Reimagining Global Health: An Introduction* (Berkeley: University of California Press, 2013).

Tracy Kidder, *Mountains Beyond Mountains: The Quest of Dr. Paul Farmer, a Man Who Would Cure the World* (New York, NY: Penguin Random House, 2009).

Andrew Lakoff, *Unprepared: Global Health in a Time of Emergency* (Berkeley and Los Angeles: University of California Press, 2017).

Jennifer Leaning, Susan Briggs, and Lincoln Chen, eds., *Humanitarian Crises: The Medical and Public Health Response* (Cambridge, MA: Harvard University Press, 1999).

Stephanie Nolen, *28 Stories of AIDS in Africa* (New York, NY: Walker Books, 2007).

Explore the state of global health at the WHO: http://www.who.int/gho/en/.

NOTES

1. World Health Organization (WHO), "Situation Report: Ebola Virus Disease," June 10, 2016. http://apps.who.int/iris/bitstream/10665/208883/1/ebolasitrep_10Jun2016_eng.pdf? ua=1.

2. Jeffrey P. Koplan et al., "Towards a Common Definition of Global Health," *The Lancet* 373 (2009): 1993–1995.

3. Robert Beaglehole and Ruth Bonita, "What Is Global Health?" *Global Health Action* 3 (2010): 1–2.

4. Andrew Lakoff, "Two Regimes of Global Health," *Humanity* 1 (2010): 59–79.

5. https://emergency.cdc.gov/agent/agentlist.asp.

6. United States National Security Council (NSC), "National Strategy for Countering Biological Threats," November 2009. https://obamawhitehouse.archives.gov/sites/default/files/National_Strategy_for_Countering_BioThreats.pdf.

7. Data available from the World Health Organization (WHO), Global Health Observatory (GHO) Data, 2017. http://www.who.int/gho/en/.

8. World Health Organization (WHO), "Children: Reducing Mortality," Media Centre Fact Sheet, 2017. http://www.who.int/mediacentre/factsheets/fs178/en/.

9. World Health Organization (WHO), "Malaria," Global Health Observatory (GHO) Data, 2017. http://www.who.int/gho/malaria/en/.

10. UNAIDS, "Topic: HIV Treatment," 2018. http://www.unaids.org/en/topic/treatment.

11. Luke Messac and Krishna Prabhu, "Redefining the Possible: The Global AIDS Response," in Paul Farmer, Jim Yong Kim, Arthur Kleinman, and Matthew Basilico, eds., *Reimagining Global Health: An Introduction* (Berkeley: University of California Press, 2013), 111–132.

12. United Nations Development Programme (UNDP), "World AIDS Day: Record Drop in Cost of HIV Treatment," November 30, 2015. http://www.undp.org/content/undp/en/home/presscenter/articles/2015/11/30/world-aids-day-record-drop-in-cost-of-hiv-treatment.html.

13. U.S. President's Emergency Plan for AIDS Relief (PEPFAR), "Program Results Achieved Through Pepfar Support," https://data.pepfar.net/.

14. Messac and Prabhu, "Redefining the Possible," 2013.

15. Gavi, the Vaccine Alliance, "Board composition." http://www.gavi.org/about/governance/gavi-board/composition/.

16. Slutkin, Okware, Naamara, et al., "How Uganda Reversed Its HIV Epidemic," *AIDS and Behavior* 10 (2006): 351–360.

17. Farmer et al., *Reimagining Global Health* (2013).

Global Environment

CONFRONTING THE CHALLENGE OF CLIMATE CHANGE

13

LEARNING OBJECTIVES

After finishing this chapter, you should be able to:

- Understand the scope of global environmental challenges.

- Distinguish between the concepts of global warming and climate change.

- Identify the main drivers of climate change.

- Focus on the main effects of climate change.

- Articulate why reaching a global climate change agreement is so difficult.

- Analyze how global forces—in particular markets, changing power, and governance— shape the climate change discussion.

Flickr/US Army Corps of Engineers

Many environmental problems are local. Fertilizer runoff might pollute a lake near you and cause dangerous algae to bloom. Garbage from your nearest city might be piled high and seep into the groundwater, or tailings from a mine might poison the land and the water table beneath it. An airborne herbicide might damage crops on a local farm.

But many environmental problems are global. Consider the problem of invasive species. In a variety of ecosystems around the world, animals and plants introduced from another part of the globe have had dramatic impacts on the local ecology. Several species of Asian carp today pose a major threat to the Great Lakes ecosystem in the United States. Introduced from Southeast Asia decades ago to clean wastewater and control algae, the carp spread into the Great Lakes system. They grow to be very large (as much as 100 pounds) and are voracious eaters. Their size, appetite, and fast rate of reproduction mean that they have seriously altered the ecosystem of the Great Lakes, depleting native fish stocks, causing discoloration of the waters, and harming the local economy that depends on existing species.[1]

The problem is not confined to North America. Native to South and Central America, the cane toad was introduced in Australia in the first half of the 20th century to control insects. These toads and their tadpoles are toxic to eat, which discourages predators. They have reproduced widely and now number some 1.5 billion in Australia.[2]

In a world with extensive global trade and economic interactions, species from one part of the world stow away or are deliberately brought to another part of the world. "Exotic" pets find homes for a while and then are discarded. A recent study in *Nature* found that invasive species threaten one sixth of the land surface of the world (see Figure 13.1). Moreover, many developing countries with weak response capacity face some of the greatest risks.

Invasive species are an example of an unwanted population boom. Population decline in important native species is the flip side of that equation. But both problems are similarly enmeshed in a global network of environmental problems. Consider commercial fishing. Across several world regions, fish stocks have declined precipitously in recent decades. Some 90% of the world's fisheries are overfished or fished at capacity, according to the United Nations Food and Agricultural Organization.[3] New technology has helped fisherman to find and harvest fish in ways that were previously impossible. Growing wealth in large developing countries has also meant growing appetite for fish. That is particularly true in China, which has invested in new fleets of long-distance fishing vessels. Traveling not only to Southeast Asia but also to the west coast of Africa, Chinese trawlers

FIGURE 13.1

Threat of Invasive Species Is Very High in Many World Regions

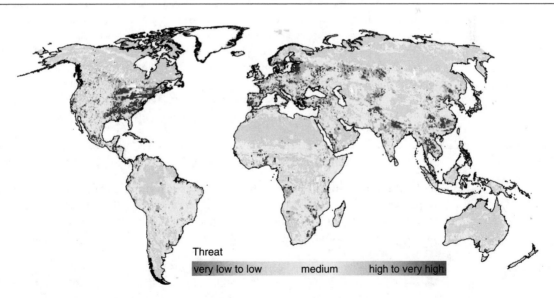

Source: Early, R. et al. Global threats from invasive alien species in the twenty-first century and national response capacities. Nat. Commun. 7: 12485, https://www.nature.com/articles/ncomms12485 licensed under CC BY-4.0 https://creativecommons.org/licenses/by/4.0/.

are contributing to overfishing in those areas. States in those regions often have a low capacity to monitor illegal fishing and to impose fines, or are vulnerable to corruption.[4] Overfishing in turn has diminished the economic prospects for West Africans and those in Southeast Asia, contributing in the former case to increased migration to Europe.[5]

As with invasive species, the problem of overfishing brings together several themes in this book: Long-haul fishing vessels sailing from one country's waters to another is a concrete form of international interaction. An inside-out force—domestic consumption in China—creates demand, which ratchets up pressure for fishermen (backed by a powerful state) to extend their reach, creating an outside-in force. That increased fishing pressure affects job security and food security in another state, which in turn affects migration patterns—with residents in the overfished state looking to leave their country because of diminished economic prospects. China's surge is a key part of the story; state weakness in West Africa and elsewhere facilitates predation; weak global governance facilitates the process but various international nongovernmental organizations (INGOs) and some United Nations (UN) offices seek to do what those organizations do best—to publicize and document the problem;[6] and declining food stocks and jobs lead to international migration from Africa to Europe, fueling populist anti-immigrant sentiment there.

Many environmental challenges share this structure. Around the world, species are in decline, leading some scholars to speak of "biological annihilation" and a "sixth mass extinction" in the world today. The causes of species extinction are many, but environmental degradation, climate change, economic growth, and invasive species are among the key factors.[7]

The world faces many global environmental challenges. They range from invasive species and overfishing to plastic waste in the oceans, access to clean water, and soil erosion. Many of these challenges are rooted in local, domestic, and international interactions. The global forces at the heart of this book in turn shape these challenges. Without paying attention to global governance, markets, and changing power around the world, it is difficult to get a handle on global environmental challenges. In the remainder of the chapter, we focus on the quintessential global environmental challenge: climate change. We provide an overview to climate change, defining it, summarizing core scientific concepts, outlining its causes, showing evidence that climate change is real, describing its global and regional effects, and discussing different responses to it. Throughout, we aim to locate the challenge in our international studies framework, both in terms of how climate change connects up with global interactions and tensions, the global forces we underline in the book, and other themes and topics discussed in the book.

WHAT IS CLIMATE CHANGE?

Of all the global environmental challenges, climate change is arguably the defining one, a challenge that is exceptionally difficult to confront and one that affects almost every living thing on the planet. As a climatic and planetary issue, by definition the topic is global in nature. Climate change is also the product of billions of local actions (from transportation, to home heating, to raising livestock) that interact over time in the atmosphere.

climate change:
natural and human-induced variability in the global climate.

Climate change refers to natural variability in the global climate or variability as a result of human activity. By and large, in the international studies context, climate change refers to the latter: to climate change that is attributed directly or indirectly to human activity and that is in addition to natural climate variability observed over comparable time periods. Such change is often called *anthropogenic climate change,* or climate change that is the result of human activity.

Herein lies some debate. There is no question that the Earth is warming and that the climate is changing. The main United Nations scientific panel discussed in detail in this chapter concludes that "warming of the climate system is unequivocal," and scientists overall consider a warming planet to be settled fact.[8]

To the extent a controversy exists around climate change, the dispute surfaces around the question of whether human activity causes the change, and how much of the change humans cause. The scientific community engaged in climate science clearly answers that question affirmatively. An intellectual historian studied more than 900 articles in peer-reviewed journals on climate change, and *not one* disputed that anthropogenic warming is happening.[9] In a 2014 report from the Climate Science Panel of the American Association for the Advancement of Science, the authors compared the scientific consensus on anthropogenic warming to the consensus linking smoking to lung cancer.[10] The main United Nations body established to monitor climate change concluded: "It is extremely likely that human influence has been the dominant cause of the observed warming since the mid-20th century."[11]

Nonetheless, some people contest the causality. They argue that the proof of human responsibility is lacking, and therefore the costly steps that would be necessary to address climate change are not the best way to approach the problem given the uncertainty. Another line of debate concerns the effects of climate change. The computer modeling that forecasts both climate change and its effects is complex. That in turn creates uncertainty about what the future holds. In the face of what would be expensive actions to reduce carbon emissions, which are the main source of anthropogenic climate change, or to adapt to the coming changes, some argue not to act until the science is clearer.

While acknowledging that the issue is not settled, the chapter will proceed by referencing the mainstream approaches to the topic, which assume that climate change is indeed a product of human activity.

EMPIRICS OF CLIMATE CHANGE

The baseline model for climate change is that certain gases collect in the atmosphere and remain there for long periods. Those gases in turn "trap" heat inside, creating what many scientists call a **greenhouse effect**. The greenhouse effect is a naturally occurring phenomenon that makes the planet inhabitable for humans. The greenhouse gases, including water, methane, and carbon dioxide, create layers that keep the heat in the atmosphere. Without them, the planet would be considerably cooler.[12]

greenhouse effect: idea that certain gases trap heat inside the atmosphere, heating the climate as windows would trap heat in a greenhouse.

The central intuition behind climate change is that since the Industrial Revolution, humans have been burning fossil fuels. The net result is an increase in greenhouse gases, primarily carbon dioxide, in the atmosphere. That creates a thicker blanket of greenhouse gases, which broadly leads to more warming. At the start of the Industrial Revolution, carbon dioxide levels were about 280 parts per million. Since then, carbon emissions have increased dramatically. Today, they are around 400 per million, and emissions are six times greater than they were in 1950. Meanwhile, the Earth has warmed on average about 0.85° Celsius mostly since 1970. The big question is how much the Earth will warm on average by the end of this century and beyond.

Key Scientific Concepts

Although the increases in greenhouse gases trap more heat and lead to a warming trend over time, most scientists prefer the term "climate change" to "global warming." Warming of the Earth's atmosphere is one of the major changes, but that change does not capture the full extent of the

radiative forcing: key metric in climate science; it refers to the net change in the energy balance of the Earth.

changes in play. Those include changing patterns of rainfall, increased numbers of extreme weather events, changing seasons, rising sea levels, melting sea ice, melting glaciers, and a variety of other changes. Climate change references this broader sense of change to weather patterns compared to global warming.

Scientists have also developed the concept of **radiative forcing** to capture the contribution of greenhouse gases to the atmosphere. Formally defined, radiative forcing is "a measure of the net change in the energy balance of the Earth system in response to some external perturbation."[13] The idea here is that the Earth absorbs a certain amount of energy from the sun and reflects a certain amount back. A variety of disturbances, however, can change the overall balance between absorption and reflection. Scientists developed a quantitative measure of radiative forcing relative to the period of the Industrial Revolution, which is typically delineated as 1750. Measures of radiative forcing are the main ways that scientists quantify the size of the contribution of different greenhouse gases—that is, to measure a change from a pre-industrial period.

In addition, there are a series of feedback mechanisms, or changes, caused by warming that in turn further affect the climate. The melting of the polar ice caps is one such mechanism. Ice deflects the heat light of the sun. When ice melts due to warming and becomes water, however, the water absorbs the heat more than the ice did, creating a knock-on effect in addition to warming caused by the greenhouse gases.

Permafrost is another example. In the northern areas of the globe, organic matter remained frozen in the ground. Warming trends—which are particularly acute in those areas—however, have meant that the areas once frozen are now melting and subject to microbial decomposition. Permafrost thawing in turn releases greenhouse gases into the atmosphere, accelerating the rate of carbon being released into the atmosphere, which contributes to planetary warming.[14]

Drivers of Climate Change

The three main heat-trapping greenhouse gases that contribute to climate change are carbon dioxide, methane, and nitrous oxide. In addition, several aerosols, such as chlorofluorocarbons, also are net contributors to climate change. Of these different contributors, the most important is carbon dioxide. Since the onset of the Industrial Revolution, there has been a huge spike of carbon dioxide measured in the atmosphere.

The main culprit is from carbon combustion, primarily through the creation of energy by burning coal, gas, and oil. Similarly, carbon combustion occurs through using petroleum products to power engines, in the case of automobiles, airplanes, and other transportation. By contrast, increases in methane and nitrous oxide are primarily the product of agricultural production and livestock rearing, as well as of fossil fuel use.

Figure 13.2 gives a breakdown of the main contributors to climate change.

Evidence of an Increase in Greenhouse Gases Since the Industrial Revolution

As noted, since the Industrial Revolution, the amount of carbon dioxide (and some of the other gases) has increased dramatically. Today, the world contributes about 10 billion metric tons of carbon per year into the atmosphere from fossil fuel use. Before the Industrial Revolution, that number was very small, and in 1900, the number was about 500 million metric tons. Figure 13.3 depicts the changes.

FIGURE 13.2

Global Greenhouse Gas Emissions by Gas

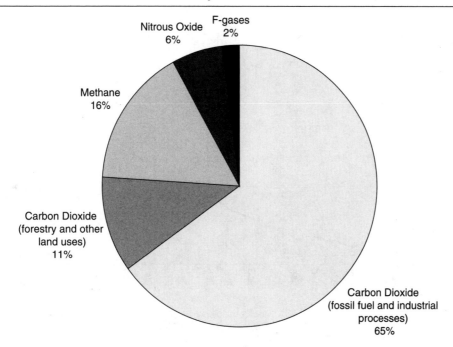

Source: Adapted from Environmental Protection Agency, "Global Greenhouse Gas Emissions Data," https://www .epa.gov/ghgemissions/global-greenhouse-gas-emissions-data.

Another way of measuring the overall contributions of greenhouse gases is through an index called the Annual Greenhouse Gas Index, which was developed at the National Oceanic and Atmospheric Administration (NOAA), which in turn has a global network of measuring stations and devices. The index creates a synthesis of the major greenhouse gases and reflects direct measurements of these. The result is expressed as net radiative forcing, relative to 1750 and to 1990, when the first climate change international treaty was created. The index shows a steady increase in overall forcing compared with the years 1750 and 1990. Indeed, since 1990 alone, the overall forcing increased about 40% compared with a 100% increase between the years 1750 and 1990. See Figure 13.4.

The NOAA index is just one measure. Authoritative data on climate change also emanate from the Intergovernmental Panel on Climate Change, or the IPCC, which provides technical support for the treaty designed to manage climate change globally. That treaty is called the UN Framework for Climate Change. On a regular basis, the IPCC releases reports that synthesize the work of hundreds of scientists. In 2013, the IPCC released its latest round of data.

The IPCC similarly calculates increases in radiative forcing by examining the contributions of different gases. Although the measure is different, the IPCC concludes that a significant increase in radiative forcing has taken place since the Industrial Revolution. The data again show a dramatic increase since 1750 but also a sharper increase in recent decades. In the IPCC's analysis, the increase

FIGURE 13.3

Global Carbon Emissions from Fossil Fuels, 1900–2014

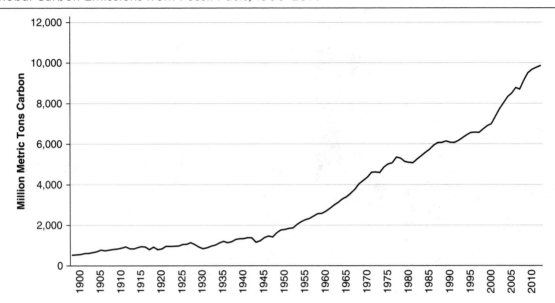

Source: Data are from T. A. Boden, G. Marland, and R. J. Andres, "Global, Regional, and National Fossil-Fuel CO2 Emissions," Carbon Dioxide Information Analysis Center, Oak Ridge National Laboratory, U.S. Department of Energy, Oak Ridge, TN, 2017. doi 10.3334/ CDIAC/00001_V2017. http://cdiac.ess-dive.lbl.gov/trends/emis/glo_2014.html.

in radiative forcing from human activity was roughly the same between 1750 and 1980 (a 230-year period) as from 1980 to 2011 (a 31-year period).[15]

Global Distribution of Drivers of Climate Change

Although climate change is a global phenomenon, the distribution of which countries contribute to the problem is uneven. The countries with the greatest levels of industrialization have contributed the greatest amount of greenhouse gases over time. In the contemporary world, that remains largely the case but with the exception of those countries with large populations that are experiencing rapid economic growth.

Today, in terms of total carbon dioxide emissions from fossil fuel burning, cement production, and gas flaring, China is the world leader, followed by the United States, India, Russia, Japan, Germany, Iran, Saudi Arabia, the Republic of Korea, Canada, Brazil, and South Africa. Of those countries, China and the United States stand out: China emits about 30% of the world total, the United States 15%.[16] The data can be visualized in Figure 13.5.

That said, the per capita amounts tell a very different story. With the world's largest population, China is the 48th largest emitter per capita of carbon dioxide, while the United States is the 14th. The top billings go to small countries: Qatar, Curacao, Trinidad and Tobago, Kuwait, and the United Arab Emirates.[17]

FIGURE 13.4

Increases in Net Radiative Forcing Since 1750

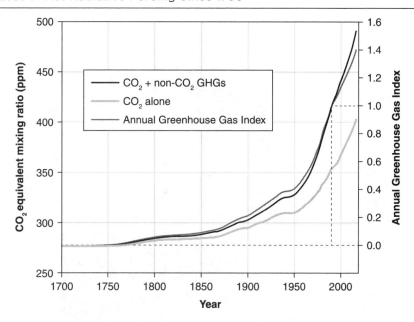

Source: NOAA, Earth System Research Laboratory, Global Monitoring Division, "The NOAA Annual Greenhouse Gas Index (AGGI), Spring 2017. https://www.esrl.noaa.gov/gmd/ccgg/aggi.html.

Note: This graph shows the steady acceleration in greenhouse gases in our atmosphere from the dawn of the Industrial Revolution to the late 1900s and a sharp escalation from 1990 to the present. The graph measures both the accumulation of atmospheric carbon dioxide (CO2) and also a broader "greenhouse gas index," which includes other gases besides carbon dioxide.

Evidence of Climate Change I: Temperature Change. The evidence of climate change is quite strong. The IPCC data on warming are particularly compelling. The report concludes that "warming of the climate system is unequivocal, and since the 1950s, many of the observed changes are unprecedented over decades to millennia. The atmosphere and ocean have warmed, the amounts of snow and ice have diminished, sea level has risen, and the concentrations of greenhouse gases have increased."[18]

According to the report, between 1880 and 2012, the warming of the Earth and ocean temperature is estimated to have increased by 0.85° Celsius. The report further finds that the Earth's surface successively warmed each of the last three decades and that the variability in weather patterns has also increased. Extreme weather events—such as monsoons, tropical storms, very heavy rains, and heat waves—are also likely to have increased since 1950.[19]

The report's figures demonstrate these weather patterns. Figure 13.6 compares annual average temperatures for land and ocean with a mean calculated from 1960 to 1991. They show quite clearly a significant increase in temperature, in particular, during the past 35 years.

Almost every world region has experienced average warming during the past 115 years. In some areas, however, the warming is more intense than in others, as Figure 13.7 shows.[20]

FIGURE 13.5

Global Carbon Dioxide Emissions From Fossil Fuel Combustion and Some Industrial Processes

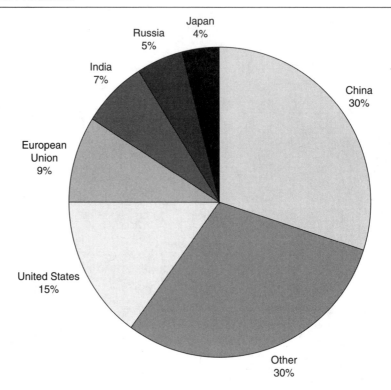

Source: Environmental Protection Agency, "Global Greenhouse Gas Emissions Data," https://www.epa.gov/ghgemissions/global-greenhouse-gas-emissions-data.

Other data sources show similar kinds of increases. The World Meteorological Organization found that 2015 and 2016 were the warmest years on record, with 2016 reflecting a 1.1° Celsius increase over pre-industrial levels.[21] The National Aeronautics and Space Administration (NASA) estimates that 2016 globally averaged temperatures were 0.99° Celsius warmer than mid-century.[22] NASA data also show a steady increase in global temperatures, with the greatest heating in and around the Arctic, South Pole, and equator.

See NASA's visualization of how the planet has warmed from 1880 forward at https://svs.gsfc.nasa.gov/vis/a000000/a004500/a004546/gistemp2016_5year_full_record_celsius_1080p.mp4.

Evidence of Climate Change II: Sea Levels, Glaciers, and Ice Sheets. Oceans are important to understanding overall climate patterns. Oceans store most of the world's energy. Rising temperatures are having a major impact on the Earth's oceans. In particular, sea levels are rising, and ocean water is becoming more acidic.

FIGURE 13.6

Evidence of Rising Land and Ocean Temperature, 1850–2012

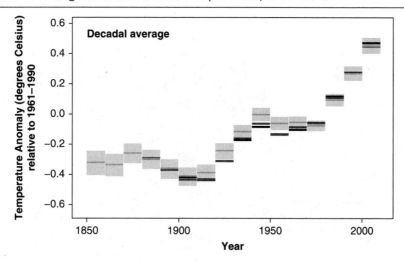

Source: Figure SPM1a. IPCC, Climate Change 2013: The Physical Science Basis: Contribution of the Working Group I to the Fifth Assessment Report of the Intergovernmental Panel on Climate Change (New York and Cambridge: Cambridge University Press, 2013), p. 6.

Note: This figure shows the average surface temperature of the Earth's land and ocean averaged across every decade since 1850. The figure shows clearly that the Earth's land and ocean surface temperatures are rising. Since 1980, the increase has been dramatic.

Sea levels rise from two main factors. The first is from increased temperature. As the ocean temperature rises, water expands. Scientists call this **thermal expansion**. The second is from melting ice and glaciers.

The data on changes to the oceans are compelling. The 2013 IPCC report concludes that the ocean's temperature is increasing, the sea level is rising, and glaciers and sea ice are decreasing. The IPCC concludes that "the rate of sea level rise since the mid-19th century has been larger than the mean rate during the previous two millennia."[23] See Figure 13.8.

The IPCC is not alone. The NOAA concludes that the rate of sea level increases has been faster in recent decades. In 2014, the global sea level was 2.6 inches higher than in 1993, and the average increase is about one eighth of an inch per year.[24] That is double the average speed from eight previous decades.[25]

A good portion of the rising sea level is due to increased water from melting glaciers and ice sheets. About 90% of the world's glaciers are shrinking. The two largest ice sheets are in Greenland and the Antarctic. Several major scientific studies show that both ice sheets are melting faster than at any other time in recorded history.[26]

Rising sea levels will have significant impacts on coastal areas around the world. A large portion of the world's population lives near a shoreline. Eight in 10 of the world's largest cities are near a coast, and rising sea levels could threaten those settlements, as well as the urban infrastructure that supports them. In addition, rising sea levels will increase the intensity of storm surges, as well as increase the frequency of flooding.

thermal expansion: expansion of water due to rising temperatures.

FIGURE 13.7

Observed Change in Surface Temperature 1901–2012

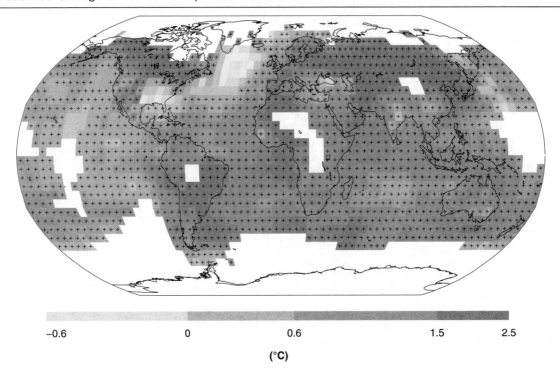

−0.6   0   0.6   1.5   2.5

(°C)

Source: Figure SPM1b. IPCC, Climate Change 2013: The Physical Science Basis: Contribution of the Working Group I to the Fifth Assessment Report of the Intergovernmental Panel on Climate Change (New York and Cambridge: Cambridge University Press, 2013), p. 6.

Evidence of Climate Change III: Precipitation and Extreme Weather Events. Other climatic changes are also in evidence. Changing temperatures affect precipitation patterns. The IPCC data show significant changes to precipitation patterns, with some areas receiving more average rainfall and others receiving less. Figure 13.9 looks at changing rainfall patterns during the past 60 and 100 years.

The IPCC report also finds that heavy precipitation events increased in the past 60 years, although it reports only low confidence of increase in droughts and tropical cyclone activity in the same period.[27] Heavy precipitation can translate into intense flooding, mudslides, and other events that have quite negative consequences for human settlements.

Climate change is also expected to make heat waves longer and more intense. One way to measure increased heat is to compare the number of record-setting hot days with the number of record-setting cold days. The number of hot days is significantly increasing. Since 1980, the number of areas of the United States that experienced very warm weather (greater than 90% compared with

FIGURE 13.8

Changes to the Ocean Level, Snow Cover, and Sea Ice

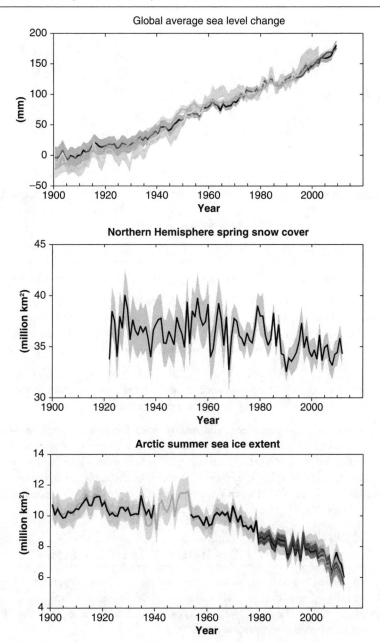

Source: Figure SPM3a,b,d IPCC, Climate Change 2013: The Physical Science Basis: Contribution of the Working Group I to the Fifth Assessment Report of the Intergovernmental Panel on Climate Change (New York and Cambridge: Cambridge University Press, 2013), p. 10.

FIGURE 13.9

Observed Change in Annual Precipitation Over Land

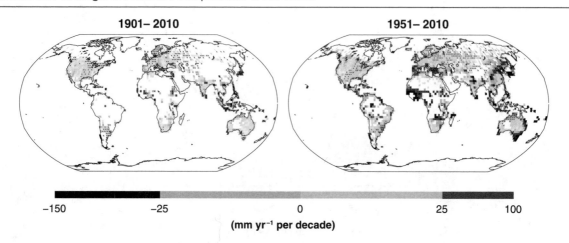

Source: Figure SPM2. IPCC, Climate Change 2013: The Physical Science Basis: Contribution of the Working Group I to the Fifth Assessment Report of the Intergovernmental Panel on Climate Change (New York and Cambridge: Cambridge University Press, 2013), p. 8.

averages in a given month) dramatically outpaced the number of very cold anomalies. In 2016, for example, 44% of the contiguous United States experienced a very hot June compared with 0% that experienced a very cold month. In 2015, the ratio was 39% to 1%. By contrast, in 1979, the ratio was 0% very hot areas and 15% very cold areas, again for June; and in 1978, it was 1% very hot and 0% very cold.

See NASA's data visualizer on record-setting hot and cold days in the United States at https://www.ncdc.noaa.gov/temp-and-precip/uspa/.

Climate change also affects wildfire frequency. Increased temperature means drier weather in many parts of the globe; it also can mean earlier snowmelts and more intense droughts. All of that contributes to increasing the flammability of certain areas, which has increased the frequency and duration of wildfires.[28] In the United States, for example, the average estimated area burned from wildfires in the early 1980s was less than 2 million acres; today that number has increased fivefold, according to the Environmental Protection Agency.[29]

PREDICTIONS ABOUT FUTURE CLIMATE CHANGE

What the future holds remains unclear. Future climate change depends to a degree on what changes occur between now and the period in question. Most forecasts look two to three generations out, to the year 2100. The consensus is that if no corrective measures are taken, the trends observed in recent decades will continue and intensify.

Globally, there is good reason to expect that the amount of greenhouse gases will increase, not decrease, over time. As readers of this book know, there is a dramatic climb out of poverty in some of the most populous countries of the world, in particular, in China, India, Brazil, Indonesia, Mexico,

Nigeria, and elsewhere. As people have more personal income, their per capita energy use likely will increase: They will want an automobile, a house with heating or air conditioning, a television, a computer, a cell phone, lighting for every room—items that most people in the United States, Canada, Europe, and Japan would consider baseline quality-of-life issues. Unless all that energy will be generated from renewable energy sources that do not contribute to greenhouse gas emission, such as solar, wind, and hydroelectric power, there will likely be a net contributor to climate change. In short, without a change in policy and/or technology, there is every reason to expect an intensification of greenhouse gases in the atmosphere and, hence, an intensification of climate change.

In practice, a continuation would mean an increase in intensity of all the changes outlined in the previous section: increased average global temperatures, a rise in sea level, warming of ocean temperatures, a decline in sea ice and glaciers, an increase in the acidity of ocean water, changes to precipitation patterns, an increase in severe weather events, longer heat waves, more wildfires, and more. The degree of change is in question.

To compensate for the uncertainty, the IPCC developed four main scenarios, known as **representative concentration pathways (RCPs).** These represent different scenarios for the concentration of greenhouse gases in the atmosphere by 2100.

One scenario (RCP 2.6) assumes a mitigation of greenhouse gases by 2100 with an average increase of 2° Celsius from pre-industrial times and about 1° Celsius from 2010. That is the optimistic scenario and target for many of the policy interventions described in this chapter. That scenario would see carbon dioxide concentrations stabilize at around 450 parts per million and then decline by the end of the century; given that the atmosphere has 400 parts per million, and adds 2 parts per million annually, a lot would need to go right for that scenario to come true.

representative concentration pathways (RCPs): models for predicting the severity of increase in greenhouse gases in the future.

FIGURE 13.10

Climate Models Predicting Future Changes in Temperature

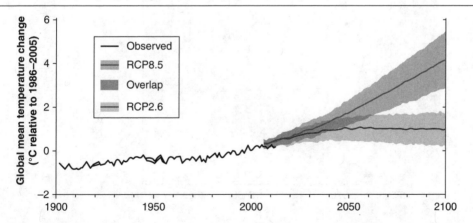

Source: Figure SPM4b. IPCC, Climate Change 2014: Impacts, Adaptation, and Vulnerability: Summary for Policymakers. Part A: Global and Sectoral Aspects. Contribution of Working Group II to the Fifth Assessment Report of the Intergovernmental Panel on Climate Change. New York: Cambridge University Press, pp. 10.

By contrast, the worst scenario (RCP 8.5) shows a predicted average increase of about 3.7° Celsius from 2010 levels or about 4.5° Celsius from pre-industrial levels. That scenario represents the path of no change or a continuation of the status quo without any concerted effort to reduce greenhouse gases over time. Figure 13.10 compares the two scenarios.

The predictions for changing sea level and the amount of sea ice are similarly dire. See Figure 13.11. Regarding sea level, the prediction under the worst scenario in the report is an average increase of 0.63 meters by 2100, or nearly two feet; under the best scenario, the predicted rise is 0.4 meters by 2100.

IMPACTS OF CLIMATE CHANGE

For many in the scientific community, the predicted impacts from climate change are alarming. The impacts will be wide ranging. Climate change will affect vegetation, animals, and human civilization in dramatic ways.

How dramatic will depend on which scenario comes true. If the worst scenario holds, and the temperature rises more than 4° Celsius by the end of the century, life as we know it is likely to change. An article in *New York* magazine, titled "The Uninhabitable Earth," looked at the worst-case

FIGURE 13.11

Climate Models Predicting Future Increases in Mean Sea Level

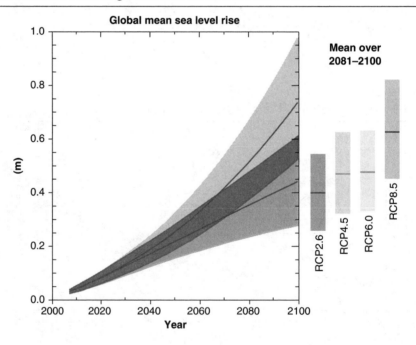

Source: Figure SPM9. IPCC, Climate Change 2013: The Physical Science Basis: Contribution of the Working Group I to the Fifth Assessment Report of the Intergovernmental Panel on Climate Change (New York and Cambridge: Cambridge University Press, 2013), p. 26.

scenario.[30] With a subtitle that read "Famine, economic collapse, a sun that cooks us: What climate change could wreak—sooner than you think" and an image of a baked skull, the article is terrifying to read. But whether the worst-case scenario will come to pass remains a question.

Next are some of the main areas where scientists expect there to be significant changes.

Effects on Flora and Fauna

Broadly speaking, changes in temperature, precipitation, and sea levels, among other effects of climate change, will have wide-ranging impacts on the conditions in which plants and animals survive. The International Union for Conservation of Nature is an international organization that focuses on species worldwide. The organization summarizes the key impacts of climate change as the following:

- A likely loss or degradation of habitat

- Changing environmental thresholds, such as temperature or water, beyond what species can tolerate

- Loss of key interactions between two unrelated species or the arrival of new, negative ones, such as diseases

- The disruption of environmental cues important for breeding or migration

- The direct loss of organisms[31]

Some species will be able to adapt to the change. They might migrate or find new patterns for survival. But for other species, the changes will spell extinction, in particular, for those species that cannot move or migrate easily.

Consider coral reefs. The National Ocean Service of NOAA calls climate change the "greatest global threat" to coral reefs. The effects on the ecosystem are multiple: increased heat leads to increased coral bleaching and infectious disease; increased sea levels lead to greater sedimentation and smothering of corals; stronger and more frequent storms destroy the reef structure; changing precipitation leads to more runoff and pollutants flowing into the sea; different ocean currents due to changing ocean temperatures will disrupt existing patterns; and ocean acidificiation could kill off plant and animal species.[32] Combined with fishing pressure and other changes, many corals are dying around the world and face severe risks of survival in the future.[33] Such a turn not only would be a tragedy for an extraordinary type of ecology but also would disrupt millions of people who depend on coral reefs for their livelihood.

Coral reefs are only one kind of fauna that are threatened through climate change. Indeed, climate change is likely to have vast impacts on a variety of different animal species. Bird and butterfly migrations, for example, are changing and likely to continue to change. Polar bears have become an iconic symbol of climate change. Polar bears are adapted to survive on sea ice that is rapidly disappearing as the globe warms, particularly so in the arctic. Indeed, the effects of climate change are likely to vary by species and ecosystem to which those animals have adapted. Some species will be able to change and adapt to new weather patterns and temperatures; others will not.

One study in the journal *Science* analyzed 131 published studies to generate a meta-prediction of the effects of climate change on species survival. The current extinction rate is about 2.8% of all species. Under the best scenario outlined earlier (RCP 2.6), which is the policy target of about

2° Celsius from pre-industrial levels, the extinction rate is likely to increase to 5.2%. In the worst scenario (RCP 8.5), however, which represents an unmitigated continuation of current trends, the extinction rate increases to 16%, or about one in six species on the planet today.

The extinction rates are not uniformly distributed. The worst risks are in South America, New Zealand, and Australia; the lowest risks are in North America and Europe. Those animals with smaller ranges—such as amphibians and reptiles—face the greatest risks.[34]

Climate change will also have major consequences on plant life. Many plants are sensitive to water and temperature. As precipitation and temperature patterns change, so will the ecosystems in which different plant species may survive. The climatic changes in turn will likely change the range in which different plant species can survive. The same is true for insects, as well as for parasites, as discussed in more detail shortly. The range of many insects and parasites depends on temperature level. As temperature warms, many insects and parasites that were once limited to tropical environments now can survive in other areas.

Effects on Human Settlements

Climate change will have wide-ranging effects on human settlements. Again, the scale of those changes will depend on how severe the average rise in temperature and the overall concentration of greenhouse gases will be.

Food. One of the major areas of concern is agriculture and, more broadly, food security. The World Food Program estimates that tens of millions of people could become food insecure in the next three decades. Many dimensions of climate change affect food production, availability, and access. Changing temperatures and rainfall patterns affect growing seasons, and in some cases, where crops are already difficult to grow, small changes can destroy plant production. Floods, heat waves, tropical storms, and other extreme events can wipe out or severely reduce the harvest in a given year. Many agricultural systems rely on runoff from glaciers. And in many areas of the world, crops are being grown on or near coastlines, which will be affected by increases in sea levels.[35]

As with many of the human effects of climate change, the risks are uneven. Some parts of the world—in particular, low-income countries that lack mechanized farming and irrigation methods—are particularly vulnerable.

See the World Food Program's Food Security and Climate Change interactive map to observe the risks under different climate scenarios around the world at http://www.metoffice.gov.uk/food-insecurity-index/.

Also true is that climate change could increase crop yields in some areas. The scientists, however, who wrote the IPCC report concluded that overall the number of places with decreasing yields will significantly outweigh those places with increased yields, as Figure 13.12 shows.[36]

Water. Climate change will also affect the availability of freshwater. Some areas of the world will become wetter, and some areas drier. Increased temperature will lead to more evaporation. More floods could deteriorate water quality. Declining snow cover and ice will affect freshwater availability in many parts of the world. Many of our existing water management systems, from dams and wells to sanitation systems, might be affected in ways that are difficult to anticipate.[37] The effects could be devastating.

FIGURE 13.12

Crop Yield Changes

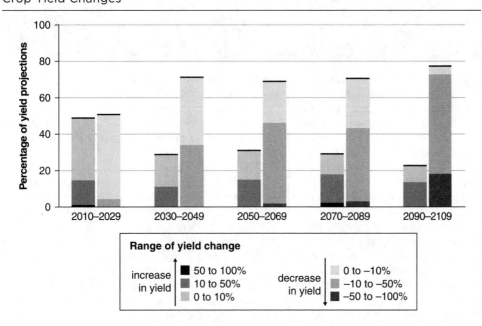

Source: Figure SPM7. IPCC, *Climate Change 2014: Impacts, Adaptation, and Vulnerability: Summary for Policymakers*. Part A: Global and Sectoral Aspects. Contribution of Working Group II to the Fifth Assessment Report of the Intergovernmental Panel on Climate Change [Field, C.B., V.R. Barros, D.J. Dokken, K.J. Mach, M.D. Mastrandrea, T.E. Bilir, M. Chatterjee, K.L. Ebi, Y.O. Estrada, R.C. Genova, B. Girma, E.S. Kissel, A.N. Levy, S. MacCracken, P.R. Mastrandrea, and L.L. White (eds.)]. New York, NY: Cambridge University Press, p. 18.

Consider the United States. According to the National Climate Assessment, an authoritative report, if climate change continues on the current path through 2050, an estimated 32% of all counties in the United States could face extreme water shortages (up from 10% today). Huge swaths of California, Texas, and Arizona, among other places, would be at risk.

See the National Climate Assessment webpage for insights into water supply issues at http://nca2014.globalchange.gov/highlights/report-findings/water-supply.

The United States is hardly alone. The IPCC estimates that some of the worst hit areas will be dry, subtropical areas. Water will become even scarcer in these areas, and its quality will also decrease.[38]

Migration. Migration is another concern. As sea levels rise, several coastal areas will likely become uninhabitable. Urban areas are expected to be particularly affected, in particular, by heat stress, heavy rains, coastal flooding, air pollution, and other issues. As documented elsewhere in the book, migration to urban areas has increased rapidly, in particular, in the developing world. But changes to urban areas from climate change may in turn pose intense risks to those in urban centers.

IS From the Outside-In

CLIMATE CHANGE, THE HIMALAYA MOUNTAINS, AND ACCESS TO CLEAN WATER

The peaks in the Hindu Kush Himalayan mountain region are not only sites of extraordinary beauty but also the primary freshwater source for some 1.3 billion people who live in South Asia and China. The mountains are crucial not only for drinking water but also for agriculture, industry, and the cultures of the area. The nickname for the Himalayas—the "Water Towers of Asia"—captures the centrality of the area for the most densely populated continent on Earth.

Yet climate change is posing a significant danger to the water supply. Across the Hindu Kush Himalayan mountain region, temperatures are rising faster than the global averages, and as a result, the glaciers that support freshwater are melting faster than they are being replenished. In addition, the weather patterns, in particular, around precipitation and monsoons are changing in duration, intensity, and predictability. That in turn is changing snow pack on the glaciers, as well as on water flows in the rivers of Asia.

The effects of these changes on the huge population in Asia is a subject of much concern. In addition to posing a long-term potential threat to water supply, the changes in water flow patterns will likely reshape agriculture, water management, and even health. In light of what appears to be a highly probable set of changes, much of the focus is on adaptation. Are there changes to water use, agriculture, sanitation, water delivery, energy consumption, and so on that can be made in anticipation of the likely changes to water supply?

Those questions are especially acute given that much of the population in the region is poor, and in general populations (and governments) with limited resources will have a difficult time with adaptation. Limited resources mean less opportunity for change and mitigation. The population is also quite diverse, ranging from mountain communities of Nepal, Afghanistan, and Bhutan, to massive dense urban spaces in India and China, to the delta or lowland regions in Bangladesh. These differences present a variety of different and difficult challenges. Large damming practices and other water use management practices further complicate the picture.

The risk that climate change poses to the communities that depend on freshwater from the Himalayas demonstrates some of the themes in this chapter. For one, climate change will have multiple, potentially devastating effects—on water, food, and human settlements. The challenge is pressing and deep. Two, there is a discrepancy between the human communities most affected and those most responsible for climate change. That creates tension and shapes discussion about efforts to cut greenhouse gases on a global scale. Three, in many ways, the management of climate change will turn out to be very local and bottom-up: How will farming communities plant? How will they anticipate and cope with severe weather? What kinds of adaptation will take place within families and communities? Through the prism of climate change, we see the ultimate outside-in force shaping and interacting with local, inside-out realities.

Reflect

In coming years, how might communities across Asia adapt to changes in access to freshwater because of climate change? What responsibility, if any, do those countries that committed the most to climate change have toward helping those communities in Asia adapt?

Sources: Shrestha, AB; Agrawal, NK; Alfthan, B; Bajracharya, SR; Maréchal, J; van Oort, B, eds., *The Himalayan Climate and Water Atlas: Impact of Climate Change on Water Resources in Five of Asia's Major River Basins.* ICIMOD, GRID-Arendal and CICERO, 2015 and BBC, "Himalayas: Water Towers of Asia," http://www.bbc.com/future/story/20130122-himalayas-water-towers-of-asia.

Some warn of "climate refugees," or people who will leave one county for another due to extreme weather events, rising sea levels, and broader patterns of environmental degradation due to climate change. That term, however, has largely fallen out of fashion. Migration may be one way of managing change, rather than being a type of forced displacement. Empirically, there does not appear to be large-scale relocations of populations yet due to environmental changes, and environmental changes seem more incremental push factors rather than sudden events, such as conflict.[39] In sum, migration is likely, but the idea of vast swells of environmental refugees is unlikely.

Conflict. The relationship to violent conflict is also complex. Some studies purport to show an increased risk of conflict due to changes induced through climate change.[40] Other studies, however, question these results, and social scientists argue that the causes of conflict are complex.[41] The IPCC concludes that evidence of a direct relationship is unclear but that climate change may exacerbate conditions that are linked to the onset of armed conflict, notably, poverty.[42]

Health. Health is another major concern. Air pollution might worsen as heat increases. Some extreme events, such as heat waves, pose clear and immediate risks, in particular, to the vulnerable. Decreases in food and water supply are also likely to have negatively affected human health. But some of the worst impacts may come in the form of infectious disease. Those parasites and insects that could not survive in colder climates are likely to expand their reach, as temperature rises. Malaria is a major concern, for example. Another major concern is that certain diseases that were frozen in the arctic might now be released as the areas thaw.

How all of these changes will unfold—from inundations, to food security, to clean water, to migration and health—are hard to predict. They depend a little on what changes occur over time and on how well humans adapt to the changes.

That said, one point of consensus is that the most vulnerable people and the poorest countries will likely suffer the most. They will have the fewest resources to adapt, and in many cases, the poorest people live in the most precarious habitats. In other words, there will be differential impacts of climate change. The World Bank estimates climate changes threatens to push 100 million people back into poverty.[43]

A way to observe the uneven distribution is to look at the capacity to respond as compared with the risks that are faced. At the University of Notre Dame, scholars developed the "Global Adaptation Index" to capture that differential. The index plots the degree of vulnerability and compares that with the degree of readiness to respond. The result is a map of the world that shows which countries are most at risk going forward. The net conclusion is that the risks fall disproportionately to countries in the Global South, which are precisely those countries that have contributed least overall to greenhouse gas emissions.

RESPONSES TO CLIMATE CHANGE: GLOBAL GOVERNANCE

Given its scale, climate change presents one of the most difficult governance challenges. Governments handle the issue at multiple and overlapping levels—from municipalities, to states and regions, to countries, to intergovernmental organizations.

United Nations Framework

At the international level, the principal policy is the **United Nations Framework Convention on Climate Change**. The Convention was adopted in 1992 at a world summit in Rio de Janeiro, Brazil, and today has near-universal ratification. Among other things, the Convention recognized climate change and established a goal to stabilize greenhouse gas concentrations in the atmosphere so as to prevent "dangerous anthropogenic interference." The Convention called on countries to monitor their emissions, and it called on some three dozen developed countries in particular to develop plans to reduce their emissions.

The initial document was followed by a set of negotiations that culminated in a second international agreement, known as the **Kyoto Protocol**, named for the city in Japan where the final round of negotiations occurred and where the language was adopted for ratification. In the Kyoto Protocol, which was adopted in 1997, countries pledged to reduce their emissions over a period of time—by 2012—to the levels below what they had in 1990.

A key aspect of the agreement, however, was that the three dozen countries named in the UN Framework Convention would take specific action to reduce their emissions below 1990 levels. The argument was that these countries had contributed more historically to producing greenhouse gases during the industrial period than had developing countries.

In practice, the Kyoto Protocol meant developed countries would commit to lowering their greenhouse gas emissions while developing countries would not. More specifically, the developed countries committed to lower their overall emissions by at least 5% below 1990 levels before 2012, but the exact number varied. For example, EU countries were supposed to reduce emissions to 8% below 1990 levels by 2012. The United States was to reduce by 7% below 1990 levels. By contrast, developing countries such as India and China did not have set standards, as they were seen not to have contributed that much to the gases that cause climate change.

The Protocol also established some market-based mechanisms. One was **Emissions trading**. A country that reduced its greenhouse gas emissions below its target could in turn sell an emissions credit to a country that did not. The main gas in question is carbon dioxide, and in effect the agreement established a "carbon market."

Another key innovation was the **Clean Development Mechanism**, which allowed a developed country to invest in a greenhouse gas reduction operation in a developing country, thereby reducing the developed country's overall burden of emissions reduction. These are often called "carbon offset projects" because an investment in one country can offset emissions in an other. Investment in renewable energy is one example—one country could help another establish a solar power facility. Another is reforestation in which one country would help plant large numbers of trees.

The Kyoto Protocols galvanized widespread ratification. Some 192 countries ratified the Treaty but not the United States. The major sticking point was the exemption to developing countries, which was opposed by labor and business, and the issue never came to a vote in the Senate (which is the legislative body that must ratify an international treaty in the United States).

Even though the treaty did not have strong punitive measures for not complying, the countries listed in the report as being required to reduce their emissions did. All but 9 of the 36 countries that participated in the Kyoto emissions reduction process met their goal of reducing the emissions by the target amount; the other 9 met their target amount through the market-based mechanisms described earlier.[44]

There is an amendment to the treaty called the "Doha Amendment," which elaborates a set of commitments for 2013–2020. This is known as the "Second Commitment" period, and countries broadly agreed to diminish their overall emissions to 18% below 1990 levels.

The next major breakthrough came in 2016 in Paris; the subsequent agreement is known as the **Paris Agreement**. The central innovation is to bring all countries into a common set of obligations to reduce greenhouse gas emissions. The agreement further sets as the global goal-reducing average to 2° Celsius below pre-industrial levels. Under the agreement, each party has its own national amount, or "nationally determined contributions," reflecting "its highest possible ambition." Those levels are still being established.

The crucial breakthrough is that the world's three greatest contributors to climate change—China, the United States, and India—each of which was not a part of Kyoto, all signed and ratified the treaty. The fourth largest individual contributor, Russia, did not. Since the treaty was ratified, however, the United States elected a president, Donald Trump, who has indicated he plans to withdraw from the agreement. At the time of this book's publishing, the fate of the Paris Agreement remains to be seen.

Paris Agreement: 2016 update to the Kyoto Protocol, which notably saw China, the United States, and India commit to reducing greenhouse gas emissions.

OTHER APPROACHES TO CLIMATE CHANGE

The UN Framework Convention and its derivatives are quintessential global governance solutions. The agreements aim to tackle an inherently global problem, climate change, through a shared set of goals and rules among the countries of the world. But as a global governance solution, the agreements are full of weaknesses. Different countries around the world have different levels of responsibilities, yet they are competing in a global marketplace. Even if countries of the Global North are disproportionately responsible for contributing to greenhouse gas concentration over time, the companies and workers in those places now compete with companies and workers located in the Global South. A differential environmental penalty on the Global North thus could hamstring those countries' economic prospects. At the same time, those countries have, until now, largely complied with the goals they set for themselves. The governments seem committed to addressing climate change, as are significant parts of their electorate.

Whatever the future holds for international treaty-based commitments, there are many approaches to climate change. These range from local- to national-level governance solutions. Municipalities or regions, such as states, have taken the lead in passing legislation aimed at addressing climate change. There is a whole range of measures that individuals can take to reduce greenhouse emissions, ranging from personal decisions to purchase electric cars, fly less, or install solar panels. The remainder of this section presents three broad responses to climate change.

Stabilization Wedges

One approach emphasizes **stabilization wedges**. Two Princeton University scholars developed the concept, which now additionally has support from major industry actors, such as Ford Motor Company and British Petroleum. Their organization is the Carbon Mitigation Initiative (CMI). The core idea is to promote a holistic, multi-effort approach. Each effort would be akin to a wedge in a pie, and taken together, the mixture of approaches could stabilize greenhouse gas emissions during the next 50 years.

stabilization wedges: idea of developing a set of specific approaches to stabilizing the amount of greenhouse gases in the atmosphere.

The proposal starts from the premise that we are on a path right now to double the amount of carbon from pre-industrial periods before the end of the century. Today there are more than 800 billion tons of carbon dioxide in the atmosphere (about 400 parts per million) compared with about 600 billion tons in the pre-industrial era (or 285 parts per million). The world currently produces some 10 billion additional tons of carbon dioxide annually. That number is likely to grow over time, such that within 50 years, the world might be producing closer to 16 billion tons per year, or more, if current trends continue (that is, under the scenario of no effective curbing of emissions). Through plant life and the oceans, the Earth absorbs about half of current carbon dioxide, which means that the net annual increase is about 4 billion tons of carbon dioxide. Doing the math, by the end of the century, the atmosphere could well have 1,200 billion tons of carbon dioxide in the atmosphere, which would be double pre-industrial levels.

The idea of a stabilization wedge is to develop different initiatives that each would reduce carbon emissions by about 1 billion tons of carbon dioxide. Taken together, the 8 to 10 wedges would total 8 to 10 billion tons of carbon dioxide per year, which would stabilize emission levels at current rates. After that period of stabilization, then the world would look to develop technologies that would permit an overall reduction.

Figure 13.13 shows the basic concept. The dotted line represents the current trajectory of emissions. The orange triangle represents the overall contribution between now and 2060 if current trends continue. By contrast, each gray line represents a "stabilization" wedge that taken together would limit the overall emissions level to what we have currently. (This graph assumes an annual increase of 8 billion tons of carbon per year, while the latest figures suggest the annual increase is about 10 billion.)

The organization divides the different available strategies into four major categories: electricity production, heating and direct fuel use, transportation, and biostorage. According to them, 15 strategies are currently available. We will look at three examples.

On transportation, for example, the CMI argues that increasing average fuel efficiency to 60 miles per gallon would account for one wedge. In CMI's estimate, a typical car has a fuel efficiency standard of 30 miles per gallon and is driven 10,000 miles per year, emitting a ton of carbon into the atmosphere annually. With about 600 million passenger cars in the world today, the expectation is that there will be two billion by 2060. If fuel efficiency were to change to an average of 60 miles per gallon, that would reduce future emissions by about 1 billion tons of carbon per year.

On energy, coal burning for energy production accounts for about one quarter of all carbon emissions. Should all coal energy plants double their efficiency—through better turbines, for example—that could account for a wedge. Alternatively, if wind energy would start to replace coal burning through an additional million windmills, that too would account for a single wedge.

Last, a wedge could be achieved through increasing the amount of vegetation that could remove carbon in the atmosphere through photosynthesis. Scientists call existing forests "natural sinks." A wedge could be achieved through halting deforestation or through increasing the amount of forest cover in the world. Through forest planting alone, about an area the size of the contiguous United States would need to be planted to achieve a wedge.[45]

Adaptation

adaptation:
process by which people and governments anticipate and prepare for the effects of climate change.

The concept of **adaptation** emerges from the reality that some aspects of climate change are irreversible, at least in the short term. Although globally the goal may be to mitigate climate change through a reduction in greenhouse gas emissions, the climate is already changing, and even

FIGURE 13.13

Stabilization Wedge

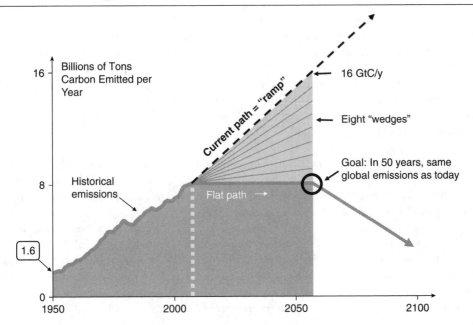

Source: Princeton University, Carbon Mitigation Initiative, "Stabilization Wedges Slides & Graphics," http://cmi
.princeton.edu/wedges/slides.php.

if the optimistic scenarios come true, the net average increase in temperature will be 1.5° Celsius. In practice, that will mean sea level rise, changes to precipitation, changes in agriculture, more extreme weather events, and all the other changes described in this chapter. Rather than simply being overtaken by these changes, many people, organizations, and governments are anticipating these changes and preparing for them. The broad umbrella concept under which these changes are grouped is adaptation.

Adaptation could take many forms. If the concern is about drought, farmers could introduce drought-resistant crops or rotate their tilled land in different ways. If the concern is about irregular rainfall, then farmers might find ways to capture and store rain when it does fall, or to irrigate. If the concern is sea level rise, then cities and countries might invest in greater seawall protection, such as storm surge barriers. Individuals might put their homes on stilts to anticipate greater ocean flooding. Governments might change zoning laws to require residents to build new homes at a greater distance from the shoreline. If the concern is increased risk of freshwater flooding, then governments could reinforce dams and levees. They could also manage water flows in reservoirs differently. They could raise the height of bridges. They could also look to widen rivers in certain places to avoid breaching. If the concern is about how increased frequency of extreme heat waves will affect the vulnerable, such as older persons, then additional monitoring systems could be put in place.

Indeed, there are many small and large changes that individuals and governments could undertake to anticipate climate change and try to manage its risks.

Large-Scale Climate Interventions

carbon dioxide removal: projects that would remove carbon dioxide from the atmosphere.

Yet another approach is to consider very large methods and technological solutions to climate change. These are often grouped under the heading of "geo-engineering" solutions to climate change, although the concept of "engineering" is probably misleading given the uncertainties involved.

The two broad approaches would either reduce the amount of carbon in the atmosphere or reflect sunlight before it reaches the Earth. The former is often called **carbon dioxide removal**, which focuses on ways to remove carbon directly from the atmosphere. This could take the form of reforestation and increasing natural sinks. But this could also take the form of chemical engineering to remove carbon dioxide from the atmosphere. Some examples include fertilizing the ocean with nutrients that would absorb more carbon. Another example is direct carbon capture from the air through chemical applications.

solar radiation management: measures that would reflect heat-causing light back into the atmosphere.

The latter approach is **solar radiation management**. The idea here is to reflect back into space the light that otherwise would heat the Earth. One example is the injection into the stratosphere if aerosols that would reflect back sunlight. Another example is brightening low-level clouds through sea-salt particles, which would also reflect back sunlight.

Although some of these solutions are appealing, they raise numerous concerns. One is cost—the interventions are very expensive. Another is effectiveness. How well each would work remains a subject for discussion. Yet another concern is the introduction of new environmental risks that could result from injecting, for example, aerosols into the atmosphere.[46] As a result, many scientists are quick to point out that these large-scale interventions are not a good solution for the problem of climate change. The best approach remains mitigation.[47]

CLIMATE CHANGE AND CROSS-CUTTING GLOBAL FORCES

Climate change is one of the most important, yet difficult, challenges facing the world today. In contrast to other global challenges, the issue has several specific difficulties. One is the issue of time. Because there is a lag between when emissions occur and when the effects of those emissions are likely to happen, the short-term pressure to take action is diffuse.

Another issue is geography. Broadly, those who contribute to the problem are not necessarily those who will suffer the most. The most developed countries of the world are those that have contributed most. But most modeling suggests that the poorest countries and the poorest people within countries are the most vulnerable to the effects of climate change. That means that the incentives to change fall the least hard on those who contribute the most to the problem.

A third issue is globality. Greenhouse gases do not stay within national boundaries. The problem requires global cooperation. If the European Union were to cut all carbon emissions by 2060, climate change would not stop as long as other countries persisted with the current status quo. That means that for there to be any real traction on the issue, you need a global, concerted effort—and achieving a global consensus of action. Yet countries have very different perspectives on this issue. Countries that are rapidly developing do not want to be hamstrung, given that their competitors in the global marketplace did not have the same restrictions when they were developing. But the same argument applies to those countries that are developed: They are still competing in a global marketplace and do not want any new disadvantages. These headwinds are what made the Paris Agreement such a landmark achievement that beat the odds (see Figure 13.14).

The global forces at the heart of this book help us understand these headwinds. The power of the *global market* clearly shapes climate change politics. Companies and states compete in the global market. If one company faces higher costs from climate change policy—through a carbon tax or some other tax on emissions—then that is a competitive disadvantage. Yet the differential contributions to climate change over time provide companies based in lower income countries with a powerful argument for why richer countries should shoulder a heavier burden. The challenge that markets pose to global cooperation may be overcome, as they were in Paris in 2015, but they remain a drag.

Global governance is fundamental to addressing climate change. Because climate change is an atmospheric problem and because its effects are transnational, countries must work together to address the problem. More broadly, climate change is such a large issue that nongovernmental actors, corporations, and governments across all levels are likely to be part of any solution.

The growth of large, developing countries is a key story line in climate change. For one thing, as citizens in China, India, Brazil, Indonesia, South Africa, and other countries increase their household income, they are likely to want the comforts of industrialization that are likely to contribute to greenhouse gas emissions. They will want personal cars, home climate regulation, air travel, and many other pleasures that those in richer countries have enjoyed for years. Moreover, the rising powers are not likely to accept limits on their growth that could potentially keep them from achieving their potential. From their perspective, the imposition of restrictions could unfairly constrain their economic expansion while locking in inequalities that already exist in the world order. The bottom line is that any solution to climate change must include the rising developing countries. They need to be part of, and now are, any global climate change agreement, and they must not see climate change policy as inimical to their economic potential. Already those changes appear to be happening. Even though China is the world's leading emitter of carbon dioxide, China is emerging as a world leader in renewable energy, such as solar paneling. With China's size and continued anticipated growth, the fate of the world's climate is related to how much of that country's energy consumption will come from renewable sources.

FIGURE 13.14

Global Forces, Interactions, and Tensions: Problems in Managing Climate Change

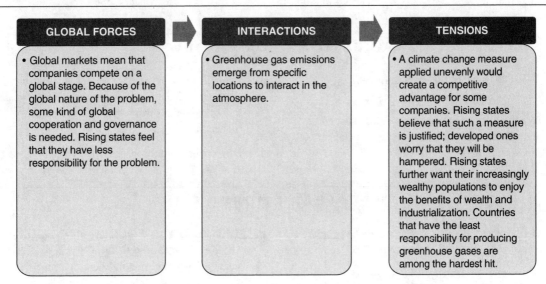

GLOBAL FORCES	INTERACTIONS	TENSIONS
• Global markets mean that companies compete on a global stage. Because of the global nature of the problem, some kind of global cooperation and governance is needed. Rising states feel that they have less responsibility for the problem.	• Greenhouse gas emissions emerge from specific locations to interact in the atmosphere.	• A climate change measure applied unevenly would create a competitive advantage for some companies. Rising states believe that such a measure is justified; developed ones worry that they will be hampered. Rising states further want their increasingly wealthy populations to enjoy the benefits of wealth and industrialization. Countries that have the least responsibility for producing greenhouse gases are among the hardest hit.

SUMMARY

The facts around climate change can be incredibly dispiriting. The Earth is warming; sea levels are rising; extreme weather events are increasing in frequency and intensity; and the path to change faces very strong headwinds. The impacts on humans, as well as other animal and plant species, are likely to be severe. As authors of this book, we do not want to paper over that reality. At the same time, the chapter aims to give you a primer on climate change. You should know what it means, what drives it, how it works, and what its likely effects will be. Climate change as a concept and reality can feel overwhelming. After you have read the chapter, we hope you feel that you can approach the topic, ask questions about it, and learn more.

Climate change also is a global challenge that illustrates the international studies framework. The gases that give rise to climate change are the product of millions of interactions, ones that start with individuals within states and accumulate in the atmosphere to affect in turn other parts of the globe. We again see here inside-out and outside-in forces at work. Global tensions are rife in this area. Many countries that had little to do with causing climate change face some of the worst consequences, yet those countries that contributed do not want to impose restrictions that would hamper them and their citizens in a global market. Climate change is also likely to disrupt food production, water access, and other essential livelihoods, which in turn will create both local and transnational tensions. How the world has and can respond to this global challenge has everything to do with global governance, global markets, and shifting centers of power globally—three key themes in this book. In sum, we hope the chapter inspires you to learn more and to develop some analytical tools to help you understand the challenge at hand.

KEY TERMS

adaptation 386
carbon dioxide removal 388
Clean Development
    Mechanism 384
climate change 366
emissions trading 384

greenhouse effect 367
Kyoto Protocol 384
Paris Agreement 385
radiative forcing 368
representative concentration
    pathways (RCPs) 377

solar radiation management 388
stabilization wedges 385
thermal expansion 373
United Nations Framework
    Convention on Climate
    Change 384

QUESTIONS FOR REVIEW

1. What are some of the main causes and consequences of climate change?

2. What are some of the main ways that states and individuals may counter and respond to climate change?

3. What are some of the main reasons why climate change is such a difficult issue on which to generate a global consensus that would lead to stronger cooperation?

4. How do global forces shape climate change?

LEARN MORE

Elizabeth Kolbert, *The Sixth Extinction: An Unnatural History* (New York, NY: Henry Holt, 2015).

Bill McKibben, ed. *The Global Warming Reader: A Century of Writing About Climate Change* (New York, NY: Penguin Random House, 2012).

Naomi Oreskes and Erik Conway, *The Collapse of Western Civilization: View From the Future* (New York, NY: Columbia University Press, 2014).

Joseph Romm, *Climate Change: What Everyone Needs to Know* (New York, NY: Oxford University Press, 2016).

Explore the data at the Intergovernmental Panel on Climate Change: http://www.ipcc.ch/.

Explore Stabilization Wedges and Play the Stabilization Wedge Game: http://cmi.princeton .edu/wedges/.

Look at NASA's Global Visualization for Climate Change: https://svs.gsfc.nasa.gov/vis/a000000/ a004500/a004546/gistemp2016_5year_full_record_ celsius_1080p.mp4.

NOTES

1. AsianCarp.org, "Asian Carp Response in the Midwest," http://www.asiancarp.us/faq.htm.

2. Ben Guarino, "Australia Is Battling a Killer Toad by Turning the Frog's Own Toxin Against It," *Washington Post*, June 14, 2016. https:// www.washingtonpost.com/news/morning-mix/ wp/2016/06/14/australian-is-battling-a-killer-toad- by-turning-the-frogs-own-toxin-against-it/? utm_ term=.ed8396b89657 and "The Biological Effects, Including Lethal Toxic Ingestion, Caused by Cane Toads (*Bufo Marinus*), April 12, 2005, http://www .environment.gov.au/biodiversity/threatened/key- threatening-processes/biological-effects-cane-toads.

3. FAO, Sustainable Development Goals, Conserve and Sustainably Use the Oceans, Seas, and Marine Resources," http://www.fao.org/sustainable- development-goals/goals/goal-14/en/.

4. Alkaly Doumbouya et al., "Assessing the Effectiveness of Monitoring Control and Surveillance of Illegal Fishing: The Case of West Africa," *Frontiers in Marine Science* 4 (2017), 1–10.

5. Andrew Jacobs, "China's Appetite Pushes Fisheries to the Brink," *New York Times*, April 30, 2017. https://www.nytimes.com/2017/04/30/world/asia/ chinas-appetite-pushes-fisheries-to-the-brink.html.

6. In addition to the FAO, the environmental NGO Greenpeace has made overfishing a theme: http://www.greenpeace.org.uk/what-we-do/ oceans/overfishing/, as has the international organization International Union for Conservation of Nature: https://www.iucn.org/news/ secretariat/201701/overfishing-threatens-food- security-africa%E2%80%99s-western-and-central- coast-many-fish-species-region-face-extinction- %E2%80%93-iucn-report.

7. Gerardo Ceballos, Paul R. Ehrlich, and Rodolfo Dirzo, "Biological annihilation via the ongoing sixth mass extinction signaled by vertebrate population losses and declines," *PNAS* 2017.

8. Joseph Romm, *Climate Change: What Everyone Needs to Know* (New York, NY: Oxford University Press, 2016), 2.

9. Elizabeth Kolbert, *Fieldnotes From a Catastrophe: Man, Nature, and Climate Change* (New York, NY: Bloomsbury, 2007), 164.

10. Romm, 2016, 9.

11. IPCC, 2013, 17.

12. Romm, 2016, 1.

13. Intergovernmental Panel on Climate Change (IPCC), *Climate Change 2013: The Physical Science Basis: Contribution of the Working Group I to the Fifth Assessment Report of the Intergovernmental Panel on Climate Change* (New York, NY, and Cambridge, U.K.): Cambridge University Press, 2013), 35.

14. E. A. G. Schuur et al., "Climate Change and the Permafrost Carbon Feedback," *Nature* 520, no. 7546 (2015): 171–179.

15. IPCC, 2014, 14.

16. Data from the Carbon Dioxide Information Analysis Center, "Fossil-Fuel CO2 Emissions by Nation," http://cdiac.ornl.gov/trends/emis/tre_coun.html.

17. Data from Carbon Dioxide Information Analysis Center, http://cdiac.ornl.gov/trends/emis/top2014.cap.

18. IPCC, 2013, 4.

19. IPCC, 2013, 5.

20. IPCC, 2013, 5.

21. World Meteorological Organization, WMO Statement on the State of Global Climate in 2016, WMP-No. 1189, 2017.

22. NASA Scientific Visualization Studio, "Five Year Global Temperature Anomalies From 1880 to 2016," https://svs.gsfc.nasa.gov/cgi-bin/details.cgi? aid=4546.

23. IPCC, 2013, 11.

24. NOAA, "Is Sea Level Rising?" https://oceanservice.noaa.gov/facts/sealevel.html.

25. Romm, 2016, 4.

26. Romm, 2016, 4–6.

27. IPCC, 2013, 7.

28. Romm, 2016, 45.

29. Environmental Protection Agency, "Climate Change Indicators: Wildfires," https://www.epa.gov/climate-indicators/climate-change-indicators-wildfires.

30. David Wallace-Wells, "The Uninhabitable Earth," *New York Magazine,* July 9, 2017. http://nymag.com/daily/intelligencer/2017/07/climate-change-earth-too-hot-for-humans.html.

31. ICUN, "Climate Change," https://www.iucn.org/theme/climate-change.

32. NOAA, "How Does Climate Change Affect Coral Reefs?" https://oceanservice.noaa.gov/facts/coralreef-climate.html.

33. Terry P. Hughes et al., "Coral Reefs in the Anthropocene," *Nature* 546 (2017): 82–90. See also Andrew D. King et al., "Australian Climate Extremes

at 1.5° C and 2.0° C of Global Warming," *Nature Climate Change* 7 (2017): 412–418.

34. Mark C. Urban, "Accelerating Extinction Risk From Climate Change," *Science* 348 (2015): 571–573. http://science.sciencemag.org/content/348/6234/571/F2.

35. World Food Program, "Climate Impacts on Food Security and Nutrition: A Review of Existing Knowledge," 2014. https://www.wfp.org/content/climate-impacts-food-security-and-nutrition-review-existing-knowledge.

36. IPCC Working Group II, 2014, 19.

37. Bryson Bates et al., "Climate Change and Water," IPCC Technical Paper VI, 2008.

38. IPCC Working Group II, 2014, 14.

39. IPCC Working Group II, 2014.

40. Solomon Hsiang and Marshall Burke, "Climate, Conflict, and Social Stability: What Does the Evidence Say," *Climactic Change* 123 (2014): 39–55.

41. H. Buhaug et al., "One Effect to Rule Them All? A Comment on Climate and Conflict," *Climactic Change* 127 (2014): 391–397.

42. IPCC Working Group II, 2014, 772–773.

43. World Bank Group, *Climate Change Action Plan 2016–2020* (Washington, DC: World Bank, 2016).

44. Igor Shishlov, Romain Morel, and Valentin Bellassen, "Compliance of the Parties to the Kyoto Protocol in the First Commitment Period," *Climate Policy* 16 (2016): 768–782.

45. Roberta Hotinski, "Stabilization Wedges: A Concept and a Game," 2015. http://cmi.princeton.edu/wedges/pdfs/teachers_guide.pdf.

46. O. Boucher et al., Summary of the Synthesis Session in IPCC Expert Meeting Report on Geoengineering in O. Edhofer et al., eds., IPCC Working Group III Technical Support Unit, Potsdam Institute for Climate Impact Research, Potsdam, Germany, 2015.

47. Romm, 2016, 163–169.

Global Food

HOW CAN WE SOLVE WORLD HUNGER?

Mall in Jakarta

Wikipedia user Jonathan McIntosh, https://commons.wikimedia.org/wiki/File:Mall_culture_jakarta90.jpg. Licensed under CC BY 2.0, https://creativecommons.org/licenses/by/2.0/legalcode.

LEARNING OBJECTIVES

After finishing this chapter, you should be able to:

- Identify the main factors behind the 2007 Global Food Crisis.

- Articulate the three major theories of global food control.

- Link the theories of global food control to the food versus fuel debate.

- Distinguish between the food security and food sovereignty approaches to hunger.

- Undertake a commodity chain analysis of one globally traded food.

Imagine you are standing up to your chin in a pool of calm water. So long as the water is calm, you breathe freely. But with only a slight ripple, the water starts to rise and fall around you. As the ripple gets higher, you breathe only intermittently. If the water rises only half a centimeter, you drown. Living with your head just barely above water is what it is like to be food insecure. Poor people in all countries, but especially in least developed countries, spend such a large share of their income on food that only a slight change in food prices can send them tumbling into extreme and fatal poverty.

In Figure 14.1, for example, we see that Nigerian households, on average, spend over 50% of their consumer expenditure just on food. We also see this statistic varies across the Global South, but generally in wealthier

FIGURE 14.1

Food Expenditure Across Countries

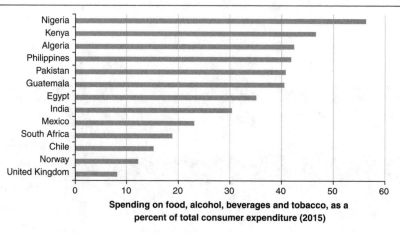

**Spending on food, alcohol, beverages and tobacco, as a
percent of total consumer expenditure (2015)**

Source: Adapted from Economic Research Service, United States Department of Agriculture.

countries, people spend less on food as a share of their income. In the United States, the share of income people spend on food has declined from 18% in 1960 to about 10% today, yet the poorest fifth of households spend over one third of their income on food.[1] With a slight change in the global price of oil or maize, food-insecure families are forced to choose between food today or vaccines tomorrow, food today or school fees next year, or food today or electricity next month.

Notes: This photo accompanied a story in *The Boston Globe* in 2015. The photo shows a food vendor in Tahrir Square in Cairo, Egypt, selling bread in the midst of the 2013 protests. The reporter quotes a retired Air Force general as saying: "The only thing we really need to worry about is a revolution of the hungry. That would be the end of us." Food prices were a causal factor in the Arab Uprising.

KHALED DESOUKI/AFP/Getty Images

The mental image of a food-insecure person barely keeping his or her head above water is important for understanding what happened when global food prices skyrocketed in 2007. Droughts in grain-producing countries such as Australia and India reduced global supply and thus increased prices, while rising oil prices meant an increased cost of agricultural inputs such as fertilizers and transportation. The deeper causes (explored later in the chapter) included rising food consumption in expanding Asian economies, the use of crops for biofuels rather than food, and speculation by hedge funds. By the end of 2007, the prices of wheat, milk, and meat had doubled while rice had reached a ten-year high (see Figure 14.2).

The immediate effect of the food crisis was on people's health, but soon politics and society were impacted. As staple foods such as maize and rice grew rapidly in price, outraged and impoverished people demanded a solution. Brazil and Argentina banned the export of rice.[2] Even COSTCO and Sam's Club in the United States limited how much rice a customer could buy.[3] Just three years later, food prices spiked again (see Figure 14.3). The effects proved even greater this time. In the Middle East and North Africa, protests and riots over food prices were a major contributor to the multicountry social movement for reform that became known as the Arab Uprisings.

This story of food insecurity, global hunger, and social turmoil is perhaps the most important aspect of food. But food is of interest to international studies for other reasons, too. For example, we are beset on all sides with impassioned pleas about food. Some books and movies alert us to the dangers of a global population that cannot feed itself, while others implore us to think and eat locally, organically, and sustainably. Anthropologists would argue that these pleas not only tell us about our globalized world but also help to create it.[4] Local festivals that celebrate the international or the global play this role. Ask yourself: If you are invited to an "international festival" next weekend, what

FIGURE 14.2

Timeline of the 2007 Global Food Crisis

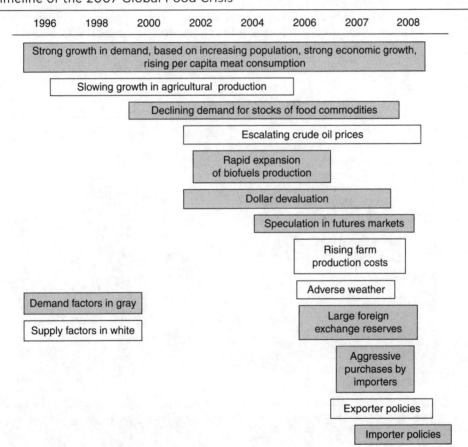

Source: Reproduced with permission from the International Food Policy Research Institute www.ifpri.org. The original figure is available online at http://ebrary.ifpri.org/utils/getfile/collection/p15738coll2/id/5724/filename/5725.pdf.

would you expect? High on your list is likely eating some international food. This is one way we think of ourselves as global citizens, by "consuming globalism." Events such as food festivals help us imagine, or construct in our minds, a world of food, which in turn makes it possible for us to act globally. Lynne Phillips argues that "food has been, and continues to be, central to the production of a global imaginary."[5] The "global consumer" eats international foods. The "modern farmer" uses advanced technologies and sells on global markets. The "modern company" has a flexible workforce and a globally diverse supply chain.

Food is thus another way that we re-create our social world. It not only reflects our global era but also constitutes Intergovernmental organizations (IGOs) play a role here. For example, when the Food and Agriculture Organization (FAO) publishes a report on boosting farm incomes in poor countries, it does so using scientific language. This enables it to appear politically neutral, as though no value judgments went into their ideas. But none of our decisions are politically neutral. For example, if an IGO said that genetically modified seeds could help poor farmers, but they did not discuss how they might affect power relations between men and women, one could say the IGO is making, however intentionally, a decision *not* to talk about gender inequality. The larger point for us is that IGOs, and "science" itself, can be used to create the idea of "global food" and "modern agriculture" in our minds.

FIGURE 14.3

Prices of Cereals and Oil, 2003–2009

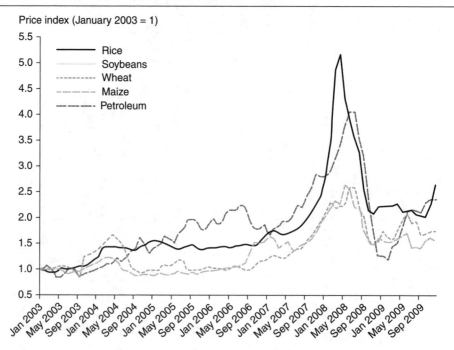

Source: Reproduced with permission from the International Food Policy Research Institute www.ifpri.org. The original figure is available online at http://ebrary.ifpri.org/utils/getfile/collection/p15738coll2/id/5724/filename/5725.pdf.

This chapter is organized around a series of questions, and we use the example of the 2007 Global Food Crisis to illustrate the tensions in global food. First, is there enough food? We will learn about the relationship between global population growth, food, and hunger. Second, why do famines occur? We will learn that famines have less to do with a lack of food and more to do with an inability of powerless people to access food. Then we will ask, how do we ensure humanity has enough to eat? We will learn about two distinct approaches to this challenge. Although the food security approach emphasizes boosting the productivity of farms, the food sovereignty approach emphasizes people's control over their food sources. This will bring us to the fifth question, who runs global food? We will learn that multinational corporations (MNCs) are the most important actors, although there are notable civil society and intergovernmental organizations. Finally, we will bring this material together with a case study of one global commodity chain: chocolate.

GLOBAL HUNGER AND A GROWING POPULATION: IS THERE ENOUGH FOOD?

The world's population has grown sevenfold in the past 200 years. As it keeps growing, will we have enough food for us all? Englishman Thomas Malthus (1766–1834) was among the first to write about the relationship between population growth and the food needed to sustain it. He observed that populations grow faster than the supply of food, yet the human population still exists. Why does this not lead to mass hunger? According to Malthus, individuals were responding to economic incentives: As food supplies went down, food prices went up, so families had fewer children and consumed less. Mass hunger would not occur since on the grounds of pure logic there could not be a point where there were more humans than there was food to support them.

Unfortunately, Malthus is invoked more often than he is read. A common misreading critiques him for assuming that the availability of food will not increase, while family sizes will not decrease. Of course, average family size has gone down over the past century while food availability has gone up. Humans have not been as reproductive as Malthus thought, while farms and fisheries have become more productive. The average number of children a woman has today is about half what she had about 200 years ago. This trend means Malthus's population-to-food tension is attenuated. Today, a person arguing that the world may run out of food would be called a neo-Malthusian, which is a sort of intellectual insult. For example, Paul Ehrlich's *The Population Bomb*[6] is a neo-Malthusian work that warned of mass starvation due to population growth. But this is a common misreading of Malthus because he did not predict that humans would run out of food. On the contrary, where Malthus went wrong is assuming that the population growth will move in tandem with the availability of food. But this is not the case. The United States, for example, produces more food than it needs and exports (or wastes) the rest. Japan is an even better example, with a very low birthrate.

Read "Can Planet Earth Feed 10 Billion People?" by Charles Mann.[7]

In the 1950s and 1960s, solutions to global hunger focused on family planning—which mostly meant birth control—and farm productivity. These solutions were technical. Poverty and hunger in the world's poorest countries was understood as rooted in the low productivity of farms. In the few decades after World War II, foreign aid (i.e., international development) focused heavily on rural livelihoods and on improving farming practices including equipment, seeds, and practices. **Food aid** became a part of foreign aid. The U.S. Food for Peace program provided food aid to billions of people worldwide. It began as a program to donate surplus food from the United States. The U.S.

food aid: type of Official Development Assistance (aka foreign aid) in which the donor country gives food to a recipient country.

government used the program to help other governments that would side with the United States against the Soviet Union.[8]

In the 1970s, many intellectuals and academics challenged the view that global hunger resulted from overpopulation. People such as Susan George and Frances Moore Lappe advanced the idea of **Food First**: Hunger was not about overpopulation but about inequality and power. Whereas the West blames poor countries for their supposed "overpopulation," in fact, global food is controlled by Western governments and corporations, while the agricultural and family policies in developing countries were often rooted in the colonial period. Food First advocates pointed to the demographic transition as a key piece of evidence against Malthus. The demographic transition shows that birth rates overwhelmingly decrease as populations industrialize and urbanize. The Food First argument also maintained that **Malthusian** ideas were a kind of victim blaming.

Although many countries were crippled with food insecurity, a group of Western and Asian scientists helped to birth revolutions in agricultural productivity in Asia. During the period now known as the **Green Revolution**, farmers used new high-yielding seeds that had been developed in laboratories.[9] An important actor was a network of research bodies spread throughout the world known as the Consultative Group on International Agricultural Research (CGIAR). Through its branches throughout the world, and in partnership with governments and philanthropic foundations, CGIAR developed and disseminated new agricultural techniques as well as new seed varieties. By the late 1960s, countries such as the Philippines were using high-yielding varieties of rice in about half of their fields and the country achieved self-sufficiency in rice production.

Into the late 1970s, Asia's Green Revolution increased food security in the region. But most developing countries did not experience a Green Revolution. By the early 1970s, many had spent years receiving food aid. The vulnerability of these countries was laid bare when a lower value of the U.S. dollar meant U.S. grains became cheaper for consumers in other industrialized countries, and grain companies could now charge more in the face of demand from wealthier customers. Between 1972 and 1974, the Soviet Union purchased record amounts of American grain, which dramatically increased prices worldwide. Developing countries that had become used to low-priced staples thanks to food aid suddenly could not afford it. Poor countries suddenly faced higher prices for imports of food. Matters were compounded when the price of oil also went up. To have enough foreign exchange to afford oil imports, many poor countries made it more expensive for their citizens to import food.[10]

IS From the Outside-In

DID POPULATION GROWTH CAUSE THE GLOBAL FOOD CRISIS?

Although the rate of population growth has declined in recent decades, the absolute number of humans is only projected to increase, while the long-term trend in agricultural production is flat when compared with long-term trends in demand.[11] The amount of global land currently under harvest has not changed much, and the growth in yields for grains and oilseeds has been low.[12] For these reasons, observers pointed to the central roles played by populous China and India in creating intense demand for food. Scholars have alerted us to the significance of the development with titles such as *Who Will Feed China?*[13] and *Will Africa Feed China?*[14] But not everyone finds the argument convincing. Headey and Fan point out that China and India are largely food secure and do not rely on significant imports of food.[15] Indeed, of the top 10 countries to have increased cereal demand the most in the 2000s, none are in Asia.[16]

Reflect

Where would you rank the importance of population growth as a contributing factor in the Global Food Crisis, relative to the factors such as biofuels and global finance discussed in the other boxes in this chapter?

Here we see major international studies concepts laid bare: interactions between states, markets, and regions, driven by political, technological and economic forces, with resultant tensions between wealthy and poor countries.

Explore this National Geographic interactive on global food consumption.[17]

This section tried to answer a basic question: Is there enough food in the world? The share of humanity that suffers from hunger has declined in recent decades, even though it spikes with occasional crises (see Figure 14.4). Economic growth over the past 50 years has seen hundreds of millions of people move out of the ranks of the world's poorest, especially in places like China. Although food has travelled long distances for thousands of years, what is new about the modern period is the variety of food, the distance traveled, the role of MNCs as the key actors in global food chains, and the dominance of liberal market-based approaches to the trade in food. In the next section, we will ask, if there is enough food in the world, why do famines occur?

FIGURE 14.4

Undernourishment Is Declining

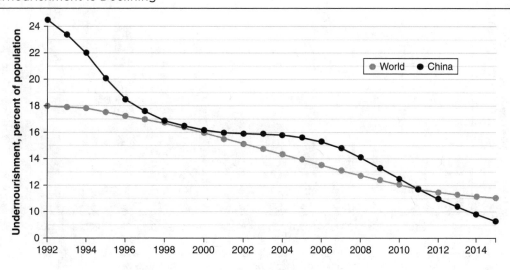

Source: Human Progress. Data from https://unstats.un.org/unsd/mdg/Data.aspx

IF THERE IS ENOUGH FOOD, WHY DO FAMINES OCCUR?

famine: severe and prolonged hunger over a large area, leading to deaths of 2 to 5 per 10,000 people as a result of starvation or hunger-related diseases.

Famine is our most tragic image of hunger.[18] Famines kill people as well as entire communities. Famines seem even more tragic in the modern period since the world produces far more than enough food. But if there is enough food, why do famines occur?

The most important social science on famines was conducted by Indian economist Amartya Sen. He showed that famines are not the result of a bad harvest or low yields. Famines even occur where there is enough food. Sen showed that famines are fundamentally political. They result from failures of government and of civil society. Factors such as low rains, high oil prices, or population pressure might make a famine more likely, but the crucial factor is the action or inaction of people in power. In modern history, famines in China (1959–1961, possibly the largest in history), the USSR (1932–1933, 1946–1947), Ethiopia (1983–1985), and South Sudan (2011–2017) had less to do with "too little food" and everything to do with government behavior.

For example, consider the Irish famine. In 1845, a fungus arrived in Ireland that attacked the potato. Thanks in part to British colonial agricultural policies, and to the suitability of the land for growing the potato, Irish communities were more reliant on potatoes for food than were other Europeans, so the potato blight had a disproportionately devastating effect. In the decade that followed, Ireland lost one third of its population: 1 million people died from starvation and disease,

FIGURE 14.5

Deaths From Large Famines, 1900–2010

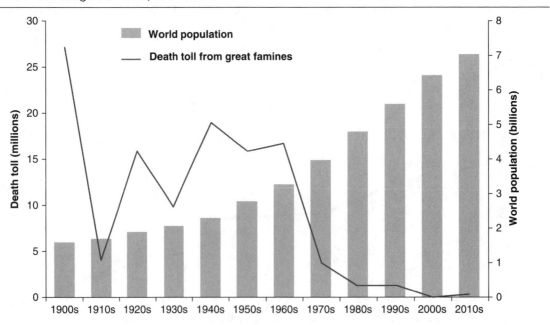

Source: Reproduced with permission from the International Food Policy Research Institute www.ifpri.org. The original figure is available online at http://ebrary.ifpri.org/utils/getfile/collection/p15738coll2/id/129681/filename/129892.pdf.

and 2 million emigrated.[19] But throughout the entire period, Ireland *exported* food to Britain. Most land was used to grow wheat, oats, and barley for export. The British government would not allow those crops to be diverted from their intended use—exports—and domestic wages had not been able to keep up with rising food costs. Thus, the Irish Famine, like others that followed, had little to do with a lack of food and much more to do with a combination of government action and inaction.[20]

We see in Figure 14.5 that deaths from major famines have declined in recent decades. Sen pointed to a free media and democratic accountability as the key to that decline. Democratic accountability allows people to punish governments for bad behavior, while civil society in the form of free media keeps people informed and tells the world about the suffering of famine victims.

REDUCING HUNGER: FOOD SECURITY OR FOOD SOVEREIGNTY

Although famines may be less common than we imagine, hunger is widespread: the United Nations (UN) estimates that over 800 million people go hungry in a given year, and this is related to the 155 million children younger than 5 who suffer from stunted growth.[21] Three groups are especially vulnerable to food insecurity.[22]

The first is traditionally marginalized groups, such as the young, older persons, and the disabled, as well as ethnic, religious, or sexual minorities. These groups are often at the mercy of the behavior of the majority of society that is able-bodied, working age, and included in their society. The second group is wage earners since these people are removed from the food they need to eat. This likely includes anyone you know who receives a paycheck, including you. Wage earners rely on markets to function, governments to govern, and farms to produce. Small changes in far corners of the world, such as inflation in Japan, lower oil exports from Venezuela, or more meat consumption in China, can affect how much of that wage can be spent on sufficient and nutritious food.

The third vulnerable group is small family farms, known as **smallholders**.[23] Of the 570 million farms in the world, more than 90% are family farms.[24] Family farms cultivate about 75% of the world's farmland and produce about 80% of the world's food: 80% of the world's farms operate on less than two hectares (about two soccer fields). So, when we speak of global food, our image should be of a small family farm.

Although small family farmers enjoy the mutual trust of a family business and have greater control over their nutrition than wage earners, these farmers are vulnerable in three ways. First, if important family members get sick, there is rarely anyone to replicate their labor or knowledge. The second challenge is market access. Smallholder farmers are often unable to take advantage of high global prices for their goods. Consumers in Detroit may be willing to spend heavily on quinoa, but a quinoa grower in rural Bolivia may not have the knowledge of the U.S. market, the means to transport the produce, or a financial institution to provide credit. Third, smallholders are at heightened vulnerability to climate change. Crop yields in Sub-Saharan Africa are projected to decline 15% to 20% by 2050 if nothing changes.[25]

So how can we ensure that all people, especially these marginalized groups, have secure nutrition? In this section, we will discuss two broad answers to the problem of global hunger. The first, **food security**, is the dominant way of thinking about global hunger among the major players: powerful states and IGOs involved with hunger, including the World Bank, International Monetary Fund (IMF), World Trade Organization (WTO), and the UN. It stresses improving the productivity of farms in developing countries, often with the use of intensive farming techniques and **genetically**

smallholders: small family-run farms.

food security: approach to global food and hunger that emphasizes boosting the productivity of farms through use of genetically modified organisms and consolidation of small farms. Associated with Bill Gates.

genetically modified organisms (GMOs): crops that have been engineered to tolerate herbicides, droughts, or insects. Actors in the food security approach are optimistic about GMOs.

modified organisms (GMOs), and managing global food in a way that enhances safety and affordability while interfering minimally with markets. The second, **food sovereignty**, is associated with Raj Patel and Vandana Shiva and is critical of the role of corporations in global food.[26] It seeks to give small farmers greater control over their own production and markets. Whereas food security is about secure *access* to food, food sovereignty is about *control* over one's food.[27]

Food Security

The food security approach to hunger emphasizes the productivity of small farms. The fact that so many of the world's farmers are smallholders is a double-edged sword. On the one hand, having control over one's source of nutrition can play a significant part in avoiding hunger. Half of the global population who suffer from hunger are on small farms, so improving the condition of small farms generally could be good for all. On the other hand, local and global food security is threatened precisely because the people upon whom we rely to produce the food are themselves suffering from deprivations.

Policy makers and researchers in the food security model tend to view small-scale farmers in developing countries as composed of two groups. The first is farmers who are slightly more efficient, interested, and committed to farming than other farmers. The second is farmers who feel trapped in the rural sector, and who should be helped to leave their farms and move to urban areas. A statement from the International Food Policy Research Institute (IFPRI) makes this clear:

> Public policy should support small family farms in either moving up to commercially oriented and profitable farming systems or moving out of agriculture to seek nonfarm employment opportunities.[28]

What would such policies look like? First, farmers need functioning private property systems to buy, sell, or rent land. This is more difficult than it may sound. It assumes an administrative competence that many governments do not have. Land must be accurately divided into defined lots, and there must be a system of certification and credentials that is widely respected and upheld. The politics is even more difficult. Millions of farmers could mean millions of land disputes, all contributing to a combustible mixture that could be easily sparked. The actors engaged in certification of ownership and transfer need to be respected and effective. The farmers need access to credit to buy or rent. They need opportunities in the nonfarm sector. This means not only decent jobs, but also schools, health facilities, religious acceptance, decent housing, and so on.

Those who remain farmers need better information about weather and market risks. This typically involves providing the kinds of public data that we

Courtesy of Jennifer Abrahamson/Landesa™ Rural Development Institute

TABLE 14.1

Two Views on Genetically Modified Organisms (GMOs)

The Food Security View	The Food Sovereignty View
GMOs can increase the productivity of family farms.	Critics of GMOs make several arguments:[29]
• By creating crops that resist insects, farmers can decrease the amount of chemicals needed to manage pests.	• The evidence that GMOs significantly increase yields is weak.
• Only GMOs can massively increase yields, which are needed to feed rapidly growing populations.	• The major challenge in the future is extreme heat from climate change, and there has been little evidence that GMOs can help with that.
• There is little to no scientific evidence that GMOs are a health risk. If there were a risk, critics would still need to factor in the risk to the world in *not* using GMOs.	• Nonorganic and industrial farms that use GMOs are actually accelerating climate change.
• The Green Revolution kept billions from starving, and would not have happened without GMOs.	• GMOs lead to "superweeds" that result in yet more chemicals to deal with new problems.
• GMOs could be especially beneficial to countries with climates or geographies that are unsuitable for farming.	• Monocultures, chemical fertilizers, and pesticides destroy biodiversity.
• GMOs allow farms to be more productive with less labor, which frees labor to work in nonfarm sectors like manufacturing.	

take for granted, such as timely and reliable weather forecasts, news on forthcoming laws, and international prices. It also means insurance markets must be able to appropriately price the risk at a level that enables farms to thrive. In some cases, it involves active government intervention to stabilize prices. Last, all concerned need public services. For example, urban areas that attract more families need improved waste disposal. Families that stay to farm more intensively will need improved access to rural schools.

Food Sovereignty

The food sovereignty model challenges the food security approach. Among its advocates are a large number of small-scale actors, including peasant and landless farmers and farm workers, women, youth, and indigenous communities. Although "the food security model is founded on, and reinforces, a model of globalization that reduces human relationships to their economic value ... the food sovereignty model considers human relations in terms of mutual dependence, cultural diversity, and respect for the environment."[30] For example, Brazil's Landless Workers Movement consists of over one million landless workers. Since the 1970s, they have peacefully occupied unused land where they engage in small-scale family farming. The movement has helped hundreds of thousands of families gain titles to their land. That legal recognition comes after years of economic and political forces engaging in coercion and violent confrontation. Now the Movement runs banking and food cooperatives, food processing plants, and environmental projects.

Watch "The Farming Movement Changing the Face of Brazil" at https://www.youtube
.com/watch?v=7Ro5opqu2Js.

Food sovereignty often adopts a human-rights approach to hunger. Advocates cite the ideas of German philosopher Thomas Pogge, who wrote about human rights in terms of negative duties. Human rights are composed of positive rights, such as the right *to* shelter, as well as of negative rights, such as the right to be *free from* religious persecution. Pogge argued that if wealthy countries, through their behavior domestically or internationally, are infringing on people's negative rights, they are denying people their fundamental human rights. Thus, if our actions affect the ability of a person to be free from hunger, we are engaging in a violation of basic human rights.

Food sovereignty is an argument for local control of production, distribution, and consumption. But it is also nonlocal in pushing for international and global change in how common resources such as water are managed. It also has a cultural component. Rather than reducing food to a matter of calories, as the food security idea does, the food sovereignty movement acknowledges that some foods are culturally significant to some societies.

The food sovereignty movement also challenges the food security idea that human progress is better served when people compete rather than cooperate. In farming, the obvious distinction is between large private companies and small family farms. Family farms are often more efficient because the workers know and trust one another, so there is less slacking or stealing. Small-scale farming is labor-intensive and brings together community members at various stages of production, distribution, and consumption. Indeed, farming is much more than the economy in agrarian societies. It provides order and social stability, continuity in traditions and cultural practices.

An example of the social and cultural importance of food is the Mexican tortilla. Maize has been central to indigenous communities for several thousand years. It is part of Mexican identity the way pasta is to Italians or hamburgers are to Americans. After World War II, the Mexican government protected maize producers and linked them to Mexico's cultural resilience as well as to its poverty reduction policies. People understood there was a market for maize, but it was not simply viewed as a commodity, something that could be easily quantified and substituted for commodities of equal value. It had *added* value, beyond the price the world market would set for it. But government control and growing industrial production of flour meant that flour tortillas began to overtake the traditional corn (maize) tortilla. In the 1980s, the country went through a debt crisis followed by structural adjustment that plunged millions more into deeper poverty.

iStock/grandriver

The leading flour tortilla producer, *Maseca*, was politically influential and in the 1980s received huge sums in government support. This cost the Mexican consumer, and the growth of *Maseca* put many small tortilla vendors out of business. Small-scale maize producers and tortilla vendors were further damaged when Mexico joined NAFTA, and cheap corn flooded the Mexican market. Since joining NAFTA in the mid-1990s, Mexico has seen several million farmers leave their land because they cannot compete with heavily subsidized American corn.[31] The decline in Mexican maize is not merely an economic phenomenon. It is tied to, and reflects, major changes in Mexican society.

Although food security activists such as Bill Gates warn that critics of GMOs are ideologues more than scientists,[32] food sovereignty activist Vandana Shiva calls Gates "the greatest threat to farmers in the developing world."[33] She argues that the Gates Foundation is too closely aligned with global agribusiness such as Monsanto, firms that directly threaten the ability of smallholders to own their own livelihoods and to engage in nonindustrial agriculture (see Table 14.1).

Many observers worry about the global growth in industrial farms since they create dependence among countries and families. Countries become vulnerable when agricultural production is centered in just a few countries. Families become **food insecure** when they are forced from their land to make way for mega-farms, as they have in Brazil. The interactive nature of global forces, and the unintended outcomes, are fully on display here:

- Global markets reward countries and farmers who produce more soybeans for biofuel.

- Governments and farmers (big and small) clear land to produce more soybeans.

- Less productive farmers become landless.

- They are pushed toward cities where they join masses in slum-like settlements, or they are pushed into less productive land.

- Their arrival stresses the farm families already on that land.

This process of forcing poor farming communities off their land is often called **de-peasantization**. De-peasantization explains how it is that a country can produce more food while seeing greater numbers of its people go hungry. This can happen because large productive farms necessarily involve many small-scale farmers leaving their land and, thus, losing access to their livelihood. Although subsistence farming might not make a family rich, it will guarantee that they will have something to eat.

Other observers worry about the political economies of biofuels in poor countries. As biofuel industries grow, so does the political power of the biofuel producers. Biofuel corporations thus come to have disproportionate political power in developing countries. Critics see this as another way in which developing countries are inserted into the global economy in ways that hurt them.

One of the most important recent events in the food sovereignty movement is *La Via Campesina* ("The Way of the Peasant"). It is a transnational advocacy network and international social movement dedicated to making global food systems work for the poor. Officially founded in 1993 with major conferences every four years, its members are small- and large-scale farmers. They advocate for changes to the production and distribution of food at national and international levels. Rather than seeing farms in poor countries as the key to feeding the world, the food sovereignty movement recognizes that much poverty is in rural areas, such that farms that can feed themselves will do much to alleviate global poverty. Movements such as *La Via Campesina* tend to be skeptical of the roles played by free trade, GMOs, and multinational agribusiness.

Read "The New Scramble for Africa" by the NGO Global Justice Now at http://www .globaljustice.org.uk/infographics/new-scramble-africa-food-monsanto-syngenta-yara/ index.htm.

Peasant and smallholder farmer movements have now spread to countries around the world, such as India (*Navdanya*), Zimbabwe (*Zimbabwe Small Holder Organic Forum*), Haiti (*Papaye Peasant Movement*), Madagascar (*Coalition Paysanne de Madagaskar*), East Timor (*Movimentu Kamponezes Timor Leste*), and Thailand (*Assembly of the Poor*). But these movements are not confined to poor

food (in)secure: defined by the 1996 World Food Summit as existing "when all people, at all times, have physical and economic access to sufficient, safe and nutritious food that meets their dietary needs and food preferences for an active and healthy life."

de-peasantization: as poor people are forced from their land and farms consolidate, they lose control of their nutrition even while the country's farms become more productive.

The 2000s was the decade in which **biofuels** took off. Governments of large economies such as Canada, China, Brazil, the EU, and the United States introduced biofuel standards for cars and other automobiles. But biofuels are controversial because they divert food for people into food for fuel. Policies to promote biofuels led to about one third of U.S. corn and EU rapeseed being diverted from food to fuel.[34] In the mid-2000s, 70% of the increase in global maize production went to ethanol.[35] Biofuel expansion is projected to increase the number of people at risk of hunger. The reason poor countries are so vulnerable is that they tend to be net importers of food. The poor are also vulnerable since they spend a larger share of their income on food and are more reliant on staples like grains and tubers than rich countries.[36]

Many reports linked the growth of biofuels to the surge in food prices around 2007–2008. Philip McMichael refers to the growth in biofuels as a "blunt reminder of the extent to which capitalism externalises its costs."[37] To externalize the costs of something means someone else pays for it. McMichael critiques biofuels for "commodity fetishism," meaning the idea that a commodity can be accurately priced without taking into account social or environmental impacts. For critics like McMichael and Walden Bello, it is useful to ask who stands to benefit if the world continues to embrace biofuels.[38] The answer for them is obvious: Western governments and corporations.

Yet others argue that biofuels were not the major contributor to the Global Food Crisis. They point out that biofuels create major export opportunities for developing countries. For example, Malaysia's palm oil is exported to Europe and the United States to be converted into biofuel. This helps Malaysia earn foreign exchange, and it does so with a crop that emits fewer greenhouse gases than biofuels such as corn. Moreover, the impact of biofuels on global food varies by crop and location. [39] The impact of Brazil's sugarcane ethanol on global food prices is likely smaller than the impact of U.S. corn.

Nevertheless, the environmental impact of biofuels is hotly debated. Although biofuels can produce energy, they also consume energy in that very production process. There have also been several cases of massive deforestation to clear the way for biofuel crops. For example, much of the palm oil exported from Malaysia is grown in areas where rainforests once stood.[40] This is important because one justification for biofuels is that they are more environmentally friendly because they do not burn fossil fuels. The burning of biofuels and fossil fuels both result in CO_2 emissions, but emissions tend to be lower for biofuels because biofuel feedstock uses atmospheric carbon to grow plant material. Thus, it remains to be proven that biofuels constitute a win–win rather than simply asserting it.

This gets to the heart of the **food-versus-fuel debate**. The question at hand is whether more harm is done when food is consumed as fuel rather than as nutrition. On balance, research makes clear that there are trade-offs when food is converted into fuel, but there is no consensus on the extent to which biofuels alone can be linked to changes in food prices or food security.

biofuels: fuels used in transport that are made from biomass materials, that is, dead plants or animals. Common biofuels include ethanol and biodiesel.

food-versus-fuel debate: debate on the economic, environmental, and human welfare consequences of using food for purposes other than human consumption.

Reflect

How would you rank the importance of biofuels as a contributing factor in the Global Food Crisis, relative to the factors such as population growth and global finance discussed in the other boxes in this chapter?

countries. The "slow food" movement has spread throughout industrialized countries. It emphasizes the social and environmental sustainability of locally grown, seasonal, and organic foods. It seeks to relink in the popular imagination the dinner table to the soil from whence the food came, and the role of the farmer as an important member of his or her community.

Read the debate: Can Biotech Food Cure World Hunger?[41]

WHO RUNS GLOBAL FOOD?

So far, we have read about the global production of food and debates surrounding famine and hunger. In this section, we will learn about the actors that matter most in global food. We will read about three theories—realism, liberalism, and structuralism—that offer different answers to the question, who runs global food? Understanding which actors matter most will help us determine in whose interests global food works. The first theory we will read—realism—says powerful states dominate global food, and that other actors such as corporations are of secondary importance. By contrast, the second theory—liberalism—will point to national and international state and nonstate actors, such as farmers' associations, multinational corporations, or intergovernmental organizations. And finally, the third theory—structuralism—will argue that food is just one of the many ways in which Western/northern states have historically dominated today's poor countries.

Realists: Powerful States Run Global Food

The United States constitutes 60% of global maize exports and 25% of wheat and is the world's third largest soybean exporter. This means that events within the United States, such as weather shocks, policy changes, or consumer behavior, all exert a powerful influence on global markets. Other actors matter, such as IGOs, multinational corporations, and civil society, but these actors are all secondary to the power of states. States regulate their own economies in ways that affect their domestic food, and to the extent that global food is at all regulated, it is so at the hands of states since they ultimately govern IGOs (see Table 14.2).

TABLE 14.2

Intergovernmental Organizations in Global Food

Intergovernmental Org	Affiliate/Parent	Based	Created	Staff[42]
Food and Agriculture Organization (FAO)*	United Nations	Italy	1946	3,500
World Food Programme (WFP)*	United Nations	Italy	1963	12,000
Agriculture and Rural Development (ARD)	World Bank	USA	1946	500
International Fund for Agricultural Development (IFAD)		Italy	1978	500
Consultative Group on International Agricultural Research (CGIAR)		USA	1971	8,000

* The Food and Agriculture Organization is the main IGO involved with global food systems. It focuses on hunger, nutrition, and agricultural development. The WFP is the main IGO concerned with food during humanitarian crises, such as war or cyclones.

Source: Organization websites.

Food also matters for international security, and realists say states care first and foremost about their security. A state that is reliant on another state for its food supply may be vulnerable to changing policies in that country. Or a state may be a food producer by way of having its farms and food supply controlled by foreign actors. For example, the Committee on Foreign Investment in the United States has the legal power to stop international business deals that raise national security concerns. Committee members include representatives from the Homeland Security and Defense departments, and its deliberations are confidential. In February 2016, the Committee ended an attempt by China's Unisplendour Corp. to buy a $4 billion stake in disk drive maker Western Digital Corp.[43] But that same year, the Committee approved a $43 billion takeover by state-owned ChemChina of the seed giant Syngenta. Outside of wealthy countries such as the United States, there are usually about 50 countries that are net importers of food, which means they import more than they export.[44] These food importers are vulnerable to forces they cannot control.

In the face of internationally competitive markets, states often protect their own farmers from imported food, or they try to increase the productivity of their farms. Consider biofuels. When oil prices spiked in the 1970s, energy importers sought protection from future shocks. In Brazil, the government expanded the sugarcane sector in the late 1970s through the use of subsidies as well as through an increased ethanol content of gasoline. Ethanol-powered cars were introduced in the 1980s using technology from public research universities. Global demand for ethanol increased in the 2000s, while Brazilian consumers added to the demand since they could choose between gasoline and ethanol at the gas station for their flex-fuel vehicles.[45]

In the United States, policies since the late 1970s have encouraged ethanol. These include subsidies for blending ethanol into gasoline, insured loans for ethanol producers, federal purchase agreements, and a tariff on imported ethanol.[46] In the 1990s, the government introduced fuel economy standards, and in the 2000s when a particular gasoline additive was banned, ethanol became more attractive once more for consumers and producers. Federal mandates in 2005 and 2007 set targets for the use of ethanol over coming years.

Other countries export more than they import, and thus, they have a major effect on the global price of food. Examples include land-abundant countries such as Australia, Brazil, and Canada. They affect the global supply of food not only through production but also by the extent to which they subsidize or protect their farmers. For example, a sugar beet farmer in the United States may receive a subsidy from the federal government. This would allow the farmer to sell his produce more cheaply than he could without the subsidy. The effect on global food might be to push down prices, but sugar beet producers in smaller countries will not be able to compete with the subsidized (i.e., artificially cheap) produce from U.S. farmers. Consumers in other countries might benefit from lower cost sugar, but their own farmers may suffer. In addition, American taxpayers would suffer since their money is what is used to subsidize their own sugar beet farmers.

Realists say that the real reason global trade negotiations have slowed in recent years is due to agriculture: Developing countries want access to food markets in industrialized countries. But states are frequently reluctant to open foreign access to their markets, especially in the case of food. Food is a security issue for states. Even if trading $1 of my corn for $1 of your paint makes economic sense, many states would still not engage in the trade because food occupies a special place in security. In a time of crisis, my country would not survive for long if I had moved my infrastructure (corn silos, fertilizer tractors, crop irrigation technology) out of the corn sector. According to realists, states understand this vulnerability and are thus reluctant to be cooperative with other countries on matters of food.

Liberals: States and Nonstate Actors, Local and Global, Run Global Food

Liberals think states are important actors in the world but that states are not the only actors that matter. Domestically, liberals point to interest groups, such as farmers or agribusinesses. Internationally, they point to IGOs, MNCs, and global civil society.

How do those actors interact? Consider the history of domestic politics in U.S. agriculture.[47] The role of the federal government in agriculture expanded dramatically with the Agricultural Adjustment Act of 1933. The Act was intended to limit the output of farms and, thereby, to keep prices artificially high. This would be bad for consumers since food would be more expensive than it would be without the Act, but it would be good for farmers. To compensate farmers for preventing them from producing as much as they would like, the government introduced price controls to boost farming incomes. But price supports only incentivized farmers to produce more from the land they were allowed to farm, and farm yields increased dramatically. The result was food surpluses, which were used in the Cold War to reward friendly governments. Thus, not only were U.S. consumers hurt, so were farmers in other countries who could not compete with cheap U.S. imports.

In *The Politics of Food Supply*, sociologist Bill Winders explains how a coalition of cotton, corn, and wheat producers was an important constituency for this agricultural policy.[48] Republicans were split in the decades after World War II between pro-market ideologues and producers from the country's Wheat Belt. Republicans in the Wheat Belt had shared economic interests with Democrats in the cotton-producing American South in having the government protect them from market forces. This coalition between cotton and wheat producers, which bridged the Republican and Democratic parties, had a major impact on the governance of global food. These interests lobbied the U.S. government when negotiating World Trade Organization deals to protect the ability of the U.S. government to subsidize agricultural exports.

Things changed when corn interests became more powerful than the cotton and wheat coalition. U.S. corn was competitive on global markets, so corn producers preferred less intervention from the U.S. government. Livestock producers also favored less government involvement since artificially low corn production meant artificially high prices, and corn was an important food for the livestock industry. The protectionist coalition between cotton and wheat producers began to fall apart as one of the partners—southern plantation owners—lost political power as America entered a post–Civil Rights era. Corn was now opposed by a wheat–cotton coalition that was falling apart.

Winders's explanation gets at the heart of the interactive nature of international studies. Wheat and cotton producers had long had a shared interest and shared ability to bend government policies in their favor. But as Southern plantations turned into large successful commercial farms, some Southern farm labor moved out of the South while many left behind became wage laborers. This changed the racial and class composition of America's North and South. Black voters became more significant forces in Southern politics and changed the face of the Democratic Party. Southern farmers began to diversify away from cotton. By the 1980s, poultry was the major commodity in the South. Thus, cotton was losing its power. Corn (and livestock) recorded a major victory in 1996 when Congress reduced limits on production.[49] But the subsidies that make American agriculture artificially cheap on global markets remained.

Structuralists: Global Food Is Characterized by Systemic Inequalities

Structuralists see historical continuities in global food and hunger. The exploitation of poor countries' commodities, including food, is a fundamental fact of colonialism, and colonialism is the fundamental historical event that explains why some countries are poor. In recent decades, the world's poorest have been increasingly pushed off their land, into semi-urban slums, and their hunger has worsened even as world food production has increased.

During the colonial period, there was a global division of labor in which the economies of today's poor countries were *intentionally reoriented* to become exporters of just one or two commodities that would be of use to northern industrial economies. This period included massive settler farming, in which Europeans took "unused" native lands. The crops sown were intended for European markets, not to serve the indigenous population.

The rise of American global power in the mid-20th century brought with it a new global food regime, centered on the U.S. government, its conflict with the Soviet Union, and the power of American chemical and agricultural companies (see Table 14.3). Under the UN's "Freedom from Hunger" campaign in the 1960s, developing countries received excess fertilizers from wealthy countries, which only increased their dependence on such inputs in later years. For example, in the early 1950s, most of Colombia's wheat was produced in the country. But a decade's worth of food aid later, the majority of wheat consumed was imported.[50]

In the 1980s, many developing countries faced debt crises and turned to the World Bank and International Monetary Fund (IMF) for help. Structuralists would say that the World Bank and IMF, as well as FAO and IFAD, were dominated by neoliberal food security thinking about food. The Bank and IMF required (liberals would say "recommended") that poor countries take advantage of strong global prices for commodities. For example, in the 1980s, Vietnam was the 42nd ranked producer of coffee globally. By 2001, it was the second ranked. But when multiple countries did this, coffee became plentiful and the price crashed, impoverishing coffee farmers with it.[51]

Structuralists would also point to the World Trade Organization as another intergovernmental organization that is biased against poor countries. Getting access to food consumers in wealthy countries represents a potentially huge benefit for poor countries, where agricultural workforces tend to be large and raw materials are a main export. As we read in Chapter 6, the WTO encourages reciprocal trade relations between member-states. Member-states, however, are only obliged to remove most trade barriers on the products and sectors contained within specific WTO agreements. Even the 1995 Agreement on Agriculture did little to lower barriers to the export of agricultural produce from poor to wealthy countries. The Agreement provided the first global rules governing the trade in food, yet in 2002, the U.S. Farm Bill actually *increased* subsidies paid to U.S. farmers. Moreover, the WTO penalizes countries that pay farmers above market rates for their crops. But in practice this hurts poor countries the most since these countries often wish to stockpile major crops to ensure domestic food security, whereas this is much less of a concern in wealthy countries. One step forward was achieved in 2015 when the WTO announced the abolition of export subsidies for agriculture.[52]

Structuralists are sympathetic to food sovereignty activists in their criticism of intellectual property in global industrial agriculture. For example, the Busy Lizzie is one of the most popular flowers in British gardens. It is a hybrid plant "created" and patented by Syngenta. It was engineered by mixing flowers from Britain with flowers indigenous to Tanzania. But communities in Tanzania were never compensated when "seed collectors" took seeds to the United Kingdom. This story is common. Rich countries possess enormous libraries of rare seeds from around the world, and many of these have their origins in the colonial period.[53] Thus, the power of Western biotech firms can often be traced to Western power during the colonial period.

Thus, in 2013, when the G8 announced an initiative to boost agricultural investment in Africa, civil society actors such as the Alliance for Food Sovereignty in Africa criticized the deal as a "new form of colonialism" in which African governments promised to make their laws on land and seeds more favorable to private investors at the expense of their own small farmers. Even the United Nations Special Rapporteur on the Right to Food described the agreement as "completely behind the screen" with "no long-term view about the future of smallholder farmers" and without their participation.[54]

Structuralists have also drawn attention to the global inequities manifest in recent **land grabs**. In 2008, South Korean electronics giant Daewoo announced a 99-year lease of 1.3 million hectares of land in Madagascar. The company "said it expected to pay nothing to farm maize and palm oil in an area of Madagascar half the size of Belgium."[55] One Daewoo manager told reporters, "We want to plant corn there to ensure our food security. Food can be a weapon in this world. We can either export the harvests to other countries or ship them back to Korea in case of a food crisis." Critics quickly cried foul, pointing out that one of the world's wealthiest countries was preying on the economic desperation of one of the world's poorest countries. At the time, the World Food Programme provided food relief to over a half a million people in Madagascar, where half of all children have stunted growth. Structuralists point out that these deals are enabled and encouraged by some major IGOs. This can be seen in even the title of the 2009 World Bank Report, *Awakening Africa's Sleeping Giant: Prospects for Commercial Agriculture in the Guinea Savannah Zone and Beyond.*

land grab: taking land from an owner or traditional occupant with unfair or no compensation.

Structuralists do not accept that markets simply need to work better. For many structuralists, markets are the problem. For example, in a functioning market, producers and investors will respond to demand for meat in growing economies. This will lead to farmland being switched to beef, which means more greenhouse gases, deforestation, and less biodiversity. It also means that the billions of

TABLE 14.3

Major Multinational Corporations in Global Food

Company	Based	Employees	Revenue
Cargill[56]	Minnesota	150,000	$120 billion
Archer Daniels Midland (ADM)[57]	Chicago	30,000	$70 billion
ConAgra[58]	Chicago	20,000	$20 billion
Monsanto[59]	St. Louis	20,000	$15 billion
Syngenta[60]	Switzerland	28,000	$13 billion

These five companies dominate markets for fertilizers, pesticides, and seeds, as well as distribution networks and processors.

Source: Data from company websites.

people who are not seeking beef in their diets will face higher prices for their own foods, as farms shift away from producing their staples like flour or sorghum. This is essentially what is happening with biofuels. Biofuels only hurt the poorest, who are in no position to take advantage of cleaner cars. What they need is cheaper food, but the biofuel industry is responding to a demand to put things like corn into cars rather than mouths.

In this section, we have learned that there is more than one answer to the question, who runs global food? We have learned that it is not a matter of identifying the particular actor (say, Germany or Japan) but the *type* of actor one thinks matters most. The difference between major

IS From the Outside-In

DID FINANCIAL MARKETS CAUSE THE GLOBAL FOOD CRISIS?

Food markets over the past century have made use of "forward contracts" between producers and buyers. These contracts reduce uncertainty by providing a guaranteed future price. But in recent years, this changed to a *futures* contract market. The difference is that a futures contract can be traded as a financial product in exchanges such as the Chicago Board of Trade Futures Exchange. This means investors can participate in agricultural markets even if they have no role in agriculture. Some observers are concerned that the interests of these nonagricultural actors are fundamentally different from the interests of the agricultural community.

Pensions funds, investment banks, and hedge funds poured billions of dollars into soybean, wheat, and corn markets in the early and mid-2000s. These investors "speculated" that these commodities would increase in price over time and thus pay a handsome return on investment. But these actors became prime targets for blame for their role in pushing up the price of food. *The Guardian* newspaper quoted Deborah Doane, director of the World Development Movement in London: "People die from hunger while the banks make a killing from betting on food."[61] Although investing is a valuable financial service, speculation is destructive gambling. It occurs when the price of a good is driven way out of line with the good's true value.

Other observers, however, say that speculation about a future price does not simply change the future price of that good: If food prices increased, and those betting on increased food prices profited, does it mean speculators *caused* the increase? One study concluded, "speculators alone have difficulty maintaining particular price levels indefinitely, and they pursue lower prices with equal vigor when market fundamentals shift. Given these findings, it is difficult to conclude that market speculation was a large factor in the overall sustained price level between 2008 and 2012."[62]

Observers who downplay the role of speculators in the Global Food Crisis say investors were responding to policy decisions made by governments, in particular, the introduction of export limits and panic buying in large countries such as India, Egypt, and China. Following India's ban on rice exports in February 2008, Saudi imports of Thai rice jumped 90%. The Philippines "panic bought" 1.3 million tons of rice in just the first four months of 2008, a sum larger than the entire 2008 import.[63] Thus, government policies affected the behavior of investors, which may have then affected prices.

Reflect

How would you rank the importance of global finance as a contributing factor in the Global Food Crisis, relative to the factors such as population growth and biofuels discussed in the other boxes in this chapter?

FIGURE 14.6
Global Forces, Interactions, and Tensions in Global Food

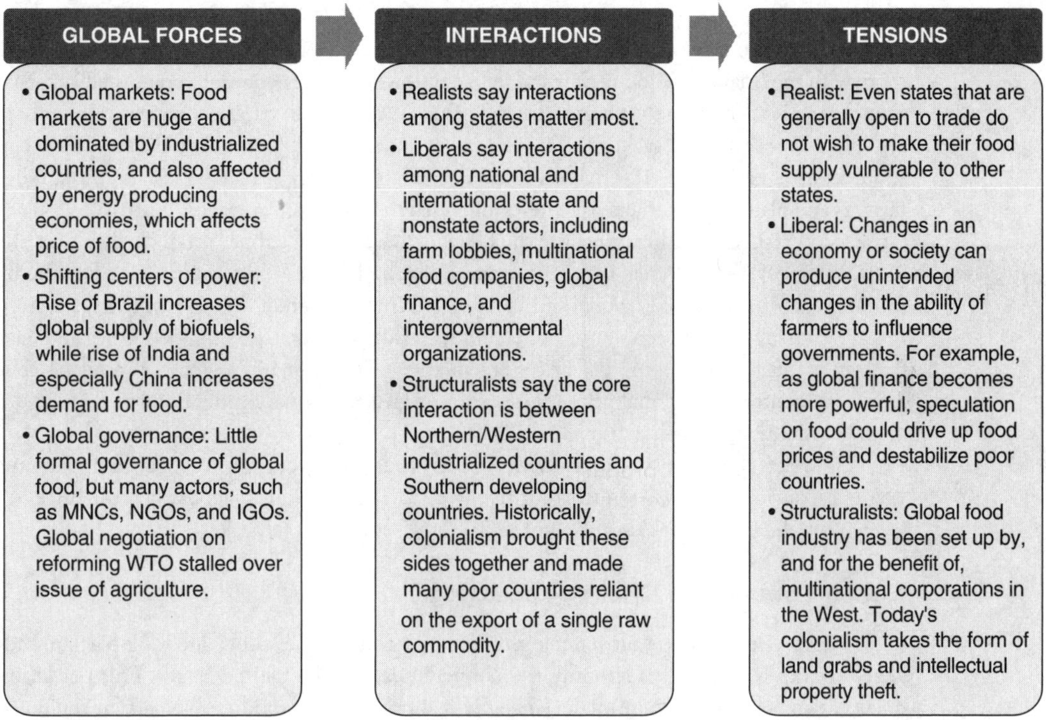

GLOBAL FORCES	INTERACTIONS	TENSIONS
• Global markets: Food markets are huge and dominated by industrialized countries, and also affected by energy producing economies, which affects price of food. • Shifting centers of power: Rise of Brazil increases global supply of biofuels, while rise of India and especially China increases demand for food. • Global governance: Little formal governance of global food, but many actors, such as MNCs, NGOs, and IGOs. Global negotiation on reforming WTO stalled over issue of agriculture.	• Realists say interactions among states matter most. • Liberals say interactions among national and international state and nonstate actors, including farm lobbies, multinational food companies, global finance, and intergovernmental organizations. • Structuralists say the core interaction is between Northern/Western industrialized countries and Southern developing countries. Historically, colonialism brought these sides together and made many poor countries reliant on the export of a single raw commodity.	• Realist: Even states that are generally open to trade do not wish to make their food supply vulnerable to other states. • Liberal: Changes in an economy or society can produce unintended changes in the ability of farmers to influence governments. For example, as global finance becomes more powerful, speculation on food could drive up food prices and destabilize poor countries. • Structuralists: Global food industry has been set up by, and for the benefit of, multinational corporations in the West. Today's colonialism takes the form of land grabs and intellectual property theft.

theories comes down to what to focus on, rather than whom. By understanding the difference between a specific actor and a type of actor, you will be better equipped to understand and act upon global food. (Figure 14.6 puts global food in our framework.)

TRACING GLOBAL FOOD: COMMODITY CHAINS

As students of international studies, we are concerned with global interactions and the tensions that result. The analysis of commodity chains illuminates how a variety of places and actors interact in the international production and consumption of food. A **commodity chain** consists of all the links between a finished consumable item and the inputs that went into it. It includes the transportation and processing of food, but it is deeper than that. It includes the inputs of labor or machinery that go into the processing stage, rather than the processing stage as one brief event. A commodity chain is more than just the study of farm-to-table since that implies a one-directional, one-time process. A commodity chain should probably be called a *commodity circle* because it is important to understand parts of the food system as a series of feedback loops.[64] Culture, law, climate, gender, labor relations, and political power all influence what happens at each of these stages. Fascinating commodity chain analyses have been carried out on tomatoes, T shirts, coffee, and cotton.[65] In this section, we will use the example of chocolate. Figure 14.8 places global chocolate into our international studies framework.

commodity chain: labor, raw materials, energy, and transit linking a raw material to its eventual life as a consumable item.

Cocoa Commodity Chain: Production

Archaeologists have found traces of cacao—the tree that produces the cocoa bean—in Central America and have traced it back to around 1,000 years ago.[66] Cacao arrived in Europe in the early 1500s, and by the 1800s, the chocolate consumer culture had taken off. Cacao went westward once more with the Spanish, who oversaw the introduction of intensive production in the Caribbean and South America. This was the period of the enormous Atlantic slave trade that saw millions of people forcibly shipped from West Africa. The plantation systems set up in the Americas and Asia began to supply consumers in industrialized countries with cacao, and they have done so ever since. Indigenous farmers and plantation workers were never intended to be the consumers of cacao. Even today, cocoa farmers in West Africa will rarely taste the Hershey, Mars, and Cadbury products they help produce.

Most cocoa today comes from the Ivory Coast and Ghana (see Table 14.4). For the biggest producers, cocoa is a major source of income for farmers, revenue for governments, and earner of foreign exchange for the economy. These countries ride this tide through good times and bad. One reason for this is that commodity prices are volatile (see Figure 14.7). Cocoa-producing countries have little control over global prices. They try to adjust their own production levels in light of the global economy, but this is extremely difficult.

This affects the ability of governments in poor countries to engage in longer term planning. For example, plans to build 100 schools over five years can be thrown into jeopardy if the price of cocoa (which supplies significant tax revenue) drops three years into the project.

Cocoa Commodity Chain: Processing

Until very recently, the processing of cocoa into consumable chocolate took place in industrialized countries, especially Germany, the Netherlands, and the United States. This put cocoa producers at an enormous disadvantage since the real profit in commodities is made at the processing stage. Historically, major cocoa producers had Cocoa Marketing Boards during the colonial period. Marketing Boards were government organizations that purchased cocoa directly from farmers at a set price, and in turn, the government sold the cocoa on world markets. In theory, the government was providing a kind of insurance by helping to soften the blow of occasional low prices. But in practice, governments gave farmers a very low price, and farmers were legally only allowed to sell

TABLE 14.4

Major Actors in Global Cocoa (2015–2016, Thousands of Tons)[67]

Top producers		Top consumers		Top processors	
Ivory Coast	1,670	United States	826	Ivory Coast	610
Ghana	970	Germany	339	Netherlands	560
Indonesia	440	UK	234	United States	425
Nigeria	260	France	225	Germany	415
Cameroon	220	Russia	202	Indonesia	440

Source: Data are from *The Economist*, "Cocoa Forecast World March 2015," https://store.eiu.com/article.aspx?productid=1884928773.

FIGURE 14.7

Volatile Cocoa Prices Since 2007

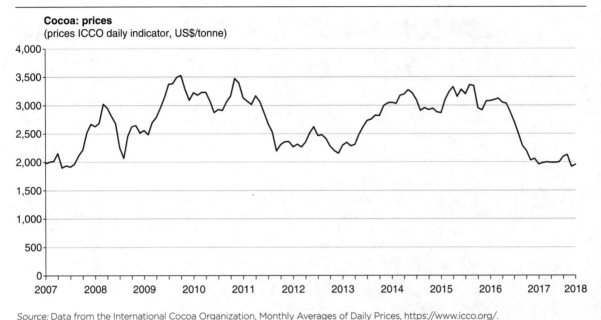

Cocoa: prices
(prices ICCO daily indicator, US$/tonne)

Source: Data from the International Cocoa Organization, Monthly Averages of Daily Prices, https://www.icco.org/.

to the Marketing Board. The government then sold the cocoa on the world market for a higher price, and the difference went into the government's bank account. Thus, governments intentionally kept cocoa farmers poor to extract a profit from their labor. In recent years, this pattern has begun to change. For example, Indonesia, Ghana, and the Ivory Coast have invested in factories to grind their cocoa beans into cocoa powder, and farmers are now offered improved prices for their goods.

Cocoa Commodity Chain: Trade and Consumption

It is more useful to think of the global trade in cocoa as dominated rather than as controlled. Cocoa is bought and sold like other commodities. There is no IGO or MNC that governs its trade. But the market is more responsive to some than others. For example, the chocolate consumption of wealthy consumers and the decisions made by major chocolate companies have a dramatic effect on cocoa prices (see Figure 14.7). Contracts to buy cocoa in the future at a specified price and date ("futures contracts") are traded in London and New York. In recent decades, major producers have tried to work together to control the supply (and thus the price) of cocoa on the world market (see Table 14.5). Such a cartel is what has enabled Organization of Petroleum Exporting Countries (OPEC) members such as Saudi Arabia to so richly profit from their oil. But cocoa producers have never been successful at building a cartel. This is likely because the major producers all wish to increase production as prices increase. Although the International Cocoa Organization is composed of 51 member-states (21 exporting and 30 importing countries), producer countries have not been able to make it a powerful organization for the joint control of global cocoa.

TABLE 14.5

Leading MNCs in Global Chocolate

Company	Based	Products	Value[68]	Employees
Nestle	Switzerland	Coffee-Mate, Cheerios	$253 billion	335,000
Mondelez	USA	Cadbury and Kraft	$67 billion	99,000
Hershey	USA	Reese's, Mounds	$24 billion	19,000
Mars	USA	M&Ms, Snickers	Privately held	75,000

Source: Data from company websites.

Tracing this commodity chain is also useful for the examples of transnational activism. One area of intense activism is fair trade chocolate, in which transnational activists raise awareness in wealthy countries of how little cocoa farmers make from the sale of chocolate. Another has been involved in the campaign to eradicate child labor while improving cocoa farm incomes. Major actors in the cocoa industry set up the International Cocoa Initiative in 2003 to oversee the eradication of child labor in cocoa production. This includes major companies as well as civil society groups such as Free the Slaves. Major producer countries now have national plans and policies that (on paper at least) seek to ensure there is no child labor at any point along the cocoa commodity chain.

FIGURE 14.8

Global Forces, Interactions, and Tensions in the Cocoa Commodity Chain

GLOBAL FORCES	INTERACTIONS	TENSIONS
• Global markets: Harvesting by West African farmers, processing by European and North American MNCs, trading by global financial actors, and consumption in mostly industrialized economies. • ICT: Civil society uses social media to reframe welfare of cocoa farmers from an economic issue to a human rights issue. • Global governance: Weak intergovernmental governance, but a vibrant community of academic researchers as well as NGOs advocating for fair trade and child-free labor.	• Historic interaction between European colonists, enslaved West Africans, and the Americas, where cacao probably originated and where plantations eventually developed. • Civil society actors struggle with chocolate companies to affect consumer perception of cocoa industry.	• Poor governments often rely on cocoa exports for taxes, but volatility in global prices makes it difficult to engage in long-term plans for investments in public health, education, and infrastructure.

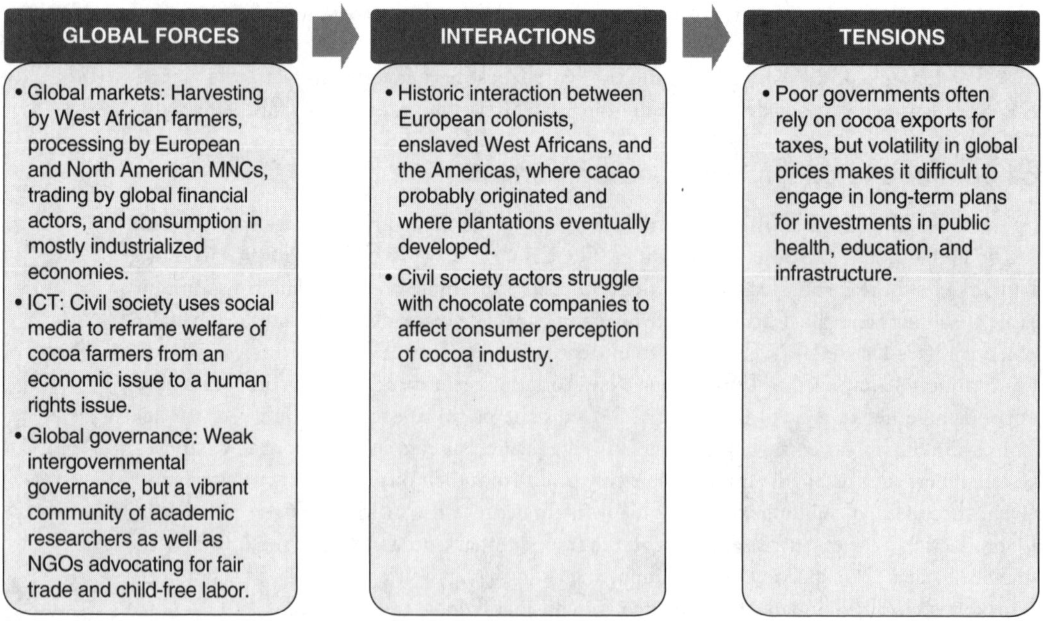

SUMMARY

In this chapter, we have learned about how different communities are linked through the production and exchange of one type of commodity: food. We have seen our global forces throughout. First, food *is* a global economic market. And what characterizes the 21st-century global market in food is the speed of interactions, not just in how quickly goods move between producers and consumers but also in the speed with which prices change and can have knock-on effects in politics and society, as we saw with the Global Food Crisis and the Arab Uprisings. Second, information and communications technology enables us to know more about food production and consumption elsewhere. This enables the global food markets, but it also affects our mental image of our world. For example, my ability to go online and watch a Mongolian chef prepare a dish might make me feel more cosmopolitan. Or, conversely, perhaps seeing how my national dish is being prepared in another continent might give me a sense that my culture is being appropriated by people who neither understand nor deserve it.

Third, we see shifting centers of power in the world in several ways. China and India have growing populations, with growing middle classes, and this profoundly affects the availability of food—and the price to be paid—for everyone else in the world. In terms of production, global food production is no longer dominated by Europe and North America. Countries such as Thailand, China, India, Brazil, Russia, and Indonesia rival the traditional agricultural powerhouses, and this affects the ability of Western countries to dictate the global food regime, which we see in the case of the WTO. Last, we see shifting centers of power in the world with the rise of global actors in agribusiness and finance, as well as in civil society organizations that advocate for the world's poorest farmers and consumers, such as Care and Caritas.

KEY TERMS

biofuels 406
commodity chain 413
de-peasantization 405
famine 400
food aid 397
Food First 398

food insecure 405
food security 401
food sovereignty 402
food-versus-fuel debate 406
genetically modified organisms
  (GMOs) 401

Green Revolution 398
land grab 411
Malthusian 398
smallholders 401

QUESTIONS FOR REVIEW

1. What is a neo-Malthusian, and how is Malthus misunderstood?

2. What are the major differences between the food security and food sovereignty approaches?

3. Which side of the food-versus-fuel debate would a structuralist support?

4. What global forces might explain why famines are less common in recent decades?

5. How could the Arab Spring be interpreted as a tension—an unintended consequence—of global food?

6. How does the recent South Sudanese famine illustrate Sen's theory of famines?

7. Why is Bill Gates criticized for supporting GMOs?

LEARN MORE

Global Hunger Index http://ghi.ifpri.org/.

Duke University's Global Value Chains Initiative www.globalvaluechains.org.

Institute of Development Studies, Innovation and Value Chains https://www.ids.ac.uk/idsresearch/innovation-and-value-chains.

USE THE DATA

FAOSTAT global dataset on agriculture http://www.fao.org/faostat/en/#data.

NOTES

1. Eliza Barclay, "Your Grandparents Spent More of Their Money on Food Than You Do," NPR.org, March 2, 2015, http://www.npr.org/sections/thesalt/2015/03/02/389578089/your-grandparents-spent-more-of-their-money-on-food-than-you-do.

2. http://therealnews.com/t2/index.php?option=com_content&task=view&id=31&Itemid=74&jumival=1408.

3. http://www.reuters.com/article/walmart-samsclub-idUSN2323679120080423.

4. Lynne Phillips, "Food and Globalization," *Annual Review of Anthropology* 35 (2006): 37–57.

5. Phillips, 2006, 43.

6. *The Population Bomb*, Rev. [& expanded] ed. (New York, NY: Ballantine Books, 1971).

7. Charles C. Mann, "Can Planet Earth Feed 10 Billion People?," *The Atlantic*, March 2018, https://www.theatlantic.com/magazine/archive/2018/03/charles-mann-can-planet-earth-feed-10-billion-people/550928/.

8. Today there is widespread admission that sending U.S. food to other countries as aid was a mistake. Following the food crisis of 2008, many wealthy countries and IGOs agreed to reduce the amount of food given as aid, and to switch to actual cash instead. Today, the U.S. government purchases food from U.S. farms in a competitive process. http://www.cbsnews.com/news/bill-clinton-we-blew-it-on-global-food/.

9. This section draws on D. John Shaw's *Global Food and Agricultural Institutions* (New York, NY: Routledge, 2008).

10. Importing food would mean exchanging domestic currency for foreign exchange currency, typically U.S. dollars. If a country is already experiencing declining exports, it needs to ration its use of foreign exchange currency.

11. Derek Headey and Shenggen Fan, *Reflections on the Global Food Crisis* (Washington, DC: IFPRI, 2010), 20.

12. Mark W. Rosegrant and Siwa Msangi, "Consensus and Contention in the Food-Versus-Fuel Debate,"

Annual Review of Environment and Resources 39 (2014): 274.

13. Lester R. Brown, *Who Will Feed China? Wake-up Call for a Small Planet* (New York, NY: W.W. Norton, 1995).

14. Deborah Brautigam, *Will Africa Feed China?* (Oxford, U.K.: Oxford University Press, 2015).

15. Headey and Fan, 2010, 20.

16. Headey and Fan, 2010, 20.

17. https://www.nationalgeographic.com/what-the-world-eats/.

18. Definition from Per Pinstrup-Andersen and Derrill D. Watson II, *Food Policy for Developing Countries: The Role of Government in Global, National, and Local Food Systems* (Ithaca, NY: Cornell University Press, 2011), 95.

19. Tim Pat Coogan, *The Famine Plot: England's Role in Ireland's Greatest Tragedy* (New York, NY: Macmillan, 2012).

20. Cormac Gráda, "Making Famine History," *Journal of Economic Literature* 45, no. 1 (2007): 5–38.

21. UN News Service, "Global Hunger Rising Again, Driven by Conflict and Climate Change — UN Report," *UN News Service Section*, September 15, 2017, http://www.un.org/apps/news/story.asp?NewsID=57526#.WlTvs5M-csm.

22. Pinstrup-Andersen and Watson, 2011, 97.

23. This section draws on IFPRI, "2014–2015 Global Food Policy Report" (Washington, DC: International Food Policy Research Institute, 2015), Chapter 4.

24. To be considered a family farm, a farm must be owned, managed, or operated by family members who also provide some farm labor.

25. IFPRI, 2015, 26.

26. Raj Patel, *Stuffed and Starved: The Hidden Battle for the World Food System—Revised and Updated*, Revised ed. (Brooklyn, NY: Melville House, 2012).

27. The following draws on William D. Schanbacher, *The Politics of Food: The Global Conflict Between Food Security and Food Sovereignty* (Santa Barbara, CA: Praeger, 2010).

28. IFPRI, 2015, 26.

29. For scientific reports critical of GMOs, see Doug Gurian-Sherman, *Failure to Yield: Evaluating the Performance of Genetically Engineered Crops* (Cambridge, MA: Union of Concerned Scientists, 2009).

30. Schanbacher, 2010, ix.

31. http://www.cbsnews.com/news/is-nafta-good-for-mexicos-farmers/.

32. http://www.reuters.com/article/us-food-security-gates-idUSTRE59E58120091015?pageNumber=1&virtualBrandChannel=11604.

33. http://www.nytimes.com/2008/10/12/magazine/12wwln-shah-t.html?_r=4&scp=1&sq=AGRA%20gates&st=cse.

34. Rosegrant and Msangi, 2014, 274.

35. Headey and Fan, 2010, 20.

36. Nicole Condon, Heather Klemick, and Ann Wolverton, "Impacts of Ethanol Policy on Corn Prices: A Review and Meta-Analysis of Recent Evidence," *Food Policy* 51 (February 2015): 63–73, https://doi.org/10.1016/j.foodpol.2014.12.007.

37. Philip McMichael, "Agrofuels in the Food Regime," *The Journal of Peasant Studies* 37, no. 4 (2010): 609–629.

38. Walden Bello, *The Food Wars*, Original ed. (New York, NY: Verso, 2009).

39. David Zilberman et al., "The Impact of Biofuels on Commodity Food Prices: Assessment of Findings," *American Journal of Agricultural Economics* 95, no. 2 (January 1, 2013): 275–281, https://doi.org/10.1093/ajae/aas037.

40. Yan Gao et al., "A Global Analysis of Deforestation Due to Biofuel Development," Working Paper (Center for International Forestry Research / CIFOR/, 2011), http://www.cifor.org/library/3506/a-global-analysis-of-deforestation-due-to-biofuel-development.

41. *The New York Times*, "Can Biotech Food Cure World Hunger?" *Room for Debate* (blog), November 26, 2009, http://roomfordebate.blogs.nytimes.com/2009/10/26/can-biotech-food-cure-world-hunger/.

42. Includes country offices.

43. Jacob Bunge et al., "Powerful U.S. Panel Clears Chinese Takeover of Syngenta," *Wall Street Journal*, August 23, 2016, sec. Business, http://www.wsj.com/articles/powerful-u-s-panel-clears-chinese-takeover-of-syngenta-1471914278.

44. Alberto Valdés and William Foster, "Net Food-Importing Developing Countries: Who They Are, and Policy Options for Global Price Volatility," Issue Paper, ICTSD Programme on Agricultural Trade and Sustainable Development (Geneva, Switzerland: International Centre for Trade and Sustainable Development, 2012).

45. Rosegrant and Msangi, 2014, 274.

46. Rosegrant and Msangi, 2014, 274.

47. This section draws on Bill Winders and James C. Scott, *The Politics of Food Supply: US Agricultural Policy in the World Economy* (New Haven, CT: Yale University Press, 2009).

48. Winders and Scott, 2009.

49. Federal Agricultural Improvement and Reform (FAIR) Act of 1996.

50. Winders and Scott, 2009, 157.

51. Gavin Fridell, *Coffee* (New York, NY: John Wiley & Sons, 2014).

52. Heinz Strubenhoff, "The WTO's Decision to End Agricultural Export Subsidies Is Good News for Farmers and Consumers," *Brookings* (blog), February 8, 2016, https://www.brookings.edu/blog/future-development/2016/02/08/the-wtos-decision-to-end-agricultural-export-subsidies-is-good-news-for-farmers-and-consumers/.

53. P. Davies, P. Francis, and T. Wyatt, eds., *Invisible Crimes and Social Harms* (New York, NY: Springer, 2014); Abena Dove Osseo-Asare, *Bitter Roots: The Search for Healing Plants in Africa*, 1st ed. (Chicago, IL: University of Chicago Press, 2014).

54. https://www.theguardian.com/global-development/2014/feb/18/g8-new-alliance-condemned-new-colonialism.

55. https://www.ft.com/content/6e894c6a-b65c-11dd-89dd-0000779fd18c.

56. http://www.cargill.com/company/glance/index.jsp.

57. http://www.adm.com/en-US/company/Facts/Pages/default.aspx.

58. http://www.conagrafoods.com/news-room/company-fact-sheet.

59. http://www.monsanto.com/whoweare/pages/default.aspx.

60. Syngenta Annual Review, 2015.

61. https://www.theguardian.com/global-development/2011/jan/23/food-speculation-banks-hunger-poverty.

62. Rosegrant and Msangi, 2014, 274.

63. Headey and Fan, 2010, 20.

64. Pinstrup-Andersen and Watson, 2011, 97. The term originated with Terence Hopkins and Immanuel Wallerstein, "Patterns of Development of the Modern World-System," *Review (Fernand Braudel Center)* 1, no. 2 (1977): 111–145. See also Jennifer Bair, "Global Capitalism and Commodity Chains: Looking Back, Going Forward," *Competition & Change* 9, no. 2 (June 1, 2005): 153–180 and Gary Gereffi and Miguel Korzeniewicz, *Commodity Chains and Global Capitalism* (Westport, CT: Praeger, 1993).

65. Deborah Barndt, *Tangled Routes: Women, Work, and Globalization on the Tomato Trail* (New York, NY: Rowman & Littlefield, 2002). Pietra Rivoli, *The Travels of a T-Shirt in the Global Economy: An Economist Examines the Markets, Power, and Politics of World Trade. New Preface and Epilogue With Updates on Economic Issues and Main Characters*, 2nd ed. (Hoboken, NJ: Wiley, 2014). Tom Standage, *A History of the World in 6 Glasses*, trade paper, later printing ed. (New York, NY: Walker, 2006). Sven Beckert, *Empire of Cotton: A Global History* (New York, NY: Alfred A. Knopf, 2015).

66. Cacao is the tree, while cocoa is the bean that comes from one of the tree's pods.

67. https://store.eiu.com/article.aspx?productid =1884928773.

68. Market capitalization.

Glossary

absolutist state: state where there is no rule of law, since the ruler is not subject to any laws.

adaptation: process by which people and governments anticipate and prepare for the effects of climate change.

African Charter on Human and People's Rights: regional human rights treaty for African states.

African Court on Human and People's Rights: regional human rights court for those countries that have ratified the African Charter of Human and People's Rights; the court is based in Arusha, Tanzania, and it hears cases brought by other states or by individuals if those individuals live in states that have ratified a special protocol allowing citizens and nongovernmental organizations to petition the court directly.

aid conditionality: donor governments require governments that receive foreign aid to take steps to become more democratic.

Alma Ata Declaration: 1978 declaration that emerged from a global meeting convened by the World Health Organization; the Alma Ata Declaration shaped the global health agenda, in particular, through last definitions, setting goals, and emphasizing primary healthcare as an anchor for global health.

American Convention on Human Rights: regional human rights treaty for the countries that are a part of the Organization of American States.

American exceptionalism: idea that the United States is special and distinct and should not subject itself to human rights global governance, even as it promotes human rights for other countries.

ASEAN Intergovernmental Commission on Human Rights (AICHR): fledgling body designed to promote human rights initially through thematic themes and drafting of a Southeast Asian declaration of human rights.

Asian Financial Crisis: in 1997, investors worried that some Southeast Asian countries might not be able to repay international loans. Panic led to massive withdrawals of investment from Thailand, South Korea, Indonesia, and Malaysia. Because some countries had fixed the value of their currency, the financial panic also led to currency crises.

Association of Southeast Asian Nations (ASEAN): regional organization designed to promote cooperation among Southeast Asian nations.

asylum seeker: migrant fleeing persecution or war and seeking refugee status in another country.

balance of payments: accounting record of an economy's transactions with the rest of the world.

Beijing Consensus: model of economic development inspired by China that competes with the (post) Washington Consensus. Emphasizes role of the state in boosting exports while downplaying need for free markets and democracy.

biofuels: fuels used in transport that are made from biomass materials, that is, dead plants or animals. Common biofuels include ethanol and biodiesel.

biothreats: idea that biological matter, such as a disease, may be intentionally used as a weapon.

bipolar: idea that global power is bifurcated between two primary holders, e.g., between the United States and the Soviet Union during the Cold War.

brain drain: idea that sending country has its resources drained when its best and brightest emigrate.

brain gain: contra the brain drain argument. Idea that sending country may benefit when some people emigrate, primarily due to remittances, personal investment in skills, and transmission of new sociopolitical values.

bottlenecks: idea that development interventions should focus on the specific local challenges in poor countries, such as corruption, weak credit, or poor communications, rather than assuming that all poor countries have the same long list of problems.

Bretton Woods Monetary System: agreement on currency exchange among mostly Western nations after World War II. Non-U.S. members set their currencies to certain values of US$, and the United States set the rate at $35 for an ounce of gold.

Bretton Woods System (BWS): economic order among mostly Western industrialized nations after World War II, providing for lower barriers to trade and investment while safeguarding the ability of member states to manage their economies even at the expense of international economic activity.

BRIC or BRICS: expression to capture four or five large countries that are rising in global power and status; BRIC stands for Brazil, Russia, India, and China; the S stands for South Africa.

capital controls: policies used to control the amount of money coming in and out of a country.

capitalism: socioeconomic system of production characterized by market-based transactions, private property, and wage labor.

carbon dioxide removal: projects that would remove carbon dioxide from the atmosphere.

Charter of the United Nations: United Nations treaty that establishes the architecture for peace and shared governance, pledging all members to achieve "universal respect for, and observance of human rights and fundamental freedoms without distinction as to race, sex, language, and religion."

circular migration: migrants moving back and forth between home and host countries. Common for migrant workers in seasonal sectors such as agriculture.

civil society: voluntary association of people outside of families, firms (companies), and states (governments). Includes nongovernmental organizations (NGOs), social movements, and transnational advocacy networks (TANs).

civil society organizations (CSOs): often used interchangeably with nongovernmental organizations (NGOs), but they can also mean NGOs as well as community-based organizations (CBOs).

civil war: armed conflict between two or more organizations actively fighting for sovereign control over the same territory.

class identity: social identity in which belonging is determined by social class.

Clean Development Mechanism: mechanism for reducing overall carbon levels in the atmosphere through development projects.

climate change: natural and human-induced variability in the global climate.

collapsed states: most territory not under state control, and maybe no government. Very rare.

Commissions of Inquiry: investigative bodies and fact-finding missions that are mandated by a variety of United Nations bodies to document and report on a specific human rights issue.

commodification: assessing something's worth in terms of its value in an economic or trading transaction.

commodity chain: labor, raw materials, energy, and transit linking a raw material to its eventual life as a consumable item.

comparative advantage: economic principle that countries should specialize in what they do best, where "best" means most efficiently.

competitive authoritarianism (or hybrid regimes): system of government that combines elements of a democracy and authoritarianism.

competitive devaluations: when a country tries to boost its exports by reducing the value of its own currency.

complementarity: principle that an international court gains jurisdiction only after domestic remedies have been exhausted or are nonexistent; the international body does not substitute for domestic judicial processes but complements them.

complex interdependence: in liberal theory, the concept that states do not pursue just one policy. Government officials and nonstate actors within a country engage in international activity in the pursuit of diverse (often conflicting) policy goals.

compulsory membership: subject to an organization's rules irrespective of consent.

conditional cash transfer (CCT) programs: programs that come with conditions, such as enrolling a child in school. An unconditional program has no strings attached.

conditionality: what an aid recipient country must do to receive aid.

conflict minerals: presence of minerals that are considered to motivate and sustain civil war.

constructivism: approach to international relations that sees states as social actors and norms as shaping the identities and wants of states.

contestation: processes of political competition and dispute.

corridors: tendency for migrants to move along specific geographic routes.

cosmopolitanism: view that cultural diversity, and thus immigration, is to be welcomed because all people share a common humanity and morality.

cost of information: price to access and disseminate information; modern information and communications technology reduces the price drastically.

Council of Europe (CoE): regional organization composed of 47 European member-states; the Council promotes common values for the continent, including democracy, human rights, and the rule of law.

counterinsurgency: coordinated actions to defeat or contain insurgency.

counterterrorism: coordinated actions to anticipate, contain, and defeat terrorism, ones that often emphasize intelligence and police action and not only military action.

creative destruction: destruction of old technologies to make way for new, including destroying the sociopolitical power of the owners of the older technology. Countries that cannot do this will stagnate.

criminal violence: organized violence to support an illicit activity, such as the drug trade.

cultural citizenship: person's sense of belonging to, or being accepted by, a host community, beyond one's legal acceptance.

culture: traditions, customs, and meanings that shape behavior and understanding.

cyberterrorism: computer-based forms of disruption and misinformation to cause fear and disorder.

cyberwarfare: computer-based forms of disruption designed to disrupt or damage a state or organization, often with a military or strategic purpose.

debt bondage: paying off a debt to a person by working for them.

democracy: system of government that means rule by the people in which citizens are allowed to associate, express, and participate in politics freely.

democracy promotion: in their foreign policy, governments encourage, and often finance, other governments to become more democratic.

democratic consolidation: process by which democracy takes root and stabilizes in a country.

democratic deficit: when elected officials no longer have control over the destiny of citizens. In this case, democratic voting is not able to hold representatives accountable because the elected officials are not making the crucial decisions.

democratic initiation: initial process that leads a country to end authoritarianism.

democratic peace: democratic states do not fight wars against each other.

democratization: process of transitioning from an authoritarian political system to a democratic one.

democratization of information: ease and decentralized nature of how individuals may access and disseminate information using modern technology.

demonstration effect (or diffusion): process by which actors in one country watch and initiate political processes in another country. Applied to democratization, the idea is that actors in one country are inspired by, learn from, and initiate challenges to authoritarianism that they observe in other countries.

de-peasantization: as poor people are forced from their land and farms consolidate, they lose control of their nutrition even while the country's farms become more productive.

dependency theory: theory that rich countries got rich at the expense of poor countries, and that the international economy has been designed to structurally favor rich countries. Raul Prebish was central figure.

development: variously defined as economic growth, improving living standards, or enhancing people's control over their own lives.

developmental states: where the state plays an active role in investing in the economy, including through the use of subsidies, credit, or limits on imports, to build the global competitiveness of national industries.

dictatorship (or authoritarianism): system of government that severely restricts association, expression, and participation in politics.

distributional effects: how distinct people or places are differentially affected by an event, such as a change in taxation or import of a product.

East Asian miracle: rapid and unprecedented growth in economies and living standards seen in several East Asian countries in the 21st century.

economic migrant: not a legally recognized term. Preferred is "migrant worker." Scholars debate whether migrant workers move voluntarily to seek better jobs or involuntarily because their home country economy or government is dysfunctional.

economic resource curse (or Dutch Disease): when investment in the energy sector drives up the exchange rate, thus hurting a country's nonenergy exporters.

ELEMENTS: acronym emerging from the Alma Ata conference; ELEMENTS emphasizes eight core tenets of primary healthcare: education, local disease control, expanded immunization, maternal and child health, essential drugs, nutrition and food supply, treatment of disease and injury, and sanitation and safe water supply.

emissions trading: market-based mechanism for incentivizing countries to reduce their greenhouse gas emissions; a country below its target level can sell its credit to a country that has not met its target.

enforcement problem: idea that human rights treaties and institutions have a weak ability to force violators to comply with human rights standards and laws.

epistemic communities: informal communities of experts with similar training, values, and ideas.

ethnicity: named human population with myths of common ancestry, shared historical memories, one or more elements of common culture, a link with a homeland, and a sense of solidarity among at least some of its members.

European Court of Human Rights: regional human rights court based in Strasbourg, France; the court hears petitions from individuals and states who are citizens within the Council of Europe.

European Union (EU): regional organization that establishes a common economic market, a common currency (the euro), joint aid policies, and a variety of other common policies; the EU has 28 member-states all of whom also are a part of the Council of Europe; the EU headquarters are in Brussels (Belgium).

export-oriented industrialization (EOI): state-led economic development model that emphasizes growing an economy by exporting ever-more sophisticated manufactured goods.

expropriation: when a government seizes a privately owned company, sometimes by force and often with little or no compensation.

extractive institutions: political institutions are extractive if they fail to be pluralistic or centralized; economic institutions are extractive when designed to allow elites to extract resources from the rest of society.

extreme poverty: also known as the "Poverty Headcount Ratio," it is the share of a country's population living on less than $1.90 a day.

failed states: significant territory not under state control. A minority of countries.

fair trade: voluntary agreement between producers of raw materials and manufacturers of consumer products to return a larger share of a final price back to the original producer, usually in a developing country.

famine: severe and prolonged hunger over a large area, leading to deaths of 2 to 5 per 10,000 people as a result of starvation or hunger-related diseases.

financial globalization: how people and places are linked through the cross-border flow of finance, such as foreign direct investment or the trading of stocks and bonds.

financial *hyper*globalization: idea that since the 1990s, allowing finance—the buying and selling of financial assets such as stocks, bonds, insurance, mortgages, or currencies— to move freely around the world has become the point of globalization rather than a means to an end. Under financial *hyper*globalization, global political and economic systems serve the interests of finance, rather than finance serving the interests of the global population.

floating currency regime: price of a currency is not formally set by a government but by global supply and demand.

food aid: type of Official Development Assistance (aka foreign aid) in which the donor country gives food to a recipient country.

Food First: theory that hunger is not caused by overpopulation but by powerlessness and inequality. Associated with Frances Moore Lappe in the 1970s.

food (in)secure: defined by the 1996 World Food Summit as existing "when all people, at all times, have physical and economic access to sufficient, safe and nutritious food that meets their dietary needs and food preferences for an active and healthy life."

food security: approach to global food and hunger that emphasizes boosting the productivity of farms through use of genetically modified organisms and consolidation of small farms. Associated with Bill Gates.

food sovereignty: approach to global food and hunger that emphasizes local community's control over local food sources. Highlights historic role of Western states and corporations in creating conditions for hunger in Global South.

food-versus-fuel debate: debate on the economic, environmental, and human welfare consequences of using food for purposes other than human consumption.

Fordism: form of capitalism characterized by mass production for mass consumption, as introduced by Henry Ford, with repetitive, semi-skill factory work in production for mass consumer markets.

foreign direct investment (FDI): ownership and management of a productive asset in another country, such as owning a factory or farm.

free rider (or public goods) problem: benefiting from someone else's work, such as using a bridge without paying for its construction.

free trade: reduction or removal of barriers to buying and selling across borders. Common barriers include tariffs or quotas on imported goods.

functionalism: when interaction generates its own dynamic and leads to deeper interaction. Example: growth of the European Union.

gender identity: social identity in which belonging is determined by gender difference.

genetically modified organisms (GMOs): crops that have been engineered to tolerate herbicides, droughts, or insects. Actors in the food security approach are optimistic about GMOs.

Gini Index of Inequality: share of national income earned by each percentage of the population.

global civil society: civil society actors working to influence global society.

global markets: arena in which goods and services are traded across borders.

global forces: particularly powerful, cross-cutting drivers of global interactions and tensions. Global forces matter on almost any global issue. They are specific to our present global age.

global health: wide range of transnational activities that promote public health for all people around the world.

global health security: framing global health concerns through a security lens, for example, as sources of threat that would endanger human populations.

global interactions: ways in which people, things, information, and ideas intersect across and within borders.

global tension: resentments, frustrations, and conflicts that arise from global interactions.

global trade: buying and selling of goods and services across borders.

globalization: multidimensional and transnational ways in which people, things, information, and ideas interact and are interconnected across space and time.

Gold Standard: agreement between countries from 1870 to 1914 that each member's currency could be exchanged for a specified amount of gold. It lasted until the early to mid-1930s, but its heyday was 1870 to 1914 because it was associated with significant international trade.

good governance: ideological belief in core features of a well-governed society, including private property, effective and impartial judiciary, low corruption, and government transparency. Good governance is not necessarily democratic governance.

governance: formal and informal institutions, systems, or relationships that manage affairs that cut across national boundaries.

government: people or political parties that govern and make laws.

Green Revolution: application of scientific agricultural research, especially genetic modification of seeds, to farming in developing countries. Associated with rapid growth in agricultural productivity in Asia from the 1960s.

greenhouse effect: idea that certain gases trap heat inside the atmosphere, heating the climate as windows would trap heat in a greenhouse.

gross domestic product (GDP): value of all goods and services in an economy, including everything produced by all people and all companies, including people's salaries.

hard power: state's ability to force actors to change their behavior.

High Commissioner for Human Rights: Geneva-based ombudsman who, through the person holding the position and the staff in the office, promotes and monitors human rights on a global scale.

horizontal inequalities: inequities between groups that are considered to cause grievances that drive civil war.

horizontal interventions: healthcare interventions that aim at improving baseline conditions, such as access to clean water, education, or clinics.

human rights: set of rights afforded to individuals on the basis of being human, i.e., irrespective of national citizenship, gender, ethnicity, or other traits.

Human Rights Council: Geneva-based United Nations (UN) body that serves to promote and monitor human rights globally; the Council is composed of 47 UN member-states.

human rights regime: modern system of human rights declarations, treaties, and institutions designed to define and promote human rights on a global scale.

humanitarian biomedicine: efforts to improve health outcomes for people who have inadequate care or resources.

ideology: theory of how the world works, how it could work, and how to get there. Examples: conservatism, communism, anarchism.

import substitution industrialization (ISI): attempt to industrialize by producing domestically what was formerly imported. Used in many developing countries from the 1940s to the 1980s.

inalienable rights: human rights are inalienable in that they cannot be removed; human rights adhere to persons by virtue of being alive.

inclusive institutions: inclusive political institutions are pluralistic (many forces may compete for power) and centralized (there is a coherent public authority, as in the modern state). Inclusive economic institutions are rules that reward investment and innovation.

information and communications technology (ICT): information technology plus a variety of audio and visual communications technology, such as smartphones and television networks.

information flows: spread of knowledge, ideas, words, and images across borders.

in-groups: people of the same group.

innovation: one way to create wealth is to make or do something new that makes more efficient use of resources.

inside-out and outside-in perspective: approach that emphasizes looking at bottom-up, within-country processes within particular places and looking at top-down, international processes that cut across national borders.

Inter-American Commission on Human Rights: investigative body that has the power to conduct country visits and report on human rights in member-states of the Organization of American States.

Inter-American Court of Human Rights: regional human rights court based in San José, Costa Rica; the court hears cases brought by states or by individuals who have first submitted their complaint to the Inter-American Commission.

intergovernmental organization (IGO): organization created and controlled by sovereign states in which the members are states.

internally displaced person (IDP): refugee within one's own country.

International Covenant on Civil and Political Rights (ICCPR): main international human rights treaty that covers civil and political rights.

International Covenant on Economic, Social, and Cultural Rights (ICESCR): main international human rights treaty that covers economic, social, and cultural rights.

International Criminal Court (ICC): permanent standing international court that is designed to prosecute individuals for exceptionally severe crimes, including genocide, crimes against humanity, and war crimes. The court is based in The Hague (the Netherlands).

international nongovernmental organization (INGO): nongovernmental organization (NGO) that has members in more than one country, typically meaning a physical office with employees.

international studies: study of global interactions, the tensions those interactions produce, and the forces and actors that play a role in them.

international treaties: binding formal agreement that establishes obligations between two or more subjects of international law, usually states.

investments: wealthy countries continuously invest in integral parts of their economy, such as physical infrastructure, healthcare, security, and childhood as well as third-level education.

kicking away the ladder: argument by Ha-Joon Chang that wealthy countries prevent poorer countries from using policies that once helped the wealthy countries industrialize.

Kyoto Protocol: 1997 update to the Framework Convention in which industrialized countries pledged to limit their greenhouse gas emissions to below their 1990 levels.

land grab: taking land from an owner or traditional occupant with unfair or no compensation.

Laws of War: humanitarian rules designed to regulate the conduct of armed conflict, in particular how civilians, prisoners of war, and other noncombatants are treated in wartime.

least developed countries (LDCs): countries with gross national income (GNI) per capita below approximately $1,000.

legitimacy: perception that something is appropriate or natural, even if not preferred.

liberalism: theory of international relations that says states are self-interested but realize that mutually beneficial relations with other states are possible, and that democracy, capitalism, and IGOs can help states cooperate with each other.

logic of appropriateness: people respond to nonmaterial things, such as norms, values, and identities. Thus, how people act reflects their understanding of appropriate behavior. Constructivists say the behavior of people and states is shaped by socially shared understandings of appropriateness.

logic of consequences: people respond to material things, such as money or threats of violence. Thus, how people act reflects the consequences they expect. Constructivists say

liberal and realist theories emphasize a logic of consequences in the behavior of states.

lump of labor fallacy: incorrect belief that there is a set number of jobs in an economy, such that an entrant into the market must deprive someone else of a job.

Malthusian: label given to a person suggesting that population growth will lead to mass hunger, based on a misreading of the work of Thomas Malthus.

Marxism: ideas of Karl Marx, that capitalism exploits labor and inequality is rooted in unequal control of means of production.

McDonaldization: idea that global capitalism driven by Western companies will homogenize global culture, with values of profit, individualism, and consumption triumphant, especially at the expense of non-Western cultures. Synonym *Disneyfication*.

mercantilism: belief that trade is only good if it strengthens a state's power as well as its economy.

microcredit: very small loans given to group small business owners to expand their business.

migrant: person who has changed his or her usual place of residence.

Millennium Development Goals (MDGs): eight goals agreed upon by UN member-states in 2000 to be reached by 2015.

modernization theory: idea attributed to Walt Rostow that there are stages of growth for each society, and that poor countries should copy what rich countries do.

monarchy: system of government in which sovereignty is vested in a single person, typically a king or queen whose entitlement to rule is assigned through hereditary traits, such as a royal lineage.

monopoly: sole ownership.

multidimensional poverty: recognition that poverty is more than income. Poverty can be experienced as poor health, education, quality of work, or violence.

multinational corporation (MNC): corporation that undertakes production in more than one country. Also known as a *transnational corporation (TNC)*.

mutual benefit: idea that states will gain jointly if each complies with the terms of an international agreement; mutual benefit creates an incentive to comply with treaties.

In human rights, the mutual benefit that would come from compliance is weak because those that suffer from human rights violations are typically not other states.

naming and shaming: process by which human rights advocates document, publicize, and condemn human rights violations.

nation: group that thinks of itself as a political community.

nation-state: where the state governs, and is governed by, people of one nation.

national identity: social identity constituted by membership in a national group.

nationalism: attitudes and emotions that individuals experience in reference to their national identity, or the desire for self-determination, the desire for a state of one's own.

negative rights: rights that are broadly about protection *from* abuse, which are the types of rights encapsulated in the International Covenant on Civil and Political Rights (ICCPR).

neoliberalism: ideological belief that free markets are desirable in an economy and in society as a whole.

next 11 or N-11: like BRICS, N-11 refers to rising powers globally, in this case Bangladesh, Egypt, Indonesia, Iran, Mexico, Nigeria, Pakistan, the Philippines, Turkey, South Korea, and Vietnam.

nongovernmental organizations (NGOs): voluntary associations, operating at local, national, or regional levels, organized in pursuit of shared interests, but not seeking profit or public office. Example: Doctors Without Borders.

nonpolarity: world in which there is no dominant power.

nonstate actors: any person, group, or organization—whether within a state or across state boundaries—that does not work in or for a state.

nonvoluntary migration: migrants moved against their will, such as an asylum seeker/refugee, an internally displaced person (IDP), or a victim of human trafficking.

norm entrepreneurs: any actor that tries to create or change a norm. Many civil society actors are, or aim to be, norm entrepreneurs.

official development assistance (ODA): loans, grants, and technical assistance given to grow economies and improve livelihoods in developing countries. Also known as foreign aid.

Organization of American States (OAS): regional organization to promote cooperation within North and South America.

out-groups: people of a different group.

Paris Agreement: 2016 update to the Kyoto Protocol, which notably saw China, the United States, and India commit to reducing greenhouse gas emissions.

participation: act of taking part in the political process, through voting, supporting organizations, and voicing concerns and preferences.

Pax Britannica: meaning "British Peace," the period of Britain's global dominance from 1815 to 1914, during which Britain's interest in increasing international trade allowed for economic cooperation between major countries.

peacebuilding: multidimensional efforts to rebuild states and societies after civil war to prevent a future armed conflict.

peacekeeping: international deployment of soldiers and police to guarantee a ceasefire or peace agreement.

political resource curse: when a government does not need to rely on citizens for revenue, it may become less accountable and may allow public institutions to deteriorate.

politically constrained: when a state is logistically able to do all types of things, but it is not *allowed* to do them.

popular sovereignty: authority to rule is vested in the general population.

portfolio investment: ownership of "paper" assets such as stocks and bonds. Does not involve managing the asset.

positive rights: rights that are broadly about entitlements *to* something, which are the types of rights encapsulated in the International Covenant on Economic, Social, and Cultural Rights (ICESCR).

Post-Fordism: late 20th century form of capitalism characterized by product quality rather than by price, with global production, flexible labor markets, and weak worker bargaining strength.

Post-Washington Consensus: updated version of the Washington Consensus, with greater emphasis on "good governance" and slightly reduced enthusiasm for free markets.

poverty trap: idea that poverty is cyclical, such that my poverty today is caused by my poverty yesterday. The solution is once-off jolts to the system in the form of rapid change or investment.

primary healthcare: essential, nonspecialized, accessible healthcare.

protectionism: government policies to favor domestic producers and discriminate against imported goods.

public good: anything that a person can use even if he or she did not contribute to it. Example: national security.

public health: wide range of activities that is concerned with health in a community; questions of prevention, the conditions that favor health, and equality of access are key for public health.

purchasing power parity (PPP): method for adjusting exchange rates to account for differences in living costs.

quasi-states: states that are legally recognized but in reality do not function because they are failed or collapsed. They exist largely "on paper."

quasi-voluntary compliance: unspoken agreement between rulers and ruled in which the ruled agree to be taxed in return for service provided by the ruler, such as police or schools.

quota: cap on the amount of imported goods.

race to the bottom: theory that countries competitively lower their labor and environmental standards in order to attract foreign investment.

radiative forcing: key metric in climate science; it refers to the net change in the energy balance of the Earth.

radicalization: process of embracing extreme ideologies and violence as a form of political action.

realism: theory of international relations that says because states are self-interested and cannot rely on others for their security, cooperation between states is the exception, and mutual distrust and conflict is the norm.

redistributive effects: when trade policies affect who gets what in society.

refugee: migrant who has been granted refugee status because the home country endangers the refugee's well-being.

regime: Rules governing how people get into power and how government works; the "rules of the game."

relative deprivation: type of grievance when individuals believe they have less than they should have.

remittances: money sent (i.e., remitted) by immigrants back to their home country.

representation: idea that citizens delegate the authority to convey their preferences to elected or appointed officials who in turn act on the citizens' behalf. In democratic politics, elected representatives are supposed to advocate and legislate in a way that accurately reflects the wishes of citizens.

representative concentration pathways (RCPs): models for predicting the severity of increase in greenhouse gases in the future.

rise of the rest: expression indicating that non-traditionally dominant powers are rising in power and status globally.

Rome Statute: international treaty that establishes the international criminal court (ICC).

rule of law: expectation that all citizens are equally subject to laws, regardless of their power or status.

Salafism: interpretation of Islam emphasizing a literalist reading of the Koran and setting an activist agenda to purify the religion of deviations and to shape the public sphere in the image of this interpretation of Islam.

slums: urban settlements characterized by poor or absent public services, poor housing quality, and weak claims of ownership to land.

smallholders: small family-run farms.

socio-economic class: grouping based on economic status.

social identity: understanding one's self in relation to a group.

social movements: collective action for social change involving very loosely organized individuals, networks, and nongovernmental organizations (NGOs). Example: Black Lives Matter.

soft power: state's ability to influence actors' behavior.

solar radiation management: measures that would reflect heat-causing light back into the atmosphere.

sovereign wealth fund: country's investment fund. Usually money from sale of energy exports, and used to invest elsewhere in the world.

sovereignty: principle that states have supreme authority within their territory.

Special Rapporteurs: independent experts appointed by the United Nations Human Rights Council to monitor, document, and promote a specific human rights issue, such as the right to food.

speed of information: rate at which information may be accessed and disseminated.

stabilization wedges: idea of developing a set of specific approaches to stabilizing the amount of greenhouse gases in the atmosphere.

state: sovereign organization with compulsory membership that claims a monopoly on the legitimate use of violence within a territory.

state actors: person, group, or organization whose ultimate authority and resources (salary, equipment, etc.) typically come from the fact that they work for, or in, a state.

state capacity: effective ability of a state to develop and execute laws and policies throughout its territory.

state-sponsored terrorism: states that fund groups that use violence to instill fear for a political purpose.

stateless persons: person with citizenship of no country.

stateness: fundamental (dis)agreements on citizenship and what/who a state covers.

strong states: high state capacity with rule of law. Common in, but not exclusive to, wealthy countries.

structural adjustment programs (SAPs): set of neoliberal reforms developing countries had to agree to in order to receive assistance from the World Bank or International Monetary Fund in the 1980s and 1990s.

structuralism: belief that global trade rules have been created by rich countries to protect their wealth. Hence, the global economy is "structurally" unfair to poor countries.

structuralist theory: also known as "dependency" theory; theory that wealthy countries got rich by making others poor. One variant, structural Marxism, believes elites in wealthy and poor countries all share a commitment to the survival of capitalism, and thus, states are tools used to ensure the dominance of capitalism.

supercitizens: small number of individuals and companies with extraordinary wealth and influence far exceeding most people and even some countries.

superpower: globally dominant state.

supranational authorities: supra means "above," so a supranational actor is above nations. These are IGOs to whom states have delegated authority to make decisions that are binding on member-states. Example: EU.

surplus economy: economy that exports more goods and services than it imports, which mathematically requires that the country also import more financial assets than it exports. China, Japan, and Germany are major surplus economies.

Sustainable Development Goals (SDGs): also known as "Global Goals," the successor to Millennium Development Goals. A total of 17 goals agreed upon by United Nations member-states in 2016 to be reached by 2030.

tariff: tax on imported goods.

technology optimists: those who believe that technology will have broad and positive impacts on society, culture, and politics.

territory: physical space including land and water.

terrorism: use or threat of use of violence against civilians to sow fear and create political change.

thermal expansion: expansion of water due to rising temperatures.

three waves of democratization: phrase coined by political scientist Samuel Huntington; clusters of countries that democratize around the same time period; in particular, the world has witnessed three big waves of change.

trafficking: migration without consent.

transaction costs: cost of doing something, above the good or service itself, such as lawyers' fees when buying a house, or the time it takes to walk to a store.

transnational advocacy network (TAN): coalition or network of people—but not a formal organization—working for change, typically narrowly focused on a specific issue. Example: Jubilee Debt Campaign.

unipolar: idea that a single power holder is dominant globally.

United Nations Framework Convention on Climate Change: Main international treaty that seeks to commit countries to target levels of greenhouse gas emissions.

Universal Declaration of Human Rights (UDHR): 1948 document that remains a touchstone for codifying human rights on a global scale; the document is a declaration, or statement of principles, not a binding legal treaty.

Varieties of Capitalism: theory that different capitalist economies have entire institutional setups designed to work for specific needs of the local variety of capitalism. Major types are liberal market economy (firms compete with each other; labor relations are poor) and coordinated market economy (firms, labor, and government cooperate).

vertical interventions: healthcare interventions that focus on addressing one specific health issue, such as a vaccine.

violence (or coercion): use or threat of physical harm. Deliberate infliction of harm against noncombatants.

voluntary migration: migrant moves without coercion.

war on terror: term that U.S. administrations have used to describe the fight against terrorism on a global scale; a war on terror implies a military fight against terrorism.

Washington Consensus: set of neoliberal assumptions shared by Western policy makers from the 1980s about what is wrong with poor countries and what ought to happen in them.

weak states: lower state capacity and some violation of rule of law. Common.

Index

Contagion, and global health security, 340
Contestation, 185
Control, as a function of a state, 57–58
Convention on Cluster Munitions, 84
Copper Rose Zambia, 144
Corridors, 301
Cosmopolitanism, 320
Cost of information, 14
Council of Europe (CoE), 221
Counterinsurgency, 292
Counterterrorism, 292
Creative destruction, 241
Criminal violence, 272
Cuban, Mark, 44
Cultural citizenship, 319
Culture, understanding, 141–148
    global challenges, 143
    globalization and, 145–147
    human intellectual and artistic activity, 142
    stereotypes, 142
    worldview, 141–142
    See also Social identities and culture
Currencies, 172–174
Currency politics, 174–176
Cyberterrorism, 293
Cyberwarfare, 293

Dahl, Robert, 185
Debt, 165–172
Debt bondage, 323
"Decline of America's Soft Power, The" (Nye), 65
Decolonization, and dependency, 33–35
de Haas, Hein, 306
DeLong, Brad, 170
Democracy, 182–207
    elections, 185
    freedom, degree of, 183–184
    international studies themes, 200–204
    quality of, 185
    See also Democratization
Democracy in America (de Tocqueville), 107
Democracy promotion, 194
Democratic consolidation, 194, 199–200
Democratic deficit, 203
Democratic initiation, 194
Democratic peace, 195
Democratic Republic of the Congo, civil war in, 280–283
Democratization, 184, 200–203

process of, 194–199
trends in, 189–194
See also Democracy
Democratization of information, 13
Demonstration effect (or diffusion), 196
Deng Xiaoping, 38–39
De-peasantization, 405
Dependency theory, 34, 154, 249
Depression, global (1929), 29–30
de Soto, Hernando, 255
de Tocqueville, Alexis, 107
de Vattel, Emmerich, 113
Development, 233–268
    as the wealth of places, 236–237
    as the welfare of people, 237–239
    countries, rich vs. poor, 240–248
    foreign aid, 256–263
    growing economies, 248–256
    measurement of, 236–239
Developmental states, 250–251
Developmental states theory, 249–251
Diamond, Jared, 243
Diana, Princess of Wales, 114
Dictatorships, 183, 186–189
Diffusion, and promotion, 194–196
Distributional effects, 10
Doane, Deborah, 412
Doha Amendment, 385
Domestic human rights organizations, 223
"Do Nongovernmental Organizations Wield Too Much Power?" (Anderson and Glasius), 123
Doomsday preppers, 21
Dougmoush, Mamoun, 299
Duflo, Esther, 260
Dutch Disease, 247
Dying for Growth (Kim), 254

East Asian miracle, 249
Easterly, William, 258–259
Economic globalization, 10, 114
Economic migrants, 302
Economic resource curse (or Dutch Disease), 247
Ehrlich, Paul, 397
Elected government, the spread of, 42–43
Elections, 185
Electoral interference, 204–205
ELEMENTS, 342
Emissions trading, 384